Embedded Systems With ARM® Cortex-M3 Microcontrollers in Assembly Language and C

Dr. Yifeng Zhu

First edition

May 1, 2015

Book covered designed by Andrew Hayford

Library of Congress Control Number: 2014946480

ISBN 978-0-9826926-2-2

Printed in the United States of America

Preface

"I hear and I forget. I see and I remember. I do and I understand."

Confucius (Chinese philosopher, 551–479 BC)

Modern embedded systems exploit a single highly integrated chip consisting of one or more general-purpose processor cores, memories, advanced peripherals, digital logic, and miniaturized sensors. Due to small power dissipation, low fabrication cost, and small size, such a System-on-Chip (SoC) becomes increasingly more popular in many embedded applications, including cellphones, MP3 players, GPS, smart watches, medical devices, fitness gadgets, and automobile control. ARM Cortex processors are of one of such successful SoC chips in industry.

This book introduces basic programming of ARM Cortex chips in assembly language and the fundamentals of embedded system design. It presents data representations, assembly instruction syntax, implementing basic controls of C language at the assembly level, and instruction encoding and decoding. The book also covers many advanced components of embedded systems, such as software and hardware interrupts, general purpose I/O, LCD driver, keypad interaction, real-time clock, stepper motor control, PWM input and output, digital input capture, direct memory access (DMA), digital and analog conversion, and serial communication (USART, I²C, SPI, and USB). The book has the following features:

- Emphasis on structured programming and top-down modular design in assembly language
- Line-by-line translation between C and ARM assembly for most example codes
- Mixture of C and assembly languages, such as a C program calling assembly subroutines, and an assembly program calling C subroutines
- Implementation of context switch between multiple concurrently running tasks according to a round-robin scheduling algorithm

Although assembly languages are used relatively less in modern embedded systems, learning assembly languages is still very important. First, an assembly language is not another programming language. It is a low-level interface between hardware and software. It provides a better understanding of how a processor executes a program. Assembly programming is the prerequisite knowledge of compilers, operating systems, and computer architecture. Secondly, assembly programs can potentially run faster than programs developed in high-level languages such as C. Compilers sometimes cannot fully exploit the hardware features of a specific processor, particularly when the processor provides specific operations that compilers do not know. Therefore, it is often that some speed-sensitive portion of an application is written in assembly language. Thirdly, some operations have to be performed in assembly language because there is no equivalent statement in high-level languages. This is why assembly programs are often embedded in operating system kernel codes to implement low-level tasks, such as booting and CPU scheduling. Finally yet importantly, understanding how high-level constructs are translated into low-level assembly instructions can help programmers to write more efficient codes in high-level languages.

The audience for this book includes those who want to gain knowledge of the inner working of a System-on-Chip (SoC), and experiences of designing embedded systems at low level. This book would serve better as text or reference material if readers have learned some basic C programming. The book covers both basic concepts and advanced topics, suitable for a wide range of audience.

I would like to thank all the people who have helped me greatly. My colleague Prof. Duane Hanselman has offered great guidance and advices on book publishing. I would like to thank Kaishuang Li for encouragement and help. I would like to thank Elyse Kahl for proofreading and Andrew Hayford for the cover design. I really appreciate all the students of ECE 271 Microcomputer Architecture and Applications class who have helped me correct many typos and gave me great improvement suggestions in my first-draft version.

Yifeng Zhu
August 4, 2014
Orono, ME

Assembly Instructions on Cortex-M3

Instruction	Operands	Description and Action
ADC, ADCS	{Rd,} Rn, Op2	Add with Carry, Rd ← Rn + Op2 + Carry, ADCS updates N,Z,C,V
ADD, ADDS	{Rd,} Rn, Op2	Add, Rd ← Rn + Op2, ADDS updates N,Z,C,V
ADD, ADDS	{Rd,} Rn, #imm12	Add Immediate, Rd ← Rn + imm12, ADDS updates N,Z,C,V
ADR	Rd, label	Load PC-relative Address, Rd ← <label>
AND, ANDS	{Rd,} Rn, Op2	Logical AND, Rd ← Rn AND Op2, ANDS updates N,Z,C
ASR, ASRS	Rd, Rm, <Rs|#n>	Arithmetic Shift Right, Rd ← Rm>>(Rs|n), ASRS updates N,Z,C
B	label	Branch, PC ← label
BFC	Rd, #lsb, #width	Bit Field Clear, Rd[(width+lsb-1):lsb] ← 0
BFI	Rd, Rn, #lsb, #width	Bit Field Insert, Rd[(width+lsb-1):lsb] ← Rn[(width-1):0]
BIC, BICS	{Rd,} Rn, Op2	Bit Clear, Rd ← Rn AND NOT Op2, BICS updates N,Z,C
BKPT	#imm	Breakpoint, prefetch abort or enter debug state
BL	label	Branch with Link, LR ← next instruction, PC ← label
BLX	Rm	Branch register with link, LR ← address of next instruction, PC ← Rm[31:1]
BX	Rm	Branch register, PC ← Rm
CBNZ	Rn, label	Compare and Branch if Non-zero; PC ← label if Rn != 0
CBZ	Rn, label	Compare and Branch if Zero; PC ← label if Rn == 0
CLREX	-	Clear local processor exclusive tag
CLZ	Rd, Rm	Count Leading Zeroes, Rd ← number of leading zeroes in Rm
CMN	Rn, Op2	Compare Negative, Update N,Z,C,V flags on Rn + Op2
CMP	Rn, Op2	Compare, Update N,Z,C,V flags on Rn – Op2
CPSID	i	Disable specified (i) interrupts, optional change mode
CPSIE	i	Enable specified (i) interrupts, optional change mode
DMB	-	Data Memory Barrier, ensure memory access order
DSB	-	Data Synchronization Barrier, ensure completion of access
EOR, EORS	{Rd,} Rn, Op2	Exclusive OR, Rd ← Rn XOR Op2, EORS updates N,Z,C
ISB	-	Instruction Synchronization Barrier
IT	-	If-Then Condition Block
LDM	Rn{!}, reglist	Load Multiple Registers increment after, <reglist> = mem[Rn], Rn increments after each memory access
LDMDB, LDMEA	Rn{!}, reglist	Load Multiple Registers Decrement Before, <reglist> = mem[Rn], Rn decrements before each memory access
LDMFD, LDMIA	Rn{!}, reglist	<reglist> = mem[Rn], Rn increments after each memory access
LDR	Rt, [Rn, #offset]	Load Register with Word, Rt ← mem[Rn + offset]
LDRB, LDRBT	Rt, [Rn, #offset]	Load Register with Byte, Rt ← mem[Rn + offset]
LDRD	Rt, Rt2, [Rn,#offset]	Load Register with two words, Rt ← mem[Rn + offset], Rt2 ← mem[Rn + offset + 4]
LDREX	Rt, [Rn, #offset]	Load Register Exclusive, Rt ← mem[Rn + offset]
LDREXB	Rt, [Rn]	Load Register Exclusive with Byte, Rt ← mem[Rn]
LDREXH	Rt, [Rn]	Load Register Exclusive with Half-word, Rt ← mem[Rn]
LDRH, LDRHT	Rt, [Rn, #offset]	Load Register with Half-word, Rt ← mem[Rn + offset]
LDRSB, LDRSBT	Rt, [Rn, #offset]	Load Register with Signed Byte, Rt ← mem[Rn + offset]
LDRSH, LDRSHT	Rt, [Rn, #offset]	Load Register with Signed Half-word, Rt ← mem[Rn + offset]
LDRT	Rt, [Rn, #offset]	Load Register with Word, Rt ← mem[Rn + offset]
LSL, LSLS	Rd, Rm, <Rs|#n>	Logic Shift Left, Rd ← Rm << Rs|n, LSLS update N,Z,C
LSR, LSRS	Rd, Rm, <Rs|#n>	Logic Shift Right, Rd ← Rm >> Rs|n, LSRS update N,Z,C
MLA	Rd, Rn, Rm, Ra	Multiply with Accumulate, Rd ← (Ra + (Rn*Rm))[31:0]
MLS	Rd, Rn, Rm, Ra	Multiply with Subtract, Rd ← (Ra - (Rn*Rm))[31:0]
MOV, MOVS	Rd, Op2	Move, Rd ← Op2, MOVS updates N,Z,C
MOVT	Rd, #imm16	Move Top, Rd[31:16] ← imm16, Rd[15:0] unaffected
MOVW, MOVWS	Rd, #imm16	Move 16-bit Constant, Rd ← imm16, MOVWS updates N,Z,C
MRS	Rd, spec_reg	Move from Special Register, Rd ← spec_reg
MSR	spec_reg, Rm	Move to Special Register, spec_reg ← Rm, Updates N,Z,C,V
MUL, MULS	{Rd,} Rn, Rm	Multiply, Rd ← (Rn*Rm)[31:0], MULS updates N,Z
MVN, MVNS	Rd, Op2	Move NOT, Rd ← 0xFFFFFFFF EOR Op2, MVNS updates N,Z,C
NOP	-	No Operation
ORN, ORNS	{Rd,} Rn, Op2	Logical OR NOT, Rd ← Rn OR NOT Op2, ORNS updates N,Z,C

ORR, ORRS	{Rd,} Rn, Op2	Logical OR, Rd ← Rn OR Op2, ORRS updates N,Z,C
POP	reglist	Canonical form of LDM SP!, <reglist>
PUSH	reglist	Canonical form of STMDB SP!, <reglist>
RBIT	Rd, Rn	Reverse Bits, for (i = 0; i < 32; i++): Rd[i] = RN[31-i]
REV	Rd, Rn	Reverse Byte Order in a Word, Rd[31:24]←Rn[7:0], Rd[23:16]←Rn[15:8], Rd[15:8]←Rn[23:16], Rd[7:0]←Rn[31:24]
REV16	Rd, Rn	Reverse Byte Order in a Half-word, Rd[15:8]←Rn[7:0], Rd[7:0]←Rn[15:8], Rd[31:24]←Rn[23:16], Rd[23:16]←Rn[31:24]
REVSH	Rd, Rn	Reverse Byte order in Low Half-word and sign extend, Rd[15:8]←Rn[7:0], Rd[7:0]←Rn[15:8], Rd[31:16]←Rn[7]*&FFFF
ROR, RORS	Rd, Rm, <Rs|#n>	Rotate Right, Rd ← ROR(Rm, Rs|n), RORS updates N,Z,C
RRX, RRXS	Rd, Rm	Rotate Right with Extend, Rd ← RRX(Rm), RRXS updates N,Z,C
RSB, RSBS	{Rd,} Rn, Op2	Reverse Subtract, Rd ← Op2 - Rn, RSBS updates N,Z,C,V
SBC, SBCS	{Rd,} Rn, Op2	Subtract with Carry, Rd ← Rn-Op2-NOT(Carry), updates NZCV
SBFX	Rd, Rn, #lsb, #width	Signed Bit Field Extract, Rd[(width-1):0] = Rn[(width+lsb-1):lsb], Rd[31:width] = Replicate(Rn[width+lsb-1])
SDIV	{Rd,} Rn, Rm	Signed Divide, Rd ← Rn/Rm
SEV	-	Send Event
SMLAL	RdLo, RdHi, Rn, Rm	Signed Multiply with Accumulate, RdHi,RdLo ← signed(RdHi,RdLo + Rn*Rm)
SMULL	RdLo, RdHi, Rn, Rm	Signed Multiply, RdHi,RdLo ← signed(Rn*Rm)
SSAT	Rd, #n, Rm{,shift #s}	Signed Saturate, Rd ← SignedSat((Rm shift s), n). Update Q
STM	Rn{!}, reglist	Store Multiple Registers
STMDB, STMEA	Rn{!}, reglist	Store Multiple Registers Decrement Before
STMFD, STMIA	Rn{!}, reglist	Store Multiple Registers Increment After
STR	Rt, [Rn, #offset]	Store Register with Word, mem[Rn+offset] = Rt
STRB, STRBT	Rt, [Rn, #offset]	Store Register with Byte, mem[Rn+offset] = Rt
STRD	Rt, Rt, [Rn,#offset]	Store Register with two Words, mem[Rn+offset] = Rt, mem[Rn+offset+4] = Rt2
STREX	Rd, Rt, [Rn,#offset]	Store Register Exclusive if allowed, mem[Rn + offset] ← Rt, clear exclusive tag, Rd ← 0. Else Rd ← 1.
STREXB	Rd, Rt, [Rn]	Store Register Exclusive Byte, mem[Rn] ← Rt[15:0] or mem[Rn] ← Rt[7:0], clear exclusive tag, Rd ← 0. Else Rd ← 1
STREXH	Rd, Rt, [Rn]	Store Register Exclusive Half-word, mem[Rn] ← Rt[15:0] or mem[Rn] ← Rt[7:0], clear exclusive tag, Rd ← 0. Else Rd ← 1
STRH, STRHT	Rt, [Rn, #offset]	Store Half-word, mem[Rn + offset] ← Rt[15:0]
STRT	Rt, [Rn, #offset]	Store Register with Translation, mem[Rn + offset] = Rt
SUB, SUBS	{Rd,} Rn, Op2	Subtraction, Rd ← Rn - Op2, SUBS updates N,Z,C,V
SUB, SUBS	{Rd,} Rn, #imm12	Subtraction, Rd ← Rn-imm12, SUBS updates N,Z,C,V
SVC	#imm	Supervisor Call
SXTB	{Rd,} Rm {,ROR #n}	Sign Extend Byte, Rd ← SignExtend((Rm ROR (8*n))[7:0])
SXTH	{Rd,} Rm {,ROR #n}	Sign Extend Half-word, Rd ← SignExtend((Rm ROR (8*n))[15:0])
TBB	[Rn, Rm]	Table Branch Byte, PC ← PC+ZeroExtend(Memory(Rn+Rm,1)<<1)
TBH	[Rn, Rm, LSL #1]	Table Branch Half-word, PC ← PC + ZeroExtend(Memory(Rn+Rm<<1, 2)<<1)
TEQ	Rn, Op2	Test Equivalence, Update N,Z,C,V on Rn EOR Operand2
TST	Rn, Op2	Test, Update N,Z,C,V on Rn AND Op2
UBFX	Rd, Rn, #lsb, #width	Unsigned Bit Field Extract, Rd[(width-1):0] = Rn[(width+lsb-1):lsb], Rd[31:width] = Replicate(0)
UDIV	{Rd,} Rn, Rm	Unsigned Divide, Rd ← Rn/Rm
UMLAL	RdLo, RdHi, Rn, Rm	Unsigned Multiply with Accumulate, RdHi,RdLo ← unsigned(RdHi,RdLo + Rn*Rm)
UMULL	RdLo, RdHi, Rn, Rm	Unsigned Multiply, RdHi,RdLo ← unsigned(Rn*Rm)
USAT	Rd, #n, Rm{,shift #s}	Unsigned Saturate, Rd←UnsignedSat((Rm shift s),n), Update Q
UXTB	{Rd,} Rm {,ROR #n}	Unsigned Extend Byte, Rd ← ZeroExtend((Rm ROR (8*n))[7:0])
UXTH	{Rd,} Rm {,ROR #n}	Unsigned Extend Half-word, Rd ← ZeroExtend((Rm ROR (8*n))[15:0])
WFE	-	Wait For Event and Enter Sleep Mode
WFI	-	Wait for Interrupt and Enter Sleep Mode

Table of Contents

CHAPTER

1

See a Program Running

This chapter shows how a machine program is generated and executed. If you do not fully understand every detail presented, do not feel discouraged. This chapter is merely meant as a general introduction. Most of the assembly programming concepts will be explained in more detail in the following chapters.

1.1 Translate a C Program into a Machine Program

Compilers translate a human readable source program written in high-level programming languages such as C, into a low-level machine understandable executable file encoded in binary form. Executable files created by compilers are usually platform dependent. An executable file compiled for one type of microprocessors, such as ARM Cortex-M3, cannot directly run on a platform with a processor that supports a different set of machine instructions, such as PIC or Atmel AVR microcontrollers. When a program written in a high-level language is migrated to a processor of a different instruction set, the source program usually has to be modified and then recompiled for the new target platform. One exception is Java executables, which leverage Java virtual machines to become platform independent.

Compilers first perform some analysis on the source program, such as identifying symbols and syntax checking, and then create an intermediate representation (IR). Compilers make a number of transformations and optimizations to the IR to improve the program execution speed or reduce the program size. For C compilers, the common intermediate program is very similar to an assembly program, as shown in Figure 1-1. Finally, compilers translate the assembly program into a machine program, also called a binary executable, which is able to run on the target platform. The machine program is composed of machine codes and data symbols.

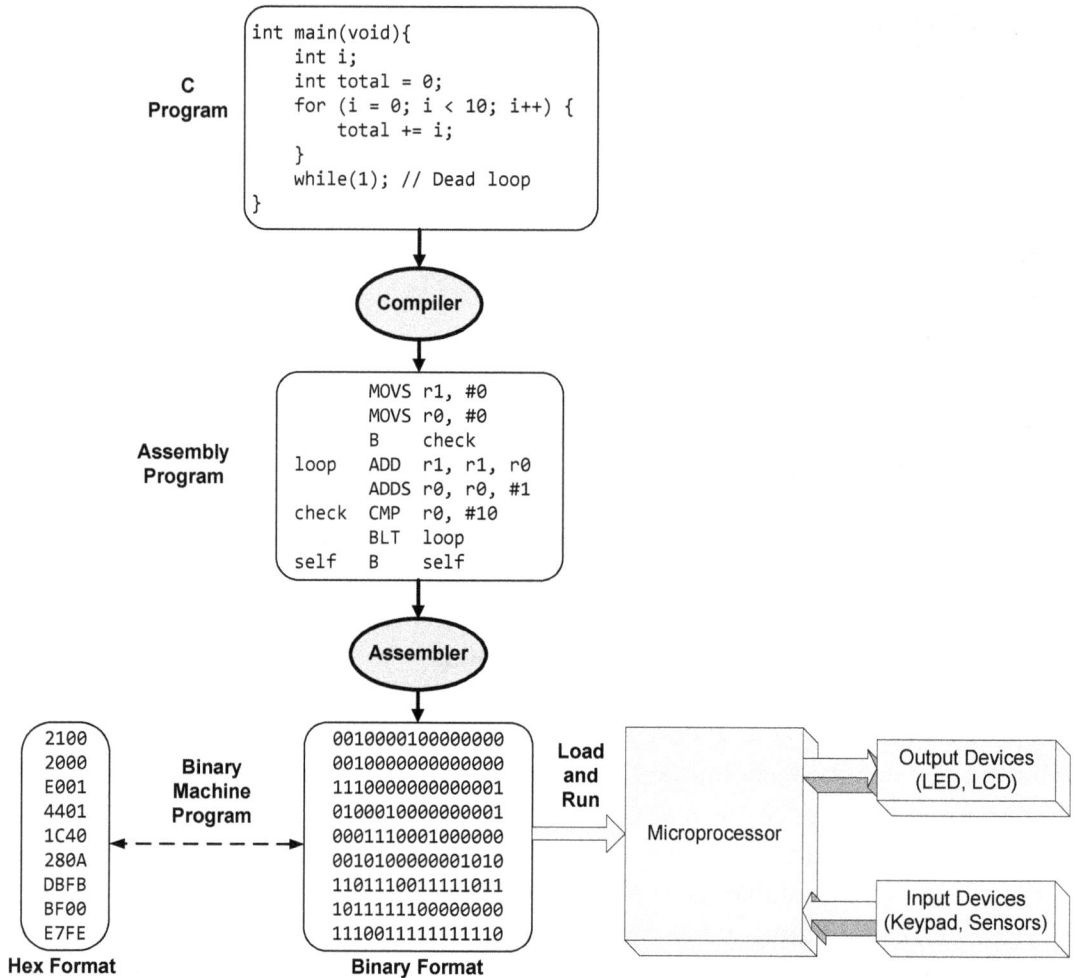

Figure 1-1. Compiling a C program into a binary executable

An assembly program consists of the following five major components. Chapter 3.5 shows a simple assembly program that annotates these components.

1. *Labels* that represent the memory addresses of application data or assembly instructions
2. *Instruction mnemonic* that represents the operation which the processor should perform, such as "ADD" and "SUB" for adding and subtracting numbers
3. *Operands* of each machine operation, which can be constant numbers or registers
4. *Program comments* that aim to improve inter-programmer communication and code readability by explicitly specifying programmers' intentions, assumptions and hidden concepts

5. *Assembly directives* that are not actual machine instructions but helpful to define data content or provide important information to assist the assembler

The binary machine program follows a standard called *executable and linkable format* (ELF), which is widely used in most Linux and UNIX systems. The UNIX System Laboratories developed and published ELF to standardize file format for most executables, shared libraries and object codes. *Object codes* are intermediate codes that are generated during the compiling stage. Object codes are linked together at the linking stage to form an executable or a software library. Most ARM-based embedded systems support the ELF format.

ELF, as its name suggests, provides two interfaces to binary files:

- A *linkable interface* that is used at static link time to combine multiple files when compiling and building a program
- An *executable interface* that is used at runtime to create a process image in memory when a program is loaded into memory and executed

Since we want to see how a program is loaded and executed, we focus only on the executable interface in the following discussion.

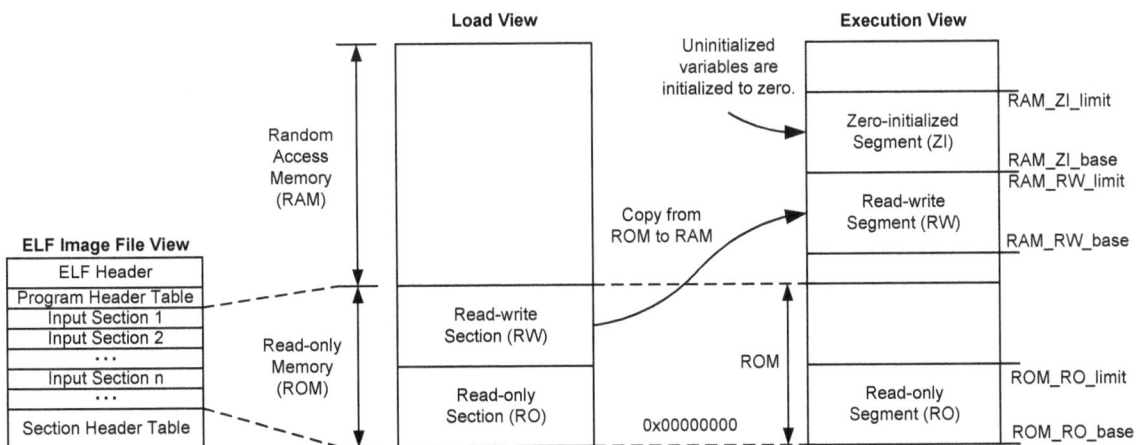

Figure 1-2. Executable interface of a binary executable file in the executable and linking format (ELF). An executable file provides two views: loading view and execution view. The loading view specifies how to load data into the memory. The execution view instructs how to initialize data regions at runtime.

In ELF, similar data, symbols, and other information are grouped into many meaningful input sections. The executable interface provides two separate logic views: the loading view and the execution view, as shown in Figure 1-2.

- The *loading view* classifies the input sections into two regions: read-write section and read-only section. The loading view also defines the base memory address of these two regions so the processor knows where these regions should be loaded into the memory.
- The *execution view* informs the processor how to load the executable at runtime. A binary machine program includes several key sections: a text segment that consists of binary machine instructions, a read-only data segment that defines value of variables unalterable at runtime, a read-write data segment that defines the initial values of statically allocated and modifiable variables, and a zero-initialized data segment that all uninitialized variables declared in the program.

1.2 Load a Machine Program into Memory

Binary executable programs are initially stored in a non-volatile storage device such as hard drives and flash memory. Accordingly, when the system loses power supply, the program is not lost and the system can restart. The instructions and data in a machine program have to be loaded into main memory before being executed. Main memory are volatile data storage devices, such as DRAM and SRAM, and all stored information in main memory is lost if power is turned off.

1.2.1   Harvard Architecture and Von Neumann Architecture

There are two types of computer architecture, *Von Neumann* architecture and *Harvard architecture*, as shown in Figure 1-3.

In the Von Neumann architecture, data and instructions share the same physical memory. There are only one memory address bus and one data transmission bus, as shown in Figure 1-4. A bus is a communication connection that allows the exchange of information between two or more parts of a computer. All sections of an executable program, including the text section (executable instructions), the read-only data section, the read-write sections, and the zero-initialized section, are loaded into the main memory. The data stream and the instruction stream share the memory bandwidth.

In the Harvard architecture, instruction memory and data memory are two physically separated memories. There are two sets of separate data transmission buses and memory address buses. When a program starts, at least the read-write data section and the zero-initialized data section are copied from the non-volatile storage to the data memory. It is optional to copy the read-only data section to the data memory. The text section usually stays in the non-volatile storage. When the program runs, the instruction stream and the data stream use separate sets of data and address buses.

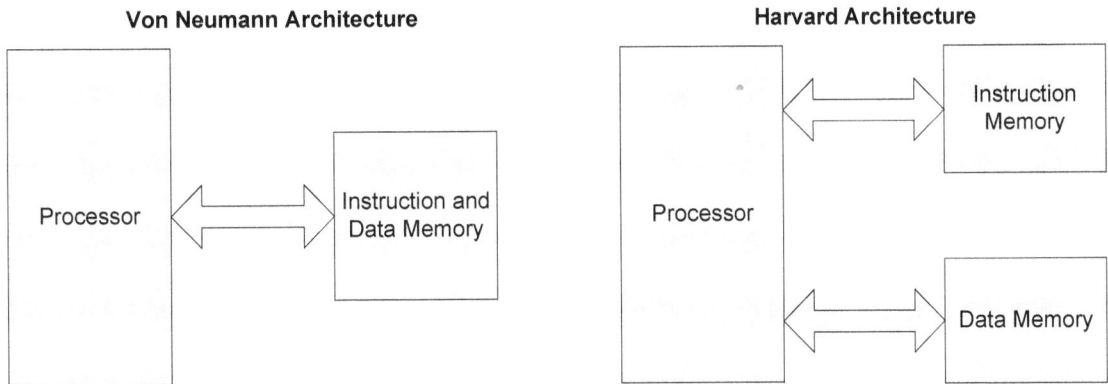

Von Neumann Architecture   **Harvard Architecture**

Figure 1-3. Two types of computer architecture. In the Von Neumann architecture, data and instructions are stored in the same memory. In the Harvard architecture, data and instructions are stored in two physically separated memories.

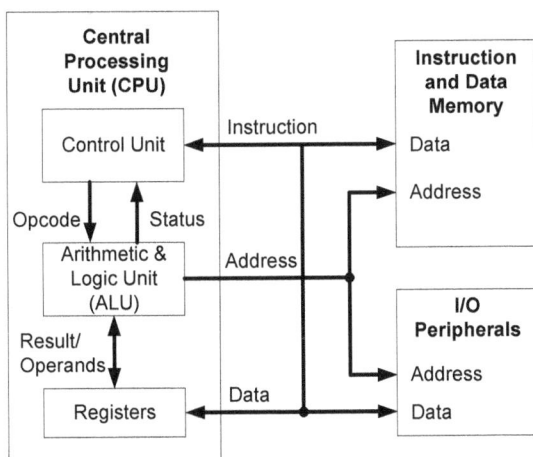

Figure 1-4. Von Neumann computer architecture. Instructions and data share the memory device. It has only one set of data bus and address bus shared by the instruction memory and data memory.

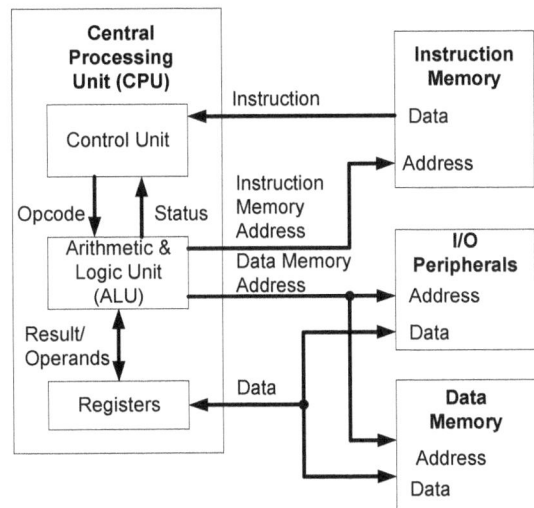

Figure 1-5. Harvard computer architecture. Instructions and data are stored in different memory devices. It has a dedicated set of data bus and address bus for the instruction memory and data memory.

In the Harvard architecture, the instruction memory and the data memory are often small enough to be placed in the same memory space. For a 32-bit processor, the memory address has 32 bits. Modern computer are byte-addressable, *i.e.* each memory address identifies a single byte of memory. When the memory address has 32 bits, the total addressable memory space includes 2^{32} bytes, *i.e.* 4 GB. Table 1-1 gives the notation of metric prefix. A 4-GB memory space is usually large enough for embedded systems.

Name	Abbr.	Size
Kilo	K	$2^{10} = 1,024$
Mega	M	$2^{20} = 1,048,576$
Giga	G	$2^{30} = 1,073,741,824$
Tera	T	$2^{40} = 1,099,511,627,776$

Table 1-1. Metric prefixes of memory size

Because the data and instruction memory are small enough to be placed in the same 32-bit memory address space, they often share the memory address bus, as shown in Figure 1-5. Suppose the data memory has 256 kilobytes (2^{18} bytes), and the instruction memory has 4 kilobytes (2^{12} bytes). In the 32-bit (*i.e.* 4 GB) memory address space, we can allocate a 4KB region for the instruction memory and a 256KB region for the instruction memory, as shown in Figure 1-6. Since there is no overlap between these two address ranges, thus the instruction memory and data memory can share the address bus.

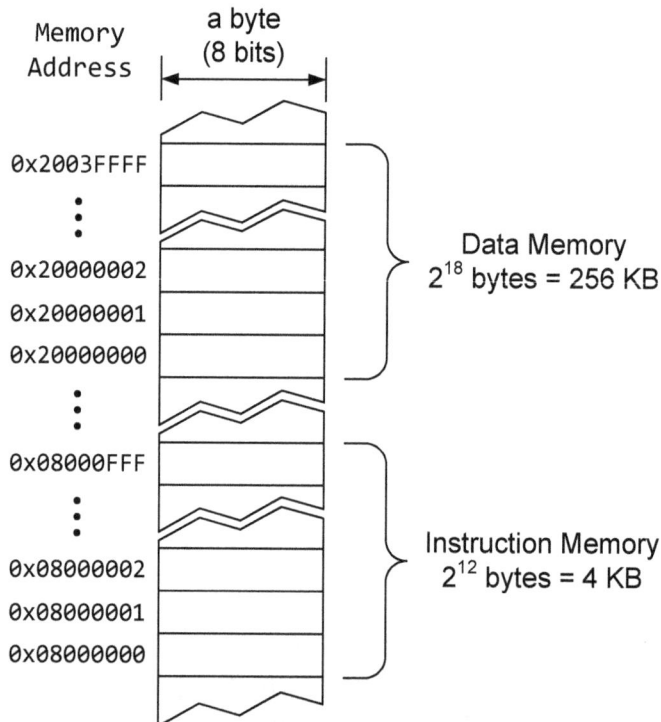

Figure 1-6. Data memory and instruction memory are placed in the same memory address space in Harvard Architecture in many embedded systems. Accordingly, the instruction memory and data memory can share the same address bus.

Each type of computer architecture has its advantages and disadvantages.

- The Harvard architecture allows the processor to access the data memory and the instruction memory concurrently whereas the Von Neumann architecture allows only one memory access at any given instant in time; either read an instruction from the instruction memory or access data in the data memory. Accordingly, the Harvard architecture can offer a faster processing speed at the same clock rate.
- The Von Neumann architecture is relatively inexpensive and simple.
- The Harvard architecture tends to be more energy efficient. To achieve the same performance, the Harvard architecture requires lower clock speeds than the Von Neumann architecture. Lower clock speeds typically result in lower power consumption rate, which is one of the most important factors in embedded systems.
- The Harvard architecture allows the width of the data transmission bus and the width of the instruction transmission bus to differ from each other. Some processors, such as digital signal processing processors, can use this feature to make the instruction transmission bus wider to reduce the number of cycles required to load an instruction.

1.2.2 Creating Runtime Memory Image

ARM Cortex-M3 microprocessors have Harvard computer architecture, and the instruction memory (flash memory) and the data memory (SRAM) are built within the processor chip, as shown in Figure 1-7. This allows concurrent accesses to instructions and data, thus improving the memory bandwidth and speeding up the processor performance. The microprocessors use two separate and isolated memories. Typically, a slower but non-volatile flash memory is used as the instruction memory, and a faster but volatile SRAM is used as the data memory.

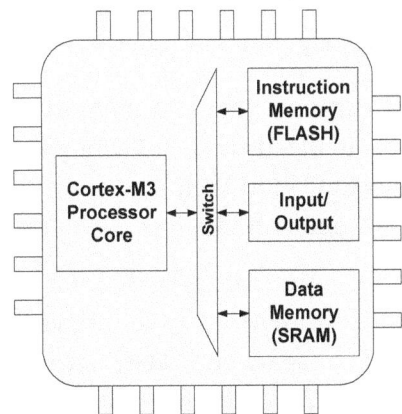

Figure 1-7. The instruction memory and the data memory are built within the processor chip.

Figure 1-8 gives a simple example that shows how a program is loaded on the Harvard architecture to start the execution. When a program is loaded, all initialized global variables, such as the integer array *a*, are copied from the instruction memory into the initialized data segment in the data memory. All uninitialized global variables, such as variable *counter*, are allocated into the zero-initialized data segment. The local variables, such as the integer array *b*, are allocated in the stack, located at the top of SRAM. Note the stack grows downward. When the processor boots successfully, the first instruction of the program is loaded from the instruction memory into the processor, and the program starts to run.

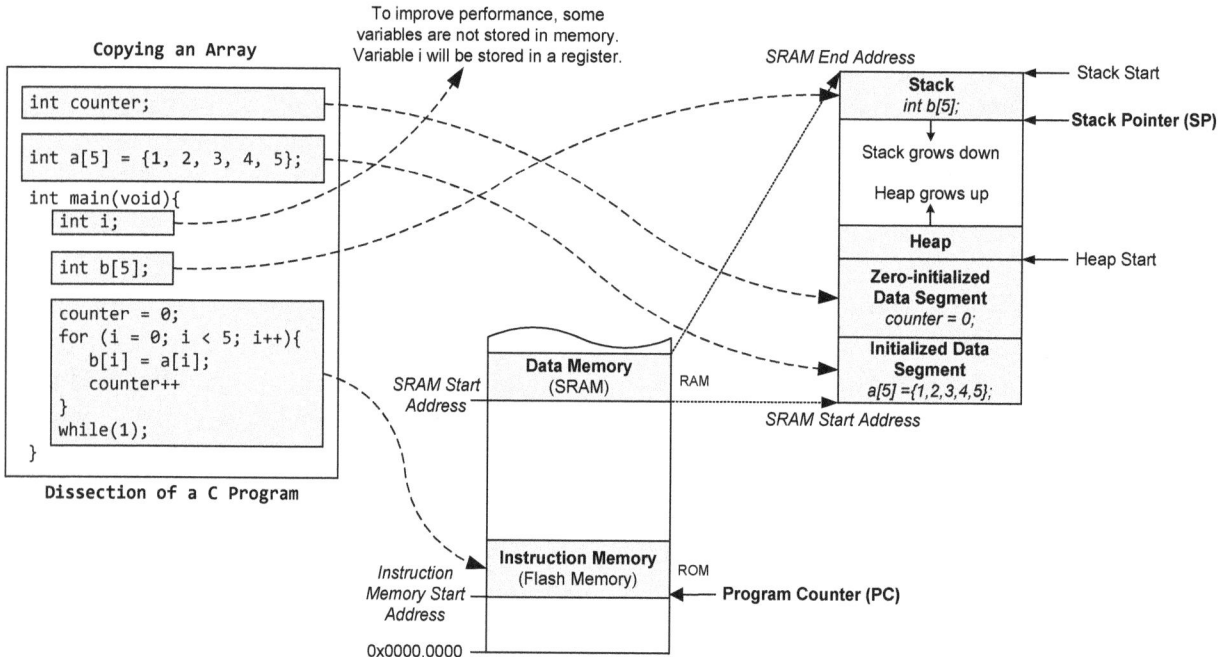

Figure 1-8. A program is loaded into two memories in a Harvard architecture.

At runtime, the data memory is divided into four segments: initialized data segment, uninitialized data segment, heap, and stack. The first two data segments are statically allocated, and their size and location remain unchanged at runtime. The size of the last two segments changes as the program runs.

- The ***initialized data segment*** contains global and static variables that are initialized with values in the program. For example, in a C declaration, "`int capacity = 100;`", if it appears outside any function (*i.e.*, it is a global variable), the capacity variable is placed in the initialized data segment with its initial value when creating a running time memory image of this C program.
- The ***zero-initialized data segment*** contains all global or static variables that are uninitialized or initialized to zero in the program. For example, a globally declared string "`char name[20];`" will be stored in the uninitialized data segment.
- The ***heap*** holds all data objects that are dynamically created at runtime. For example, all data objects created by dynamic memory allocation library functions like *malloc()* or *calloc()* in C or by the *new* operator in C++ are placed in

the heap. A *free*() function in C or a *delete* operator in C++ will remove a data object from the heap and the memory allocated to this data objected is freed up. The heap is placed immediately after the zero-initialized segment and it grows upward (toward higher addresses).

- The **stack** is used to hold local variables of subroutines (including *main*()), to preserve the runtime environment, and to pass arguments to a subroutine. A stack is a *first-in-last-out* (FILO) memory region, and it is placed on the top of the data memory. When a subroutine declares a new variable, it is pushed onto the stack. When a subroutine exits, all variables pushed onto the stack by this subroutine should be popped out of the stack. In addition, when a caller calls a subroutine, the caller may pass parameters to the subroutine via the stack. As subroutines are called and returned, the stack grows downward or shrinks upward correspondingly.

The heap and the stack are placed at the opposite end of a memory region and they grow in opposite directions, as shown in Figure 1-8. In a free memory region, the stack starts from the top and the heap starts from the bottom. The size of the heap and stack changes at runtime as variables are dynamically allocated or removed from the heap or stack. The heap grows up toward the large memory address, and the stack grows down toward the small memory address. This allows the heap and stack to take full advantage of available memory. When the stack meets the heap, free memory space is exhausted.

Figure 1-9 shows an example memory map of the 4GB memory space in a Cortex-M3 microprocessor. The memory map is pre-defined by the chip manufacturer and is not programmable usually. Within this 4GB linear memory space, instruction memory, data memory, internal and external peripheral devices, and external RAM are also allocated with no overlapping.

- The on-chip flash memory, used for the instruction memory, has 4 KB and its address starts at 0x08000000.
- The on-chip SRAM, used for the data memory, has 256 KB and its memory address starts at 0x20000000.
- The external RAM allows the processor to expand the data memory capacity.
- Memory addresses are allocated for each internal or external peripheral. This allows the processor to interface a peripheral in a convenient way. A peripheral usually have a set of registers, such as data registers for exchange data between the peripheral and the processor, control registers for the processor to configure or control the peripheral, and status registers to indicate the operation states of the peripheral. A peripheral may also contain a small memory. The registers

and memory of all peripherals are mapped to the same memory address space of the instruction and data memory. To interface a peripheral, the processor uses normal memory access instructions to read or write to those special memory addresses predefined for this peripheral. The processor interfaces all peripheral in the way as if they were part of the memory.

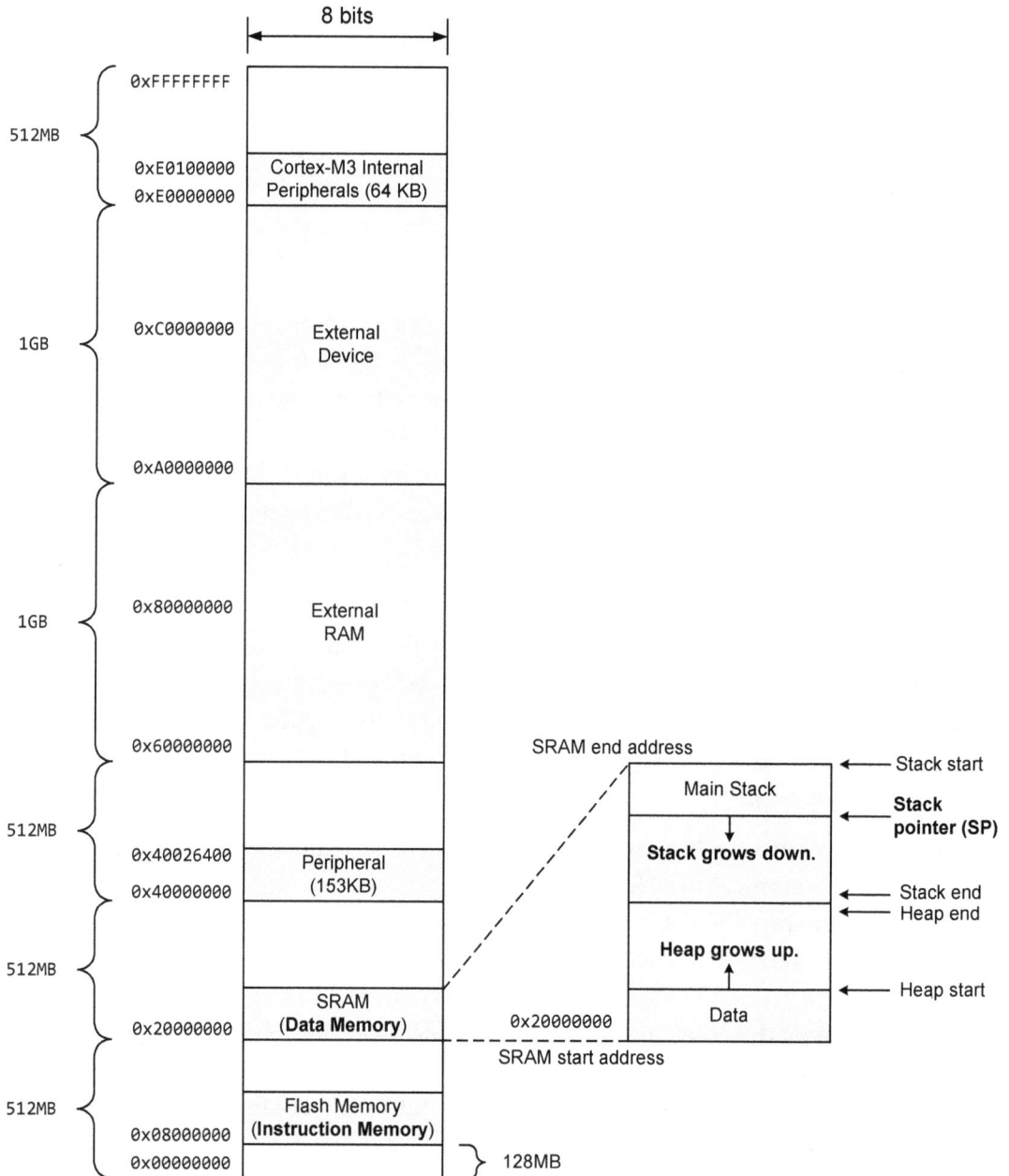

Figure 1-9. Example memory map of a 4GB memory space. The address space is shared between memories and peripherals. The memory map is fixed and contains unused region.

1.3 Registers

Before we illustrate how a microprocessor executes a program, let us first introduce one important component of microprocessors - hardware registers. A processor contains a small set of registers to store digital values. Registers are the fastest data storage in a computing system.

All registers are of the same size and typically hold 16, 32, or 64 bits. All bits in a register are read and written simultaneously. Registers store the content of the operands for logic or arithmetic operations performed by the processor, or the memory address and offset when data are stored into or fetched from the memory.

Registers are divided into two groups: general-purpose registers and special-purpose registers. While general-purpose registers store the operands and intermediate results during the execution of a program, special-purpose registers have a pre-determined usage, such as representing the processor status. Special-purpose registers have more usage restrictions than general-purpose registers. For example, some of them require special instructions or privileges to access them.

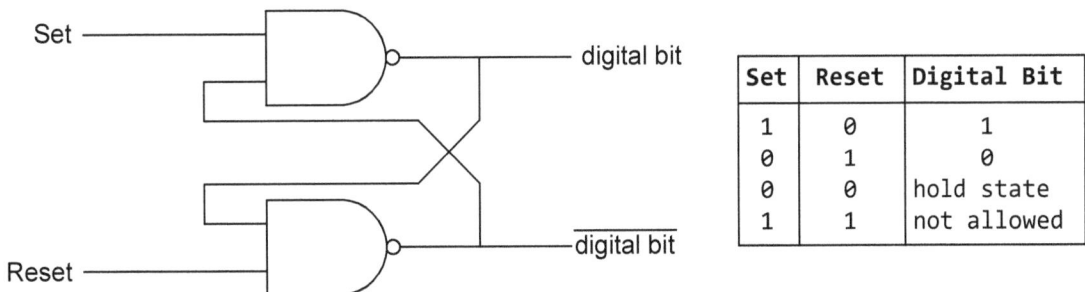

Set	Reset	Digital Bit
1	0	1
0	1	0
0	0	hold state
1	1	not allowed

Figure 1-10. Logic diagram and truth table of a basic flip-flop constructed by using two Negated AND (NAND) gates

A register consists of a set of flip-flops in parallel to store binary bits. A 32-bit register has 32 flip-flops side by side.

Figure 1-10 shows a simple implementation of a flip-flop by using a pair of Negated AND (NAND) gates. In this example, the flip-flop does not include a clock control signal. When the set or the reset is true, a digital value of true or false is stored, respectively. When both the set and the reset are false, the digital value stored remains unchanged. The set and reset signals cannot be true simultaneously since the result produced is random.

1.3.1   Reusing Registers to Improve Performance

The access speed of these registers is much faster than data memory. The processor speed is improved if data to be accessed are stored in registers instead of memory. In most programs, the probability that a data is accessed is not uniform. It is a common phenomenon that a program accesses some data much more frequently than other data. In addition, data that is accessed at one point in time is likely to be accessed again in the near future. This phenomenon is called temporal locality. Therefore, most compilers try to place the value of frequently or recently accessed data and memory addresses in registers whenever possible to optimize the performance. Software programs also have spatial locality. When data at a particular memory location is accessed, data stored at nearby memory locations are likely to be accessed in the near future. Spatial locality is also exploited in processor and software design (such as caching and prefetch) to speed up the application performance.

Analogy Example

Temporal Locality: **You tend to read the same book repeatedly from the library when preparing an exam.**

Spatial Locality: **You tend to read books on the same bookshelf in the library when preparingan exam.**

The number of registers available on a processor is often very small, typically between four and sixteen, for two important reasons.

- Many experimental measurements have shown that registers often exhibit the highest temperature compared to the other hardware components of a processor. Reducing the number of registers helps mitigate the thermal problem.
- A small number of registers available reduce the length of a binary instruction, consequently decreasing code size and memory bandwidth requirement. For example, if a processor has 16 registers, 4 bits are required to address each register. To encode an assembly instruction with two operand registers and one destination register, such as "add r3, r1, r2" (r3 = r1 + r2), 12 bits are used for locating registers when encoding this instruction into a binary machine instruction. However, if a processor has only eight registers, only 9 bits are required to encode the addresses of these three register operands.

Register allocation is a process that assigns variables and constants to general-purpose registers. It is often the case that we have more variables and constants than registers. Register allocation decides whether a variable or constant should reside in a processor register or at some location in the data memory. Register allocation is performed either automatically by compilers if a high-level language is used, or manually by programmers if the program is written in an assembly language.

For a given program, finding the optimal register allocation that minimizes the number of memory accesses is a challenging problem. Register allocation becomes further complicated in Cortex-M3 processors. For example, some instructions can only access registers with small addresses (low registers). Some instructions, such as multiplication, place a possibly large result into two registers.

When writing an assembly program, we can follow three basic steps to allocate registers. Chapter 7.2 gives a detailed example.

1. We inspect the live range of a variable. A variable is live if its value will be used at some later point in the program.
2. If the live range of two variables overlaps, we should not allocate them into the same register. Otherwise, we can assign them to the same register.
3. We map frequently used variables to registers and map least frequently used variables to memory if necessary to avoid making frequent memory accesses.

1.3.2 Processor Registers

As shown in Figure 1-11, registers are divided into two groups: general-purpose registers and special-purpose registers.

- There are 13 general-purpose registers (r0 - r12) available for program data operations. The first eight registers (r0 - r7) are called low registers and the other five (r8 - r12) are called high registers. Some of 16-bit assembly instructions in Cortex-M3 can only access the low registers.
- *Stack point* (SP) r13 holds a memory address that points to the top of the stack. Cortex-M3 processors provide two different stacks: main stack and process stack. As a result, there are two stack pointers: the main stack pointer (MSP) and the process stack pointer (PSP). While PSP is used for regular user program execution, MSP is used for interrupts or privileged accesses. The stack pointer (SP) is a shadow register of either MSP or PSP depending on the processor's mode setting. When a processor starts, it assigns MSP to SP.
- *Link register* (LR) r14 points to the instruction that needs to be executed immediately after a subroutine completes. During the execution of an interrupt service routine, LR holds a special value to indicate whether MSP or PSP is used.
- *Program counter* (PC) r15 holds the memory address (location in memory) of the next instruction to be fetched from the instruction memory.

- *Special-purpose program status register* (xPSR) records status bit flags of application program, interrupt, and processor execution. Example flags include negative, zero, carry, and overflow. Chapter 9 gives detailed introduction.
- *Base priority mask register* (BASEPRI) defines the priority threshold that an exception should have the same or lower priority value in order to be executed.
- *Control register* (CONTROL) sets the choice of main stack or process stack, and the choice of privileged or unprivileged mode. The CONTROL register will be discussed in Chapter 23.
- *Priority mask register* (PRIMASK) is used to disable all interrupts excluding hard faults and non-maskable interrupts (NMI). If an interrupt is masked, this interrupt is ignored (*i.e.* disabled) by the processor. Chapter 12 introduces interrupts in detail.
- *Fault mask register* (FAULTMASK) is used to disable all interrupts excluding non-maskable interrupts (NMI).

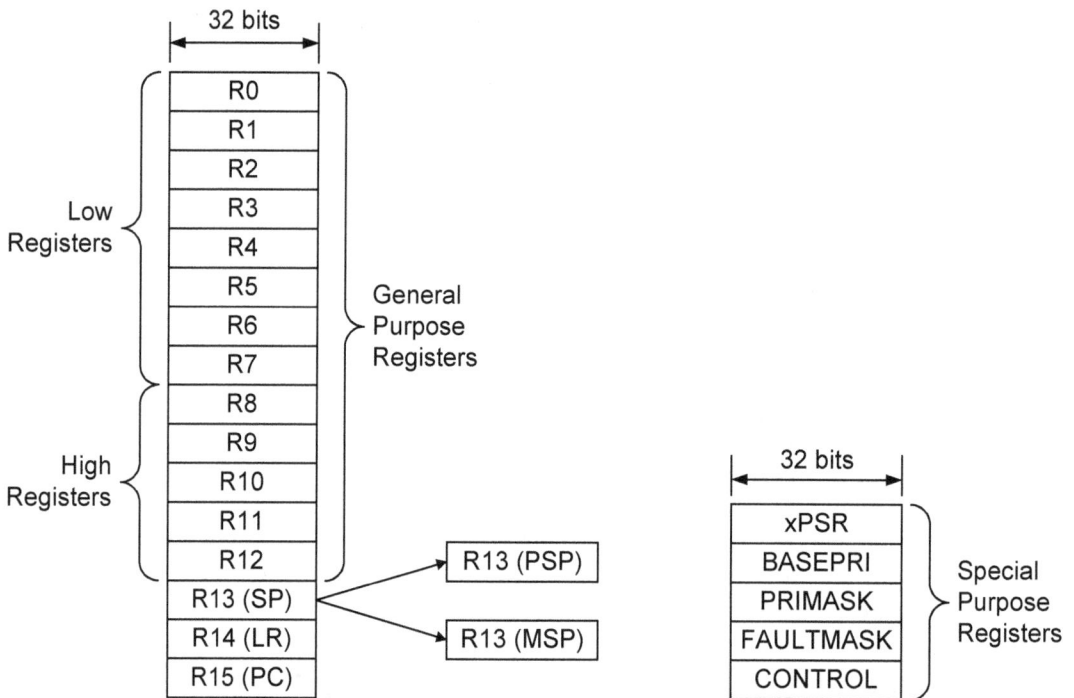

Figure 1-11. Registers of ARM Cortex-M3 processor.
PC = program counter, LR = link register, SP = stack pointer, MSP = main stack pointer, PSP = program stack pointer, xPSR = special-purpose program status register

The program counter (PC) stores the memory address of the next instruction to be loaded into the processor from the instruction memory. Typically, instructions in the memory are executed sequentially. Therefore, instructions are usually fetched sequentially from the instruction memory and thus the program counter is automatically incremented to point to the next instruction. In Cortex-M3, an instruction has either 16 or 32 bits. Accordingly, except in cases of branching, the processor automatically increases the program counter by two or four, depending on the size of the current instruction.

However, branch instructions, interrupts, subroutine calls, and subroutine returns can change the program flow by setting the program counter to the memory address of the target instruction.

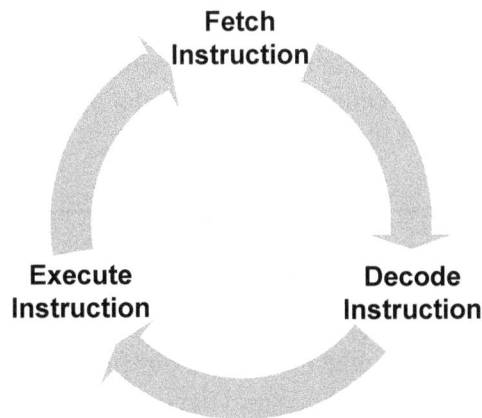

Figure 1-12. Life cycle of an instruction. An instruction pointed by the program counter is fetched, decoded, and executed. PC is automatically incremented after each instruction fetch.

Each instruction takes three stages to complete, as shown in Figure 1-12.

- At the first stage, the processor fetches one instruction from the instruction memory and increases the program counter. After each instruction is fetched, the program counter points to the next instruction to be fetched.
- At the second stage, the processor decodes the instruction and finds out what operations are to be carried out.
- At the last stage, the processor reads operand registers, carries out arithmetic and logic operation, accesses data memory (if necessary) and updates target registers (if necessary).

This fetch-decode-execution process repeats for each instruction until the program completes. As shown in Figure 1-13, three stages of the life cycle of each instruction are executed in a pipelined fashion similar to an automobile assembly line. Pipelining allow multiple instructions to run simultaneously, thus increasing the utilization of hardware resources and improving the processor performance. Special considerations need to be taken when a branch instruction runs in the pipeline.

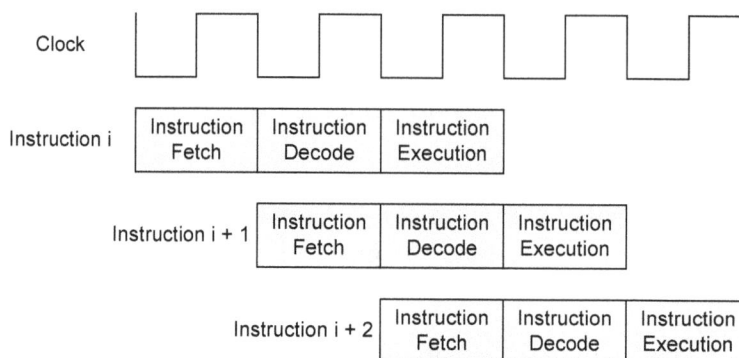

Figure 1-13. Three-stage fetch-decode-execution pipeline. This allows hardware resources to be fully utilized. The program counter (PC) points the instruction currently being fetched.

1.4 Executing a Machine Program

This section illustrates how a C program is executed on a Cortex-M3 processor. We use a simple C program given in Table 1-2 as an example. The program calculates the sum of two global integer variables (a and b) and saves the result into another global variable c. Since most software programs in embedded systems never exit, there is an endless loop at the end of the C program.

C Program	Assembly Program	Machine Program	
		Binary	Hex

int a = 1;
int b = 2;
int c = 0;
 	
int main(){
  c = a + b;
  while(1);
}
 	
	AREA myCode, CODE
	EXPORT __main
	ALIGN
	ENTRY
	__main LDR r1, =a
	     LDR r2, [r1]
	     LDR r3, =b
	     LDR r4, [r3]
	     ADDS r5, r2, r4
	     LDR r6, =c
	     STR r5, [r6]
	stop B stop
	
	     AREA myData, DATA
	     ALIGN
	a DCD 1
	b DCD 2
	c DCD 0
	     END
		0100100100000011
		0110100000001010
		0100101100000011
		0110100000011100
		0001100100011001
		0100111000000011
		0110000000111001
		1110011111111110
		0000000000000000
		0010000000000000
		0000000000000100
		0010000000000000
		0000000000001000
		0010000000000000
			0x4903
			0x680A
			0x4B03
			0x681C
			0x1915
			0x4E03
			0x6035
			0xE7FE
			0x0000
			0x2000
			0x0004
			0x2000
			0x0008
			0x2000

Table 1-2. Comparison of C program, assembly program, and machine program

A C compiler translates the C sample program into an assembly program similar to the one given in Table 1-2. Different C compilers might generate assembly programs that differ from each other. Even the same C compiler can generate different assembly programs from the same C program if different compilation options (such as optimization levels) are used.

The assembler then produces the machine program based on the assembly program. The machine program includes two parts: data and instructions. Table 1-2 only lists the instructions. The prefix "0x" represents a hexadecimal number. A number represented in hexadecimal format is more readable than its representation in binary. Chapter 2 introduces the representation and conversion of numbers in detail.

1.4.1   Loading a Program

When the program is executed in the Harvard architecture, its instructions and data are loaded into the instruction and data memory, respectively. Table 1-3 gives an example image of the instruction and data memory.

Memory Region	Memory Address	Binary Instruction	Assembly Instruction	Comments
Instruction Memory	0x08000160	0x4903	LDR r1, [pc,#12]	; @0x08000170
	0x08000162	0x680A	LDR r2, [r1]	; r2 = a
	0x08000164	0x4B03	LDR r3, [pc,#12]	; @0x08000174
	0x08000166	0x681C	LDR r4, [r3]	; r4 = b
	0x08000168	0x1915	ADDS r5, r2, r4	; r5 = a + b
	0x0800016A	0x4E03	LDR r6, [pc,#12]	; @0x08000178
	0x0800016C	0x6035	STR r5, [r6]	; save c
	0x0800016E	0xE7FE	B 0x0800016E	; stop
	0x08000170	0x0000	DCW 0x0000	
	0x08000172	0x2000	DCW 0x2000	; 0x20000000
	0x08000174	0x0004	DCW 0x0004	
	0x08000176	0x2000	DCW 0x2000	; 0x20000004
	0x08000178	0x0008	DCW 0x0008	
	0x0800017A	0x2000	DCW 0x2000	; 0x20000008
	. . .	. . .	. . .	
Data Memory	0x20000000	0x0001	DCW 0x0001	
	0x20000002	0x0000	DCW 0x0000	; 0x00000001
	0x20000004	0x0002	DCW 0x0002	
	0x20000006	0x0000	DCW 0x0000	; 0x00000002
	0x20000008	0x0000	DCW 0x0000	
	0x2000000A	0x0000	DCW 0x0000	; 0x00000000
	. . .	. . .	. . .	

Table 1-3. Memory image when a program is loaded into instruction and data memory

Depending on the processor hardware setting, the starting address of the instruction and data memory might differ from this example. Each instruction in this example happens to take two bytes in the instruction memory. The data memory holds three integers (*a*, *b*, and *c*), and each integer takes four bytes.

Each instruction takes three clock cycles (fetch, decode and execute) to complete on an ARM Cortex-M3 processor: (1) Fetch the instruction from the instruction memory, (2) Decode the instruction, and (3) Execute the arithmetic or logic operation, update the program counter for a branch instruction, or access the data memory for a load or store instruction.

Note the assembly instruction "LDR r1, =a" is a pseudo instruction, which is translated into real machine instructions by the assembler, as discussed in detail in Chapter 5.4.4. This instruction sets the content of register r1 to the memory address of variable *a*. The pseudo instruction is translated into "LDR r1, [pc, #12]". The memory address of variable *a* is stored at the memory location "[pc, #12]". This

> *Pseudo Instructions are not real machine instructions.*

is a general approach to load a large irregular number into a register. We will introduce the PC-relative addressing in Chapter 3.

1.4.2   Starting the Execution

After the processor is booted and initialized, the program counter (PC), which points to the next instruction to be fetched from the instruction memory, is set as 0x08000160. After executing an instruction, PC is automatically incremented by two and points to the next instruction in this specific example. In this example, each instruction happens to take only two bytes (16 bits) in the instruction memory. There are many instructions that take four bytes (32 bits), as discussed in Chapter 13.

Each processor has a special program called *boot loader*, which sets up the runtime environment after completion of self-testing. The boot loader sets PC to the first instruction of a user program. For a C program, PC points to the first statement in the main function. For an assembly program, PC points the first instruction of the __main function (See Table 1-2).

Figure 1-14 shows the values of registers, the layout of instruction memory and data memory when the sample program is loaded. When the program starts, PC is set to 0x08000160. Note each memory address specifies the location of a byte in memory. Since each instruction takes 16 bits in this example, the memory address of the next instruction is 0x08000162. Variables *a*, *b*, and *c* are declared as integers and each of them takes four bytes in memory.

PC stores the memory address of the next instruction to be fetched from the instruction memory. When one instruction starts the execution, the program counter is incremented automatically by the hardware, pointing to the next instruction to be fetched. When the program starts, PC initially points to the first instruction of the program.

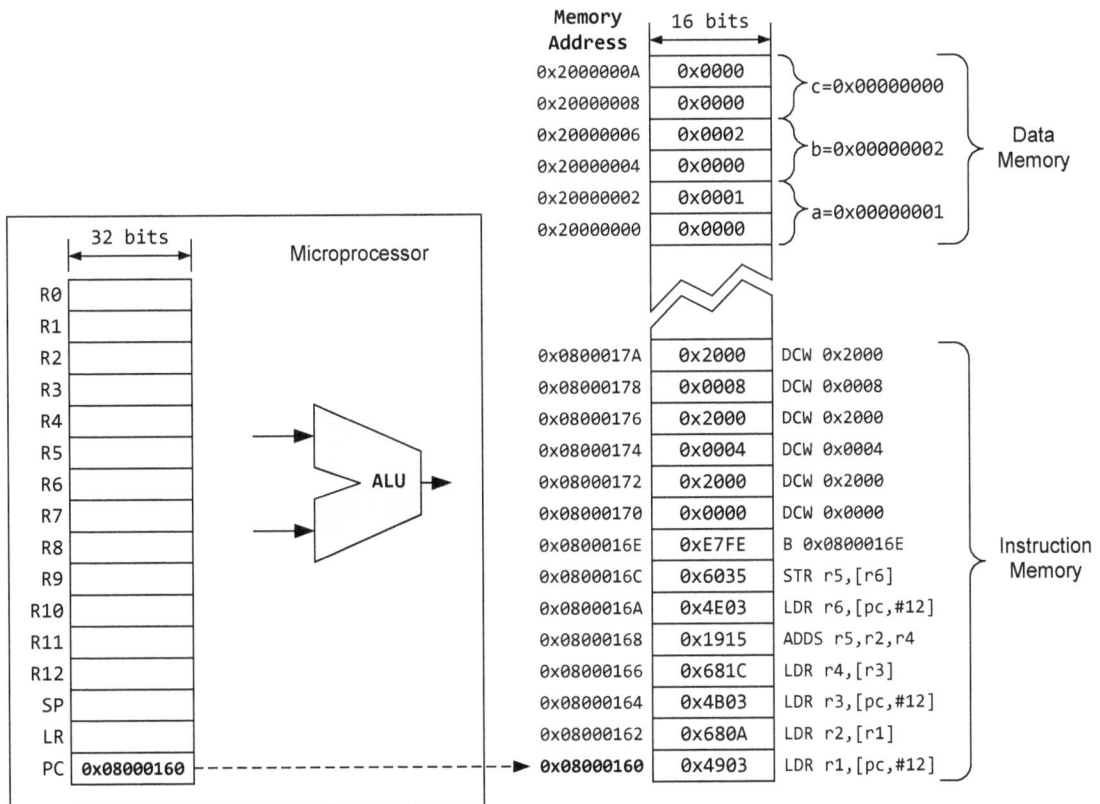

Figure 1-14. Memory image when the example program is loaded. The program counter points to the next instruction to be loaded. Variables *a*, *b*, and *c* are stored in the data memory.

Registers hold values to be operated by the arithmetic and logic unit (ALU). All registers can be accessed simultaneously, without causing any extra delay. A variable can be stored in the memory or a register. When a variable is stored in the data memory, the value of this variable has to be loaded into a register because arithmetic and logic instructions cannot directly operate on a value stored in the memory. If a variable is stored in memory, the processor must follow the *load-modify-store* sequence to update this

A load-modify-store sequence is required to update a memory value.

variable:

1. Load the value of the variable from the data memory into a register,
2. Modify the value of the register by using ALU, and
3. Store the value of this register back into the data memory.

This assembly program given in Table 1-2 involves the following four key steps:

1. Load the value of variable *a* from the data memory into register r2.
2. Load the value of variable *b* from the data memory into register r4.
3. Calculate the sum of r2 and r4 and save the result into register r5.
4. Save the content of register r5 at the memory address of variable *c*.

The following explains the execution of each assembly instruction line by line. To facilitate the discussion, we list the memory address where the instruction is stored, the binary machine instruction, the assembly instruction that the binary machine instruction represents, and comments.

1. `0x08000160: 0x4903`
   `LDR r1, [pc, #12]`
   `; Load memory address of global variable a into register r1`

   The processor fetches two bytes located at `0x08000160` from the instruction memory. After these two bytes (`0x4903`) are retrieved from the instruction memory, the processor decodes the binary instruction `0x4903` as "`LDR r1, [pc, #12]`", where the constant number 12 is an offset, which denotes the distance between a base address and a specific target address. This instruction loads a 32-bit data (a word) stored at the memory address pc + 4 + 12 into register r1. Since the content of PC at this moment is `0x08000160`, the target data memory address of this load instruction is pc + 4 + 12, *i.e.* `0x08000170`. The 32-bit data stored at the memory address `0x08000170` is `0x20000000`. Because of this load register instruction (LDR), register r1 is set to `0x20000000`. At the end, PC is automatically incremented by two and the new PC value is `0x08000162`, pointing to the next instruction to be fetched.

2. `0x08000162: 0x680A`
   `LDR r2, [r1]`
   `; Load value of global variable a from data memory into r2`

   The binary instruction pointed by PC is `0x680A`. This instruction is to load integer variable *a*, stored in the data memory, into register r1. Each integer variable takes four bytes in memory. After this instruction completes, the content of register r2 is `0x00000001` and PC is `0x08000164`.

3. 0x08000164: 0x4B03
   LDR r3, [pc, #12]
   ; Load memory address of global variable b into register r3

The next instruction fetched from the instruction memory is 0x4B03. It loads the memory address of variable *b* into register r3. PC is 0x08000164 and thus the target memory address is PC + 4 + 12, *i.e.* 0x08000174. After loading 32-bit data located at 0x08000174, r3 is 0x20000004 and PC is 0x08000166.

4. 0x08000166: 0x681C
   LDR r4, [r3]
   ; Load value of global variable b into register r4

The machine instruction 0x681C instructs the processor to load 32-bit data at memory location 0x20000004 into register r4. Register r3 holds the memory address of variable *b*. After the execution, r4 is 0x00000002 and PC is 0x08000168.

5. 0x08000168: 0x1915
   ADDS r5, r2, r4
   ; Add the values of a and b

The machine instruction 0x1915 asks the processor to add two integers stored in register r2 and r4, and save the result into register r5. Register r2 and r4 hold the values of variable *a* and *b*, respectively. After the add operation completes, r5 is 0x00000003 and PC is 0x0800016A.

6. 0x0800016A: 0x4E03
   LDR r6, [pc, #12]
   ; Load memory address of global variable c into register r6

This instruction loads the memory address of variable *c* into register r6. After completion, r6 is 0x20000008 and PC is 0x0800016C.

7. 0x0800016C: 0x6035
   STR r5, [r6]
   ; Store sum into variable c located in data memory

This instruction stores the 32-bit content of register r5 into the memory address pointed by register r6. This saves the content of variable *c* into the data memory located at 0x20000008. After completion, the content of the data memory located at 0x20000008 is 0x00000003, and PC is 0x0800016E.

8. 0x0800016E: 0xE7FE
   B 0x0800016E
   ; Dead loop

This instruction (0xE7FE) is a branch instruction that sets PC to 0x0800016E, which points to the instruction itself. The 11-bit branch offset is 0x7FE, *i.e.* -2. Thus, PC = PC + 4 + 2 × offset = PC + 4 − 4 = PC. Consequently, the same instruction is repeatedly executed, which creates an endless loop. This corresponds to the *while(1)* loop of the C program.

1.4.3   Program Completion

Figure 1-15 shows the values of all registers and the data memory when the program reaches the dead loop. The 32-bit result is stored in the data memory, and the program counter (PC) keeps pointing to the instruction 0xE7FE repeatedly. Variable *c* stored at the data memory address 0x20000008 has a value of 3, which is the sum of *a* and *b*.

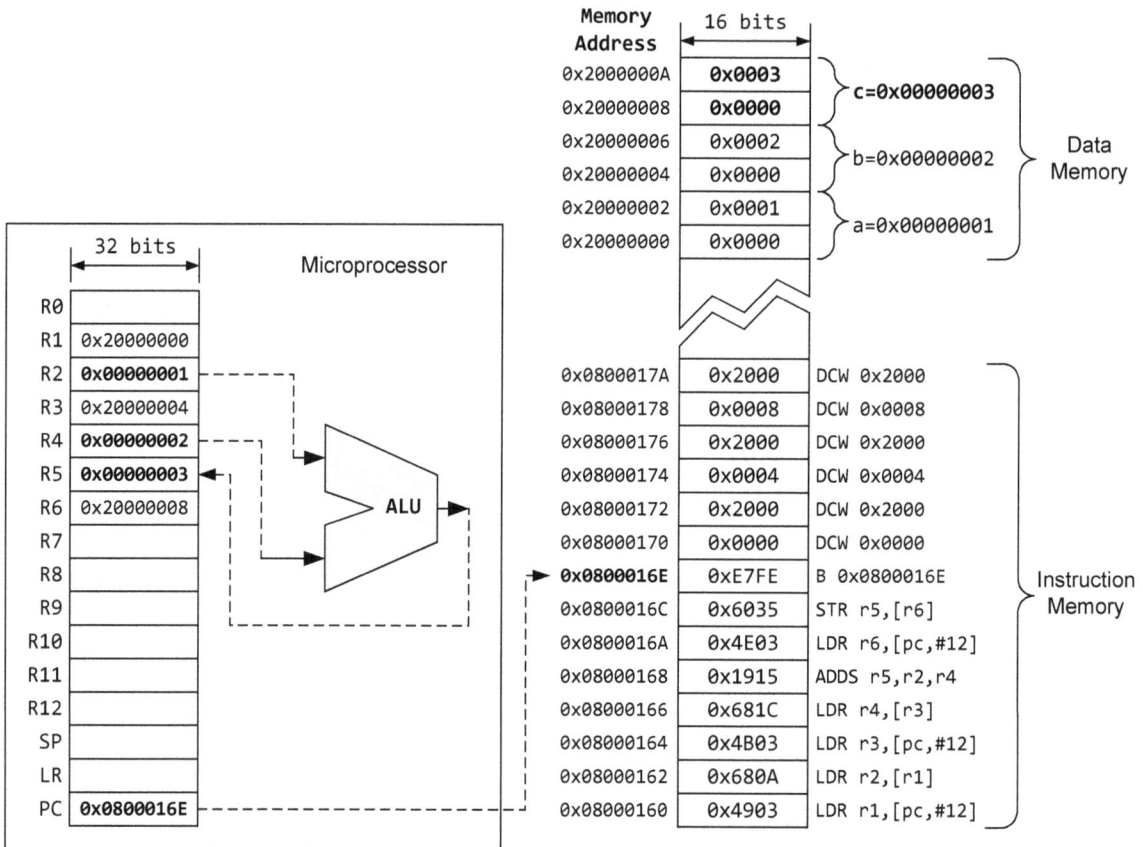

Memory (16 bits), Data Memory

Memory Address	Value	
0x2000000A	0x0003	c=0x00000003
0x20000008	0x0000	
0x20000006	0x0002	b=0x00000002
0x20000004	0x0000	
0x20000002	0x0001	a=0x00000001
0x20000000	0x0000	

Microprocessor (32 bits)

R0	
R1	0x20000000
R2	0x00000001
R3	0x20000004
R4	0x00000002
R5	0x00000003
R6	0x20000008
R7	
R8	
R9	
R10	
R11	
R12	
SP	
LR	
PC	0x0800016E

ALU

Instruction Memory

Address	Value	Instruction
0x0800017A	0x2000	DCW 0x2000
0x08000178	0x0008	DCW 0x0008
0x08000176	0x2000	DCW 0x2000
0x08000174	0x0004	DCW 0x0004
0x08000172	0x2000	DCW 0x2000
0x08000170	0x0000	DCW 0x0000
0x0800016E	0xE7FE	B 0x0800016E
0x0800016C	0x6035	STR r5,[r6]
0x0800016A	0x4E03	LDR r6,[pc,#12]
0x08000168	0x1915	ADDS r5,r2,r4
0x08000166	0x681C	LDR r4,[r3]
0x08000164	0x4B03	LDR r3,[pc,#12]
0x08000162	0x680A	LDR r2,[r1]
0x08000160	0x4903	LDR r1,[pc,#12]

Figure 1-15. Processor and memory status when the program reaches the dead loop. The program counter (PC) points to the branch instruction. The ALU can take any general-purpose registers as the source operands and destination operand. To change the value stored in the data memory, a load-modify-store sequence has to be performed.

1.5 Exercises

1. Identify the processor type and manufacturer of five different devices excluding servers, laptops, and desktops. How many bits does a machine instruction have? How many bits does the memory address have? What is the maximum memory capacity they can support? Are they Harvard architecture and the Von Neumann architecture?

2. The program counter (PC) points to the memory address of the next instruction to be loaded from the memory. How does the PC value change after fetching a 32-bit instruction? How does PC change after fetching a 16-bit instruction?

3. An arithmetic and logic unit (ALU) performs integer and logic operations. Implement the logic of a simple ALU that performs 2-bit addition and subtraction. Assume the operands are $A_1 A_0$ and $B_1 B_0$, and the output is $C_1 C_0$. The operation code O has only one bit, which selects addition or subtraction.

4. A register is the fastest data storage element within a processor. A 32-bit register consists of a set of flip-flops to store 32 bits of information. Design a 4-bit register by using flip-flops.

5. Suppose the memory address in most embedded systems has 32 bits. How many unique memory locations can this 32-bit address access? On desktop or servers, usually virtual memory is deployed, which allows a process to allocate and use a memory space that is larger than the physical memory. Why is virtual memory often not used in embedded systems?

6. Executable and linkable format (ELF) is a standard used for Linux operating systems and many other embedded systems. Compile a C program in Linux into a binary executable and use the *readelf* command to display the information of a binary executable. Identify the data sections and instruction/data sections of a binary executable program.

7. Suppose a processor of the Harvard architecture has 4MB instruction memory and 32MB data memory. If the memory address bus is shared between instruction memory and data memory, design a memory allocation scheme for this processor (*i.e.* address range for the instruction memory and the data memory).

[This page is intentionally left blank.]

CHAPTER

2

Data Representation

All data are stored in a computer as a sequence of binary bits. This chapter focuses on digital representation of integers and text strings. Chapter 11 will introduce digital representation of a real number.

2.1 Bit, Byte, Half-word, Word, and Double-word

A bit is the smallest quantity of information. Each bit has a value of either one or zero, and thus it is called a binary bit. However, it is more efficient for computers to load, process, store, and transmit a group of bits simultaneously. Therefore, bits are divided into a sequence of fixed-length logic units. A byte is a group of 8 bits, a half-word consists of 16 bits (or 2 bytes), a word has 32 bits (or 4 bytes), and a double-word is equal to 64 bits (or 8 bytes), as shown in Figure 2-1. The most significant bit (MSB) and the least significant bit (LSB) of a byte are the bit at the left-most and right-most position, respectively. Usually this is also true for half-word, word, and double-word. However, MSB and LSB may be located at some other positions in these units (See big endian and little endian in Chapter 5.2 for details).

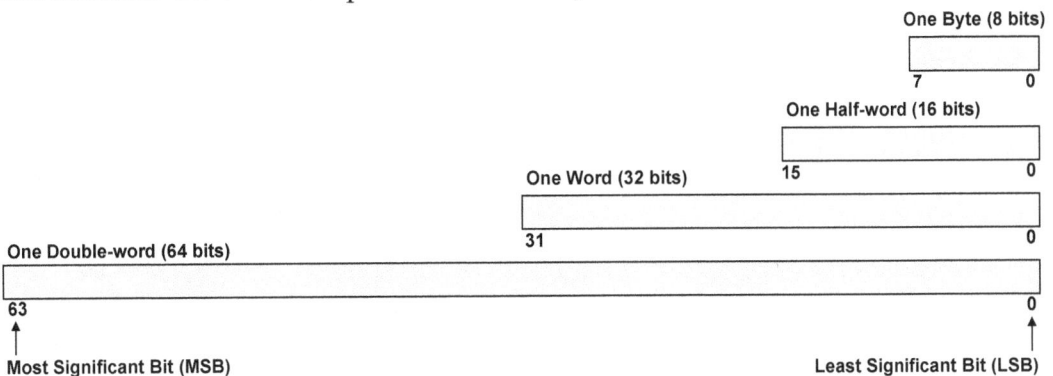

One Byte (8 bits)

7   0

One Half-word (16 bits)

15   0

One Word (32 bits)

31   0

One Double-word (64 bits)

63   0

↑   ↑
Most Significant Bit (MSB)   Least Significant Bit (LSB)

Figure 2-1. Size of a byte, half-word, word, and double-word

Standard C specifies the minimum size of different basic data types. While the actual size of a variable varies by the implementation of C compilers, Table 2-1 gives the typical size of commonly used data bytes. A pointer in C is a special variable that holds the memory address of a variable stored in memory. On a 32-bit processor, a pointer has 32 bits. As introduced previously, each register of the ARM processor has 32 bits. Accordingly, a register can hold a memory address or all the basic data types listed in Table 2-1 except a double data type. Two registers are required to store the value of a double data type.

Basic data type of C language	Typical size in memory
char	1 byte
short	2 bytes or 1 half-word
signed/unsigned integer	4 bytes or 1 word
signed/unsigned long	4 bytes or 1 word
signed/unsigned long long	8 bytes or 1 double word
float	4 bytes or 1 word
double	8 bytes or 1 double word

Table 2-1. Size of C variables in memory

A byte is the smallest unit that can be transferred into or out of memory. Each byte in memory has its own memory address. A half-word, word, and double-word spans 2, 4, and 8 consecutive bytes in memory, respectively. When a variable takes multiple bytes in memory, the lowest memory address of these bytes is used as the memory address of this variable by convention. For example, if a C integer variable takes four bytes in memory (0x20000000 - 0x20000003), the memory address of this integer variable is 0x20000000. To access a bit in memory, the computer has to load at least a byte from the memory and then operate on individual bits.

History of Binary Representation
Modern binary systems were inspired from *"Yi Jing"* (also known as book of changes), one of the oldest classic texts dating back to 2852 - 2738 B.C. It used *Yin* (a broken line, --) and *Yang* (a solid line, —) to represent two contrast but complementary natural phenomena, such as heaven and earth, fire and water, and wind and thunder. It uses a set of eight special symbols (called trigrams): ☷ (000), ☶ (001), ☵ (010), ☴ (011), ☳ (100), ☲ (101), ☱ (110), and ☰ (111). Two trigrams from this set form a hexagram. Therefore, there are 64 possible hexagrams, forming sophisticated tools in analyzing and predicting patterns applicable to all human affairs.

Figure 2-2. Yin Yang Ba Gua.
Courtesy: Image from
wikipedia.org

2.2 Binary, Octal, Decimal, and Hexadecimal Numbers

An integer can be represented with different base values. Four commonly used bases are binary (base 2), octal (base 8), decimal (base 10) and hexadecimal (base 16). In general, an n-digit integer N in the base b has the following form:

$$a_{n-1}a_{n-2}a_{n-3}\cdots a_1 a_0$$

The decimal value is calculated as follows:

$$N = a_{n-1} \times b^{n-1} + a_{n-2} \times b^{n-2} + a_{n-3} \times b^{n-3} + \cdots + a_1 \times b + a_0$$

For example, in the decimal system (base 10), the number 2014_{10} means

$$2014_{10} = 2 \times 10^3 + 0 \times 10^2 + 1 \times 10^1 + 4$$

Similarly, in the octal system (base 8), the number 1375_8 represents

$$1375_8 = 1 \times 8^3 + 3 \times 8^2 + 7 \times 8^1 + 5 = 765_{10}$$

Table 2-2 shows the conversion of a decimal number between 0 and 15 to its equivalent in decimal, binary, octal and hexadecimal (hex for short). Since binary numbers are verbose, programmers often use hex numbers in programs. A binary is converted into its hex equivalent by separating binary bits into a group of four bits and then using Table 2-2 to substitute each four digits with their corresponding hex digit.

Decimal	Binary	Octal	Hexadecimal
0	0000	00	0x0
1	0001	01	0x1
2	0010	02	0x2
3	0011	03	0x3
4	0100	04	0x4
5	0101	05	0x5
6	0110	06	0x6
7	0111	07	0x7
8	1000	010	0x8
9	1001	011	0x9
10	1010	012	0xA
11	1011	013	0xB
12	1100	014	0xC
13	1101	015	0xD
14	1110	016	0xE
15	1111	017	0xF

Table 2-2. Conversion between decimal, binary, octal and hexadecimal

In C, a prefix "0" represents octal, and a prefix "0x" or "0X" represents hexadecimal. The following gives examples of using constant numbers in a C program. Most C compilers do not support directly declaring a binary number. However, in this book, a prefix "0b" represents binary.

```
int k;
k = 0xA;      // hex constant, k = 10 in decimal
k = 0XA;      // 0X is the same as 0x
k = -0xA;     // hex constant, k = -10 in decimal
k = 012;      // octal constant, k = 10 in decimal
k = 0b1010;   // binary constant. Most compilers do not support it.
```

2.3 Unsigned Integers

How many different symbols can be represented with n binary bits? Since each bit has two possible values, either one or zero, n bits can represent a total of 2^n different symbols. For example, 5 bits can represent 2^5, *i.e.* 32 symbols, including 0b00000, 0b00001, 0b00010, ..., and 0b11111. In order to use these symbols to represent different numbers, we need to decide the mapping between these symbols onto the numbers to be represented.

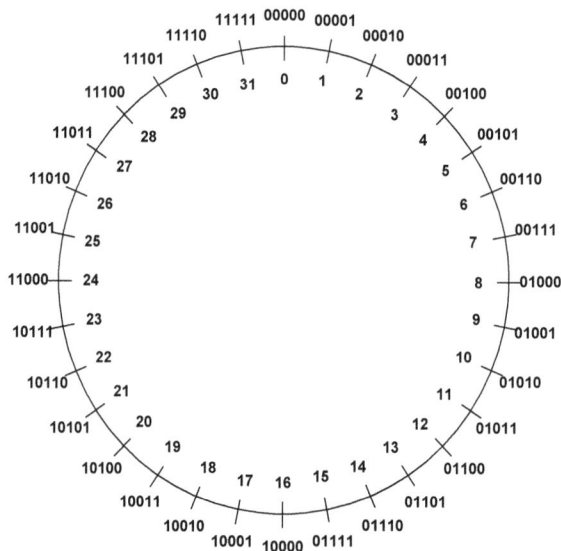

Figure 2-3. Representing unsigned numbers in a five-bit system

Let us first look at unsigned numbers. A natural approach is to use its binary presentation to represent an unsigned integer. Figure 2-3 shows the mapping between unsigned numbers and all binary symbols in a five-bit system. In general, an n-bit string can represent any unsigned number in the range $[0, 2^n - 1]$, including zero and $2^n - 1$ positive numbers.

Converting a binary number to an unsigned integer

Since binary numbers have a base of 2, the conversion from binary to unsigned decimal is the same as the one presented in Chapter 2.2. The equivalent unsigned decimal integer of a binary number is the sum of the product between each binary digit and the power of 2 this binary bit represents. The exponent of each power is incremented by 1 for each binary digit, starting from the right-most digit. For example, the binary value 0b1011 represents:

$$1011_2 = 1 \times 2^3 + 0 \times 2^2 + 1 \times 2^1 + 1 \times 2^0$$
$$= 8 + 2 + 1$$
$$= 11$$

Converting an unsigned integer to a binary number

An unsigned decimal can be converted to its binary equivalent by repeatedly dividing the decimal number by 2 until the quotient becomes zero. The binary equivalent is the combination of all remainders, with the first remainder as the least-significant bit (LSB). For example, the binary of 52 and 32 are 0b110100 and 0b100000 respectively, as shown below.

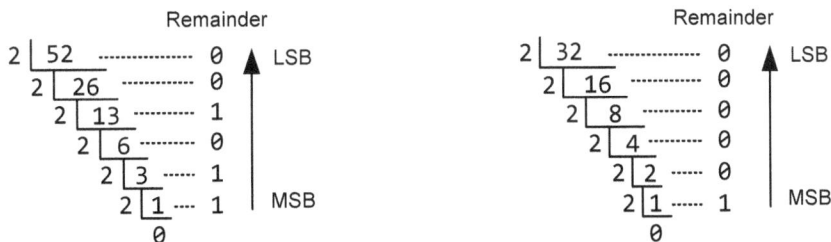

Figure 2-4. Converting a decimal number to binary by repeatedly dividing it by 2. Read the binary from the bottom to the top (52_{10} = 110100_2, and 32_{10} = 100000_2).

2.4 Signed Integers

There are different ways to map binary symbols to signed integer numbers. Examples include sign-and-magnitude, one's complement, and two's complement. One common characteristic of these three numeral systems is that the most significant bit (also called the right most bit) indicates the sign of the number. The most significant bit is also called a sign bit. The number is non-negative if the sign bit is zero and negative if it is one.

Table 2-3 shows three different approaches to map 4-bit binary symbols to different signed integers. These approaches are called sign-and-magnitude, one's complement, and two's complement. While we will present these three different representations for signed numbers in detail later, we give a brief summary below.

- Sign-and-magnitude uses the most significant bit to represent the sign and the rest bits to represent the magnitude.
- One's complement represents a negative number by inverting every bit of its positive equivalent.
- Two's complement represents a negative number by adding one to the equivalent one's complement.

Binary Bit String	Sign-and-Magnitude	One's Complement	Two's Complement
0000	+0	+0	0
0001	1	1	1
0010	2	2	2
0011	3	3	3
0100	4	4	4
0101	5	5	5
0110	6	6	6
0111	7	7	7
1000	-0	-7	-8
1001	-1	-6	-7
1010	-2	-5	-6
1011	-3	-4	-5
1100	-4	-3	-4
1101	-5	-2	-3
1110	-6	-1	-2
1111	-7	-0	-1

Table 2-3. Decimal values represented by a four-bit binary string

Based on Table 2-3, we make the following summary if the bit string has n bits. The range means the largest and the smallest vales that these bit strings can represent.

	Sign-and-Magnitude	One's Complement	Two's Complement
Range	$[-2^{n-1} + 1, 2^{n-1} - 1]$	$[-2^{n-1} + 1, 2^{n-1} - 1]$	$[-2^{n-1}, 2^{n-1} - 1]$
Zero	Two zeroes (± 0)	Two zeroes (± 0)	One zero
Unique Numbers	$2^n - 1$	$2^n - 1$	2^n

Table 2-4. Data range of three different representation methods

In C, the range that a signed integer variable can represent depends on its data type. An integer variable of "signed char," "signed short," "signed int," and "signed long long" has at least 8, 16, 32, and 64 bits in size, respectively.

Two's complement is the one used in almost all modern computers to represent signed integers because it simplifies the hardware design from two aspects: (1) the hardware for two's complement subtraction is the same as two's complement addition, and (2) the hardware implementation for addition, subtraction, and multiplication of signed numbers are identical to those for unsigned numbers.

2.4.1 Sign-and-Magnitude

The sign-and-magnitude is a simple way to represent signed integers. It uses the most significant bit to indicate the sign, with one being negative and zero being positive. The rest n-1 bits represent the value.

Sign-and-Magnitude

$$value = (-1)^{sign} \times Magnitude$$

For example, in a five-bit system, as shown in Figure 2-5, 0b10111 is -7, and 0b00111 is 7. There are two ways to represent zero: 0b00000 for +0 and 0b10000 for -0.

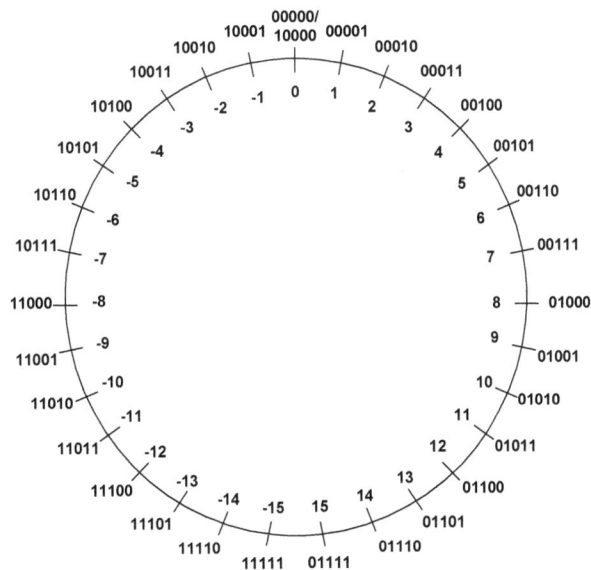

Figure 2-5. Sign-and-magnitude representation in a five-bit system

The sign-and-magnitude representation is not used in many computer systems because of two major shortcomings.

- First, it is difficult for the hardware to perform addition or subtraction since the signs of both operands have to be specially considered in order to obtain correct results. If we add two numbers in a straightforward way, such as 00011 (3) + 11011 (-3), we get a wrong result, 11110 (-14).
- Second, there are two representations of zero: positive zero and negative zero. This complicates the circuit for checking numbers for equality or requires programmers to pay special attention.

2.4.2   One's Complement

The one's complement representation of a negative binary number is the bitwise NOT of its positive counterpart. For example, in a five-bit system, the one's complement of 0b00001(+1) is 0b11110(-1), as shown in Figure 2-6. Arithmetically, in an n-bit system, if the one's complement of a binary α is denoted as $\tilde{\alpha}$, we have:

> One's Complement ($\tilde{\alpha}$):
>
> $$\alpha + \tilde{\alpha} = 2^n - 1$$

$$\tilde{\alpha} = 2^n - 1 - \alpha.$$

The word "complement" means that two counterparts complete the whole. Specifically, the one's complement representation of a positive number and its negative counterpart adds to 2^n-1. For example, adding 0b00001(+1) and 0b11110(-1) leads to 0b11111, which is in fact negative zero.

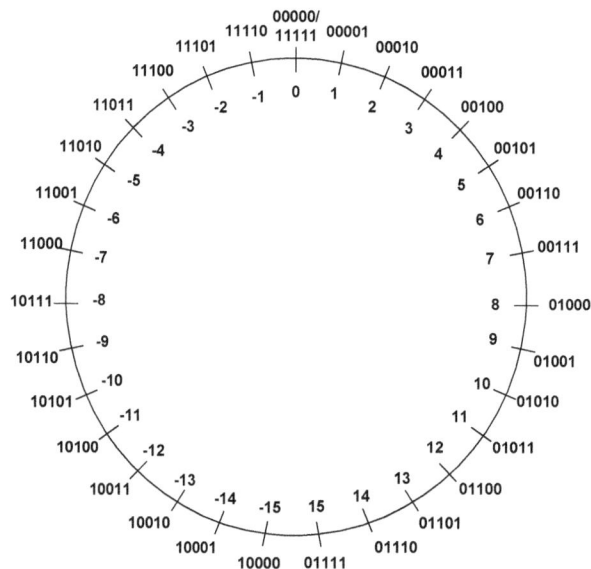

Figure 2-6. One's complement representation in a five-bit system

A simple way to find the one's complement of α is to toggle every bit of α. In C, the bitwise NOT operator (~) is also called the one's complement operator.

```
y = ~y;    // Take one's complement in a C program
```

One's complement was used in processors such as CDC Cyber 18 in the 1980s. However, it is seldom used in modern computer systems.

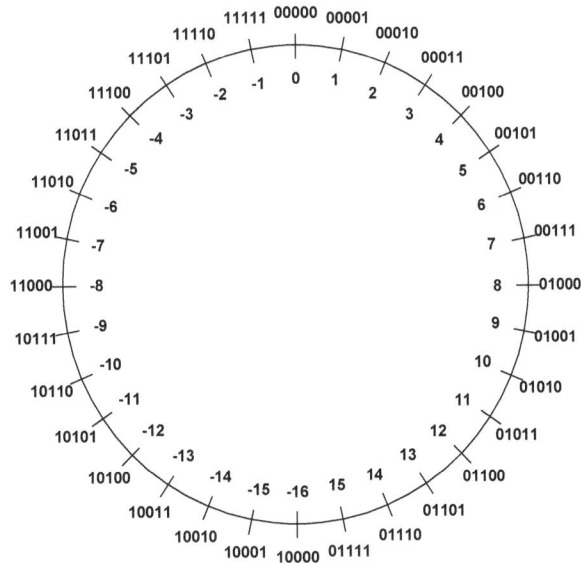

Figure 2-7. Two's complement representation in a five-bit system

2.4.3   Two's Complement

The two's complement (TC) representation of a negative number can be obtained by the bitwise NOT of its positive counterpart plus one. In two's complement representation, there is only one representation of zero, such as 0b00000 in a five-bit system, as shown in Figure 2-7.

> *Two's Complement*
>
> $$\alpha + \bar{\alpha} = 2^n$$

Arithmetically, in an n-bit system, if the two's complement of a binary α is denoted as $\bar{\alpha}$, we have $\bar{\alpha} = \tilde{\alpha} + 1 = 2^n - \alpha$. A simple way to find the two's complement of a binary α is to first toggle every bit and then add 1. In C, it can be implemented as follows:

```
y = ~y;    // Take one's complement
y += 1;    // Find two's complement
```

For example, the two's complement of 0b00011 is 0b11101, and the calculation is as follows:

	Binary	Decimal
Original number	0b00011	3
Step 1: Invert every bit	0b11100	
Step 2: Add 1	+ 0b00001	
Two's complement	0b11101	-3

Similarly, we can find the two's complement of 0b11101 is 0b00011.

	Binary	Decimal
Original number	0b11101	-3
Step 1: Invert every bit	0b00010	
Step 2: Add 1	+ 0b00001	
Two's complement	0b00011	3

2.4.3.1   *Carry Flag for Unsigned Addition or Subtraction*

Cortex-M3 processors automatically maintain a status hardware register that holds a collection of flag bits, particularly including a carry flag (C), an overflow flag (V), a zero flag (Z) and a negative flag (N), indicating the information of the result of data processing operations, such as arithmetic instructions and logical instructions. Each flag is stored as one bit in the status register.

Application programs rely on these flags bits to evaluate whether any abnormal phenomena occurs during an arithmetic operation. Cortex-M3 processors also rely on these flags to implement branch instructions. For example, the following if-else statement will check N, V, C and Z flag bits to decide whether "$c = a - b$" or "$c = b - a$" should be executed. Chapter 6.1 gives a detailed description of how these flag bits are used to implement conditional branch instructions.

```
if ( a > b ) {
    c = a - b;
} else {
    c = b - a;
}
```

Example 2-1. Depending on whether *a* and *b* are signed or unsigned, different assembly instructions are used to implement the if-else statement.

In the following, we will focus only on how a processor sets up the carry flag and the overflow flag when adding and subtracting numbers. The carry flag is for arithmetic and logic operations on unsigned numbers, and the overflow flag is for arithmetic operations on signed numbers. Let us first review simple addition and subtraction on numbers with only one bit. The carry flag and the borrow flag are set as shown in Table 2-5.

Addition	Subtraction
0 + 0 = 0, Carry = 0	0 - 0 = 0, Borrow = 0
1 + 0 = 1, Carry = 0	1 - 0 = 1, Borrow = 0
0 + 1 = 1, Carry = 0	0 - 1 = 1, Borrow = 1
1 + 1 = 0, Carry = 1	1 - 1 = 0, Borrow = 0

Table 2-5. Settings of carry and borrow on binary addition and subtraction

When adding two unsigned numbers in an n-bit system, a carry occurs if the result is larger than the maximum unsigned integer that can be represented (*i.e.* $2^n - 1$). When two unsigned numbers are subtracted, borrow occurs if the result is negative, smaller than the smallest unsigned integer that can be represented (*i.e.* 0).

While an addition generates a carry flag, a subtraction generates a borrow flag. On ARM Cortex-M3 processors, the carry flag and the borrow flag are physically the same flag bit in the status register, thus the borrow flag is in fact called the carry flag.

> *For an unsigned subtraction, Carry = NOT Borrow*

On Cortex-M3, the carry/borrow flag is set as follows:

- When adding two unsigned integers, the carry flag is set to 1 if a carry occurs, *i.e.* the result is too large (greater than or equal to 2^{32} in 32-bit processors); otherwise, the carry flag is reset to 0.
- When subtracting two unsigned integers, the carry bit is set to 1 if no borrow occurs, implying the result is positive or zero. On the contrary, the carry bit is cleared when the result is negative.

Figure 2-8 and Figure 2-9 show two examples of finding the value of the carry flag. The result of addition and subtraction can be obtained by traversing the number circle clockwise and counter-clockwise, respectively. The following rule is used to set the carry flag.

> *If the traverse crosses the boundary between 0 and $2^n - 1$, the carry flag is set on addition and is cleared on subtraction.*

Example: 28 + 6

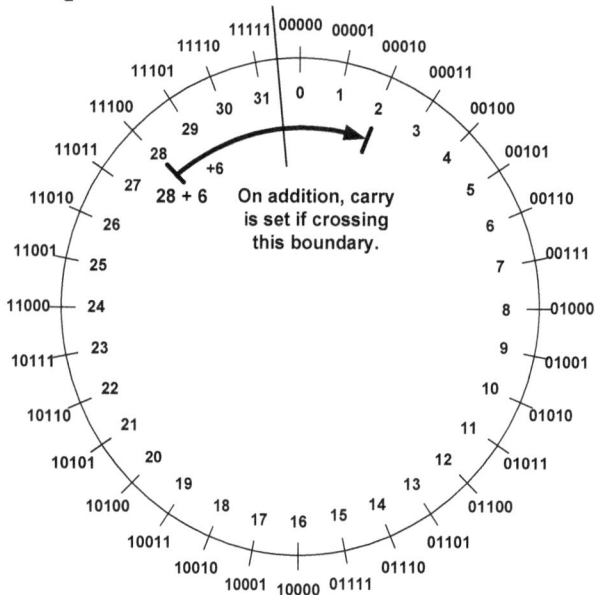

Figure 2-8. Carry flag is set if the result of an unsigned addition is larger than 2^5 - 1.

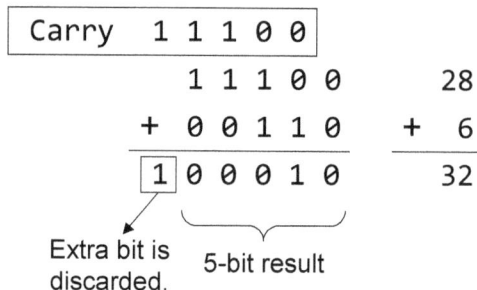

```
Carry   1 1 1 0 0

          1 1 1 0 0        28
      +   0 0 1 1 0      +  6
      ┌─┐ ─────────      ────
      │1│ 0 0 0 1 0        32
      └─┘
```

Extra bit is discarded.   5-bit result

- Carry flag = 1, indicating carry has occurred on unsigned addition.
- The carry flag is 1 because the result crosses the 31-0 boundary

Example: 3 – 5

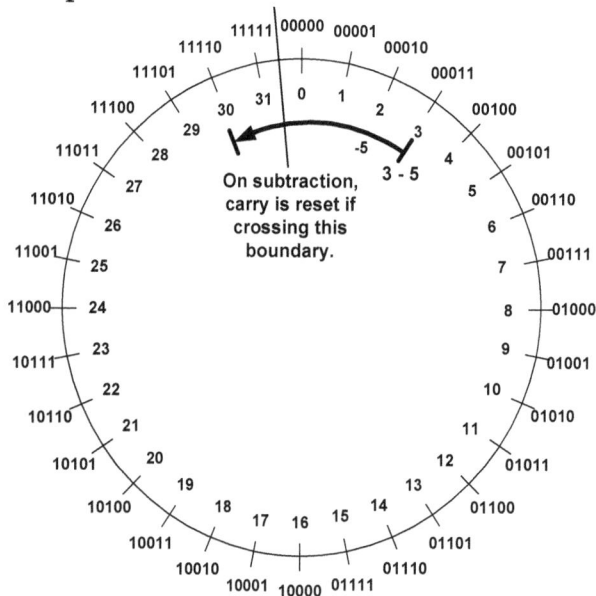

Figure 2-9. Carry flag is cleared if the result of an unsigned subtraction should be negative.

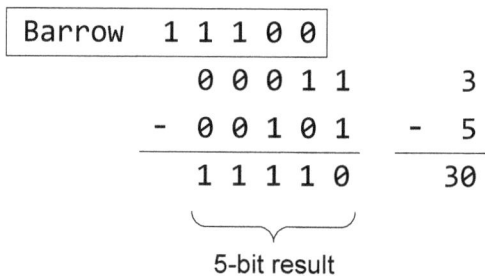

```
Barrow   1 1 1 0 0

           0 0 0 1 1         3
       -   0 0 1 0 1      -  5
           ─────────      ────
           1 1 1 1 0        30
```

5-bit result

- Carry flag = 0, indicating borrow has occurred on unsigned subtraction.
- For subtraction, carry = NOT borrow.

2.4.4   Overflow Flag for Signed Addition or Subtraction

While the carry flag is for unsigned arithmetic operations, the overflow flag is for signed arithmetic operations. Overflow occurs when the result produced by an arithmetic operation falls outside the representable range $[-2^{n-1}, 2^{n-1} - 1]$ of two's complement.

- When adding signed numbers represented in two's complement, overflow occurs only in two scenarios: (1) adding two positive numbers but getting a non-positive result, or (2) adding two negative numbers but yielding a non-negative result.
- Similarly, when subtracting signed numbers, overflow occurs in two scenarios: (1) subtracting a positive number from a negative number but getting a positive result, or (2) subtracting a negative number from a positive number but producing a negative result.
- Overflow cannot occur when adding operands with different signs or when subtracting operands with the same signs.

Detection of overflow on addition can be achieved by checking sign bits. When the signs of the operands of an addition are the same but the sign of the result is different, overflow has occurred. We can use the number circle to illustrate the concept. On the number circle, if the boundary between -2^{n-1} and $2^{n-1} - 1$ is crossed on addition, the overflow flag is set, as shown in Figure 2-10 and Figure 2-11.

Example: 12 + 5

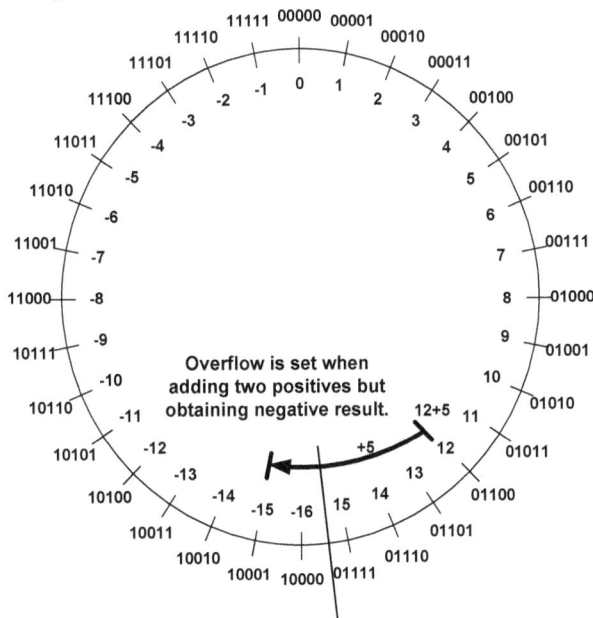

```
  0 1 1 0 0        12
+ 0 0 1 0 1      +  5
-----------      -----
  1 0 0 0 1       -15
```

5-bit result

- On addition, overflow occurs if $sum \geq 2^4$ when adding two positives.
- On addition, overflow never occurs when adding two numbers with different signs.

Figure 2-10. Overflow example

Example: (–13) + (–7)

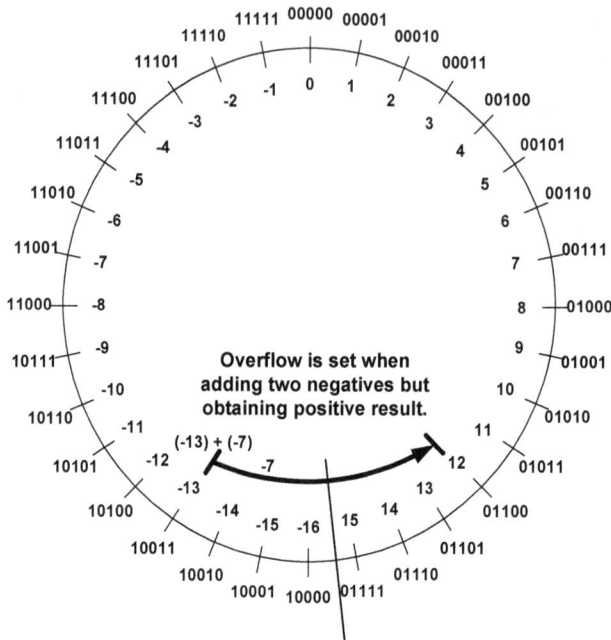

$$\begin{array}{rr} 1\ 0\ 0\ 1\ 1 & -13 \\ +\ \ 1\ 1\ 0\ 0\ 1 & +\ -7 \\ \hline \boxed{1}\ 0\ 1\ 1\ 0\ 0 & 12 \end{array}$$

Extra bit is discarded.   5-bit result

- On addition, overflow occurs if $sum < -2^4$ when adding two negatives.

Figure 2-11. Overflow example

Detecting overflow on subtraction can be converted to detecting overflow of an addition when two's complement representation is used. A subtraction can be converted into an addition. Algebraically, we have

$$A - B = A + (-B)$$
$$= A + TC(B)$$

where *TC(B)* is the two's complement of *B*. As a result, instead of performing subtraction, we add the negation of *B* to *A*. Therefore, the overflow flag of the original subtraction is set or unset based on the addition result. When adding a negative number, the number circle is traversed counter-clockwise.

Subtraction example: 0b10111 - 0b00110, *i.e.* -9-6

In a five-bit two's complement system, we have 0b10111 = -9 and 0b00110 = 6. The two's complement of -6 is invert(0b00110) + 0b00001 = 0b11010.

$$-9 - 6 = -9 + (-6) = 0b10111 + 0b11010 = 0b10001$$

The hardware adder produces 0b10001, which equals -15 in two's complement, as shown in Figure 2-12. This shows that a signed subtraction can be successfully converted to a signed addition by taking the two's complement of the second source operand. When adding 0b10111 and 0b11010, no overflow has occurred. Therefore, the overflow flag for the signed subtraction `0b10111` - `0b00110` is 0.

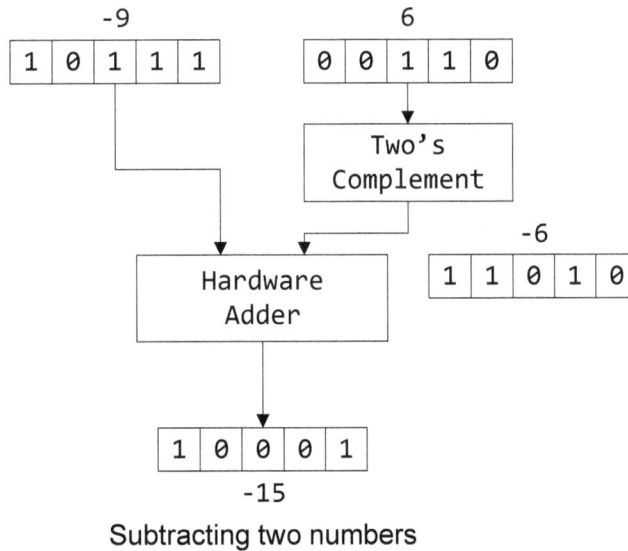

Subtracting two numbers

Figure 2-12. Signed subtraction can be converted to signed addition. No overflow occurs on addition in this example. Therefore, the overflow flag of the signed subtraction is 0.

Besides using the number circle to identify the overflow flag status, here is another method: *Overflow occurs on signed addition if the carry into the sign bit differs from the carry out of the sign bit*. Otherwise, there is no overflow.

Example: 12 + 5

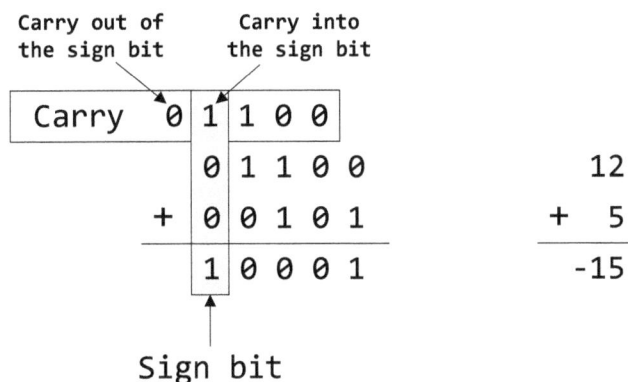

When adding 12 and 5, the carry into the sign bit is 1 but the carry out of the sign bit is 0. Thus an overflow has occurred.

Example: $(-13) + (-7)$

```
       Carry out of        Carry into
       the sign bit        the sign bit
                  ╲              ╱
        ┌───────────────────────────┐
        │ Carry  1 │0│0 1 1          │
        └───────────────────────────┘
                    1 0 0 1 1              -13
                +   1 1 0 0 1           +  -7
                  ─────────────          ──────
                    0 1 1 0 0              12
                        ↑
                    Sign bit
```

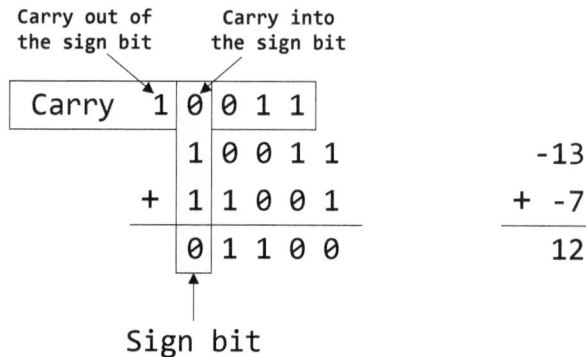

When adding -13 and -7, the carry into the sign bit is 0 but the carry out of the sign bit is 1. Thus an overflow has occurred.

2.4.4.1 Interpreting the Carry and Overflow Flags

Suppose in a five-bit system, the binary values of two variables are set as follows:

$$a = 0b10000$$

$$b = 0b10000$$

> *Is 0xFFFFFFFF a signed or unsigned number? A processor does not know it at all.*

When adding these two numbers in an assembly program, should these two binary values represent signed or unsigned integers?

- If a and b are unsigned integers, we have:
    $a = 16,$
    $b = 16,$ and
    $a + b = 32 > 2^5 - 1.$
  Thus carry has occurred if a and b are unsigned integers.

- If a and b are signed integers, we have:
    $a = -16,$
    $b = -16,$ and
    $a + b = -32 < -2^4.$
  Thus overflow has occurred if a and b are signed integers.

Should the processor set up the carry flag or the overflow flag when a and b are added?

In fact, when adding these two numbers in an assembly program, the processor does not know whether a and b are signed or unsigned integers. Thus, the processor simply sets both the overflow flag and the carry flag. It is the assembly programmer's responsibility to interpret the flag results. Programmers should appropriately choose to check either the overflow flag or the carry flag in assembly instructions, depending on the programmer's intention of using them as signed or unsigned integers. For example, in order to evaluate the logical expression $a + b > 10$, we should use different assembly instructions to

> *A processor sets up both the carry flag and overflow flag.*

check either the carry or overflow flag depending on whether a and b are unsigned or signed integers (Chapter 6.1).

	Carry Flag	Overflow Flag
Sign or unsigned $c = a + b$ $c = a - b$	Unsigned arithmetic, assuming a, b, and c are all unsigned numbers	Signed arithmetic, assuming two's complement is used to represent a, b and c
Addition $c = a + b$	**Method 1**: Carry = 1 if true result > 2^n-1. **Method 2**: Both a and b are unsigned. Carry is set if $c < a$ or $c < b$.	**Method 1**: Overflow = 1 if true result > 2^{n-1}-1 or true result < -2^{n-1}. **Method 2**: Overflow = 1 if • $a > 0$ and $b > 0$ but $c < 0$ • $a < 0$ and $b < 0$ but $c > 0$
Subtraction $c = a - b$	Carry = Not Borrow. Carry is set if $a \geq b$. (meaning no borrow)	**Method 1**: Subtraction is transformed to addition. Overflow is set based on addition. **Method 2**: Overflow = 1 if • $a > 0$ and $b < 0$ but $c < 0$ • $a < 0$ and $b > 0$ but $c > 0$
Correctness	If carry is 1 on unsigned addition, the result is incorrect; otherwise, the result is correct. If carry is 1 on unsigned subtraction, the result is correct; otherwise, the result is incorrect.	Overflow flag has the same meaning for signed addition and signed subtraction. If overflow is 1, the result is incorrect.
Shift operations	Shift operations can change the carry flag.	Shift operations cannot change the overflow flag.

Table 2-6. Summary of the carry flag and the overflow flag

When interpreting the carry flag and overflow flag, be careful that they have different meanings. If the carry flag is set, it means the result is incorrect for addition but correct subtraction. If the overflow is set, it means the result is incorrect for both addition and subtraction. Table 2-6 summarizes the carry flag and the overflow flag for unsigned and signed addition/subtraction.

In C, variables *a* and *b* are declared explicitly either signed or unsigned by the programmer, such as "unsigned int a" or "int a", and thus the corresponding assembly program translated from the C program can correctly choose either the carry flag or the overflow flag to interpret the result.

Example: Translating C statement "if (a > b)" into assembly
An *if*-statement in C will be translated into a set of assembly instructions involving comparison and conditional branch. When translating "if (a > b)", C compilers have to choose appropriate branch instructions by considering whether the logic expression compares two signed numbers or two unsigned numbers. When performing comparison, the processor does not know whether they are signed or unsigned. Therefore, the processor hardware will write a value to the carry flag by assuming they are unsigned and simultaneously write a value to the overflow flag by assuming they are signed. The software has to choose the appropriate instructions to evaluate the carry flag or the overflow flag, according to the following rules. (Explanation that is more detailed is given in Chapter 6.2.)

- If variables *a* and *b* are declared as unsigned in C, the compiler uses the HI condition suffix on the branch instruction, which checks the carry flag.
- On the other hand, if they are declared as signed in C, the compiler uses the GT suffix on the branch instruction, which checks the overflow flag.

Although an if-statement is correctly translated into assembly, most C compilers ignore the occurrence of overflow and carry when an integer result falling out of the representable range is stored during data operations. In Example 2-2, the leading bytes of variable *i* are truncated but the compiler might not generate any error message to abort compiling. This often leads to an unexpected or erroneous result and behavior. Failing to consider overflow and carry is a software bug often made by programmers.

```
signed int i = 0x89ABCDEF;   // 32-bit signed integer
signed short s = i;          // overflow, s=0xCDEF, i is truncated
signed char c = i;           // overflow, c=0xEF, i is truncated
...
```
Example 2-2. Overflow and carry are ignored in C.

2.4.4.2 Two's Complement Simplifies Hardware Implementation

Two's complement simplifies the logic implementation of arithmetic functions. Binary data to be processed may be signed or unsigned integers. If two's complement is used to represent signed numbers, the hardware implementation becomes simple. The hardware does not need to worry about whether these numbers are signed or unsigned, performs exactly the same addition, subtraction, or multiplication, and still obtains the correct result.

Two's complement addition

The hardware adder designed for adding two unsigned numbers also works correctly for adding two signed numbers. For example, if two binary numbers, 0b10111 and 0b00110, are added in a five-bit system, the hardware adder performs a simple addition by treating them as unsigned numbers, such as the ones shown in Figure 2-13. We obtain the sum as 0b11101.

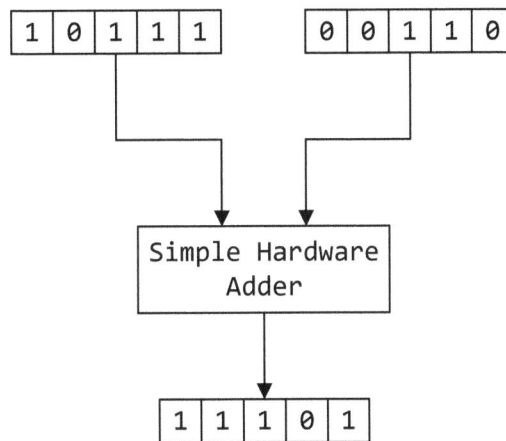

Figure 2-13. A simple adder works for both unsigned addition and signed addition.

In fact, the binary number 0b11101 equals 29 if it is an unsigned number, and -3 if it represents a signed number in two's complement. This implies that a simple adder, which does not distinguish the sign of operands, can obtain the correct result. Therefore, the same hardware adder works correctly for both signed addition and unsigned addition.

```
  Simple Addition      Unsigned    Signed
   (ignore sign)       Addition    Addition
   1  0  1  1  1           23         -9        addend
+  0  0  1  1  0        +   6      +   6      + addend
   ─────────────        ──────     ──────      ────────
   1  1  1  0  1           29         -3           sum
```

Proposition 1. Suppose X and Y are two unsigned integers that two n-bit strings represent, and x and y are two signed integers that these bit strings represent in two's complement. Prove the following:

$$X + Y = x + y \quad \text{(modulo } 2^n\text{)}.$$

Proof. We give the proof in four cases.

1. If $x \geq 0$ and $y \geq 0$, apparently $X + Y = x + y$ (modulo 2^n);
2. If $x < 0$ and $y \geq 0$, then $X + Y = (2^n + x) + y = x + y$ (modulo 2^n);
3. If $x \geq 0$ and $y < 0$, apparently $X + Y = x + (y + 2^n) = x + y$ (modulo 2^n);
4. If $x < 0$ and $y < 0$, apparently $X + Y = (x + 2^n) + (y + 2^n) = x + y$ (modulo 2^n);

Two's complement subtraction

The same subtraction hardware works correctly for both signed subtraction and unsigned subtraction. For example, when we subtract 0b00110 from 0b10111, in a five-bit system, we obtain 0b10001, as shown in Figure 2-14.

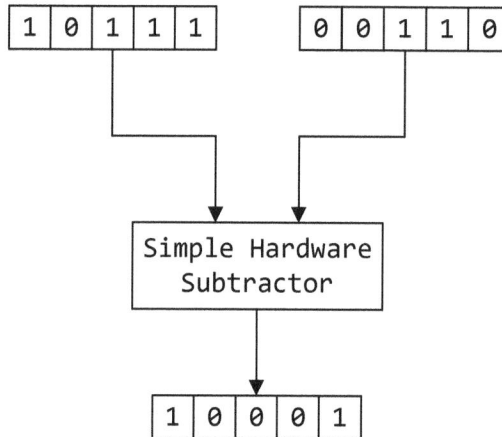

Figure 2-14. A simple subtractor works for both unsigned subtraction and signed subtraction.

The binary result 0b10001 represents 17 if it is unsigned and -15 if it is signed in two's complement. As illustrated below, the simple subtraction hardware can successfully achieve the correct result no matter if the operands are signed or unsigned.

```
Simple Subtraction      Unsigned       Signed
   (ignore sign)       Subtraction   Subtraction
     1 0 1 1 1              23            -9          minuend
  -  0 0 1 1 0         -     6        -     6       - subtrahend
     1 0 0 0 1              17           -15          difference
```

Proposition 2. Suppose X and Y are two unsigned integers that two n-bit strings represent, and x and y are two signed integers that these bit strings represent in two's complement. Prove the following:

$$X - Y = x - y \quad \text{(modulo } 2^n).$$

Proof. We give the proof in four cases.
1. If $x \geq 0$ and $y \geq 0$, apparently $X - Y = x - y$ (modulo 2^n);
2. If $x < 0$ and $y \geq 0$, then $X - Y = (2^n + x) - y = x - y$ (modulo 2^n);
3. If $x \geq 0$ and $y < 0$, apparently $X + Y = x - (y + 2^n) = x - y$ (modulo 2^n);
4. If $x < 0$ and $y < 0$, apparently $X + Y = (x + 2^n) - (y + 2^n) = x - y$ (modulo 2^n);

Two's complement multiplication

If the product is required to keep the same number of bits as operands, unsigned multiplication hardware works correctly for signed numbers. Given two binary numbers: `0b00011` and `0b11101`, the hardware performs a simple multiplication, as shown below. Since the product has to be five bits, the product obtained is `0b10111`, with extra leading bits truncated.

- If both operands are signed, then in two's complement we have two operands as `0b00011` = 3, `0b11101` = -3, and the result as `0b10111` = -9.
- On the other hand, if both operands are unsigned, then we have two operands `0b00011` = 3 and `0b11101` = 29, and the result `0b10111` = 23. While the result is incorrect, it does not mean the hardware has failed. It is only because the result is too large and cannot be fully expressed with 5 bits. In order to avoid this issue, a more complex multiplication instruction should be used to multiply two large numbers, as discussed in Chapter 4.4 (Refer to UMULL and SMULL instructions).

```
            0 0 0 1 1        multiplicand
        ×   1 1 1 0 1      ×   multiplier
        _____   _____
            0 0 0 1 1
          0 0 0 0 0 0
        0 0 0 0 1 1
      0 0 0 0 1 1
    0 0 0 1 1
    _____      _____
    0 0 1 0 1 0 1 1 1          product
```

On many processors, multiplication instructions do not affect the carry and overflow flags. On ARM Cortex-M3, a multiplication instruction leaves the carry flag undefined and the overflow flag unchanged.

Proposition 3. Suppose X and Y are two unsigned integers that two n-bit strings represent, and x and y are two signed integers that these bit strings represent in two's complement. Prove the following:

$$X \bullet Y = x \bullet y \quad (\text{modulo } 2^n).$$

Proof. We give the proof in four cases.

1. If $x \geq 0$ and $y \geq 0$, apparently $X \bullet Y = x \bullet y \quad (\text{modulo } 2^n)$;
2. If $x < 0$ and $y \geq 0$, then $X \bullet Y = (2^n + x) \bullet y = 2^n \bullet y + x \bullet y = x \bullet y \quad (\text{modulo } 2^n)$;
3. If $x \geq 0$ and $y < 0$, apparently $X \bullet Y = x \bullet (y + 2^n) = x \bullet y + 2^n \bullet x = x \bullet y \quad (\text{modulo } 2^n)$;
4. If $x < 0$ and $y < 0$, apparently $X + Y = (x + 2^n) \bullet (y + 2^n) = x \bullet y + 2^n \bullet x + 2^n \bullet y + 2^{n+1} = x \bullet y \quad (\text{modulo } 2^n)$;

Two's complement division

However, signed and unsigned division cannot directly share the same division hardware. For example, we divide -10 (`0b10110` in two's complement) by 2 (`0b00010` in two's complement) by using traditional division technique, the quotient obtained is 11 (`0b01011` in two's complement). Apparently, conventional division for unsigned integers does not work for signed integers.

```
                     0  1  0  1  1      quotient
     divisor    1  0 │1  0  1  1  0      dividend
                     1  0
                        0  1
                        0  0
                           1  1
                           1  0
                              1  0
                              1  0
                              ───────
                                 0      remainder
```

Signed division is more difficult than unsigned division. A general method of signed division is to first convert both signed numbers to positive numbers, then execute unsigned division, and finally change the result into signed form. Therefore, there are two 32-bit integer division instructions in Cortex-M3 processors, one for signed integers, and the other for unsigned integers.

Summary of two's complement arithmetic operations

Two's complement can simplify the hardware design. The same addition, subtraction, and multiplication hardware work for both signed and unsigned integers.

1. When adding or subtracting two integers, the hardware does not know whether they are signed or unsigned. As a result, the hardware will set up both the overflow and carry flags.
    a. The hardware assumes both operands are unsigned and sets the carry flag to the appropriate value.
    b. At the same time, the hardware also assumes both operands are signed, and sets up the overflow flag.

2. It is the software's responsibility to decide whether to use either the carry flag or overflow flag in the assembly code. Whether the carry flag or the overflow flag should be used depends on the programmer's intention.
    a. If the programmer intends to use the binary value stored in a register as an unsigned integer, then the carry flag should be used.
    b. If the programmer intends to use it as a signed integer, then the overflow flag should be used.
    c. When programming in high-level languages such as C, the compiler automatically chooses to use the carry or overflow flag based on how this integer is declared in source code ("int" or "unsigned int").

3. The same multiplication hardware works for both signed and unsigned multiplication if the product obtained has the same length as the operands.

4. The same division hardware cannot work correctly for both signed division and unsigned division.

2.5 Character String

The American Standard Code for Information Interchange (ASCII) defines 7-bit encoding standard for 128 characters, including 33 control characters (0x00-0x19, plus 0x7F) and 95 printable characters (0x20-0x7E). Note 0x20 is the space character, which is a printable character. The first ASCII was published in 1963 and many of its control characters have become obsolete. However, ASCII is still widely used for computers to store a text document and data, such as a C or assembly program code.

Dec	Hex	Char	Dec	Hex	Char	Dec	Hex	Char	Dec	Hex	Char
0	00	NUL	32	20	SP	64	40	@	96	60	`
1	01	SOH	33	21	!	65	41	A	97	61	a
2	02	STX	34	22	"	66	42	B	98	62	b
3	03	ETX	35	23	#	67	43	C	99	63	c
4	04	EOT	36	24	$	68	44	D	100	64	d
5	05	ENQ	37	25	%	69	45	E	101	65	e
6	06	ACK	38	26	&	70	46	F	102	66	f
7	07	BEL	39	27	'	71	47	G	103	67	g
8	08	BS	40	28	(	72	48	H	104	68	h
9	09	HT	41	29	)	73	49	I	105	69	i
10	0A	LF	42	2A	*	74	4A	J	106	6A	j
11	0B	VT	43	2B	+	75	4B	K	107	6B	k
12	0C	FF	44	2C	,	76	4C	L	108	6C	l
13	0D	CR	45	2D	-	77	4D	M	109	6D	m
14	0E	SO	46	2E	.	78	4E	N	110	6E	n
15	0F	SI	47	2F	/	79	4F	O	111	6F	o
16	10	DLE	48	30	0	80	50	P	112	70	p
17	11	DC1	49	31	1	81	51	Q	113	71	q
18	12	DC2	50	32	2	82	52	R	114	72	r
19	13	DC3	51	33	3	83	53	S	115	73	s
20	14	DC4	52	34	4	84	54	T	116	74	t
21	15	NAK	53	35	5	85	55	U	117	75	u
22	16	SYN	54	36	6	86	56	V	118	76	v
23	17	ETB	55	37	7	87	57	W	119	77	w
24	18	CAN	56	38	8	88	58	X	120	78	x
25	19	EM	57	39	9	89	59	Y	121	79	y
26	1A	SUB	58	3A	:	90	5A	Z	122	7A	z
27	1B	ESC	59	3B	;	91	5B	[	123	7B	{
28	1C	FS	60	3C	<	92	5C	\	124	7C		
29	1D	GS	61	3D	=	93	5D	]	125	7D	}
30	1E	RS	62	3E	>	94	5E	^	126	7E	~
31	1F	US	63	3F	?	95	5F	_	127	7F	DEL

Table 2-7. ASCII table

A string consists of an array of ASCII characters, in which the last character is NULL. The ASCII value of the NULL character is 0x00 and it is a reserved character used to signify the termination of a string. Note NULL differs from ZERO. The ASCII value of the ZERO character is 0x30 while the ASCII of the NULL character is 0x00.

When a C program declares a string, the compiler automatically adds a NULL terminator at the end of the string. Each character takes one byte in memory and all characters are stored in consecutive memory addresses. The first character of the string is stored at the lowest memory address. Example 2-3 shows the memory layout of a string "ARM Assembly". The compiler automatically appends a NULL character at the end and thus the string size is 13, including the terminator.

Memory Address	Memory Content	Letter
str + 12 →	0x00	\0
str + 11 →	0x79	y
str + 10 →	0x6C	l
str + 9 →	0x62	b
str + 8 →	0x6D	m
str + 7 →	0x65	e
str + 6 →	0x73	s
str + 5 →	0x73	s
str + 4 →	0x41	A
str + 3 →	0x20	space
str + 2 →	0x4D	M
str + 1 →	0x52	R
str →	0x41	A

```
char str[13] = "ARM Assembly";
// The length has to be at least 13
// even though it has 12 letters. The
// NULL terminator should be included.
```

Example 2-3. All strings are null-terminated. While "ARM Assembly" has 12 characters, the string should be declared with a length of 13 characters to include NULL.

Characters are compared based on their ASCII values. For example, character 'B' is larger than 'A' because ASCII of 'B' is 0x42 and ASCII of 'A' is 0x41. Similarly, we have 'z' > 'a' > 'Z' > 'A' > '9' > '1' > '0' > '!' > ' '.

Strings are compared by alphabetical order. If two strings are of different length, the shorter one is assumed to have one or more NULL (0x00) characters appended to make the length equal. Then the strings are compared by character starting with the first one. When a character in one string is smaller than the corresponding one in the other string, the former string is then smaller than the latter one. For example, we have the following string comparison results:

- "j" < "jar" < "jargon" < "jargonize"
- "CAT" < "Cat" < "DOG" < "Dog" < "cat" < "dog"
- "12" < "123" < "2" < "AB" < "Ab" < "ab" < "abc"

The following code gives a few commonly used string functions written in C language:

isDigit: Test for a decimal digit (0 through 9). If the given character is one of the 10 decimal digits, the function returns 1; otherwise, returns 0. The ASCII values of decimal digits are from 48 to 57, with 48 representing '0' and 57 representing '9'.

C Implementation	Simplified C Implementation
```int isDigit(char c){ if(c >= '0' && c <= '9') return 1; return 0; }```	```int isDigit(char c){ return (c >= '0' && c <= '9'); // or: return (c >= 48 && c <= 57); }```

isLower: Test for a lower-case character (a through z). The ASCII values of lower-case characters are between 97 and 122.

```
int isLower(char c){
    return(c >= 'a' && c <= 'z');      // or: return (c >= 97 && c <= 122);
}
```

isUpper: Test for an upper-case character (A through Z). The ASCII values of upper-case characters are between 65 and 90.

```
int isUpper(char c){
    return(c >= 'A' && c <= 'Z');      // or: return(c >= 65 && c <= 90);
}
```

isWhitespace: Test for a whitespace character, including space (ASCII 32), horizontal tab (ASCII 9), line feed (ASCII 10), and form feed (ASCII 12).

```
int isWhitespace(char c) {
    return(c == ' ' || c == '\t' || c == '\n' || c == '\12');
    // or: return(c == 32 || c == 9 || c == 10 || c == 12);
}
```

strlen: Find the length of a string, excluding the null terminator. It checks all characters of a string array one by one. If the loop reaches the end of the string array, *pStr*[i] has a value of 0, making the while condition false and thus terminating the loop.

```
int strlen (char *pStr){
    int i = 0;
    while( pStr[i] )    // loop until pStr[i] is NULL
        i++;
    return i;
}
```

toUpper: Convert all alphabetic characters in a string to its lower case. The difference between the ASCII value of a lower-case character and its corresponding upper case is 32. The following provides two different implementations, one based on dereferencing a pointer (*i.e.* get the value stored at the pointer address), and the other based on a numeric index.

Pointer dereference operator *	Array subscript operator []
| ```
void toUpper(char *pStr){
  for(char *p = pStr; *p; ++p){
    if(*p >= 'a' && *p <= 'z')
      *p -= 'a' - 'A';
      //or: *p -= 32;
  }
}
``` | ```
void toUpper(char *pStr){
  char c = pStr[0];
  for(int i = 0; c; i++, c = pStr[i];) {
    if(c >= 'a' && c <= 'z')
      pStr[i] -= 'a' - 'A';
      // or: pStr[i] -= 32;
  }
}
``` |

toLower: Convert all alphabetic characters in a string to its upper case. Adding 32 to the ASCII value of a lower-case character converts it to its corresponding upper case. Similar to the toUpper function, the following provides two different implementations.

Pointer dereference operator *	Array subscript operator []
| ```
void toLower(char *pStr){
  for(char *p = pStr; *p; ++p) {
    if(*p >= 'A' && *p <= 'Z')
      *p += 'a' - 'A';
      // or: *p += 32;
  }
}
``` | ```
void toLower(char *pStr){
  int i;
  char c= pStr[0];
  for(i = 0; c; i++, c = pStr[i]) {
    if(c >= 'A' && c <= 'Z')
      pStr[i] += 'a' - 'A';
      // or: pStr[i] += 32;
  }
}
``` |

2.6 Exercises

1. For the six-bit binary values given below, find the equivalent decimal values when the data is interpreted as signed or unsigned integers, respectively.

    010000, 100001, 010111, 111000, 111001,
    001111, 101011, 110110, 101010, 100011

2. Complete the following arithmetic operations in two's complement representation. What are the value of the carry flag and overflow flag? (Assume a six-bit system)
    *   -7 + (-29)
    *   31 + 11
    *   15 – 19
    *   -7 × (-3)
    *   -7 × (3)
    *   21 ÷ 3
    *   21 ÷ (-3)

3. To check for the signed greater or equal (GE) condition, we evaluate whether the negative flag is equal to the overflow flag. If they are equal, then GE condition is true. Explain the reasons why this works.

4. For Cortex-M3, there are separate division instructions for signed integers and unsigned integers. Does the same division instruction work for both signed and unsigned integers? If yes, approve it. If not, show an example.

5. What are the overflow and carry flags of the following operations? (Assume a four-bit system.)

	Carry	Overflow
1101 + 1100		
1101 - 1100		
1100 + 1010		
0100 - 0110		
0100 + 0010		
0100 + 0110		
1100 - 0110		

6. Given the following two 32-bit binary unsigned numbers A and B, find the logic expression of the carry flag when A and B are added. The result is R.

$$A = a_{31}a_{30}a_{29}\cdots a_2a_1a_0$$

$$B = b_{31}b_{30}b_{29}\cdots b_2b_1b_0$$

$$R = r_{31}r_{30}r_{29}\cdots r_2r_1r_0$$

7. Find the logic expression of the carry flag when B is subtracted from A, where A and B have the same format as Question 5.

8. Suppose A and B are signed numbers and they have the same format as Question 5, find the logic expression of the overflow flag when A and B are added.

9. Suppose A and B are signed numbers and they have the same format as Question 5, find the logic expression of the overflow flag when B is subtracted from A.

10. If a string is stored at the memory address 0x20008000 and the string is "Cortex-M3", show the memory content in hex format starting at 0x20008000. How many bytes does this string take in the memory?

11. Write a C program that implements the standard function
                    char * strrchr(const char *str, int c)
    that returns the pointer of the last instance of c in string str. Return a NULL pointer if c is not found in the string.

12. Write a C program that implements the standard function
                    char * strstr(char *str1, char *str2)
    that returns the pointer of the first instance of string $str2$ in string $str1$. Return a NULL pointer if string $str2$ is not found in string $str1$.

CHAPTER 3

ARM Instruction Set Architecture

This chapter gives an overview of ARM assembly instructions and presents basic ARM instruction format.

3.1 ARM Assembly Instruction Sets

ARM processors support mainly four different assembly instruction sets: Thumb, Thumb-2, ARM32, and ARM64. Figure 3-1 shows their history.

- *Thumb*. The objective of the Thumb instruction set is to improve the code density. Since an instruction in Thumb has only 16 bits in length, the size of their executable files is small. The space saving is achieved by reducing the possibilities of operands and limiting the number of registers that are accessible by an instruction. Reducing the size of instruction memory benefits many embedded systems demanding for low cost and long battery life.

- *ARM32*. An instruction in ARM32 has 32 bits and provides more coding flexibility than a Thumb instruction because more operand options, more flexible memory addressing, larger immediate numbers, and more addressable registers can be encoded in a 32-bit word. In addition, ARM32 instructions run faster than Thumb because more operations can be encoded in one instruction. However, the disadvantage is its code density.

- *Thumb-2*. It provides an outstanding compromise between ARM32 and Thumb. It optimizes the tradeoff between code density and processor performance. It consists of 16-bit Thumb instructions and a subset of 32-bit ARM32 instructions. The goal of Thumb-2 is to achieve high code density similar to Thumb and fast processor performance comparable to ARM32.

- *ARM64*. Recently 64-bit ARM processors are released to support desktops and servers. These processors support a set of 64-bit assembly instructions.

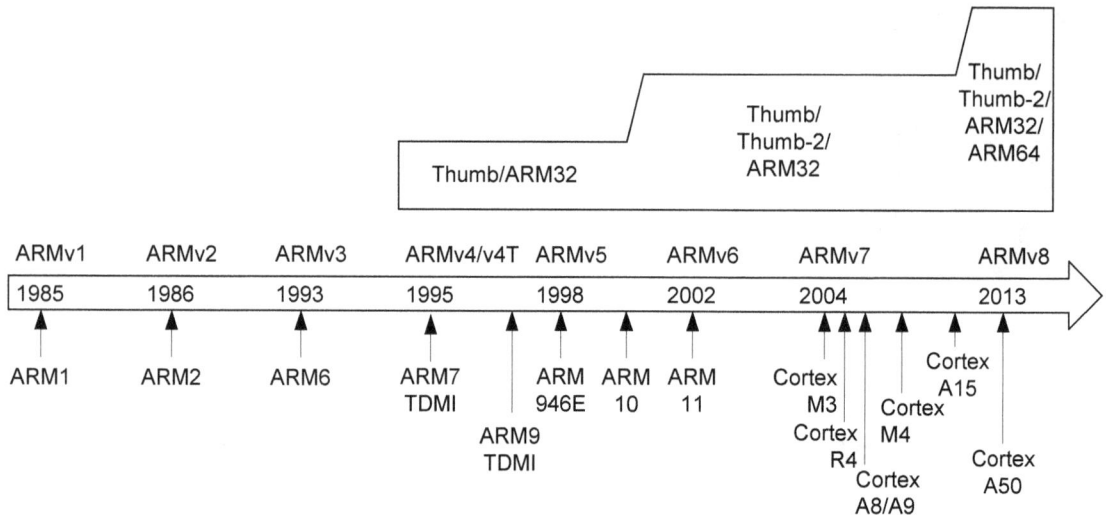

Figure 3-1. History of ARM architecture and instruction sets

One important ARM family is Cortex processors, which have three groups: Cortex-M series for microcontrollers (M stands for microcontroller), Cortex-R series for real-time embedded systems (R stands for real-time), and Cortex-A series for high-performance application processors (A stands for application).

The Cortex-M family includes Cortex-M0, Cortex-M1, Cortex-M3, and Cortex-M4. The first two are Von Neumann architecture and the latter two are Harvard architecture. Cortex-M4 supports more instructions than Cortex-M3, while Cortex-M3 supports more than Cortex-M0 and Cortex-M1. However, these processors are backward compatible. For example, a binary program of Cortex M3 can be executed on Cortex-M4 without any modification.

This book focuses on Cortex-M3 processors, which are the ARMv7-M architecture. Cortex-M3 only supports the Thumb-2 instruction set and does not support ARM32. Cortex-M3 processors are low cost and energy efficient, and they are used in a wide range of devices, such as wireless sensor network, automotive systems, motor control, and input devices for human-computer interaction. Conventional ARM processors are required to switch to the Thumb state to execute a 16-bit

Thumb-2 optimizes the tradeoff between code density and application speed.

instruction and to the ARM state to execute a 32-bit instruction. Cortex-M3 processors can execute a mix of 16-bit Thumb2 instructions and 32-bit Thumb2 instructions without changing the processor state, thus eliminating the overhead of state switching.

3.2 ARM Cortex-M3 Organization

An ARM Cortex-M3 processor chip consists of a Cortex-M3 core licensed by ARM, on-chip peripheral devices implemented by chip manufacturers, and buses and bridges for the communication between the core and peripheral devices. Examples of peripheral devices integrated into a Cortex-M3 chip are LCD hardware driver, serial communication (I²C, SPI, and USART), USB, digital-to-analog converter (DAC), and analog-to-digital converter (ADC). Different manufacturers may add various peripheral devices to the chip.

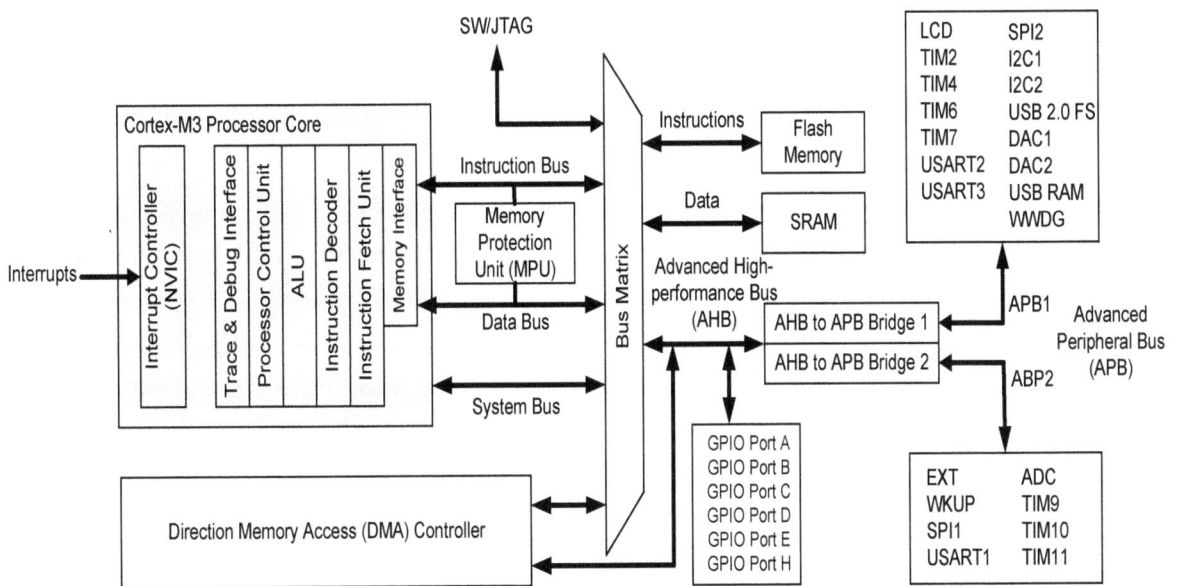

Figure 3-2. Organization of STM32L ARM Cortex-M3 processor

Figure 3-2 shows the core and peripheral devices integrated into the STM32L Cortex-M3 chip.

- The core processor communicates with the flash memory (used as instruction memory), SRAM (used as data memory), Direct Memory Access (DMA) controller, and general-purpose input/output (GPIO) ports via a bus matrix (also called crossbar switch).
- The bus matrix allows concurrent data streams between devices connected to the bus matrix, thus providing a high communication bandwidth.
- Peripheral devices are connected to the bus matrix via bus bridges linking the advanced high-performance bus (AHB) and the advanced peripheral bus (APB).

Generally, AHB is for high-bandwidth communication, and APB is for low-bandwidth communication.

- GPIO pins can be configured by software based on the application needs. It can be used in a simple way as digital input or output, or in an advanced way as analog-to-digital converter, serial communication, timer functions, and so on. Note different SoC chips may have different GPIO functions, depending on the chip manufacturers.

A bus is a set of physical wires that are shared between two or more hardware components for transferring data or control signals. A communication protocol or agreement must be in place to coordinate the usage of a bus. The bandwidth of a bus is mainly determined by the width of the bus (usually specified in bits) and the clock speed supported. Various buses exist within the chip to communicate internal and external hardware components. A bus bridge can connect two similar or dissimilar buses together.

Fundamental components of a Cortex-M3 processor core include the arithmetic logic unit (ALU), the processor control unit, the interrupt controller (NVIC), the instruction fetching and decoding unit, and the interfaces for memory and debug.

- ALU carries out logical (such as logic AND), and integer arithmetic operations (such as add). ALU has two data inputs (called operands) and one data output.
- The processor control unit generates control signals for internal digital circuits (such as selection signal of multiplexer, control signal of the ALU) and coordinates all components of the processor core.
- The interrupt controller (NVIC) allows the processor core to stop the execution of the current task and immediately respond to special events or signals generated by software or by peripheral devices. Detailed introduction to interrupts are given in Chapter 12.
- The instruction fetching and decoding unit reads one machine instruction from the instruction memory pointed by the program counter and decodes the instruction to figure out what operations the processor core should perform. The processor control unit then generates corresponding control signals based on the decoding result. Chapter 13 introduces how to encode and decode an instruction.
- The memory interface supports the access to memory devices (such as SRAM and flash).
- The debug interface allows a programmer to use a host computer to start or stop a software program on a Cortex-M3 processor, and monitor or modify processor registers, peripheral registers and memory in real-time.

3.3 Going from C to Assembly

Before we study the syntax (grammar) and semantics (meaning) of assembly instructions, let us first examine the key differences between C and assembly. C, like many other high-level programming languages, makes strong abstraction of computer hardware in order to hide from programmers the details of how a computation is actually be implemented. High-level languages make the program codes more concise, more portable, and easier to develop and debug. However, the assembly language, a low-level programming language, offers programmers not only almost complete fine-grained control of underlying hardware but also the flexibility of specifying how a computation should be carried out. Hence, it is often that a well-written assembly program is more efficient than its C counterpart is. Besides abstracting a microprocessor at different levels, some assembly instructions have no equivalent implementation in C, as described later in this book.

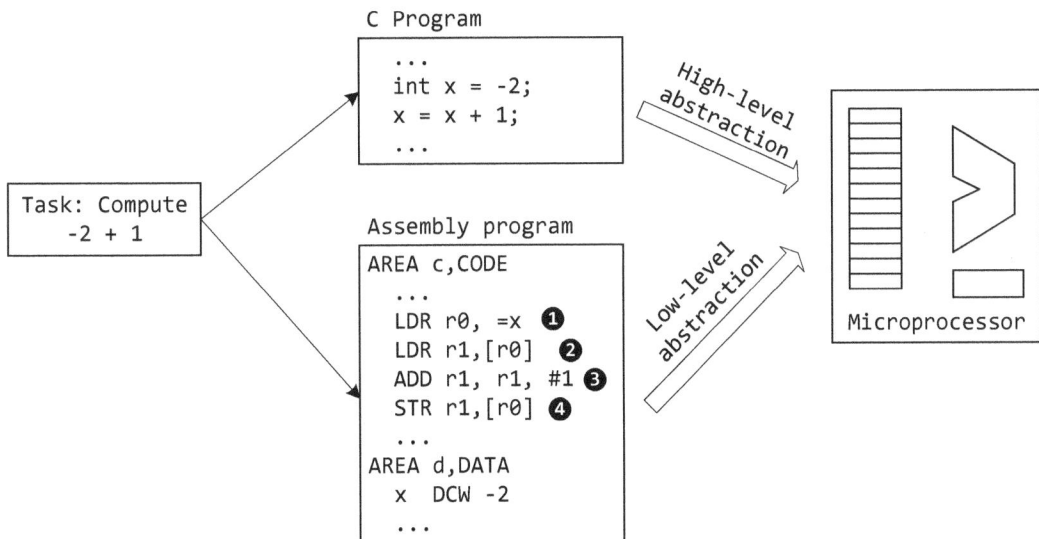

Figure 3-3. Comparison of C and assembly in abstracting microprocessors

 In Figure 3-3, we use a simple example, which computes the sum of two signed integers (1 and -2), to compare the hardware abstraction of C and assembly. We assume variable x is stored in memory. Note a variable may be placed in a register instead of in memory to order to improve the computation speed.

- C abstracts away much detail of complex low-level computing operations. Accordingly, C provides a friendly and convenient programming interface to programmers. Because of strong abstraction, the same C program can be recompiled for two different hardware platforms, as given below:

	Platform 1	Platform 2
Signed integer representation	Two's complement	One's complement
Size of an integer (bits)	32	16
Can operands be immediate number?	No	Yes
Data endian (see Chapter 5.1)	Big endian	Little endian

Table 3-1. A C program can be compiled for two different hardware platforms.

- In contrast, assembly language requires programmers to understand low-level details of the instruction set that this specific microprocessor supports. For example, how many bits does an integer take in memory? What is the data layout of the signed integer x in memory? How are memory locations specified? How is the integer x retrieved from memory? How many operands can an addition can support? How is an overflow or carry handled on an addition?

The instruction set supported by all processors can be classified into three categories:

- **Accumulator-based instruction set**. One of the ALU source operands is implicitly stored in a special register called accumulator and the ALU result is saved into the accumulator. The programmer does not have to specify this operand and the destination register in the program. The accumulator-based instruction set was popular in the 1950s.
- **Stack-based instruction set**. All ALU operands are assumed be on top of the stack and the ALU result is also placed on top of the stack. The stack is a special region of memory. Thus, programmers need to push the value of operands into the stack before an ALU operation is called. The stack-based instruction set was used in the 1960s.
- **Load-store instruction set**. ALU operands can be any generic-purpose registers. Most modern processors are based on a load-store instruction set.

In the load-store instruction set, many arithmetic and logic instructions typically support two source operands that are stored in registers. The second operand of some instructions can also be a constant number, encoded directly in the instruction. Compared with the other two types of instruction sets, the major advantage of load-store instruction set is that it is faster. The accumulator-based instruction set always has to make an extra copy to store one of the source operands in the accumulator. The

> *Load-store instruction set allows effective use of registers.*

performance of a stack-based instruction set is undermined by the performance of memory because ALU has to access the memory repeatedly. However, since there are many general-purpose registers available, the load-store instruction set can take full advantage of temporal locality exhibited in almost all applications, effectively reducing the number of accesses to slow memory.

In a load-store instruction set, data stored in memory cannot be ALU operands directly. Therefore, if we want to change the value of some data stored in memory, we need to perform a sequence of load-modify-store operations:

1. load target data from the memory to a register,
2. change the value of the register, and
3. store the updated value stored in the register back to the memory.

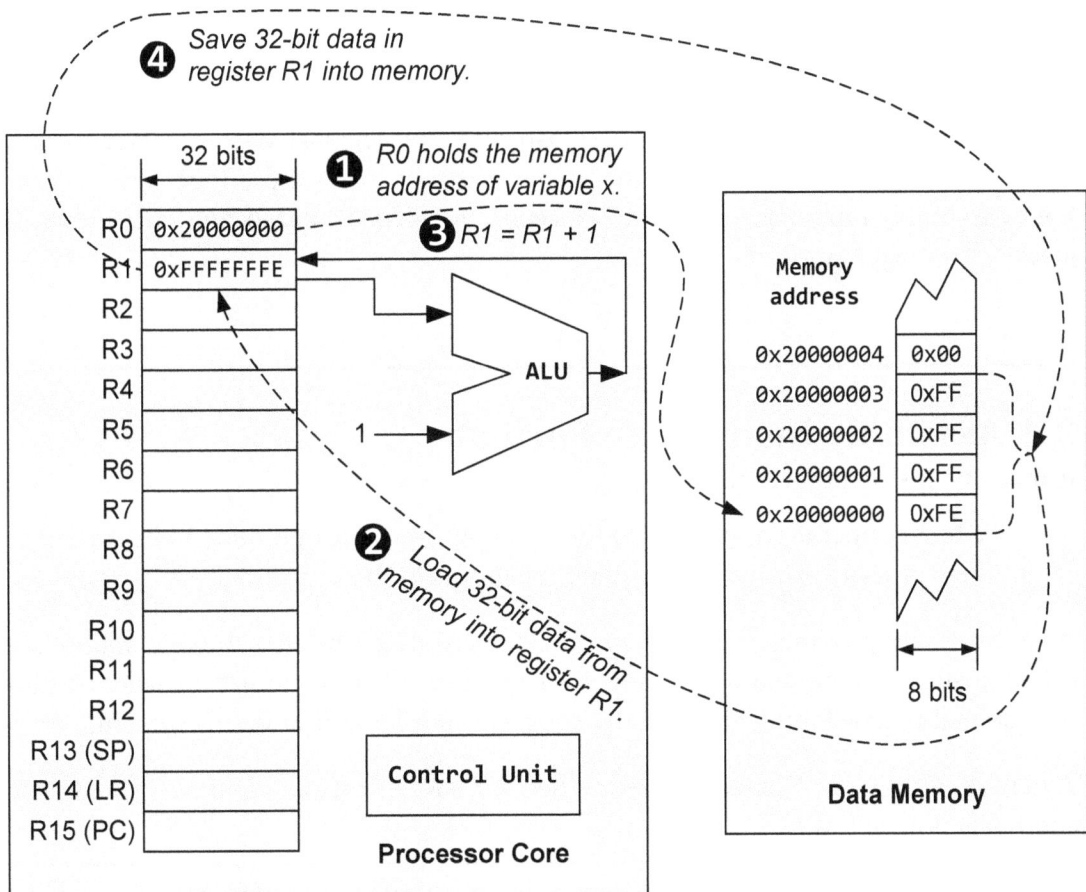

Figure 3-4. A sequence of load-modify-store in assembly equivalent to "x = x + 1;" in C. Note variable *x* has an initial value of -2, *i.e.* 0xFFFFFFFE in two's complement.

As Figure 3-4 shows, in order to increment the value of variable *x* stored in the memory by one, a load-modify-store sequence is carried out in four steps in a sequential order:

1. set up the memory address,
2. load data from memory,
3. perform addition, and
4. store new value back to memory.

While we will examine the detailed syntax of assembly instruction later, we can briefly show the assembly program to illustrate the load-modify-store concept.

```
LDR r1, [r0]      ; Load    (Assuming r0 holds the memory address of x)
ADD r1, r1, #1    ; Modify  (Increase the value of register r1 by 1)
STR r1, [r0]      ; Store   (Save the content of register r1 into memory)
```

Note an integer takes four bytes in memory. The 32-bit two's complement representation of -2 is 0xFFFFFFFE. Assume this number is stored in contiguous memory locations, starting at 0x20000000. The second LDR instruction will load this 32-bit integer into register r0 (LDR stands for load register). The last step is to save the 32-bit result (0xFFFFFFFF, *i.e.* -1) back to the memory region. After these four steps complete, the byte stored at memory location 0x20000003, 0x20000002, 0x20000001 and 0x20000000 is 0xFF, 0xFF, 0xFF, and 0xFF.

3.4 Assembly Instruction Format

A machine instruction consists of:

- a binary operation code (opcode) denoting a specific operation to be carried out
- zero or more operands specifying the inputs of the operation

In an assembly program, each binary opcode is replaced by its symbolic abbreviation, called instruction **mnemonic**. Using human readable mnemonics instead of binary opcode makes developing an assembly program simpler and more convenient.

A generic format of an assembly instruction for ARM RealView and Keil (MDK-ARM) compilers is as follows:

```
label        mnemonic operand1, operand2, operand3    ; comments
```

- The *label* is a reference to the memory address of this instruction. The assembler either replaces the label with the actual numeric memory address or memory address offset when generating the binary executable. The label is optional and must be unique within the same assembly program file. The label should starts at the beginning of a line, without any leading whitespace. The instruction can start a newline, as shown below:

```
label
        mnemonic operand1, operand2, operand3    ; comments
```

- The *mnemonic* represents the operation to be performed.
- The number of *operands* varies, depending on each specific instruction. Some instructions have no operands at all. The comma mark "," is used to separate operands. Some instruction allows constant numbers (also called immediate numbers) as operands.
- Typically, the first operand (operand1) is the *destination register*, and operand2 and operand3 are *source operands*. The second operand (operand2) is usually a register. The last operand (operand3) may be a register, an immediate number, a register shifted to a constant amount of bits (using the Barrel shifter introduced in Chapter 4.5), or a register plus an offset (used for memory access).
- Everything after the semicolon ";" is a *comment*, which is an annotation explicitly declaring programmers' intentions or assumptions.

For GNU compilers, the instruction format is slightly different. All assembly instructions presented in this book follow the ARM format, not the GNU format.

The GNU format is shown below.

```
label:        mnemonic operand1, operand2, operand3    /* comment */
```

The following gives five examples of ARM assembly instructions.

Example 1: Adding two registers

```
    ADD r0, r2, r3    ; r0 = r2 + r3
```

"ADD" is a mnemonic for arithmetic addition, register r0 is the destination operand, and registers r2 and r3 are two source operands.

Example 2: Subtracting an immediate number

```
    SUB r3, r0, #3    ; r3 = r0 - 3
```

"SUB" is a mnemonic for subtraction, register r3 is the destination operand, register r0 is the minuend, and the immediate number 3 is the subtrahend.

Example 3: Setting the value of a register

```
    MOV r0, #'M'    ; r0 = ASCII value of 'M', i.e. 0x4D
```

"MOV" instruction sets the value of r0 to the ASCII value of character M. A constant number has prefix '#'.

Example 4: Variants of the ADD instruction

```
ADD r1, r2, r3     ; r1 = r2 + r3
ADD r1, r3         ; r1 = r1 + r3
ADD r1, r2, #4     ; r1 = r2 + 4
ADD r1, #15        ; r1 = r1 + 15
```

The number of operands in an instruction varies. If the destination operand (operand1) is the same as the first source operand (operand2), the destination operand can be omitted. The second operand (operand2) is often written as Op2 in the instruction description. For example, the add instruction is described as follows:

```
ADD {Rd,} Rn, Op2   ; Rd = Rn + Op2
```

The curly brackets "{ }" mean the destination operand Rd is optional if Rn is the same as Rd.

Example 5: Inline Barrel shifter

```
ADD r0, r2, r1, LSL #2  ; r0 = r2 + r1 << 2 = r2 + 4 × r1
MOV r0, r2, ASR #2      ; r0 = r2/4 (signed division)
MOV r0, r0, ROR #16     ; Swap the top and bottom half-word
```

In many instructions, the last operand (operand2 or operand3) can have different formats. It can use the Barrel shifter to shift or rotate the last operation. Refer to Chapter 4.5 for details.

3.5 Anatomy of an Assembly Program

Let us take a quick look at a complete assembly program, as shown in Figure 3-5. The program copies a string to another string. An assembly program includes labels, directives, assembly instructions, and program comments.

1. A *label*, such as *strcpy*, *stop*, *srcStr*, and *dstStr*, represents the memory address of the data or instruction marked by that label. The assembler will replace each label with its memory address or its memory address offset when generating the executable. *A label must start with the beginning of a line without any leading space.* A label can be a function name (such as "__main" as in the example), which is the memory address of the first instruction of a function. The "__main" label is exported to allow the linker to find it and resolve this label.

2. The *directives* provide important information to assist the assembler, such as declaring the start and end of an assembly function (PROC and ENDP), the end

of an assembly program file (END), defining code or data regions (AREA), designating the initial entry to the program (ENTRY), specifying memory address alignment (ALIGN), and allocating and defining data (DCB) in this example.

3. An *assembly instruction* is a machine command that controls the program flow or manipulates data. Some instructions are pseudo instructions, which are not real machine commands but are allowed in assembly language code. A pseudo instruction, such as "LDR r1, =srcStr" in the example code, will be translated into a real instruction by the assembler. Pseudo instructions make the job of writing this assembly language code easier.

4. A *comment* is a text annotation that explains programmer's intentions or assumptions. It aims to improve inter-programmer communication and code readability. A comment in an assembly program starts with a semicolon. Assemblers ignore everything after the semicolon until the end of that line.

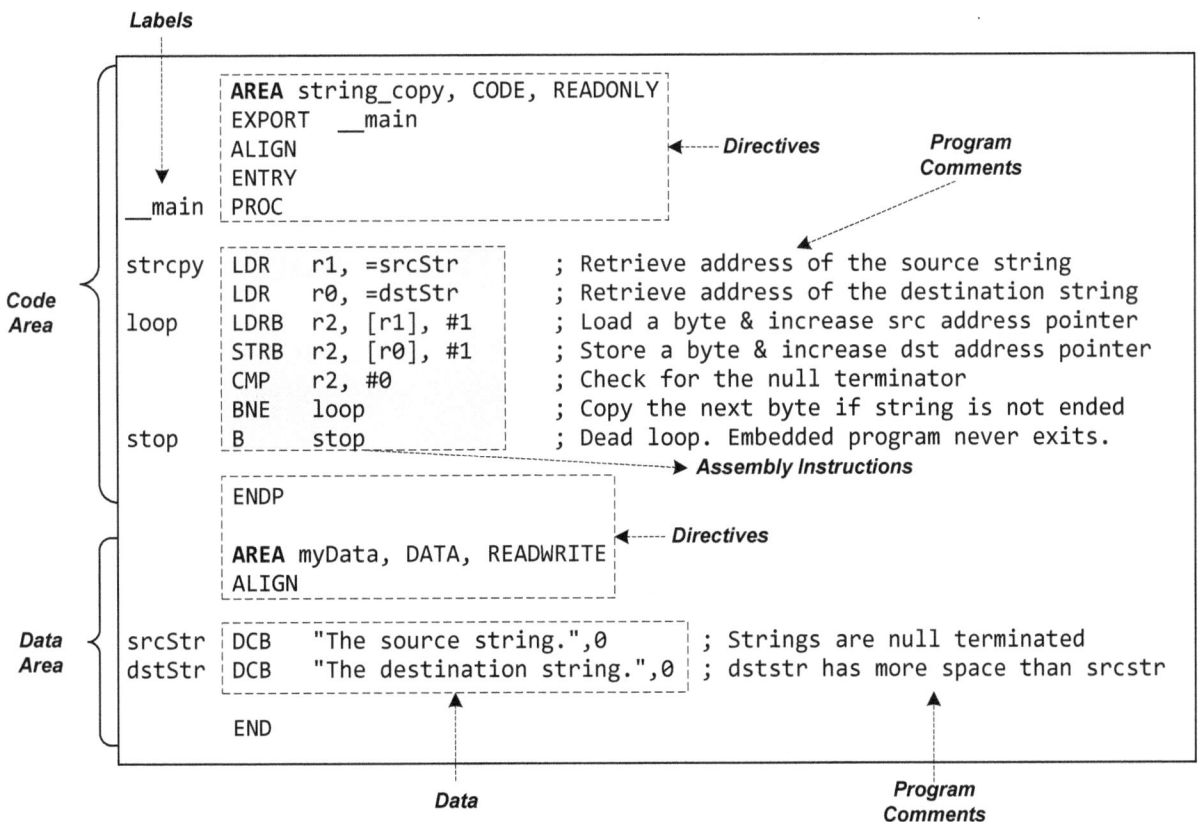

```
Labels

                    AREA string_copy, CODE, READONLY
                    EXPORT   __main
                    ALIGN                              <----- Directives    Program
                    ENTRY                                                   Comments
          __main    PROC

          strcpy    LDR    r1, =srcStr    ; Retrieve address of the source string
                    LDR    r0, =dstStr    ; Retrieve address of the destination string
          loop      LDRB   r2, [r1], #1   ; Load a byte & increase src address pointer
                    STRB   r2, [r0], #1   ; Store a byte & increase dst address pointer
                    CMP    r2, #0         ; Check for the null terminator
                    BNE    loop           ; Copy the next byte if string is not ended
          stop      B      stop           ; Dead loop. Embedded program never exits.
                                          -----> Assembly Instructions
                    ENDP
                                             <----- Directives
                    AREA myData, DATA, READWRITE
                    ALIGN

          srcStr    DCB    "The source string.",0      ; Strings are null terminated
          dstStr    DCB    "The destination string.",0 ; dststr has more space than srcstr

                    END
```

Code Area

Data Area

Data   Program Comments

Figure 3-5. An example assembly program

The example assembly program, shown in Figure 3-5, includes two areas: a data area and a code area.

- The data area defines two strings: *srcStr* and *dstStr*. Both strings are allocated with space and have initial values. All stings should be terminated with NULL.
- The code area includes a function (or called subroutine) named __*main*, which is equivalent to the *main()* function in a C program. The program copies string *strStr* to string *dstStr*.

Most assembly instructions can be classified into the following four categories: (1) arithmetic and logic instructions, (2) data movement instructions, (3) compare and branch instructions, and (4) miscellaneous instructions. Detailed explanation of these instructions will be given later in this book.

(1) *Arithmetic and logic instructions*

Shift, logic, and bit instructions	**Shift:** *LSL* (logic shift left), *LSR* (logic shift right), *ASR* (arithmetic shift right), *ROR* (rotate right), *RRX* (rotate right with extend)
	Logic: *AND*(bitwise and), *ORR*(bitwise or), *EOR* (bitwise exclusive or), *ORN* (bitwise or not), *MVN* (move not)
	Bit set/clear: *BFC* (bit field clear), *BFI* (bit field insert), *BIC* (bit clear), *CLZ* (count leading zeroes)
	Bit/byte reordering: **RBIT** (reverse bit order in a word), **REV** (reverse byte order in a word), **REV16** (reverse byte order in each half-word independently), **REVSH** (reverse byte order in the bottom halfword, and sign extend to 32 bits)

Arithmetic instructions	**Addition:** *ADD*, *ADC* (add with carry)
	Subtraction: *SUB*, *RSB* (reverse subtract), *SBC* (subtract with carry)
	Multiplication: *MUL* (multiply), *MLA* (multiply with accumulate), *MLS* (multiply with subtract), *SMULL* (signed long multiply), *SMLAL* (signed long multiply, with accumulate), *UMULL* (unsigned long multiply), *UMLAL* (unsigned long multiply, with subtract)
	Division: *SDIV* (signed), *UDIV* (unsigned)
	Saturation: *SSAT* (signed), *USAT* (unsigned)
	Sign extension: *SXTB* (signed), *SXTH, UXTB, UXTH*
	Bit field extract: *SBFX* (signed), *UBFX* (unsigned)

(2) Data movement instructions

Memory access instructions	**Read data memory:** *LDRB* (load byte), *LDRH* (load half-word), *LDR* (load word), *LDRD* (load double-word) *LDRSB* (load signed byte), *LDRSH* (load signed half-word) *LDM, LDMDB, LDMFD* (load multiple words) *LDREXB, LDREXH, LDREX* (load register exclusive with a byte, half-word, and word) *LDRT* (load in privileged modes) *POP* (load registers from stack)
	Write data memory: *STRB* (store byte), *STRH* (store half-word), *STR* (store word), *STRD* (store double-word) *STRSB* (store signed byte), *STRSH* (store signed half-word) *STM, STMDB, STMFD* (store multiple words) *STREXB, STREXH, STREX* (store register exclusive with a byte, half-word, and word) *STRT* (store in privileged modes) *PUSH* (store registers into stack)
Data copy instructions	*MOV* (move), *MOVT* (move top), *MOVW* (move half-word), *MRS* (move from coprocessor), *MSR* (move to coprocessor)

(3) Compare and branch instructions

Data compare instructions	*CMP* (compare), *CMN* (compare negative), *TST* (test), *TEQ* (test equivalent), *IT* (if-then)
Branch instructions	**B** (branch), **CBZ** (compare and branch on zero), **CBNZ** (compare and branch on non-zero), **TBB** (table branch byte), **TBH** (table branch half-word)
Subroutine instructions	*BL* (branch with link), *BLX* (branch with link and exchange), *BX* (branch and exchange)

(4) Miscellaneous instructions

Miscellaneous instructions	*BKPT* (breakpoint), *NOP* (no operation), *SEV* (set event), *WFE* (wait for event), *WFI* (wait for interrupt), *CPSID* (interrupt disable), *CPSIE* (interrupt enable), *DMB* (data memory barrier), *DSB* (data synchronization barrier), *ISB* (instruction synchronization barrier)

3.6 Assembly Directives

In assembly programs, directives are not actual commands. Instead, they are used to provide key information to compile the source program, such as declaring constants and symbolic names, defining data layout, allocating memory space, and specifying the program structure and entry point. Table 3-2 lists some commonly used directives.

AREA	Make a new block of data or code
ENTRY	Declare an entry point where the program execution starts
ALIGN	Align data or code to a particular memory boundary
DCB	Allocate one or more bytes (8 bits) of data
DCW	Allocate one or more half-words (16 bits) of data
DCD	Allocate one or more words (32 bits) of data
SPACE·	Allocate a zeroed block of memory with a particular size
FILL	Allocate a block of memory and fill with a given value.
EQU	Give a symbol name to a numeric constant
RN	Give a symbol name to a register
EXPORT	Declare a symbol and make it referable by other source files
IMPORT	Provide a symbol defined outside the current source file
INCLUDE/GET	Include a separate source file within the current source file
PROC	Declare the start of a procedure
ENDP	Designate the end of a procedure
END	Designate the end of a source file

Table 3-2 Directives commonly used in ARM assembly language

Table 3-3 gives a typical skeleton frame of an assembly program, which highlights all directives used.

```
        AREA myData, DATA, READWRITE ; Define a data section
Array   DCD 1, 2, 3, 4, 5            ; Define an array with five integers

        AREA myCode, CODE, READONLY  ; Define a code section
        EXPORT  __main               ; Make __main visible to the linker
        ENTRY                        ; Mark the entrance to the entire program
__main  PROC                         ; PROC marks the begin of a subroutine
        ...                          ; Assembly program starts here.
        ENDP                         ; Mark the end of a subroutine
        END                          ; Mark the end of a program
```

Table 3-3. A simple skeleton of an ARM assembly program.

(1) The AREA directive

An application consists of one or multiple data and code areas. The AREA directive indicates to the assembler the start of a new data or code section. A code section contains the list of instructions and a data section includes the declaration and initialization of variables.

Areas are the basic independent and indivisible unit processed by the linker. Each area is identified by a name and areas within the same source file cannot share the same name. An assembly program must have at least one code area. By default, a code area can only be read (READONLY) and a data area may be read from and written to (READWRITE).

(2) The ENTRY directive

The ENTRY directive marks the first instruction to be executed within an application. There must be one and only one entry directive in an application, no matter how many source files the application has. When there is no entry directive, the linker will generate an error message. When there are multiple entry directives, the assembler will generate an error message. For applications written in C or C++, the entry point is usually located in some library, not directly visible to programmers.

> *There should be only one entry for the whole application, even if it has multiple source files.*

(3) The END directive

The END directive indicates the end of a source file. Each assembly program must end with this directive. When a source file is included by using the GET or INCLUDE directive, the assembler returns to the parent source file after reaching the END directive of the current source file, and continue to assemble the rest of the parent. The END directive of the top-level file informs the assembler to end the application.

(4) Function or subroutine definition: PROC and ENDP

PROC and ENDP are to mark the start and end of a function (also called subroutine or procedure). They stand for "procedure" and "end of procedure." A single source file can contain multiple subroutines, with each of them defined by a pair of PROC and ENDP. PROC and ENDP cannot be nested. We cannot define a subroutine within another subroutine.

A C program must have at least one function, *i.e. main()*. Similarly, an assembly program also must have at least one subroutine named "__main".

(5) Data allocation directive: DCB, DCW, DCD, DCQ, SPACE, and FILL

An assembly program needs to reserve space in data memory for variables and set their initial contents. Table 3-4 lists commonly used data allocation directives.

Directive	Description	Memory Space
DCB	Define Constant Byte	Reserve 8-bit values
DCW	Define Constant Half-word	Reserve 16-bit values
DCD	Define Constant Word	Reserve 32-bit values
DCQ	Define Constant	Reserve 64-bit values
SPACE	Defined Zeroed Bytes	Reserve a number of zeroed bytes
FILL	Defined Initialized Bytes	Reserve and fill each byte with a value

Table 3-4. Directives for data allocation and initialization

Example 3-1 shows how to declare an initialized string, initialized integer arrays, a zeroed memory region, and a few variables in different formats.

```
        AREA    myData, DATA, READWRITE
hello   DCB     "Hello World!",0    ; Allocate a string that is null-terminated
dollar  DCB     2,10,0,200          ; Allocate integers ranging from -128 to 255
scores  DCD     2,3.5,-0.8,4.0      ; Allocate 4 words containing decimal values
miles   DCW     100,200,50,0        ; Allocate integers between -32768 and 65535
p       SPACE   255                 ; Allocate 255 bytes of zeroed memory space
f       FILL    20,0xFF,1           ; Allocate 20 bytes and set each byte to 0xFF
binary  DCB     2_01010101          ; Allocate a byte in binary
octal   DCB     8_73                ; Allocate a byte in octal
char    DCB     'A'                 ; Allocate a byte initialized to ASCII of 'A'
```

Example 3-1. Data definition by using data allocation directive

(6) The EQU and RN directive

The EQU and RN are to make an assembly program easier to understand. The EQU directive associates a symbolic name to a numeric constant. Similar to the use of #define in a C program, the EQU can be used to define a constant in an assembly code.

```
; Interrupt Number Definition (IRQn)
; ********* Cortex-M3 Processor Exceptions Numbers **************
BusFault_IRQn   EQU   -11    ; Cortex-M3 Bus Fault Interrupt
SVCall_IRQn     EQU    -5    ; Cortex-M3 Supervisor (SV) Call Interrupt
PendSV_IRQn     EQU    -2    ; Cortex-M3 Pend SV Interrupt
SysTick_IRQn    EQU    -1    ; Cortex-M3 System Tick Interrupt
```

Example 3-2. EQU is equivalent to "define" in a C program.

The RN directive gives a symbolic name to a specific register.

```
Dividend        RN    6      ; Defines dividend for register 6
Divisor         RN    5      ; Defines divisor for register 5
```

Example 3-3. "RN" gives a special meaningful name to a register.

(7) The EXPORT and IMPORT directive

The EXPORT and IMPORT directives define and locate symbols externally defined in different source files. The EXPORT declares a symbol and makes this symbol visible to the linker. The IMPORT gives the assembler a symbol that is not defined locally in the current assembly file. The IMPORT is similar to the "extern" keyword in C.

(8) The ALIGN directive

In order to achieve optimal performance, many processors require the starting memory address of a program instruction or a data variable to be a power of 2. For example, a memory address aligned to words must be divisible by 4, *i.e.* 2^2. If instruction or data are not appropriately aligned in memory, some processors might generate a misalignment fault signal and abort the memory access. Cortex-M3 processors allow unaligned memory accesses at the sacrifice of performance. Multiple memory accesses are required to fetch a misaligned data item or instruction. Chapter 10.1 introduces data alignment in detail.

```
      AREA example, CODE, ALIGN = 3   ; Memory address begins at a multiple of 8
      ADD r0, r1, r2                  ; Instructions start at a multiple of 8

      AREA myData, DATA, ALIGN = 2    ; Address starts at a multiple of four
a     DCB 0xFF                        ; The first byte of a 4-byte word
      ALIGN 4, 3                      ; Align to the last byte of a word
b     DCB 0x33                        ; Set the fourth byte of a 4-byte word
c     DCB 0x44                        ; Add a byte to make next data misaligned
      ALIGN                           ; Force the next data to be aligned
d     DCD 12345                       ; Skip three bytes and store the word
```

Example 3-4. Data alignment in assembly language

(9) The INCLUDE or GET directive

The INCLUDE or GET directive is to include an assembly source file within another source file. It is useful to include constant symbols defined by using EQU and stored in a separate source file. In Example 3-5, all constants are defined by using EQU directives and are stored in a separate assembly file called "*constants.s*". In order to include these constants, we can use a simple statement "INCLUDE constants.s".

```
        INCLUDE constants.s        ; Load Constant Definitions
        AREA main, CODE, READONLY
        EXPORT  __main
        ENTRY
__main  PROC
        ...
        ENDP
        END
```

Example 3-5. Using "INCLUDE" to load constants defined in a separate file

3.7 Exercises

1. Find five devices that use an ARM processor. Identify the instruction set they support (ARM32, Thumb, Thumb-2, or ARM64).

2. Identify two ARM-Cortex M3 processors and find what I/O peripherals are built in the processor chip.

3. Identify key differences between Cortex-M3 and Cortex-M4.

4. An assembly program must have a subroutine named "__main". Find why it has to be named as "__main". (Hints: Look at the boot loader source code, which is used to initialize the processor when the processor starts.)

5. What does "ALIGN 8, 5" mean? Draw the data memory layout assuming that the data memory starts at 0x20000000.

```
        AREA    myData, Data
        ALIGN   4
a       DCB     1
b       DCB     1
c       DCB     1
        ALIGN   8,5
d       DCB     2
```

6. What are incorrect in the following assembly program?

```
        AREA myData, DATA, READWRITE
String DCB "ABCDE"
Array  DCD 1, 2, 3, 4, 5
        END

        AREA myCode, CODE, READONLY
        EXPORT  __main2
__main  PROC
        ...

sum     PROC
        ...
        ENDP

        ENDP
        END
```

7. How to define a float or double variable of C in assembly?

CHAPTER

4

Arithmetic and Logic

Data processing instructions can be classified into seven categories: arithmetic instructions, reorder instructions, extension instructions, bitwise logic instructions, shift instructions, comparison instructions, and data copy instructions. In this chapter, we will focus on assembly instructions for arithmetic and logic operations.

4.1 Program Status Register

Cortex-M3 processors have five status flags: negative (N), zero (Z), overflow (O), carry (C), and saturation (Q).

- Negative flag (**N**) is set to 1 if the result of ALU is negative (*i.e.* bit[31] is 1) and reset to 0 otherwise.
- Zero flag (**Z**) is set to 1 if the result of ALU is zero and reset to 0 otherwise.
- Carry flag (**C**) is set to 1 if a carry occurs for unsigned addition and reset to 0 otherwise. For unsigned subtraction, it is set to 1 if no borrow has occurred, and reset to 0 otherwise.
- Overflow flag (**V**) is set to 1 if an overflow occurs when performing a signed addition or subtraction, and reset to 0 otherwise.
- Saturation flag (**Q**) is set to 1 if an SSAT or USAT instruction causes saturation and reset to 0 otherwise.

On Cortex-M3 processors, most data processing instructions have an option to update these ALU status flags. These flags are stored in the program status register (PSR). The program status register is a combination of three special registers: application program status register (APSR), interrupt program status register (IPSR), and execution program status register (EPSR). Since these three special registers have no overlap in bit fields, they are combined into one register as shown in Figure 4-1, to allow convenient access.

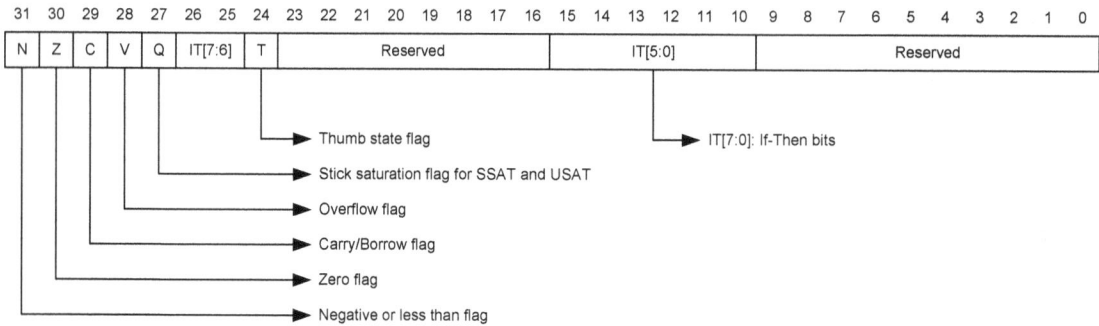

Figure 4-1. Program status register (PSR)

The T flag indicates whether the processor is in Thumb state or ARM32 state. Since Cortex-M3 processors only support Thumb-2/Thumb instructions, the T flag has a fixed value of 1 in Cortex-M3.

The IT bit fields (IT[7:6] and IT[5:0]) collectively hold a 8-bit interrupt number when an interrupt occurs. With a total of eight bits to represent the interrupt number, Cortex-M3 can support up to 256 different interrupts. Chapter 12 introduces the concept of interrupts.

4.2 Updating Program Status Flags

It is an option for an instruction to set those status flags depending on the result. To update the ALU status flags, the S suffix is added to an instruction mnemonic. For example, the ADDS instruction sets the N, V, C, and Z flags when performing mathematic addition. On the contrary, ADD cannot change these flags. If an instruction does not update these flags, the existing value of each flag, set by a previous instruction, is preserved.

ADD *vs* ADDS

Data comparison instructions (introduced in Chapter 4.9), such as CMP (compare), CMN (compare negative), TST (test), and TEQ (test equivalence), set these flags even though they do not have the S suffix.

Let us look at ADD instructions with and without the S suffix.

```
ADD  r1, r2, r3  ; r1 = r2 + r3, but won't update N, Z, C, and V flags
ADDS r2, r2, r3  ; r1 = r2 + r3, and update N, Z, C, and V flags
```

While the first instruction will not change the N, Z, C, and V flags, the second instruction will set these flags as follows: ALU updates

(1) the overflow flag by assuming that the contents of r2 and r3 are signed integers represented in two's complement,
(2) the carry flag by assuming that r2 and r3 hold unsigned integers,
(3) the zero flag by checking whether the result saved in destination register r1 is zero or not, and
(4) the negative flag by checking the sign bit of r1 (the most significant bit of r1).

If the Barrel shifter is used, the source operand may update the program status flags. Barrel shifter is introduced in Chapter 4.5. For example, the bitwise logical ANDS instruction can update the N, Z, and C flags. In the following example, the N flag is set if the most significant bit of r1 is 1, and the Z flag is set if r1 equals 0.

```
ANDS   r1, r2, r3              ; r1 = r2 AND r3
```

It is easy to understand that most logical instructions do not update the overflow flag. How would a logical instruction update the carry flag? The answer lies in the second operand of a logical instruction. If the second operand uses the Barrel shifter, then the carry flag is then updated based on the shift or rotation result.

```
ANDS   r1, r2, r3, LSL #3    ; r1 = r2 AND (r3 << 3)
```

When Barrel shifter is used in a MOVS instruction, the Z, N, and C flags will also be updated.

```
MOVS     r2, r1, LSR #3
```

However, the Barrel shifter will not change the flags if it is used in an arithmetic instruction. For example, in the following instruction, the flags depend on the result of addition, instead of logical shift left.

```
ADDS   r1, r2, r3, LSL #3    ; r1 = r2 AND (r3 << 3)
```

If the program is written in assembly, it is the programmers' responsibility to correctly interpret and use these flags. For programs written in high-level languages, compilers automatically interpret these flags. As introduced in Chapter 2.4.3, if the ALU is to update the status flags when performing an arithmetic addition or subtraction, both the carry flag and the overflow flag will be updated. It must be clear to programmers whether the numbers stored in the registers are signed or unsigned.

4.3 Shift and Rotate

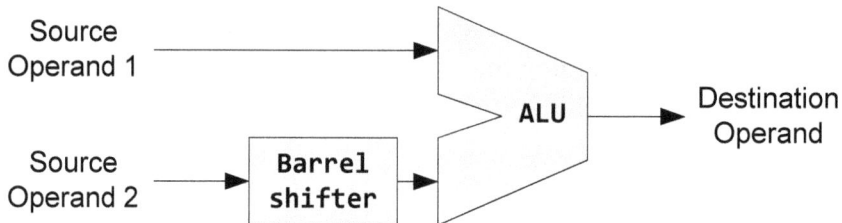

Figure 4-2. Barrel shifter is added to the second source operand. Barrel shifter is special hardware that performs fast shift and rotation operations.

As shown in Figure 4-2, one of the ALU operands is equipped with a Barrel shifter, which is a special digital circuit for fast shift and rotation. Barrel shifters are usually not available on other processors such as PIC and AVR. There are five types of shift and rotate operations: LSL, LSR, ASR, ROR, and RRX, as shown in Figure 4-3.

- **LSL** (logical shift left) n bits moves all bits of a register value left by n bits and zeros are shifted in at the right end. LSL is equivalent to multiplication by 2^n ("<<" operation in C).
- **LSR** (logical shift right) n bits moves all bits of a register value right by n bits and zeros are shifted in at the left end. LSR equals unsigned division by 2^n (">>" operation on unsigned numbers in C).
- **ASR** (arithmetic shift right) n bits moves all bits right by n bits and copies of the left most bit (the sign bit) are shifted in at the left end. ASR is equivalent to signed division by 2^n. (">>" operation on signed numbers in C).
- **ROR** (rotate right) is the circular shift, in which all 32 bits are shifted right simultaneously as if the right end of the register is joined with its left end. The bit shifted out from the right end of the register can be copied into the carry bit. The carry bit can be optionally used to update the carry flag of the processor status register.
- **RRX** (rotate right with extend) works similarly to ROR except that the carry bit joins the rotate circle and RRX can rotate the data by only one bit.

Below gives a few examples of shift and rotation instructions.

```
LSL r1, r2          ; r1 = r1 << r2
LSL r1, #3          ; r1 = r1 << 3
LSL r1, r2, #3      ; r1 = r2 << 3
LSL r1, r2, r3      ; r1 = r2 << r3
ROR r1, r2          ; r1 = rotate r1 by r2 bits
RRX r1, r2          ; rotate r2 right by one bit (with extension)
```

LSL : Logical Shift Left

LSR : Logical Shift Right

ASR: Arithmetic Shift Right

ROR: Rotate Right

RRX: Rotate Right Extended

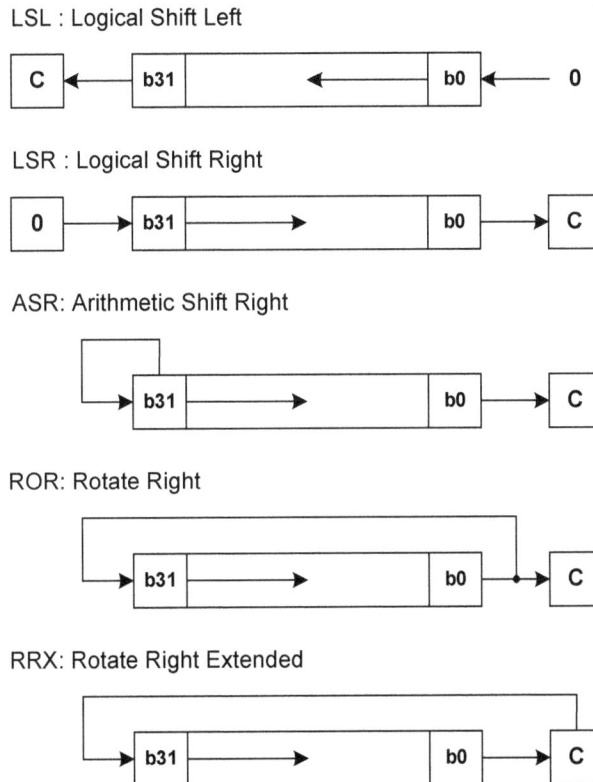

Figure 4-3. Shift and rotate operations

C language does not directly provide rotate operations (ROR and RRX). The compiler will automatically use a rotation instruction if it can improve the performance. In addition, there is no rotate left operation. However, a rotate left by n bits can be replaced with a rotate right by $32 - n$ bits, which takes the same amount of execution time. For example, rotating left by 6 bits has the same result as rotating right by 26 bits.

Note the carry bit shown in Figure 4-3 is not the carry flag of the processor status register. Therefore, none of these shift and rotate instructions updates the flags by default. In order to update the flags, the suffix S has to be specified. In addition, the overflow flags cannot be updated by these instructions.

```
LSL  r1, #3      ; r1 = r1 << 3, but won't update the flags
LSLS r1, #3      ; r1 = r1 << 3, and update the N, Z, C flags
                 ; LSLS will not update V flag
```

The Barrel shifter is often used to replace slow multiplication and division instructions to improve the processor speed, as shown in the following two example instructions.

```
ADD r0, r2, r1, LSL #1   ; r0 = r2 + r1 << 1 = r2 + 2 × r1
ADD r1, r0, r0, LSR #3   ; r1 = r0 + r0 >> 3 = r0 + r0/8
```

When the Barrel shifter is used in a move (MOVS and MVNS), logical (such as ANDS, ORRS, or EORS) or bitwise operation (such as BICS) instruction with the S suffix, the carry flag can be updated. Detailed discussions are introduced later in this chapter.

4.4 Arithmetic Instructions

Table 4-1 lists arithmetic instructions producing 32-bit results.

ADD {Rd,} Rn, Op2	Add. $Rd \leftarrow Rn + Op2$
ADC {Rd,} Rn, Op2	Add with carry. $Rd \leftarrow Rn + Op2 + Carry$
SUB {Rd,} Rn, Op2	Subtract. $Rd \leftarrow Rn - Op2$
SBC {Rd,} Rn, Op2	Subtract with carry. $Rd \leftarrow Rn - Op2 + Carry - 1$
RSB {Rd,} Rn, Op2	Reverse subtract. $Rd \leftarrow Op2 - Rn$
MUL {Rd,} Rn, Rm	Multiply. $Rd \leftarrow (Rn \times Rm)[31:0]$
MLA Rd, Rn, Rm, Ra	Multiply with accumulate. $Rd \leftarrow (Ra + (Rn \times Rm))[31:0]$
MLS Rd, Rn, Rm, Ra	Multiply and subtract, $Rd \leftarrow (Ra - (Rn \times Rm))[31:0]$
SDIV {Rd,} Rn, Rm	Signed divide. $Rd \leftarrow Rn / Rm$
UDIV {Rd,} Rn, Rm	Unsigned divide. $Rd \leftarrow Rn / Rm$
SSAT Rd, #n, Rm {,shift #s}	Signed saturate
USAT Rd, #n, Rm {,shift #s}	Unsigned saturate

Table 4-1. Arithmetic instructions with 32-bit results

Addition and subtraction instructions

Most of these instructions take two source operands, and the 32-bit result is saved into a destination register. While the first source operand is a register, the second source operand is flexible and can be a register, an immediate constant, or an inline Barrel shifter.

Examples of three register operands:

```
SUB r3, r2, r1    ; r3 = r2 - r1
SBC r3, r2, r1    ; r3 = r2 - r1 + Carry - 1
RSB r3, r2, r1    ; r3 = r1 - r2
```

Examples of immediate number operand:

```
SUB r3, r2, #987    ; r3 = r2 - 987
RSB r3, r2, #987    ; r3 = 987 - r2
```

Examples of inline Barrel shifter:

```
RSB r0, r0, r0, LSL #5     ; r0 = r0 << 5 - r0 = 31 × r0
ADD r0, r0, r0, LSL #3     ; r0 = r0 + r0 << 3 = 9 × r0
```

The Barrel shifter will be introduced in details in the next section.

If an instruction has three operands, the second operand cannot be a constant number in most instructions (except SSAT and USAT). For example, the SUB instruction below has a syntax error.

```
SUB r0, #1, r3     ; This is not allowed and causes syntax error.
RSB r0, r3, #1     ; r0 = 1 - r3. RSB is for reverse subtraction.
```

Example 4-1 given below shows the implementation of subtracting two 96-bit integers by using SUB and SBC. A 96-bit integer is saved in three registers.

$$C(r8:r7:r6) = A(r2:r1:r0) - B(r5:r4:r3)$$

The program uses the LDR instruction, which is introduced in Chapter 5.1. The LDR instruction sets a register to a constant value.

```
; C = A - B
; Subtracting two 96-bit integers A (r2:r1:r0) and B (r5:r4:r3).
; Result C (r8:r7:r6)
; A = 00001234,00000002,FFFFFFFF
; B = 12345678,00000004,00000001
LDR r0, =0xFFFFFFFF   ; A's lower 32 bits (See LDR in Chapter 5.1)
LDR r1, =0x00000002   ; A's middle 32 bits
LDR r2, =0x00001234   ; A's upper 32 bits

LDR r3, =0x00000001   ; B's lower 32 bits
LDR r4, =0x00000004   ; B's middle 32 bits
LDR r5, =0x12345678   ; B's upper 32 bits

; Subtract A from B
SUBS r6, r0, r3 ; C[31:0] = A[31:0] - B[31:0], update carry
; Carry flag is 1 if no borrow has occurred in the previous subtraction
SBCS r7, r1, r4 ; C[64:32] = A[64:32] - B[64:32] + carry - 1, update carry
SBC  r8, r2, r5 ; C[96:64] = A[96:64] - B[96:64] + carry - 1
```

Example 4-1. Subtracting two 96-bit integers

Short multiplication and division instructions

The results of multiplications may have more than 32 bits. However, only the least significant 32 bits (LSB32) of the result are saved into the destination register.

```
MUL   r6, r4, r2        ; signed multiply, r6 = LSB32( r4 × r2 )
UMUL  r6, r4, r2        ; unsigned multiply, r6 = LSB32( r4 × r2 )
MLA   r6, r4, r1, r0    ; r6 = LSB32( r4 × r1 ) + r0
MLS   r6, r4, r1, r0    ; r6 = LSB32( r4 × r1 ) - r0
```

```
SDIV r3, r2, r1      ; signed divide, r3 = r2/r1
UDIV r3, r2, r1      ; unsigned divide, r3 = r2/r1
```

Long multiplication instructions

Table 4-2 lists long multiplication instructions that produce 64-bit results.

UMULL RdLo, RdHi, Rn, Rm	Unsigned long multiply. $RdHi, RdLo \leftarrow unsigned(Rn \times Rm)$
SMULL RdLo, RdHi, Rn, Rm	Signed long multiply. $RdHi, RdLo \leftarrow signed(Rn \times Rm)$
UMLAL RdLo, RdHi, Rn, Rm	Unsigned multiply with accumulate. $RdHi, RdLo \leftarrow unsigned(RdHi, RdLo + Rn \times Rm)$
SMLAL RdLo, RdHi, Rn, Rm	Signed multiply with accumulate. $RdHi, RdLo \leftarrow signed(RdHi, RdLo + Rn \times Rm)$

Table 4-2. Long multiplication instructions

Two registers are used to store a result, with the high register (RdHi) holding the most significant 32 bits, and the low register (RdLo) holding the least significant 32 bits. UMULL and UMLAL assume the operands Rn and Rm, and the 64-bit multiplication result are unsigned integers, while SMULL and SMLAL treats all as signed integers. UMLAL and SMLAL also perform accumulation.

```
UMULL r3, r4, r0, r1   ; r4:r3 = r0 × r1, r4 = MSB bits, r3 = LSB bits
SMULL r3, r4, r0, r1   ; r4:r3 = r0 × r1
UMLAL r3, r4, r0, r1   ; r4:r3 = r4:r3 + r0 × r1
SMLAL r3, r4, r0, r1   ; r4:r3 = r4:r3 + r0 × r1
```

Saturation instructions

The saturation instructions limit a given input to a configurable signed or unsigned range. When the input value exceeds the specified range, its output is then set as the maximum or minimum value of the selected range. Otherwise, the output is equal to the input. The saturate instructions take one immediate source operand and one register source operand.

- SSAT saturates a signed integer x to the signed range $-2^{n-1} \leq x \leq 2^{n-1} - 1$.

$$SSAT(x) = \begin{cases} 2^{n-1} - 1 & if\ x > 2^{n-1} - 1 \\ -2^{n-1} & if\ x < 2^{n-1} \\ x & otherwise \end{cases}$$

- USAT saturates a signed integer x to the unsigned range $0 \leq x \leq 2^n - 1$.

$$USAT(x) = \begin{cases} 2^n - 1 & if\ x > 2^n - 1 \\ x & otherwise \end{cases}$$

The following gives two examples in which n is 11. Note the second operand is an immediate numbers in SSAT and USAT.

```
SSAT    r2, #11, r1    ; output range: -2^10 ≤ r2 ≤ 2^10
USAT    r2, #11, r3    ; output range: 0 ≤ r2 ≤ 2^11
```

4.5 Barrel Shifter

Typically, Barrel shifters are implemented as a cascade of parallel 2-to-1 multiplexers. Figure 4-4 gives an example implementation of a four-bit Barrel shifter that performs rotate right. The S_1S_0 indicates the amount of rotation. The implementation of logic shift is similar except a zero bit is shifted in either from right or the left end.

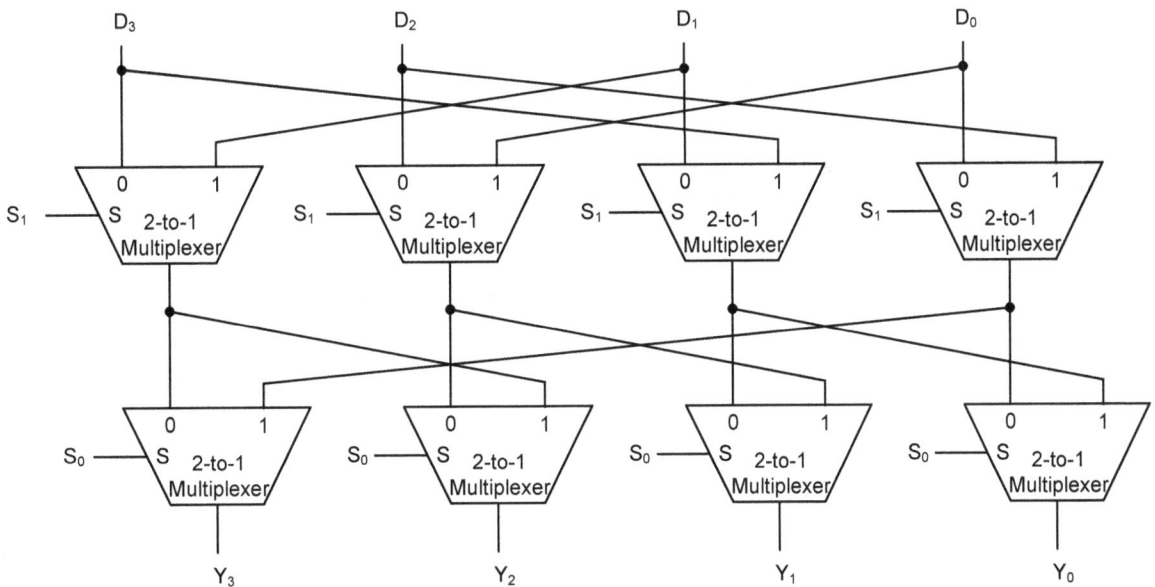

Figure 4-4. Example four-bit Barrel shifter that performs rotate right

As shown in Figure 4-2, the Barrel shifter is special hardware that can perform shift and rotation on the second ALU source operand. Therefore, not only can these shift and rotation instructions be used as standalone assembly instructions, but they can also be used in other instructions to make changes to the second source operand.

S_1	S_0	Y_3	Y_2	Y_1	Y_0
0	0	D_3	D_2	D_1	D_0
0	1	D_0	D_3	D_2	D_1
1	0	D_1	D_0	D_3	D_2
1	1	D_2	D_1	D_0	D_3

Table 4-3. Truth table of rotation right

For example,

```
ADD r1, r0, r0, LSL #3    ; r1 = r0 + r0 << 3 = r0 + 8 x r0
ADD r1, r0, r0, LSR #3    ; r1 = r0 + r0 >> 3 = r0 + r0/8 (unsigned)
ADD r1, r0, r0, ASR #3    ; r1 = r0 + r0 >> 3 = r0 + r0/8 (signed)
```

We can take advantage of Barrel shifter to speed up the application. Without Barrel shifter, two separate instructions would be required to perform each of the above instructions. This would not only increase the size of a binary program but also take more processor cycles to complete the same task. In addition, Barrel shifter is also used to replace slow multiplication instructions, as shown in the following example.

```
ADD r1, r0, r0, LSL #3   ⟺   MOV r2, #9     ; r2 = 9
                             MUL r1, r0, r2   ; r1 = r0 * 9
```

4.6 Bitwise Logic

There are four commonly used bitwise operations: AND, OR, Exclusive OR ($\oplus$), and negation (not). Table 4-4 shows their truth table.

a	b	a and b	a or b	a $\oplus$ b	not a
0	0	0	0	0	1
0	1	0	1	1	1
1	0	0	1	1	0
1	1	1	1	0	0

Table 4-4. Truth table of logic operations

The bitwise assembly instructions supported in Cortex-M3 are listed in Table 4-5.

AND {Rd,} Rn, Op2	Bitwise logic AND. $Rd \leftarrow Rn \,\&\, operand2$
ORR {Rd,} Rn, Op2	Bitwise logic OR. $Rd \leftarrow Rn \mid operand2$
EOR {Rd,} Rn, Op2	Bitwise logic exclusive OR. $Rd \leftarrow Rn \,\wedge\, operand2$
ORN {Rd,} Rn, Op2	Bitwise logic NOT OR. $Rd \leftarrow Rn \mid (NOT\ operand2)$
BIC {Rd,} Rn, Op2	Bit clear. $Rd \leftarrow Rn \,\&\, NOT\ operand2$
BFC Rd, #lsb, #width	Bit field clear. $Rd[(width+lsb-1):lsb] \leftarrow 0$
BFI Rd, Rn, #lsb, #width	Bit field insert. $Rd[(width+lsb-1):lsb] \leftarrow Rn[(width-1):0]$
MVN Rd, Op2	Move NOT, logically negate all bits. $Rd \leftarrow 0xFFFFFFFF\ EOR\ Op2$

Table 4-5. Bitwise Logic Instructions

These instructions operate at the bit level. The logic operation is performed on each pair of bits that are at the same position in two inputs.

For example, suppose r0 = 0xD5755755 and r1 = 0xAABAAAA9, the following shows the result of various bitwise logic operations.

```
AND r2, r0, r1   ; r2 = r0 bitwise AND r1 ⟹ r2 = 0x80300201

         r0    1 1 0 1 0 1 0 1 0 1 1 1 0 1 0 1 0 1 0 1 0 1 1 1 0 1 0 1 0 1 0 1
         r1    1 0 1 0 1 0 1 0 1 0 1 1 1 0 1 0 1 0 1 0 1 0 1 0 1 0 1 0 1 0 0 1
         r2    1 0 0 0 0 0 0 0 0 0 1 1 0 0 0 0 0 0 0 0 0 0 1 0 0 0 0 0 0 0 0 1

ORR r2, r0, r1   ; r2 = r0 bitwise OR r1 ⟹ r2 = 0xFFFFFFFD

         r0    1 1 0 1 0 1 0 1 0 1 1 1 0 1 0 1 0 1 0 1 0 1 1 1 0 1 0 1 0 1 0 1
         r1    1 0 1 0 1 0 1 0 1 0 1 1 1 0 1 0 1 0 1 0 1 0 1 0 1 0 1 0 1 0 0 1
         r2    1 1 1 1 1 1 1 1 1 1 1 1 1 1 1 1 1 1 1 1 1 1 1 1 1 1 1 1 1 1 0 1

EOR r2, r0, r1   ; r2 = r0 bitwise Exclusive OR r1 ⟹ r2 = 0x7FCFFDFC

         r0    1 1 0 1 0 1 0 1 0 1 1 1 0 1 0 1 0 1 0 1 0 1 1 1 0 1 0 1 0 1 0 1
         r1    1 0 1 0 1 0 1 0 1 0 1 1 1 0 1 0 1 0 1 0 1 0 1 0 1 0 1 0 1 0 0 1
         r2    0 1 1 1 1 1 1 1 1 1 0 0 1 1 1 1 1 1 1 1 1 1 0 1 1 1 1 1 1 1 0 0

ORN r2, r0, r1   ; r2 = r0 bitwise NOT OR r1 ⟹ r2 = 0xD5755757

         r0    1 1 0 1 0 1 0 1 0 1 1 1 0 1 0 1 0 1 0 1 0 1 1 1 0 1 0 1 0 1 0 1
         r1    1 0 1 0 1 0 1 0 1 0 1 1 1 0 1 0 1 0 1 0 1 0 1 0 1 0 1 0 1 0 0 1
     NOT r1 0 1 0 1 0 1 0 1 0 1 0 0 0 1 0 1 0 1 0 1 0 1 0 1 0 1 0 1 0 1 1 0
         r2    1 1 0 1 0 1 0 1 0 1 1 1 0 1 0 1 0 1 0 1 0 1 1 1 0 1 0 1 0 1 1 1

BIC r2, r0, r1   ; r2 = bit clear r0 according to r1 ⟹ r2 = 0x55455554

         r0    1 1 0 1 0 1 0 1 0 1 1 1 0 1 0 1 0 1 0 1 0 1 1 1 0 1 0 1 0 1 0 1
         r1    1 0 1 0 1 0 1 0 1 0 1 1 1 0 1 0 1 0 1 0 1 0 1 0 1 0 1 0 1 0 0 1
     NOT r1 0 1 0 1 0 1 0 1 0 1 0 0 0 1 0 1 0 1 0 1 0 1 0 1 0 1 0 1 0 1 1 0
         r2    0 1 0 1 0 1 0 1 0 1 0 0 0 1 0 1 0 1 0 1 0 1 0 1 0 1 0 1 0 1 0 0

MVN r2, r1       ; r2 = NOT r1 ⟹ r2 = 0x55455556

         r1    1 0 1 0 1 0 1 0 1 0 1 1 1 0 1 0 1 0 1 0 1 0 1 0 1 0 1 0 1 0 0 1
         r2    0 1 0 1 0 1 0 1 0 1 0 0 0 1 0 1 0 1 0 1 0 1 0 1 0 1 0 1 0 1 1 0
```

Bit mask

We often use bit masks to manipulate conveniently a specific subset of binary bits in a single bitwise operation. For a given integer N, its bit mask is constructed as follows:

- The mask has the same number of bits in binary as the integer N.
- Bit mask(i) is set to 1 if bit N(i) is to be operated; otherwise mask(i) is 0.

The mask can separate the binary bits of an integer into two parts: one part that will be examined or modified, and the other part that will be ignored. For example, a mask of 0b00110100 (0x34) would select bits 2, 4, and 5 of the target variable. The following gives example C and assembly programs to set, clear, toggle and check these bits.

- N = 0xa2 = 0b10100010
- Mask = 0x34 = 0b00110100

Bitwise Operators	Symbol	Example
AND	&	C = N & Mask; // C = 0b00100000 = 0x20
OR	|	C = N | Mask; // C = 0b10110110 = 0xb6
EXCLUSIVE-OR	^	C = N ^ Mask; // C = 0b10010111 = 0x97
NOT	~	C = ~N; // C = 0b01011101 = 0x5D
SHIFT RIGHT	>>	C = N >> 2; // C = 0b00101000 = 0x28
SHIFT LEFT	<<	C = N << 2; // C = 0b10001000 = 0x88

Example 4-2. Bit 0, 2, 4, and 5 are selected by the mask.

Checking a bit

C Program	Assembly Program 1	Assembly Program 2

char a = 0x34
char mask = 1<<5;
char b;
// Check bit 5
b = a & mask;
	LDR r0,#0x34 ; r0 = a
	LDR r1,#(1<<5) ; r1 = mask
	ANDS r2,r0,r1 ; r2 = b
		LDR r0,#0x34 ; r0 = a
		ANDS r2,r0,#(1<<5)

Setting a bit

C Program	Assembly Program 1	Assembly Program 2

char a = 0x34
char mask = 1<<5;
// Set bit 5
a |= mask;
	LDR r0,#0x34 ; r0 = a
	LDR r1,#(1<<5) ; r1 = mask
	ORR r0,r0,r1
		LDR r0,#0x34 ; r0 = a
		ORR r0,r0,#(1<<5)

ORR a bit with 1 sets this bit to 1. ORR a bit with 0 does not change it. Therefore, ORR a variable with the mask sets all bits marked by the mask, while keeping all the other bits unchanged.

Clearing a bit

C Program	Assembly Program 1	Assembly Program 2

char a = 0x34
char mask = 1<<5;
// Reset bit 5
a &= ~mask;
	LDR r0,#0x34 ; r0 = a
	LDR r1,#(1<<5) ; r1 = mask
	MVN r1,r1 ; NOT
	EOR r0,r0,r1
		LDR r0,#0x34 ; r0 = a
		BIC r0,#(1<<5)

AND a bit with 0 clears this bit to 0. AND a bit with 1 does not change it. Therefore, AND a variable with the mask clears all bits marked by the mask, while keeping all the other bits unchanged.

Toggling a bit

C Program	Assembly Program 1	Assembly Program 2

char a = 0x34
char mask = 1<<5;
// Toggle bit 5
a ^= mask;
	LDR r0,#0x34 ; r0 = a
	LDR r1,#(1<<5) ; r1 = mask
	EOR r0,r0,r1
		LDR r0,#0x34 ; r0 = a
		EOR r0,r0,#(1<<5)

The result of exclusive OR between 1 and a data bit can invert the data bit. On the contrary, exclusive OR between 0 and a data bit keeps the value of the data bit, as illustrated in Table 4-6. Therefore, excluding a data with a mask toggles every data bit specified in the mask, keeping all the other bits unchanged.

Data bit	Mask bit	Data bit ⊕ Mask bit
0	1	1
1	1	0
0	0	0
1	0	1

Table 4-6. Truth table of Exclusive OR

In C, the Boolean operations are **A && B** (Boolean and), **A||B** (Boolean or), and **!B** (Boolean not), which are different from the above bitwise operations. The Boolean operators perform word-wide operations, not bitwise. For example, "0x10 & 0x01" equals 0x00, but "0x10 && 0x01" equals 0x01. Bitwise negation expression "~0x01" equals 0xFFFFFFFE, but Boolean NOT expression "!0x01" equals 0x00.

Using EQU to define a mask in assembly

In order to make the program codes easier to read, we often give a special name to a mask. For example, the following defines the bit masks for the clock enable and disable bits for GPIO Port A, B and C.

```
RCC_AHBENR_GPIOAEN   EQU (0x00000001)  ; GPIO port A clock enable
RCC_AHBENR_GPIOBEN   EQU (0x00000002)  ; GPIO port B clock enable
RCC_AHBENR_GPIOCEN   EQU (0x00000004)  ; GPIO port C clock enable

LDR r7,=RCC_BASE                       ; Address of reset and clock control (RCC)
LDR r1,[r7,#RCC_AHBENR]                ; Load RCC from memory into r1
ORR r1,r1,#RCC_AHBENR_GPIOAEN          ; Enable clock of GPIO port A
ORR r1,r1,#RCC_AHBENR_GPIOBEN          ; Enable clock of GPIO port B
ORR r1,r1,#RCC_AHBENR_GPIOCEN          ; Enable clock of GPIO port C
STR r1,[r7,#RCC_AHBENR]                ; Save RCC
```

By using EQU, the program defines three constants (such as RCC_AHBENR_GPIOAEN). These constants are actually bit masks, which make it easier to manipulate individual bits. It is not recommended to directly set or clear bits by using constants instead of a named mask, such as the following instruction.

```
ORR r1, r1, #0x7  ; Set bits 0, 1, and 2
```

Updating program status flags

The logic operations with S suffix, including ANDS, ORRS, EORS, ORNS, and MVNS will update N, Z, C flags. None of them affects V flag. In addition, BFC and BFI do not update any of these four flags.

It is understandable that the negative and zero flags are updated by a logic operation. You may wonder why the carry flag is updated. The carry flag is updated when the second operand uses the Barrel shifter. For example,

```
ANDS r0, r1, LSL #3
```

The carry flag of the AND operation is set as the carry of the "LSLS r2, #3" operation.

4.7 Order of Bits and Bytes

Instructions for reversing the bit or byte orders are useful, particularly when data exchanged between two systems have different formats. For example, the REV instruction can be used to convert data that are exchanged between systems with different endian settings.

RBIT Rd, Rn	Reverse bit order in a word. *for (i = 0; i < 32; i++) Rd[i] ← RN[31– i]*
REV Rd, Rn	Reverse byte order in a word. *Rd[31:24] ← Rn[7:0], Rd[23:16] ← Rn[15:8],* *Rd[15:8] ← Rn[23:16], Rd[7:0] ← Rn[31:24]*
REV16 Rd, Rn	Reverse byte order in each half-word. *Rd[15:8] ← Rn[7:0], Rd[7:0] ← Rn[15:8],* *Rd[31:24] ← Rn[23:16], Rd[23:16] ← Rn[31:24]*
REVSH Rd, Rn	Reverse byte order in bottom half-word and sign extend. *Rd[15:8] ← Rn[7:0], Rd[7:0] ← Rn[15:8],* *Rd[31:16] ← Rn[7] & 0xFFFF*

Table 4-7. Instructions for changing the order of bits or bytes

Reverse bits (RBIT)

31	30	29	28	27	26	25	24	23	22	21	20	19	18	17	16	15	14	13	12	11	10	9	8	7	6	5	4	3	2	1	0

0	1	2	3	4	5	6	7	8	9	10	11	12	13	14	15	16	17	18	19	20	21	22	23	24	25	26	27	28	29	30	31

Reverse byte order in a word (REV)

Byte 3	Byte 2	Byte 1	Byte 0

Byte 0	Byte 1	Byte 2	Byte 3

Reverse byte order in each half-word (REV16)

Byte 3	Byte 2	Byte 1	Byte 0

Byte 2	Byte 3	Byte 0	Byte 1

Reverse byte order in bottom half-word and sign extension (REVSH)

Byte 3	Byte 2	Byte 1	Byte 0

Sign Extension of Byte 0 (16 bits)		Byte 0	Byte 1

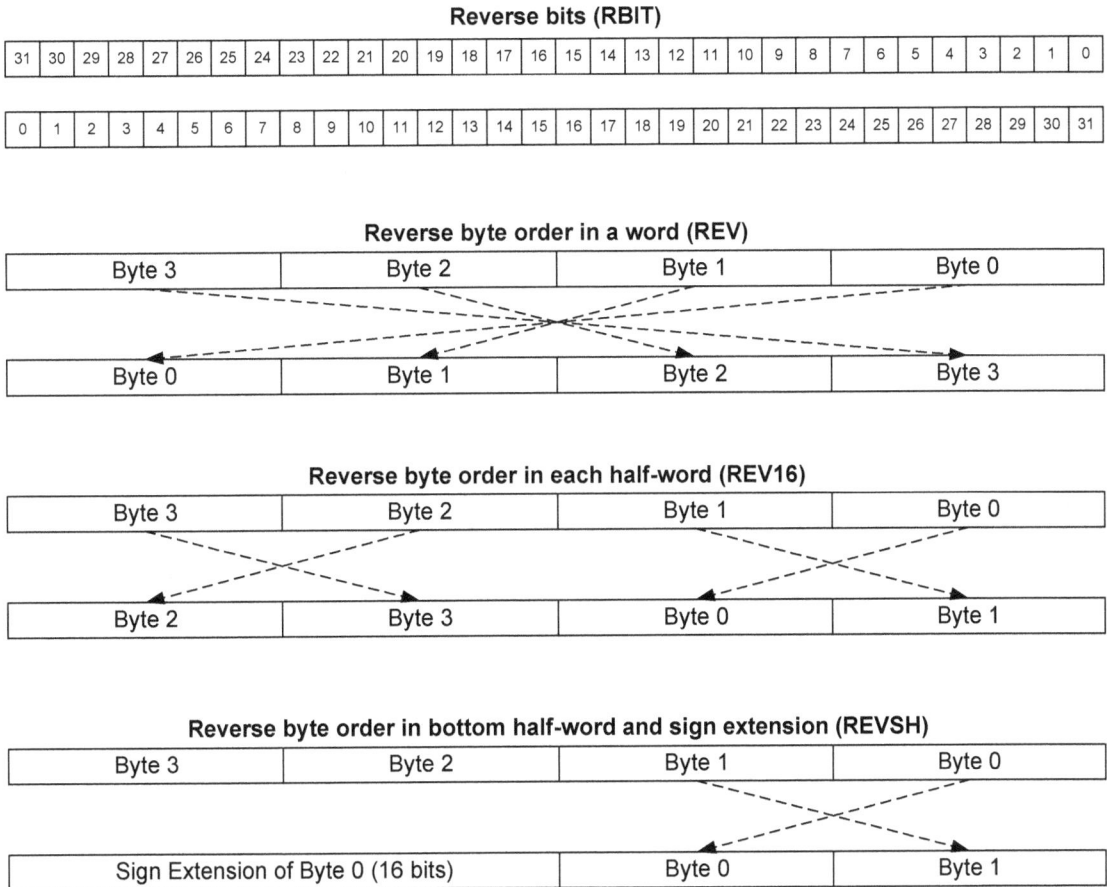

Figure 4-5. Reverse bit or byte order

The following gives a few examples of changing the bit or byte order of a value stored in register r0.

```
LDR  r0, =0x12345678    ; r0 = 0x12345678
RBIT r1, r0             ; Reverse bits, r1 = 0x1E6A2C48

LDR  r0, =0x12345678    ; r0 = 0x12345678
REV  r1, r0             ; Reverse byte order, r1 = 0x78563412
REV16 r2, r0            ; Reserve byte order in half-word, r2 = 0x34127856

LDR  r0, =0x33448899    ; r0 = 0x33448899
REVSH r1, r0            ; Reverse bytes in lower half-word and extend sign
                        ; r0 = 0xFFFF9988
```

Example 4-3. Assembly codes to change the order of bits or bytes.

4.8 Sign and Zero Extension

Signed integers are represented in two's complement in computers. When a signed integer is converted to another signed integer with more bits, the sign bit (*i.e.* the most significant bit or the left-most bit) should be duplicated to maintain the integer's sign. This operation is called sign extension.

In the following C example, when variable a or b is assigned to variable c, sign extension should be performed. The int_8, int_16, and int_32 are standard integer data types defined in the header file *stdint.h*. They define 8-, 16- and 32-bit signed integers, respectively. Their corresponding unsigned integer definition is uint_8, uint_16, and uint32_t, respectively.

```
int_8  a = -1;    // a signed 8-bit signed integer,  a = 0xFF
int_16 b = -2;    // a signed 16-bit signed integer, b = 0xFFFE
int_32 c;         // a signed 32-bit signed integer

c = a;            // sign extension required, c = 0xFFFFFFFF
c = b;            // sign extension required, c = 0xFFFFFFFF
```
Example 4-4. Example of sign extension performed in a C program

Table 4-8 lists assembly instructions that perform sign and zero extension.

SXTB {Rd,} Rm {,ROR #n}	Sign extend a byte.
	$Rd[31:0] \leftarrow Sign\ Extend((Rm\ ROR\ (8 \times n))[7:0])$
SXTH {Rd,} Rm {,ROR #n}	Sign extend a half-word.
	$Rd[31:0] \leftarrow Sign\ Extend((Rm\ ROR\ (8 \times n))[15:0])$
UXTB {Rd,} Rm {,ROR #n}	Zero extend a byte.
	$Rd[31:0] \leftarrow Zero\ Extend((Rm\ ROR\ (8 \times n))[7:0])$
UXTH {Rd,} Rm {,ROR #n}	Zero extend a half-word.
	$Rd[31:0] \leftarrow Zero\ Extend((Rm\ ROR\ (8 \times n))[15:0])$

Table 4-8. Instructions for zero and sign extension

The following program gives a few examples of sign and zero extension. Register r0 is assumed to have a value of 0x11228091.

```
; r0 = 0x11228091:
SXTB r1, r0       ; r1 = 0xFFFFFF91, sign extend a byte
SXTH r1, r0       ; r1 = 0xFFFF8091, sign extend a half-word
UXTB r1, r0       ; r1 = 0x00000091, zero extend a byte
UXTH r1, r0       ; r1 = 0x00008091, zero extend a half-word
```
Example 4-5. Example code of sign and zero extension

4.9 Data Comparison

There are four different data comparison instructions.

CMP Rn, Op2	Compare	Set flags on Rn – Op2
CMN Rn, Op2	Compare negative	Set flags on Rn + Op2
TST Rn, Op2	Test	Set flags on Rn AND Op2
TEQ Rn, Op2	Test equivalence	Set flags on Rn EOR Op2

Table 4-9. Data comparison instructions

- The CMP instruction subtracts the value of Op2 from the value in Rn. It is the same as a *SUBS* instruction, except the result is discarded. The CMP instruction will update the N, Z, C, and V flags according to the subtraction result.
- The CMN instruction adds the value of Op2 to the value in Rn. "CMN Rn, Op2" is similar to "ADDS Rn, Op2", except the result is discarded. The N, Z, C, and V flags are updated.
- The TST instruction performs a bitwise AND operation on the value in Rn and the value of Op2. "TST Rn, Op2" performs "ANDS Rn, Op2", except the result is discarded. The N and Z flags are updated. If Op2 uses the Barrel shifter, TST also updates the C flag during the calculation of Op2. However, it does not affect the V flag.
- The TEQ instruction performs a bitwise exclusive OR operation on the value in Rn and the value of Op2. "TEQ Rn, Op2" is the same as "EOR Rn, Op2" except the result is discarded. Similar to TST, TEQ updates the N, Z, and C flags.

Note TEQ and TST have different usages. TEQ is to check whether two values are equal and TST is to check whether target bits set by the second operand are clear. After TEQ completes, the zero flag is set if two operands are equal; otherwise, the zero flag is clear. Note TEQ instruction cannot check the equivalence of two operands. For example, when r0 = 0b1010 and r1 = 0b0101, the instruction "TST r0, r1" sets the zero flag since the exclusive result is 0. However, these two operands are not equal.

The following gives a few examples of data comparison.

```
CMP r0, #3            ; Compare r0 with 3
CMN r0, #10           ; Compare r0 with -10
CMP r0, r1            ; Compare r0 and r1
TEQ r0, #'?'          ; Compare r0 with ASCII value of '?' (0x3F)

MOV r1, #1, LSL #31   ; r1 = 0x80000000
TST r0, r1            ; check whether the sign bit is 1.
```

4.10 Data Movement Between Registers

Data movement between registers can be classified into two categories:

- move data between two general-purpose registers (r0 – r12)
- move data between a general-purpose register and a special-purpose register

MOV (move) and MVN (move not) are used to copy data between two general-purpose registers.

MRS and MSR are used to move contents between special registers and general registers. Special registers include APSR, IPSR, EPSR, IEPSR, IAPSR, EAPSR, PSR, MSP, PSP, PRIMASK, BASEPRI, BASEPRI_MAX, FAULTMASK, and CONTROL.

MOV	Rd ← operand2
MVN	Rd ← NOT operand2
MRS Rd, spec_reg	Move from special register to general register
MSR spec_reg, Rm	Move from general register to special register

Table 4-10. Data copy instructions

Note MOV and MVN can also load an immediate number into a register, as introduced in Chapter 5.4.4. The following are a few examples of MOV and MVN.

```
MOV r4, r5            ; Copy r5 to r4
MVN r4, r5            ; r4 = bitwise logical NOT of r5
MOV r1, r2, LSL #3    ; r1 = r2 << 3
MOV r0, PC            ; Copy PC (r15) to r0
MOV r1, SP            ; Copy SP (r14) to r1
```

The follow shows examples of copying program status registers (PSR) into a general register.

```
MRS r0, APSR    ; Read flag state into r0
MRS r0, IPSR    ; Read exception/interrupt state into r0
MRS r0, EPSR    ; Read execution state into r0
MRS r0, PSR     ; Copy combined CPSR, EPSR, and SPSR into r0
```

The follow shows how to copy a register into program status registers (PSR).

```
MSR APSR, r0      ; Write flag state
MSR BASEPRI, r0   ; Write base priority mask register; it prevents
                  ; the activation of all exceptions with the same
                  ; or lower priority level
```

4.11 Exercises

1. LSL (logic shift left) can be used to speed up the multiplication because LSL runs much faster than MUL. Use LSL to implement the following C statements.
   - (1) $x = 31 * x$;
   - (2) $x = 38 * x$;
   - (3) $x = 17 * x$;

2. Suppose r0 = 0x0F0F0F0F, and r1 = 0xFEDCBA98, find the result of the following operations.
   - (1) EOR r3, r1, r0
   - (2) ORR r3, r1, r0
   - (3) AND r3, r1, r0
   - (4) BIC r3, r1, r0
   - (5) MVN r3, r1
   - (6) MVN r3, r0
   - (7) MVN r3, r0
        ADD r3, r1, r3

3. Suppose r0 = 0x56789ABC, find the result of the following operation.
   - (1) RBIT r1, r0
   - (2) REV   r1, r0
   - (3) REV16 r1, r0
   - (4) REVSH r1, r0

4. Translate the following C statement into an assembly program, assuming 16-bit signed integers x, y and z (*i.e.* signed short) are stored in 32-bit register r0, r1, and r2, respectively.
$$x = x * y + z - x;$$

5. Translate the following C statement into an assembly program, assuming 16-bit unsigned integers x and y (*i.e.* unsigned short) are stored in register r0, and r1, respectively.
$$x = x \% y;$$

6. Write an assembly program that calculates the value of the following given polynomial, assuming signed integers x and y are stored in register r0 and r1, respectively.
$$y = 3x^3 - 7x^2 + 10x - 11.$$

7. Write an assembly program that calculates the remainder of the division between two unsigned 32-bit integers.

8. Explain why Cortex-M3 processors do not provide any rotation left instructions. They only provide ROR (rotate right) and RRX (rotate right extended).

9. Explain the difference of the Barrel shifter's role in the following two instructions:
   - ANDS r1, r2, r3, LSL #3
   - ADDS r1, r2, r3, LSL #3

10. Write an assembly program that reverses the byte order of a register without using the REV instruction.

11. Write an assembly program that swaps the upper half-word and the lower half-word of a register.

12. Implement the BIC (bitwise clear) instruction by using other assembly instructions.

13. Suppose Mask = 0x00000F0F and P = 0xABCDABCD. What are the results of the following bitwise operations?
    (1) Q = P & Mask;
    (2) Q = P | Mask;
    (3) Q = P ^ Mask;
    (4) Q = ~Mask;
    (5) Q = P & ~Mask;

14. Suppose r0 = 0xFFFFFFFF, r1 = 0x00000001, and r2 = 0x00000000. Initially the N, Z, C, and V flags are zero. Find the value of the N, Z, C, and V flags of the following instructions. (Assume each instruction runs individually, *i.e.* these instructions are not part of a program.)
    (1) ADD r3, r0, r2
    (2) SUBS r3, r0, r0
    (3) ADDS r3, r0, r2
    (4) LSL r3, r0, #1
    (5) LSRS r3, r1, #1
    (6) ANDS r3, r0, r2

15. Suppose we have a hypothetical processor, of which each register has only five bits. r0 = 0b11101 and r1 = 0b10110. What are the N, Z, C, and V flags of the following instructions? Assume initially N = 0, Z = 0, C = 1, V = 0, and these instructions are executed independently (*i.e.* they are NOT part of a program)
    (1) ADDS r3, r0, r1
    (2) SUBS r3, r0, r1
    (3) EOR r3, r0, r1
    (4) ANDS r3, r1, r1, LSL #3

CHAPTER

5

Load and Store

A load instruction sets a register to a specific value. The value might be a constant directly specified in the program or a value that is stored in the memory. A store instruction saves the value held in a register to the memory.

5.1 Load Constant into Registers

Many constant numbers, often called immediate numbers, can directly be used in assembly instructions. One command usage is to set a register to a specific constant value.

MOV Rd, #<immed_8>	Move 8-bit immediate value (0-255) to register
MVN Rd, #<immed_8>	Move the bitwise inverse of 8-bit immediate value (0-255) to register
MOVT Rd, #<immed_16>	Move 16-bit immediate value to top half-word [31:16] of register. Bottom half-word unaltered.
MOVW Rd, #<immed_16>	Move 16-bit immediate value to bottom half-word [15:0] of register and clear top half-word [31:16]
LDR Rt, =#<immed_8>	Equivalent to MOV
LDR Rt, =#<immed_32>	A pseudo instruction

Table 5-1. Instructions for loading constants into a register.

5.1.1 Data Movement Instruction MOV and MVN

All immediate numbers start with a "#" sign. If the immediate number is less than 8 bits, we can use MOV to set the register value.

```
MOV r0, #0xFF          ; Set r0 to the hexadecimal value 0xFF
MOV r0, #0b10011100    ; Set r0 to the binary value 10011100
MOV r0, #54            ; Set r0 to the decimal value 54
```

```
MOV r0, #0d54            ; Set r0 to the decimal value 54
```

If the immediate number has 32 bits, we can use MOV to set the register value if the immediate number can be obtained by using the following format:

```
#immed_32 = #immed_8 ROR (2 × #immed_4)
```

where ROR is the circular right rotate. For example, right rotating 0xAF by 24 bits can get 0x0000AF00.

```
0x0000AF00 = 0xAF ROR (2×12)
```

Some other 32-bit values with special regular patterns, such as 0xABABABAB, 0x00AB00AB, and 0xAB00AB00, can also be directly used in the MOV assembly instruction.

5.1.2   Pseudo Instruction LDR and ADR

A pseudo instruction is an instruction that is available to use in an assembly program but not directly supported by the microprocessor. It is translated to one or multiple actual machine instructions when the assembler builds the program into an executable. Pseudo instructions are provided for the convenience of programmers.

The LDR instruction can also be used as a pseudo instruction to load an immediate number into a register. A pseudo instruction is not a real machine instruction but it provides convenience for assembly programmers and improves the readability of the program. The assembler translates a pseudo instruction into one or multiple real machine instructions.

```
LDR   r0, =myArray     ; A pseudo instruction
LDR   r1, [r0]         ; This LDR is not a pseudo instruction
ADD   r1, r1, #1       ; Increment myArray[0] by 1
STR   r1, [r0]         ; Save value to memory

AREA myData, DATA      ; Directive: Declare a data area
ALIGN                  ; Directive: Align on a word boundary
                       ; Paddle bytes if necessary to make myArray
                       ; to start at an address that is a multiple of 4
myArray  DCW  1, 2, 3, 4, 5
```

Example 5-1. Using LDR pseudo instruction to load a memory address into a register.

Another widely used pseudo instruction in ARM assembly language is ADR (stands for address), which allow programmers to set a register to a large constant number. Both can be used to load a 32-bit memory address into a register. Note the syntax difference. LDR needs an equal sign ("=") but ADR does not.

In addition, the pseudo instruction LDR is different from the LDR instruction for accessing memory. For example, "LDR r1, =0x12345678" is a pseudo instruction, and

"LDR r1, [r0]" is a real machine instruction that loads a word from the memory. The assembler can distinguish them by checking the format of the operands specified in the LDR instruction.

```
        ADR  r0, myArray      ; A pseudo instruction
        LDR  r1, [r0]         ; Load myArray[0]
        ADD  r1, r1, #1       ; myArray[0]++
        STR  r1, [r0]         ; Store myArray[0]

        AREA myData, DATA     ; Declare a data area
        ALIGN                 ; Align on word boundaries: address divisible by 4
myArray DCW 1, 2, 3, 4, 5     ; Define and allocate an integer array
```

Example 5-2. Using ADR pseudo instruction to load a memory address into a register

5.1.3   Comparison of LDR, ADR and MOV

While ADR can only be used to load a memory address label into a register, LDR is more versatile and can load an immediate number up to 32 bits. The real instructions translated from the LDR pseudo instruction depend on the immediate number.

LDR can load a 32-bit constant to a register.

MOV can only load an 12-bit constant into a register.

ADR can load a memory address.

- If the constant number can fit into the 12-bit immediate number format used by a MOV or MVN instruction, the LDR pseudo instruction is translated to MOV or MVN.
- Otherwise, it is translated into a regular LDR instruction that uses PC-relative memory address.

In the latter case, the immediate numbers are directly stored together with instruction code in the machine executable, and thus a load instruction with a PC-relative memory address is used to load the immediate number from the binary executable. Chapter 5.4.3 introduces PC-relative addressing in details.

```
    LDR r1, =2          ; Translated to:  MOV r1, #2
    LDR r2, =-2         ; Translated to:  MVN r0, #1
    LDR r3, =0x12345678 ; Translated to:  LDR r2, [pc, #offset1]
    LDR r4, =myAddress  ; Translated to:  LDR r2, [pc, #offset2]
                        ; LDR with a PC-relative address
```

Example 5-3. Compilers translate a pseudo LDR to MOV, MVN, or PC-relative LDR.

Note the syntax of the constant number in MOV and LDR are different.

```
    LDR r0, =0xFF       ; '=' before the constant
    MOV r0, #0xFF       ; '#' before the constant
```

5.2 Big Endian and Little Endian

Cortex-M3 processors can be configured as big endian or little endian. The endian specifies the byte order if a data element has multiple bytes, as shown in Figure 5-1.

- Little endian means the low-order byte of the number is stored in memory at the lowest address, and the high-order byte at the highest address. (The little end comes first.)
- Big endian means the high-order byte of the number is stored in memory at the lowest address, and the low-order byte at the highest address. (The big end comes first.)

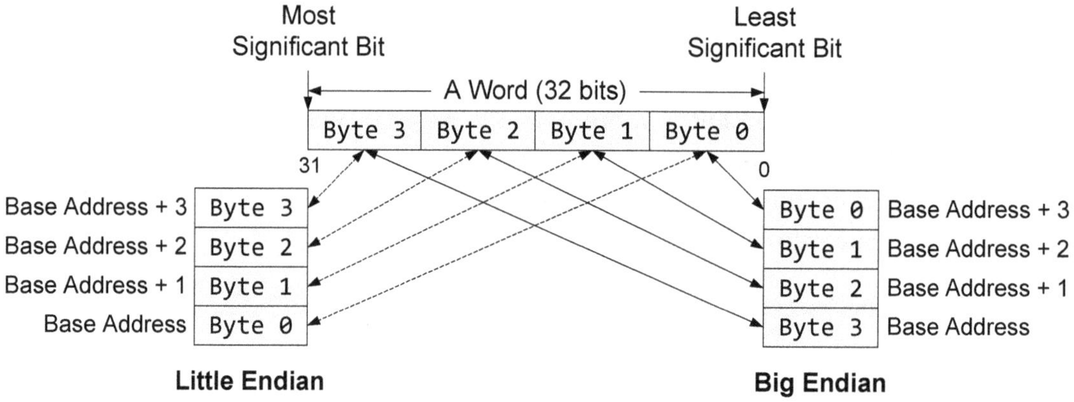

Figure 5-1. Comparison of little endian and big endian

In the example given in Figure 5-2, the assembly instruction "LDR r1, [r0]" loads a 32-bit value from the memory address 0x20008000 to register r1. Register r1 will have different results, depending on whether the big or little endian is used.

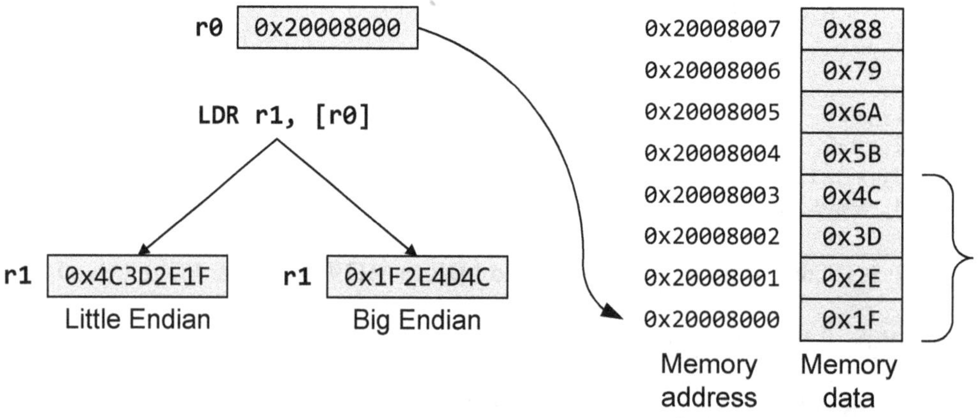

Figure 5-2. After loading, r1 is 0x4C3D2E1F if little endian, and 0x1F2E3D4C if big endian.

5.3 Accessing Data in Memory

A load instruction is used to retrieve data stored at the specified memory address and save the data in a specific register. A store instruction is the opposite: It saves the content of a register to the memory at a given memory address.

To access data in the memory, the memory address must be stored in a register. Example 5-4 puts the memory address into register r0 and then loads a word into register r1. In addition, it stores a decimal value 123 into the memory.

```
; Suppose r0 = 0x82000004
LDR r1, [r0]     ; r1 = a word (4 bytes) in memory starting at 0x82000004
MOV r2, #123     ; Set the value of register r2 to 123
STR r2, [r0]     ; Save 4 bytes into memory starting at 0x82000004
```
Example 5-4. Loading a word from the memory

5.4 Memory Addressing

5.4.1 Pre-index, Post-index, and Pre-index with Update

ARM microprocessors support flexible memory addressing and provide three memory address modes: pre-index, post-index, and pre-index with update. Each index format includes a base memory address and an offset in terms of bytes. In the pre-index format, the target memory address is calculated as the base memory address plus the offset.

1. In the pre-index format with update, three steps are involved: (1) calculating the target memory address as the base plus the offset; (2) accessing the data at the target memory address; and (3) and updating the base memory.
2. In the post-index format, two steps are involved: (1) updating the base memory address as the sum of the base memory address and offset, and (2) accessing the data by using the updated base memory address.

Index Format	Example	Equivalent
Pre-index	LDR r1, [r0, #4]	r1 ← memory[r0 + 4], r0 is unchanged
Pre-index with update	LDR r1, [r0, #4]!	r1 ← memory[r0 + 4] r0 ← r0 + 4
Post-index	LDR r1, [r0], #4	r1 ← memory[r0] r0 ← r0 + 4

Table 5-2. Comparison of three addressing formats

We will use three examples, as listed in Table 5-2, to compare these three addressing modes. Suppose register r0 has an initial value of 0x20008000, the values of different memory locations are given in Figure 5-3, the little endian is used to store a word in memory.

LDR r1, [r0, #4]   ; Pre-index

> As shown in Figure 5-3, the value of register r0 is not updated. After loading the word stored at memory address 0x20008004, the content of register r1 is 0x88796A5B.

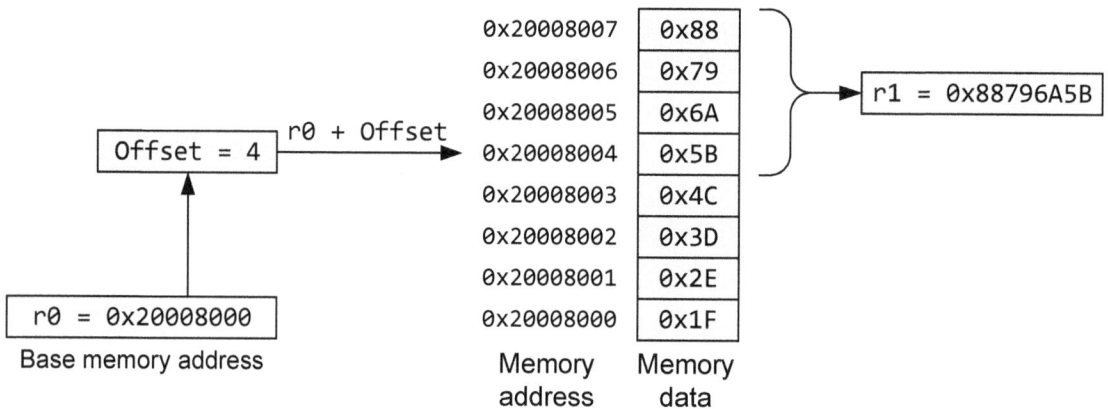

Figure 5-3. Pre-index (r1 ← memory[r0 + 4], r0 is unchanged)

LDR r1, [r0], #4   ; Post-index

> As shown in Figure 5-4, the value of register r0 is incremented by the offset after loading. Register r1 is fetched from the memory address 0x20008000.

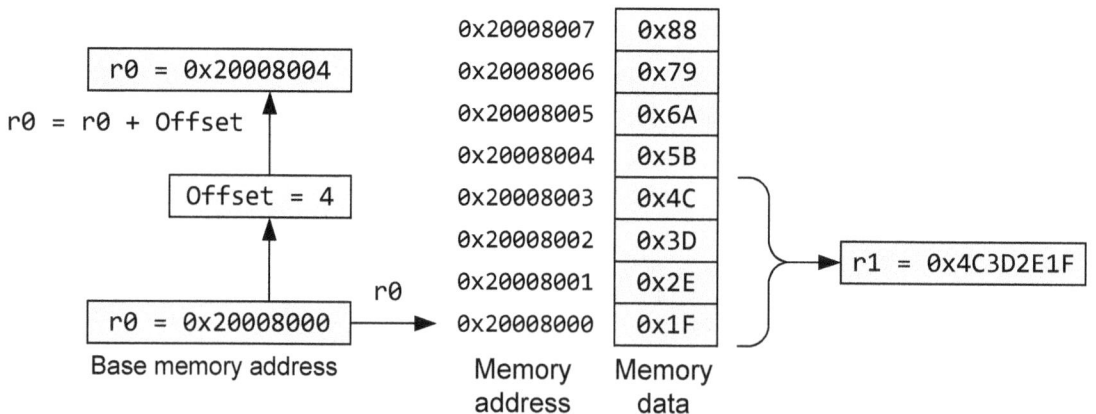

Figure 5-4. Post-index (r1 ← memory[r0], r0 ← r0 + 4)

```
LDR r1, [r0, #4]!    ; Pre-index with update
```

As shown in Figure 5-5, the value of register r0 is incremented by the offset after loading. Different with the post-index, the pre-index with update retrieves the word from the memory address 0x20008004, instead of 0x20008000.

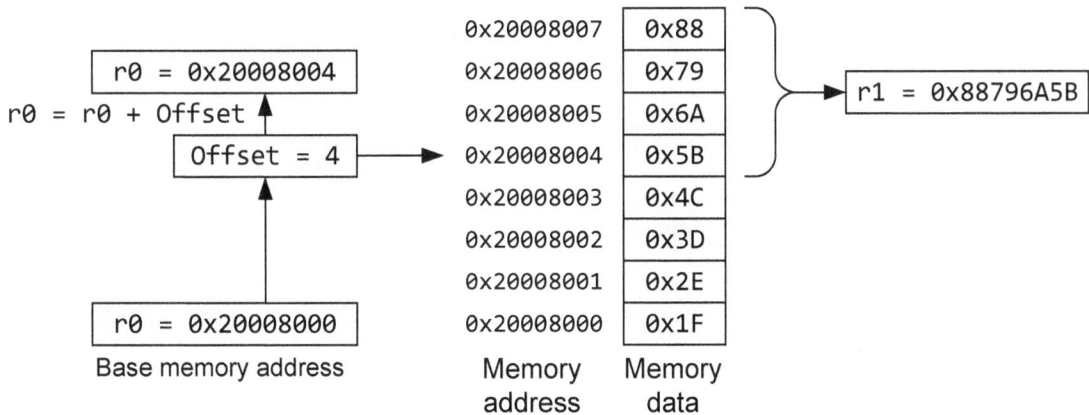

	Memory address	Memory data	
	0x20008007	0x88	
r0 = 0x20008004	0x20008006	0x79	r1 = 0x88796A5B
r0 = r0 + Offset	0x20008005	0x6A	
Offset = 4 →	0x20008004	0x5B	
	0x20008003	0x4C	
	0x20008002	0x3D	
	0x20008001	0x2E	
r0 = 0x20008000	0x20008000	0x1F	
Base memory address	Memory address	Memory data	

Figure 5-5. Pre-index with update (r1 ← memory[r0 + 4], r0 ← r0 + 4)

Table 5-2 summarizes the results of load instructions with three addressing modes described above.

Instruction	Result of r0	Result of r1	Comment
LDR r1, [r0,#4]	0x20008000	0x88796A5B	Pre-index
LDR r1, [r0],#4	0x20008004	0x4C3D2E1F	Post-index
LDR r1, [r0,#4]!	0x20008004	0x88796A5B	Pre-index with update

Table 5-3. Example of three addressing modes

5.4.2 Load and Store Instructions

While there are three different memory addressing formats, Table 5-4 and Table 5-5 use the pre-index format to illustrate different types of load and store instructions, respectively. The other two address index formats can also be used for these instructions.

When a byte or half-word is loaded into a 32-bit register, attention should be drawn to whether the data in memory represents a signed or unsigned number. If it is signed, LDRSB or LDRSH should be used to preserve the number's sign and value. LDRSB and LDRSH perform sign extension, which duplicates the sign bit.

Note in the LDM and STM instructions, the order in which registers are listed does not matter. The lowest-numbered register is loaded from the lowest memory address, through to the highest-numbered register from the highest memory address.

LDR Rt, [Rn, #offset]	Load word, $Rt \leftarrow mem[Rn + offset]$
LDRB Rt, [Rn, #offset]	Load byte, $Rt \leftarrow mem[Rn + offset]$
LDRH Rt, [Rn, #offset]	Load half-word, $Rt \leftarrow mem[Rn + offset]$
LDRSB Rt, [Rn, #offset]	Load signed byte, $Rt \leftarrow Sign\ Extend\ (mem[Rn + offset])$
LDRSH Rt, [Rn, #offset]	Load signed half-word, $Rt \leftarrow Sign\ Extend\ (mem[Rn + offset])$
LDM Rn, register_list	Load multiple words

Table 5-4. Load data of different sizes from memory to a register

STR Rt, [Rn, #offset]	Store word, $mem[Rn + offset] \leftarrow Rt$
STRB Rt, [Rn, #offset]	Store lower byte, $mem[Rn + offset] \leftarrow Rt$
STRH Rt, [Rn, #offset]	Store lower half-word, $mem[Rn + offset] \leftarrow Rt$
STM Rn, register_list	Store multiple words

Table 5-5. Store value of a register in memory

5.4.3   PC-relative Addressing

PC-relative addressing is widely used in ARM processors to locate nearby instructions and data. Even if the original assembly codes did not use it, the compiler may translate a memory index by using PC-relative addressing in order to achieve position independent addressing. The target memory address is as the following:

$$Target\ Memory\ Address = PC + 4 + Offset$$

If a Thumb assembly instruction reads the program counter (PC), the value read is the address of the instruction plus 4 bytes.

PC-relative addressing is often used to set a register to a complicated value. For example, the program needs to set register r1 to 0xF1234567. We cannot use the instruction "MOV r1, #0xF1234567" because the constant number is too large. Instead, we use the following pseudo LDR instruction.

```
LDR r1, =0xF1234567
```

The compiler will translate the above LDR pseudo instruction into a PC-relative LDR instruction. Suppose the constant 0xF1234567 is stored at the memory location 0x08000144. The compiler will use the PC-relative addressing for the load word instruction. If the memory address of the load-word (LDR) instruction is 0x0800012C, the difference between 0x08000144 and 0x0800012C is 24 in decimal. As a result, the memory address is written as [pc, #20].

The following shows the translated PC-relative load instruction.

0x0800012C	LDR	r1,[pc,#20] ; @0x08000144
...	...	
0x08000144	DCW	0x4567
0x08000146	DCW	0xF123

Example 5-5. Using PC-relative addressing to load a large constant number into a register

5.4.4 Example of Accessing an Array

The following examples illustrate how to iterate through an array of five 32-bit integers by using three different memory-addressing modes.

Suppose we want to load an array of five integers into registers r1, r2, r3, r4, and r5. We will use three different address modes to access the array and calculate the sum of the array. The array is defined as follows:

```
        AREA myData, DATA, READWRITE
array   DCD 1, 2, 3, 4, 5
```

(1) Iterate an array by using pre-index

```
        LDR r0, =array      ; Using LDR pseudo instruction, r0 = array address
        LDR r1, [r0]        ; r1 = array[0]. After loading, r0 = array
        LDR r2, [r0, 4]     ; r2 = array[1]. After loading, r0 = array + 4
        LDR r3, [r0, 8]     ; r3 = array[2]. After loading, r0 = array + 8
        LDR r4, [r0, 12]    ; r4 = array[3]. After loading, r0 = array + 12
        LDR r5, [r0, 16]    ; r5 = array[4]. After loading, r0 = array + 16
```

(2) Iterate an array by using post-index

```
        LDR r0, =array      ; Using LDR pseudo instruction, r0 = array address
        LDR r1, [r0], 4     ; r1 = array[0]. After loading, r0 = array + 4
        LDR r2, [r0], 4     ; r2 = array[1]. After loading, r0 = array + 8
        LDR r3, [r0], 4     ; r3 = array[2]. After loading, r0 = array + 12
        LDR r4, [r0], 4     ; r4 = array[3]. After loading, r0 = array + 16
        LDR r5, [r0], 4     ; r5 = array[4]. After loading, r0 = array + 20
```

(3) Iterate an array by using pre-index with update

```
        LDR r0, =array      ; Using LDR pseudo instruction, r0 = array address
        LDR r1, [r0]        ; r1 = array[0]. After loading, r0 = array
        LDR r2, [r0, 4]!    ; r2 = array[1]. After loading, r0 = array + 4
        LDR r3, [r0, 4]!    ; r3 = array[2]. After loading, r0 = array + 8
        LDR r4, [r0, 4]!    ; r4 = array[3]. After loading, r0 = array + 12
        LDR r5, [r0, 4]!    ; r5 = array[4]. After loading, r0 = array + 16
```

The above example codes only work well for a short array. If the length of the array is long, then the assembly program needs to use conditional branch instructions (introduced in Chapter 6) to implement a loop in order to iterate the array.

5.5 Exercises

1. Suppose r0 = 0x8000, and the memory layout is as follows:

Address	Data
0x8007	0x79
0x8006	0xCD
0x8005	0xA3
0x8004	0xFD
0x8003	0x0D
0x8002	0xEB
0x8001	0x2C
0x8000	0x1A

   a) What is the value of r1 after running LDR r1, [r0] if the system is little endian or big endian?

   b) Suppose the system is set as little endian. What are the values of r1 and r0 if the instructions are executed separately?

   - LDR r1, [r0, #4]
   - LDR r1, [r0], #4
   - LDR r1, [r0, #4]!

2. Write an assembly program that converts a 32-bit integer stored in the memory from little endian to big endian, without using the REV instruction. Make sure the result is saved back to the memory.

3. Suppose r0 = 0x20000000 and r1 = 0x12345678. All bytes in memory are initialized to 0x00. Suppose the following assembly program has been executed successfully. Draw a table to show the memory value if the processor uses little endian.

```
STR r1, [r0], #4
STR r1, [r0, #4]!
STR r1, [r0, 4]
```

4. What is the memory value of Question 3 if the processor uses big endian?

CHAPTER 6

Branch and Conditional Execution

Normally instructions of an assembly program are executed in the same sequential order as they are listed in the program. When one instruction completes, the program counter is incremented by the control unit within the processor and ordinarily points to the next instruction. However, modifying the program counter at runtime can dynamically change the execution order. This is called changing the flow of control. There are four major approaches to change the flow of control:

1. branch instructions,
2. conditional execution,
3. calling a subroutine, and
4. interrupts.

In this chapter, we will focus on the first two approaches. Chapter 8 will discuss subroutines and Chapter 12 will present interrupts.

6.1 Condition Testing

Most assembly instructions can be selectively executed based on the N, Z, C, and V flags of the application program status register (APSR). Table 2-3 lists the condition flags for comparing signed and unsigned numbers.

Compare	Signed	Unsigned	Relationship Tested
==	EQ	EQ	Equal to
!=	NE	NE	Not equal to
>	GT	HI	Greater than
≥	GE	HS	Greater than or equal to
<	LT	LO	Less than
≤	LE	LS	Less than or equal to

Table 6-1. Summary of the comparison suffix for signed and unsigned numbers

These condition flags provide convenience for programmers and improve the code readability. For example, the following two assembly instructions calculate the absolute value of a signed integer stored in register r1. The second instruction RSB is only executed when r1 is less than 0. The condition flag "LT" tests the negative flag and the RSB instruction is ignored by the processor if the negative flag is 0.

```
CMP   r1, #0       ; CMP updates N, Z, C, and V flags
RSBLT r1, r1, #0   ; Run r1 = 0 - r1 if r1 < 0. LT = signed Less Than.
```

Cortex-M3 processors have 15 condition flags, as summarized in Table 6-2. These condition flags check whether N, Z, C, and V meet specific requirements. When an instruction has no conditional flag, it defaults to "AL" and is always executed.

Suffix	Description	Flags tested	Logic Implementation
EQ	EQual	$Z = 1$	Z
NE	Not Equal	$Z = 0$	$\bar{Z}$
CS/HS	unsigned Higher or Same	$C = 1$	C
CC/LO	unsigned LOwer	$C = 0$	$\bar{C}$
MI	MInus (negative)	$N = 1$	N
PL	PLus (positive or zero)	$N = 0$	$\bar{N}$
VS	oVerflow Set	$V = 1$	V
VC	oVerflow Clear	$V = 0$	$\bar{V}$
HI	unsigned HIgher	$C = 1\ \&\ Z = 0$	$C\bar{Z}$
LS	unsigned Lower or Same	$C = 0$ or $Z = 1$	$\bar{C} + Z$
GE	signed Greater or Equal	$N = V$	$NV + \bar{N}\bar{V}$
LT	signed Less Than	$N\ != V$	$N\bar{V} + \bar{N}V$
GT	signed Greater Than	$Z = 0\ \&\ N = V$	$Z(NV + \bar{N}\bar{V})$
LE	signed Less than or Equal	$Z = 1$ or $N\ != V$	$Z + N\bar{V} + \bar{N}V$
AL	ALways		

Table 6-2. Summary of flag testing for various signed and unsigned comparisons

The CMP instruction "CMP r0, r1" is equivalent to the subtraction operation r0 - r1, except the result is discarded.

When two registers in the instruction "CMP r0, r1" represent unsigned integers,

- the carry flag is set if no borrow occurs during the subtraction, *i.e.* r0 ≥ r1, and
- the carry flag is cleared if borrow does occur during the subtraction, *i.e.* r0 < r1.

Therefore, the HS, LO, HI and LS suffix checks the zero flag (if necessary) and the carry flag.

When two registers in the instruction "CMP r0, r1" represent signed numbers, Table 6-3 summarizes the meaning of all four possible combinations of the negative flag (N) and the overflow flag (V).

	N = 0	N = 1
V = 0	r0 ≥ r1	r0 < r1
V = 1	r0 < r1	r0 ≥ r1

**Table 6-3. Meaning of the overflow and negative flags of "CMP r0, r1"
if r0 and r1 hold signed numbers.**

Table 6-4 gives the detailed explanation of how to get the conclusions listed in Table 6-3.

- When two signed numbers are subtracted, there are two possible scenarios in which overflow occurs: (1) the result of subtracting a positive number from a negative number is positive, or (2) the result of subtracting a negative number from a positive number is negative.
- When subtracting two numbers with the same sign, no overflow would occur.

In sum, if overflow occurs, the result is incorrect and its sign indicated by the N flag is opposite to the sign of the true result.

	N = 0	N = 1
V = 0	No overflow has occurred, implying the result is correct. The result is non-negative. Thus, r0 – r1 ≥ 0, *i.e.* r0 ≥ r1.	No overflow has occurred, implying the result is correct. The result is negative. Thus, r0 – r1 < 0, *i.e.* r0 < r1.
V = 1	Overflow occurred, implying the result is incorrect. The result is mistakenly reported as non-negative but it should be negative. Thus, r0 – r1 < 0 in reality, *i.e.* r0 < r1.	Overflow has occurred, implying the result is incorrect. The result is mistakenly reported as negative but it should be non-negative. Thus, r0 – r1 ≥ 0 in reality, *i.e.* r0 ≥ r1.

Table 6-4. The signed greater or equal (GE) checks whether V equals N.

According to Table 6-4, we can get the following conclusions:

- If N = V, then r0 is signed greater than or equal to r1.
- If N ≠ V, then r0 is signed less than r1.

Therefore, the signed greater or equal (GE) and signed greater than (GT) check whether the N flag is the same as the V flag.

6.2 Branch Instructions

A branch instruction is used to change the flow of program execution from a normal sequential order. It allows the microprocessor to begin execution a different set of instructions. There are two types of branch instructions: unconditional and conditional.

- An unconditional branch instruction always loads the memory address of the designated instruction into the program counter and starts to execute the new program flow. The designated instruction is usually identified by using a label in assembly language.
- A conditional branch instruction first checks whether a specific condition is satisfied or not. If the condition is met, the processor then starts to execute the designated instruction, instead of the next sequential instruction. A conditional branch instruction is equivalent to "if condition is true, then go to label." When the program jumps away, we say the branch is taken. Otherwise, the branch is not taken.

The condition can be coded to the branch instruction "B" to form different conditional branch instructions, as summarized in Table 6-5. For example, "BEQ" compares two register values and the branch is taken if they are equal.

	Instruction	Description	Flags tested
Unconditional Branch	B *Label*	Branch to label	
Conditional Branch	BEQ *Label*	Branch if **EQ**ual	$Z = 1$
	BNE *Label*	Branch if **N**ot **E**qual	$Z = 0$
	BCS/BHS *Label*	Branch if unsigned **H**igher or **S**ame	$C = 1$
	BCC/BLO *Label*	Branch if unsigned **LO**wer	$C = 0$
	BMI *Label*	Branch if **MI**nus (Negative)	$N = 1$
	BPL *Label*	Branch if **PL**us (Positive or Zero)	$N = 0$
	BVS *Label*	Branch if o**V**erflow **S**et	$V = 1$
	BVC *Label*	Branch if o**V**erflow **C**lear	$V = 0$
	BHI *Label*	Branch if unsigned **HI**gher	$C = 1 \;\&\; Z = 0$
	BLS *Label*	Branch if unsigned **L**ower or **S**ame	$C = 0 \text{ or } Z = 1$
	BGE *Label*	Branch if signed **G**reater or **E**qual	$N = V$
	BLT *Label*	Branch if signed **L**ess **T**han	$N \mathbin{!=} V$
	BGT *Label*	Branch if signed **G**reater **T**han	$Z = 0 \;\&\; N = V$
	BLE *Label*	Branch if signed **L**ess than or **E**qual	$Z = 1 \text{ or } N = !V$

Table 6-5. List of unconditional and conditional branch instructions

Note some ARM processors can directly support all branch instructions listed above. However, Cortex-M3 processors do not directly support all branch instructions with a condition suffix. Instead, these branch instructions excluding "B" are translated to If-then-else (IT) instructions. The IT instruction performs the same flag testing as presented in the above table.

Program flow control structures such as if-then, if-then-else, for loop, and while loop use the CMP instruction followed by a branch instruction. Table 6-6 summarizes conditional branch instructions for the comparison of signed numbers and unsigned numbers.

Comparison	Signed	Unsigned
==	BEQ	BEQ
!=	BNE	BNE
>	BGT	BHI
≥	BGE	BHS
<	BLT	BLO
≤	BLE	BLS

Table 6-6. Comparison of branch instructions used for signed and unsigned comparison

Example:　Go to the labeled instruction if two numbers are equal:

```
CMP r1, r2
BEQ Label
```

When comparing 0xFFFFFFFF or 0x00000001, which is greater? When they are unsigned integers, the first number is larger. However, if they are signed numbers, the second one is larger. When the program is written in assembly, it is the programmer's responsibility to tell the processor how to interpret data. If written in C, their corresponding variables are declared explicitly by programmers as signed or unsigned integers.

When two numbers are unsigned integers, unsigned condition code should be used.

C Program	Assembly Program

unsigned int x, y, z;
x = 0x00000001;
y = 0xFFFFFFFF;
if (x > y)
　z = 1;
else
　z = 0;
	MOV　r5, #0x00000001 ; x
	　　　MOV　r6, #0xFFFFFFFF ; y
	　　　CMP　r5, r6
	　　　BLS　else　　; branch if ≤
	then　MOV　r7, #1　; z = 1
	　　　B　　endif　; skip the next instruction
	else　MOV　r7,#0　; z = 0
	endif

Example 6-1. Implementation of if-statement that compares two unsigned integers

When these two numbers are signed integers, signed condition code should be used.

C Program	Assembly Program

`signed int x, y, z;`
`x = 1;  // 0x00000001`
`y = -1;  // 0xFFFFFFFF`
`if (x > y)`
`  z = 1;`
`else`
`  z = 0;`
	`        MOVS  r5, #0x00000001 ; x`
	`        MOVS  r6, #0xFFFFFFFF ; y`
	`        CMP   r5, r6`
	`        BLE   then        ; branch if signed ≤`
	`        MOVS  r7, #1       ; z = 1`
	`        B     endif       ; skip the next instruction`
	`then    MOVS  r7,#0        ; z = 0`
	`endif`

Example 6-2. Implementation of if-statement that compares two signed integers

It is often that an assembly program compares against zero and checks whether the branch should be taken or not. CBZ (compare and branch on zero) and CBNZ (compare and branch on non-zero) are available to improve the program performance of this common case by reducing one instruction. One limitation is that CBZ and CBNZ can only branch forward and the branch destination must be within 4 to 130 bytes after the instruction. The following shows example usages and their equivalent implement.

`CBZ   r1, label`   ⟹

`CMP   r1, #0`	
`BEQ   label   ; branch if equal`	

`CBNZ r1, label`   ⟹

`CMP   r1, #0`	
`BNE   label   ; branch if not equal`	

In addition, the following instructions are used to call a subroutine.

- "BL label" instruction copies the memory address of the instruction immediately after the BL instruction into the link register (r14), and then branches to the instruction addressed by the label.
- "BX Rm" is similar to "BL label" except the target instruction address is saved in register Rm.
- "BLX Rm" first places the address of the next instruction after the BLX instruction into the link register and then branches to the address held in Rm.

Detailed description and examples are given in Chapter 8.1.

Instruction	Operands	Brief description
BL	label	Branch with link
BLX	Rm	Branch indirect with link
BX	Rm	Branch and exchange

Table 6-7. Branch instructions that calls a subroutine.

6.3 Conditional Execution

Besides four data comparison instructions (CMP, CMN, TEQ, and TST), most instructions can update the program status flags (N, Z, C, and V) if the suffix S is added. One of the salient features of ARM assembly language is that an instruction can optionally be executed based on the program status flags. This feature is often not supported in other assembly languages.

The condition flags introduced in Chapter 6.1 can be a postfix of almost all instructions to implement conditional execution. The conditional branch instructions presented in the previous section is a special case of conditional execution.

We take the add instruction as an example to illustrate conditional execution. By default, the instruction "ADD r3, r2, r1" is always executed no matter what value the program status flags are. The conditional flag, such as "EQ", can be appended to "ADD" to form a conditionally executed instruction "ADDEQ", as shown in Table 6-8.

Add instruction	Condition	Flag tested
ADDEQ r3, r2, r1	Add if **EQ**ual	Add if Z = 1
ADDNE r3, r2, r1	Add if **N**ot **E**qual	Add if Z = 0
ADDHS r3, r2, r1	Add if Unsigned **H**igher or **S**ame	Add if C = 1
ADDLO r3, r2, r1	Add if Unsigned **LO**wer	Add if C = 0
ADDMI r3, r2, r1	Add if **MI**nus (Negative)	Add if N = 1
ADDPL r3, r2, r1	Add if **PL**us (Positive or Zero)	Add if N = 0
ADDVS r3, r2, r1	Add if o**V**erflow **S**et	Add if V = 1
ADDVC r3, r2, r1	Add if o**V**erflow **C**lear	Add if V = 0
ADDHI r3, r2, r1	Add if Unsigned **HI**gher	Add if C = 1 & Z = 0
ADDLS r3, r2, r1	Add if Unsigned **L**ower or **S**ame	Add if C = 0 or Z = 1
ADDGE r3, r2, r1	Add if Signed **G**reater or **E**qual	Add if N = V
ADDLT r3, r2, r1	Add if Signed **L**ess **T**han	Add if N != V
ADDGT r3, r2, r1	Add if Signed **G**reater **T**han	Add if Z = 0 & N = V
ADDLE r3, r2, r1	Add if Signed **L**ess than or **E**qual	Add if Z = 1 or N = !V

Table 6-8. Conditionally executed ADD instruction

Conditionally executed instructions can help facilitate the implementation of the selection and loop control structures. An example is given below.

```
CMP r1, r0
ADDSPL r3, r3, #1    ; increment r3 by 1 and update flags if r1 ≥ r0
```

6.4 If-then Statement

An *if-then* statement in C selectively executes a block of code based on whether a given Boolean condition is true or false. If the condition is true or nonzero, the block is executed. Otherwise, the block is skipped, and the control returns to the first statement after the if-then statement.

The following example calculates the absolute value of a signed integer a and increases variable x by 1.

```
C Program
if (a < 0 ) {
    a = 0 - a;
}
x = x + 1;
```

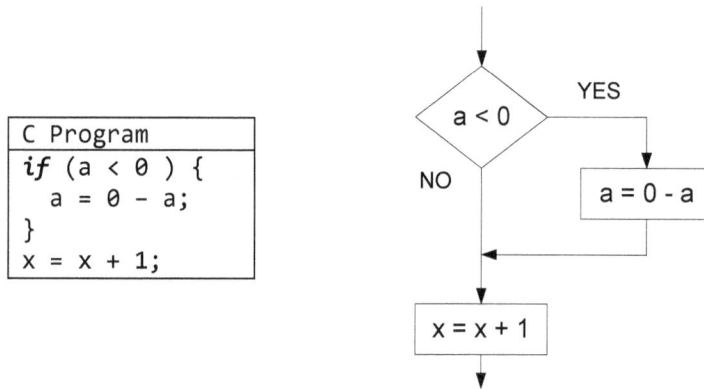

Assuming variable a and x are stored in register r1 and r1, respectively, the following gives two assembly implementations equivalent to the above C code. An if-then statement can be implemented by using a conditional branch instruction (Example 6-3) or a conditionally executed instruction (Example 6-4).

```
         ; r1 = a, r2 = x
         CMP r1, #0          ; Compare a with 0
         BGE endif           ; Go to endif if a ≥ 0
then     RSB r1, r1, #0      ; a = - a
endif    ADD r2, r2, #1      ; x = x + 1
```

Example 6-3. An if-then statement can be implemented by using conditional branch instructions

```
         ; r1 = a, r2 = x
         CMP   r1, #0        ; Compare a with 0
         RSBLT r1, r1, #0    ; a = 0 - a if a < 0
         ADD   r2, r2, #1    ; x = x + 1
```

Example 6-4. An if-then statement can be implemented by using conditional execution

Compared with conditional branch instructions, conditionally executed instructions are concise and provide convenience for programmers. However, conditionally executed instructions are only used when the if-statement body is short. In addition, in nested-if statement, conditional branches are often preferred.

Compound Boolean expression

In mathematics, a Boolean (or logical) condition can be a compound expression combined by logical operators AND, OR, and NOT. C language uses three special symbols as logical operators: **&&** (AND), **||** (OR), and **!** (NOT). In C, we write a Boolean condition like this:

```
x > 20 && x < 25
x == 20 || x == 25
!(x == 20 || x == 25)
```

The NOT operator (!) has higher precedence than the AND operator (&&), which has higher precedence than the OR operator (||).

If-then statement with a compound logical OR expression

A compound logical expression combined by logical OR can be implemented by multiple comparison instructions that test each simple logical expression. Example 6-5 show how to implement an if-statement with a compound logic OR expression.

C Program	Assembly Program

`// x is a signed integer`
`if(x <= 20 || x >= 25){`
`   a = 1`
`}`
	`         ; r0 = x`
	`     CMP  r0, #20    ; compare x and 20`
	`     BLE  then       ; go to then if x ≤ 20`
	`     CMP  r0, #25    ; compare x and 25`
	`     BLT  endif      ; go to endif if x < 25`
	`then MOV  r1, #1     ; a = 1`
	`endif`

Example 6-5. A generic approach to implement if-then with a compound logical OR

Example 6-6 gives a simplified implementation that uses conditionally executed instructions.

C Program	Assembly Program

`// x is a signed integer`
`if(x <= 20 || x >= 25){`
`   a = 1;`
`}`
	`       ; r0 = x, r1 = a`
	`   CMP   r0, #20  ; compare x and 20`
	`   MOVLE r1, #1   ; a=1 if less or equal`
	`   CMP   r0, #25  ; CMP if greater than`
	`   MOVGE r1, #1   ; a=1 if greater or equal`
	`endif`

Example 6-6. Conditional execution can be used to implement a compound logical OR.

Sometimes conditional comparison (such as CMPNE) and conditional execution can simplify the program, as shown below.

C Program	Assembly Program

`if( x == 20 || x == 25){`
`    a = 1;`
`}`
	`; r0 = x, r1 = a`
	`CMP   r0, #20  ; compare x and 20`
	`CMPNE r0, #25  ; CMP if r0 ≠ 25`
	`MOVEQ r1, #1   ; r1 = 1 if Z = 1`

Example 6-7. Conditional comparison (such as CMPNE) tests a compound expression

However, using conditional branch and execution can only implement an if-then statement in which the actions performed are simple. A generic approach to implement an if-then structure with a compound logic OR expression is to use conditionally branch instructions.

If-then statement with a compound logical AND expression

It is more difficult to test in assembly a compound logical expression combined by AND. De Morgan's laws are often used to break a logical AND compound expression into a logical OR expression.

$$\overline{A \text{ and } B} = \overline{A} \text{ or } \overline{B}$$

For example:

$$\overline{x > 20 \text{ and } x < 25} = \overline{x > 20} \text{ or } \overline{x < 25}$$
$$= x \leq 20 \text{ or } x \geq 25$$

Therefore, when the condition of the if-statement is x > 20 && x < 25, in the assembly implementation given in Example 6-8, we test whether $x \leq 20$ or $x \geq 25$.

C Program	Assembly Program

`if ( x > 20 && x < 25){`
`    a = 1;`
`}`
	`; Assume r0 = x, r1 = a`
	`CMP   r0, #20  ; compare x with 20`
	`BLE   endif    ; go to endif if x ≤ 20`
	`CMP   r0, #25  ; compare x with 25`
	`BGE   endif    ; go to endif if x ≥ 25`
	`MOVS r1, #1    ; a = 1`

	`endif`

Example 6-8. Using De Morgan's laws to convert a logical AND to a logical OR

If-then statement with a compound logical AND and OR expression

When a compound logical expression includes both AND and OR operators, the techniques introduced previously must be combined.

```
if ( x == 5 || (x > 20 && x < 25) )
     a = 1;
```

The following gives an example implementation.

```
; Assume r0 = x, r1 = a
CMP   r0, #5     ; compare x with 5
BEQ   then       ; if x == 5, go to then

CMP   r0, #20    ; compare x with 20
BLE   endif      ; go to endif if x ≤ 20

CMP   r0, #25    ; compare x with 25
BGE   endif      ; go to endif if x ≥ 25

then    MOVS r1, #1    ; a = 1
endif
```

Example 6-9. Assembly implementation of a logic expression with both AND and OR

6.5 If-then-else Statement

The *if-then-else* statement selects one of two alternative set of statements to execute. It first evaluates the given Boolean condition. If the condition is true, the statements following the *if* statement are executed. Otherwise, the statements following the *else* statement are executed.

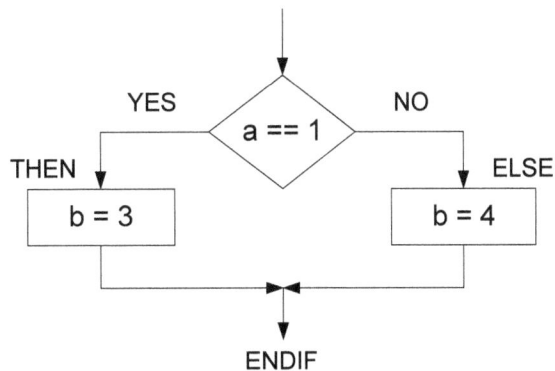

In the sample C program shown above, variable *b* is set to 3 if *a* is 1; oherwise, *b* is set to 4.

Assume the content of variable *a* is stored in r1, and *b* in r2, the following gives two equivalent implementations of the above if-else C program. In order to make assembly code easy to understand, we should give each label a meaningful name, such as "then", "else", and "endif".

Assembly Program 1	Assembly Program 2

`; r1 = a, r2 = b`
`        CMP r1, #1    ; compare a and 1`
`        BNE else      ; go to else if a ≠ 1`
`then    MOV r2, #3    ; b = 3`
`        B   endif     ; go to endif`
`else    MOV r2, #4    ; b = 4`
`endif`
	`; r1 = a, r2 = b`
	`        CMP   r1, #1   ; compare a and 1`
	`        MOVEQ r2, #3   ; b = 3 if a = 1`
	`        MOVNE r2, #4   ; b = 4 if a ≠ 1`

6.6 For Loop

The *for* loop repeatedly executes a specific block of codes as long as a particular condition is satisfied. A for loop contains three expressions, as shown below.

- The initial expression is executed only once often to initialize loop indices.
- The condition expression is tested before each iteration is executed. The loop body is executed if the condition expression is true. Note the loop body is skipped if the condition expression is false at the very first time it is evaluated.
- The loop expression is often used to increment loop indices after each loop.

```
for (initial_expression; condition_expression; loop_experssion) {
    // loop body

}
```

The following C program calculates the sum of the first 10 integers.

C Program

`int i;`
`int sum = 0;`
`for(i = 0; i < 10; i++){`
`    sum += i;`
`}`

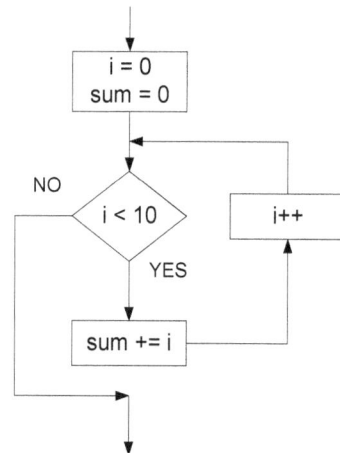

Assume r0 = *i* and r2 = *sum*, the following gives three different approaches to translate the above for loop program into assembly.

Assembly Program 1	Assembly Program 2	Assembly Program 3
``` MOV r0, #0 ; i MOV r1, #0 ; sum B check loop ADD r1, r1, r0 ADD r0, r0, #1 check CMP r0, #10 BLT loop endloop ```	``` MOV r0, #0 ; i MOV r1, #0 ; sum loop CMP r0, #10 BGE endloop ADD r1, r1, r0 ADD r0, r0, #1 B loop endloop ```	``` MOV r0, #0 ; i MOV r1, #0 ; sum loop CMP r0, #10 ADDLT r1, r1, r0 ADDLT r0, r0, #1 BLT loop endloop ```

6.7 While Loop

A *while* loop tests the condition expression before executing the loop body. If the condition expression is true, the loop body is then executed. Otherwise, the loop is terminated. Thus, the loop body may not be executed at all.

```
while (condition_expression) {
    // loop body
    ...
}
```

The following C program uses a *while* loop to calculate the sum of the first 10 integers, starting with 0.

```
C Program
int i = 10;
int sum = 0;
while( i > 0 ){
    sum += i;
    i--;
}
```

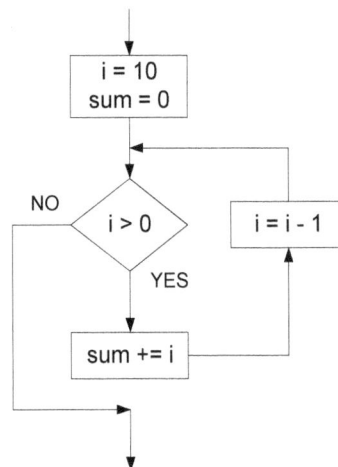

Assume variable *i* is save in r0 and variable *sum* is saved in r1, the following gives three different assembly implementations of the above while loop.

Assembly Program 1	Assembly Program 2	Assembly Program 3
``` MOV r0, #10 ; i MOV r1, #0 ; sum B check loop ADD r1, r1, r0 SUB r0, r0, #1 check CMP r0, #0 BGT loop endloop```	``` MOV r0, #10 ; i MOV r1, #0 ; sum loop CMP r0, #0 BLE endloop ADD r1, r1, r0 SUB r0, r0, #1 B loop endloop```	``` MOV r0, #10 ; i MOV r1, #0 ; sum loop CMP r0, #0 ADDGT r1, r1, r0 SUBGT r0, r0, #1 BGT loop endloop```

The first implementation checks the condition expression at the end of the loop. The second and third implementations check the conditional expression at the beginning of the loop. Since the loop body is not large, the last implementation uses conditionally executed instructions.

6.8 Do While Loop

The *do-while* loop is similar to the *while* loop. The key difference is that the condition expression is evaluated before executing the loop body in the while loop, whereas the condition expression is evaluated at the end of each iteration. Therefore, the while loop executes the loop body zero or multiple times, whereas the do-while loop executes the loop body at least once.

```
do {
    // loop body
    ...
} while (condition_expression)
```

Again, we calculate the sum of the first 10 integers, starting with 0. The implementation in C is given below.

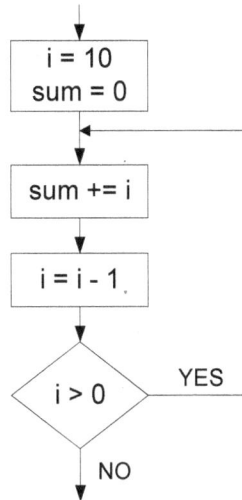

```
C Program
int sum = 0;
int i = 10;
do{
    sum += i;
    i--;
} while( i > 0 );
```

The following gives two implementations equivalent assembly codes (r0 = i, r1 = sum).

Assembly Program 1	Assembly Program 2

`        MOV r0, #10    ; i = 10`
`        MOV r1, #0     ; sum = 0`
 	
`loop    ADD r1, r1, r0 ; sum += i`
`        SUB r0, r0, #1 ; i--`
`        CMP r0, #0`
`        BGT loop`
`endloop`
	`        MOV  r0, #10    ; i = 0`
	`        MOV  r1, #0     ; sum = 0`
	
	`loop    ADD  r1, r1, r0 ; sum += i`
	`        SUBS r0, r0, #1 ; i--`
	`        BGT  loop`
	`endloop`

The second implementation uses SUBS that performs subtraction and updates the NZCV flags. Therefore, there is no need to use CMP before the BGT instruction.

6.9 Continue Statement

A *continue* statement in a loop is to skip the remaining statements in the current iteration and transfer the control to the next iteration of the loop. The following program calculates the sum of all integers between 0 and 9, excluding 5. The assembly program uses the condition code "NE" to skip the add instruction if r0 equals 5. The continue statement is simply implemented as a branch instruction in the assembly code.

C Program	Assembly Program

`int i;`
`int sum = 0;`
 	
`for(i = 0; i < 10; i++) {`
`    if (i == 5) // skip 5`
`        continue;`
`    sum += i;`
`}`
	`          MOVS  r0, #0      ; i = 0`
	`          MOVS  r1, #0      ; sum = 0`
	
	`loop      CMP   r0, #10`
	`          BGE   endloop`
	`          CMP   r0, #5`
	`          ADDNE r1, r1, r0  ; sum += i`
	`          ADD   r0, r0, #1  ; i++`
	`          B     loop`
	`endloop`

6.10 Break Statement

A *break* statement is to exit the current loop, including for, while, and do-while. It is useful when the number of iterations in a loop cannot be predetermined. When there are nested loops, the break statement terminates the nearest enclosing loop. It is easy to confuse the break and continue statements.

The following two C programs illustrate the difference between break and continue.

Example code for break	Example code for continue

`for(int i = 0; i < 5; i++){`
`  if (i == 2) break;`
`  printf("%d, ", i)`
`}`
`Output: 0, 1,`
	`for(int i = 0; i < 5; i++){`
	`  if (i == 2) continue;`
	`  printf("%d, ", i)`
	`}`
	`Output: 0, 1, 3, 4`

The break statement is translated to a conditional or unconditional branch statement in assembly. The following examples show how the break statement is implemented by a combination of CBNZ and B instructions.

C Program	Assembly Program

`// Find string length`
`char str[] = "hello";`
`int len = 0;`
 	
`for( ; ; ) {`
`    if (*str == '\0')`
`        break;`
`    str++;`
`    len++;`
`}`
	`; r0 = string memory address`
	`; r1 = string length`
	`          MOV  r1, #0       ; len = 0`
	
	`loop      LDRB r2, [r0]`
	`          CBNZ r2, notZero`
	`          B    endloop`
	`notZero   ADD  r0, r0, #1   ; str++`
	`          ADD  r1, r1, #1   ; len++`
	`          B    loop`
	`endloop`

6.11 Switch Statement

A *switch* statement in C allows the program to make multiple choices based on a switch expression. If the value of the expression matches one of the predetermined set of integer values defined in the program, the program branches accordingly. When there are many choices, the switch statement makes the program more structured and easier to read than a combination of if-then or if-then-else statements.

The body of a switch structure consists of an optional default label, a series of case labels and case expressions, and lists of statements for each case. The switch expression must be evaluated to an integer or a character. If the switch expression does not match any of the case constants, the default label is then selected. A break statement in the switch structure is used to exit the switch and execute the instruction immediately after the switch structure.

Instruction	Operands	Brief description
TBB	[Rn, Rm]	Table branch byte
TBH	[Rn, Rm, LSL #1]	Table branch half-word

Table 6-9. Table branch instructions

The assembly code can use the table branch byte (TBB) instruction to implement the switch statement.

```
TBB [pc, r0]        ; pc = pc + 4 + 2 × BranchTable[r0]
```

TBB relies on the branch table defined immediately after the TBB instruction. In the branch table, each table item takes one byte, and it represents the offset in half-words between the current PC and the memory address of the target instruction. The memory address of the instruction that the program should branch to calculated as follows:

$$\mathtt{target = pc + 4 + 2 \times BranchTable[r0]}$$

As a result, the program counter (pc) is

$$\mathtt{pc = pc + 4 + 2 \times BranchTable[r0]}$$

The table branch half-word (TBH) instruction is similar to TBB. However, each item in the branch table takes half-words.

```
TBH [pc, r0]        ; pc = pc + 4 + 2 × BranchTable[r0]
```

We use a simple example to illustrate how to use TBB or TBH instruction to implement a switch statement in assembly. This example converts a numeric score to its corresponding letter grade.

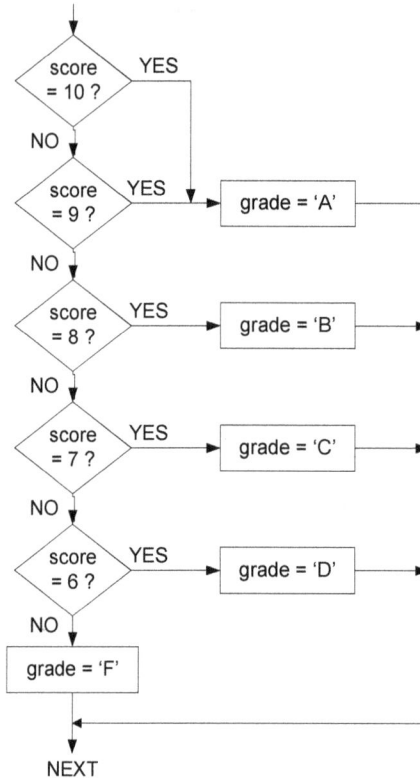

Figure 6-1. Flowcharts of an example switch program

The following assembly code uses TBB to implement a switch statement, which converts a numeric score to its corresponding letter grade.

C Program	Assembly Program
`unsigned int score;`	`  ; r0 = numeric score ( 0 ≤ r0 ≤ 10)`
`char grade;`	`  ; r1 = letter grade`
`switch (score){`	
`  case 10:`	`  SUBS r2, r0, #6    ; r6 is branch index`
`  case 9:`	`  CMP  r2, #5`
`    grade = 'A';`	`  BHS  default      ; branch if unsigned r6 ≥ 5`
`    break;`	
`  case 8:`	`  ; r6 is the index;`
`    grade = 'B';`	`  ; pc = pc + 4 + 2 × BranchTable[r6]`
`    break;`	`  TBB  [pc, r2]    ; Table Branch Byte`
`  case 7:`	
`    grade = 'C';`	`BranchTable`
`    break;`	`  DCB  (case_6 - BranchTable)/2    ; index = 0`
`  case 6:`	`  DCB  (case_7 - BranchTable)/2    ; index = 1`
`    grade = 'D';`	`  DCB  (case_8 - BranchTable)/2    ; index = 2`
`    break;`	`  DCB  (case_10_9 - BranchTable)/2 ; index = 3`
`  default:`	`  DCB  (case_10_9 - BranchTable)/2 ; index = 4`
`    grade = 'F';`	`  ALIGN`

```
      break;
 }                                  case_10_9
                                        MOV  r1, #0x41      ; ASCII 'A' = 0x41
                                        B    exit

                                    case_8
                                        MOV  r1, #0x42      ; ASCII 'B' = 0x42
                                        B    exit

                                    case_7
                                        MOV  r1, #0x43      ; ASCII 'C' = 0x43
                                        B    exit

                                    case_6
                                        MOV  r1, #0x44      ; ASCII 'D' = 0x44
                                        B    exit

                                    default
                                        MOV  r1, #0x46      ; ASCII 'F' = 0x46

                                    exit
```

6.12 Exercises

1. Translate the following code into a C program and explain what it does.

```
f        MOV r2, #1
         MOV r1, #1
loop     CMP r1, r0
         BGT done
         MUL r2, r1, r2
         ADD r1, r1, #1
         B   loop
done     MOV r0, r2
```

2. Conversion between 32-bit little endian and big endian numbers can be performed by using the REV instruction. Write an assembly program that uses bitwise operators, such as &, |, ^, <<, and >>, to implement the endian conversion without using the REV instruction.

3. Define an array with 10 unsigned integers in assembly code, and write an assembly program that calculates the mean of these 10 integers (truncating the result to an integer).

4. Define an array with 10 unsigned integers a_i $(0 \le i \le 9)$ in assembly code, and write an assembly program that calculates the sum of the cube of these 10 unsigned integers.

$$sum = \sum_{i=0}^{9} a_i^3$$

The array is defined in data memory as the following

```
        AREA myData, DATA
array   DCD 2, 4, 7, 3, 1, 2, 10, 11, 5, 13
size    DCD 10
```

5. Write an assembly program that converts all lower-case letters to their corresponding upper cases.

6. Write an assembly program that calculates the kinetic energy (E), E = MC², where the mass (M) is 15kg and is stored in r0. C is the speed of light (299,792,458 m/s) and is stored in r1. The result E has 32-bit and stored in register r2.

7. Write an assembly program that calculates the value of the following integer expression: $7x^2 + 9xy + \frac{3x}{y} + 11x + 13y + 5$, where unsigned integers $x = 4$ and $y = 2$.

8. Test for complex roots in solution to the following quadratic equation:

$$ax^2 + bx + c = 0$$

The solution has complex roots if $b^2 - 4ac$ is smaller than 0 and real roots otherwise. Suppose a, b, and c are signed integers and they are stored in register r0, r1, and r2. Write an assembly program that set register r3 to 1 if the solution has complex roots and 0 otherwise.

9. Write an assembly program that calculates the following function. Assume the signed integer input x is stored in register r0 and the result $f(x)$ is saved in register r1.

$$f(x) = \begin{cases} -1 & if \ x < 0 \\ 0 & if \ x = 0 \\ 1 & if \ x > 0 \end{cases}$$

10. Write an assembly program that calculates the following cost function. Assume the unsigned integer input x is stored in register r0 and the cost is in register r1.

$$cost(x) = \begin{cases} 9x & if\ x \leq 10 \\ 8x & if\ x > 10\ and\ x \leq 100 \\ 7x & if\ x > 100\ and\ x \leq 1000 \\ 6x & if\ x > 1000 \end{cases}$$

11. Translate the following C program into an assembly program. The C program finds the minimal value of three signed integers. Assume a, b, and c is stored in register r0, r1, and r3, respectively. The result min is saved in register r4.

```
if (a < b && a < c) {
    min = a;
} else if (b < a && b < c){
    min = b;
} else {
    min = c;
}
```

12. Assume two dates are stored in the memory as follows. Write an assembly program to compare these two dates. If date1 comes before date2, set register r0 to 1; Otherwise, set r0 to -1.

```
           AREA myData, DATA
date1   DCD   12, 31, 2014    ; month, day, year
date2   DCD   01, 20, 2013    ; month, day, year
```

13. Write an assembly program that calculates the sum as given below. Variable n is saved in register r0 and the *sum* is saved in register r1.

$$sum = \sum_{i=1}^{n} i^2 = 1^2 + 2^2 + \cdots + n^2$$

14. Write an assembly program that calculates the factorial of a non-negative integer n. Assume n is given in register r0 and the result is saved in register r1.

$$f(n) = \prod_{i=1}^{n} i = n \times (n-1) \times (n-2) \times \cdots \times 3 \times 2 \times 1$$

15. When a two-dimension (2D) matrix is declared in a C program, the matrix in fact is stored as a one-dimensional array in the memory. C program uses a row-major approach to convert a 2D matrix into a 1D array. The following gives an example of storing a 3-by-3 matrix in the memory.

Index	(0, 0)	(0, 1)	(0, 2)	(1, 0)	(1, 1)	(1, 2)	(2, 0)	(2, 1)	(2, 2)
Content	1	2	3	4	5	6	7	8	9
Memory offset in bytes	0	4	8	12	16	20	24	28	32

1st Row   2nd Row   3rd Row

Translate the following C program into an assembly program. Your assembly program must consist of two nested loops.

```
int a[4][3] = {
    {11, 12, 13},     // first row
    {21, 22, 23},     // second row
    {31, 32, 33},     // third row
    {41, 42, 43}      // fourth row
};

void main(void) {
    int i, j;
    for(i = 0; i < 4; i++)
        for(j = 0; j < 3; j++)
            a[i][j] = 2*a[i][j];
    return;
}
```

16. Write an assembly program that transpose the matrix defined in the previous question. Your assembly program should have two nested loops. In linear algebra, the transpose of a matrix $[a_{ij}]_{m \times n}$ is $[a_{ji}]_{n \times m}$.

$$[a_{ij}]_{m \times n}^{T} = [a_{ji}]_{n \times m}$$

For example:

$$\begin{bmatrix} 11 & 12 & 13 \\ 21 & 22 & 23 \\ 31 & 32 & 33 \\ 41 & 42 & 43 \end{bmatrix}^{T} = \begin{bmatrix} 11 & 21 & 31 & 41 \\ 12 & 22 & 32 & 42 \\ 13 & 23 & 33 & 43 \end{bmatrix}$$

CHAPTER 7

Structured Programming

Structured programming has been widely supported in high-level programming languages such as C to provide the clarity, simplicity, and ease of maintenance of programs. Structured programming is a technique that utilizes a top-down hierarchical method to solve a problem. It only uses sequence, selection, and loop control structures to implement programs. In particular, a *goto* statement, which was available in high-level languages, is prohibited. Although assembly language is not a structured programming language intrinsically, we can still apply basic principles of structured programming to simplify the complexity and increase the ease of programming.

This chapter introduces the basic idea of top-down design and gives example assembly programs to illustrate how to realize structured programming by using three basic control structures. We use one useful tool, *i.e.* program flowcharts, to facilitate structured programming.

7.1 Basic Control Structures

A software program solves a problem by using an appropriate combination of three basic control structures: sequence, selection, and loop. A sequence is a set of instructions that are completed in a sequential order. A selection lets the computer choose two alternatives based upon whether a logic condition is true or false. A loop executes a sequence of instructions repeatedly as long as a logic condition is satisfied. One common characteristic of these control structures is that each has only one entry point and one exit point. A control structure can be nested or imbedded in another one to form a compound structure. It has been mathematically proven that any program can be written by using only these three control structures.

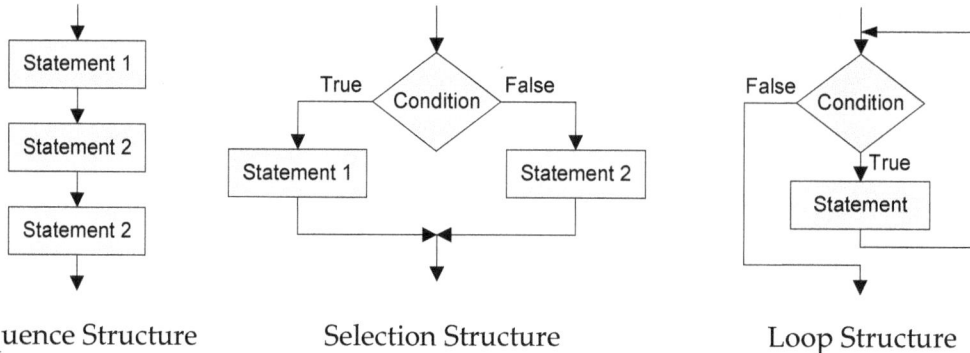

Sequence Structure   Selection Structure   Loop Structure

Figure 7-1. Three basic control structures in structured programming

To solve a large complex problem, the first step is to break down this large problem into a set of simpler and more manageable sub-problems. This divide-and-conquer strategy effectively reduces the difficulty of problem solving since each sub-problem is easier to solve, and the solution requires less time to develop, verify and maintain. Our next step is to design a solution for each sub-problem. Usually we make the solution to a sub-problem as a subroutine (or function). These subroutines communicate with each other by passing parameters (or arguments) and returning values. In this chapter, we will focus on how to develop a simple program, and we will introduce how to build a subroutine in the next chapter.

> *"Nothing is particularly hard if you divide it into small jobs."*
>
> Henry Ford, Founder of Ford Motor

The three control structures (sequence, selection, and loop) almost are implemented in every structured programming language.

- *Sequence.* All statements or instructions of a software program are implicitly assumed to be completed in a sequential order, even though on modern processors they might be executed out of order. In addition, a function (or called subroutine) can be part of a sequence.
- *Selection.* The *"if"*, *"if else"* and *"switch"* statements are selection control structure. Although the *"if"* statement is sufficient to implement any selection structure, the *"if else"* and *"switch"* are provided for the convenience of programming.
- *Loop.* The loop in C includes *"for"*, *"while"* and *"do while"*. Two statements (*"break"* and *"continue"*) are built in C to change the normal control flow of the loop. The *"break"* statement makes an immediate exit from the innermost *"for"*, *"switch"*, *"while"*, and *"do while"* in which it appears. The *"continue"* statement is

used to skip the remaining statements in the current loop body and begin the next iteration of the loop.

Top-Down Design

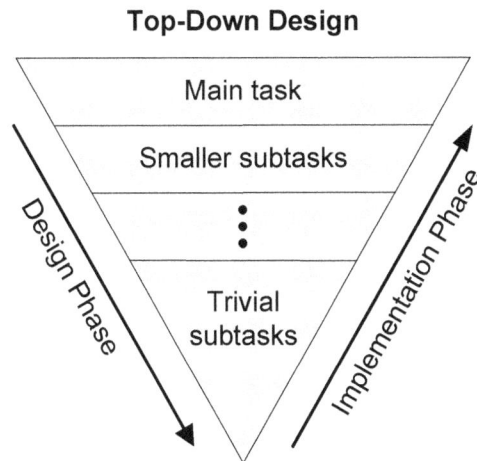

Figure 7-2. Top-down design (also called stepwise refinement)

Programming using hierarchical or nested control structures as well as subroutines in high-level languages is called *structured programming*. The key process of structured programming is stepwise refinement, which is about solving a problem by making a series of design decisions. Each successive refinement logically decomposes a task into a number of subtasks. The stepwise process stops until all subtasks can be described by using three basic control structures. Examples of the final subtask include "if P is true, then do X else do Y", or "while C is true, do Z". The final program code can be naturally written based on the result of the last decomposition.

However, assembly language itself is not a structured programming language since it does not directly support selection and loop structures. An assembly program relies on conditional or unconditional branch instructions to implement the high-level selection and loop structure. A branch instruction in assembly is equivalent to a *goto* statement in a high-level language. Structured programming languages discourage the usage of goto statements. That is why some high-level languages have eliminated goto and most textbooks do not cover it. Edsger Dijkstra, a famous computer scientist, published a letter titled "Goto Considered Harmful" in 1968.

In assembly languages, we have to use branch instructions that are equivalent to goto. In spite of this, we can still extend the principle of structured programming to assembly language. We should still follow the stepwise refinement approach to solve a problem in assembly language. While the basic control structures are not directly available, they can be readily implemented. Structured programming in assembly language involves two steps:

1. Top-down logical design. It performs stepwise refinement and constructs program flow by using high-level control structures.
2. Implementing the high-level structures identified in the previous step in assembly language. Instruction labels should be meaningfully named in order to demonstrate clearly their corresponding control structures. Branch instructions should be carefully used to ensure there are only one entry and one exit into each structure. If possible, the assembly instructions should be broken into subroutines to make the program more modularized.

These two steps separate the process of logic construction and low-level coding. In other words, we think in high-level structured language but write code in low-level assembly language.

An indispensable tool that can help us use structured programming techniques in assembly language is program flowcharts. A program flowchart visually organizes the program logic flow and steps by using a few graphic symbols. A flowchart not only serves as valuable program documentation, but also more importantly as an aid of top-down design and analysis during the problem-solving phase and an effective guideline during the software development phase. Detailed example flowcharts will be given later in this section.

Example: Find all Armstrong numbers less than 10,000.

Given a positive integer that has n digits, it is an Armstrong number if the sum of the nth powers of its digits equals the number itself. For example, 371 is an Armstrong number since we have $371 = 3^3 + 7^3 + 1^3$. Our task is to print out all Armstrong numbers less than 10,000.

The tasks can be divided into 10,000 subtasks, and each subtask checks whether a given integer is an Armstrong number or not. Apparently, a loop structure is needed to execute these 10,000 subtasks iteratively. There should be one in and one out to the loop structure. We can further refine the subtask by using a selection structure, which prints the number if it is an Armstrong number.

The subtask of checking whether a number is Armstrong can be implemented as a subroutine that returns YES or NO for a given input integer. In general, using subroutines in a program can help decompose a complex task into smaller and simpler subtasks, making program design, verification, and maintenance easier.

This top-down design process is illustrated in Figure 7-3.

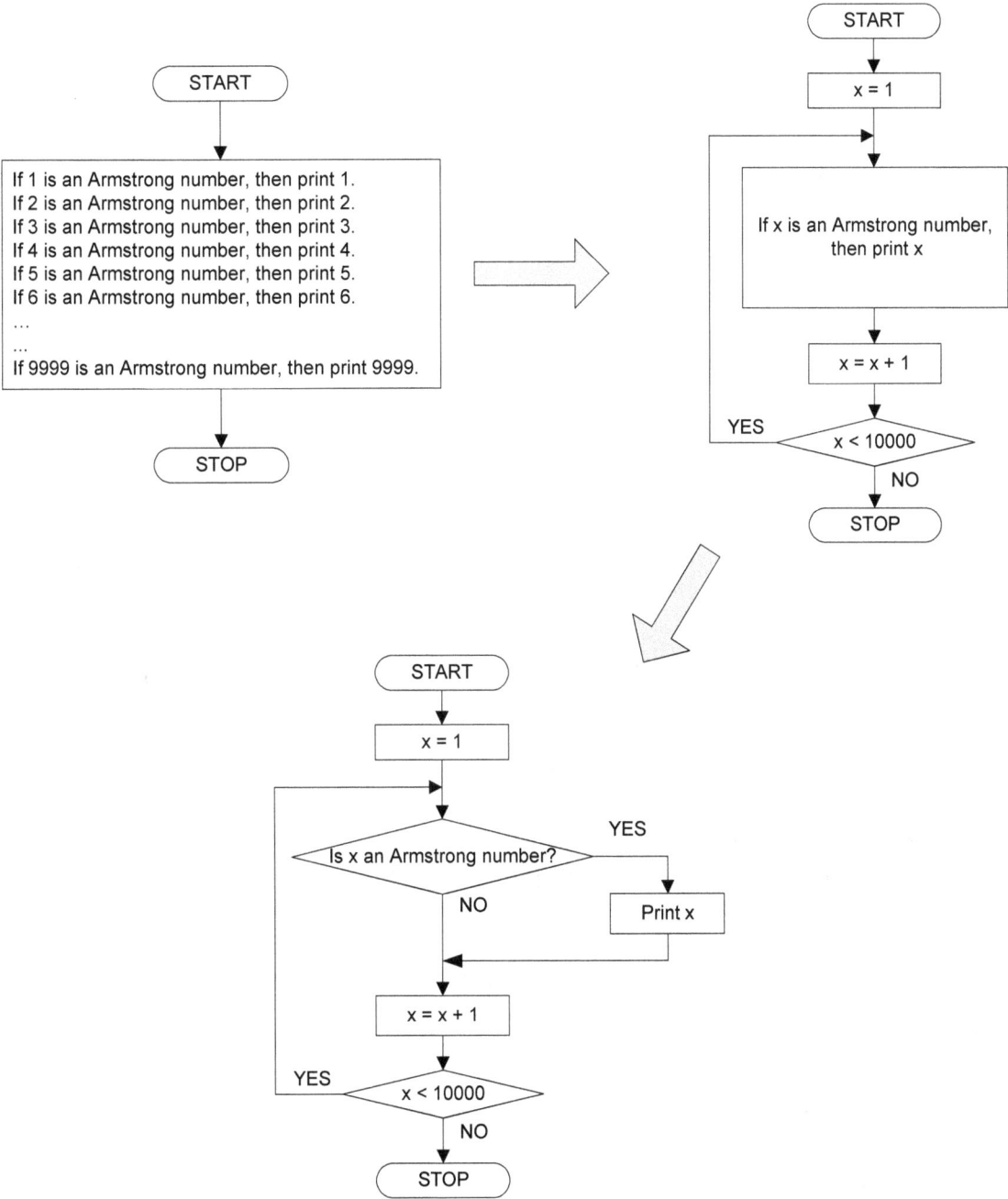

Figure 7-3. Example of top-down design to find Armstrong numbers less than 10,000

This subtask, however, is still complex. We can further decompose it into four smaller subtasks, as in Figure 7-4. The first three of them are still not simple, and we can implement them as subroutines. Within each subroutine, the above decomposition process repeats if necessary to break a subtask into smaller subtasks to the level that they can be expressed by using the three basic control structures. Chapter 7.6 shows the flowchart and program of identifying the number of digits an integer has, and Chapter 7.9 gives an example of implementation checking whether a number is an Armstrong number.

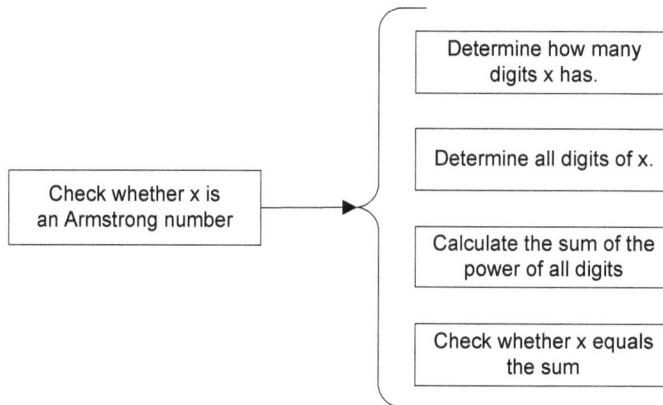

Figure 7-4. Break a complex task to smaller subtasks.

7.2 Register Reuse

There are always a limited number of physical registers available on a microprocessor. However, it is often that a large number of variables are defined in a program. Therefore, we need to minimize the number of registers used for each chunk of codes in order to save registers for other chunks of codes.

If the program runs out of registers, we need to save the value of some registers back to memory to make registers free to use. When these variables are used later on, we need to load their value back from the memory again. Reducing the number of registers used by a piece of code can help eliminate some memory accesses, thus speeding up the application performance.

A register should be reused if possible in order to minimize the footprint of registers. One simple strategy is that *a register can be reused outside its live range*. A live range of a register in a program is defined as the interval between the instruction that writes to the register and the last instruction that reads the register before it is written again.

The following example illustrates how this strategy works. Assuming global variables are allocated in the data memory starting at the address of 0x20000000. The assembly program needs to load variables B, C, and D from the memory into registers first, then calculate the results, and finally save the result in the memory. A simple assembly implementation, as shown in Figure 7-5, uses eight registers.

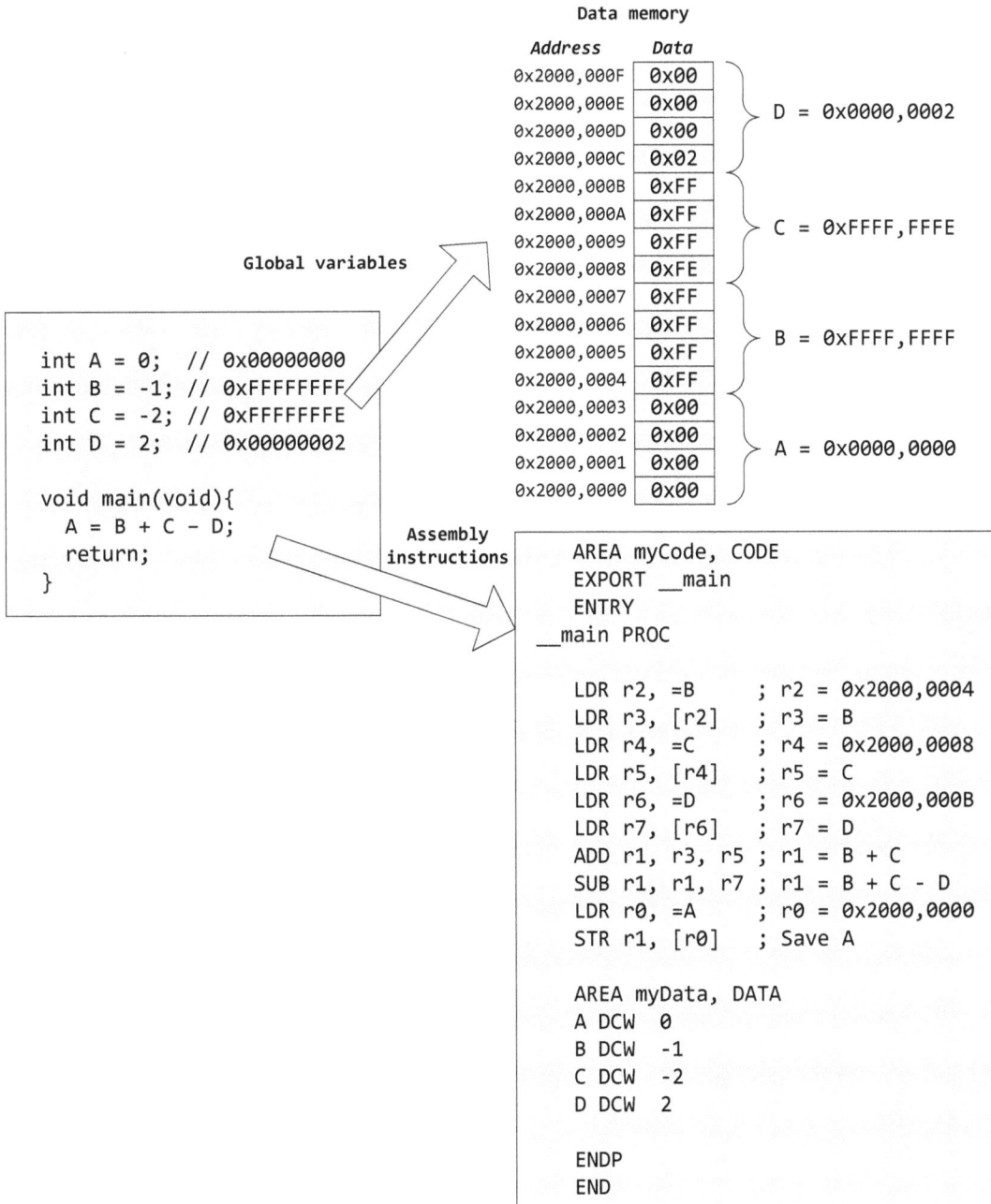

Figure 7-5. Simple assembly implementation and data memory layout

In order to reuse registers, first we need to determine the live range of each register. A register may have multiple live ranges in a program. However, no live ranges of a register overlap with each other. A register can be reused outside its live range.

Figure 7-6 shows the process of renaming registers to reduce the number of registers used in the above program.

- During the first step, we can replace register r4, r6, and r0 by register r2, and replace r1 by r3. This reduces the total number of registers used by the program from eight to four.
- During the second step, we replace register r7 by r2, and the total number of registers is then further reduced to three.
- This process repeats if necessary.

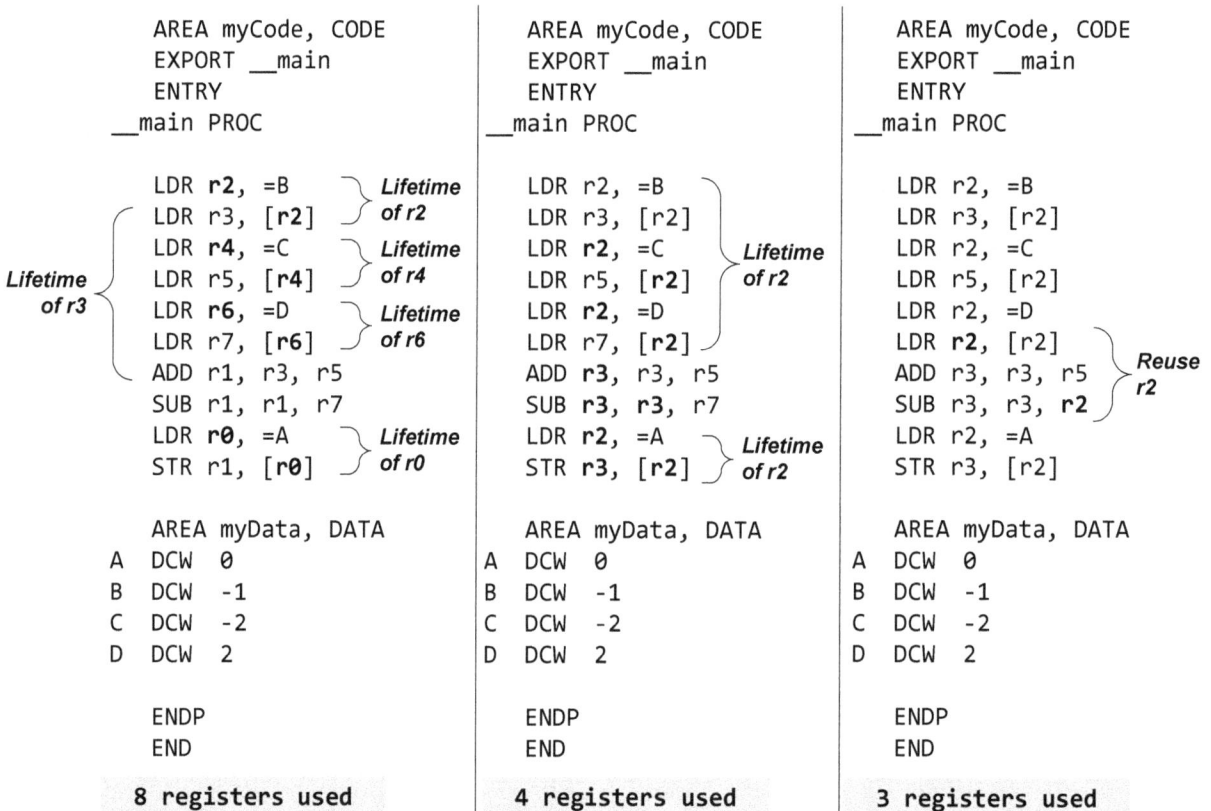

```
        AREA myCode, CODE              AREA myCode, CODE              AREA myCode, CODE
        EXPORT __main                  EXPORT __main                  EXPORT __main
        ENTRY                          ENTRY                          ENTRY
   __main PROC                    __main PROC                    __main PROC

        LDR r2, =B      Lifetime       LDR r2, =B                     LDR r2, =B
        LDR r3, [r2]    of r2          LDR r3, [r2]                   LDR r3, [r2]
        LDR r4, =C      Lifetime       LDR r2, =C      Lifetime       LDR r2, =C
        LDR r5, [r4]    of r4          LDR r5, [r2]    of r2          LDR r5, [r2]
        LDR r6, =D      Lifetime       LDR r2, =D                     LDR r2, =D
        LDR r7, [r6]    of r6          LDR r7, [r2]                   LDR r2, [r2]       Reuse
        ADD r1, r3, r5                 ADD r3, r3, r5                 ADD r3, r3, r5     r2
        SUB r1, r1, r7                 SUB r3, r3, r7                 SUB r3, r3, r2
        LDR r0, =A      Lifetime       LDR r2, =A      Lifetime       LDR r2, =A
        STR r1, [r0]    of r0          STR r3, [r2]    of r2          STR r3, [r2]

        AREA myData, DATA              AREA myData, DATA              AREA myData, DATA
   A    DCW  0                    A    DCW  0                    A    DCW  0
   B    DCW  -1                   B    DCW  -1                   B    DCW  -1
   C    DCW  -2                   C    DCW  -2                   C    DCW  -2
   D    DCW  2                    D    DCW  2                    D    DCW  2

        ENDP                           ENDP                           ENDP
        END                            END                            END

    8 registers used               4 registers used               3 registers used
```

(Lifetime of r3 spans from LDR r3, [r2] through ADD r1, r3, r5 in the first column)

Figure 7-6. Reduce the total number of registers used by reusing registers based on their live range.

7.3 Example of Factorial Numbers

The factorial of a non-negative number n, denoted as $n!$, is the product of all positive integers less or equal to n, shown in the following equation. There is one special case: $0! = 1$.

$$n! = \prod_{i=1}^{n} i = n \times (n-1) \times (n-2) \cdots \times 2 \times 1$$

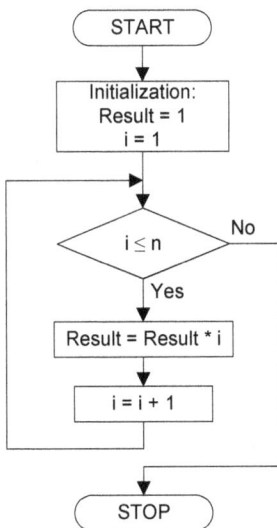

Figure 7-7. Flowchart of factorial program

This example illustrates how to implement a *for* loop in an assembly program.

- An unconditional branch instruction "B loop" implements a loop.
- At the beginning of the loop body, a condition check instruction (CMP in this example) is executed to set up the NZCV flags.
- A conditional branch (BGT in this example) is used to exit the loop.

C Program	Assembly Program
| | ```
AREA factorial, CODE, READONLY
        EXPORT __main
        ENTRY
__main PROC
``` |
| `int main(void) {`<br>`  int result, n, i;`<br>`  result = 1;`<br>`  n = 5;`<br>`  for (i = 1; i <= n; i++)`<br>`    result = result * i;`<br><br><br><br>`  while(1);`<br>`}` | ```
        MOV  r0, #1       ; r0 = result
        MOV  r1, #5       ; r1 = n
        MOV  r2, #1       ; r2 = i = 1
loop    CMP  r2, r1       ; compare i and n
        BGT  stop         ; if i > n, stop
        MULS r0, r2, r0   ; result *= i
        ADD  r2, r2, #1   ; i++
        B    loop
stop    B    stop
        ENDP
        END
``` |

7.4 Example of Counting Ones in a Word

In this example, we count the number of 1-bits in a 32-bit word. One application of this code is to calculate the Hamming distance, which is defined as the number of different bits in two words. Given two words A and B, let $C = A \oplus B$, then the Hamming distance of A and B equals the number of 1-bits in C. Hamming distance has a wide range of applications in information coding and cryptography.

The assembly implementation is given below. The assembly program checks two bits every time, and one of them is stored in the carry flag set by the "MOVS" instruction.

However, the C language cannot directly access the carry flag. To test whether carry has occurred, we can use an *if*-statement that compares x and x << 2. If x is smaller than x << 2, then carry has occurred, implying the bit being shift out has a value of 1; otherwise, the bit shifted out has a value of 0.

> *The C language cannot directly check the carry flag. This shows an advantage of assembly language over C language.*

C Program	Assembly Program

```// Count the number ones in x```
 ```// Result saved in counter```
 	
 ```int main(void){```
 ```   unsigned int x = 0xAAAAAAAA;```
 ```   unsigned int y, z;```
 	
 ``` unsigned int counter = 0;```
 ``` counter = x >> 31;```
 	
 ``` while (x > 0) {```
 ```   y = x << 2;```
 ```   z = y >> 31;```
 ```   if (x < y)   // check carry```
 ```   counter += z + 1;```
 ```   else```
 ```   counter += z;```
 ```   x = y;```
 ``` }```
 ``` while(1);```
 ```}```
	``` AREA Count_Ones, CODE```
	 ``` EXPORT __main```
	 ``` ALIGN```
	 ``` ENTRY```
	 ```__main PROC```
	 ``` ; r0 = Input = x```
	 ``` ; r1 = Number of ones = counter```
	
	 ``` LDR r0, =0xAAAAAAAA```
	
	 ``` ; r1 = r0 >> 31```
	 ``` MOV r1, r0, LSR #31```
	
	 ``` ; r0 = r0 << 2 and change Carry```
	 ```loop MOVS r0, r0, LSL #2```
	
	 ``` ; r1 = r1 + r0 >> 31 + Carry```
	 ``` ADC r1, r1, r0, LSR #31```
	 ``` BNE loop```
	
	 ```stop B stop```
	 ``` ENDP```
	 ``` END```

The following shows the initialization and the execution of the first loop. Note the ADC instruction does not update the carry flag. At the end of the first loop, we have r1 = bit[31] + bit[30] + bit[29].

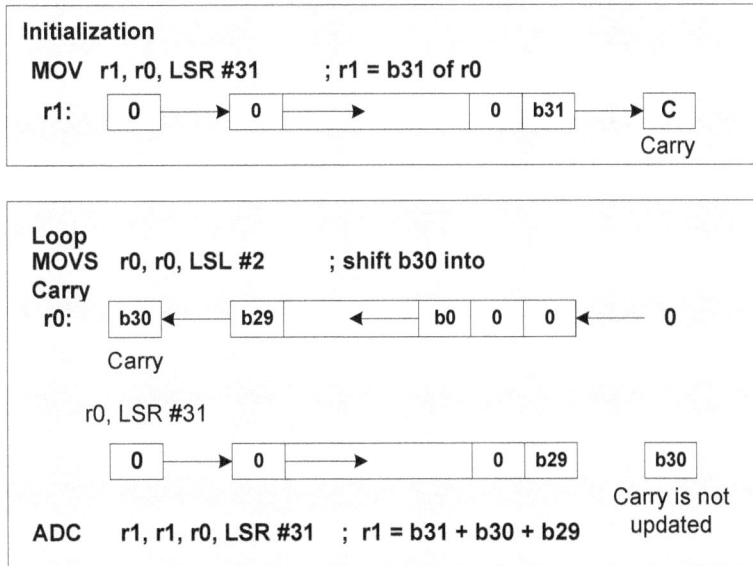

At the end of the first loop: r1 = b31 + b30 + b29

Figure 7-8. Illustration of the result of the first loop. The input data is stored in register r0. The counting result is saved in register r1.

The loop body is executed 16 times and each loop checks two bits. The following gives a detailed illustration of the above example to show the key idea.

1. Initially we have r0 = 0xAAAAAAAA. Note 0xA = 0b1010.
2. The counter r1 is initially set to r0>>31, *i.e.* 0x00000001.
3. During the first iteration of the loop:
    a) MOVS r0, r0, LSL #2 $\Longrightarrow$ Carry = 0 and r0 = 0xAAAAAAAC
    b) ADC r1, r1, r0, LSR #31 $\Longrightarrow$ r1 = 1 + 0x00000000 + Carry = 1
    c) Since r0 does not equal zero, the loop is executed again.
4. During the second iteration of the loop:
    a) MOVS r0, r0, LSL #2 $\Longrightarrow$ Carry = 0 and r0 = 0xAAAAAAA0
    b) ADC r1, r1, r0, LSR #31 $\Longrightarrow$ r1 = 1 + 0x00000000 + Carry = 2
    c) Since r0 does not equal zero, the loop is executed again.
5. During the third iteration of the loop:
    a) MOVS r0, r0, LSL #2 $\Longrightarrow$ Carry = 0 and r0 = 0xAAAAAAC0
    b) ADC r1, r1, r0, LSR #31 $\Longrightarrow$ r1 = 1 + 0x00000000 + Carry = 3
    c) Since r0 does not equal zero, the loop is executed again.
6. The loop is executed 16 times, and finally we have r1 = 16.

7.5 Example of Finding the Maximum of an Array

In order to find the maximum value and its location in a given signed integer array, the program needs to traverse the array and keep track of the maximum value and its location or index. The program updates the maximum value variable if a larger value is found during the loop. If there are multiple maximum values in this array, only the first one is identified. This method is often called linear search.

The program flowchart is given in Figure 7-9. At the beginning, the program assumes the maximum value is the first integer of this array and correspondingly *maxLocation* is set to 0. It uses a *for* loop to iterate through the array. The loop index *i* starts with 0 and is incremented by 1 in the loop body. In each loop, the program loads an integer of this array and updates *maxValue* and *maxLocation* when a larger value is found when iterating through the array.

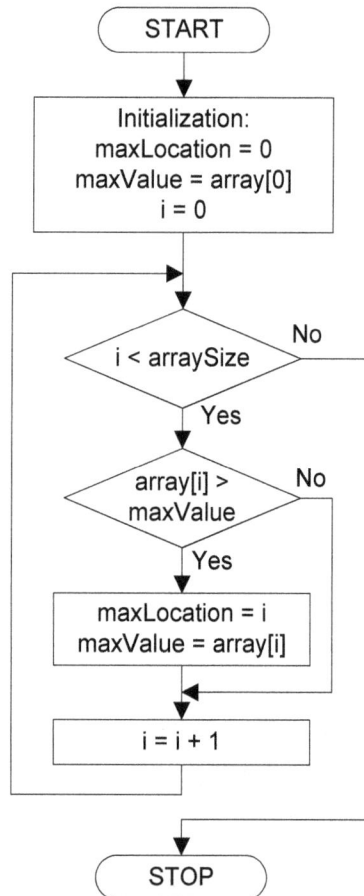

Figure 7-9. Flowchart of finding the maximum value of an integer array

The following shows the implementation of finding the maximum value in C and assembly. Since the array and size are initialized global variables in the C program, the corresponding assembly program places them in the initialized data area, defined by using the directive AREA. The assembly program starts to identify the array size and the memory address where the array is stored. Variables i, *maxLocation*, and *maxValue* are local variables and are stored in r2, r0, and r1, respectively. The assembly program initializes r0 to the first integer of the array, and r1 to 0.

The memory address of the first integer of this array, which we also call the memory address of this array, is stored in register r4. The following statement loads *array[i]* into register r5. Since each integer takes 4 bytes in memory, the memory address of *array[i]* is $r4 + r2 \times 4$.

```
LDR r5,[r4,r2,LSL #2]
```

C Program	Assembly Program

`int array[10] = {-1, 5, 3, 8, 10,`
`23, 6, 5, 2, -10};`
 	
`int size = 10;`
 	
`int main(void) {`
`  int i, maxLocation, maxValue;`
	`        AREA myData, DATA`
	`        ALIGN`
	`array   DCD -1,5,3,8,10,23,6,5,2,-10`
	`size    DCD 10`
	
	`        AREA findMax, CODE`
	`        EXPORT __main`
	`        ALIGN`
	`        ENTRY`
	`__main PROC`
	`        ; Identify the array size`
	`        LDR   r3, =size`
	`        LDR   r3, [r3]    ; array size`
	`        SUB   r3, r3, #1`

`  // Initialize max and location`
`  maxLocation = 0;`
`  maxValue = array[0];`
	`        ; Initialize max value and location`
	`        LDR   r4, =array`
	`        LDR   r0, [r4]    ; r0 = default max`
	`        MOV   r1, #0     ; r1 = max location`

`  // loop over the array`
`  for (i = 0; i < size; i++){`
`    if (array[i] > maxValue) {`
`      maxValue  = array[i];`
`      maxLocation = i;`
`    }`
`  }`
	`        ; loop over the array`
	`        MOV   r2, #0          ; loop index i`
	`loop    CMP   r2, r3           ; compare i & size`
	`        BGE   stop            ; stop if i ≥ size`
	`        LDR   r5, [r4,r2,LSL #2]   ; array[i]`
	`        CMP   r5, r0          ; compare with max`
	`        MOVGT r0, r5          ; update max value`
	`        MOVGT r1, r2          ; update location`
	`        ADD   r2, r2, #1      ; update index i`
	`        B     loop`

`  while(1); //dead loop`
 	
`}`
	`stop    B     stop            ; dead loop`
	`        ENDP`
	`        END`

7.6 Example of Counting Digits

Given a decimal integer, find how many decimal digits this number has. For example, the decimal number 9578 has four digits.

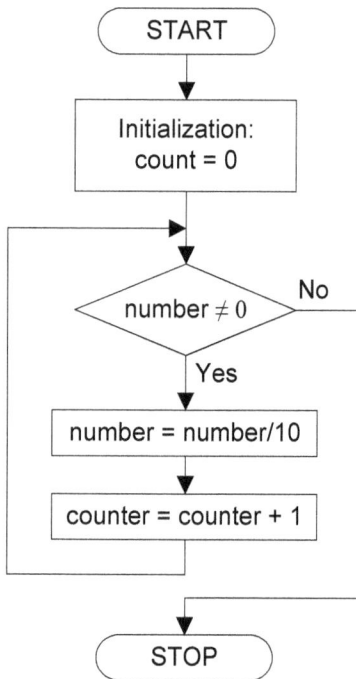

Figure 7-10. Flowcharts of counting decimal digits

The C program uses a simple while loop that repeatedly executes a block of code until a given Boolean condition becomes false.

The implementation of a *while* loop in assembly language is similar to a *for* loop. It often relies on a comparison instruction (CMP, CMN, TEQ, and TST) and a conditional branch instruction. However, CBZ (compare and branch if zero) and CBNZ (compare and branch if nonzero) is an efficient combination instruction of two operations.

When integers are divided, any fractional part of the result is discarded, which is often called "truncation toward zero." For example, the result of 9/10 is zero. Note if either operand is negative, the result truncates toward 0 rather than flooring. For example, the result of -8/3 is -2, not -3.

C Program	Assembly Program
	AREA countDigits, CODE, READONLY
	EXPORT __main
int main(void){	ENTRY
int number, count;	__main PROC
number = 123456;	LDR r0, =123456 ; input integer number
count = 0;	MOV r1, #0 ; number of digits
	MOV r2, #10 ; set r2 to 10
while(number){	loop CBZ r0, stop ; if r0 = 0, stop
number = number/10;	SDIV r0, r0, r2 ; r0 = r0 / 10
count++;	ADD r1, r1, #1 ; count++
}	B loop ; loop again
while(1);	stop B stop
}	ENDP
	END

7.7 Example of Parity Bit

The parity bit of a binary number indicates whether it contains an odd or even number of ones. Parity bit is widely used in communication and digital systems to detect data corruption when there are an odd number of bit errors.

There are two parity schemes: even parity and odd parity. In the even parity, the parity bit is set to 1 if there are an odd number of ones in the data; otherwise, it is set to 0. As a result, the number of ones in the data and the parity bit is always even. This scheme is called odd parity. On the other hand, the odd parity always keeps the total number of ones in the entire data set (including the parity) an odd number. The exclusive OR of all bits in the entire dataset including the parity bit should always be zero in the even parity scheme, and always be one in the odd parity scheme.

	Data bits	Parity bit	Total # of 1-bits (including parity)
Even Parity	10101010	0	4 (An even number of ones)
	10101011	1	6 (An even number of ones)
Odd Parity	10101010	1	5 (An odd number of ones)
	10101011	0	5 (An odd number of ones)

Table 7-1. Examples of even and odd parity

The following example implements a simple bit-counting algorithm that computes the odd parity. The key idea, proposed in reference [13], is to repetitively reset one of the 1-bits to zero and invert the parity bit until all bits are zero. The reset operation is achieved by the bitwise logic AND operation between n and $n - 1$. The following gives two examples.

Example 1: n = 11 (0b1011)

	Step 1	Step 2	Step 3
n	1011	1010	1000
n-1	1010	1001	0111
n & (n-1)	1010	1000	0000
Parity	0	1	0

Example 2: n = 15 (0b1111)

	Step 1	Step 2	Step 3	Step 4
n	1111	1110	1100	1000
n-1	1110	1101	1011	0111
n & (n-1)	1110	1100	1000	0000
Parity	0	1	0	1

This algorithm is based on the observation that the bitwise AND operation of $n \& (n - 1)$ always unset one of the 1-bits to zero. This can easily be proven. When we examine the least significant two bits, there are four possible scenarios. In each of the four scenarios, $n \& (n - 1)$ unsets a 1-bit. The number of steps required to complete this algorithm does not depend on the total number of bits, but instead the number of ones in the tested data.

Cases	Bits[1:0]	$n \& (n - 1)$	Observation
1	11	10	A 1-bit is reset.
2	10	00	A 1-bit is reset.
3	01	00	A 1-bit is reset.
4	00	Either the algorithm stops or the last 1 on the right most is reset to 0.	A 1-bit is reset.

The C program and assembly program of calculating the odd parity are shown below. In this example, we calculate the parity of a 32-bit integer, which is 0x11 in decimal, and 0b1011 in binary. The total number of 1-bits in this integer is an odd number; therefore, its parity bit, saved in register r1, is cleared to 0.

C Program	Assembly Program
	AREA parity, CODE, READONLY EXPORT __main ENTRY
int main(void){	__main PROC

unsigned int n = 11;
  int parity = 0;
  while (n) {
    parity = !parity;
 	
    n = n & (n - 1);
  }
 	
  while(1);
}
	MOVS r0, #11 ; number to be checked
	        MOVS r1, #0 ; parity
	loop CBZ r0, stop ; branch to stop if zero
	        CMP r1, #0 ; flip parity bit
	        MOVEQ r1, #1 ; if r1 = 0, set it
	        MOVNE r2, #0 ; if r1 ≠ 0, clear it
	        SUBS r2, r0, #1 ; (n-1)
	        ANDS r0, r0, r2 ; n = n & (n-1)
	        B loop
	stop B stop
	        ENDP
	        END

The CBZ instruction can be replaced by these two instructions.

```
CMP r0, #0
BEQ stop
```

Another approach to implement the C statement "parity = !parity;" is as follows:

```
MVN  r1, r1      ; negate all bits
AND  r1, r1, #1  ; clear all bits except bit[0]
```

7.8 Example of Perfect Numbers

If the sum of all proper divisors of a positive number equals the number itself, this number is called a perfect number. For example, 6 is a perfect number since the sum of its proper divisors including 1, 2, and 3 equals 6. Other examples are 28, 496, and 8128. We will write a program to check whether a given positive number is perfect or not.

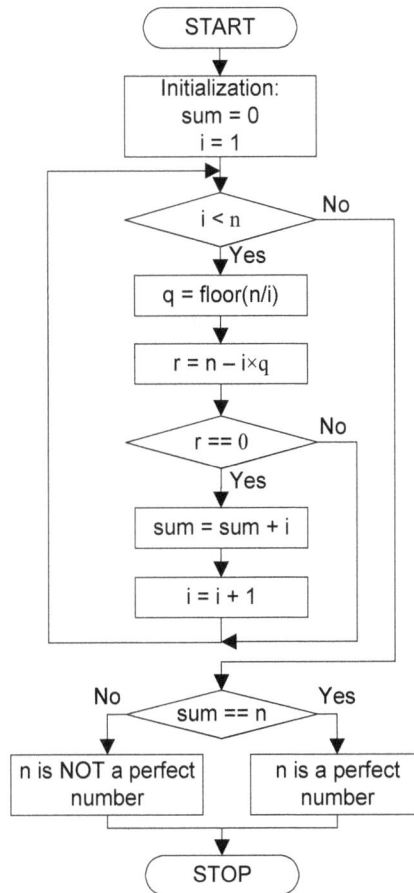

```
            ( START )
               │
               ▼
      ┌──────────────────┐
      │  Initialization:  │
      │     sum = 0       │
      │     i = 1         │
      └──────────────────┘
               │
    ┌─────────►▼
    │      ╱ i < n ╲ ──── No ───┐
    │      ╲       ╱            │
    │         │ Yes            │
    │         ▼                │
    │   ┌─────────────┐        │
    │   │ q = floor(n/i)│      │
    │   └─────────────┘        │
    │         ▼                │
    │   ┌─────────────┐        │
    │   │ r = n − i×q │        │
    │   └─────────────┘        │
    │         ▼                │
    │      ╱ r == 0 ╲ ── No ───┤
    │      ╲        ╱           │
    │         │ Yes            │
    │         ▼                │
    │   ┌──────────────┐       │
    │   │ sum = sum + i │      │
    │   └──────────────┘       │
    │         ▼                │
    │   ┌──────────────┐       │
    │   │  i = i + 1   │       │
    │   └──────────────┘       │
    └─────────│◄───────────────┘
              ▼
  No      ╱ sum == n ╲     Yes
   ┌──────╲          ╱──────┐
   ▼                        ▼
┌──────────────┐      ┌──────────────┐
│ n is NOT a   │      │ n is a perfect│
│   perfect    │      │    number    │
│   number     │      └──────────────┘
└──────────────┘              │
         │                    │
         └────────►( STOP )◄──┘
```

Figure 7-11. Checking whether _n_ is a perfect number

For a given positive integer n, the program loops over the _loop_ variable i from 1 to $n - 1$, checks whether i is a divisor of n, and adds to _sum_ if yes. After the loop completes, the program evaluates whether _sum_ equals n. If yes, then n is a perfect number; otherwise, n is not. In order to check whether i is a divisor of n, the program performs a modulo operation, which is simple in C (use % operator). However, this modulo operations takes several steps in assembly. First, it uses truncated division to find the quotient q, _i.e._

$q = \left\lfloor \frac{n}{i} \right\rfloor$, and then the remainder is calculated as $r = n - q \times i$. If the remainder is zero, then i is a divisor of n.

In the following program, the number to be checked is stored in variable *num*, which is assigned to register r1 in the assembly program. The flag indicating whether the integer is a perfect number or not is stored in register r0.

C Program	Assembly Program

`int main(void){`
`  unsigned int i, flag;`
`  unsigned int num, sum;`
 	
`  num = 28;`
`  sum = 0;`
 	
`  for(i = 1; i < num; i++){`
`    if( num % i == 0)`
`      sum += i;`
`  }`
 	
`  if (sum == num)`
`    flag = 1;`
`  else`
`    flag = 0;`
 	
`  while(1);`
`}`
	` ` `AREA perfectNumber, CODE`
	` ` `EXPORT __main`
	` ` `ALIGN`
	` ` `ENTRY`
	`__main PROC`
	
	` ` `MOV   r1, #28        ; number to check`
	` ` `MOV   r2, #0         ; sum = 0`
	` ` `MOV   r3, #1         ; i = 1`
	`loop  CMP   r3, r1        ; compare i & num`
	` ` `BHS   check          ; if i ≥ num, exit`
	` ` `UDIV  r4, r1, r3     ; r4 = num/i`
	` ` `MLS   r4, r3, r4, r1 ; r4 = num - i*r4`
	` ` `CMP   r4, #0         ; num % i`
	` ` `ADDEQ r2, r2, r3     ; sum += i`
	` ` `ADD   r3, r3, #1     ; i++`
	` ` `B     loop           ; loop again`
	
	`check CMP   r2, r1        ; compare sum & num`
	`yes   MOVEQ r0, #1        ; flag = 1`
	`no    MOVNE r0, #0        ; flag = 0`
	
	`stop  B     stop`
	` ` `ENDP`
	` ` `END`

The "CMP r3, r1" instruction updates the N, Z, C, and V flags according to the results of subtraction r3 − r1. The following BHS (Branch if unsigned higher or same) instruction checks the C flag and it makes PC to branch away if the C flag is set, indicating no borrowing has occurred during the subtraction.

The "MLS r4, r3, r4, r1" instruction performs the following operation: r4 = r3 − r4 × r1. Note the product of r4 and r1 might have 64 bits and the most significant 32 bits are discarded.

The C statement "num % i" is translated into two assembly statements.
```
    UDIV  r4, r1, r3     ; r4 = num ÷ i
    MLS   r4, r3, r4, r1 ; r4 = num - i × r4
```

7.9 Example of Armstrong Numbers

An n-digit number is Armstrong if the sum of the nth powers of its digits equals the number itself. For example, 371, 1634, 54748, and 1741725 are Armstrong numbers since

$$371 = 3^3 + 7^3 + 1^3$$

$$1634 = 1^4 + 6^4 + 3^4 + 4^4$$

$$54748 = 5^5 + 4^5 + 7^5 + 4^5 + 8^5$$

$$1741725 = 1^7 + 7^7 + 4^7 + 1^7 + 7^7 + 2^7 + 5^7$$

The following C and assembly programs check whether a given three-digit number is Armstrong. The program checks whether the sum of cubes of individual digits of this three-digit number is equal to the number itself.

C provides a modulus operator (%) that calculates the remainder of an integer division. However, there are no modulus instructions in assembly. The modulus operation (r2 = r1 % r3) can be performed by using the following two instructions.

```
        SDIV    r6, r1, r3      ; r2 = remainder
        MLS     r2, r3, r6, r1  ; r2 = r1 - r3 * r6,
```

C Program	Assembly Program		
		AREA	Armstrong, CODE, READONLY
int main(void) {		EXPORT	__main
int number, sum, r;		ENTRY	
int flag, t;	__main	PROC	
number = 371;		LDR r0, =371	; number to be checked
sum = 0;		MOV r4, #0	; sum = 0
t = number;		MOV r1, r0	; save a copy, r1=number
while(t != 0) {		MOV r3, #10	
r = t % 10;	loop	CBZ r1, check	; if t = 0, exit loop
sum = sum + r*r*r;		SDIV r6, r1, r3	; r2 = remainder
t = t / 10;		MLS r2, r3, r6, r1	; r2 = r1 - 10*r6
}		MUL r3, r2, r2	; remainer^2
		MLA r4, r3, r2, r4	; r4 = 10*r2 + r4
		MOVS r3, #10	
		SDIV r1, r1, r3	; t = t/10
		CBNZ loop	
if (number == sum)	check	CMP r0, r4	
flag = 1;	yes	MOVEQ r0, #1	; Armstrong
else	no	MOVNE r0, #0	; not Armstrong
flag = 0;			
while(1);	stop	B stop	
}		ENDP	
		END	

7.10 Example of Palindrome String

A string is a palindrome if the string is read the same forward and backward. For example, "rats live on no evil star" is a palindrome. Write a program to check whether a given string is a palindrome.

The assembly program uses two memory pointers (r1 and r2), which are initially set to the memory address of the first letter and the last letter of the string to be checked. The program loads two characters pointed by r1 and r2, and compares them whether they are the same. If yes, the program updates the memory pointers and continues the comparison until r2 becomes larger or equal to r1.

The assembly program uses the post-index memory address mode, which automatically updates the memory pointer after loading data from memory. For example,

```
    LDRB   r4,[r1],-1
```
is equivalent to two instructions:
```
    LDRB   r4,[r1]
    SUB    r1, r1, 1
```

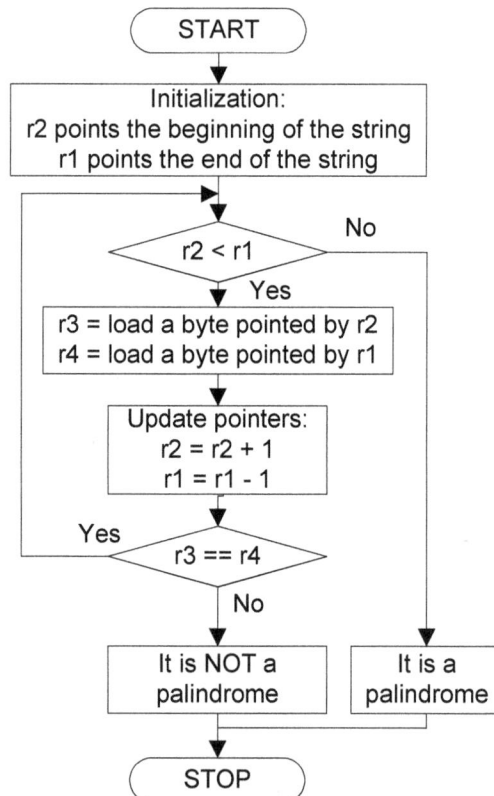

Figure 7-12. Check whether a given string is palindrome.

A character string is an array of ASCII characters terminated with a null character ('0x00', called NULL in ASCII) in assembly, with each character (including the null terminator) taking one byte in memory. In a C program, the compiler automatically adds a null character at the end of each string. In an assembly program, the string can be defined by using the DCB (define constant byte) directive and the programmer should explicitly add "0" at the end of a string.

Note "LDR r6, =str" is a pseudo instruction, which is not a real instruction and is translated into a PC-relative load. It loads a 32-bit memory address, identified by the label *str*, into register r6. The LDR pseudo instruction provides convenience for assembly programmers.

C Program	Assembly Program
	`            AREA  myData, DATA`
	`            ALIGN`
`char str[26] = "rats live on no evil star";`	`str         DCB   "rats live on no evil star",0`
	`            AREA  palindrome, CODE`
	`            EXPORT __main`
`int main(void) {`	`            ALIGN ENTRY`
`  int i = 0, j = 0;`	`__main  PROC`
`  int len = 0, flag = 1;`	`            LDR   r6, =str`
`  // find the string length`	`            ; find the string length`
`  while(str[i++]!='\0')`	`            MOV   r1, #0     ; len`
`    len++;`	`            MOV   r5, r6     ; r5 = str`
	`strLen  LDRB  r2, [r5], 1 ; post-index`
	`            CMP   r2, #0     ; check NULL`
	`            ADDNE r1, r1, #1 ; len++`
	`            BNE   strLen     ; loop again`
`  // if the string is not a`	`            ; check palindrome`
`  // palindrome, clear the flag`	`            SUB   r1, r1, 1   ; len - 1`
	`            ADD   r1, r6, r1  ; &str[len-1]`
`  for(i=0,j=(len-1); i<j; i++,j--){`	`            MOV   r2, r6      ; &str`
`    if(str[j] != str[i]) {`	`cmpStr  LDRB  r3, [r2], 1 ; str[i]`
`        flag = 0;`	`            LDRB  r4, [r1],-1 ; str[len-1-i]`
`        break;`	`            CMP   r3, r4    ; compare`
`    }`	`            MOVNE r0, #0    ; not Palindrome`
`  }`	`            BNE   stop      ; stop`
`}`	`            CMP   r1, r2    ; compare i & j`
	`            BLT   cmpStr    ; loop again`
	`            MOV   r0, #1    ; Palindrome`
`  while(1);`	`stop        B     stop      ; dead loop`
`}`	`            ENDP`
	`            END`

7.11 Example of Converting String to Integer (atoi)

A character takes one byte in the memory and it is represented by the corresponding ASCII value, shown in the following table. To convert the character "9" to its numeric value, the program needs to subtract 0x30 from its ASCII value. The *atoi* function in C converts a numeric string to an integer.

Letter	0	1	2	3	4	5	6	7	8	9
ASCII	0x30	0x31	0x32	0x33	0x34	0x35	0x36	0x37	0x38	0x39

In order to implement the multiplication with 10, we can use the multiplication instruction:

```
MOV r4,#10
MUL r3,r2,#10
ADD r2,r0,r3           ; r2 = 10*r2 + r0
```

However, a more efficient implementation is to use the shift operations since the MUL instruction is slow.

```
ADD r3,r2,r2,LSL #2    ; r3 = r2 + r2*4 = 5*r2
ADD r2,r0,r3,LSL #1    ; r2 = 2*r3 + r0 = 10*r2 + r0
```

C Program	Assembly Program

`char str[] = "123456";`	`        AREA myData, DATA`
	`        ALIGN`
	`str   DCB   "123456",0`

`int main(){`
`  char *p = str;`
`  int value = 0;`
 	
`  while( *p != '\0' ){`
`    // ASCII of '0' = 0x30`
`    // ASCII of '9' = 0x39`
`    if( *p<0x30 || *p>0x39)`
`      return 0;`
`    else`
`      value = \`
`        value*10 + (*p-0x30);`
 	
`    p++;`
`  }`
`  while(1); //dead loop`
`}`
	`        AREA atoi, CODE`
	`        EXPORT    __main`
	`        ALIGN`
	`        ENTRY`
	`__main PROC`
	`        LDR   r1, =str`
	`        MOVS r2, #0          ; r2 = value`
	
	`loop LDRB r0, [r1], 1    ; r0 = *p; p = p + 1`
	`        CBZ   r0, stop       ; check null terminator`
	`        CMP   r0, #0x30      ; 0x30 = '0'`
	`        BLT   stop           ; stop if < '0'`
	`        CMP   r0, #0x39      ; 0x39 = '9'`
	`        BGT   stop           ; stop if > '9'`
	`        SUBS r0, r0, #0x30 ; r0 = *p-48`
	`        ADD   r3, r2, r2, LSL #2   ; r3 = 5*r2`
	`        ADD   r2, r0, r3, LSL #1   ; r2 = 10*r2 + r0`
	`        B     loop`
	
	`stop B     stop`
	`        ENDP`
	`        END`

7.12 Example of Binary Search

If an array is already sorted in an ascending order, we can use the binary search to locate a specific value in this array. It uses a divide-and-conquer approach, which divides the array in half and checks the middle point. If the middle is the target, the search completes successfully. If the middle is larger than the target, then it searches the first half of the array. Otherwise, it searches the second half. This procedure repeats until the size of the remaining array is reduced to zero. The following gives the flowchart of binary search.

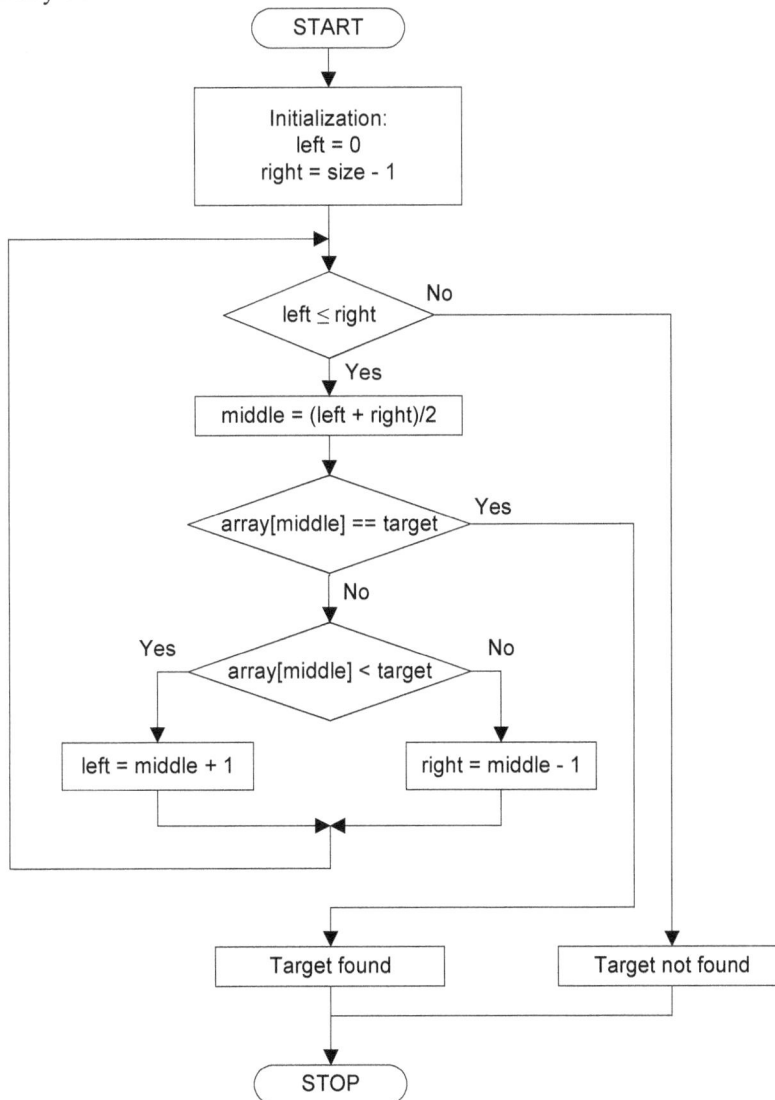

Figure 7-13. Flowchart of binary search over an ascending sorted array

For example, suppose the array consists of six integers, including 11, 12, 13, 14, 15, and 16 in order. The target number to be searched is 12. Note the index of an array in C language starts with 0.

- During the first round of the while loop, variable *left* is 0 and variable *right* is 5. As a result, the *middle* is (*left* + *right*)/2 = (0 + 5)/2 = 2. Note C language uses truncation instead of rounding for integer arithmetic. Since array[middle], *i.e.* array[2], is 13, which is larger than the target 12, we have *right* = *middle* − 1 = 2 − 1 = 1.
- During the second loop, *middle* = (*left* + *right*)/2 = (0 + 1)/2 = 0. Since array[0] is smaller than the target, we have *left* = *middle* + 1 = 0 + 1 = 1.
- During the third loop, the *middle* is (*left* + *right*)/2 = (1 + 1)/2 = 1; since array[1] is equal to the target, the target has been found and the while loop stops.

C Program	Assembly Program

`int array[6] =`
`   {11, 12, 13, 14, 15, 16};`
`int size = 6;`
 	
`int main( void ) {`
 	
`  int left, right, middle;`
`  int target = 12;`
`  int targetLocation = -1;`
 	
`  left  = 0;`
`  right = size - 1;`
 	
`  while( left <= right ){`
`    middle = (left + right)/2;`
`    if(array[middle]==target){`
`      targetLocation = middle;`
`      break;`
`    }`
`    if(array[middle] < target)`
`      left = middle + 1;`
`    else`
`      right = middle - 1;`
`  }`
`  while(1); // dead loop`
`}`
	`        AREA myData, DATA`
	`        ALIGN`
	`array   DCD 11,12,13,14,15,16`
	`size    DCD 6`
	
	`        AREA binarySearch, CODE`
	`        EXPORT __main`
	`        ALIGN`
	`        ENTRY`
	`__main  PROC`
	`        MOVS r3, #12      ; Search target`
	`        MOVS r5, #-1      ; Location`
	`        LDR  r12, =array`
	`        MOVS r1, #0       ; r1 = left`
	`        LDR  r2, =size`
	`        LDR  r2, [r2]`
	`        SUB  r2, r2, #1   ; r2 = right`
	`loop    ADD  r0, r1, r2   ; r0 = left + right`
	`        LSR  r0, r0, #1   ; middle = r0/2`
	`        LDR  r4, [r12,r0,LSL #2] ; array[middle]`
	`        CMP  r4, r3       ; compare with target`
	`        SUBGT r2, r0, #1  ; right = middle - 1`
	`        ADDLT r1, r0, #1  ; left = middle + 1`
	`        BEQ  found`
	`        CMP  r1, r2       ; compare left & right`
	`        BLE  loop         ; loop if left ≤ right`
	`found   MOVEQ r5, r0`
	
	`stop    B stop`
	`        ENDP`
	`        END`

7.13 Example of Bubble Sort

Bubble sort is a simple and well-known sorting algorithm that iterates through an array to be sorted, repeatedly compares each pair of adjacent elements in this array, and swaps them if they are in reverse order. In each iteration, the heaviest or largest element within the unsorted portion of the array sinks to the tail of this array for sorting in ascending order, and to the head of this array for sorting in descending order.

Assuming we want to sort an array of signed integers into ascending order:

1. The program has a pair of nested loops. In the outer loop i, the ith largest number of the array is identified and moved toward the tail. The inner loop j iterates through unsorted portion of the array and moves the largest number in the unsorted portion to its proper place.

2. In the first iteration of the outer loop (loop over i), we will find the largest number in this array and store it at array[size-1]. This is achieved by the following sequential steps: comparing array[0] and array [1], comparing array[1] and array[2], ..., and comparing array[size-2] and array[size-1]. If array[j-1] is larger than array[j], then they are swapped.

3. In the second iteration of the outer loop, we will find the largest number in the subarray from array[0] to array[size-2], and store it into the position array[size-2].

4. In each iteration, the size of the subarray to be sorted is reduced by one.

5. The above process repeats until the subarray size is reduced to zero. At the end, all numbers in this array are sorted in ascending order.

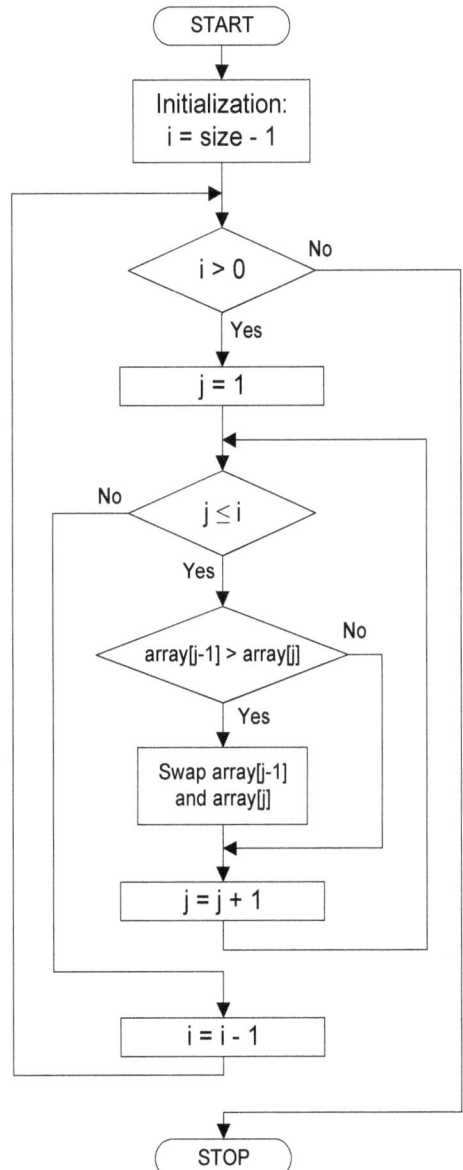

Figure 7-14. Flow chart of bubble sort

The implementation of bubble sort in C and assembly are given in the following. In the assembly implementation, loop variable i is stored in register r1, and loop variable j is stored in register r0. While the outer loop iterates n times, the inner loop is always executed in each pass of the outer loop. During the first iteration of the outer loop, the inner loop iterates n times; during the second outer loop, the inner loop iterates $n-1$ times, and so on. Therefore the total number of comparisons when sorting an array of n integers, is $(n-1) + (n-2) + (n-3) + \cdots + 1 = n(n+1)/2$. Note bubble sort is simple but not efficient. There are faster sorting algorithms, such as quick sort and heap sort.

C Program	Assembly Program

<pre>int array[12] = {12, 11, 10,
9, 8, 7, 6, 5, 4, 3, 2, 1};
 	
int size = 12;
 	
int main(void) {
  int i, j, temp;
 	
  for(i=(size-1); i > 0; i--){
 	
    for (j = 1; j <= i; j++) {
 	
      if (array[j-1]>array[j]){
        // swap them
        temp = array[j-1];
        array[j-1] = array[j];
        array[j] = temp;
      }
    }
  }
 	
  while(1);
}</pre>
	<pre> AREA myData, DATA
	            ALIGN
	array DCD 12,11,10,9,8,7,6,5,4,3,2,1
	size DCD 12
	
	            AREA bubbleSort, CODE
	            EXPORT __main
	            ALIGN
	            ENTRY
	__main PROC
	            LDR r5, =array
	            LDR r6, =size
	            LDR r6, [r6] ; array size
	
	            SUB r1, r6, #1 ; r1 = i = size -1
	loop_i CMP r1, #0 ; check for i > 0
	            BLE stop ; exit the loop i
	            MOV r0, #1 ; r0 = j = 1
	loop_j CMP r0, r1 ; compare j and i
	            BGT exit_j ; exit the loop j
	            SUB r2, r0, #1 ; r2 = j - 1
	            LDR r3, [r5,r2,LSL #2] ; array[j-1]
	            LDR r4, [r5,r0,LSL #2] ; array[j]
	            CMP r3, r4
	            STRGT r4, [r5,r2,LSL #2] ; array[j-1]
	            STRGT r3, [r5,r0,LSL #2] ; array[j]
	            ADD r0, r0, #1 ; j++
	            B loop_j
	exit_j SUB r1, r1, #1 ; i--
	            B loop_i
	stop B stop
	            ENDP
	            END</pre>

7.14 Exercises

1. Write an assembly program that converts all characters of a string to upper case.

2. Write an assembly program that finds the least common multiple (LCM) of two integers. For example, LCM(4, 6) = 12.

3. Write an assembly program that calculates the result of x raised to the power of y, i.e. x^y, where x and y are two signed integers.

4. Write an assembly program that checks whether a given year is a leap year. A leap year is a year containing one additional day in February. A leap year meets one of the following requirements.

    - divisible by 400, or
    - only divisible by 4 not by 100.

5. Write an assembly program that removes all vowel letters (a, e, i, o, u, A, E, I, O, U) from a string.

6. Let n be a positive integer. Integers a and b are congruent modulo n if they have the same remainder when divided by n. For example, 39 and 19 are congruent modulo 10. Write an assembly program that checks whether two unsigned integers, a and b, are congruent modulo n.

7. Write an assembly program that checks whether an unsigned number is a prime number or not.

8. Write an assembly program that reverses all bits of a 32-bit number without using the RBIT instruction.

9. Write an assembly program that checks whether an unsigned integer is a square of some unsigned integer. For example, $25 = 5^2$.

10. Write an assembly program that calculates the number of words in a string. The string is terminated with NULL and words are separated by space.

11. Write an assembly program that finds the day of the week for a given date. Suppose the year is stored in r0, the month in r1, and the day of the month in r2. The day of the week is saved in r3 (0 = Sunday, 1 = Monday, etc.). The following method was published by Michael Keith and Tom Craver in 1990.

```
int day_of_week(int y, int m, int d)    {
    static int t[] = {0, 3, 2, 5, 0, 3, 5, 1, 4, 6, 2, 4};
    y -= m < 3;
    return (y + y/4 - y/100 + y/400 + t[m-1] + d) % 7;
}
```

12. Write an assembly program that calculates the variance of an unsigned integer array, defined as follows:

$$\bar{x} = \frac{1}{n}\Sigma_i^n x_i \qquad var = \frac{1}{n}\Sigma_i^n(x_i - \bar{x})^2$$

13. Write an assembly program that calculates the sum of diagonal elements of n-by-n integer matrix. The following gives an example matrix definition.

```
        AREA myData, DATA
size    DCD 4
matrix DCD 1,2,3,4,5,6,7,8,9,10,11,12,13,14,15,16
```

14. Write an assembly program that calculates the dot product of two integer vectors of the equal number of elements. The dot product is the sum of the products of the corresponding elements of the two vectors, as shown below.

$$product = A \cdot B = \sum_{i=1}^{n}(a_i \times b_i) = a_1 b_1 + a_2 b_2 + \cdots + a_n b_n$$

```
        AREA myData, DATA
size    DCD 8
A_Array DCD 1,2,3,4,5,6,7,8
B_Array DCD 9,10,11,12,13,14,15,16
Product DCD 0
```

15. Write an assembly program that performs matrix multiplication.

$$C_{(m \times n)} = A_{(m \times p)} \cdot B_{(p \times n)}$$

The (i, j) element of the product matrix is calculated as follows:

$$c_{ij} = \sum_{k=1}^{p}(a_{ik} \times b_{kj}) = a_{i1}b_{1j} + a_{i2}b_{2j} + \cdots + a_{ip}b_{pj}$$

where $1 \le i \le m$ and $1 \le j \le n$.

```
      AREA myData, DATA
m     DCD   4
p     DCD   3
n     DCD   4
AM    DCD   1,2,3,4,5,6,7,8,9,10,11,12
BM    DCD   1,2,3,4,5,6,7,8,9,10,11,12
CM    SPACE 64      ; Reserve 16 words
```

CHAPTER
8

Subroutines

One key motivation of subroutines is to enable the reuse of a portion of program code that carries out a specific task. In addition, using subroutines can increase the quality and reliability of a large program. A subroutine is also often called a procedure, a function, or a routine.

One mistake inexperienced software programmers often make is to duplicate code within a program by copy-and-paste. This programming style makes the program less modularized and difficult to read and debug. It increases the cost of developing and maintaining a large software project substantially.

> *"One of my most productive days was throwing away 1000 lines of code."*
>
> Ken Thompson, early developer of UNIX OS

Breaking the program codes into subroutines has two important advantages. First, it decomposes a complex task into several simpler and more manageable subtasks, which makes the design, development, and debugging of each subtask much easier. Programmers can develop and test each individual subtask separately, making it easier to find errors. Second, subtasks can be reused in a program or other subtasks repeatedly without duplicating any code, which saves time and effort by eliminating redundant development work.

A subroutine usually takes some input arguments and may return a result when the subroutine exits. For example, a subroutine that finds the maximum of an array of elements may take two arguments, the memory address (a pointer in C language) of the array and the number of elements in this array, and return the maximum value or its location. Using arguments makes a subroutine versatile and suitable for a variety of uses.

Implementing a subroutine using a high-level programming language such as Java, C, or C++ differs significantly from using an assembly language. Specifically, when a programmer develops a subroutine in assembly, two special issues need to be considered.

1. Preserve the processor environment. The subroutine should be non-intrusive and avoid destroying the content of important registers, which are still meaningful for the caller. A typical approach is to preserve the environment by pushing registers to be used in the subroutine into the stack at the beginning of the subroutine, and then popping the content out from the stack to these registers at the end of the subroutine.
2. Follow the standard of application binary interface, which specifies the protocol of passing input arguments to a subroutine and returning result back to the caller. Subroutines programmed in assembly may need to be used by a C program or another assembly program developed by different programmers.

8.1 Calling a Subroutine

The branch and link (BL) instruction is used to call a subroutine. The BL instruction performs two operations: (1) set the link register (LR) as the sequentially next value of the program counter (PC + 4 in Cortex-M3), and (2) set the program counter (PC) as the memory address of the very first instruction of the subroutine.

In fact, LR stores the memory address of the instruction to be executed immediately after a subroutine exits. The address held by LR is also called return address. The return address should be the memory address of the instruction immediately after the BL instruction. Since a BL instruction takes 32 bits (*i.e.* 4 bytes) in memory, the memory address of the instruction after the BL instruction is PC + 4.

There are two different approaches to return from a subroutine.

- The first one is to run the branch and exchange instruction "BX LR".
- The second one is to directly pop the LR value out of the stack into PC, *i.e.* "POP {PC}", if the LR has already been pushed into the stack.

Figure 8-1 shows an example in which the main program calls the *foo* subroutine, and the *foo* subroutine then calls the *bar* subroutine. Because a BL instruction has 32 bits, the memory address of the instruction immediately after a BL instruction is PC + 4. When the *foo* subroutine is called, PC is set as the memory address of the *foo* subroutine and LR is set as PC_1 + 4. When the *foo* subroutine returns by executing "BX LR", the content of LR is copied to PC, making the next instruction after "BL foo" in the main program to start the execution.

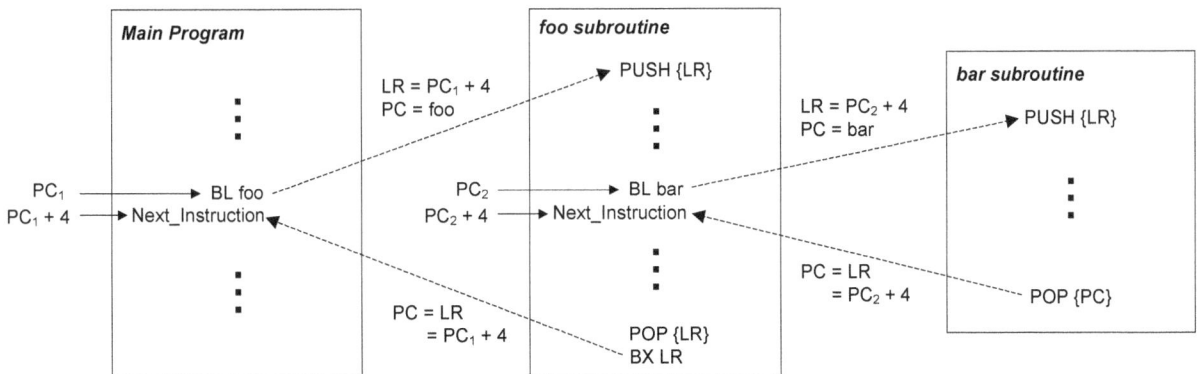

Figure 8-1. An example of calling subroutines. A subroutine should preserve the link register (LR) in the stack if this subroutine calls any subroutines.

When a subroutine calls another subroutine, register LR should be preserved into the stack at the beginning of the subroutine. In the example shown in Figure 8-1, when *foo* calls *bar*, the instruction "BL bar" sets LR as PC_2 + 4. If *foo* did not preserve LR, the "BX LR" instruction at the end of *foo* would not be able to return correctly the control to the main program because PC would be mistakenly set as PC_2 + 4, instead of PC_1 + 4. Therefore, LR has to be pushed into the stack before this subroutine calls any subroutines.

Preserve LR in a subroutine.

8.2 Stack

A stack, a last-in-first-out (LIFO) data structure, is used to preserve the processor environment in subroutines. On Cortex-M3 processors, a stack is a pre-defined special memory region, and the address of the top of the stack is stored in the stack pointer (SP). According to the direction in which the stack grows, a stack can be either descending or ascending.

- *Descending stack.* When the content of a register is pushed into the stack, the stack pointer (SP) is decreased by 4 if it is a descending stack. The stack grows downward, *i.e.* in the direction toward low memory addresses, as shown in Figure 8-3.
- *Ascending stack.* When pushing a register into the stack, SP is increased by 4. The stack grows toward high memory addresses.

In addition, a stack can be either a *full stack* or an *empty stack*.

- If the memory pointed by SP holds a valid stack item, then it is called a full stack.
- If the memory pointed by SP is an empty spot and can store a new stack item, then it is called an empty stack.

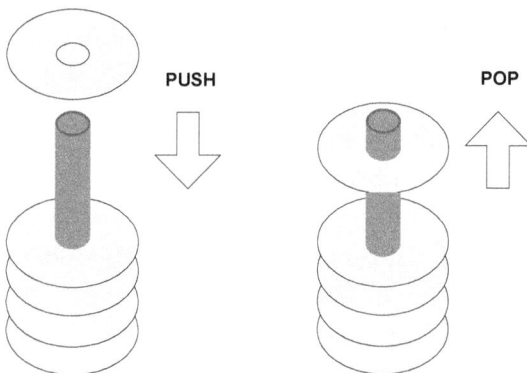

Figure 8-2. A stack is last-in-first-out (LIFO).

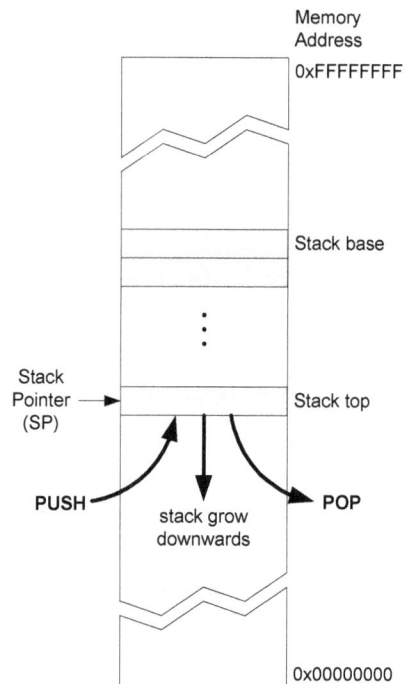

Figure 8-3. Cortex-M3 processors use the descending stack that grows toward lower memory addresses.

ARM Cortex-M3 uses *full descending* stacks, as shown in Figure 8-3. In fact, a Cortex-M3 processor supports two stacks: one main stack and one process stack. Therefore, there are two stack pointers: MSP and PSP. The stack pointer (SP) is a shadow of MSP or PSP. Chapter 23.1 discusses the usage of these two stacks. The initial values of the stack pointers can be programmed. Typically, the system stack is placed in the top region of the system memory region.

8.3 Preserving Runtime Environment via Stack

If a register is used in a subroutine to hold the value of local variables, it is often preserved in the stack at the beginning of the subroutine and recovered from the stack when the subroutine exits. This process is to preserve the runtime environment of the caller.

Example 8-1 shows the motivation why the runtime environment should be preserved. The caller uses register r4 as a loop variable looping from 0 to 100. The loop body calls a subroutine named *foo*. However, the subroutine *foo* also uses register r4 as a local variable. If the subroutine does not perverse the content of register r4, r4 will be mistakenly set as 10 after the subroutine completes. As a result, the loop in the caller will not perform as desired.

Caller Program	Subroutine/Callee
<pre> MOV r4, #100
  ...
  BL foo
  ...
  ADD r4, r4, #1 ; r4 = 101, not 11</pre>	<pre>foo PROC
    ...
    MOV   r4, #10 ; foo changes r4
    ...
    BX   LR
    ENDP</pre>

Example 8-1. The loop in the caller program is not executed as desired.

In order to solve this issue, the subroutine stores the value of r4 into the stack before executing any other code, and then restores the content to r4 immediately before the subroutine is returned. This is implemented by the stack push and pop operation, as illustrated below.

Caller Program	Subroutine/Callee
<pre> MOV r4, #100
  ...
  BL foo
  ...
  ADD r4, r4, #1 ; r4 = 101, not 11</pre>	<pre>foo PROC
    PUSH {r4}   ; preserve r4
    ...
    MOV   r4, #10 ; foo changes r4
    ...
    POP   {r4}   ; Recover r4
    BX   LR
    ENDP</pre>

Example 8-2. A subroutine preserves register values in the stack at the beginning and recovers register values from the stack before the subroutine exits.

The ARM embedded application binary interface (EABI) requires that a subroutine must preserve the content of registers r4 - r11 and r13 (SP) if their content is to be changed in this subroutine. However, a subroutine is not required to preserve registers r0-r3, also called scratch registers. Thus, if the caller has to store values that should not be changed by a subroutine in registers r0-r3, the caller should push them into the stack before it calls the subroutine.

Table 8-1 summarizes the register usage. Except r0-r3, a subroutine also does not preserve the intra-procedure-call register r12 (IP) and the link register r14 (LR). Register r9 is platform dependent and can be used for different purposes. For example, r9 can be used as variable register 6 to hold a local variable.

- Register IP allows a routine and any subroutine it calls to share an intermediate value. When a BL instruction is executed, the value of IP may be changed if the memory address of the destination instruction is beyond the range of the BL instruction. Therefore, it should not be used as a general-purpose register to hold important values.
- It is not required to preserve register LR. However, if a subroutine calls on to yet another subroutine, LR has to be preserved in the stack, as discussed in Chapter 8.1.

Register	Usage	Subroutine Preserved	Notes
r0	Argument 1 and return value	No	If return has 64 bits, then r1:r0 hold it. If 1st argument has 64 bits, r1:r0 hold it. r1 is upper word, r0 is bottom word.
r1	Argument 2	No	
r2	Argument 3	No	The If the return has 128 bits, r0-r3 hold it. If 2nd argument has 64 bits, r3:r2 hold it.
r3	Argument 4	No	If more than 4 arguments, use the stack
r4	General-purpose V1	Yes	Variable register 1 holds a local variable.
r5	General-purpose V2	Yes	Variable register 2 holds a local variable.
r6	General-purpose V3	Yes	Variable register 3 holds a local variable.
r7	General-purpose V4	Yes	Variable register 4 holds a local variable.
r8	General-purpose V5	YES	Variable register 5 holds a local variable.
r9	Platform specific/V6	No	Usage is platform-dependent.
r10	General-purpose V7	Yes	Variable register 7 holds a local variable.
r11	General-purpose V8	Yes	Variable register 8 holds a local variable.
r12 (IP)	Intra-procedure-call register	No	It holds intermediate values between a procedure and the sub-procedure it calls.
r13 (SP)	Stack pointer	Yes	SP has to be the same after a subroutine has completed.
r14 (LR)	Link register	No	LR does not have to contain the same value after a subroutine has completed.
r15 (PC)	Program counter	N/A	Do not directly change PC

Table 8-1. Standard of register usage of a subroutine

When using the push instruction to push multiple registers into the stack, as shown in Example 8-3, the order that the registers are listed in the bracket does not matter. The compiler sorts the registers in the descending order according to their numbers, pushes the largest register first during the push operation, and pops the smallest register first during the pop operation.

Push and pop multiple registers	Equivalent assembly code
MOV r4, #4	MOV r4, #4
MOV r5, #5	MOV r5, #5
MOV r6, #6	MOV r6, #6
PUSH {r4, r5, r6}	; equivalent code
; The order in the bracket does not matter.	PUSH {r6}
; The assembler sorts the register list,	PUSH {r5}
; and pushes the largest register first.	PUSH {r4}
POP {r6, r4, r5}	; equivalent code
; The order in the bracket does not matter.	POP {r4}
; The assembler sorts the register list,	POP {r5}
; and pops the smallest register first.	POP {r6}
; result: r4=4, r5=5, r6=6	; result: r4=4, r5=5, r6=6

Example 8-3. Push and pop operations of the stack

8.4 Passing Arguments to Subroutine via Registers

In order to allow an assembly subroutine to be used by a standard C program or by assembly programs developed independently by different programmers, the subroutine must follow the ARM EABI protocol in passing arguments and returning a result, defined as follows:

- When up to four 32-bit arguments are passed to a subroutine, these arguments are stored in registers r0 - r3.
- When up to two 64-bit arguments, such as "long long" and "double" variables in C, are passed, the first argument is then passed via registers r0 and r1, and the second one via registers r2 and r3.
- When a 128-bit argument is passed, the argument is contained in registers r0-r3.
- When there are more than four arguments, the first four arguments are stored in registers r0 – r3, respectively, and the rest of the arguments have to be passed through the stack.

When a subroutine returns a 32-bit value, the return value is stored in register r0. If the result has 64 bits, it is stored in register r0 and r1. If the return has 128 bits, it is stored in registers r0, r1, r2, and r3.

R0	R1	R2	R3
32-bit Argument 1	32-bit Argument 2	32-bit Argument 3	32-bit Argument 4

Extra arguments are pushed to the stack by the caller. The caller is responsible to pop them out of the stack after the subroutine returns.

R1(MSB32)	R0(LSB32)	R3(MSB32)	R2(LSB32)
64-bit Argument 1		64-bit Argument 2	

R3(MSB32)	R2	R1	R0(LSB32)
128-bit Argument			

Subroutine

R0
32-bit Return Value

R1(MSB32)	R0(LSB32)
64-bit Return Value	

R3(MSB32)	R2	R1	R0(LSB32)
128-bit Return Value			

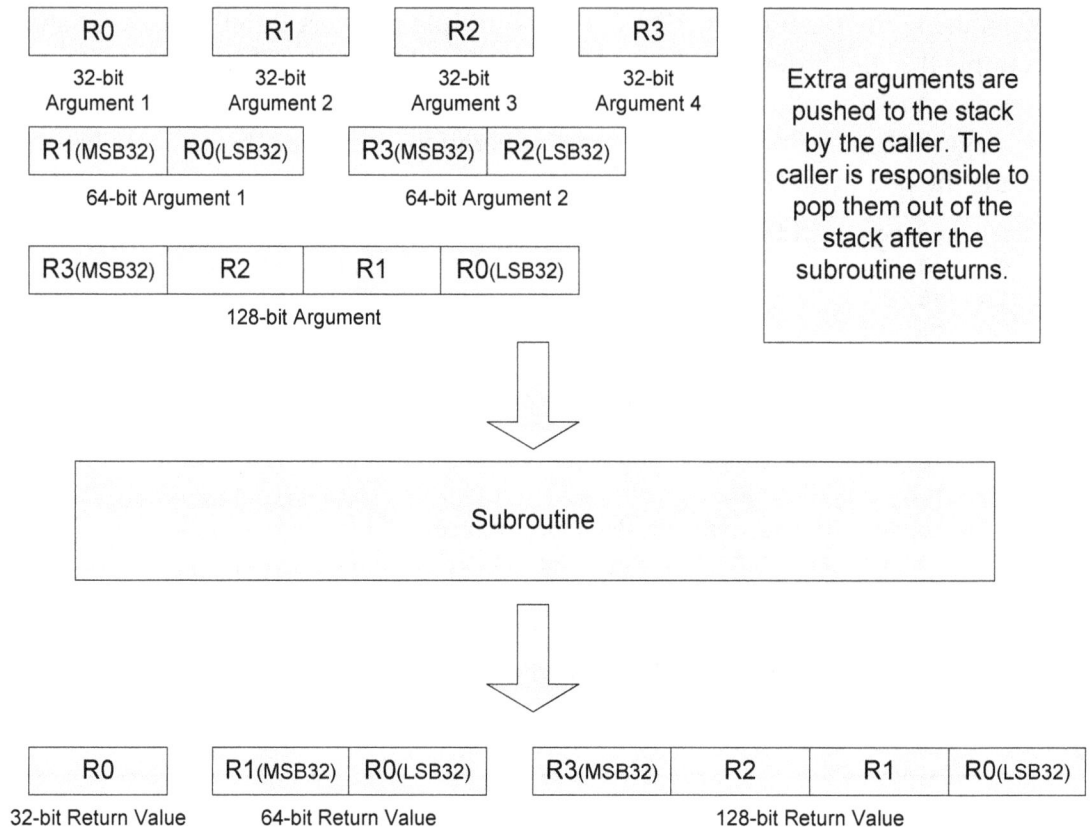

Figure 8-4. Passing arguments and returning a value. If a value takes multiple registers, the most significant bits (MSB) are stored in the highest numbered register.

8.4.1   Pass a Variable by Value and by Reference

We can pass arguments to a subroutine by value or by reference. In C, arguments are always passed by value. However, C can use memory points to emulate passing a variable by reference.

- Passing a variable by value is to make a copy of the variable. After the subroutine exits, the value of the variable always remains the same in the caller program. The subroutine cannot change the variable value of the caller.
- Passing a variable by reference is achieved by making a copy of the memory address of the variable. The value of the variable can be changed by the subroutine since the subroutine can directly change values stored in the memory.

Example 8-4 shows a simple example that compares passing a variable to a subroutine by value and by reference. We can better understand their differences by looking at the assembly programs into which a C compiler translates them, as illustrated in Figure 8-5 and Figure 8-6.

Pass by Value	Pass by Reference
| ```c
void fun(int n){
  n = 1;    // won't update callee' n
}


int main(void){
  int n = 0;
  fun(n);    // pass value of n
  printf("%d", n);
}
``` | ```c
void fun(int *n){
  *n = 1;    // dereference and
            // update memory
}

int main(void){
  int n = 0;
  int *p = &n;
  fun(p);        // pass pointer
  printf("%d", n);
}
``` |
| Output: 0 | Output: 1 |

Example 8-4. Comparison of passing a variable by value and by reference in C

When a C program is compiled, the compiler can assign a local variable to a register or store it in the heap region of the data memory, as discussed in Chapter 7.2. Suppose variable n in Example 8-4 is stored in the memory.

- When a variable is passed by value, the key operations of the corresponding assembly code are illustrated in Figure 8-5. The value of variable n is loaded from the memory to register r0 since this is only one argument to be passed in this example. While the subroutine changes the value of register r0, the value stored in the memory remains unchanged. Therefore, the in-memory variable cannot be changed by a subroutine if it is passed by value.
- When a variable is passed by reference, the key operations of its assembly implementation are given in Figure 8-6. The memory address of variable n is loaded into register r0 and is passed to the subroutine. Register r0 serves as a pointer to variable n. Since the memory address is passed to the subroutine, the subroutine can change the value of the variable by using the store register instruction (STR). When the subroutine exits, the value of variable n in the memory has been changed.

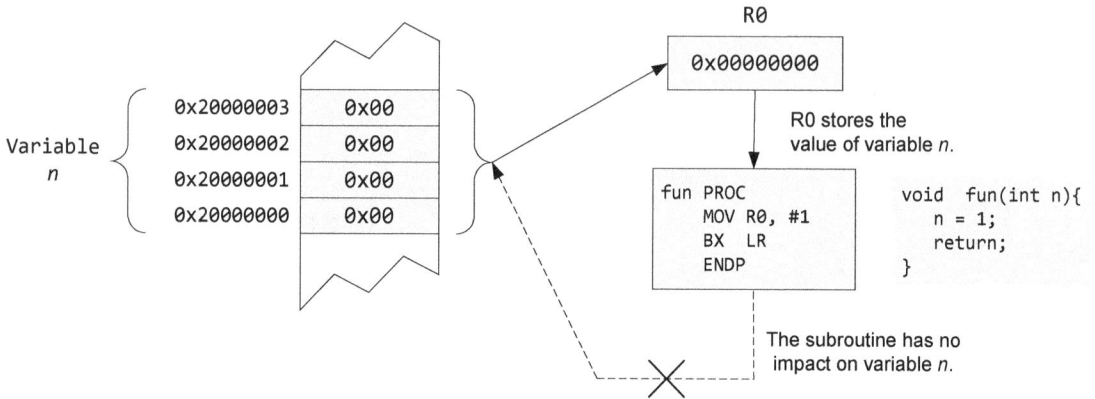

Figure 8-5. Example of passing a variable by value. If variable *n* is passed by value, the subroutine cannot change the variable value stored in the memory. This is because the subroutine only knows the value but not the memory address of variable *n*. Therefore, after the fun subroutine exits, the value of *n* stored in memory is still 0, not 1.

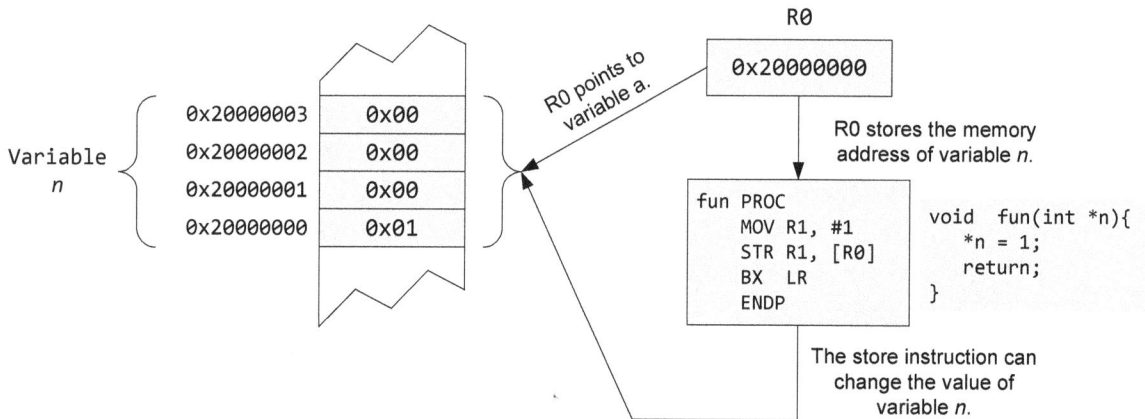

Figure 8-6. Example of passing a variable by reference. If variable *n* is passed by reference, the memory address of variable *n* is passed. Therefore, the subroutine can change the value of variable *n*. After the subroutine exits, the value of *n* in the memory is changed to 1.

8.4.2 Example of Passing by Value

In Example 8-5, two 32-bit integers are passed to the subroutine *sum2*. According to the application binary interface (ABI) protocol, the assembly program should meet the following requirements.

- The value of variable *a1* is passed in register r0, and *a2* in register r1. An integer in C has 32 bits. Therefore, only one register is required to hold *a1*.
- The caller program assumes the subroutine saves the result *total* in register r0.
- Registers r0, r1, r2, and r3 are scratch registers, and the subroutine does not have to preserve them in the stack. If the caller wishes to preserve the value of these registers, the caller has to push them into the stack before the subroutine is called, and pop them out of the stack after the subroutine completes.
- If a subroutine does not call any other subroutine, the subroutine is required to preserve the link register (LR) in the stack. Otherwise, the subroutine should preserve LR on entry and recover it on exit.

C Program	Assembly Program
| int t;<br>int sum2(int a1, int a2);<br><br>int main(){<br>  t = sum2(1, 2);<br>  while(1);<br>}<br><br><br><br><br><br><br><br><br><br>int sum2(int a1, int a2){<br>  int total;<br>  total = a1 + a2;<br>  return total;<br>} | ```
        AREA sum, CODE
        EXPORT __main
        ALIGN
        ENTRY
__main PROC
        MOV  r0, #1    ; 1st argument
        MOV  r1, #2    ; 2nd argument

        BL   sum2      ; result returned in r0
                       ; LR points to LDR

        LDR  r1, =t    ; memory address of t
        STR  r0, [r1]  ; save the sum

stop    B    stop
        ENDP
sum2    PROC           ; name of procedure
        ; r0 = 1st argument
        ; r1 = 2nd argument

        ADD  r0, r0, r1 ; r0 = r0 + r1

        ; r0 = result to be returned

        BX   lr        ; set PC to LR
        ENDP           ; end of procedure
        AREA myData, DATA
t       DCD 0
        END            ; end of program
``` |

Example 8-5. Passing two arguments to a subroutine
```

In the following, we illustrate how to pass a 64-bit value into a subroutine. In C, a long long variable takes 64 bits in the memory. When this variable is passed to a subroutine, two registers, r0 and r1, are used to hold the value of this variable, with r1 holding the most significant 32 bits and r0 holding the least significant 32 bits. For example, if the long long variable has a value of -2, then register r0 is 0xFFFFFFFE and register r1 is 0xFFFFFFFF.

A 64-bit result is returned from a subroutine in register r1 and r0. In the following example, the 64-bit sum should be 3. Thus, when the subroutine returns, r1 is 0x00000000 (the upper word) and r0 is 0x00000003 (the lower word). Two store register instructions are used to save the 64-bit result in the memory.

C Program	Assembly Program

`long sum2(long long a1,`
`long long a2);`
 	
`int main(){`
`  long long t;`
`  t = sum2(1, 2);`
`  while(1);`
`}`
	` ` `AREA sum, CODE`
	` ` `EXPORT __main`
	` ` `ALIGN`
	` ` `ENTRY`
	`__main PROC`
	` ` `MOV  r0, #1   ;`
	` ` `MOV  r1, #0   ; 1`st` 64-bit argument`
	` ` `MOV  r3, #2   ;`
	` ` `MOV  r4, #0   ; 2`nd` 64-bit argument`
	` ` **`BL   sum2`**`    ; result in r1:r0`
	` ` `              ; LR points to stop`
	` ` `LDR  r3, =t   ; memory address of t`
	` ` `STR  r0, [r3] ; save lower 32 bits`
	` ` `STR  r1, [r3, 4]  ; save upper 32 bits`
	` ` `              ; r0 = 3, r1 = 0 in`
	` ` `              ; this example`
	`stop B    stop`
	` ` `ENDP`

`long long `**`sum2`**`(long long`
`a1, long long a2){`
`  long long total;`
`  total = a1 + a2;`
`  return total;`
`}`
	`sum2` ` PROC            ; name of procedure`
	` ` `; r0 = 1`st` argument`
	` ` `; r1 = 2`nd` argument`
	
	` ` `ADDS r0, r0, r3 ; Add lower 32 bits`
	` ` `ADC  r1, r1, r3 ; Add upper 32 bits`
	
	` ` `; r1:r0 = 64-bit return value`
	
	` ` `BX   lr         ; set PC to LR`
	` ` `ENDP            ; end of procedure`
	
	` ` `AREA myData, DATA`
	`t    DCQ 0           ; allocate 8 bytes`
	` ` `END             ; end of program`

Example 8-6. Passing two 64-bit arguments to a subroutine

8.4.3   Write a Subroutine in Different Files

In addition, subroutines may be written in separate source files. These source files are compiled separately and linked together when building an executable. This approach improves the clarity and makes code more manageable when the source code is large. If a source file contains the implementation of subroutines, the names of subroutines have to be exported to allow other files to reference it. The caller has to import the subroutine names defined elsewhere.

Example 8-7 shows how an assembly program calls a subroutine implemented in a separate assemble source file.

- In the *sum2.s* file, "EXPORT sum2" is used to declare a symbol *sum2* that may be referred to in other source files. The directive "EXPORT" in assembly is similar to "EXTERN" in C.
- In the *main.s* file, "IMPORT sum2" is used to tell the assembler that the symbol *sum2* is located in other files.

Source file *sum2.s*	Source file *main.s*

`        AREA sum, CODE`
`        EXPORT sum2`
`        ALIGN`
 	
`sum2    PROC`
`        ADD r0, r0, r1  ; return r0`
`        BX  lr          ; set PC to LR`
`        ENDP`
 	
`        END`
	`        AREA program, CODE`
	`        EXPORT  __main`
	`        IMPORT sum2`
	`        ALIGN`
	`        ENTRY`
	
	`__main  PROC`
	`        MOV r0, #1   ; 1`st` argument`
	`        MOV r1, #2   ; 2`nd` argument`
	`        BL  sum2     ; result in r0`
	
	`stop    B    stop`
	`        ENDP`
	`        END`

Example 8-7. Implementing a subroutine stored in a separate file. The keywords IMPORT and EXPORT are used to call a subroutine stored in a separate source file.

A symbol can be the name of a subroutine or a data variable. All symbols are resolved at the linking stage in which various pieces of code and data are combined into a single executable file. A linker performs the linking process. The EXPORT directive makes a symbol visible to all modular files during the linking stage. By default, the linker tries to locate a symbol locally within the current source file or included files. The IMPORT directive informs the linker that a specific symbol is defined or implemented in a different file.

8.4.4   Example of Passing by Reference

Pass-by-reference in C is a method that passes the memory address of a variable to the subroutine and thus allows the subroutine to change the variable value. Argument passed by reference must be declared as a pointer type. In the following swap subroutine, two arguments are passed by reference.

C program	Assembly Program
``// swap two characters
void swap (char *x, char *y) {
char t;
t = *x;
*x = *y;
*y = t;
}
``	```; swap routine
swap   PROC
LDRB r2, [r0]
LDRB r3, [r1]
STRB r3, [r0] ; [r1] into [r0]
STRB r2, [r1] ; [r0] into [r1]
BX   lr
ENDP
``

Example 8-8. Implementation of passing by reference in assembly language

Example 8-9 shows how to call a subroutine to swap the first and the last character of a string. For example, the swap subroutine changes the character string from "abcde" to "ebcda".

```
char str[6] = "abcde";    // Include the NULL terminator into the length
int main(void){
    swap(str, str+4);     // The result is "ebcda".
}
```

Example 8-9. A C program calls a subroutine implemented in assembly language.

In contrast to passing by reference, another method is to pass by value. Their key difference is that any variables passed by value are not changed by the subroutine. The following gives an example of passing by value. The variables that are passed by value are made a copy by the subroutine and are local variables of this subroutine. These variables remain unchanged after the subroutine returns. However, Example 8-10 fails to swap the characters of this string. The subroutine call "swap(str[0], str[4])" will not affect the content of the string at all.

C program (Incorrect code)	Assembly Program (Incorrect code)
``// swap two characters
void swap (char x, char y) {
char t;
t = x;
x = y;
y = t;
}
``	```; swap routine
swap   PROC
MOVS r2, r0
MOVS r1, r0
MOVS r2, r1
BX   lr
ENDP
``

Example 8-10. A subroutine implemented in C and assembly language fails to swap two characters when pass by value is used. In this example, pass by reference should be used.

8.4.5   Example of Greatest Common Divisor

This example gives a subroutine that calculates the greatest common divisor (GCD) of two positive integers. Figure 8-7 shows the flowchart of the *gcd* subroutine. The subroutine uses Euclid's algorithm, *i.e.* $gcd(a,b) = gcd(b, a \bmod b)$. The subroutine swaps a and b if a is smaller than b. It then repeatedly finds the GCD of the remainder $(a \bmod b)$ and b. Note the remainder becomes smaller and smaller and this process continues until the remainder becomes zero.

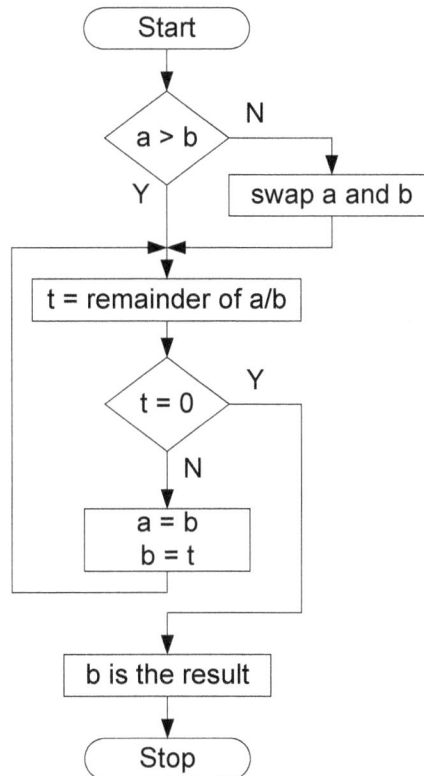

Figure 8-7. Flowchart of GCD subroutine

For illustration, suppose $a = 2310$ and $b = 483$. The program takes the following iterations:

1. $a = 2310$ and $b = 483$. Since $2310 = 4 \times 483 + 378$, the remainder of a/b is 378.
2. $a = 483$ and $b = 378$. Since $483 = 1 \times 378 + 105$, the remainder of a/b is 105.
3. $a = 378$ and $b = 105$. Since $378 = 3 \times 105 + 63$, the remainder of a/b is 63.
4. $a = 105$ and $b = 63$. Since $105 = 1 \times 63 + 42$, the remainder of a/b is 42.
5. $a = 63$ and $b = 42$. Since $63 = 1 \times 42 + 21$, the remainder of a/b is 21
6. $a = 42$ and $b = 21$. Since $42 = 2 \times 21$, the remainder of a/b is 0.
7. The program stops, and the GCD of 2310 and 483 is 21.

According to the ARM EABI protocol, the two input arguments are saved in register r0 and r1 respectively, and GCD identified is returned from the subroutine via register r0.

Since this *gcd* subroutine does not call any other subroutines, LR is not saved into the stack. In addition, the subroutine only uses registers r0, r1, r2, and r3, there is no need to save any of them into the stack.

C Program	Assembly Program

`int gcd(int a, int b);`
`int result;`
 	
`int main(void){`
`  result = gcd(21, 28);`
`  while(1);`
`}`
	`        AREA myData, DATA`
	`        ALIGN`
	`result  DCW 0                   ; allocate four bytes`
	
	`        AREA GCD, CODE`
	`        EXPORT __main`
	`        ALIGN`
	`        ENTRY`
	`__main PROC`
	`        MOV    r1, #21          ; 1`st` argument`
	`        MOV    r0, #28          ; 2`nd` argument`
	`        BL     gcd              ; call subroutine`
	`        ; GCD is returned in r0`
	`        LDR    r2, =result      ; r2 = memory address`
	`        STR    r0, [r2]         ; save result`
	`stop    B      stop`
	`        ENDP`

`int gcd(int a, int b) {`
`  int t; // temp variable`
 	
`  // swap a and b if a < b`
`  if( a < b ) {`
`    t = a;`
`    a = b;`
`    b = t;`
`  }`
 	
`  while( b != 0 ){`
`    t = a % b;`
`    a = b;`
`    b = t;`
`  }`
`  return a;`
`}`
	`gcd     PROC`
	`        ; r0 = 1`st` argument = a`
	`        ; r1 = 2`nd` argument = b`
	`        CMP    r0, r1           ; compare a & b`
	`        MOVLT r2, r0            ; if a < b, swap a & b`
	`        MOVLT r0, r1`
	`        MOVLT r1, r2`
	
	`loop    CBZ    r1, exit         ; if b = 0, exit`
	`        SDIV   r3, r0, r1       ; r3 = r0/r1`
	`        MLS    r2, r1, r3, r0   ; r2 = r1 - r3*r0`
	`        MOV    r0, r1           ; a = b`
	`        MOV    r1, r2           ; b = remainder`
	`        B      loop             ; loop again`
	
	`exit    BX     lr               ; return in r0`
	
	`        ENDP`
	`        END`

Example 8-11. Implementation of finding the greatest common divisor (GCD)

8.4.6 Example of Concatenating Two Strings

When a string is concatenated to anther string, the destination string must have enough extra memory space to hold the source string. Otherwise, the data stored immediately after the destination string may be modified by mistake. Thus in the data region, the statement "str1_ SPACE 20" reserves 20 bytes of memory space to hold the source string.

Each string ends with a null character. The string uses the post index memory addressing. For example,

```
LDRB   r3,[r1],#1
```

is equivalent to the following two instructions:

```
LDRB, r3, [r1]
ADD r1, r1, #1
```

C Program	Assembly Program

`void strcat(char *s1, char *s2);`
 	
`char s1[20] = "Shaking";`
`char s2[10] = " hands";`
 	
`int main(){`
`  strcat(s1, s2);`
`  while(1);`
`}`
	`          AREA  myData, DATA`
	`          ALIGN`
	`str1  DCB   "Shaking",0`
	`str1_ SPACE 20        ; reserve space`
	`str2  DCB   " hands",0`
	`          AREA my_strcat, CODE`
	`          EXPORT __main`
	`          ALIGN`
	`          ENTRY`
	`__main PROC`
	`          LDR  r0, =str1   ; 1st argument`
	`          LDR  r1, =str2   ; 2nd argument`
	`          BL   strcat`
	`stop  B    stop`
	`          ENDP`

`// Concatenate two strings`
`void strcat(char *dest, char *src){`
 	
`  while(*dest != '\0')`
`    dest++;`
 	
`  while((*dest++ = *src++)!= '\0');`
 	
`}`
	`; Concatenate two strings`
	`strcat PROC`
	`loop  LDRB  r2, [r0]   ; load a byte`
	`      CBZ   r2, copy   ; null ending`
	`      ADD   r0, r0, #1`
	`      B     loop`
	
	`copy  LDRB  r3, [r1], #1 ; post-index`
	`      STRB  r3, [r0], #1 ; post-index`
	`      CBNZ  r3, copy`
	
	`      BX    lr`
	`      ENDP`
	`      END`

Example 8-12. Implementation of concatenating two strings in C and assembly

8.4.7 Example of Comparing Two Strings

The *strcmp* subroutine compares two null-terminated strings and returns a positive, zero, or negative integer if the first string is greater than, equal to, or less than the second string. The comparison starts with the first character and continues with the following pairs if they are equal. When a pair is found different, *strcmp* returns the difference between these two characters. For example:

- strcmp("their", "there") returns -9 because the ASCII code of "i" and "r" is 105 and 114, respectively.
- strcmp("their", "the") returns 105. All strings are terminated with the NULL character. The ASCII value of "i" is 105 and the NULL terminator is 0.
- strcmp("the", "there") returns -114. In ASCII, NULL is 0 and 'r' is 114.
- strcmp("their", "their") returns 0.

C Program	Assembly Program

<pre>char str1[] = "dog";
char str2[] = "cat";
int result;
 	
int main(void){
   int result;
   result = strcmp(str1, str2);
   while(1);
}</pre>
	<pre> AREA myData, DATA
	        ALIGN
	str1 DCB "dog",0 ; NULL terminated
	str2 DCB "cat",0 ;
	result DCW 0 ; allocate one word
	
	        AREA my_strcmp, CODE
	        EXPORT __main
	        ALIGN
	        ENTRY
	__main PROC
	        LDR r0, =str1 ; address of str1
	        LDR r1, =str2 ; address of str2
	        ; r0 and r1 are arguments to strcmp
	        BL strcmp ; call subroutine
	        LDR r1, =result; address of result
	        STR r0, [r1] ; save the result
	stop B stop ; dead loop
	        ENDP</pre>

<pre>// Compare two strings
int strcmp(char *s, char *t){
   while(*s == *t){
      if (*s == '\0') return 0;
      s++;
      t++;
   }
   return *s - *t;
}</pre>
	<pre>; Compare two strings
	strcmp PROC
	        ; r0 = s, r1 = t
	loop LDRB r2, [r0], 1 ; post-index
	        LDRB r3, [r1], 1 ; post-index
	        CBZ r2, exit ; NULL terminator
	        CMP r2, r3 ; if *s == *t
	        BEQ loop ; Compare again
	exit SUB r0, r2, r3 ; r0 = *s - *t
	        BX lr ; return r0
	        ENDP
	        END</pre>

Example 8-13. Implementation of comparing two strings in C and assembly

8.4.8 Example of Inserting an Integer into a Sorted Array

The insert subroutine takes three arguments, saved in registers r0, r1, and r2. The subroutine preserves registers r4 and LR. The return of the subroutine is implemented by popping LR into PC.

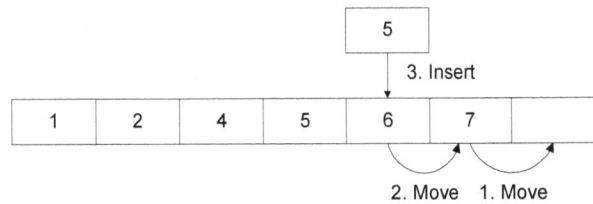

Suppose the array has been sorted in ascending order. The program starts with the last element (*i.e.* the largest one) of the array and compares the input integer with each array element one by one. If the element is larger than the input integer, this element is moved to the right by one; otherwise, the input integer is inserted at the current position.

C Program	Assembly Program

`int a[10] = {1, 2, 4, 5, 6, 7};`
 	
`void insert(int, int *, int);`
 	
`int main(void){`
  `insert(3, a, 5);`
  `while(1);`
`}`
	`        AREA myData, DATA`
	`        ALIGN`
	`a       DCD 1,2,4,5,6,7`
	
	`        AREA insert_array, CODE`
	`        EXPORT __main`
	`        ALIGN`
	`        ENTRY`
	`__main PROC`
	`        MOV r0, #3    ; 1`st` argument, value`
	`        LDR r1, =a    ; 2`nd` argument, array`
	`        MOV r2, #5    ; 3`rd` argument, size`
	`        BL  insert    ; call subroutine`
	`stop   B   stop`
	`        ENDP`

`// input: value, pointer, size`
`void insert(int v, int *a, int s){`
  `int i;`
  `for (i=s; i>0 && v<a[i-1]; i--){`
    `a[i] = a[i-1];`
  `}`
  `a[i] = v;`
`}`
	`; r0 = value, r1 = array, r2 = size`
	`insert PROC`
	`        PUSH {r4, lr}`
	`        loop    CMP r2, #0  ; check i > 0`
	`        BLE done            ; done if i ≤ 0`
	`        SUB r4, r2, #1      ; r4 = i - 1`
	`        LDR r4, [r1,r4,LSL #2]   ; a[i-1]`
	`        CMP r0, r4     ; compare v & a[i-1]`
	`        BGE done       ; done if v ≥ a[i-1]`
	`        STR r4, [r1,r2,LSL #2]   ; a[i]`
	`        SUB r2, r2, #1           ; i--`
	`        B   loop`
	`done   STR r0, [r1,r2,LSL #2]   ; a[i] = v`
	`        POP {r4, pc}             ; exit`
	`        ENDP`
	`        END`

Example 8-14.Implementation of inserting an integer into a sorted array in C and assembly

8.4.9 Example of Converting Integer to String (itoa)

The C function *itoa* converts an integer to a string. To convert a digit d ($0 \leq d \leq 9$) to its ASCII value of the corresponding letter *ch[1]*, we can

$$ch[0] = d + 0x30$$

or

$$ch[0] = d + '0'$$

Letter	0	1	2	3	4	5	6	7	8	9
ASCII	0x30	0x31	0x32	0x33	0x34	0x35	0x36	0x37	0x38	0x39

For a given unsigned integer, such as 12345, we extract the digits backwards. We start with the least significant digit, which can be obtained by using modulo operation to find the remainder of division of 12345 by 10, *i.e.* mod(12345, 10). We append this digit to a string. The modulo operation continues until all digits have been obtained. At the end, we get a string of "54321". We need to reverse the string order and move the least significant digit from the first position to the end of the string.

Quotient/10	Quotient	Remainder	Reverse
12345/10 =	1234	5	
1234/10 =	123	4	
123/10 =	12	3	⇑
12/10 =	1	2	
1/10 =	0	1	
	If quotient is 0, stop	Result="54321"	Result="12345"

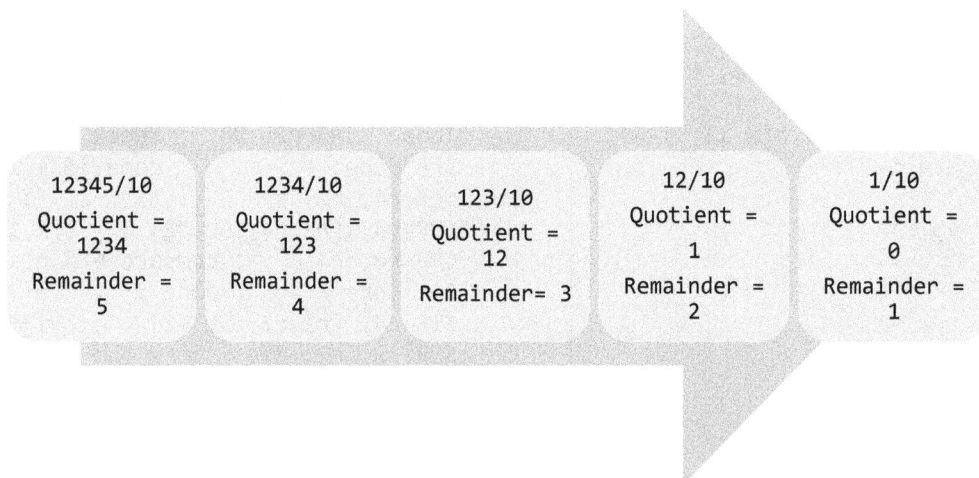

Figure 8-8. Basic steps of obtaining all digits of an integer

C Program	Assembly Program
`char str[20];`	<pre> AREA myData, DATA ALIGN str SPACE 20</pre>

`void itoa(unsigned int, char *);`	<pre> AREA my_itoa, CODE
	        EXPORT__main
	        ALIGN
	        ENTRY</pre>

<pre>int main(void){
  itoa(12345, str);
  while(1);
}</pre>
	<pre>__main PROC
	        MOV r0, #12345
	        LDR r1, =str
	        BL itoa
	stop B stop
	        ENDP</pre>

<pre>void itoa(unsigned int n,
char *s) {
 	
  char * p = s, temp;</pre>
	<pre>itoa PROC
	        PUSH {r4-r6, lr}
	        MOV r2, r0 ; r2 = n
	        MOV r3, r1 ; r3 = s</pre>

<pre> // Build the string backward
  for (; n != 0; n /= 10){
    *p = n % 10 + '0';
    p++;
  }
  *p = '\0';</pre>
	<pre> ; Build the string backward
	        MOV r6, #10
	loop1 CBZ r2, done ; done if n = 0
	        UDIV r5, r2, r6 ; r5 = n/10
	        MLS r4, r6, r5, r2 ; r4 = r2-10*r5
	        ADD r4, r4, #0x30 ; n%10 + '0'
	        STRB r4, [r3], 1 ; *p = n%10+'0'
	        UDIV r2, r2, r6 ; n /= 10
	        B loop1
	done MOV r4, #0
	        STRB r4, [r3] ; *p = '\0';</pre>

<pre> // Reverse the string
  p--;   // skip NULL
 	
  for(; p > s; s++, p--){
    temp = *p;
    *p = *s;
    *s = temp;
  }
}</pre>
	<pre> ; Reverse the string
	        SUB r3, r3, #1 ; skip NULL
	loop2 CMP r3, r1 ; compare p & s
	        BLE exit ; exit if p ≤ s
	        LDRB r4, [r3] ; swap
	        LDRB r5, [r1]
	        STRB r4, [r1]
	        STRB r5, [r3]
	        ADD r1, r1, #1 ; s++
	        SUB r3, r3, #1 ; p--
	        B loop2
	exit POP {r4-r6, pc}
	        ENDP
	        END</pre>

Example 8-15. Implementation of converting an integer to a string in C and assembly

8.4.10 Example of Matrix Transpose

In linear algebra, the transpose of a matrix $[a_{ij}]_{m \times n}$ is $[a_{ji}]_{n \times m}$. In C, a two-dimension (2D) matrix in fact is stored as a one-dimensional array in memory. C uses a row-major approach to convert the 2D matrix into a 1D array, and it stores the matrix row by row contiguously in the memory. For example, a 3×3 matrix is stored as a simple 1D array in the memory, as shown in Figure 8-9. We assume each element is an integer and takes four bytes. Note since a memory address is always in terms of bytes, the memory offset is expressed in bytes.

Index	(0, 0)	(0, 1)	(0, 2)	(1, 0)	(1, 1)	(1, 2)	(2, 0)	(2, 1)	(2, 2)
Content	1	2	3	4	5	6	7	8	9
Memory offset in bytes	0	4	8	12	16	20	24	28	32

1st Row   2nd Row   3rd Row

Figure 8-9. Linear layout of a two-dimensional matrix in the memory

Multiplication is often optimized by using shift operations. For example, the following instructions

```
MOV r1, #3
MUL r4, r0, r1
```

can be replaced by a single instruction "ADD r4, r0, r0, LSL #1", in which r4 = r0 + r0<<1 = 3 × r0. The shift and addition operations are much faster than the multiplication instruction.

Figure 8-10 gives an example of matrix transpose. Note the items on the diagonal do not change. Therefore, the program only needs to swap items in the upper right triangle matrix with the lower left triangle matrix.

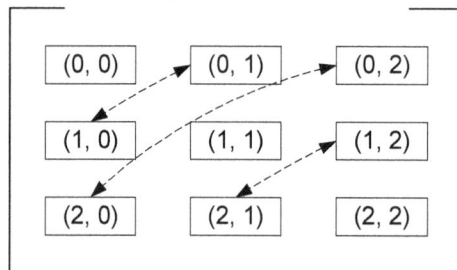

Figure 8-10. Demonstration of matrix transpose. None-diagonal elements are swapped.

C Program	Assembly Program
```int a[3][3] = { { 1, 2, 3 }, { 4, 5, 6 }, { 7, 8, 9} };```	``` AREA myData, DATA ALIGN matrix DCD 1, 2, 3, 4, 5, 6, 7, 8, 9```
```void transpose(int *p); int main(void){ int *p = &a[0][0]; transpose(p); while(1); }```	``` AREA Matrix_Transpose, CODE EXPORT __main ALIGN ENTRY __main PROC LDR r0, =matrix BL transpose stop B stop ENDP```
```void transpose(int *p){ int i, j, t; for(i=0; i<3; i++){ for (j=i+1; j<3; j++){ t=*(p + 3*i + j); *(p + 3*i + j)=*(p + 3*j + i); *(p + 3*j + i)=t; } } }```	```transpose PROC PUSH {r4-r7, lr} MOV r1, #0 ; r1 = i; loop_i CMP r1, #3 BGE exit ADD r2, r1, #1 ; j = i + 1 loop_j CMP r2, #3 BGE exit_j ; r4 = p + (3*i + j)*4 ADD r4,r1,r1,LSL #1 ; 3 * i ADD r4,r0,r4,LSL #2 ; 4 * r4 ADD r4,r2,LSL #2 ; r5 = p + (3*j + i)*4 ADD r4,r2,r2,LSL #1 ; 3 * j ADD r4,r0,r4,LSL #2 ; 4 * r4 ADD r4,r1,LSL #2 ; swap LDR r6, [r4] LDR r7, [r5] STR r7, [r4] STR r6, [r5] ADD r2, r2, #1 B loop_j ; for loop j exit_j ADD r1, r1, #1 ; i++ B loop_i ; for loop i exit_i POP {r4-r7, lr} ENDP END```

Example 8-16. Implementation of transposing a matrix in C and assembly

8.4.11 Example of Removing a Character from a String

This example subroutine removes a specific character from a string. The subroutine starts to compare each character from the beginning and shift all following characters left one if this character is the same as the target characters. Note a null terminator is appended at the end when all characters have been checked.

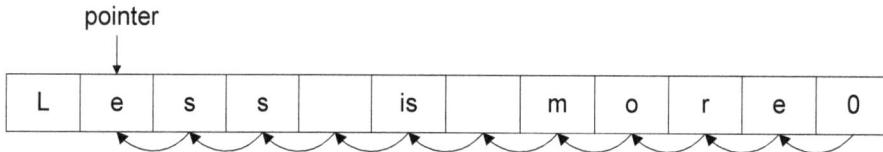

pointer

| L | e | s | s | | is | | m | o | r | e | 0 |

Figure 8-11. All following characters have to be moved left when a character is removed.

C Program	Assembly Program

`char s[15] = "Less is more";`
`void remove(char *s, char c);`
 	
`int main(void){`
`  // remove letter 'e' from string`
`  remove(s, 'e');`
`  while(1);`
`}`
	` ` `AREA myData, DATA`
	`str    DCB    "Less is more",0`
	
	` ` `AREA removeChar, CODE`
	` ` `EXPORT__main`
	` ` `ALIGN`
	` ` `ENTRY`
	`__main PROC`
	` ` `LDR    r0, =str   ; memory address`
	` ` `MOVS   r1, #'e'   ; ASCII of 'e'`
	` ` `; r0 and r1 are arguments`
	` ` `BL     remove`
	`stop   B      stop       ; dead loop`
	` ` `ENDP`

`// Remove the character c`
`// from the string s`
`void remove(char *s, char c){`
`  char *t = s;`
`  for(; *s != '\0'; s++) {`
`    if (*s != c){`
`      *t = *s;`
`      t++;`
`    }`
`  }`
`  *t = '\0';`
`}`
	`remove PROC`
	` ` `; r0 = s, r1 = c`
	` ` `MOV    r2, r0     ; r2 = t = s`
	
	`loop   LDRB   r3, [r0]   ; r3 = *s`
	` ` `CBZ    r3, exit   ; null ending`
	` ` `CMP    r3, r1     ; compare *s & c`
	` ` `LDRBNE r3, [r0]   ; get byte *s`
	` ` `STRBNE r3, [r2]   ; store to *t`
	` ` `ADDNE  r2, r2, #1 ; t++`
	` ` `ADD    r0, r0, #1 ; s++`
	` ` `B      loop       ; do it again`
	
	`exit   STRB   r3, [r2]   ; *t = '\0';`
	` ` `BX     lr         ; return`
	
	` ` `ENDP`
	` ` `END`

Example 8-17. Implementation of removing a character from a string

8.4.12 Example of Finding Unique Numbers in an Array

This example removes any duplicate numbers in an array. It finds all unique numbers of an array. The program uses three loops over the array. The outer loop based on loop variable i selects a character to be compared with. The middle loop based on loop variable j compared the following characters with $array[i]$. The inner loop based on loop variable k is used to shift all following characters to the left by one position if $array[j]$ is equal to $array[i]$. The following figure shows a simple example when $i = 0$. When a duplicate is found at position 2 ($j = 2$), the third loop over k is used to shift all following numbers left by one to remove $array[2]$.

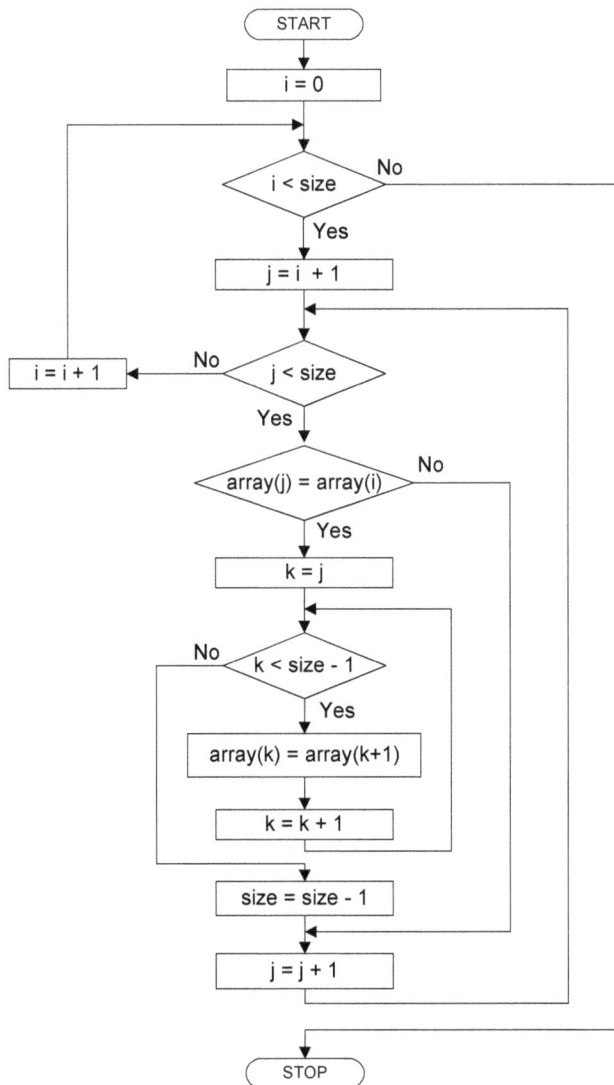

Figure 8-12. Flowchart of removing duplicates in an array

C Program	Assembly Program

```
int array[50] = {                         AREA myData, DATA
  7, 1, 7, 2, 1,                          ALIGN
  3, 1, 2, 4, 5,                  array   DCD 7, 1, 7, 2, 1
  2, 3, 2, 6, 7,                          DCD 3, 1, 2, 4, 5
  2, 3, 2, 6, 7};                         DCD 2, 3, 2, 6, 7
                                          DCD 2, 3, 2, 6, 7
int size = 20;                    size    DCD 20


                                          AREA remove_duplications, CODE
int remove_dup(int *, int);               EXPORT __main
                                          ALIGN
int main(){                               ENTRY
 int i;                           __main PROC
                                          LDR r0, =array
 size = remove_dup(array, size);          LDR r1, =size
                                          LDR r1, [r1]
                                          BL  remove_dup

 for (i = size; i < 50; i++)              MOV r4, r0     ; r0 = size returned
  array[i] = 0;                   loop    CMP r4, #50
                                          BGE stop
                                          MOV r0, #0
                                          STR r0, [r1,r4,LSL #2] ; array[i]
                                          ADD r4, r4, #1
 while(1);                                B    loop
}                                 stop    B    stop
                                          ENDP


int remove_dup( int *array, int   remove_dup PROC
size) {                                   ; r0 = array pointer
 int i, j, k;                             ; r1 = size
 int *p;                                  PUSH {r4-r8,lr}
 i = 0;                                   ; r5 = i, r6 = j, r7 = k
 while(i < size){                         MOV r5, #0     ; r5 = i
   j = i + 1;                     Li      CMP r5, r1     ; compare i and size
   while(j < size) {                      BGE exit
    if( *(p+i)==*(p+j) ){                 ADD r6, r5, #1 ; r6 = j, j = i + 1
      for(k=j; k<size-1; k++)     Lj      CMP r6, r1     ; compare j and size
        *(p+k)=*(p+k+1);                  BGE Ej
      size--;                            LDR r8, [r0,r5,LSL #2]  ; r8 = *(p+i)
    } else                               LDR r4, [r0,r6,LSL #2]  ; r4 = *(p+j)
      j++;                               CMP r8, r4     ; *(p+i) and *(p+j)
   }                                     BNE Ek2
   i++;                                  MOV r7, r6     ; r7 = k
 }                                       SUB r4, r1, #1 ; r4 = size - 1
 return size;                     Lk     CMP r7, r4     ; compare k and size-1
}
```

```
                                BGE Ek1
                                ADD r8, r0,r7,LSL #2
                                LDR r8, [r8, #4]        ; r8 = *(p+k+1)
                                STR r8, [r0,r7,LSL #2]  ; *(p+k)
                                ADD r7, r7, #1          ; k++
                                B   Lk                  ; loop k
                        Ek1     SUB r1, r1, #1          ; size--
                                B   Lj                  ; loop j
                        Ek2     ADD r6, r6, #1          ; j++
                                B   Lj                  ; loop j
                        Ej      ADD r5, r5, #1          ; i++
                                B   Li                  ; loop i
                        exit    MOV r0, r1              ; return size
                                POP {r4-r8, pc}
                                ENDP
                                END
```

Example 8-18. Implementation of removing duplicates in an integer array in C and assembly

Figure 8-13 shows an example to illustrate the basic idea of using three nested loops to remove all duplicates in a given array.

- The first loop indexed by i starts with the first element.
- The second loop indexed by j iterates through all elements between (i+1) and the end of the array.
- When a duplicate is found, the third loop indexed by k is used to shift all numbers after the jth number left by 1. In this example, when the duplicate "7" is found, all numbers after the "7" is moved left by one.

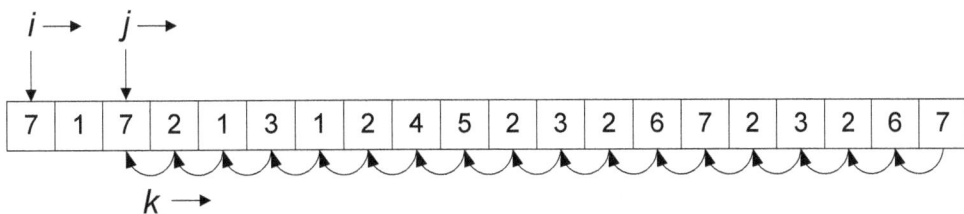

Figure 8-13. Variable i, j, and k are indices of three nested loops.
Loop k is to shift numbers left after a duplicate is found.

8.5 Passing Arguments Through Stack

Up to four arguments can be directly passed by using registers. When more than four arguments are passed to a subroutine, extra parameters have to be passed through the stack.

Suppose we have a simple subroutine named *sum6* that takes six 32-bit integers and calculates their sum. The C and assembly implementation are given in Example 8-19.

C Program	Assembly Program

`int sum6(int, int, int, int, int, int);`	`        AREA sum, CODE`
	`        EXPORT __main`
	`        ALIGN`
	`        ENTRY`

`int main(){`
`  int t;`
`  t = sum6(1, 2, 3, 4, 5, 6);`
`  while(1);`
`}`
	`__main PROC`
	`        MOV   r0, #5   ; 5`[th]` argument`
	`        MOV   r1, #6   ; 6`[th]` argument`
	`        MOV   r2, #3   ; 3`[rd]` argument`
	`        MOV   r3, #4   ; 4`[th]` argument`
	`        PUSH {r0, r1} ; push 5`[th]` and 6`[th]
	`        MOVS r1, #2    ; 1`[st]` argument`
	`        MOVS r0, #1    ; 2`[nd]` argument`
	`        BL    sum6`
	`stop    B     stop`
	`        ENDP`

`int sum6(int a1, int a2, int a3,`
`        int a4, int a5, int a6) {`
 	
`  int total;`
`  total = a1 + a2 + a3 + a4 + a5 + a6;`
`  return total;`
 	
`}`
	`sum6    PROC`
	`        PUSH {r4-r7, lr}`
	`        MOV   r4, r0`
	`        ; LDRD = Load a double-word`
	`        LDRD r5, r6, [sp,#20]`
	`        ADD   r7, r4, r1`
	`        ADD   r7, r7, r2`
	`        ADD   r7, r7, r3`
	`        ADD   r7, r7, r5`
	`        ADD   r0, r7, r6`
	`        POP   {r4-r7, pc}`
	`        ENDP`
	`        END`

Example 8-19. Example of passing 6 arguments in C and assembly

The caller puts the first four arguments in registers r0, r1, r2, and r3 and pushes the last two arguments into the stack. When the subroutine is called, it first has to preserve any non-scratch registers used in this subroutine. In this example, registers r4 - r7 and lr are pushed into the stack by the subroutine.

The subroutine then uses a load double-word instruction (LDRD) to load these two arguments by using SP-relative addressing.

```
LDRD r5, r6, [sp, #20]        ⟺    LDR r5, [sp, #20]
                                   LDR r6, [sp, #24]
```

Note when multiple registers are pushed into the stack by using a single push instruction, the compiler sorts the registers according to their register names and pushes the largest register first, as introduced in Example 8-3. On the contrary, when multiple registers are popped out from the stack by using a single pop instruction, the value is popped into the register with the smallest register number.

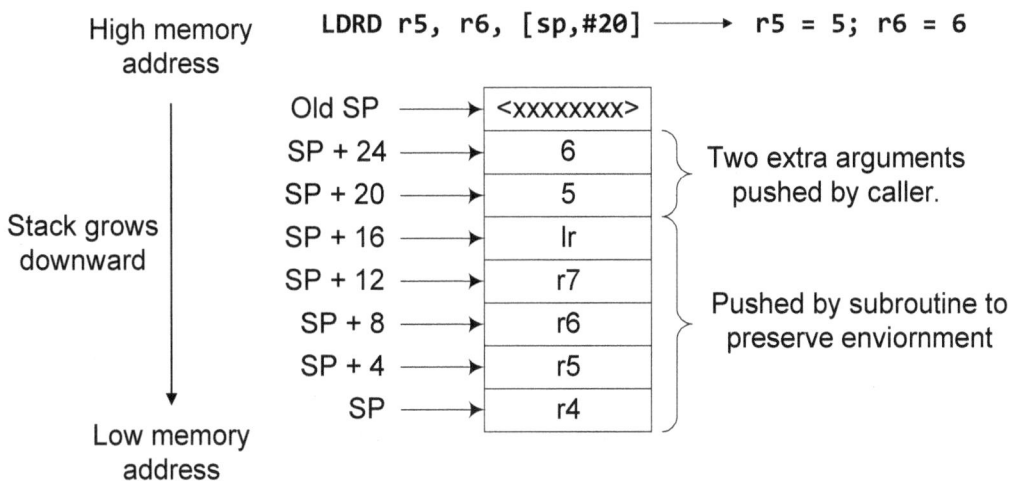

Figure 8-14. Memory layout after the subroutine preserves the environment

The LDRD instruction transfers two contiguous words starting at the memory address sp + 20 to two destination registers. The first destination register holds the word of the lower memory address. It can be replaced by using the following two load register instructions:

```
LDR r5, [#sp, #20]
LDR r6, [#sp, #24]
```

Note the subroutine does not pop the fifth and sixth arguments out from the stack. According to the application binary interface standard, the stack pointer (SP) has to remains the same immediately before and after a subroutine is executed. Therefore, the subroutine should not pop out these two arguments.

Example 8-20 gives a slightly more efficient implementation. The key idea is to reuse register r0 and therefore the subroutine does not need to push any registers into the stack. In addition, since the sum6 subroutine does not call any other subroutines, the link register (LR) is not preserved in the stack.

```
sum6 PROC
     ADD  r0, r0, r1   ; add 1st and 2nd arguments
     ADD  r0, r0, r2   ; add 3rd argument
     ADD  r0, r0, r3   ; add 4th argument
     LDRD r2, r3, [sp] ; load 5th and 6th arguments
     ADD  r0, r0, r2   ; add 5th argument
     ADD  r0, r0, r3   ; add 6th argument
     BX   LR
     ENDP
```

Example 8-20. Improved implementation of the sum6 subroutine by reusing register r0

8.6 Recursive Functions

A recursive function is a function that calls itself directly or indirectly. If *foo*() calls *bar*() and *bar*() calls *foo*(), *foo*() calls itself indirectly. A recursive function solves a task by calling itself on smaller pieces of input data.

For example, quick sort is a recursive function. It randomly picks an element from an array and partitions the array into two subarrays, one with all elements smaller than the chosen element, and the other with all elements larger than the chose element. This process repeats on each subarray until there are only one or two elements in each subarray. The result is a combination of these sorted subarrays.

Recursive function is an effective divide-and-conquer tactic that divides a large problem into smaller sub-problems of the same type as the original problem, then solves those sub-problems, and finally combines the results to form the solution of the original problem.

Any problem that can be solved by using a recursive function can also be solved by using a traditional iterative function based on loops. The advantages of recursive functions over iterative functions are twofold. A recursive function more naturally resembles the problem to be solved. In addition, recursive function is easier to program and debug. However, a recursive function usually is slow and requires more memory than its corresponding iterative function.

Example 8-21 shows a classic recursive and iterative functions that calculates the factorial. Figure 8-5 shows the call graph of the recursive function when calculating *factorial*(5).

Recursive Function	Iterative Function
```int factorial(int n) { if(n==1) return 1; else return n * factorial(n-1); } int main(void){ int y; y = factorial(5); return 0; }```	```int factorial(int n) { result = 1; for (int i = 1; i < n; i++) result *= i; return result; } int main(void){ int y; y = factorial(5); return 0; }```

Example 8-21. Factorial function implemented by using recursive and iterative function

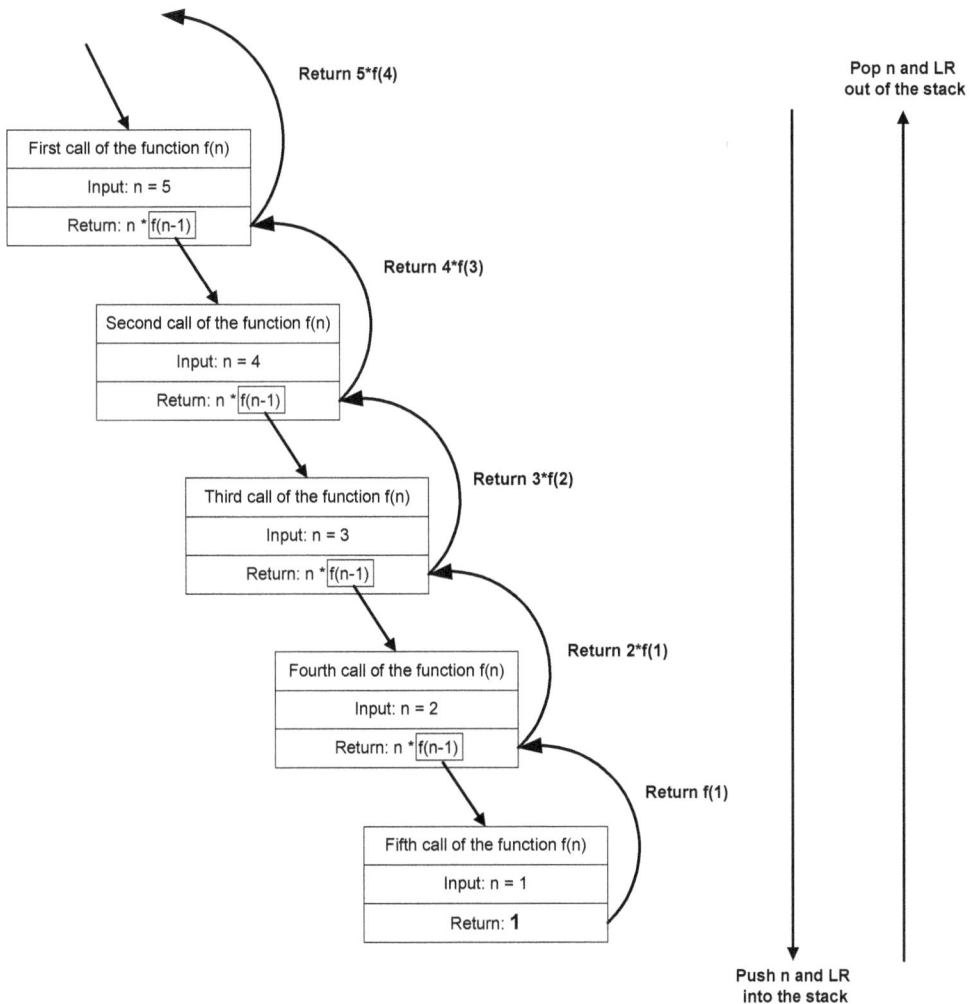

Figure 8-15. Call graph of the recursive factorial function

An exit condition, also called a stopping case, is a critical component of a recursive function. For example, the statement of "if (n == 1) return 1;" is the exit condition, which ensures that the recursive function does not go into an infinite loop.

Figure 8-5 shows how *factorial*(5) is performed step by step.

- The function *factorial* (5) calls *factorial*(4), and
- *factorial*(4) calls *factorial*(3), and
- *factorial*(2) calls *factorial*(1).

After calculating *factorial*(1), the result is returned backwards to calculating previously pending results.

Recursive functions rely on the stack to preserve the runtime environment and keep track of different call instances of the recursive functions. When programming in assembly, in particular, the link register (LR) has to be preserved in a recursive function.

In the example of recursively calculating the factorial number, the subroutine has to LR and the input *n* into the stack. The stack keeps growing as data are pushed onto it in each call. After the exit condition is met, the stack begins to shrink as data are popped out of the stack upon each function return.

In sum, when programming a recursive function in assembly, the stack needs to be carefully managed to ensure the correction and avoid infinite loop or stack overflow.

8.6.1   Example of Factorial Numbers

We will illustrate how the stack grows when a recursive function is called and how the stack shrinks when a recursive function is returned.

Suppose SP is 0x20000600 and r4 is 0 immediately before the factorial recursive function is called. When the function is called, r4 and LR are pushed onto the stack. Recall that the BL instruction puts the memory address of the instruction immediately after the BL instruction into LR. The subroutine copies r0 to r4 since r0 has to be used to pass the argument when it calls itself.

Table 8-2 shows the stack content immediately after *factorial*(1) completes. The stack grows down toward address 0. Register r4 represents the input *n* to the subroutine of the last call instance. The result of the factorial operation is stored in register r0. When the factorial subroutine is called recursively, LR points to the multiplication instruction "MUL r0, r4, r0", which multiples *n* and *factorial* (*n*-1).

Memory Address	Memory Content
0x20000600	
0x200005FC	0x08000134 (LR)
0x200005F8	0 (r4)
0x200005F4	0x08000148 (LR)
0x200005F0	5 (r4)
0x200005EC	0x08000148 (LR)
0x200005E8	4 (r4)
0x200005E4	0x08000148 (LR)
0x200005E0	3 (r4)
0x200005DC	0x08000148 (LR)
0x200005D8	2 (r4)
0x200005D4	0x08000148 (LR)
0x200005D0	

Table 8-2. Stack content immediately after factorial (1) completes.

C Program	Address	Assembly Program
		AREA main, CODE, READONLY
int factorial(int n);		EXPORT __main
		ENTRY
int main(void){		__main PROC
factorial(5);	0x0800012E	MOV r0, #0x03
return 0;	0x08000130	BL factorial
}	0x08000134	stop B stop
		ENDP
int **factorial**(int n) {		**factorial PROC**
int f;	0x08000136	PUSH {r4, lr} ; preserve
if(n==1)	0x08000138	MOV r4, r0 ; r4 = n
f = 1;	0x0800013A	CMP r4, #1
else	0x0800013C	BNE else ; if n ≠ 1
f = n***factorial**(n-1);	0x0800013E	MOV r0, #1 ; f = 1
return f;	0x08000140	loop POP {r4, pc} ; return
}	0x08000142	else SUB r0, r4, #1 ; n - 1
	0x08000144	**BL factorial** ; r0 is input
	0x08000148	**MUL r0, r4, r0** ; n*f(n-1)
	0x0800014C	B loop
		ENDP
		END

Example 8-22. Implementation of calculating factorial number in C and assembly

8.6.2   Example of Reversing a String

If a string is "ABCD", its reverse is "DCBA". The following shows the implementation of the reverse function as a recursive function. The key idea is to swap the first and last character and reverse the substring excluding the first and the last characters. This process repeats for each substring.

C Program	Assembly Program
<pre>char str[20] = "Reverse me, please!";
void swap (char *x, char *y);
void reverse(char *, int, int);

int main() {
  reverse(str, 0, 20);
  while(1);
}</pre> | <pre>   AREA myData, DATA
        ALIGN
str   DCB   "Reverse me, please!",0
        AREA reverse_string, CODE
        EXPORT __main
        ALIGN
        ENTRY
__main PROC
        LDR r0, =str   ; 1st argument
        MOV r1, #0   ; 2nd argument
        MOV r2, #20   ; 3rd argument
        BL   reverse   ; Recursive call
stop   B   stop
        ENDP</pre> |
| <pre>; swap two characters in a string
void swap (char *x, char *y) {
    char temp;
    temp = *x;
    *x = *y;
    *y = temp;
}</pre> | <pre>; Swap routine
swap   PROC
        LDRB r2, [r0]   ; temp = *x
        LDRB r3, [r1]   ;
        STRB r3, [r0]   ; *x = y
        STRB r2, [r1]   ; *y = temp
        BX   lr
        ENDP</pre> |
| <pre>; recursive function for reversion
void reverse(char *str,
             int start,
             int end)
{
   if (start == end)
      return;
   swap (str + start, str + end);
   start++;
   end--;
   reverse(str, start, end);
}</pre> | <pre>reverse PROC
        PUSH {r4-r6, lr}
        MOV r6, r0   ; string pointer
        MOV r4, r1   ; start position
        MOV r5, r2   ; end position
        CMP r4, r5   ; check start <= end
exit   POPEQ {r4-r6, pc} ; exit
        ADD r0, r6, r4   ; [str + start]
        ADD r1, r6, r5   ; [str + end]
        BL   swap
        ADD r4, r4, #1 ; start++
        SUB r5, r5, #1 ; end--
        MOV r0, r6   ; 1st argument
        MOV r1, r4   ; 2nd argument
        MOV r2, r5   ; 3rd argument
        BL   reverse
        POP {r4-r6, pc}
        ENDP
        END</pre> |

Example 8-23. Implementation of reversing a string in C and assembly

8.6.3   Example of String Permutation

The following code finds all possible permutations of the characters in a string. For example, the permutation of "ABC" includes "ABC", "ACB", "BAC", "BCA", "CAB", and "CBA". All permutations are stored in a string named result, separated by a space. The permute function uses two subroutines: *strcat* that concatenates two strings (given in Chapter 8.4.6) and *swap* that swaps two characters in a string (given in Chapter 8.6.2). As shown in Figure 8-16, the permutation of a string is found by recursively permuting all new substrings. New substrings are formed by swapping the first letter with all letters in the original string (excluding the first letter of each new string).

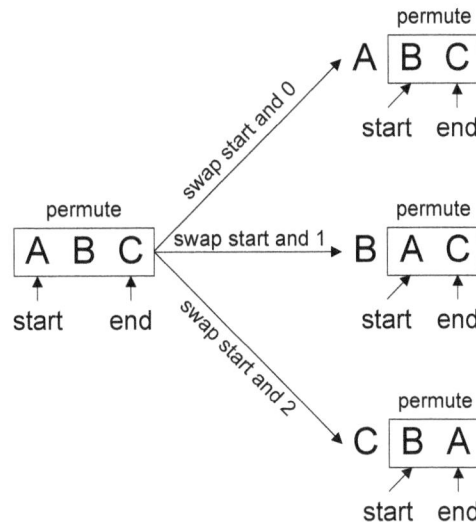

Figure 8-16. Permutation is achieved by swapping the first letter to every letter and permuting all substrings excluding the first letter of all new strings.

C Program	Assembly Program

<pre>char str[4] = "ABC";
char result[200];
char sep[2] = " ";
 	
void strcat(char *, char *);
void swap(char *, char *);
void permute(char *, int, int);
 	
int main() {
   permute(str, 0, 2);
   while(1);
}</pre>
	<pre> AREA myData, DATA
	       ALIGN
	str DCB "ABC",0
	result SPACE 200
	sep DCB " ",0
	
	       AREA permute, CODE
	       EXPORT __main
	       ALIGN
	       ENTRY
	__main PROC
	       LDR r0, =str
	       MOV r1, #0 ; start
	       MOV r2, #2 ; end
	       BL permute
	stop B stop
	       ENDP</pre>

<pre>// recursive permute function
void **permute**(char *str,
              int start,
              int end)
{
  int i;
  if (start >= end){
    strcat(result, sep);
    strcat(result, str);
  } else {
    for (i=start; i<=end; i++){
      swap(str + start, str + i);
      permute(str, start+1, end);
      swap(str + start, str + i);
    }
  }
 	
}</pre>
	<pre>; recursive permute function
	permute PROC
	         PUSH {r4-r7, lr}
	         MOV r4, r0 ; r0 = *str
	         MOV r5, r1 ; r1 = start
	         MOV r7, r2 ; r2 = end
	
	         CMP r5, r7 ; start >= end (?)
	         BLT skip
	         LDR r0, =result
	         LDR r1, =sep
	         BL strcat ; result + set
	         LDR r0, =result
	         MOV r1, r4 ; r1 = str
	         BL strcat ; result + str
	         B exit
	
	skip MOV r6, r5 ; r6 = variable i
	loop ADD r0, r4, r5 ; r0 = str+start
	         ADD r1, r4, r6 ; r1 = str+i
	         BL swap
	         MOV r0, r4 ; str
	         ADD r1, r5, #1 ; start + 1
	         MOV r2, r7 ; end
	         BL permute
	
	         ADD r0,r4,r5 ; str + start
	         ADD r1,r4,r6 ; str + i
	         BL swap
	
	         ADD r6, r6, #1 ; i++
	check CMP r6, r7 ; compare i & end
	         BLE loop
	
	exit POP {r4-r7,pc}
	
	         ENDP
	         END</pre>

Example 8-24. Implementation of string permutation in C and assembly

8.7 Exercises

1. Write a subroutine that checks whether a given number is a prime number. The subroutine takes one argument and returns true or false. Find all prime numbers between 100 and 200.

2. Write a subroutine that takes 8 integer arguments and computes the product of these integers. Note extra arguments should be passed to the subroutine via the stack.

3. Implement a subroutine of the Caesar shift encryption. It is a simple substitution encryption algorithm, in which each letter is replaced by a letter with a fixed number of offset down in the alphabet. For example, with a shift offset of 3, A would become D, and B would be replaced by E, and so on.

4. Write a subroutine called *MoviePrice* that calculates the movie ticket price based on the input argument called age. If the age is 12 or under, the price is $6.00. If the age is between 13 and 64, the price is $8.00. If the age is 65 or over, the price is $7.00.

5. Write a subroutine that calculates the value of the following expression based on two input arguments a and n.

$$S_n(a) = a + aa + aaa + \cdots + \overbrace{aa \ldots a}^{n}$$

For example, when $a = 3$ and $n = 5$, we have

$$S_5(3) = 3 + 33 + 333 + 3333 + 33333$$

6. Write a program that calculates $\sum_{n=0}^{10} n!$. The program should use two subroutines. One subroutine calculates the factorial $n!$, and the other subroutine calculates the sum of the factorials.

7. Write a program that uses a subroutine to find how many 1-bits exists in a 32-bit number.

8. Write a program that uses a subroutine to find how many bits differ in two 32-bit numbers.

9. Mathematically, the cardinality of an array is defined as the number of unique elements in an array. Write a subroutine that calculates the cardinality of an integer array.

10. When PC is 0x08000100 in the following assembly program, the stack pointer (SP) is 0x20002000. Show the value of link register (LR) and the whole stack content when PC = 0x08000120.

Memory Address	Instruction	
0x08000100		MOV R0,#2
0x08000104		BL QUAD
0x08000108		B ENDL
0x0800010C	SQ1	PUSH {LR}
0x08000110		MUL R0,R0
0x08000114		BL SQ2
0x08000118		POP {PC}
0x0800011C	SQ2	PUSH {LR}
0x08000120		MUL R0,R0
0x08000124		POP {PC}
0x08000128	QUAD	PUSH {LR}
0x0800012C		BL SQ1
0x08000130		POP {LR}
0x08000134		BX LR
0x08000138	ENDL	...

11. Write an assembly subroutine named f that calculates the following value

$$f(x,y) = ax^2 + bxy + c$$

where a, b, and c are constant integers, x and y are the input integers. Assuming a, b, and c are defined in data memory, x and y are input arguments of this subroutine.

12. Write a recursive assembly subroutine that calculates the Fibonacci number.

$$F(n) = \begin{cases} 0 & if\ n = 0 \\ 1 & if\ n = 1 \\ F(n-1) + F(n-2) & otherwise \end{cases}$$

13. Write a recursive assembly subroutine that checks whether a given string is a palindrome.

14. Write a recursive assembly subroutine that calculates the Kth power of 2, *i.e.* 2^K.

15. Compared with iterative methods, what are the advantages and disadvantages of recursive methods?

CHAPTER 9

64-bit Data Processing

The Cortex-M3 is a 32-bit processor and the operands of almost all instructions cannot exceed 32 bits. There are a few exceptions, such as UMULL (unsigned multiply), UMLAL (unsigned multiply with accumulate), SMULL (signed multiply), and SMLAL (signed multiply with accumulate). It is often that an embedded system performs arithmetic operations based on integers that are larger than $2^{32} - 1$. One important example is fixed-point arithmetic, which will be introduced in Chapter 11.1. This chapter focuses on how to implement 64-bit operations based on 32-bit instructions.

9.1 64-bit Addition

As discussed in Chapter 2.4.4.2, when signed numbers are represented by two's complement, the adder works in exactly the same way for both unsigned and signed additions. In other words, the same add assembly instruction works for both signed integers and unsigned integers.

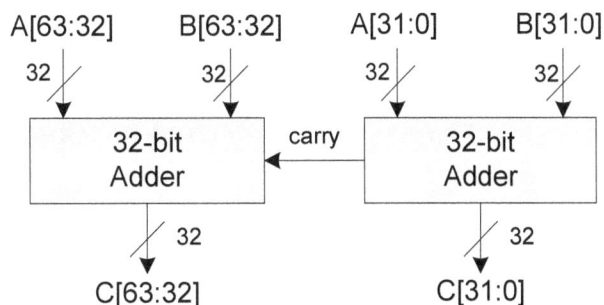

Figure 9-1. Adding two 64-bit integers

Suppose we are adding two 64-bit integers *A* and *B*, either signed or unsigned. A 64-bit number is stored in a pair of registers (r1:r0), with the most significant 32 bits stored in register r1, and the least significant bits stored in r0. The following gives an example assembly code for 64-bit addition.

```
; Adding two 64-bit integers A (r1:r0) and B (r3:r2)
; C (r5:r4) = A (r1:r0) + B (r3:r2)
; A = 00002222FFFFFFFF, B = 0000044400000001
LDR   r0, =0xFFFFFFFF    ; A's lower 32 bits
LDR   r1, =0x00002222    ; A's upper 32 bits
LDR   r2, =0x00000001    ; B's lower 32 bits
LDR   r3, =0x00000444    ; B's upper 32 bits

; Add A and B
ADDS  r4, r2, r0         ; C[31:0] = A[31:0] + B[31:0], update Carry
ADC   r5, r3, r1         ; C[64:32] = A[64:32] + B[64:32] + Carry
```

9.2 64-bit Subtraction

No matter whether the two operations are signed or unsigned, the following program performs 64-bit subtraction. This is similar to the 64-bit addition except the subtraction starts with the upper word. The carry flag is set if no borrow occurs during the subtraction.

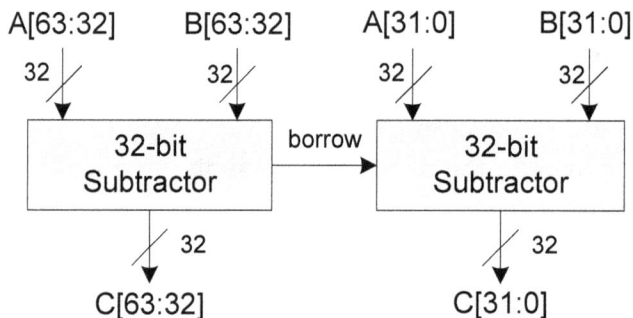

Figure 9-2. Subtracting two 64-bit integers

```
; Subtracting two 64-bit integers A (r1:r0) and B (r3:r2).
; C (r5:r4) = A (r1:r0) - B (r3:r2)
; A = 00000002FFFFFFFF, B = 0000000400000001
LDR r0, =0xFFFFFFFF    ; A's lower 32 bits
LDR r1, =0x00000002    ; A's upper 32 bits
LDR r2, =0x00000001    ; B's lower 32 bits
LDR r3, =0x00000004    ; B's upper 32 bits

; Subtract A from B
SUBS r4, r0, r2        ; C[31:0] = A[31:0] - B[31:0], update Carry
SBC  r5, r1, r3        ; C[64:32] = A[64:32] - B[64:32] + Carry - 1
```

9.3 64-bit Counting Leading Zeroes

The following program counts the number of leading zero bits before the first significant one in a 64-bit integer. The key instruction used is CLZ (Count Leading Zeroes). It is useful to normalize an integer by removing all leading zeroes and making the most significant bit as 1.

When counting the leading zeroes of a 64-bit number that is stored in two registers, there are two scenarios:

1. The upper word is not zero. Then the number of leading zeroes of the 64-bit number equals the number of leading zeroes of the upper word.
2. The upper word is zero. Then the number of leading zeroes of the 64-bit number equals the number of leading zeroes of the lower word plus 32.

```
; 64-bit input data = (r1:r0), r1 = upper word, r0 = lower word
; r2 = # of leading zero bits in the 64-bit data

; Counting # of leading zeroes in upper word
CLZ   r2, r1          ; CLZ = Count leading zeroes

; Counting # of leading zeroes in lower word
CMP    r2, #32
CLZEQ  r3, r0         ; if r2 == 32, then count leading zero
                      ; bits of the lower word
ADDEQ  r2, r2, r3     ; if all bits of the upper word are zero,
                      ; add the leading zeroes of the lower word
```

9.4 64-bit Sign Extension

When a 32-bit signed integer is extended to 64 bits, we must preserve the number's sign (either positive or negative) and value by duplicating the sign bit to the upper word. If the most significant bit (MSB) of the 32-bit signed integer is 1, the upper word of the 64-bit number must of 0xFFFFFFFF.

```
; r0 = Lower word of 64-bit data
; r1 = Upper word of 64-bit data

TST r0, 0x80000000     ; Check the sign bit
LDREQ r1, =0xFFFFFFFF  ; If MSB is 1, duplicate 1 in upper word
LDRNE r1, =0x00000000  ; If MSB is 0, duplicate 0 in upper word
```

9.5 64-bit Logic Shift Left

When a 64-bit number is shifted left, some of the bits in the lower word have to be shifted into the upper word.

Figure 9-3. Logic shift left of a 64-bit number stored in two registers

The following gives an example of shifting a 64-bit number left by 3 bits. The most significant three bits of the lower word are shifted into the upper word. If the shift amount is larger than 32 bits, the lower word becomes zero.

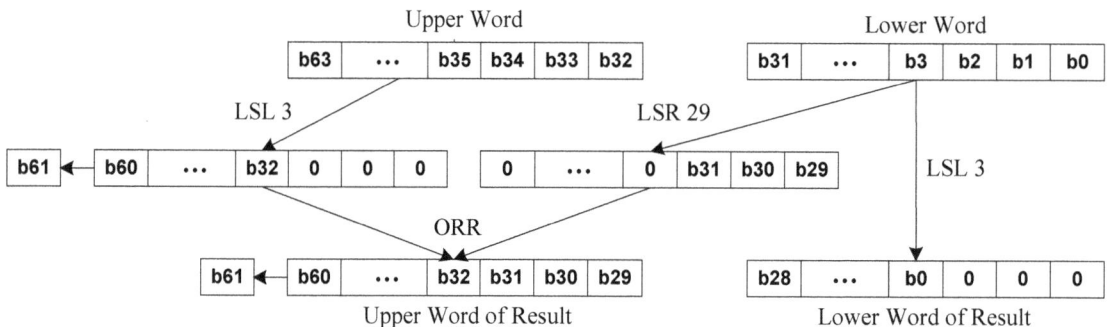

Figure 9-4. Shifting left a 64-bit number by 3 bits

```
; r0 = Lower word of 64-bit data, r1 = Upper word of 64-bit data
; r2 = Shift amount

MOV   r3, r0                  ; Backup the lower word
MOV   r1, r1, LSL r2          ; Shift left the upper word
MOV   r0, r0, LSL r2          ; Shift left the lower word

; Shift bits of the lower into the upper
CMP   r2, #32

; if r2 < 32
RSBLO   r5, r2, #32           ; r5 = 32 - r2
LSR     r4, r3, r5           ; r4 = r3 >> (32 - r2)
ORRLO   r1, r1, r4           ; upper |= lower >> (32 - r2)

; if r2 ≥ 32
SUBHS   r5, r2, #32           ; r5 = r2 - 32
LSLHS   r1, r3, r5           ; upper = lower << (r2 - 32)
```

9.6 64-bit Logic Shift Right

When a 64-bit number is shifted right, the least significant bits of the upper word are shifted into the lower word, as shown in Figure 9-5.

Figure 9-5. Logic shift right of a 64-bit number stored in two registers

The following example shows logic shift right of a 64-bit number by 3 bits. The least significant three bits of the upper word are shifted into the lower word. If the shift amount is larger than 32 bits, the upper word becomes zero.

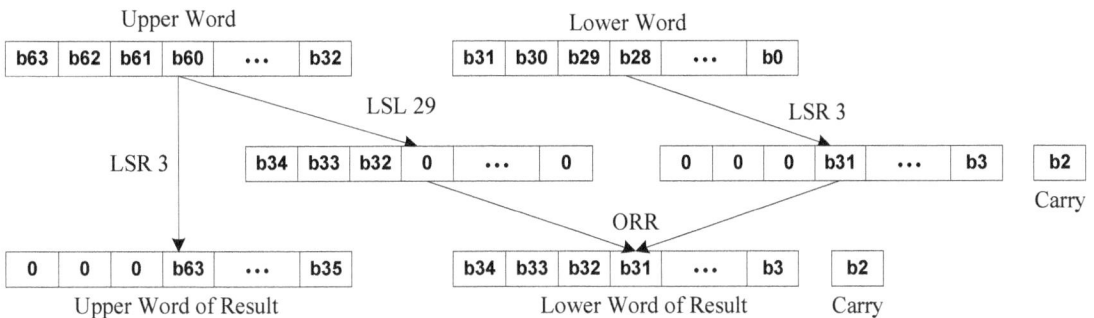

Figure 9-6. Shifting right a 64-bit number by 3 bits

```
; r0 = Lower word of 64-bit data
; r1 = Upper word of 64-bit data
; r2 = Shift amount

MOV   r3, r1                    ; Backup the upper word

MOV   r1, r1, LSR r2           ; Shift right the upper word
MOV   r0, r0, LSR r2           ; Shift right the lower word

; Shift bits of the upper into the lower
CMP   r2, #32

; if r2 < 32
RSBLO   r5, r2, #32            ; r5 = 32 - r2
ORRLO   r0, r0, r3, LSL r5     ; lower |= upper << (32 - r2)

; if r2 ≥ 32
SUBHS   r5, r2, #32            ; r5 = r2 - 32
LSRHS   r0, r3, r5             ; lower = upper >> (r2 - 32)
```

9.7 64-bit Multiplication

We can use long multiply instructions (32-bit by 32-bit, 64-bit result) and the multiply accumulate instruction (MLA) to multiply two 64-bit numbers.

```
; product (r5:r4) = multiplier (r1:r0) × multiplicand (r3:r2)
; (r5:r4) = r0 × r2 + 2^32 × (r1 × r2 + r0 × r3) + 2^64 × r1 × r3
; The last item exceeds 64 bits and thus it is ignored.

UMULL r4, r5, r0, r2    ; (r5:r4) = r0 * r2
MLA   r5, r1, r2, r5    ; r5 = r5 + r1 * r2
MLA   r5, r0, r3, r5    ; r5 = r5 + r0 * r3
```

Note UMULL is for multiplication of two 32-bit unsigned integers, and SMULL is for multiplication of two 32-bit signed integers. However, the above code also works correctly for multiplying two 64-bit signed numbers. For example, when multiplying (-2) and (-3), the above code can obtain the correct result, *i.e.* 6.

```
; A (r1:r0) = -2 = FFFF,FFFF,FFFF,FFFE
; B (r3:r2) = -3 = FFFF,FFFF,FFFF,FFFD

UMULL   r4,r5,r0,r2    ; r5:r4 = FFFF,FFFE × FFFF,FFFD = FFFF,FFFB,0000,0006
MLA     r5,r1,r2,r5    ; r5 = FFFF,FFFB + FFFF,FFFF × FFFF,FFFD = FFFF,FFFE
MLA     r5,r0,r3,r5    ; r5 = FFFF,FFFE + FFFF,FFFE × FFFF,FFFF = 0000,0000
                       ; r5:r4 = 0000,0000,0000,0006
```

The reason why it also works for signed numbers is simple. Given two 32-bit negative numbers A and B, their two's complement is $2^{64} - A$ and $2^{64} - B$, respectively.

$$(2^{64} - A)(2^{64} - B) = 2^{128} - 2^{64} \times (A + B) + A \times B$$

The first two items are larger than 2^{64} and thus are discarded. As a result, we have

$$(2^{64} - A)(2^{64} - B) = A \times B$$

9.8 64-bit Unsigned Division

We will show the implement of 64-bit unsigned division. A 64-bit integer has to be stored in two registers. For example, when a 64-bit integer is stored in (r1:r0), the most significant 32 bits stored in register r1, and the least significant 32 bits are stored in r0.

```
1. Initialization
      •  Quotient(r9:r8)  = 0;
      •  Remainder(r1:r0) = Dividend(r1:r0)

2. Loop over the following steps if remainder (r1:r0) ≥ divisor (r3:r2)
      (1) a_64_bit = remove leading zeroes of remainder(r1:r0),
            • x = number of leading zero bits removed
            • CLZ instruction counts the number of leading zero bits
      (2) b_64_bit = remove leading zeroes of divisor(r3:r2),
            • y = number of leading zero bits removed
      (3) g_32_bit = MSB_32(a_64_bit) / MSB_16(b_64_bit)
            • MSB: Most significant bits
            • UDIV can be used for the 32-bit division
      (4) r6:r11 = unsign_extend_to_64_bits(g_32_bit << (y - 16)) >> x;
      (5) Quotient(r9:r8)  = Quotient(r9:r8) + (r6:r11)
      (6) Remainder(r1:r0) = Remainder(r1:r0) - (r6:r11) * Divisor(r3:r2)
      (7) If the remainder (r1:r0) is smaller than zero,
            • g_32_bit = MSB_32(a_64_bit) / (MSB_16(b_64_bit) + 1), and
              go to step c.

3. Copy the results
      •  Quotient(r1:r0) = Quotient(r9:r8)
      •  Remainder(r3:r2) = Remainder(r1:r0)
```

Table 9-1. Basic steps of dividing two 64-bit unsigned integers

The program assumes inputs are stored in registers r0-r3, including the 64-bit dividend stored in registers (r1:r0) and the 64-bit divisor stored in register (r3:r2). The program has two 64-bit outputs: the 64-bit quotient in registers (r1:r0) and the 64-bit remainder in registers (r3:r2). The basic idea of this program is in Table 9-1.

Example of 64-bit division

We use a simple example to illustrate the basic idea of the above algorithm. Assuming the dividend and the divisors are given as follows:

- Dividend(r1:r0) = 0x0000,FFFF,FFFF,FFFF
- Divisor(r3:r2) = 0x0000,0000,0000,0001

The algorithm starts to initialize the quotient and the remainder, shown as follows:

- Quotient(r9:r8) = 0;
- Remainder(r1:r0) = Dividend(r1:r0) = 0x0000,FFFF,FFFF,FFFF

```
Loop 1:
   •  a_64_bit = 0xFFFF,FFFF,FFFF,0000           x = 16
   •  b_64_bit = 0x8000,0000,0000,0000           y = 63
   •  g_32_bit = MSB_32(a_64_bit) / MSB_16(b_64_bit)
```

```
                    = 0xFFFF,FFFF / 0x0000,8000,
                    = 0xFFFF,FFFF / 2^15
                    = 0x0001,FFFF
  •  r6:r11    = unsign_extend_to_64_bits(g_32_bit << (y - 16)) >> x
               = unsign_extend_to_64_bits(0x0001,FFFF << (63 - 16)) >> 16
               = unsign_extend_to_64_bits(0x0001,FFFF << 47) >> 16
               = 0x0001,FFFF << 31
               = 0x0000,FFFF,8000,0000
  •  Quotient(r9:r8)  = Quotient(r9:r8) + (r6:r11)
                      = 0 + 0x0000,FFFF,8000,0000
                      = 0x0000,FFFF,8000,0000
  •  Remainder(r1:r0) = Remainder(r1:r0) - (r6:r11) * Divisor(r3:r2)
                      = 0x0000,FFFF,FFFF,FFFF - 0x0000,FFFF,8000,0000 * 1
                      = 0x0000,0000,7FFF,FFFF
```

```
Loop 2:
  •  a_64_bit = 0xFFFF,FFFE,0000,0000                    x = 33
  •  b_64_bit = 0x8000,0000,0000,0000                    y = 63
  •  g_32_bit = MSB_32(a_64_bit) / MSB_16(b_64_bit)
             = 0xFFFF,FFFE / 0x0000,8000
             = 0x0001,FFFF
  •  r6:r11    = unsign_extend_to_64_bits(g_32_bit << (y - 16) ) >> x
               = unsign_extend_to_64_bits(0x0001,FFFF << (63 - 16)) >> 33
               = unsign_extend_to_64_bits(0x0001,FFFF << 47 ) >> 33
               = 0x0000,0000,7FFF,C000
  •  Quotient(r9:r8)  = Quotient(r9:r8) + (r6:r11)
                      = 0x0000,FFFF,8000,0000 + 0x0000,0000,7FFF,C000
                      = 0x0000,FFFF,FFFF,C000
  •  Remainder(r1:r0) = Remainder(r1:r0) - (r6:r11) * Divisor(r3:r2)
                      = 0x0000,0000,7FFF,FFFF - 0x0000,0000,7FFF,C000 * 1
                      = 0x0000,0000,0000,3FFF
```

```
Loop 3:
  •  a_64_bit = 0xFFFC,0000,0000,0000                    x = 50
  •  b_64_bit = 0x8000,0000,0000,0000                    y = 63
  •  g_32_bit = MSB_32(a_64_bit) / MSB_16(b_64_bit)
             = 0xFFFC,0000 / 0x0000,8000
             = 0x0001,FFF8
  •  r6:r11    = unsign_extend_to_64_bits(g_32_bit << (y - 16)) >> x
               = unsign_extend_to_64_bits(0x0001,FFF8 << (63 - 16)) >> 50
               = unsign_extend_to_64_bits(0x0001,FFF8 << 47) >> 50
               = 0x0000,0000,0000,3FFF
  •  Quotient(r9:r8)  = Quotient(r9:r8) + (r6:r11)
                      = 0x0000,FFFF,FFFF,C000 + 0x0000,0000,0000,3FFF
                      = 0x0000,FFFF,FFFF,FFFF
  •  Remainder(r1:r0) = Remainder(r1:r0) - (r6:r11) * Divisor(r3:r2)
                      = 0x0000,0000,0000,3FFF - 0x0000,0000,0000,3FFF * 1
                      = 0x0000,0000,0000,0000
```

9.9 64-bit Signed Division

The following program shows the algorithm of 64-bit signed division. Each 64-bit number is stored in two 32-bit registers. For example, the most significant 32 bits of the dividend is stored in register r1 and the least stored in register r0.

```
; Signed Division Algorithm: (r1:r0)/(r3:r2)
; Inputs:
;       Dividend (64 bits): r1:r0
;       Divisor (64 bits): r3:r2
; Return:
;       Quotient (64 bits): r1:r0
;       Remainder (64 bits): r3:r2

        PUSH {r4, lr}
        ASRS r4, r1, #1         ; if r1 >= 0, r4[31:30] = 00;
                                ; otherwise r4[31:30] = 11
        EOR r4, r4, r3, LSR #1  ; if r3 >= 0, shift result[31:30] = 00;
                                ; otherwise shift result[31:30] = 01

        ; If r1 >= 0 and r3 >= 0, r4[31:30] = (00)^(00) = 00
        ; If r1 >= 0 and r3 < 0,  r4[31:30] = (00)^(01) = 01
        ; If r1 < 0 and r3 >= 0,  r4[31:30] = (11)^(00) = 11
        ; If r1 < 0 and r3 < 0,   r4[31:30] = (11)^(01) = 10
        ; Bit r4[31] represents whether dividend >= 0
        ; Bit r4[30] represents whether dividend and divisor
        ; are both positive or both negative

        ; Convert dividend (r1:r0) to a positive number if it is negative
        BPL Test1               ; check whether dividend >= 0,
        RSBS r0, r0, #0         ; if dividend < 0, r0 = -r0
        RSB  r1, r1, #0         ; if dividend < 0, r1 = -r1
        IT CC                   ; Carry clear (CC) = Unsigned lower;
        SUBS r1, r1, #1         ; If borrow occurs

        ; Convert divisor(r3:r2) to a positive number if it is negative
Test1   TST r3, r3              ; check whether divisor >= 0; bitwise AND
        BPL uldiv               ; branch if positive or zero
        RSBS r2, r2, #0         ; if divisor is negative, r2 = -r2
        RSB  r3, r3, #0         ; if divisor is negative, r3 = -r3
        IT CC
        SUBS r3, r3, #1         ; If borrow occurs

        ; perform unsigned division (r1:r0)/(r3:r2)
uldiv   BL unsigned_devision_64_bits
        ; If dividend and divisor are not both positive or both negative,
        ; then convert the quotient to a negative number
Test2   TST r4, #0x40000000     ; 0100, bitwise AND
```

```
        BEQ Test3                   ; Branch if ZERO is set
                                    ; i.e. branch if dividend >=0
        RSBS r0, r0, #0             ; r0 = -r0
        RSB  r1, r1, #0             ; r1 = -r1
        IT CC                       ;
        SUBS r1, r1, #1             ; If borrow occurs


        ; If dividend (r1:r0) < 0,
        ; then convert the remainder to a negative number
Test3   TST r4, #0x80000000         ; 1000, bitwise AND
        BEQ exit                    ; Branch if ZERO is set
        RSBS r2, r2, #0             ; r2 = -r2
        RSB  r3, r3, #0             ; r3 = -r3
        IT CC                       ;
        SUBS r3, r3, #1             ; If borrow occurs

exit    POP {r4, pc}
```

Table 9-2. Implementation of 64-bit unsigned integer division

9.10 Exercises

1. Write an assembly program that performs 64-bit rotation right.

2. Write an assembly program that calculates the sum of an array of 64-bit integers.

3. Write an assembly program that multiplies a 32-bit unsigned integer and a 64-bit unsigned integer. The result is limited to 64 bits.

4. Write an assembly program that divides a 64-bit unsigned integer and a 32-bit unsigned integer. The result is limited to 32 bits.

5. Write an assembly program that uses the subtraction-based Euclid's algorithm to compute the greatest common divisor of two 64-bit integers.

```
uint64_t gcd(uint64_t a, uint64_t b) {
    while (a != b) {
        if (a > b)
            a = a - b;
        else
            b = b - a;
    }
    return a;
}
```

CHAPTER

10

Mixing C and Assembly

Occasionally it is required to write a program in both C and assembly language. There are several possible reasons.

- First, an experienced programmer might want to optimize a performance-critical function manually in assembly, instead of relying on compilers. Many profiling tools can identify the most time-consuming functions and compilers often have limited intelligence in optimizing these functions. A handcrafted assembly code can out-perform high-level languages, such as C.
- Second, writing a program in assembly allows a programmer to use processor-specific instructions. For example, a test-and-set atomic assembly instruction can be used to implement locks and semaphores. Another example is that standard C compilers do not use some operations available on Cortex-M3 processors, such as ROR (rotate right) and RRX (rotate right extended).
- Third, assembly allows direct accesses to hardware, which is particularly helpful for device drivers and processor booting code.

The embedded application binary interface (EABI) briefly introduced in Chapter 8.2 defines low-level standards of interfacing separately compiled program modules, no matter whether these modules are written in C or assembly. The EABI specifies (1) standards for data types, data alignments, and executable file formats, and (2) conventions for function calls, parameter passing, registers usage, and stack frame. If a program is written in C, compilers ensure that these standards are strictly followed. However, if a program is written in assembly, it is the

> *"The good thing about standards is that there are so many to choose from."*
>
> **Andrew Tanenbaum, famous computer scientisit**

programmer's responsibility to adhere to these standards. The standard allows programmers to mix C and assembly in the application.

10.1 Data Types and Access

While the size of a basic data type in the C language depends on the compilers and platforms, the following table lists the typical size of commonly used data types in the C language.

Data Type	Size (bits)	Alignment	Data Range
bool	8	byte	0 or 1. Bits 1 – 7 are ignored
char	8	byte	-128 – 127 (signed) or 0 – 255 (unsigned)
int	32	word	-2,147,483,648 – 2,147,483,647(signed) or 0 – 4,294,967,296(unsigned)
short int	16	half-word	-32,768 – 32,767 (signed) or 0 – 65,536 (unsigned)
long int	32	word	same as int
long long	64	word	-9,223,372,036,854,775,808 - 9,223,372,036,854,775,807 (signed) or 0 - 18,446,744,073,709,551,616 (unsigned)
float	32	word	+/- 1.4023 x 10^{-45} to 3.4028 x 10^{+38}, always signed
double	64	word	+/- 4.9406 x 10^{-324} to 1.7977 x 10^{308}, always signed
long double	96	word	very large range
pointer	32	word	0 – 4,294,967,296

Table 10-1. Data size and alignment of basic data types in C

10.1.1 Signed or Unsigned Integers

When programming in an assembly language, it is the programmer's responsibility to interpret whether a data item is signed or unsigned. For example, when loading an 8-bit data into a 32-bit register, the program should use LDRSB (load register with signed byte) for a signed character and LDRB (load register with byte) for an unsigned character.

- The LDRSB loads a byte from the memory into a register and performs sign extension. The sign extension duplicates the sign bit of the 8-bit data to all bits at the most significant side of a register to preserve the positive or negative sign.
- The LDRB loads a byte from the memory into a register and simply pads the left of the register with zeroes.

For example, when an 8-bit binary data 0x88 (+136 for unsigned or -120 for signed) is loaded from the memory into a 32-bit register, should the register be 0xFFFFFF88 or

0x00000088? It depends on the programmer's intention. If these 8 bits represent a signed number, the LDRSB instruction should be used to preserve the number's sign. If they represent an unsigned number, the LDRB instruction should be used. Similarly, LDRSH (load register with signed half-word) and LDRB (load register with byte) load a 16-bit signed and unsigned number into a register, respectively. Table 10-2 summarizes these load instructions.

Variable	Instruction	Description	Sign Extension
unsigned char	LDRB	Load register with byte	No
unsigned short	LDRH	Load register with half-word	No
unsigned/signed int	LDR	Load register with word	No
char	LDRSB	Load register with signed byte	Yes
short	LDRSH	Load register with signed half-word	Yes

Table 10-2. ARM assembly instructions for accessing various basic integer data types.

Note STRB (store register byte) and STRH (store register half-word) can correctly store either a signed number or an unsigned number into the memory. Loading or storing a 32-bit or 64-bit integer does not need to take care of the sign. A 64-bit integer has to be stored in two registers and it can be loaded by using two separate LDR instructions or a single LDRD (load registers with double words).

C Program	Assembly Program
| signed long long x = -1; | ```
LDR r3, =x
LDRD r0, r1, [r3] ; r0 lower word, r1 higher word

x   DCW   0xFFFFFFFF, 0xFFFFFFFF  ; allocate 8 bytes
``` |

10.1.2 Data Alignment

Most computer systems have some alignment requirement on the starting memory address of a variable. The memory address of a C variable often has to be aligned, as listed in Table 10-1. The smallest unit that can be retrieved from or written to the memory is a byte (8 bits) and thus the memory address is always in terms of bytes.

A variable is n-byte aligned in memory if its starting memory address is some multiple of n. Typically, n is a power of 2, such as 2 (half-word aligned), 4 (word aligned), and 8 (double word aligned). Suppose a 32-bit variable is word aligned. If the address of the next available byte in memory is 0x8001, the variable is then stored in a continuous span of 4 bytes from 0x8004 to 0x8007. Three meaningless bytes are paddled at memory addresses 0x8001, 0x8002, and 0x8003.
```

Enforcing data alignment is to improve the memory performance. A memory system consists of multiple units and data are usually distributed among these units in a round-robin fashion. Because the number of pins available on a processor is limited, these memory units have to share some pins in the memory address bus. In order to allow these memory units to transfer data concurrently, the target data stored in all memory units needs to share a portion of their memory addresses. The data alignment ensures that all data of a variable stored in different memory units meet this requirement. When loading this variable into the processor, only one access is required to transfer to the data out of these memory units. Otherwise, two separate memory accesses might be required, which may significantly slow down the memory performance.

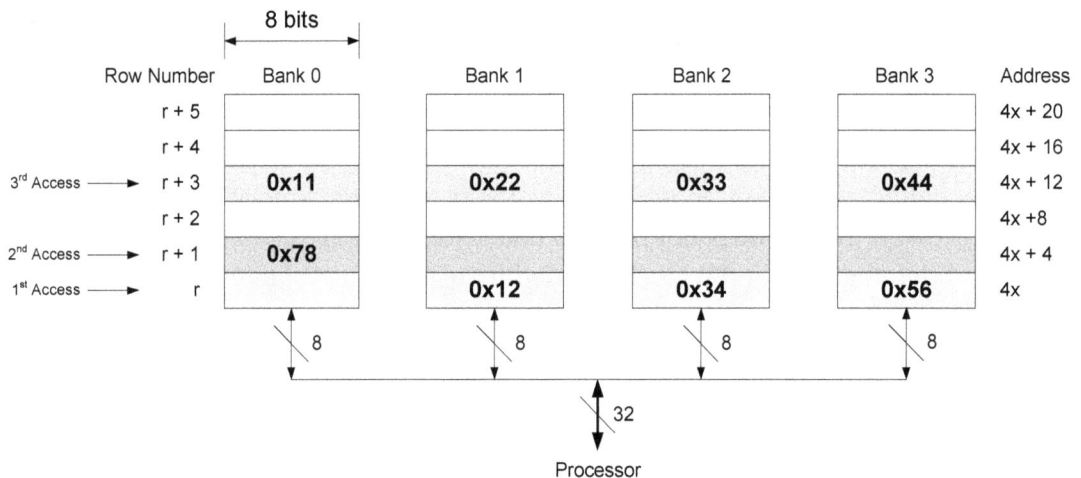

Figure 10-1. Loading unaligned data 0x78563412 takes two accesses if unaligned memory accesses are not supported. Loading aligned data 0x44332211 takes only one access.

Suppose the data bus from the memory to the processor has 32 bits, as shown in Figure 10-1. The memory is organized into banks, and four banks can feed the data bus. Four bytes on the same row, with one from each bank, can be loaded into the processor concurrently with only one access. In this example, data 0x78563412 is not aligned by words, and it takes two memory accesses to be loaded to the processor. However, it takes only one memory access to load data 0x44332211.

As introduced in Chapter 3.6, the "ALIGN" directive can be used to instruct data alignment requirements to compilers. The syntax is "ALIGN boundary, offset", where the boundary has a value of power of 2 with a default value of 4, and the offset specifies a byte offset with a default value of 0.

```
        AREA myData, DATA, ALIGN=2
        ; word aligned

a       DCB   0x11

        ALIGN 4
        ; word aligned
b       DCD   0x12345678

        ALIGN 4,3
        ; word aligned with an offset of 3
c       DCB   0x22

        ALIGN 4,2
        ; word aligned with an offset of 2
d       DCW   0xAABB
```

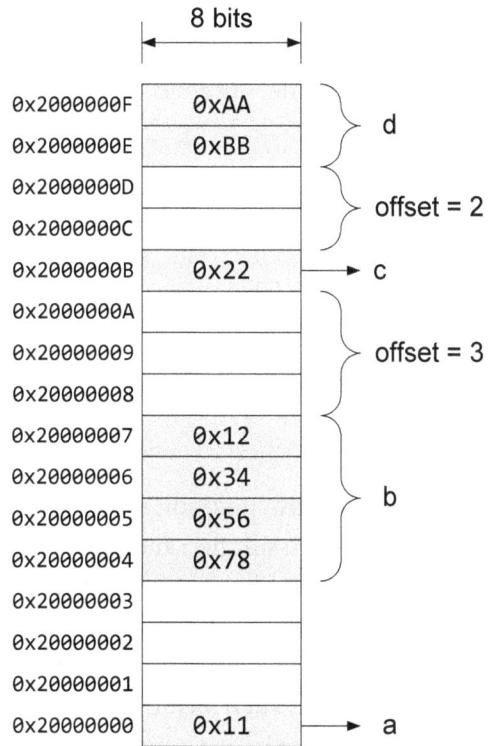

Figure 10-2. Memory layout

10.1.3 Data Structure Padding

A data structure defined in C language aggregates multiple basic variables into a single complex entity. By default, compilers ensure that all basic variables in a structure are aligned to their required memory boundaries. In a structure array, compilers also ensure that all variables in this array meet their alignment requirements. Therefore, bytes might be padded between structure variables. Figure 10-3 gives an example of an unpacked structure.

C language also supports packed structures in which variables are not memory aligned. Therefore, no padding bytes are inserted into a data structure. Packed structures are often used in standard communication protocols (such as USB) to save transmission time. Figure 10-4 gives an example of a packed structure.

In Figure 10-3, the compiler inserts three padding bytes into the structure position. The first padding byte is added after variable *x* in order to make the following integer variable *time* aligned to a word boundary. In a structure array, the compiler also ensures that all variables in this array meet their alignment requirements. Therefore, two additional bytes are added at the end of the data structure to make the size of the Position structure a multiple of four. This makes the variables in this array, particularly the time variable, aligned properly. In fact, the following structure definitions are equivalent.

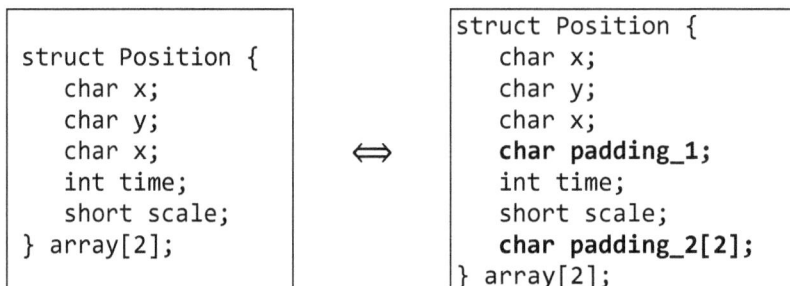

<table>
<tr><td>

```
struct Position {
    char x;
    char y;
    char x;
    int time;
    short scale;
} array[2];
```
</td><td>⟺</td><td>

```
struct Position {
    char x;
    char y;
    char x;
    char padding_1;
    int time;
    short scale;
    char padding_2[2];
} array[2];
```
</td></tr>
</table>

In Figure 10-4, the position structure uses the type modifier "__packed" to the compiler to produce an unaligned memory layout. Specifically, the integer variable (time) is not aligned to a word boundary and the short variable (scale) is not aligned to a half-word boundary. Therefore, there is no padding between structure members or at the end of the structure. The __unpack modifier is often used to map a structure to a special data area in memory, such as a USB communication package received in a memory buffer.

Generally, packed structures are not often used. No ARM processors released before ARM V6 support unaligned memory accesses. The instruction "LDR r1, [r0]" would generate an alignment exception if the memory address stored in r0 were not a multiple of four. The Cortex-M3 processors do support unaligned memory accesses. However, unaligned accesses are still slower than aligned memory accesses and thus it is recommended to avoid using unaligned accesses.

Unpacked Structure	Packed Structure

`struct Position {`
`    char x;`
`    char y;`
`    char x;`
`    int time;`
`    short scale;`
`} array[2];`
	`__packed struct Position {`
	`    char x;`
	`    char y;`
	`    char x;`
	`    int time;`
	`    short scale;`
	`} array[2];`

Packed structures and unpacked structures are not compatible to each other. We cannot assign or cast one to the other. The only way to assign a packed structure to an unpacked structure is to copy each structure members one by one.

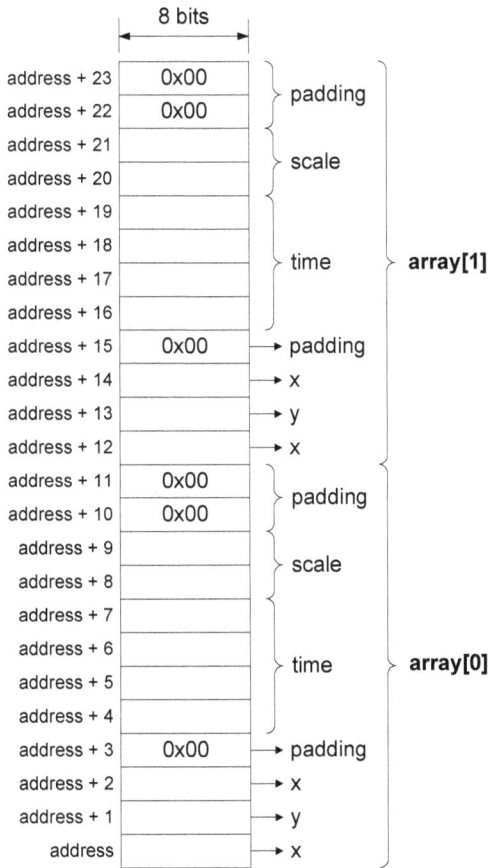

Figure 10-3. In an unpacked structure, variables
are aligned. Specifically the integer variable
and the structure are aligned in words.

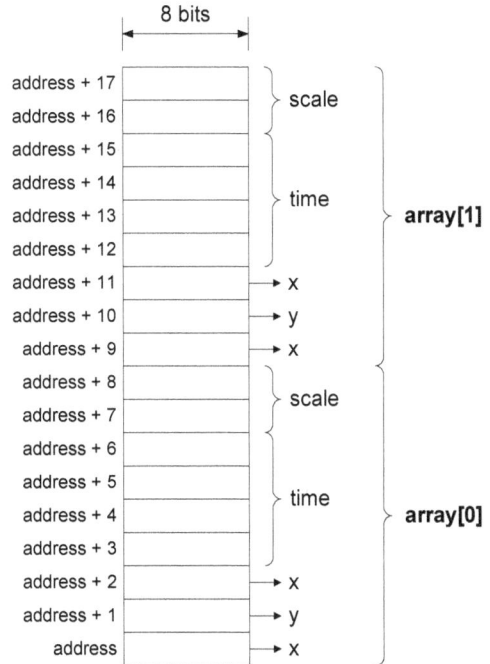

Figure 10-4. In a packed structure, variables
are not aligned. Cortex-M3 processors
support unaligned access in the following
instructions: LDR/STR, LDRT/STRT,
LDRH/STRH, and LDRHT/STRHT.

Suppose we want to set *array[0].time* to 1234. The following compares the assembly
codes to update the *time* variable of the unpacked and packed structure.

Unpacked Structure	Packed Structure

LDR r0, =array   ; load base address
LDR r1, [r0, #4] ; array[0].time
LDR r2, #1234
STR r2, [r0, #4] ; array[0].time
	LDR r0, =array ; load base address
	LDR r1, [r0, #3] ; array[0].time
	LDR r2, #1234
	STR r2, [r0, #3] ; array[0].time

In the unpacked structure, access to *array[0].time* is aligned. However, in the packed
structure, the access is misaligned. While the misaligned accesses "LDR r1, [r0, #3]"
and "STR r2, [r0, #3]" are supported in Cortex-M3, their access speed is much slower
than the aligned accesses "LDR r1, [r0, #4]" and "STR r2, [r0, #4]".

10.2 Special Variables

This section discusses two special types of variables in C: static variables and volatile variables.

10.2.1 Static Variables

> *A static variable is initialized only once. Its lifetime is across its entire program runtime.*

Different from local variables, a *static* C variable has a lifetime over the entire program runtime. A static variable declared within a C function is initialized only once at the compiling time no matter how many times this function is called. This static variable is visible only in this function.

A static variable can be either global or local. A local static variable can only be accessed within the scope of the function in which this variable is declared. A global static variable can only be accessed within the source file in which it was declared. It cannot be accessed by other source files.

A static variable is preferred to a global variable in C because a local or global static variable has a narrower access range. A program should avoid global variables whenever possible. A global variable can be accessed by source codes in any file of a software system. The major problem of using global variables is that they create hidden coupling between different software modules that is difficult to identify and understand, thus increasing the risk of software bugs. Because of the implicit interference created by global variables, a bug in one software module might cause the failure of another seemly-unrelated module, making the debug process difficult.

> *Always avoid global variables.*

One effective way to avoid global variables is to use static variables. As shown in Example 10-1, the counter is declared as a static global variable, instead of a global variable. Therefore, the counter can only be accessed within in that source file. Codes in other source files cannot access the counter variable.

If a global variable is only accessed by one subroutine, it can be declared as a local static variable within that subroutine. The access scope of a local static variable is the subroutine that declares it. When that subroutine is called successively, the value of the local static variable is retained.

```
static int counter = 0;

void increase(void){
    counter++;
}

void decrease(void){
    counter--;
}
```

Example 10-1. Example of using static global variable, instead of global variables.

Example 10-2 and Example 10-3 compare how a local static variable and a local regular variable are accessed in assembly. All static variables are allocated in the data memory. However, a local variable is often stored in a register or in the heap region of the data memory. A static variable is always loaded from the memory first, and then is stored back to the memory before exiting the subroutine. Therefore, if the subroutine is called again, the static variable keeps its previous value, instead of its initial value.

Example of a local non-static variable

C Program	Assembly Program

`int foo();`	`        AREA static_demo, CODE`
	`        EXPORT __main`
	`        ALIGN`
	`        ENTRY`

`int main(void) {`
`    int y;`
`    y = foo();  // y = 6`
`    y = foo();  // y = 6`
`    y = foo();  // y = 6`
`    while(1);`
`}`
	`__main  PROC`
	`        BL   foo     ; r0 = 6`
	`        BL   foo     ; r0 = 6`
	`        BL   foo     ; r0 = 6`
	`stop    B    stop`
	`        ENDP`

`int foo() {`
`    int x = 5;  // x is a local variable`
`    x = x + 1;`
`    return(x)`
`}`
	`foo     PROC`
	`        MOV  r0,#5`
	`        ADD  r0,r0,#1`
	`        BX   lr`
	`        ENDP`
	`        END`

Example 10-2. If x is not declared as static, *foo*() always returns the same value.

In the program given in Example 10-2, variable *x* is not declared as static. Thus, *foo* returns the same value each time it is called. From the assembly implementation, we can notice that the local variable x is always reinitialized when *foo* is called. In addition, in this example, x is stored in a register and its value is lost (not saved in the data memory) after *foo* exits.

Example of a local static variable

C Program	Assembly Program

`int foo();`	`        AREA myData, DATA`
	`        ALIGN`
	`        // Reserve space for x`
	`x       DCD   5`
	
	`        AREA static_demo, CODE`
	`        EXPORT __main`
	`        ALIGN`
	`        ENTRY`

`int main(void) {`
`  int y;`
`  y = foo();  // y = 6`
`  y = foo();  // y = 7`
`  y = foo();  // y = 8`
`  while(1);`
`}`
	`__main PROC`
	`        BL  foo      ; r0 = 6`
	`        BL  foo      ; r0 = 7`
	`        BL  foo      ; r0 = 8`
	`stop    B   stop`
	`        ENDP`

`int foo() {`
`  // x is initialized only once`
`  static int x = 5; // local static variable`
`  x = x + 1;`
`  return(x)`
`}`
	`foo     PROC`
	`        ; load address of x`
	`        LDR  r1,=x`
	`        ; load value of x`
	`        LDR  r0,[r1]`
	`        ADD  r0,r0,#1`
	`        ; save value of x`
	`        STR  r0,[r1]`
	`        BX   lr`
	`        ENDP`
	`        END`

Example 10-3. When x is declared as static, the *foo*() function returns different values.

In the program given in Example 10-3, variable x is declared as static locally within the *foo* function.

- The local static variable x is only initialized once. The initialization is performed at compile time instead of at runtime. As you see from the assembly code, the variable is defined in the data region with an initial value of 5. No matter how many times *foo* is executed, variable x is never re-initialized.
- When *foo* needs to increase the value of the local static variable x, the value of variable x is read from the memory at the beginning of *foo* and is saved into the memory before *foo* exits. Therefore, *foo* returns a different result each time it is called. On the contrary, *foo* in Example 10-2, in which x is not static, always returns the same value.

Example 10-4 gives another example of using static variables. The program uses the static variable *sum* to check whether an integer number is a palindrome number. A palindrome number remains the same if all digits are reversed.

C Program	Assembly Program

`int isPal(int);`	`        AREA myData, DATA`
	`        ALIGN`
	`sum     DCD 0`

`int main(){`
`    int n;`
`    n = isPal(12321);`
`    while(1);`
`}`
	`        AREA palindrome, CODE`
	`        EXPORT __main`
	`        ALIGN`
	`        ENTRY`
	`__main PROC`
	`        LDR   r0,=12321`
	`        BL    isPal`
	`stop    B     stop`
	`        ENDP`

`// Check palindrome number`
`int isPal(int n){`
	`; Recursively check palindrome`
	`isPal  PROC`
	`        PUSH  {r4, lr}`

`    static int sum = 0;`	`        MOV   r4, r0` `        CBZ   r4, done        ; if n is zero, done`

`    int r;`	`        MOV   r2, #10`
	`        SDIV  r1, r4, r2      ; r1 = n/10`
	`        MLS   r3, r1, r2, r4  ; r3 = n - r1 * 10;`

`    if(n!=0) {`
`      r = n % 10;`
`      sum = sum*10 + r;`
`      isPal (n/10);`
`    }`
	`        LDR   r1, =sum`
	`        LDR   r1, [r1]        ; r1 = sum`
	`        ADD   r1, r1,r1,LSL #2 ; r1 = 5*sum`
	`        ADD   r1, r3,r1,LSL #1 ; sum = sum*10 + r;`
	`        LDR   r2, =sum`
	`        STR   r1, [r2]        ; save sum`
	`        MOV   r2, #10`
	`        SDIV  r0, r4, r2      ; r0 = n/10`
	`        BL    isPal          ; recursive call`

`    if (sum == n)`
`      return 1;`
`    else`
`      return 0;`
`}`
	`done    LDR   r1, =sum`
	`        LDR   r1, [r1]`
	`        CMP   r1, r4`
	`        BNE   no`
	`yes     MOV   r0, #1          ; if palindrome`
	`        B     exit`
	`no      MOV   r0, #0          ; if not palindrome`
	`exit    POP   {r4, pc}`
	`        ENDP`
	`        END`

Example 10-4. Example of using a local static variable *sum* in a function

10.2.2 Volatile Variables

When the compiler optimizes a software program, a hard-to-find hidden error is that the program mistakenly reuses the value of a variable stored in a register, instead of reloading it from memory each time. In order to avoid such compilation error, a variable can be declared as volatile, such as:

For a variable that is concurrently updated, volatile prevents a compiler from mistakenly reusing a variable value instead of always reloading the value from memory.

volatile int variable;

The keyword volatile forces the compiler to generate an executable, which always loads the variable value from the memory whenever this variable is accessed.

Example 10-6 gives a simple example to illustrate the necessity of declaring a variable counter, shared by two concurrently running tasks (*main* function and *SysTick_Handler*), as volatile. In this example, the main program uses the SysTick to implement a time delay. It sets up the SysTick timer and then waits until the SysTick interrupt service routine reduces the counter to 0. The SysTick decrements the counter by one when a system timer interrupt occurs. Chapter 12.4 gives the implementation of *SysTick_Init()*.

Main Program (*main.c*)	Interrupt Service Routine (*isr.s*)

`// volatile unsigned int counter;`
`unsigned int counter;`
`extern void task();`
`extern void SysTick_Init();`
 	
`int main(void) {`
`   counter = 10;`
`   SysTick_Init();`
`   while(counter != 0);  // Delay`
`   // Continue the task`
`   while(1);`
`}`
	`        AREA ISR, CODE, READONLY`
	`        IMPORT counter`
	`        ENTRY`
	
	`SysTick_Handler PROC`
	`        EXPORT SysTick_Handler`
	`        LDR r1,=counter`
	`        LDR r0,[r1]     ; load counter`
	`        SUB r0,r0,#1    ; counter--`
	`        STR r0,[r1]     ; save counter`
	`        BX  LR          ; exit`
	`        ENDP`
	`        END`

Example 10-5. A C variable is not declared as *volatile* while it should be.

Compilers often attempt to optimize the program but sometimes can cause troubles. The compiler observes that, after the counter is initialized to 10, the value of the counter variable is not modified directly by *main()* or indirectly by any subroutine called by *main()*. Because loading data from memory is much slower than retrieving data from registers, the compiler decides to reuse the value of the counter stored in a register, instead of fetching the counter value again from the memory when the counter is accessed in the while loop. Example 10-6 compares the assembly program generated by the compiler when the counter variable is declared as volatile or non-volatile.

- If the counter is not declared as volatile, the while loop is a dead loop. *SysTick_Handler* periodically decrements the counter and stores its value into the memory. However, the main program repeatedly checks register r0, without reloading the latest value of the counter from the memory.
- If the counter is declared as volatile, the dead loop problem is avoided.

If counter is not declared as volatile	If counter is declared as volatile

<pre>__main PROC
        LDR r1,=counter
        MOV r0,#10
        STR r0,[r1]
 	
        BL   SysTick_Init
 	
wait   CMP r0,#0 ; r0 does not hold
                   ; latest counter value
        BNE wait ; Thus, a dead loop
 	
stop   B   stop
        ENDP</pre>
	<pre>__main PROC
	        LDR r1,=counter
	        MOV r0,#10
	        STR r0,[r1]
	
	        BL SysTick_Init
	
	wait LDR r1,=counter
	        LDR r0,[r1]
	        CMP r0,#0
	        BNE wait
	
	stop B stop
	        ENDP</pre>

Example 10-6. Comparison of assembly instructions generated by compiler when the counter variable is declared as volatile and non-volatile.

The C keyword volatile should also be used for memory-mapped I/O registers. In embedded systems, a variable is often used to access a hardware register that is updated directly by hardware. Memory-mapped I/O has been widely used to access peripheral devices. Data and control registers of external devices are mapped to specific memory addresses, and a program can use memory pointers to access these hardware registers, such as the following:

```
unsigned int *p = (unsigned int *) 0x60002400;
```

In order to prevent the compiler from optimizing out these memory pointers incorrectly, these pointers must be declared as volatile. The following example uses a memory pointer to access a 32-bit hardware register mapped to the memory address 0x60002400.

```
volatile unsigned int *p = (unsigned int *) 0x60002400;
```

In general, a variable should be declared as volatile to prevent the compiler from optimizing it away when (1) this variable is updated by external memory-mapped hardware, or (2) this variable is global and is changed by interrupt handlers or by multiple threads.

10.3 Inline Assembly

A block of assembly code, called inline assembly, can be directly embedded in a C program. It is convenient to programmers since it does not require separate assemble and link process. Another advantage of inline assembly is that it can flexibly access C variables without export and import operations, which would be required if the assembly code were written as an assembly subroutine.

10.3.1 Assembly Functions in a C Program

When a function is declared with "__asm ", the assembly code of this function has to preserve the environment.

When a block of assembly code is embedded within a function by using "__asm", the assembly code does not need to preserve the environment.

Inline assembly can be implemented by using the "__asm" keyword. It has two different uses. The first is to specify a function that is completely implemented in assembly. The second is to specify multiple lines of assembly code within a C function. When "__asm" is used to declare a function, the assembly code must preserve the runtime environment via the stack and recover the environment before exiting from the subroutine. The assembly code can directly access the registers and must follow the procedure call protocol, with up to four arguments saved in registers r0-r3 and the return result saved in register r0. Example 10-7 and Example 10-8 give two examples of implementing a function of C in assembly.

```
__asm int sum4(int a, int b, int c, int d){
    ; arguments stored in r0, r1, r2, r3
    PUSH {r4, lr}      ; preserve environment in stack
    MOV r4, r0         ; r0 = 1st argument
    ADD r4, r4, r1     ; r1 = 2nd argument
    ADD r4, r4, r2     ; r2 = 3rd argument
    ADD r0, r4, r3     ; r3 = 4th argument, r0 = return
    POP {r4, pc}       ; recover environment from stack
}

int main(void){
    int s = sum4(1, 2, 3, 4);
    while(1);
}
```

Example 10-7. Using inline assembly to implement a subroutine that adds four integers.

```
char a[25] = "Hello!";
char b[25];

__asm void strcpy(char *src, char *dst){
loop    LDRB  r2, [r0], #1      ; 1st argument, r0 = src, post-index
        STRB  r2, [r1], #1      ; 2nd argument, r1 = dst, post-index
        CMP   r2, #0
        BNE   loop
        BX    lr
}

int main(void){
        strcpy(a, b);
        while(1);
}
```

Example 10-8. Using inline assembly to copy a string.

When a function is declared with "__asm", the compiler only creates the interface of this function and does not provide any actual implementation. Therefore, in the above example, the PUSH and POP instructions are used to preserve and recover the running environment.

10.3.2 Inline Assembly Instructions in a C Program

When "__asm" is used to declare a block of assembly code within a C function, the assembly code cannot directly access registers and does not need to preserve the runtime environment via the stack. The compiler is responsible for generating assembly code to preserve the environment. The assembly code treats each C variable as a register. These C variables, called virtual registers, can be directly used in an assembly instruction. Compilers replace these virtual registers with real registers. In addition, the comment has to be in C style, not in assembly style. The following gives an example of embedding assembly code in a C function.

```
int sum4(int a, int b, int c, int d){
        int t;
        __asm {
          ADD t, a, b;   // t, a, and b are virtual registers
          ADD t, c;      // Cannot directly access r0 - r15
          ADD t, d;      // Have to use comment style of C
        }
        return t;
}

int main(void){
        int s = sum4(1, 2, 3, 4);
        while(1);
}
```

Example 10-9. Using "__asm" to declare a block of assembly instructions in a C function.

10.4 Calling Assembly Subroutines from a C Program

In a large application, program code is often saved in multiple small source files, instead of a single monolithic file. This technique not only improves the software modularity and maintainability, but also reduces the compilation time. These files can be compiled separately so that unmodified files do not need to be recompiled.

This section shows how a C program calls assembly subroutines that are stored in separate source files.

- In the assembly code, the names of all subroutines that are accessed by the C program must be declared as global by using the directive "EXPORT" or "GLOBAL". This makes these subroutine names visible outside this source code module so that the compiler can locate them when linking the object files generated from the source codes.
- In the C program, these functions have to be declared by using the keyword "extern".

10.4.1 Example of Calling an Assembly Subroutine

In the following example, the C program calls the assembly subroutine *strlen*, which calculates the length of a string. The C program and the assembly program are stored in two separate source files: *main.c* and *strlen.s*.

C Program (*main.c*)	Assembly Program (*strlen.s*)

char str[25] = "Hello!";
 	
extern void strlen(char* s);
 	
int main(void){
    int i;
    i = strlen(str);
    while(1);
}
	` ` `AREA stringLength, CODE`
	` ` `EXPORT strlen      ; make strlen visible`
	` ` `ALIGN`
	`strlen PROC`
	` ` `PUSH {r4, lr}       ; preserve r4 and lr`
	` ` `MOV  r4, #0         ; initialize length`
	`loop  LDRB r1, [r0, r4] ; r0 = string address`
	` ` `CBZ  r1, exit       ; branch if zero`
	` ` `ADD  r4, r4, #1     ; length++`
	` ` `B    loop           ; do it again`
	`exit  MOV  r0, r4         ; place result in r0`
	` ` `POP  {r4, pc}       ; exit`
	` ` `ENDP`

Example 10-10. A C program calls an assembly routine stored in a different file.

- The assembly subroutine follows the procedure call protocol defined in ARM embedded-application binary interface (EABI) and assumes argument *str* is passed in register r0. In addition, the caller expects that the assembly subroutine returns a 32-bit result in register r0 and a 64-bit result in registers r1:r0.

- The C program declares the assembly function to be used by using the keyword "extern" to inform the compiler that the implementation of this function is in another file.
- The assembly subroutine uses "EXPORT strlen" to make the symbol strlen visible to the linker. Note all symbols are case-sensitive.

10.4.2 Example of Accessing C Variables in Assembly

An assembly program can access global variables that are defined in a C program or a separate assembly source file. When an assembly program accesses a global variable defined elsewhere, it needs to import that variable name by using the directive "IMPORT". A imported variable name, or called a symbol, will be resolved at link time. In the following example, the global variable *counter* is declared in the C program. The assembly code uses "IMPORT counter" to read and write this global variable.

C Program (*main.c*)	Assembly Program (*count.s*)

``int counter;
 	
extern int getValue();
extern void setValue(int c);
 	
void increment();
 	
int main(void) {
    int c = 0;
    setValue(1);
    increment();
    c = getValue();
    while(1);
}
 	
void increment(){
    counter += 2;
}```
	`` AREA count, CODE
	            IMPORT counter
	            ALIGN
	setValue PROC
	            EXPORT setValue
	            LDR r1, =counter
	            STR r0, [r1]
	            BX lr
	            ENDP
	
	getValue PROC
	            EXPORT getValue
	            LDR r1, =counter
	            LDR r0, [r1]
	            BX lr
	            ENDP
	
	increment PROC
	            EXPORT increment [WEAK]
	            LDR r1, =counter
	            LDR r0, [r1]
	            ADD r0, r0, #1
	            STR r0, [r1]
	            BX lr
	            ENDP
	            END```

Example 10-11. Example of accessing a C variable in assembly routines

Note in the assembly program, the *increment* symbol is exported with weak specified. By default, all symbols are strong. During linking, a strong symbol replaces a weak symbol of the same name. The linker reports a fatal error if there more than one strong instances of the same symbol name. Since the symbol *increment* defined in the assembly code is weak but the one defined in the C program is strong, the increment function defined in C overrides the one defined in the assembly. Accordingly, when the increment function is called, the counter variable is incremented by two, instead of one.

10.5 Calling C Functions from Assembly Programs

An assembly program can call functions implemented in C. The assembly program needs to follow the procedure call protocol defined in ARM embedded-application binary interface (EABI). The assembly program needs to place the input arguments of a C function in registers r0-r1 before it calls the function. The assembly program should also expect the result is saved in register r0 if the C function returns a value less than 32 bits. If the result has more than 32 bits, registers r0 – r4 will be used.

10.5.1 Example of Calling a C Function

In the following example, the assembly program calls the *strlen* function implemented in C. The C function returns the length of the string in register r0 to the assembly program. In the assembly code, the C function names have to be imported to avoid linking errors.

Assembly Program (*main.s*)	C Program (*strlen.c*)
```AREA my_strlen, CODE EXPORT __main IMPORT strlen ALIGN ENTRY __main PROC LDR r0, =str BL strlen stop B stop ENDP AREA myData, DATA ALIGN Str DCB "12345678",0 END```	```int strlen(char *s){ int i = 0; while(s[i] != '\0') i++; return i; }```

Example 10-12. Example of an assembly program that calls a C subroutine

If "WEAK" is specified in the import directive, the linker will not produce any error if the symbol is not defined externally. Instead, the linker then replaces the symbol with zero or some appropriate value. For example, if the label is not defined in the project, the linker then replaces it with the address of the next instruction after the branch.

```
IMPORT label [WEAK]
...
B label
...
```

Example 10-13. A symbol declared with weak prevents the linker from fatal linking error.

10.5.2 Example of Accessing Assembly Data in a C Program

In the C program, in order to access variable *counter* defined in the assembly code, the C program has to use "extern int counter" to inform the compiler that this variable is defined outside this C program. The memory space of the counter variable is allocated by the assembly program and the C program only needs to indicate the existence of this variable without performing any memory allocation. Without the "extern" keyword, variable *counter* would be allocated again in the C program, thus producing an error of duplicated variables at the link stage.

Assembly Program	C Program

`        AREA main, CODE`
`        EXPORT  __main`
`        IMPORT getValue`
`        IMPORT increment`
`        IMPORT setValue`
`        ALIGN`
`        ENTRY`
 	
`__main  MOVS   r2,#0`
`        MOVS   r0,#1`
`        BL     setValue`
`        BL     increment`
`        BL     getValue`
`        MOV    r2,r0`
`stop    B      stop`
 	
`        AREA myData, DATA`
`        EXPORT counter`
`counter DCD    0`
`        END`
	`extern int counter;`
	
	`int getValue() {`
	`    return counter;`
	`}`
	
	`void increment() {`
	`    counter++;`
	`}`
	
	`void setValue(int c) {`
	`    counter = c;`
	`}`

Example 10-14. Example of C routines that access a variable defined in assembly program.

10.6 Exercises

1. Write a subroutine in assembly that removes all occurrences of a given character in a string. The subroutine takes two parameters: the string pointer, and the character to be removed. Write a C code that calls this subroutine. The string is defined in the C code as global.

2. Suppose we have the following *strcat* function written in C, which concatenates the second string to the first string. Write an assembly program that calls the strcat function. The two strings are allocated in the data area in the assembly code.

```
void strcat (char * dst, char * src) {
    while(*dst++);
    while(*dst++ = *src++);
}
```

3. Write a subroutine *swap* in assembly that swaps two strings, and a C program that calls the swap subroutine. The two strings are defined in C program. (Hint: There is no need to swap all characters in the strings, and swapping the memory pointers in the assembly is sufficient.)

4. Write an assembly program that calls the following C subroutine that returns the memory address of the last occurrence of a given character in a string.

```
char * search (char * s, char c) {
    char *p = NULL;
    for(; *s; s++)
        if (*s == c)
            p = s;
    return p;
}
```

5. Suppose the following structure array is defined as global in a C program. Write an assembly program that iterates through the array and find the total scores.

```
struct Student_T {
    char c1;
    char c2;
    int score;
    char c3;
} students[10];
```

6. Write a subroutine *max4* in assembly to find the maximum value among four signed integers. These integers are passed to the subroutine via registers. Write a C program to test the *max4* subroutine.

7. Write a subroutine in assembly that checks whether a given integer is a palindrome number. For example, 9, 11, 1234321, 141, 1221, and 120021 are palindrome numbers. Write a C program that calls the assembly subroutine. The integer is the input argument, and the return is either 1 if the number is a palindrome or 0 if not.

8. Identify and correct the errors in the following inline assembly program that calculates the sum of four integers.

```
__asm int sum4(int a, int b, int c, int d){

        // arguments stored in r0 - r3
        MOV r4, r0       ; r0 = 1st argument
        ADD r4, r4, r1   ; r1 = 2nd argument
        ADD r4, r4, r2   ; r2 = 3rd argument
        ADD r0, r4, r3   ; r3 = 4th argument, r0 = return

}

int main(void){
        int s = sum4(1, 2, 3, 4);
        while(1);
}
```

9. Identify and correct the errors in the following inline assembly codes that calculate the sum of four integers.

```
int sum4(int a, int b, int c, int d){
        int t;
        __asm {
            ADD t, r0, r1;
            ADD t, r2;
            ADD t, r3;
        }
        return t;
}

int main(void){
        int s = sum4(1, 2, 3, 4);
        while(1);
}
```

10. Identify and correct the errors in the following two programs.

C Program (*main.c*)	Assembly Program (*strcpy.s*)

```char src[25] = "Hello!";```
 ```char dst[25];```
 	
 ```int main(void){```
 ```   strcpy(dst, src);```
 ```   while(1);```
 ```}```
	``` AREA stringCopy, CODE```
	 ``` ALIGN```
	 ```strcpy PROC```
	 ```loop LDRB r2, [r1] ; Load a byte, r1 = *src```
	 ``` STRB r2, [r0] ; Store a byte, r0 = *dst```
	 ``` ADD r1, #1 ; Increase memory pointer```
	 ``` ADD r0, #1 ; Increase memory pointer```
	 ``` CMP r2, #0 ; Zero terminator```
	 ``` BNE loop ; Loop if not null terminator```
	 ``` ENDP```
	 ``` END```

CHAPTER

11

Fixed-point and Floating-point Arithmetic

Let us review how real numbers work. In general, a real number can often be written in the following format:

$$\pm d_0. d_1 d_2 d_3 d_4 d_5 \cdots d_{n-1} \cdots \times b^e$$

where b is the base (or radix) and each d_i is a digit ($0 \leq d_i < b$). The number of digits may be infinite.

The decimal system, the most widely used number system in daily life, is based on powers of 10. Each digit represents the coefficient that multiplies the power of 10 represented by its position. For example,

$$654.321_{10} = 6 \times 10^2 + 5 \times 10^1 + 4 \times 10^0 + 3 \times 10^{-1} + 2 \times 10^{-2} + 1 \times 10^{-3}$$

All information is stored in the form of binary numbers in composters. A binary real number works in a similar way to a decimal real number.

$$101.011_2 = 1 \times 2^2 + 0 \times 2^1 + 1 \times 2^0 + 0 \times 2^{-1} + 1 \times 2^{-2} + 1 \times 2^{-3}$$

If we convert it to the decimal notation, we get

$$101.011_2 = 4 + 0 + 1 + 0 + 0.25 + 0.125 = 5.375$$

There are two common ways to represent an approximation of a real number: fixed-point format and floating-point format. It is an approximation because not all real numbers can be represented by a finite number of digits. For example, the true value of 1/3 is 1.333333…, which has an infinite number of digits. Whereas the fixed-point format has a fixed number of digits after the decimal point as introduced previously, the floating-point format can have a various number of digits after the decimal point depending on the scale of the real number.

While fixed-point arithmetic has fixed resolution for a given representation range and simple math allowing easy and fast computation, floating-point arithmetic trades manufacturing cost and computation efficiency for better precision and a wider range of representation. A special hardware, called floating-point unit (FPU), is often added within the processor to speed up floating-point processing. In embedded systems, not all microcontrollers have FPU on the chip. In the absence of FPU, fixed-point arithmetic is often preferred since software implementation of floating-point arithmetic is much more complex than the fixed-point arithmetic. In addition, if the dynamic data range of an application's data set is small, fixed-point format is preferred to improve the computational performance and accuracy. For example, fixed-point arithmetic is often used for video processing since pixel values have a fixed and regular format. On the contrary, audio systems often deploy floating-point arithmetic since the value of audio signals changes over a wide range.

> *There's no sense in being precise when you don't even know what you're talking about.*
>
> John von Neumann
>
> mathematician, computer scientist

While most desktops and servers use floating-point systems, the decision of using fixed-point or floating-point in an embedded system is sometimes difficult to make, as the cost of on-chip FPU has decreased sharply. For small applications running on limited computation capability or requiring long battery lifetime, fixed-point arithmetic is often preferred for simplified computation and improved energy efficiency. However, floating-point arithmetic can represent a wider dynamic range, and it is easier to program since complex floating-point functions have been implemented in hardware and the software runs floating-point instructions supported by the hardware.

11.1 Fixed-point Arithmetic

As its name suggests, a fixed-point number assumes there are a predefined number of binary bits to the right of the binary point. For processors, a fixed-point number is treated as a normal integer so integer arithmetic can directly be used to operate on these numbers. However, for programmers, there is a virtual decimal place at a fixed location of the binary representation. When two fixed-point numbers are added or subtracted, their bit strings can be treated as two integers and can be directly added or subtracted because their virtual decimal points are naturally aligned. However, when two fixed-point numbers are multiplied or divided, shift operations are required to fit the result into the same format as the operands.

11.1.1 Fixed-point Representation

Fixed-point numbers often use the $Qm.n$ notation, where m is the number of bits used to represent the integer portion and n is the number of bits used to represent the fractional portion.

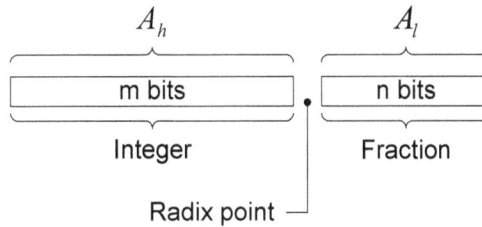

Figure 11-1. $Qm.n$ representation of fixed-point numbers

In the $Qm.n$ notation, the decimal value of a fixed-point number is calculated as follows:

$$f = A_h + A_l \times 2^{-n}$$

where A$_h$ and A$_l$ are the integer value of the integer portion and the fraction portion (h stands for high, l stands for low), respectively. In the following example, the integer portion A$_h$ = 10101_2 = 21, and the fraction portion A$_l$ = 101_2 = 5.

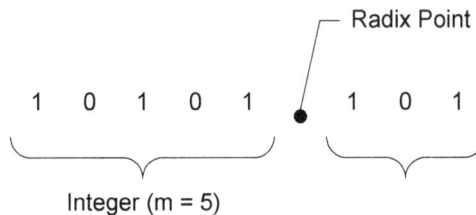

Figure 11-2. An example fixed-point number.

$$10101.101_2 = A_h + A_l \times 2^{-3} = 21 + 5 \times 2^{-3} = 21.625$$

We need to convert a fixed-point number f_A to an integer to facilitate the computation. We define the integer I_A as the value of the bitstring of f_A if the binary point is ignored.

$$I_A = f_A \times 2^n = (A_h + A_l \times 2^{-n}) \times 2^n = A_h \times 2^n + A_l$$

In the above example, we have $I_A = 10101101_2 = 173$.

11.1.2 Fixed-point Range and Resolution Tradeoff

$Qm.n$ uses $m + n$ bits for unsigned fixed-point numbers. For unsigned fixed-point numbers, an extra sign bit is used and thus a total of $m + n + 1$ bits are used. If the total number of bits available is given, the fixed-point representation has to play a tradeoff between the range and resolution, depending on the application's needs.

The resolution is defined as the smallest non-zero real number representable. It equals the gap between two consecutive numbers that can be represented in fixed-point format. The resolution of $Qm.n$ format is 2^{-n}. For example, the resolution of Q3.3 is 2^{-3}, i.e. 0.125.

Note resolution differs from accuracy. Resolution is the smallest change that can be represented in the digital system.

- *Accuracy* refers to the closeness of a numeric representation of a number to its true value. For example, when representing a real number, such as π, in Q16.16, the error is the difference between the true value and the value of the approximation in Q16.16. Naturally, the maximum error is less than the resolution 2^{-n}.
- *Resolution* is used to describe precision. The precision or resolution does not measure how close a representation is from its true value, instead it measures how close the values of different representations in the same format can be from each other.

The range is defined as the difference between the maximal and minimal values that can be represented.
- *Range of unsigned fixed numbers*
  The range of unsigned integers represented by using $m + n$ bits is $[0, 2^{m+n} - 1]$. Therefore, the range of unsigned fixed-point numbers that can be represented is $[0, 2^{m+n} - 1] \times 2^{-n}$, i.e. $[0, 2^m - 2^{-n}]$.
- *Range of signed fixed numbers*
  The range of signed integers, represented in two's complement by using $m + n + 1$ bits, is $[-2^{m+n}, 2^{m+n} - 1]$. Therefore, the range of signed fixed-point numbers that can be represented is $[-2^{m+n}, 2^{m+n} - 1] \times 2^{-n}$, i.e. $[-2^m, 2^m - 2^{-n}]$.

The fixed-point representation has to play a tradeoff between range and resolution. If n is too small, then we have a poor resolution but a large representation range. On the other hand, if n is too large, then we have a good resolution but a small representation range and high risk of overflow. For unsigned fixed numbers, we can choose to use Q16.16. However, if we need a larger range, we may use Q20.12; if we need a higher resolution, we may use Q12.20.

If the dynamic range of application's data set does not fit in the representation range of a given $Qm.n$ format, a predefined linear scaling and offsetting operation is often used to transform the application's data set into the representation range. When the arithmetic operation completes, a reverse scaling and shifting might be needed to recover the original data. The linear scaling and offsetting is performed as follows. If the actual value of an application's data is V, and the represented approximation is $\tilde{V}$, then we have

$$\tilde{V} = V \times 2^{scale} + offset$$

where $scale$ and $offset$ are two constants (can be positive or negative value) predefined by the application to ensure $\tilde{V}$ falls in the available fixed-point range.

11.1.3 Fixed-point Addition and Subtraction

Suppose f_A, f_B and f_C are three fixed-point numbers in the Q16.16 format and we have

$$f_C = f_A + f_B$$

In the following, we show how to calculate f_C. If the radix point (or binary point) is ignored, the integer that is represented by the bit string of f_A, f_B and f_C is I_A, I_B and I_C, respectively. In addition, the conversion between them is below:

$$\begin{cases} I_A = f_A \times 2^{16} \\ I_B = f_B \times 2^{16} \\ I_C = f_C \times 2^{16} \end{cases} \Longleftrightarrow \begin{cases} f_A = I_A \times 2^{-16} \\ f_B = I_B \times 2^{-16} \\ f_C = I_C \times 2^{-16} \end{cases}$$

Thus, the fixed-point addition $f_A + f_B$ can be calculated as follows:

$$\begin{aligned} f_C &= f_A + f_B \\ &= I_A \times 2^{-16} + I_B \times 2^{-16} \\ &= (I_A + I_B) \times 2^{-16} \end{aligned}$$

Since

$$f_C = I_C \times 2^{-16}$$

Thus, we have the following equation:

$$I_C \times 2^{-16} = (I_A + I_B) \times 2^{-16}$$

To solve this simple equation, we have

$$I_C = I_A + I_B$$

This shows that f_C can be directly obtained by adding the two bit strings that represent f_A and f_B. The addition of two fixed-point numbers is performed exactly the same way as if these two bit-strings were representing two integers.

Similarly, for the fixed-point subtraction $f_C = f_A - f_B$, we have $I_C = I_A - I_B$. Therefore, the representation of the subtraction result is the same as the representation of the result of integer subtraction between the bit strings representing f_A and f_B.

In sum, the addition and subtraction are simple. While bit strings represent fixed-point numbers, we can treat them as integers during subtraction and addition. In other words, although they are fixed-point numbers, we can use integer "add" and "sub" instructions to calculate the addition and subtraction of two fixed-point numbers. The following code shows the implementation.

```
; r0 = Q16.16 representation of a fixed-point number fa
; r1 = Q16.16 representation of a fixed-point number fb
; r2 = Q16.16 representation of a fixed-point number fc
add    r2, r0, r1    ; fc = fa + fb
sub    r2, r0, r1    ; fc = fa + fb
```

Example 11-1. Adding and subtracting two fixed-point numbers in Q16.16 format

11.1.4 Fixed-point Multiplication

This following example shows how to calculate the fixed-point multiplication of f_A and f_B, i.e.

$$f_C = f_A \times f_B$$

where f_A, f_B and f_C are fixed-point numbers in Q16.16 notation.

Mathematically, we have

$$\begin{aligned} f_C &= f_A \times f_B \\ &= (I_A \times 2^{-16}) \times (I_B \times 2^{-16}) \\ &= (I_A \times I_B) \times 2^{-32} \end{aligned}$$

We also know that

$$f_C = I_C \times 2^{-16}$$

Therefore, we get

$$I_C = (I_A \times I_B) \times 2^{-16}$$

This shows that we can treat fixed-point numbers f_A and f_B as integers first and calculate the product of these two integers. Note, multiplying two 32-bit integers can yield to a 64-bit product, which is stored in two registers. The result that we want is the middle 32 bits of the 64-bit product. Therefore, we need to shift the 64-bit product right by 16 bits, and the product is the least significant 32 bits of the shifted product.

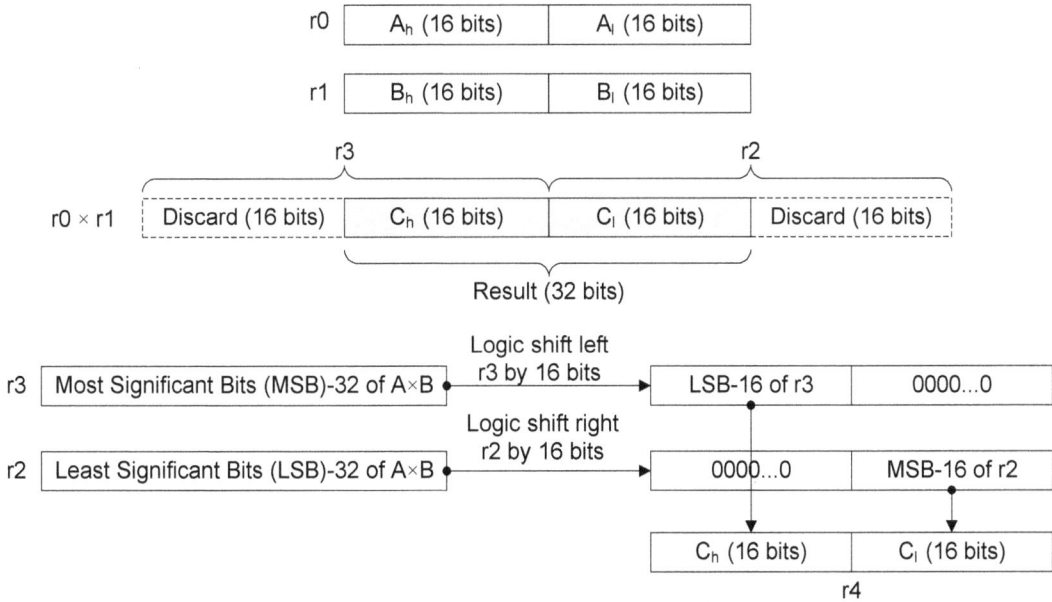

Figure 11-3. Multiplying two fixed-point numbers in Q16.16 format

```
; r0 = fixed-point number A
; r1 = fixed-point number B
; r4 = fixed-point product = A × B

SMULL  r2, r3, r0, r1   ; r2 = low word, r3 = high word
LSLS   r3, r3, #16      ; shift left high word
LSRS   r2, r2, #16      ; shift right low word
ORR    r4, r2, r3       ; pack them
```

Example 11-2. Multiplying two fixed-point numbers in Q16.16 format

Note: **SMULL** treats two source operands r0 and r1 as two's complement signed integers. It multiplies these integers and places the least significant 32 bits into register r2 and the most significant 32 bits into register r3. For unsigned numbers, UMULL can be used.

11.1.5 Fixed-point Division

The following shows how to calculate the fixed-point division of f_A and f_B, i.e.

$$f_C = f_A \div f_B$$

where f_A, f_B and f_C are fixed-point numbers in Q16.16 notation.

Mathematically we have,

$$\begin{aligned} f_C &= f_A \div f_B \\ &= (I_A \times 2^{-16}) \div (I_B \times 2^{-16}) \\ &= I_A \div I_B \end{aligned}$$

We also know that

$$f_C = I_C \times 2^{-16}$$

Therefore, we have

$$I_C = (I_A \div I_B) \times 2^{16} = (I_A \times 2^{16}) \div I_B$$

This shows that we can treat fixed-point numbers f_A and f_B as integers first. Then we shift the dividend I_A left by 16 bits to make it a 64-bit number. After that, we divide this 64-bit number by the 32-bit divisor I_B. The 32-bit quotient is the result.

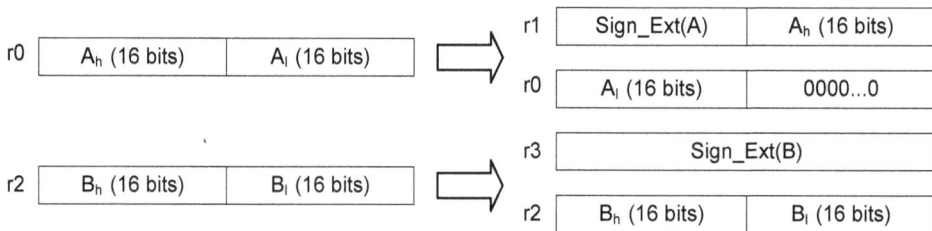

Figure 11-4. Dividing two fixed-point numbers in Q16.16 format

```
; r0 = fixed-point number A
; r2 = fixed-point number B
; r4 = fixed-point quotient = A ÷ B

ASRS   r1, r0, #31            ; r1[31:0] = sign bits of A
LSLS   r1, r1, #16            ; put sign bits in upper half word
ORR    r1, r1, r0, LSR #16    ;
LSLS   r0, r0, #16            ; [r1:r0] stores sign extended A
ASRS   r3, r2, #31            ; [r4:r3] stores sign extended B
BL     division_64_bits       ; Take four input register(r0:r1, r3:r4)
MOV    r4, r0                 ; division_64_bits places result in r0
```

Example 11-3. Dividing two fixed-point numbers in Q16.16 format

Note ARM does not have any instructions that perform 64-bit integer division. The implementation of 64-bit integer division is introduced in Chapter 9.9.

11.2 Floating-point Arithmetic

The IEEE standard for floating-point arithmetic (IEEE 754) is a *de facto* standard to store real numbers in computers. It aims to provide portability across different platforms by defining a shared method of representing floating-point numbers and implementing floating-point operations. IEEE 754 has been widely supported by numerous processors with FPU and by many software libraries written for processors without FPU.

11.2.1 Floating-point Representation

The IEEE 754 standard uses a normalized notation, which includes three fields: the sign bit, the fraction, and the true exponent, as shown in Figure 11-5. We call it true exponent in order to differ from the biased exponent introduced later in this section. The normalized notation implicitly assumes there is only one digit before the decimal point and this digit has to be 1. This bit is also called the hidden bit or the hidden 1 in IEEE 754.

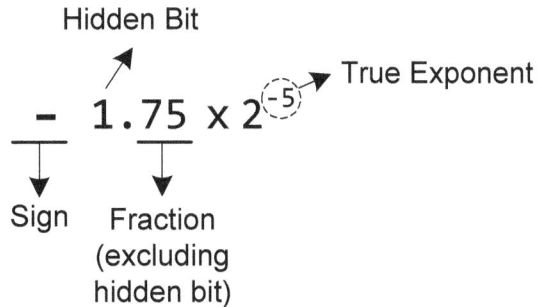

Figure 11-5. Normalized notation.

The following numbers are not in normalized format: 10.746×2^6, 5.023×2^3, -0.5×2^{-7}, and 0.05×2^9, because their integer part (all digits to the left of the decimal point) is not exactly 1. In addition, 1.025×10^3 is not in normalized format because the exponential part is based on 10, instead of 2.

We can convert 10.746×2^6 to normalized format as follows:

$$10.746 \times 2^6 = \frac{10.746}{8} \times 8 \times 2^6 = 1.34325 \times 2^9$$

Single precision and double precision, defined in IEEE 754, are two of the most commonly used formats. The single-precision uses 32 bits to store a floating-point number and the double-precision uses 64 bits. In C, the statement "float x;" declares a single-precision variable, and "double y;" declares a double-precision variable.

Compared with single precision, double precision has higher accuracy and can represent a much wider range of numbers. However, double precision takes more memory space and bandwidth, and is less computationally efficient. While most scientific applications running on desktops or servers use double precision, many embedded systems use single precision in order to reduce the hardware cost and improve the energy efficiency.

Single Precision (32 bits)

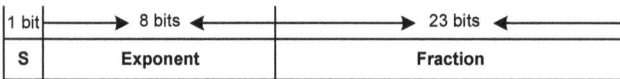

1 bit	8 bits	23 bits
S	Exponent	Fraction

Double Precision (64 bits)

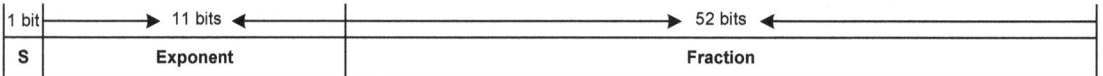

1 bit	11 bits	52 bits
S	Exponent	Fraction

Figure 11-6. IEEE 754 single-precision and double-precision format

Each format has three fields. As shown in Figure 11-6, the single-precision has 1 sign bit, an 8-bit *biased* exponent, and a 23-bit fraction. The double precision has 1 sign bit, an 11-bit *biased* exponent, and a 52-bit fraction. Each field is discussed below.

- The sign bit indicates whether the number is positive or negative. A value of 0 in the sign bit stands for a positive number, whereas a value of 1 denotes a negative one.
- The biased exponent is defined as the sum of the true exponent and a bias constant. In other words, the true exponent equals the biased exponent minus the bias constant. The bias constant is defined as 127 for single precision and 1203 for double precision. For single precision, the true exponent can have a positive or negative value falling between -127 and 128, and therefore the biased exponent is always non-negative, ranging from 0 to 255. You may wonder why the exponent field does not use two's complement of the true exponent, instead of the biased exponent. The key reason is that comparing two unsigned numbers can be executed much faster than comparing two signed numbers represented in two's complement. This can speed up floating-point comparison.
- The fraction field consists of all bits to the right of the binary point. In the normalized format, as shown in Figure 11-5, the leading bit (the bit to the left of the decimal point) is always 1. This hidden bit is therefore not stored in the fraction field. When calculating the decimal value of a binary format, the hidden bit should be included. For example, if the fraction field is `0b0100101` in binary, the actual fraction is `1.0100101` in binary, which includes the fraction bits and the hidden leading bit with a value of 1.

The floating-point number represented in IEEE 754 format can be calculated as follows:

$$(-1)^S \times (1 + Fraction) \times 2^{Exponent - Bias}$$

where the Bias constant is 127 for single precision and 1023 for double precision. In the following gives two examples of converting the binary representation of a floating-point number in IEEE 754 single-precision format and the standard decimal representation.

Example 1: decoding `0xC1FF0000` into a floating-point number

We need to convert the hex value into a 32-bit binary bit string. The bits are divided into three groups: with bit 31 (the leftmost bit) being the sign bit, bits 30-23 (the next eight bits) being the exponent, and bits 22-0 (the rest) being the fraction.

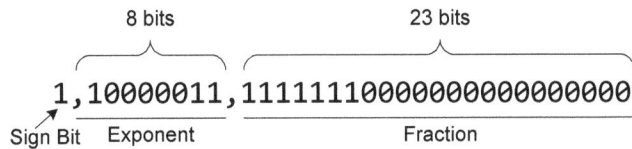

1. The first step is to check the sign bit, which is the leading bit of the bit string. In this case, we have S = 1.

2. Convert the exponent `10000011` into a decimal integer.

$$10000011_2 = 131$$

3. Convert the fraction `11111110000000000000000` into a decimal real number.

$$0.1111111_2 = 1 \times 2^{-1} + 1 \times 2^{-2} + 1 \times 2^{-3} + 1 \times 2^{-4} + 1 \times 2^{-5} + 1 \times 2^{-6} + 1 \times 2^{-7}$$
$$= 0.5 + 0.25 + 0.125 + 0.0625 + 0.03125 + 0.015625 + 0.078125$$
$$= 0.9921875$$

4. Calculate the represented real number as follows:

$$f = (-1)^S \times (1 + Fraction) \times 2^{Exponent-127}$$
$$= (-1)^S \times (1 + 0.9921875) \times 2^{131-127}$$
$$= -1 \times 1.9921875 \times 2^4$$
$$= -31.875$$

Example 2: encoding 14.5 into single-precision IEEE 754 format

The encoding involves the following five steps:

1. First, set up the sign bit. The sign bit S is set to 0 for a positive number and 1 for a negative number. Therefore, S = 1 in this case.

2. Rewrite the floating number in base-2 normalized format. Since 14.5 is larger than 2, we can repeatedly divide it by 2 until the quotient is smaller than 2 but larger than 1. Note if the floating-point number to be converted is smaller than 1, we will multiply it by 2, instead of dividing it by 2.

$$14.5 \div 2 = 7.25$$
$$7.25 \div 2 = 3.625$$
$$3.625 \div 2 = 1.8125$$

Therefore, we have

$$14.5 = 1.8125 \times 2^3$$
$$= (1 + 0.8125) \times 2^3$$

3. Calculate the exponent by adding the true exponent and the bias. The bias is 127 for the single-precision.

$$Exponent = 3 + 127 = 130 = 1000010_2$$

4. Calculate the fraction by converting 0.8125 into binary. This is achieved by repeatedly multiplying the fraction part (all digits to the right of the decimal point) of the product with 2 until the product becomes 1.

$$0.8125 \times 2 = 1.625 = 1 + 0.625$$
$$0.625 \times 2 = 1.25 = 1 + 0.25$$
$$0.25 \times 2 = 0.5 = 0 + 0.5$$
$$0.5 \times 2 = 1$$

Thus, the binary representation of 0.8125 is 0.1101, which combines the leading digit of the products (the digit to the left of the decimal point) of the above multiplications. The following can help you understand why the above conversion process works.

$$
\begin{aligned}
0.8125 &= \frac{1}{2} \times (1 + 0.625) \\
&= \frac{1}{2} \times \left(1 + \frac{1}{2} \times (1 + 0.25) \right) \\
&= \frac{1}{2} \times \left(1 + \frac{1}{2} \times \left(1 + \frac{1}{2} \times (0 + 0.5) \right) \right) \\
&= \frac{1}{2} \times \left(1 + \frac{1}{2} \times \left(1 + \frac{1}{2} \times \left(0 + \frac{1}{2} \times 1 \right) \right) \right) \\
&= 1 \times \left(\frac{1}{2} \right)^{-1} + 1 \times \left(\frac{1}{2} \right)^{-2} + 0 \times \left(\frac{1}{2} \right)^{-3} + 1 \times \left(\frac{1}{2} \right)^{-4} \\
&= 2^{-1} + 2^{-2} + 2^{-4} \\
&= 0.1101_2
\end{aligned}
$$

As a result, the fraction is `11010000000000000000000`, which appends 0 to the result to make the length of the fraction bit string 23 bits.

5. The single-precision floating-point format of 14.5 is `01000001011010000000000000000000` in binary and `0x41680000` in hex.

11.2.2 Special Values

Distinctive bit patterns are required to represent some special values, as shown in Figure 11-7.

- A value of zero cannot be directly represented in IEEE 754 format, and a special pattern in which all bits of exponent and fraction are cleared is used to represent zero. Note there is a positive zero and negative zero, and they should be treated as equal.
- Positive infinity and negative infinity are denoted with all exponent bits being 1 and all fraction bits being *NaN* (Not any Number), meaning that a floating-point arithmetic is invalid, is represented with an exponent of all ones and any non-zero fraction. For example, the following operations produce NaN: 0. 0/0.0, -∞ + ∞, 0 × (±∞), ±∞/±∞, *sqrt*(-1.0), and *log*(-10.0). There are two types of NaN: *QNaN* (Quiet NaN) and *SNaN* (Signaling NaN). A SNaN will generate a hardware exception signal to let the software handle the anomaly, and a QNaN does not raise such a hardware signal.

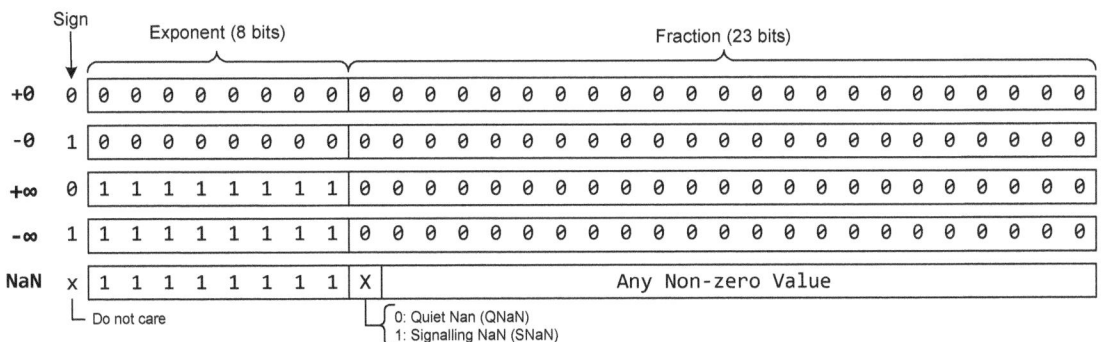

Figure 11-7. Special values in IEEE 754 single-precision

Floating operations normally use QNaN and let the NaN result propagate through most of all following arithmetic operations. For example, 0×NaN = NaN, *sqrt*(NaN) = NaN, logic expressions "0 < NaN", "0 > NaN", and "0 == NaN" are false, but "0 != NaN" is true. Many processors, including ARM Cortex-M3, are configurable so the same operation can produce either a QNaN or a SNaN to meet the application's need. In the default setting, QNaN is preferred over SNaN.

11.2.3 Overflow and Underflow

Now let us find the smallest and largest values that the single-precision format can represent.

- *Numbers closest to zero.* Since 00000000 is reserved, the minimal value of the exponent is 00000001. The fraction can be as small as 000...00. Thus the numbers closest to zero are

$$(-1)^S \times (1 + 0) \times 2^{1-127} = \pm 2^{-126} \approx \pm 1.18 \times 10^{-38}$$

- *Numbers farthest from zero.* The maximum value of the exponent is 11111110 because 11111111 is reserved. The fraction can be as large as 111...111. As a result, the largest finite values are

$$(-1)^S \times \left(1 + (1 - 2^{-23})\right) \times 2^{254-127} = \pm(2^{128} - 2^{104}) \approx \pm 3.40 \times 10^{38}$$

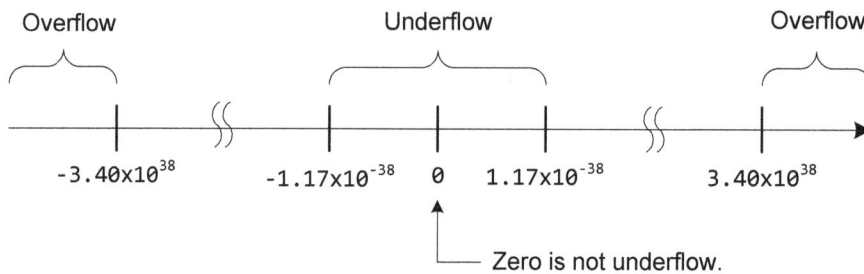

Figure 11-8. Representation range of IEEE 754 single-precision

If the true result is non-zero but smaller than the smallest value that can be represented, an underflow occurs, which may cause a loss of precision and create a large computation error. If the true result is finite but exceeds the largest representable value, an overflow happens, which is another common cause of software failures.

When a processor detects an underflow or overflow, the hardware returns zero or the maximum number, respectively, and simultaneously generates an exception signal to provide an opportunity for the software to handle anomalies.

Overflow and underflow can cause mysterious and unexpected software failures that can be disastrous. On June 4, 1996, the Ariane 5 rocket veered off the designed course and destructed itself because an overflow occurred when assigning a floating-point number to an integer. That simple software failure caused an estimated loss of $370 million.

At the hardware level, overflow and underflow can be detected by checking whether the exponent of a floating-point arithmetic operation is too large or too small. The processor can generate a special hardware signal upon overflow or underflow.

However, it is difficult for programmers to write software to handle the anomaly because the signal can be raised at any point of the program. For example, in the following simple C statement, if the subtraction causes an underflow, most processors automatically return zero as the result of the subtraction. As a result, a divide-by-zero anomaly takes place though the following *if*-statement aims to prevent it.

```
if (a != b)
     c = 1/(a - b);     // Divide-by-zero can still occur.
```

Example 11-4. An if-statement fails to prevent divide-by-zero error.

11.2.4 Subnormal Numbers

IEEE 754 standard also defines a subnormal format for a class of floating-point numbers filling between 0 and the minimum positive number that the normalized format can represent. Upon an underflow in the normalized presentation, the data can be "deformalized" to the subnormal format to trade the numeric range for accuracy. Formerly the subnormal format was called *denormal* format. A bit string is a subnormal format if all bits of the exponent are zero but at least one bit of the fraction is non-zero. Specifically, the decimal value it represents can be calculated as follows for single-precision:

$$(-1)^S \times Fraction \times 2^{-126}$$

Note the subnormal format differs from the normalized format introduced previously in two major aspects:

1. The subnormal allows a leading zero in front of the decimal point in the fraction, while the normalized format assumes the fraction always has a leading hidden 1 to the left of the decimal point. Thus when calculating the decimal values, the normalized format uses (*1 + Fraction*) while the subnormal uses *Fraction* only.
2. All subnormal floating numbers have the same exponent, which is always 0.

The smallest positive number that a subnormal format can represent in single-precision is

```
0,00000000,00000000000000000000001,
```

whose fraction value is 2^{-23}.

Therefore, the smallest positive number is

$$2^{-23} \times 2^{-126} = 2^{-149}$$
$$\approx 1.40^{-45}$$

The largest positive number of single-precision subnormal format is

$$0,00000000,11111111111111111111111,$$

whose fraction value is $1 - 2^{-23}$.

Therefore, the largest positive number is

$$(1 - 2^{-23}) \times 2^{-126} = 2^{-126} - 2^{-149}$$
$$\approx 1.175 \times 10^{-38}$$

11.2.5 Tradeoff between Numeric Range and Resolution

Compared with fixed-point numbers, the floating-point numbers can represent a larger numeric range but at the cost of degrading the resolution. Specifically, all floating-point numbers are not distributed uniformly across the represented range. If the total number of bits is given, the fixed-point format has to play a tradeoff between the representation range and the representation resolution. It has either a large range but inferior resolution, or a narrow range but superior resolution.

Let us consider a hypothetical floating-point system that is similar to the IEEE 754 standard. This system has only five bits: the sign bit, an exponent with two bits and a fraction with two bits. The bias for the normalized representation is 1. Therefore, the corresponding decimal value is as follows:

$$(-1)^S \times (1 + Fraction) \times 2^{Exponent-1}$$

For example, if the binary is 10110, its corresponding floating-point number is

$$(-1)^1 \times (1 + 0.10)_2 \times 2^{2-1} = -3/4$$

If the exponent is zero but the fraction is not zero, then it is in subnormal format and its decimal value is

$$(-1)^S \times Fraction \times 2^0 = (-1)^S \times Fraction$$

For example, if the binary is 10010, the decimal is then

$$(-1)^1 \times (0.10)_2 = -1/2$$

We assume the fixed-point numbers have a format of Q3.2, with three bits set aside for integer portion and two bits used for the fractional portion. The integer portion uses two's complement. For fair comparison, we also require the fixed-point uses the same bit patterns to represent special values, including $\pm\infty$, QNaN, and SNaN. Table 11-1 lists the values for all 32 possible bit strings.

Binary	Floating-point	Notation for floating-point	Fixed-point
00000	0.0	Reserved	0.0
00001	¼	$(0.01)_2$	¼
00010	½	$(0.10)_2$	½
00011	¾	$(0.11)_2$	¾
00100	1.0	$(1+0.00)_2 \times 2^{1-1}$	1.0
00101	1¼	$(1+0.01)_2 \times 2^{1-1}$	1¼
00110	1½	$(1+0.10)_2 \times 2^{1-1}$	1½
00111	1¾	$(1+0.11)_2 \times 2^{1-1}$	1¾
01000	2.0	$(1+0.00)_2 \times 2^{2-1}$	2.0
01001	2½	$(1+0.01)_2 \times 2^{2-1}$	2¼
01010	3.0	$(1+0.10)_2 \times 2^{2-1}$	2½
01011	3½	$(1+0.11)_2 \times 2^{2-1}$	2¾
01100	$+\infty$	Reserved	$+\infty$
01101	QNaN	Reserved	QNaN
01110	SNaN	Reserved	SNaN
01111	SNaN	Reserved	SNaN
10000	-0.0	Reserved	-0.0
10001	-¼	$-(0.01)_2$	-¼
10010	-½	$-(0.10)_2$	-½
10011	-¾	$-(0.11)_2$	-¾
10100	-1.0	$-(1+0.00)_2 \times 2^{1-1}$	-1.0
10101	-1¼	$-(1+0.01)_2 \times 2^{1-1}$	-1¼
10110	-1½	$-(1+0.10)_2 \times 2^{1-1}$	-1½
10111	-1¾	$-(1+0.11)_2 \times 2^{1-1}$	-1¾
11000	-2.0	$-(1+0.00)_2 \times 2^{2-1}$	-2.0
11001	-2½	$-(1+0.01)_2 \times 2^{2-1}$	-2¼
11010	-3.0	$-(1+0.10)_2 \times 2^{2-1}$	-2½
11011	-3½	$-(1+0.11)_2 \times 2^{2-1}$	-2¾
11100	$-\infty$	Reserved	$-\infty$
11101	QNaN	Reserved	QNaN
11110	SNaN	Reserved	SNaN
11111	SNaN	Reserved	SNaN

Table 11-1. Resolution and range comparison of floating-points and fixed-points

Figure 11-9 plots the representable floating-point and fixed-point numbers listed in the above table in the same axis.

1. The fixed-point has a smaller window of real numbers that can be represented than the floating-point. In other words, the fixed-point can represent a wider range of real data.
2. The fixed-point representation uniformly distributes representable numbers across the representable range, with equal gap between any two consecutive numbers. As a result, the resolution remains fixed. The resolution means the closeness of two consecutive numbers. However, the gap of two consecutive numbers in the floating-point becomes larger as the exponent increases, and accordingly its resolution degrades gradually. When considering the subnormal numbers, the resolution of the floating-point becomes reasonable.

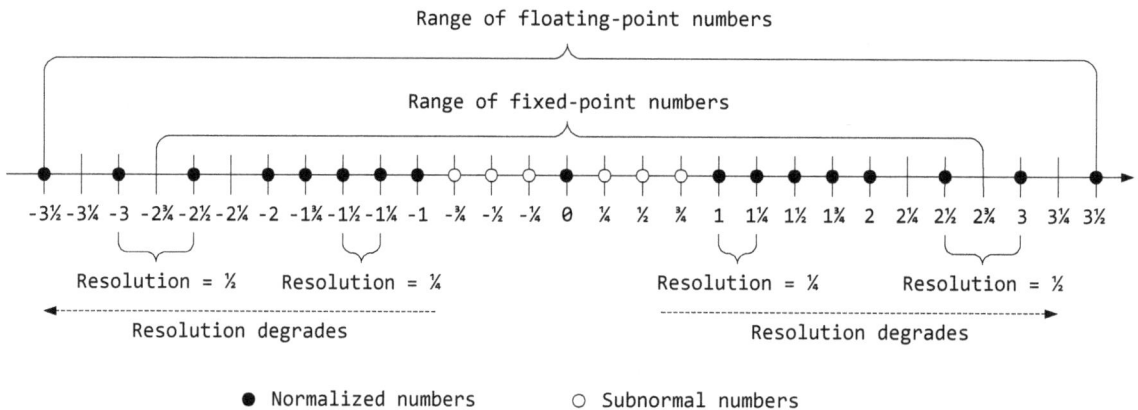

Figure 11-9. An example of the distribution of floating-point numbers. Resolution degrades as the exponent increases since the gap between two consecutive floating numbers increases.

11.2.6 Rounding Rules

As introduced in the previous section, not all real numbers can be accurately represented by using a finite number of binary digits without any error. Therefore, we have to find an approximate representation of the actual real number. The process of finding an approximation, which is representable, is called rounding.

IEEE 754 defines four different rounding rules:

- round to the nearest value,
- round toward zero (truncation),
- round toward plus infinity (rounding up), and
- round toward negative infinity (rounding down).

In rounding to nearest, if the data is exactly halfway between the two nearest numbers, the system chooses the one whose least significant bit of the fraction field is zero.

We use decimal numbers to illustrate the four rounding rules. In order to simplify the presentation, we assume only 5 digits are allowed after the decimal point and Table 11-2 gives the rounded result of four rounding modes.

Rounding Rule	Data	Rounded Result
Nearest	+0.123456	+0.12346
	-0.123456	-0.12346
Truncate	+0.123456	+0.12345
	-0.123456	-0.12345
Rounding up	+0.123456	+0.12346
	-0.123456	-0.12345
Rounding down	+0.123456	+0.12345
	-0.123456	-0.12346

Table 11-2. Four different rounding rules

Rounding to the nearest is the default and most widely used rounding rule. The other three rounding rules are statistically biased. For example, when adding a set of randomly generated positive numbers, the sum of these numbers when rounded based the rounding down tends to be consistently smaller than the true sum. For a set of negative numbers, it tends to be consistently larger.

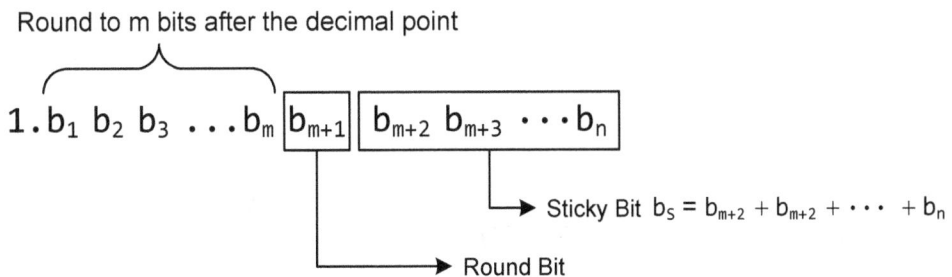

Round to m bits after the decimal point

$$1.b_1\ b_2\ b_3\ \ldots b_m\ |b_{m+1}|\ |b_{m+2}\ b_{m+3}\ \cdots b_n|$$

Sticky Bit $b_S = b_{m+2} + b_{m+2} + \cdots + b_n$

Round Bit

Figure 11-10. A binary number that is to rounded m bits after the decimal point

Rounding to the nearest in binary can be implemented as follows. Suppose we want to keep m bits to the right of the binary point. As shown in Figure 11-10, the algorithm checks three bits: (1) bit b_m, (2) the round bit b_{m+1}, and (3) a sticky bit which is the bitwise logical OR of all bits to the right of the round bit.

There are three different scenarios:

1.   When the round bit is zero, rounding down (truncation) should be used.

2. When the round bit is one and the sticky bit is also one, rounding up should be used.

3. When the round bit is one and the sticky bit is zero, this is a tie and the value has an equal distance to two nearest neighboring numbers. The tie is broken by using the "round to even" rule, *i.e.* choose the one that has zero as its least significant bit.

Table 11-3 is the algorithm of "rounding to the nearest."

```
1. If b_{m+1} = 0, directly truncate and remove bits b_{m+1}b_{m+2}b_{m+2}...b_n
2. If b_{m+1} = 1 and b_S = 1, round up
3. If b_{m+1} = 1 and b_S = 0, round to even
   •  If b_m = 0,   directly truncate and remove b_{m+1}b_{m+2}b_{m+2}...b_n
   •  If b_m = 1,   round up
```

Table 11-3. Algorithm of rounding to the nearest

Table 11-4 gives a few examples to illustrate the above nearest rounding algorithm. Suppose we want to keep two binary digits after the binary point.

Binary Value	Round bit	Sticky Bit	Rounded Result	Round Method
0.000001	0	-	0.00	Truncate
0.000011	0	-	0.00	Truncate
0.000101	0	-	0.00	Truncate
0.000111	0	-	0.00	Truncate
0.011000	1	0	0.10	Round to Even
0.001000	1	0	0.00	Round to Even
0.001011	1	1	0.01	Round up
0.001101	1	1	0.01	Round up
0.001111	1	1	0.01	Round up

Table 11-4. Example of nearing rounding

11.2.7 Floating-point Addition

In general, suppose we add the following two floating numbers with the same sign:

$$f_1 = (-1)^S \times (1 + F_1) \times 2^{E1}$$

and

$$f_2 = (-1)^S \times (1 + F_2) \times 2^{E2}$$

where $E1 \geq E2$. Then mathematically, the addition is performed as follows:

$$f_1 + f_2 = (-1)^S \times (1 + F_1) \times 2^{E1} + (-1)^S \times (1 + F_2) \times 2^{E2}$$
$$= (-1)^S \times \left((1 + F_1) + (1 + F_2) \times 2^{E2-E1} \right) \times 2^{E1}$$
$$= (-1)^S \times \left((1 + F_1) + \frac{1 + F_2}{2^{E1-E2}} \right) \times 2^{E1}$$

The division operation in the above equation can easily be implemented by using shift operations. As shown in Figure 11-11, the basic procedure of adding two floating-point numbers involves the following steps: (1) shift the smaller fraction to match the larger one, (2) add or subtract the fraction based on its sign bits, (3) normalize the sum, (4) round the sum to appropriate bits, and (5) detect overflow and underflow.

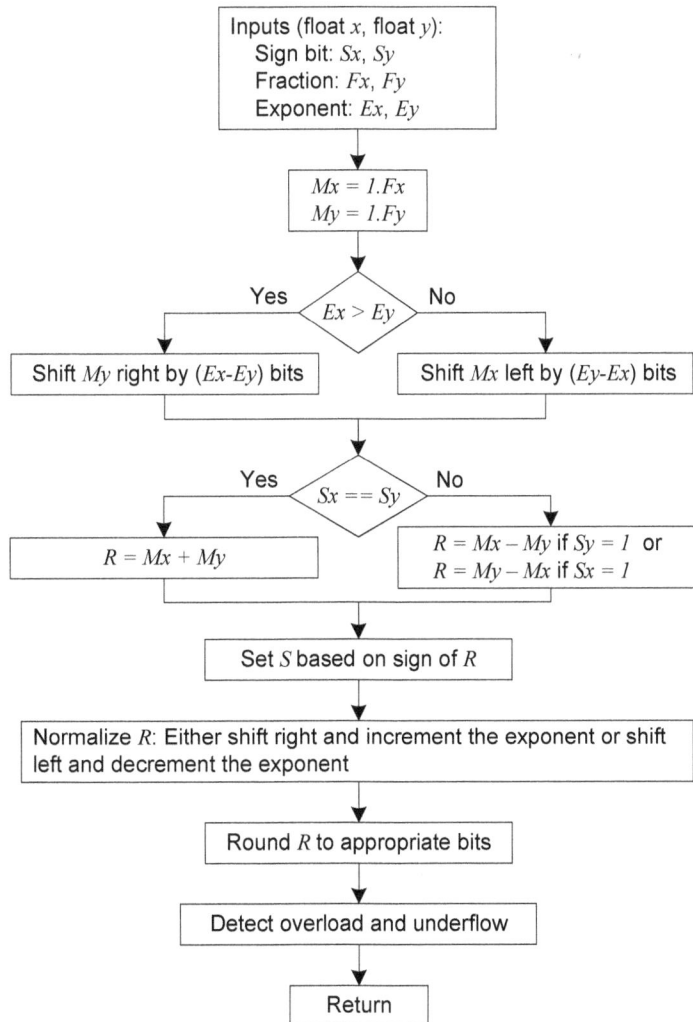

Figure 11-11. Flowchart of adding two floating numbers

We will illustrate the above algorithm by using a simple example. Suppose we are adding x and y,

$$x = (1.1011011101)_2 \times 2^4$$

and

$$y = (1.1110101111)_2 \times 2^5$$

First, since the exponent of y is larger than x, we shift the fraction of x right by one bit to make the exponent match the larger one. Note we should not shift left the fraction of the operand with a larger exponent to match the lower exponent. The reason is that we may create a large computational error if a larger operand causes an overflow when it is shifted.

$$x = (0.11011011101)_2 \times 2^5$$

Then we perform a simple addition. We do not need to worry about the alignment of the decimal points since both fraction bit strings have the same length.

```
    x =     0 . 1 1 0 1 1 0 1 1 1 0 1
    y =     1 . 1 1 1 0 1 0 1 1 1 1 0
x + y = 1 0 . 1 1 0 0 0 1 1 1 0 1 1
```

As a result, we get the sum:

$$x + y = (10.11000111011)_2 \times 2^5$$

The next step is to normalize the sum. In this case, we shift the sum right since the integer part of the fraction of the sum has more than one bit. If the fraction of the sum has many leading zeroes, including the integer part, then we should shift the fraction of sum left and reduce the exponent accordingly. The following is the sum after normalization.

$$x + y = (1.011000111011)_2 \times 2^6$$

During the normalization, the hardware can detect overflow or underflow by checking whether the result falls out of the representable data range.

While the implementation is complex because it needs to consider special inputs, such as $\pm\infty$ and NaN, we will show a simplified implementation below which ignores special inputs and does not detect overflow and underflow.

```
; Adding two floating-point numbers
; Input: r0 = first operand, r1 = second operand
; Output: r0 holds the sum
; For each register,
```

```
;    bits[31] = sign (1 bit)
;    bits[30-23] = exponent (8 bits)
;    bits[22:0] = fraction (23 bits)

fadd PROC
  ; If inputs have different signs, flip the sign bit of the second operand
  ; and call the subtraction function.
  TEQ      r0,r1                    ; Are they both positive or both negative?
                                    ; If r0 and r1 the same sign bit, then N = 0;
                                    ; Otherwise N = 1
  EORMI    r1,r1,#0x80000000        ; If N = 1, flip sign bit of second operand
  BMI      fsub                     ; call subtraction, return r0 - (-r1)

  ; r0 and r1 are guaranteed to have the same sign
  ; If r0 < r1 (unsigned comparison), swap them
  SUBS     r2,r0,r1                 ; r2 = r0 - r1
  SUBSCC   r0,r0,r2                 ; if r0 < r1, swap r0 and r1
  ADDSCC   r1,r1,r2                 ; Guarantee r0 > r1

  ; Find the difference of exponents
  ; Now it has guaranteed that r0 > r1 (unsigned comparison)
  ; r3[8:0] = [sign:exponent] of r0 - [sign:exponent] of r1
  LSR      r2,r0,#23                ; r2[8:0] = [sign:exponent] of r0
  SUB      r3,r2,r1,LSR #23         ; r3 = difference of exponents

  ; Shift right the fraction of the smaller operand (r1) to make
  ; their exponents match and then add the fractions
  MOV      r12,#0x80000000          ; Set the leading hidden 1
  ORR      r0,r12,r0,LSL #8         ; r0 = 1:fraction:0000,0000
  ORR      r1,r12,r1,LSL #8         ; r1 = 1:fraction:0000,0000
  LSR      r12,r1,r3                ; r12 = r1 >> difference between exponents
  ADDS     r12,r0,r12               ; r12 = sum of both fractions
  BCS      fraction_Too_Large       ; If fraction sum is 11.xxxx or 10.xxxx, skip

  ; Pact final result into r0
  ; The true value of the fraction sum is 1.xxxxx
  LSRS     r0,r12,#8                ; r0[22:0] = first 23 bits of fraction of sum
                                    ; Guard bit is shifted into carry
  ADC      r0,r0,r2,LSL #23         ; r0[31:23] = [sign:exponent] of sum,
                                    ; also add guard bit into r0
  BXCC     lr                       ; if guard bit is 0, return truncated result

fraction_Too_Large
  ; The true value of the fraction sum is 11.xxxxx or 10.xxxxx
  RRX      r0,r12,r1                ; Shift carry back into r0
```

```
; If guard bit is 1, perform rounding to even or round up
; and pack final result into r0
RSB       r3,r3,#0x20           ; r3 = 32 - r3, r3 = diff of exponents
LSLS      r1,r1,r3              ; r1 = all sticky bits
BICEQ     r0,r0,#0x01           ; Clear the round bit if all sticky bits
                                ; are zero (round to even)
LSRS      r0,r0,#8              ; r0[22:0] = first 23 bits of fraction of sum
                                ; Guard bit is shifted into carry
ADC       r0,r0,r2,LSL #23      ; r0[31:23] = [sign:exponent] of sum
                                ; also add guard bit into r0
BX        lr                    ; return

ENDP
```

Example 11-5. Simplified implementation of adding two floating-point numbers

Note the sum of adding two aligned fraction parts (including their leading hidden 1 bit) can have three possible results, 1.xxxxx, 10.xxxxx, or 11.xxxxx. When the integer part has two bits (10.xxxxx or 11.xxxxx), we need to shift the leading bit back to the fraction of the sum, which is achieved with the instruction "RRX r0, r12, #1".

In addition, when the result is packed into the single-precision format by using the statement "ADC r0,r0,r2,LSL #23", the leading bit of the fraction sum is added into the exponent part because the leading bit is removed from the fraction sum before the packing. Therefore, if the fraction sum is 10.xxxxx or 11.xxxxx, then the "ADC" instruction automatically increases the exponent of the result by 1.

As the standard suggests, nearest rounding should be used as the default rounding scheme. When packing the results, "ADC" instead of "ADD" is used. The carry bit is added to the fraction part of the result. This is to achieve nearest rounding. The carry bit actually holds the guard bit. If the guard bit is 0, extra bits are truncated by the "LSRS r0,r0,#8" instruction. If all sticky bits are 0, then the round bit (the least significant bit of the fraction sum) is set to zero. If the sticky bits are not all zero, the guard bit is 1 and is added into the result.

11.2.8 Floating-point Multiplication

Suppose we multiply the following two floating-point numbers:

$$f_1 = (-1)^{S1} \times (1 + F_1) \times 2^{E1}$$

and

$$f_2 = (-1)^{S2} \times (1 + F_2) \times 2^{E2}$$

Mathematically, the product of two floating-point numbers

$$f_1 \times f_2 = \left((-1)^{S1} \times (1 + F_1) \times 2^{E1} \right) \times \left((-1)^{S2} \times (1 + F_2) \times 2^{E2} \right)$$
$$= (-1)^{S1+S2} (1 + F_1) \times (1 + F_2) \times 2^{E1+E2}$$

As the above equation indicates, the multiplication involves the following steps:

- Identify the sign of the product.
- Add the exponents together.
- Multiply the fractions including the leading hidden one.
- Normalize the result to standard format.

The following gives a simplified implementation of multiplying two single-precision floating-point numbers. The program does not handle special cases, such as overflow, underflow, and input of infinity and NaN.

The trick is handling the multiplication of two fractions. Two fractions include their hidden leading 1. When multiplying two fractions of the same length, *i.e.* 1.xx...x × 1.yy...y (where x and y is either 1 or 0), their product has to be truncated into the same length. Suppose each fraction has n bits, their product has either 2n or 2n − 1 bits because the leading bit of both fractions is 1. We can use $n = 2$ as a simple example to illustrate. In binary, we have three different scenarios:

$$1.1 \times 1.1 = 10.11$$

$$1.1 \times 1.0 = 01.10$$

$$1.0 \times 1.0 = 01.10$$

In other words, the most significant two bits of the product of 1.xx...x and 1.yy...y can only be either 10 or 01. If the most significant bits are 01, we need to remove the leading zero bit. If the most significant bits are 10, we need to renormalize the result by shifting the fraction product right by one bit and then increasing the exponent by 1.

```
; Function of multiplying two single-precision floating-point numbers
; Input: r0 = first operand, r1 = second operand
; Output: r0 = product
; For each register,
;     bits[31] = sign (1 bit)
;     bits[30-23] = exponent (8 bits)
;     bits[22:0] = fraction (23 bits)

fmul PROC
  ; Add two exponents
  MOV      r12,#0x000000FF        ; mask
  ANDS     r2,r12,r0,LSR #23      ; r2[7:0] = exponent of r0
  ANDS     r3,r12,r1,LSR #23      ; r3[7:0] = exponent of r1
```

```
ADD        r2,r2,r3                    ; r2[7:0] = sum of both exponents

; If operands have different signs, set the product as negative
TEQ        r0,r1                       ; check whether r0 and r1 have the sign
ORRMI      r2,r2,#0x100                ; i.e. r2[8] = 1
                                       ; It will be shifted to r0[31] later on.

; Multiply fractions
MOV        r12,#0x80000000             ; Mask for leading hidden 1
ORR        r0,r12,r0,LSL #8            ; r0 = 1:Fraction:00000000 (binary)
ORR        r1,r12,r1,LSL #8            ; r1 = 1:Fraction:00000000 (binary)
UMULL      r1,r3,r0,r1                 ; r1:r3 = product of both fractions
                                       ; r1 = low word, r3 = high word

; Perform rounding up and discard lower 32 bits of the fraction product
CMP        r1,#0x00                    ; Are tailing 32 bits of the product
                                       ; of two fractions are zero?
ORRNE      r3,r3,#0x01                 ; if r1 ~= 0, round up, set r3[0] = 1

; Remove leading zero bit of fraction product
; Note there is at most one leading zero bit in the product
LSLS       r3,r3,#1                    ; r3<<1, shift out leading bit
RRXCS      r3,r3,#1                    ; If leading bit was 1, recover it

; Pack final result into r0
LSRS       r12,r3,#8                   ; r12 = 0000,0000:24-bit fraction (binary)
                                       ; Guard bit is shifted into carry
ADC        r0,r12,r2,LSL #23          ; pack result into r0
                                       ; r2[8:0] = [sign:exponent] of product
                                       ; Guard bit (carry bit) is added to fraction
BXCC       lr                          ; If the guard bit is 0, return

LSL        r12,r3,#24                  ; r12 = [guard bit:all sticky bits]
CMP        r12,#0x80000000             ; if guard bit is zero and sticky bits are
                                       ; zero, clear the last bit of fraction
BICEQ      r0,r0,#0x01                 ; round to even by setting r0[0] = 0;
BX         lr                          ; return

ENDP
```

Example 11-6. Simplified implementation of multiplying two floating-point numbers

11.3 Exercises

1. Suppose we are given two real numbers A and B in Q16.16 format. Show the basic procedure to calculate the product C. $C = A \times B$. Note C is also in Q16.16 format. List all key operations and write an assembly program to conduct the multiplication.

2. Convert 3.1415 to Q8.8 format.

3. Convert the binary real number `1111.1101` to decimal.

4. Write an assembly program that calculates the sum of an array of Q8.8 numbers.

5. Write an assembly program that calculates the sum of an array of Q16.16 numbers.

6. Convert 3.1415 to IEEE 754 single-precision format.

7. Convert `0xC1F54000` to IEEE 754 single-precision decimal

8. Manually subtract the following two IEEE 754 single-precision numbers:

    `0xC1D15053 - 0xC3FD5053`

9. Manually add the two IEEE 754 single-precision numbers given in the previous question.

10. Manually multiply the following IEEE 754 single-precision numbers.

    `0xC0D40000 × 0x41C20000`

11. Manually divide the following IEEE 754 single-precision numbers.

    `0xC0D40000 ÷ 0x41C20000`

12. Write an assembly program that performs subtraction of two single-precision floating-point numbers in IEEE 754 format.

13. Write an assembly program that performs addition of two single-precision floating-point numbers in IEEE 754 format.

14. Write an assembly program that performs multiplication of two single-precision floating-point numbers in IEEE 754 format.

15. Write an assembly program that performs division of two single-precision floating-point numbers in IEEE 754 format.

16. Write an assembly program that performs subtraction of two double-precision floating-point numbers in IEEE 754 format.

17. Write an assembly program that performs addition of two double-precision floating-point numbers in IEEE 754 format.

18. Write an assembly program that performs multiplication of two double-precision floating-point numbers in IEEE 754 format.

19. Write an assembly program that performs division of two double-precision floating-point numbers in IEEE 754 format.

CHAPTER
12

Interrupt

This chapter introduces the basic concepts of *interrupts* and *interrupt service routines*. Use of interrupts is illustrated by using the system timer, external interrupt, and software interrupt.

12.1 Introduction to Interrupt

An interrupt is a specific signal that utilizes a combination of software and hardware implementation to force the processor to stop the current activity and start to execute a specific piece of code, called interrupt service routine (ISR). The ISR responds to an event generated by either hardware or software. When the ISR completes, the processor automatically resumes the activity that has been halted. This process is transparent to the interrupted activity, as if nothing had happened.

Interrupts are widely used in microcontrollers for applications to respond to hardware requests efficiently. There are two major motivations for a processor to support interrupts: (1) informing a program of some timely external events and (2) providing fast response to human inputs or mission critical events.

Interrupts allow a microcontroller to perform multiple tasks simultaneously. At any specific time instant, only one program activity is served on a microcontroller. However, multiple computation tasks can be alternatively served in a multiplexing fashion. There are two scenarios: preemptive and non-preemptive. In the preemptive scenario, a task with a higher priority can stop the current task with relatively lower priority without requiring any cooperation and take over the control of the processor. The old task can be resumed after the new task completes. In the non-preemption scenario, the current task cannot be interrupted until it voluntarily gives the control to other tasks. The non-preemptive system often relies on the system timer, described later in this chapter, to serve multiple tasks periodically in a round-robin fashion.

Interrupts enable a microcontroller to respond to human inputs or latency-sensitive events rapidly. An alternative to interrupt in response to an event is periodic polling. In the polling scheme, the processor continually queries the I/O devices to check whether a specific event has happened, and provides corresponding service if needed. In the interrupt scheme, the processor provides a hardware mechanism that allows an internal or external device to generate a signal actively to inform the processor of occurring events.

We use a telephone as an example to compare the efficiency of polling and interrupt. Suppose you are expecting a call at home. In the polling scheme, you pick up your telephone every 10 seconds to check whether there is anyone on the line calling you. In the interrupt scheme, you continue to perform whatever tasks you are supposed to complete. When the telephone rings, *i.e.* an interrupt signal is generated most likely by the hardware, you can stop your current task and answer the phone call. The polling is much less efficient than the interrupt, since much precious time has been spent on grabbing the telephone without successfully receiving any calls.

12.2 Interrupt Service Routine (ISR)

When the microcontroller is turned on or reset, the processor fetches the first two words from the memory, one word at the address 0x00000000 to initialize the main stack pointer (MSP) and the other at the address 0x00000004 to initialize the program counter (PC). The word stored at 0x00000004 is the memory address of the first instruction of the *reset_handler*() procedure, which is determined by the compiler and link script. Typically the *reset_handler*() procedure calls the *main*() procedure, which is the user's application code. After PC is initialized, the program starts the execution.

While the very first word in the memory stores the memory address used to initialize MSP, the following words starting at 0x00000004 represent a vector table, which store the memory address of the first instruction of all interrupt and exception handling routines.

All interrupts are managed by the nested vectored interrupt controller (NVIC). NVIC allows applications to enable specific interrupts and program their priority levels dynamically if needed. All interrupts are served based on their priority levels. The current running interrupt handler is stopped if a new interrupt with a higher priority occurs. The current lower-priority task is preempted by the new interrupt task and resumes the computation when the handler of the new interrupt completes. A higher value of interrupt priority number actually represents a lower priority. The *reset_handler*() has the highest priority and it has a priority number of -3.

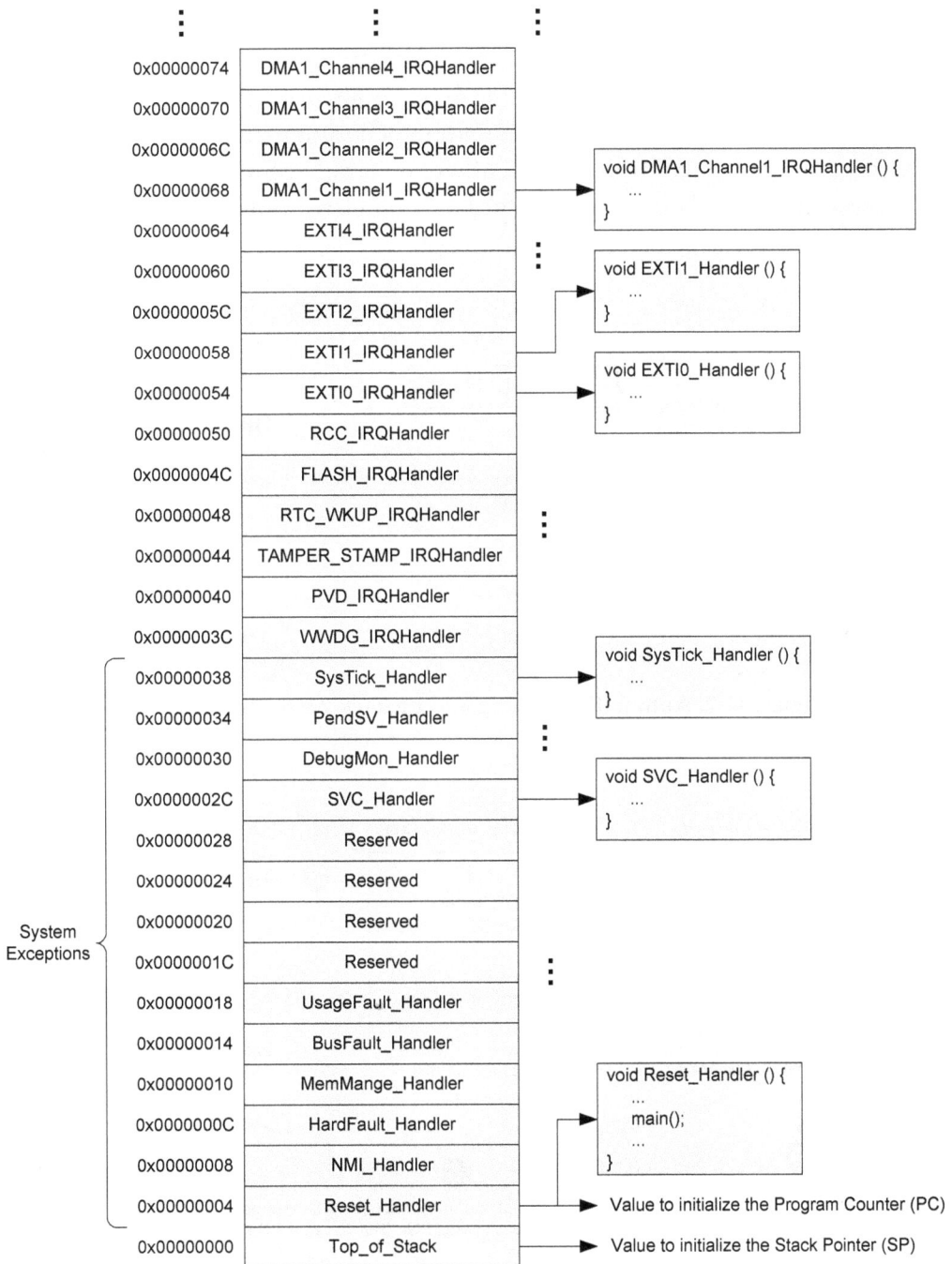

Figure 12-1. Interrupt vector table

Among all interrupts defined in the interrupt vector table, the first 15 interrupts are to support systems, called system exceptions, while the others (interrupt number 16 and above) are to support peripherals, called external interrupts. Examples for system exceptions include fault-handling interrupt (bus faults for prefetch and memory management, memory management fault, instruction usage fault, hard faults), supervisor call interrupt, and system timer interrupt. The others, such as ADC interrupts, USB interrupt, and serial communication interrupt (SPI, I²C, and USART), are to inform the microcontroller efficiently of external events. Without these interrupts, the microcontroller then would rely on inefficient polling to check peripherals repeatedly, wasting precious computation cycles.

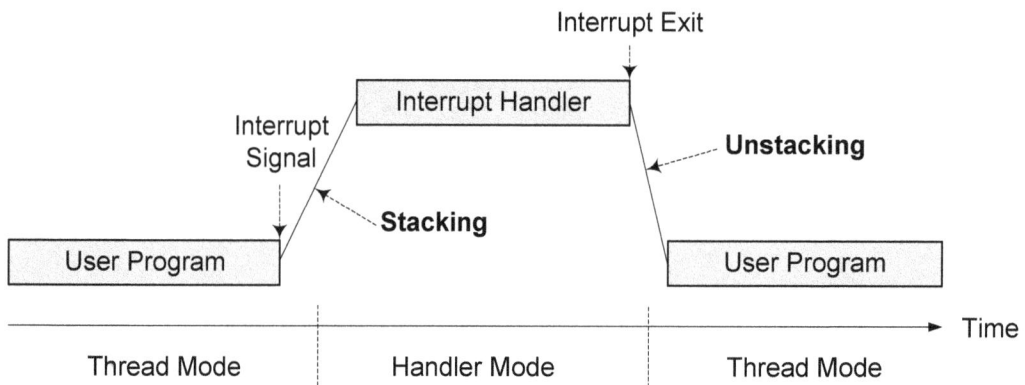

Figure 12-2. Automatic stacking and unstacking for interrupt handler

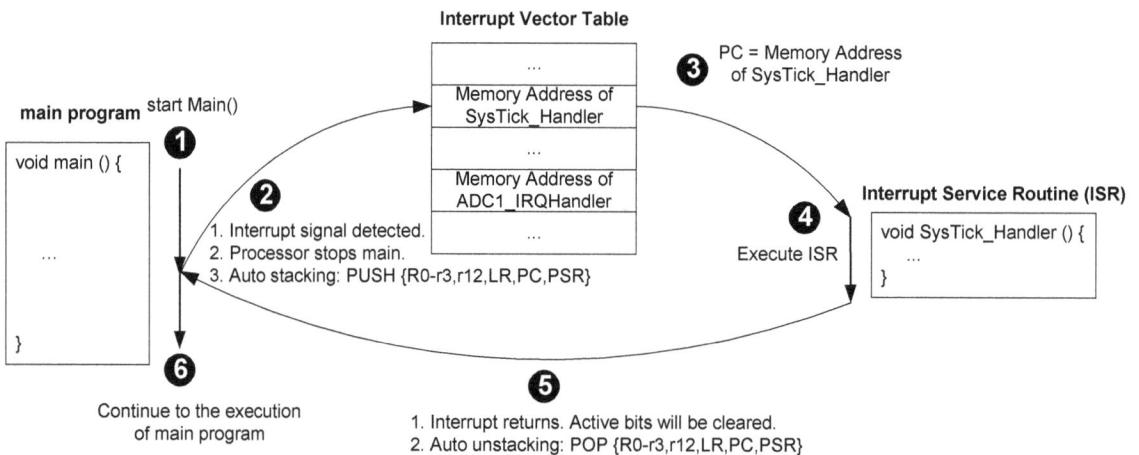

Figure 12-3. Steps of stacking and unstacking for interrupt handler

When serving an interrupt, the Cortex-M3 microcontroller performs automatic stacking and unstacking.

- **Interrupt Stacking.** Before executing the interrupt handler, the stacking process spontaneously pushes eight registers to preserve the running environment, including the lowest four registers (r0, r1, r2, and r3) and four other registers (r12, LR, PSR, and PC).
- **Interrupt Unstacking.** After the interrupt handler completes, the unstacking process automatically pops the values of these eight registers out of the stack to recover the environment to the time instant immediately before this interrupt handler is called. At the same time, corresponding NVIC status registers will also be automatically updated. Specifically, the active bits are cleared.

Since an interrupt may occur at any time instant, the program counter (PC) is preserved during interrupt stacking and is recovered during interrupt unstacking. As a result, the processor can successfully continue executing the computation process that has been interrupted.

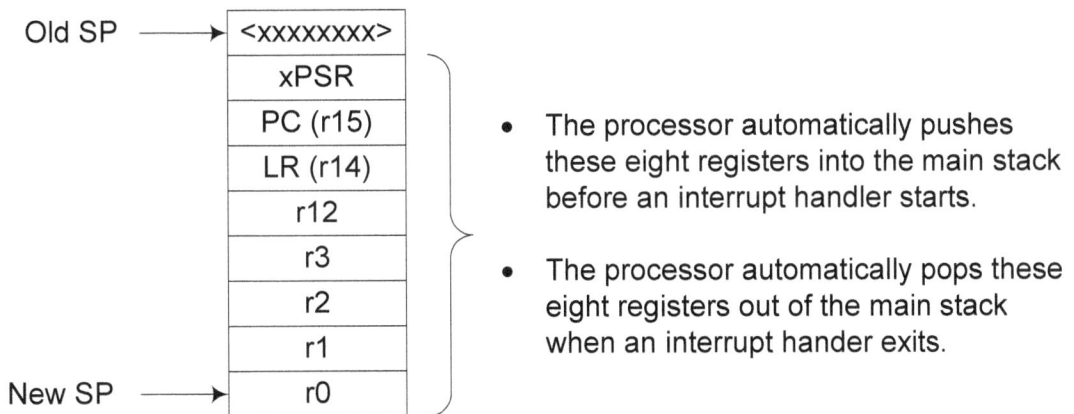

Figure 12-4. Stacking and unstacking when an interrupt handler starts or exits

The interrupt service routine exits by running "BX LR". Note that LR in an interrupt service routine has a meaning different from LR in a regular subroutine.

- LR in a regular subroutine represents the return address to the caller. When a regular subroutine is executed, LR holds the memory address of the instruction to be processed after exiting the subroutine. The value of LR is copied to PC when a regular service routine exits.
- LR in an interrupt service routine indicates whether the main or process stack should be used to push and pop operations. Since the interrupt service routine

preserves and recovers PC via stacking and unstacking, the LR register is not used to set PC when an interrupt service routine exits. Instead, the LR register is set to be a special value (either 0xFFFFFFF9 or 0xFFFFFFFD) to indicate whether the processor should unstack from the main stack (MSP) or the process stack (PSP). Chapter 23.1 gives detailed explanation of LR for interrupts.

12.3 Nested Vectored Interrupt Controller (NVIC)

The nested vectored interrupt controller (NVIC) is built in Cortex-M3 cores to manage all interrupts. It offers three key functions:

1. Enable and disable interrupts
2. Set the preemption priority and sub-priority of a specific interrupt
3. Set and clear the handing bit of a specific interrupt

Depending on the manufacturer, the process can support multiple interrupts. The Cortex-M3 microcontroller supports up to 256 interrupts, in which the first 16 interrupts are system exceptions and the rest 240 interrupts are peripheral interrupts. The number of interrupts supported by a microcontroller is stored in the read-only interrupt controller type register (ICTR).

Each interrupt has six control bits, as listed in Table 12-1.

Interrupt control bit	Corresponding register (32 bits)
Enable bit	Interrupt set enable register (ISER)
Disable bit	Interrupt clear enable register (ICER)
Pending bit	Interrupt set pending register (ISPR)
Un-pending bit	Interrupt clear pending register (ICPR)
Active bit	Interrupt active bit register (IABR)
Software trigger bit	Software trigger interrupt register (STIR)

Table 12-1. Interrupt control bits

Each interrupt has an interrupt number, ranging from 0 to 256 for Cortex-M3 processors. A Cortex-M3 processor includes 16 system interrupts (0-15) defined by ARM. System interrupts are also called system exceptions or processor exceptions. The rest 240 interrupts are peripheral interrupts (also called non-system interrupts), which are defined by chip manufacturers. Note that in the Cortex-M3 code library, the interrupt number of peripherals starts with 0.

Cortex-M3 defines eight registers for each control bit. For example, there are ISER0, ISER1, ..., and ISER7, which can enable 256 interrupts.

1. *Enable and disable an interrupt.* Writing an enable bit to 1 can enable the corresponding interrupt. Writing an enable bit to 0 does not disable the corresponding interrupt. Write a disable bit to 1 can disable the interrupt. Writing a disable bit to 0 has no impacts on the related interrupt. This allows us to disable an interrupt conveniently without affecting other interrupt enable states.

2. *Pend and clear an interrupt.* If an interrupt occurs, the corresponding pending bit will be set if the microcontroller cannot process this interrupt immediately. Writing the clear pending bit to 1 will remove the corresponding interrupt from the pending list. When an interrupt is disabled but its pending bit has already been set, this interrupt instance remains active and will be serviced before it is disabled.

3. *Trigger an interrupt.* Setting an active bit by software or hardware will activate the related interrupt, and the microcontroller will start the corresponding interrupt handler. If software writes a trigger bit of the software trigger interrupt register (STIR) to 1, the related interrupt will also be activated. Most system exceptions can only be activated by hardware.

12.3.1 Enable and Disable Peripheral Interrupts

Cortex-M3 has eight 32-bit ISER registers (ISER0 – ISER7) and eight 32-bit ICER registers. Figure 12-5 shows ISER0 and ISER1 registers for enabling a peripheral interrupt for STM32L processors. Each bit in an ISER register can enable one peripheral interrupt. The interrupt number of peripheral interrupts ranges from 0 to 240. Not all peripheral interrupts are used. For example, STM32L has only 45 peripheral interrupts. Note that all NVIC registers are little endian regardless of whether big endian or little endian is used by the processor.

The following C program can enable a peripheral interrupt whose interrupt number is IRQn.

```
WordOffset = IRQn >> 5;                  // Word Offset = IRQn/32
BitOffset = IRQn & 0x1F;                 // Bit Offset = IRQn mod 32
NVIC->ISER[WordOffset]  =  1 << BitOffset;   // Enable interrupt
```

Since each ISER register has 32 bits, the ISER register array index is obtained by shifting right the interrupt number IRQn by five bits. Note that the peripheral interrupt number starts with 0. For example, the interrupt number of Timer 7 is 44. Therefore, the following code can enable the Timer 7 interrupt:

```
NVIC->ISER[1] = 1 << 12;                    // Enable Timer 7 interrupt
```

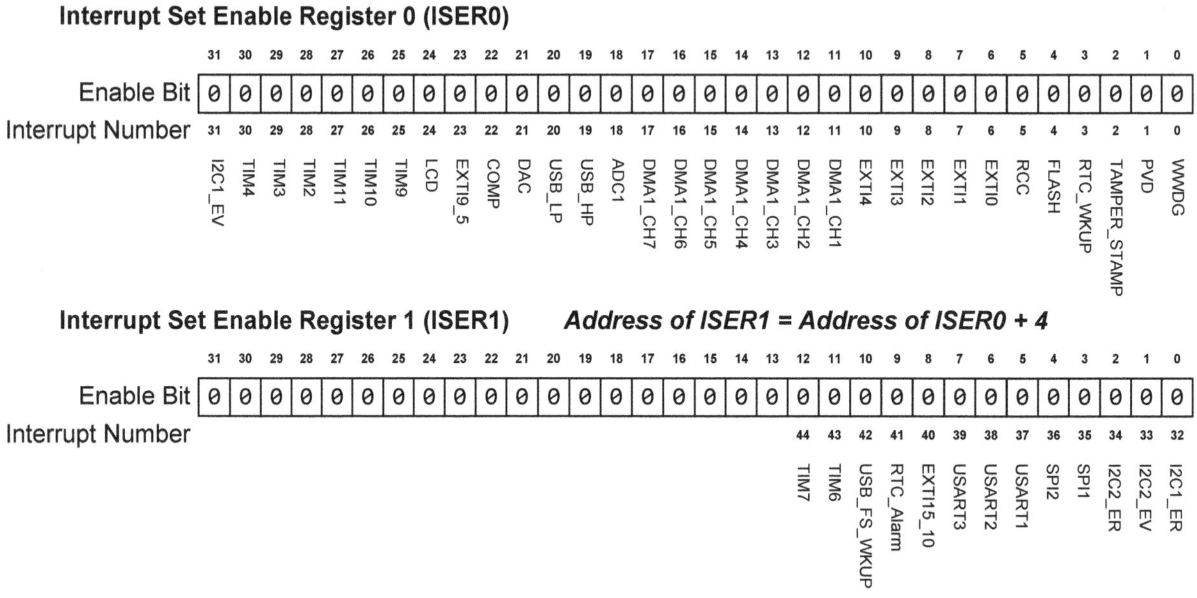

Interrupt Set Enable Register 0 (ISER0)

Bit	31	30	29	28	27	26	25	24	23	22	21	20	19	18	17	16	15	14	13	12	11	10	9	8	7	6	5	4	3	2	1	0
Enable Bit	0	0	0	0	0	0	0	0	0	0	0	0	0	0	0	0	0	0	0	0	0	0	0	0	0	0	0	0	0	0	0	0

Interrupt Number (31 → 0):
31 = I2C1_EV, 30 = TIM4, 29 = TIM3, 28 = TIM2, 27 = TIM11, 26 = TIM10, 25 = TIM9, 24 = LCD, 23 = EXTI9_5, 22 = COMP, 21 = DAC, 20 = USB_LP, 19 = USB_HP, 18 = ADC1, 17 = DMA1_CH7, 16 = DMA1_CH6, 15 = DMA1_CH5, 14 = DMA1_CH4, 13 = DMA1_CH3, 12 = DMA1_CH2, 11 = DMA1_CH1, 10 = EXTI4, 9 = EXTI3, 8 = EXTI2, 7 = EXTI1, 6 = EXTI0, 5 = RCC, 4 = FLASH, 3 = RTC_WKUP, 2 = TAMPER_STAMP, 1 = PVD, 0 = WWDG

Interrupt Set Enable Register 1 (ISER1)   *Address of ISER1 = Address of ISER0 + 4*

Bit	31	30	29	28	27	26	25	24	23	22	21	20	19	18	17	16	15	14	13	12	11	10	9	8	7	6	5	4	3	2	1	0
Enable Bit	0	0	0	0	0	0	0	0	0	0	0	0	0	0	0	0	0	0	0	0	0	0	0	0	0	0	0	0	0	0	0	0

Interrupt Number (44 → 32):
44 = TIM7, 43 = TIM6, 42 = USB_FS_WKUP, 41 = RTC_Alarm, 40 = EXTI15_10, 39 = USART3, 38 = USART2, 37 = USART1, 36 = SPI2, 35 = SPI1, 34 = I2C2_ER, 33 = I2C2_EV, 32 = I2C1_ER

Figure 12-5. Interrupt Set Enable Registers for Peripheral Interrupts in STM32L

Similarly, the following C program can disable the interrupt IRQn.

```c
WordOffset = IRQn >> 5;                        // WordOffset = IRQn/32
BitOffset = IRQn & 0x1F;                       // BitOffset = IRQn mod 32
NVIC->ICER[WordOffset]  =  1 << BitOffset;     // Disable interrupt
```

```
; Input arguments:
;     r0: interrupt number of a peripheral interrupt
;     r1: 1 = Enable, 0 = Disable

Peripheral_Interrupt_Enable    PROC
      PUSH  {r0-r4, lr}
      AND   r2,r0,#0x1F      ; Bit offset in a word
      MOV   r3,#1
      LSL   r3,r3,r2         ; r3 = 1 << (IRQn & 0x1F)
      LDR   r4,=NVIC_BASE
      CMP   r1,#0
      LDRNE r1,=NVIC_ISER0   ; Enable register base address
      LDREQ r1,=NVIC_ICER0   ; Disable register base address
      ADD   r1,r4,r1         ; Address of NVIC->ISER0 or NVIC->ICER0
      LSR   r2,r0,#5         ; Memory offset (in bytes): IRQn >> 5
      STR   r3,[r1,r2]       ; Enable/Disable interrupt
      POP   {r0-r4, pc}
      ENDP
```

Example 12-1. Enable and disable a peripheral interrupt

Example 12-1 shows the assembly implementation of enabling a peripheral interrupt. Note that when calculating the memory address offset of ISER and ICER, we only shift right IRQn by five bits. This is because the register array index is based on words in the above in C code, and in the assembly code, the STR instruction is based on the memory address, which is always in terms of bytes.

$$Memory\ Address\ Offets\ (in\ bytes) = Interrupt\ Number \div 32$$

12.3.2 Interrupt Priority

The order of interrupts to be serviced is determined by priority. Each interrupt has an interrupt priority register (IP), which has a width of 8 bits. Each consists of two fields: the preemption priority number and the sub-priority number. *A lower value of a priority number represents a higher priority or a higher urgency.*

Priority value 0 has the highest urgency.

Usually the peripheral interrupts have a positive interrupt level while a microcontroller core interrupt can have negative priority numbers, not changeable by software. When there are multiple pending interrupts, the interrupt that has the lowest interrupt number will be serviced by the processor.

Preemption is a widely used technique that allows a time-sensitive and urgent computation task to take control of the processor from a relatively less urgent computation task. The preemption priority number defines the priority for preemption. If the processor receives a new interrupt that has a preemption priority number lower than the preemption priority number of the current interrupt in progress, the current interrupt will be stopped and the processor starts to serve the new interrupt. The preempted interrupt will be resumed after the new interrupt handler routine completes.

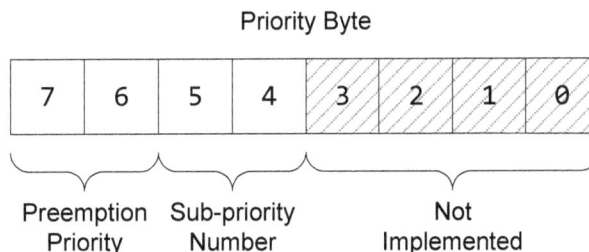

Priority Byte

| 7 | 6 | 5 | 4 | 3 | 2 | 1 | 0 |

Preemption Priority   Sub-priority Number   Not Implemented

Figure 12-6. Interrupt Priority Byte

While Cortex-M3 uses eight bits to store the priority number, STM32L processors only implement four bits. As a result, The STM32L microcontroller only supports 16 interrupt priority levels, ranging from 0 to 15. Priority value 0 has the highest priority (or the highest urgency).

STM32L processors allow five different schemes to split the four-bit priority number. If we uses n bits for the preempt priority number, then the sub-priority number has $4 - n$ bits, where $n = 0, 1, 2, 3,$ or 4. By default, two bits are used for the preempt priority number, and two bits are used for the sub-priority number, as shown in Figure 12-6.

For a system interrupt IRQn, its priority can be set as follows. Note that SHP (System Handler Priority) is defined as a byte array, instead of a word array.

```
// Set the priority of a system interrupt IRQn
SCB->SHP[(IRQn) & 0xF) - 4] = (priority << 4) & 0xFF;
```

SCB is the base memory address of System Control Block (SCB), and SHP is the System Handler Priority register. Cortex-M3 has three SHP registers, as shown in Figure 12-7.

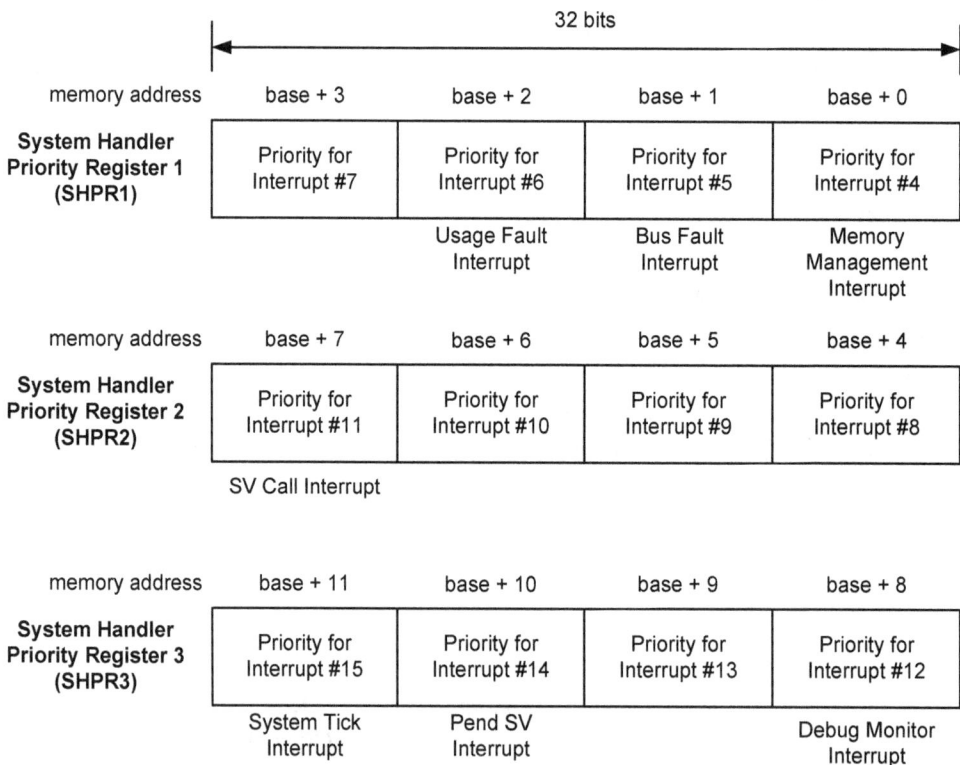

			32 bits	
memory address	base + 3	base + 2	base + 1	base + 0
System Handler Priority Register 1 (SHPR1)	Priority for Interrupt #7	Priority for Interrupt #6	Priority for Interrupt #5	Priority for Interrupt #4
		Usage Fault Interrupt	Bus Fault Interrupt	Memory Management Interrupt

memory address	base + 7	base + 6	base + 5	base + 4
System Handler Priority Register 2 (SHPR2)	Priority for Interrupt #11	Priority for Interrupt #10	Priority for Interrupt #9	Priority for Interrupt #8
SV Call Interrupt				

memory address	base + 11	base + 10	base + 9	base + 8
System Handler Priority Register 3 (SHPR3)	Priority for Interrupt #15	Priority for Interrupt #14	Priority for Interrupt #13	Priority for Interrupt #12
	System Tick Interrupt	Pend SV Interrupt		Debug Monitor Interrupt

Figure 12-7. Priority registers for system interrupts

For a peripheral interrupt IRQn, its priority can be set as follows. Note that the interrupt priority (IP) array is defined as an array of bytes, not words.

```
// Set the priority of a peripheral interrupt IRQn
NVIC->IP[IRQn] = (priority << 4) & 0xFF;
```

Figure 12-8 shows the memory layout of interrupt priority registers for the first 16 peripheral interrupt. For example, the following code changes the priority of EXTI Line 0, whose interrupt number is 6, to the lowest priority.

```
// Set the priority for EXTI 0 (Interrupt number 6)
NVIC->IP[6] = 0xF0;
```

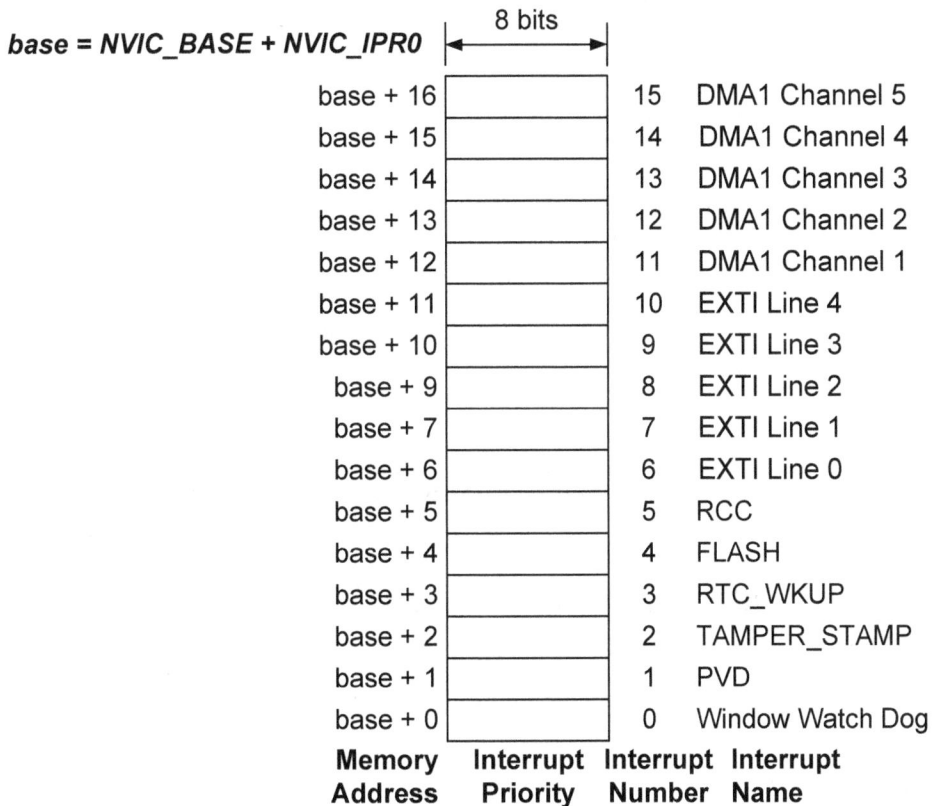

Figure 12-8. Example of interrupt priority (IP) registers for the first 16 peripheral interrupts.

Example 12-2 and Example 12-3 give two example assembly functions that set the priority of a system interrupt and a peripheral interrupt, respectively. Note that both functions use the STRB (store a byte) instruction, instead of the STR (store a word) instruction.

```
; Input arguments:
;     r0: Interrupt Number IRQn
;     r1: Interrupt Priority

Set_System_Interrupt_Priority PROC
        PUSH {r0-r4, lr}
        CMP   r0,#0
        LSL   r2,r1,#4          ; r2 = priority << 4
        LDR   r3,=SCB_BASE      ; System control block base address
        LDR   r4,=SCB_HP_1_12   ; System handlers priority registers
        ADD   r3,r3,r4
        AND   r4,r0,#0x0F
        SUBS  r4,r4,#4
        STRB  r2,[r3,r4]        ; Save priority; Note don't use STR
        POP   {r0-r4, pc}
        ENDP
```

Example 12-2. Setting priority of system interrupts

```
; Input arguments:
;     r0: Interrupt Number IRQn
;     r1: Interrupt Priority

Set_Peripheral_Interrupt_Priority PROC
        PUSH {r0-r4, lr}
        LSLS r2,r1,#4          ; r2 = priority << 4
        LDR   r3,=NVIC_BASE     ; NVIC base address
        LDR   r4,=NVIC_IPR0     ; Interrupt priority register
        ADD   r3,r3,r4
        STRB  r2,[r3,r0]        ; Save priority; Note don't use STR
        POP   {r0-r4, pc}
        ENDP
```

Example 12-3. Setting priority of peripheral interrupts

12.3.3 Global Interrupt Enable and Disable

Except of using NVIC to configure individual interrupts, the Cortex-M3 processors also allow us to enable and disable a group of interrupts by using change processor state (CPS) instructions.

The priority mask register (PRIMASK) is used to enable or disable all interrupts excluding hard faults and non-maskable interrupts (NMI). The fault mask register (FAULTMASK) is used to enable or disable all interrupts excluding non-maskable interrupts (NMI).

When the base priority mask register (BASEPRI) is non-zero, all interrupts with a priority value lower than or equal to BASEPRI are disabled. In this case, we also say that interrupts with a priority value lower than BASEPRI are masked (*i.e.* enabled). Note that a larger priority value represents lower priority.

In the equivalent instructions, the MSR instruction transfers the content of a general-purpose register to a special-purpose register. These special registers cannot be accessed by using the MOV or MOVS instruction.

Instruction	Action	Equivalent Instructions
CPSID i	Disable interrupts and configurable fault handlers	MOVS r0, #0 MSR PRIMASK, r0
CPSID f	Disable interrupts and all fault handlers	MOVS r0, #1 MSR FAULTMASK, r0
CPSIE i	Enable interrupts and configurable fault handlers	MOVS r0, #1 MSR PRIMASK, r0
CPSIE f	Enable interrupts and fault handlers	MOVS r0, #0 MSR FAULTMASK, r0
	Disable interrupts with priority 0x05 – 0xFF	MOVS r0, #5 MSR BASEPRI, r0

Table 12-2. Instructions for enabling or disabling interrupts excluding hard faults and NMI

12.4 System Timer

The system tick timer (SysTick) is a simple 24-bit down counter to produce a small fixed-time quantum, which can generate periodic interrupts or create time delays. The timer counts down from N-1 to 0 and generates a SYSTICK interrupt once the counter reaches zero. The counter loads an automatic reload value and counts down again after reaching zero. The SysTick timer does not stop counting down when the processor is halted. The processor still generates SysTick interrupts during the process of debugging.

The SysTick timer is a useful hardware timer for providing timekeeping functions to real-time operating systems (RTOS) and CPU task schedulers. When there are multiple tasks running concurrently, the processor allocates a time slot to each task according to some CPU scheduling policy, such as round robin, and early deadline first. To achieve that, the processor relies on a hardware timer to generate interrupts at regular time intervals to inform the processor to stop the current task, save the context registers of the current task to the stack, and then select a new task in the job-waiting queue to serve. The SysTick timers are often protected by operation systems and are not modifiable by user applications or tasks.

There are four key registers for configuring system timers:

- SysTick control and status register (CTRL)
- SysTick reload value register (LOAD)
- SysTick current value register (VAL)
- SysTick calibration register (CALIB)

Their basic memory addresses and offsets are listed in the following table. Refer to *"Cortex-M3 Devices Generic User Guide"* for the details.

```
SysTick_BASE  EQU (0xE000E010) ; SysTick base address
SysTick_CTRL  EQU (0xE000E010) ; SysTick control and status register
SysTick_LOAD  EQU (0xE000E014) ; SysTick reload value register
SysTick_VAL   EQU (0xE000E018) ; SysTick current value register
SysTick_CALIB EQU (0xE000E01C) ; SysTick calibration register
```

Table 12-3. Address location of registers for SysTick

SysTick control and status register (SysTick_CTRL)

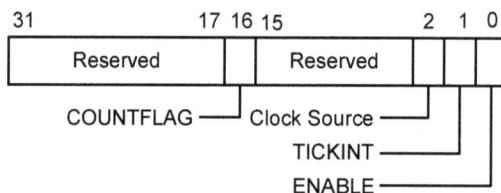

CLKSOURCE indicates the clock source:
   0 = external clock
   1 = processor clock

TICKINT enables SysTick interrupt request:
   0 = counting down to zero does not assert the SysTick interrupt request
   1 = counting down to zero asserts the SysTick interrupt request

ENABLE enables the counter:
   0 = counter disabled
   1 = counter enabled

To enable SysTick interrupt, the program needs to set up three bits: (1) Set the TICKINT bit of SysTick_CTRL to enable SysTick interrupt. (2) Enable SysTick interrupt in the NVIC vector. Note that SysTick interrupt is enabled by default in the NVIC vector. (3) Set the ENABLE bit of SysTick_CTRL to enable the SysTick timer.

The COUNTFLAG is set to 1 once the counter transitions from 1 to 0; therefore, it activates every $n+1$ clock ticks. Reading the COUNTFLAG status bit clears it to 0. For each SysTick interrupt, the user program should check COUNTFLAG to ensure that the SysTick event had occurred.

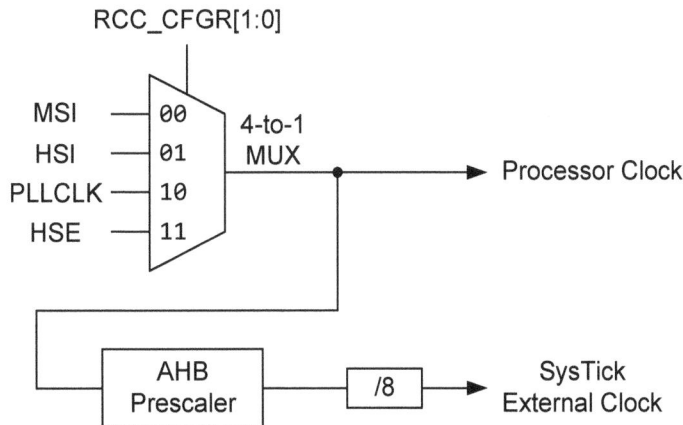

Figure 12-9. Two different clock sources for SysTick on STM32 processor. The default AHB prescaler is 1. The selection of MSI, HSI, PLLCLK, and HSE can be configured by the RCC_CFGR register.

SysTick reload value register (SysTick_LOAD)

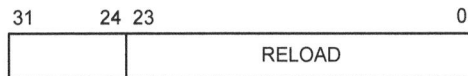

If the SysTick interrupt is required every N clock pulses, set RELOAD to N-1. Software has to write a desired value to this register, depending on the time interval required, before the SysTick is enabled. The SysTick Reload Value register supports 24-bit values ranging between 1 and `0x00FFFFFF`. If a system timer is required to generate an interrupt for each 100 clock cycles, the SysTick reload value register should be set as 99.

SysTick current value register (SysTick_VAL)

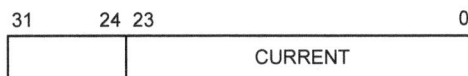

When SysTick is enabled, the current value register is initialized to the value stored in the SysTick reload value register. However, this valued of this register is arbitrary on reset. This register is decremented at each clock pulse.

SysTick calibration register (SysTick_CALIB)

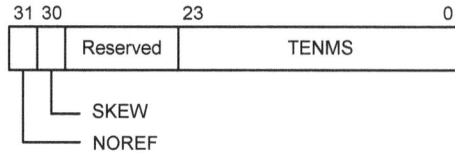

The value in the calibration register (stored in the TENMS field) is the required preload value for generating a time interval of 10ms, *i.e.* a timer of 100Hz.

Example of calculating the system timer interval

Figure 12-10 shows an example of how to calculate the time interval between two consecutive SysTick interrupts. In this example, the SysTick_LOAD register is 6. If the processor clock is 1MHz and it is used to drive the SysTick counter, then the SysTick interrupt period is calculated as follows:

$$SysTick\ Interrupt\ Period = (1 + SysTick_{Load}) \times \frac{1}{SysTick\ Counter\ Clock\ Frequency}$$

$$= (1 + 6) \times \frac{1}{1MHz}$$

$$= 7\mu s$$

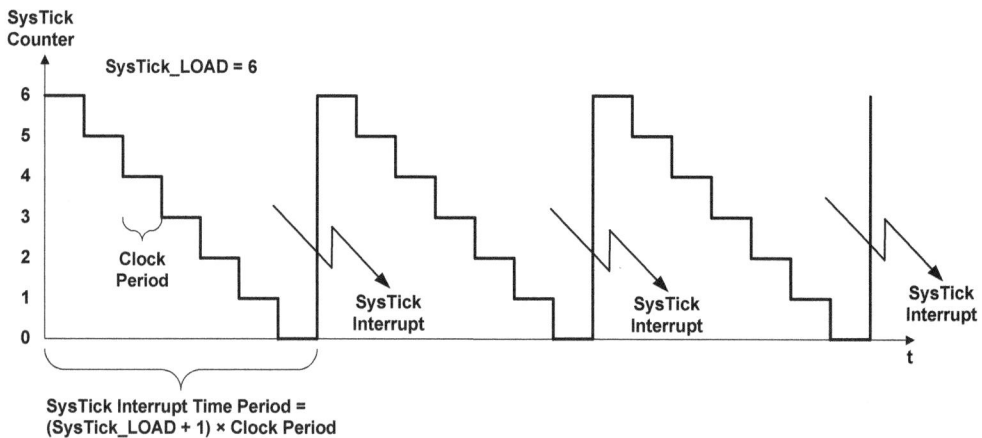

Figure 12-10. Example of SysTick interrupt when SysTick_LOAD is 6.

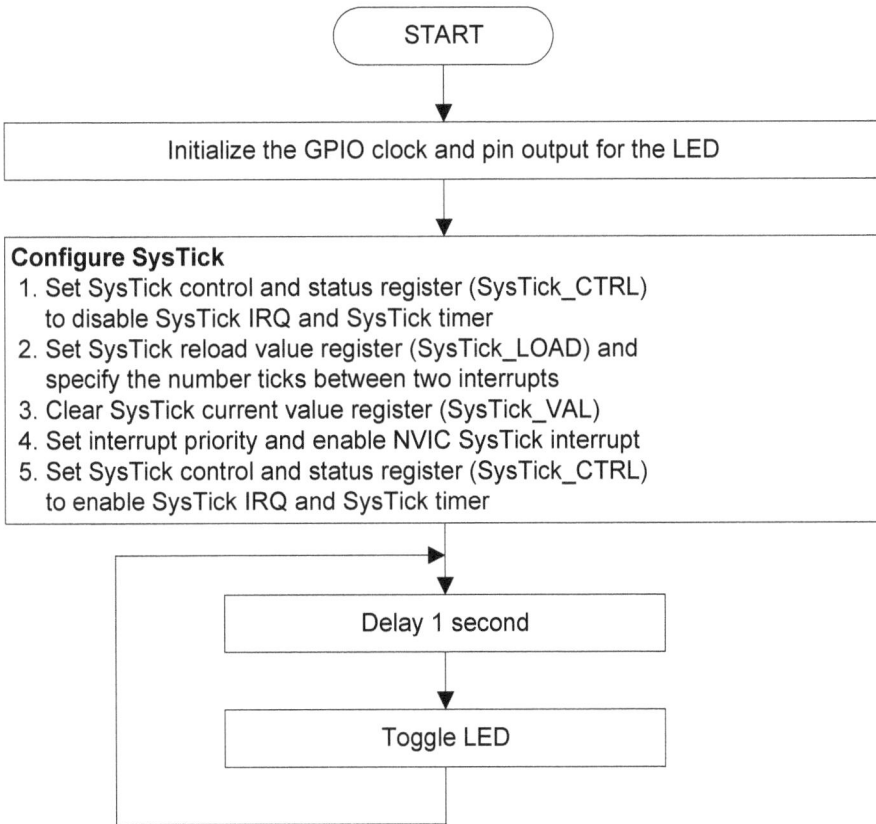

Figure 12-11 Flowchart of the main program to toggle an LED periodically

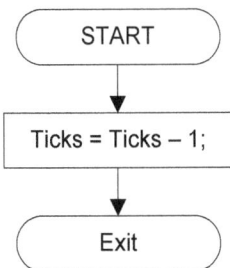

Figure 12-12. Flowchart of SysTick interrupt handler

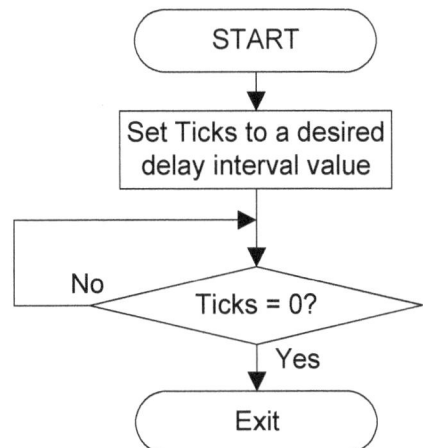

Figure 12-13. Flowchart of delay function

Figure 12-11 shows the flowchart of the SysTick initialization and an endless loop that use the delay function. The SysTick interrupt handler shown in Example 12-5 and the delay function shown in Example 12-6 are executed concurrently.

The interrupt handler decrements the *ticks* variable by one whenever a SysTick interrupt is generated. The delay function constantly checks whether the value of ticks and exits when the ticks variable has been decreased to zero by the SysTick handler. In order to delay one second, the *ticks* variable should be initialized to 1000 if a SysTick interrupt is generated every *1ms*.

The following shows the key data structure and example functions in C language to show how to set up the SysTick timer and perform time delay. The SysTick data structure includes four control registers introduced previously. As shown below, a specific memory address pre-defined by the chip manufacturer is converted to a pointer to the SysTick structure.

```
// Memory mapping structure for SysTick
typedef struct
{
   __IO uint32_t CTRL;      //  SysTick control and status register
   __IO uint32_t LOAD;      //  SysTick reload value register
   __IO uint32_t VAL;       //  SysTick current value register
   __I  uint32_t CALIB;     //  SysTick calibration register
} SysTick_Type;

#define SysTick_BASE          0xE000E010
#define SysTick               ((SysTick_Type *) SysTick_BASE)
```

Table 12-4. Data structure of SysTick

The following *SysTick_Initialize* function sets the SysTick timer to generate interrupts at a fixed-time interval. The input parameter *ticks* equals the time interval divided by the clock period.

```
// Input:  ticks = number of ticks between two interrupts
void SysTick_Initialize (uint32_t ticks) {

   // Disable SysTick IRQ and SysTick counter
   SysTick->CTRL = 0;

   // Set reload register
   SysTick->LOAD  = ticks - 1;

   // Set Priority
   NVIC_SetPriority (SysTick_IRQn, (1<<__NVIC_PRIO_BITS) - 1);

   // Reset the SysTick counter value
   SysTick->VAL   = 0;

   // Select processor clock
   // 1 = processor clock;  0 = external clock
```

```
    SysTick->CTRL |= SysTick_CTRL_CLKSOURCE;

    // Enable SysTick IRQ and SysTick timer
    SysTick->CTRL |=  SysTick_CTRL_ENABLE;

    // Enables SysTick exception request
    // 1 = counting down to zero asserts the SysTick exception request
    // 0 = counting down to zero does not assert the SysTick exception request
    SysTick->CTRL |= SysTick_CTRL_TICKINT;
}
```
Example 12-4. Generating an interrupt periodically with a fixed-time interval in C

The system timer interrupt service routine decrements the *TimingDelay* variable, as shown below.

```
void SysTick_Handler (void) { // SysTick interrupt service routine

    if (TimingDelay != 0) // prevent it from being negative
        TimingDelay--;

}
```
Example 12-5. SysTick Interrupt Handler in C

The Delay function initializes the *TimingDelay* variable and waits until *TimingDelay* is decremented to zero by SysTick_Handler.

```
void Delay(uint32_t nTime) {
  // nTime: specifies the delay time length
  TimingDelay = nTime;
  while(TimingDelay != 0);    // Busy wait
}
```
Example 12-6. Delay function in C

The following shows the complete codes in assembly to initialize the system timer.

```
SysTick_Initialization PROC

    ; Set SysTick_CTR to disable SysTick IRQ and SysTick timer
    LDR    r1,=SysTick_BASE

    LDR    r2,[r1,#SysTick_CTRL]
    BIC    r2,r2,#1                 ; Clear ENABLE
    STR    r2,[r1,#SysTick_CTRL]

    LDR    r2,[r1,#SysTick_CTRL]
    BIC    r2,r2,#0x01<<1           ; Disable SysTick interrupt
    STR    r2,[r1,#SysTick_CTRL]

    // Select clock source
```

```
        LDR    r2,[r1,#SysTick_CTRL]
        BIC    r2,r2,#0x01<<2              ; Select external clock
        STR    r2,[r1,#SysTick_CTRL]

        ; Set SysTick_LOAD and specify the number of clock cycles
        ; between two interrupts
        LDR    r3,=262
        STR    r3,[r1,#SysTick_LOAD]

        ; Clear SysTick current value register (SysTick_VAL)
        MOV    r2,#0
        STR    r2,[r1,#SysTick_VAL]

        ; Set interrupt priority and enable NVIC SysTick interrupt
        LDR    r3,=NVIC_BASE
        LDR    r4,[r3,#NVIC_ISER0]
        BIC    r4,r4,#(0x03<<0x0F)
        ORR    r4,r4,#(0x01<<0x0F)
        STR    r4,[r3,#NVIC_ISER0]

        LDR    r4,[r3,#NVIC_IPR0]
        BIC    r4,r4,#0xFF
        STR    r4,[r3,#NVIC_IPR0]

        ; Set SysTick_CTRL to enable SysTick timer and SysTick interrupt
        LDR    r2,[r1,#SysTick_CTRL]
        ORR    r2,r2,#1                        ; Enable SysTick counter
        STR    r2,[r1,#SysTick_CTRL]

        LDR    r2,[r1,#SysTick_CTRL]
        ORR    r2,r2,#1<<1                     ; Enable SysTick interrupt
        STR    r2,[r1,#SysTick_CTRL]

        BX     lr
```

Example 12-7. Setting SysTick timer in assembly

The *SysTick_Handler()* in assembly is implemented as follows. It decreases the TimingDelay variable (saved in register r10) by one each time a SysTick interrupt is generated, *i.e.* the SysTick counter counts down to zero.

```
SysTick_Handler    PROC
        EXPORT SysTick_Handler
        ; Auto-stacking eight registers r0 - r3, r12, LR, PSR, and PC
        SUB  r10, r10, #1       ; Decrement TimingDelay
        BX  lr                  ; Exit and trigger auto-unstacking
        ENDP
```

Example 12-8. SysTick interrupt handler in assembly

The *delay* function given in Example 12-9. Register r0 is the input argument and represents the amount of delay in time units set by the SysTick_Handler. The function deploys a busy-waiting loop which exits only when the TimingDelay variable has been decreased to zero by the SysTick interrupt handler *SysTick_Handler*().

```
delay PROC
      ; r0 is the TimingDelay input
      MOV  r10, r0        ; Make a copy of TimingDelay
loop  CMP  r10, #0        ; Wait for TimingDelay = 0
      BNE  loop           ; r10 is decreased periodically by SysTick_Handler
      BX   lr             ; Exit
      ENDP
```

Example 12-9. Delay subroutine in assembly

12.5 External Interrupt

The GPIO pins with the same pin number in all GPIO ports map to the same external interrupt as shown in Figure 12-14. For example, GPIO pin PA 0 can be mapped to EXTI 0, PA 1 to EXTI 1, PA 2 to EXTI 2, and so on. In addition, only one external interrupt on the same GPIO pin number out of all GPIO ports. For example, if the pin PA 3 has an external interrupt on it, then the pins PB 3, PC 3, PD 3, and PE 3 cannot be used for external interrupts.

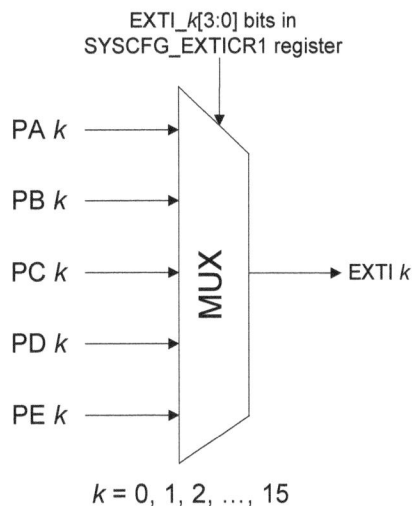

Figure 12-14. Mapping between external interrupt (EXTI) and GPIO pins

To configure the hardware interrupt for EXTI input line *k*, the general procedure is as follows:

1. Enable the clock of SYSCFG and the clock of corresponding GPIO port.
2. Configure the GPIO pin k as input.
3. Configure the SYSCFG external interrupt configuration register (EXTI_CR) to map the GPIO pin k to the external interrupt input line k.
4. Select a signal change that will trigger EXTI k. The trigger signal can be a rising edge, a falling edge, or both. This is configured by the EXTI rising edge trigger selection register (EXTI_RTSR) and the EXTI falling edge trigger selection register (EXTI_FTSR).
5. Set the kth bit in EXTI interrupt mask register (EXTI_IMR) and EXTI event mask register (EXTI_EMR) to enable the EXTI interrupt and the EXTI event for input line k, respectively.
6. Configure the enable and mask bit that controls the NVIC interrupt channel mapping to EXTI k.
7. Write the interrupt handler for EXTI k. The EXTI pending register (EXTI_PR) records the source of the interrupt. The function name of the interrupt handler is given by the startup assembly file. For example, the handler for EXTI 0 is called *EXTI0_IRQHandler()*.
8. In the interrupt handler, the corresponding pending bit needs to be cleared by software to avoid mistakenly reentering the interrupt service routine. Surprisingly, writing it to 1 is to clear a pending bit.

The following shows an example program that uses the external hardware interrupt to light up the LED when the user push button is pushed.

Example 12-10 shows the initialization for connecting the EXTI line 0 to the pin 0 of GPIO port A.

```
// Enable SYSCFG clock
RCC->APB2ENR |= RCC_APB2ENR_SYSCFGEN;

// EXTIx: PA[x] = 0000, PB[x] = 0001, PC[x] = 0010, PD[x] = 0011
SYSCFG->EXTICR[0]  &= ~(0x000F);    // Select PA.0 for EXTI line 0

// Select trigger edge for EXTI 0
// 0: Rising edge trigger disabled; 1: Rising edge trigger enabled
EXTI->RTSR |= EXTI_RTSR_TR0;       // Set interrupt trigger to rising edge

// Enable EXTI 0 interrupt
// Interrupt mask register: 0 - masked; 1 - not masked
// "Masked" means that it is ignored by the system.
EXTI->IMR  |= EXTI_IMR_MR0;        // Enable EXTI line 0

// Enable and set EXTI line 0 interrupt to the lowest priority
NVIC_SetPriority(EXTI0_IRQn, 1);   // Set EXTI0 priority to 1
```

```
NVIC_EnableIRQ(EXTI0_IRQn);              // Enable EXTI0 interrupt
```

Example 12-10. Initialize EXTI line 0 to pin A.9 in C

Example 12-11 shows the code of the external interrupt handler for line 0, which toggles an LED when PA.0 generates an external interrupt.

```
void EXTI0_IRQHandler(void) {
  if (EXTI->PR & (1<<0)) {              // Check for EXTI0 interrupt flag
    GPIOB->ODR ^= 1<<6;                 // Toggle the LED (PB.6)
    EXTI->PR   |= (1<<0);               // Clear EXTI0 pending interrupt
  }
}
```

Example 12-11. External interrupt handler for EXTI 0 in C

Note that some EXTI lines are connected for other peripherals. For example, on the STM32L microcontrollers, the following EXTI input lines are to support the event detection of other peripherals. Therefore, when the interrupts of these peripherals are used, make sure to enable the corresponding EXTI interrupt.

EXTI Line Number	Peripherals
16	PVD output
17	RTC alarm event
18	USB device FS wakeup event
19	RTC tamper and time stamp events
20	RTC wakeup event
21	Comparator 1 wakeup event
22	Comparator 2 wakeup event
23	Comparator channel acquisition interrupt

Table 12-5. Definition of external interrupt number

12.6 Software Interrupt

Interrupt signals can be generated by hardware, such as hardware timers and peripheral hardware devices. Interrupt signals can also be generated by software by setting the interrupt pending registers or by using special instructions.

There are two major usages of software interrupts: exception handling and privilege hardware access.

Exception Handling

When exceptional conditions occur during execution, such as division by zero, illegal opcode, and invalid memory access, the processors have to handle these abnormal situations to potentially correct software errors. Two software faults, including division by error and unaligned memory access, can be captured if these fault captures are enabled. A software interrupt invoked by software faults are often called a trap.

The following program gives an example of enabling the trap of dividing by zero.

```
    LDR   r2,=SCB_Base       ; Base address of system control block (SCB)
    LDR   r3,[r2,#SCB_CCR]   ; Configuration and Control Register
    ORR   r3,r3,#0x10        ; Enable trap on dividing by 0
    STR   r3,[r2,#SCB_CCR]

    MOV   r0,#0
    MOV   r1,#1
    UDIV  r1,r1,r0           ; Invoke hard fault
```

Example 12-12. A trap that handles abnormal situations

After the division-by-zero trap is enabled, the above division instruction (UDIV) generates a trap, halts the processor, and invokes the hard fault handler shown below. The fault handler may print out the error message or simply reboot the processor.

```
HardFault_Handler PROC
    EXPORT HardFault_Handler

    ; Handle the error of division by 0
    ; For example, force the processor to reboot
    BL NVIC_SystemReset     ; Reboot the system using AIRCR register

    ENDP
```

Example 12-13. Hard fault interrupt handler

Privilege Hardware Access

When a user application runs in unprivileged mode and needs to access a hardware resource that is only accessible in privileged mode, a special instruction (supervisor call) generates a software interrupt and makes the processor switch from the unprivileged mode to the privilege mode. A detailed introduction of the supervisor call (SVC) is introduced in Chapter 23.2.

12.7 Exercises

1. Compare two methods of responding external events: polling and interrupts. Discuss the advantage and disadvantage of each approach.

2. Give two example instructions that make an interrupt service routine exit.

3. The MSI (multi-speed internal) oscillator clock is used as system clock source after startup from Reset, wake-up from Stop or Standby low power modes. The MSI clock has seven optional frequency ranges available: 65.536 kHz, 131.072 kHz, 262.144 kHz, 524.288 kHz, 1.048 MHz, 2.097 MHz (default value) and 4.194 MHz. Write an assembly program that selects MSI 4.094 MHz as the system clock.

4. If the MSI 4.094 MHz clock is used as the system clock and the SysTick selects it as the clock, what should the SysTick_LOAD register be in order to generate a SysTick interrupt every microsecond? What is the SysTick_LOAD value in order to generate a SysTick interrupt every millisecond?

5. Suppose the default MSI (2.097 MHz) is used to drive the system timer (SysTick). Can you use this MSI to generate a SysTick interrupt every minute? If yes, show how do you set up the system timer registers. If not, give a solution to solve this problem.

6. Is it possible to use the SysTick Timer to generate an interrupt once every 12 seconds if there is only a clock of 2.097 MHz? If not, name two ways that you can solve this problem. If yes, how to set up the timer registers?

7. Suppose register i (i ≤ 12) is initialized to have a value of i (e.g. r0 = 0, r1= 1, r2 = 2, r3 = 3, etc.). Assume the main stack (MSP) is used. In addition, in the interrupt handler, if LR = 0xFFFFFFF9, then the main stack (MSP) is used. If LR = 0xFFFFFFFD, then the process stack (PSP) is used. The program status register (PSR) = 0x00000020, PC = 0x08000020, and LR = 0x20008020, when the interrupt occurs.

    a. Show the stack content immediately before the PUSH instruction is executed. Suppose the stack pointer SP, *i.e.* MSP in this case, was 0x20000600 immediately before the system timer interrupt occurs.

```
SysTick_Handler PROC
        PUSH        {r4,r5,r6}
        ADD         r0, r0, #1
        ADD         r1, r1, #1
        ADD         r2, r2, #1
        ADD         r3, r3, #1
        ADD         r4, r4, #1
        ADD         r5, r5, #1
        ADD         r6, r6, #1
        ADD         r7, r7, #1
        ADD         r8, r8, #1
        ADD         r9, r9, #1
        ADD         r10, r10, #1
        ADD         r11, r11, #1
        ADD         r12, r12, #1
        POP         {r4,r5,r6}
        BX LR
        ENDP
```

b. What are the values of these registers (R0-R12, LR, SP, and PC) immediately after the interrupt exits?

8. Suppose the SysTick interrupt occurs when PC = 0x08000044, XPSR = 0x00000020, SP = 0x20000200, LR = 0x08001000, and register $R_i = i$, $i = 0, 1, 2, \ldots,$ 12.

Memory Address	Instruction
	__main PROC
	...
0x08000044	MOV r3,#0
	...
	ENDP
	SysTick_Handler PROC
	EXPORT SysTick_Handler
0x0800001C	ADD r3, #1
0x0800001E	ADD r4, #1
0x08000020	BX lr
	ENDP

a. Show the stack content and the value of PC and SP when immediately entering the SysTick interrupt service routine.

b. When executing the instruction "BX LR", how does the processor know whether it is exiting a standard subroutine or an interrupt service routine? What operations are performed when exiting a standard subroutine? What operations are performed when exiting an interrupt service routine?

CHAPTER

13

Instruction Encoding and Decoding

Several different instruction sets exist. The legacy ARM instruction set includes 32-bit instructions. All instructions in the Thumb instruction set have only 16 bits. The Thumb-2 consists of all 16-bit Thumb instructions as well as many 32-bit instructions, as shown in Figure 13-1. The Cortex-M family has a series of processors that are backwards compatible. The Cortex-M3 series extends Cortex-M0 series by adding more instructions for advanced data processing and bit field manipulations. The Cortex-M4 extends the Cortex-M3 by adding digital signal processing and floating-point arithmetic instructions. This book focuses primarily on Cortex-M3.

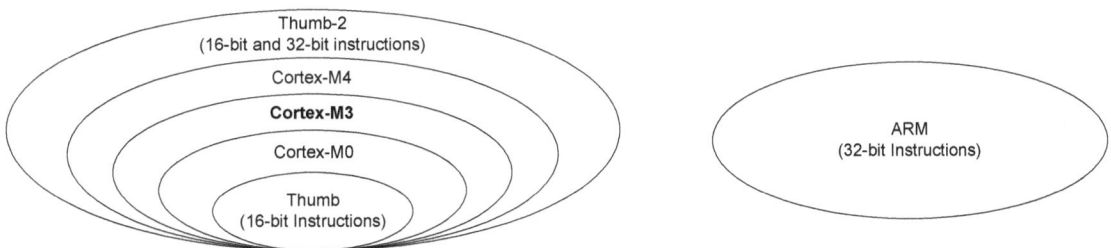

Figure 13-1. Comparison of Thumb, Thumb-2 and ARM instruction sets

13.1 Tradeoff between Code Density and Performance

These instruction sets play different tradeoff between code density and performance, as shown in Figure 13-2. Code density measures the size of a binary executable program. A high code density means that the binary program has a less number of bytes. A high code density is often preferred in embedded systems because less memory is required, thereby directly reducing cost and power consumption.

The 16-bit Thumb instructions decrease the size of program code and accordingly reduce the memory capacity requirement. The 32-bit legacy ARM instructions increase the flexibility of encoding, such as directly encoding large immediate numbers and including more operands, thus improving the performance. The Thumb-2 instruction set, consisting of a mix of 16-bit and 32-bit instructions, provides a good tradeoff between the code size and performance. Accordingly, the performance and code size ratio of Thumb-2 is the highest.

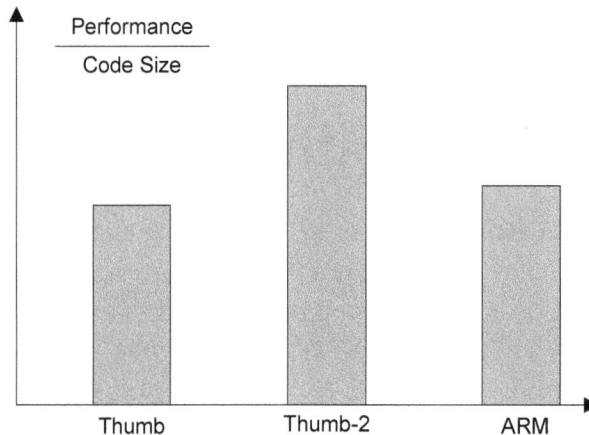

Figure 13-2. Thumb-2 plays a good tradeoff between the code density and performance.

13.2 Dividing Bit Streams into 16- or 32-bit Instructions

The processor fetches a 16-bit half-word (two bytes) from the instruction memory addressed by the program counter.

- If the most significant five bits are 11101, 11110, or 11111, then this half-word is the least significant two bytes of a 32-bit instruction and accordingly the processor continues to fetch the next two bytes, forming a 32-bit instruction. In this case, PC is incremented by 4 automatically, pointing to the next instruction;
- Otherwise, this half-word is a 16-bit instruction and accordingly PC is incremented by 2.

"Looking at a program written in machine language is vaguely comparable to looking at a DNA molecule atom by atom."

Douglas Hofstadter, cognitive scientist

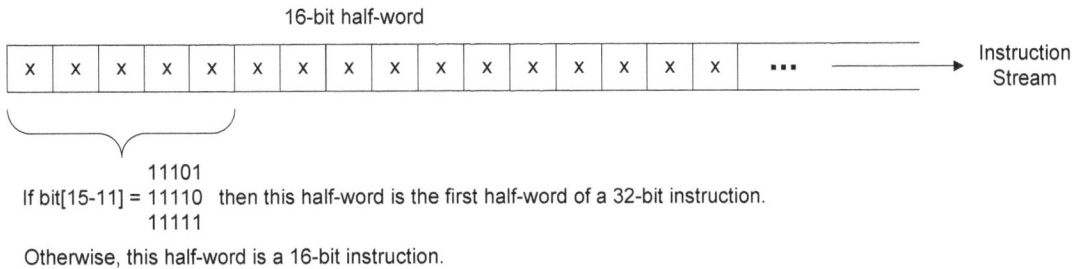

16-bit half-word

11101
If bit[15-11] = 11110   then this half-word is the first half-word of a 32-bit instruction.
11111

Otherwise, this half-word is a 16-bit instruction.

Figure 13-3. Identification of 16-bit and 32-bit Thumb instructions

Each machine instruction consists of a binary operation code (opcode) and zero or more operands.

- The opcode specifies the operation to be carried out. The total number of bits in an opcode varies, depending on specific instructions. An opcode sometimes is divided into two bit-fields: a major opcode that specifies the major category of this instruction, and a minor opcode that identifies a specific option to be performed.
- If the operand is a register, generally four bits are required to represent a register since there are 16 registers. Most 16-bit instructions can only access the lower registers (r0 – r7), because only three bits are used to address a register operand in a 16-bit instruction.
- If the operand is an immediate number, 16-bit instructions usually limit it to 5 or 8 bits, and 32-bit instructions limit it to 8, 16, or 24 bits. Some 32-bit immediate numbers with special bit patterns can be directly encoded in the 32-bit instructions.

The encoding of immediate number is complex in ARM. Let us look at 12-bit immediate number. ARM uses a combination of a 4-bit rotation and an 8-bit immediate number to decode a 12-bit immediate number stored in the instruction. It is impossible to use the 4-bit rotation to place the 8-bit immediate number to all 32 possible positions in a word. The tradeoff is that the 8-bit immediate number can only be rotated to even positions, i.e., the rotation amount is multiplied by two. For example, if the 8-bit immediate number is 0b11001100, and the 4-bit rotation amount is 0b1001, the 32-bit immediate encoded is obtained as follows:

```
0b11001100 ROR 2 x 0b1001 = 0b00110011,00000000,00000000,00000000.
```

Note that not all immediate numbers can be directly encoded in an instruction.

13.3 Encoding 16-bit Thumb Instructions

The following table lists the major opcode of 16-bit thumb instructions. A detailed list of all 16-bit instructions is given in Appendix A.

15	14	13	12	11	10	9	8	7	6	5	4	3	2	1	0	
0	0	minor opcode														Shift, add, subtract, move, & compare
0	1	0	0	0	0	minor opcode		Rm/Rn			Rd/Rn					Data processing
0	1	0	0	0	1	minor opcode		Rm			Rd/Rn					Special data instructions & branch
0	1	0	0	1	x	minor opcode										Load from Literal Pool
0	1	0	1	x	x											Load/store single data item
0	1	1	x	x	x											Load/store single data item
1	0	0	x	x	x											Load/store single data item
1	0	1	0	0	Rd			imm8								Generate PC-relative address
1	0	1	0	1	Rd			imm8								Generate SP-relative address
1	0	1	1	minor opcode												Miscellaneous 16-bit instructions
1	1	0	0	0	Rd			register list								Store multiple registers
1	1	0	0	1	Rd			register list								Load multiple registers
1	1	0	1	minor opcode		offset-8										Conditional branch, & supervisor call
1	1	1	0	0	offset-11											Unconditional branch

The minor opcode of data processing instructions in which the destination operand is also one of the source operands has four bits, *i.e.* bits[9-6], as listed below.

	Bits [7-6]			
Bit[9-8]	00	01	10	11
00	AND	EOR	LSL	LSR
01	ASR	ADC	SBC	ROR
10	TST	RSB	CMP	CMN
11	ORR	MUL	BIC	MVN

For example, the minor opcode for the bitwise logic OR instruction is 1100 in binary, and thus the instruction of "ORR r1, r0" is encoded 0x4301, shown as follows. Note that register r0 is both the source operand and destination operand.

15	14	13	12	11	10	9	8	7	6	5	4	3	2	1	0	
0	1	0	0	0	0	1	1	0	0	0	0	0	0	0	1	ORR r1, r0
		major opcode				minor opcode				Rn			Rd			

When there are three different register operands, a 32-bit instruction may have to be used. For example, "ORR r2, r1, r0" cannot be encoded by a 16-bit instruction.

13.4 Encoding 32-bit Instructions

The decoding scheme of 32-bit instructions is summarized in the table on the next page. For example, the major opcode of data processing instructions with registers as operands is `1110101`. The minor opcode and the bit fields are defined in the following table. The format of 32-bit instructions is given in Appendix B.

31 - 25	24 - 21	20	19 - 16	15	14-12	11 - 8	7	6	5	4	3 - 0	
major opcode	minor opcode	S	Rn	0	imm3	Rd	imm2				Rm	
1110101	0000	S	Rn	0	imm3	Rd	imm2		type		Rm	AND
1110101	0000	1	Rn	0	imm3	1111	imm2		type		Rm	TST
1110101	0001	S	Rn	0	imm3	Rd	imm2		type		Rm	BIC
1110101	0010	S	Rn	0	imm3	Rd	imm2		type		Rm	ORR
1110101	0011	S	Rn	0	imm3	Rd	imm2		type		Rm	ORN
1110101	0011	S	1111	0	imm3	Rd	imm2		type		Rm	MVN
1110101	0100	S	Rn	0	imm3	Rd	imm2		type		Rm	EOR
1110101	0110	S	Rn	0	imm3	Rd	imm2	tb	T		Rm	PKHBT, PKHTB
1110101	1000	S	Rn	0	imm3	Rd	imm2		type		Rm	ADD
1110101	1000	1	Rn	0	imm3	1111	imm2		type		Rm	CMN
1110101	1010	S	Rn	0	imm3	Rd	imm2		type		Rm	ADC
1110101	1011	S	Rn	0	imm3	Rd	imm2		type		Rm	SBC

Table 13-1. Major and minor opcode of commonly used 32-bit instructions

Example: Encoding "ORRS r3, r1, r0, LSL #2" into binary format

According to Table 13-1, we find that the minor opcode is `0010`. According to the instruction format presented in Appendix B, the 32-bit ORR instruction, that has three register operands, has a format presented in Table 13-2. In addition, the S bit is set to 1 to update the NZCV flags since the instruction has the "S" suffix. The shift type is 00, representing logic shift left (LSL). The five-bit shift amount (imm3:imm2) is `00010`.

31 - 25	24 - 21	20	19 - 16	15	14 - 12	11 - 8	7 6	5 4	3 - 0
major opcode	minor opcode	S	Rn	0	imm3	Rd	imm2	type	Rm
1110101	0010	1	0001	0	000	0011	10	00	0000

Table 13-2. Instruction format of the 32-bit ORR instruction with three registers

Therefore, the binary encoding of "ORRS r3,r1,r0,LSL #2" is
`1110,1010,0101,0001,0000,0011,1000,0000`, which is `0xEA510380` in hex.

13.5 Calculating Target Memory Address

PC-relative addresses are used for branch and load/store instructions for two important reasons. First, PC-relative addressing helps to achieve position-independent code, which allows the instructions to be placed in different memory regions. Second, PC-relative addressing helps to store in instruction memory complicated immediate numbers, which cannot be directly encoded in an instruction.

In PC-relative addressing, the target memory address is calculated as following.

$$\text{target address} = PC + 4 + \text{offset}$$

where PC is the memory address of the current branch or load/store instruction. Note that Thumb instructions are always half-word aligned and thus the least significant bit of the PC is always 0.

Example: Decoding 0100101000000110

The above 16-bit instruction is decoded as "LDR Rt, [pc, #imm8<<2]", where #imm8 is 6 (00000110 in binary), according to 16-bit instruction format given in Appendix A. The offset is equal to #imm8 << 2, *i.e.* 24. Therefore, we can decode it as "LDR r2, [pc, #24]". If the memory address of this instruction is 0x080001CC, then the above instruction will load a word stored at the following target memory address:

$$\text{target address} = PC + 4 + \text{Offset} = 0x080001CC + 4 + 24 = 0x80001E8$$

Example: Decoding 1101101111110111

This 16-bit branch instruction is decoded as "B(cond) #imm8<<1", where the conditional code is 1011, representing "Less Than (LT)" (see Table 13-4), and #imm8 is 11110111. The offset is equal to 1111011<<1 = 111110110, representing -18 in two's complement. Suppose the memory address of this branch instruction is 0x080001E2, then this branch instruction will jump to the instruction stored at the following target address if the comparison result is "Less Than".

$$\text{target address} = PC + 4 + \text{Offset} = 0x080001E2 + 4 + (-18) = 0x080001D4$$

If we put a label, such as "loop", on the instruction stored at 0x080001D4, then we can translate this binary instruction to "BLT loop".

Encoding of 32-bit Thumb2 Instructions

31	30	29	28	27	26	25	24	23	22	21	20	19	18	17	16	15	14	13	12	11	10	9	8	7	6	5	4	3	2	1	0	
1	1	1	0	1	0	0	op		0	W	L	Rn				Register list																Load/store multiple
1	1	1	0	1	0	0	op1		1	op2		Rn				x																Load/store dual or exclusive, table branch
1	1	1	0	1	0	1	op				S	Rn				x	imm3			Rd				imm2		op3		Rm				Data processing (shifted register)
1	1	1	0	1	1	1	op1					Rn				x				coproc						op						Coprocessor instructions
1	1	1	1	0	x	0	op					Rn				0	imm3			Rd				imm8								Data processing (modified immediate)
1	1	1	1	0	x	1	op					Rn				0	imm3			Rd				imm8								Data processing (plain binary immediate)
1	1	1	1	0			op									1	op1															Branches and miscellaneous control
1	1	1	1	1	0	0	0	op1			0	Rn				x				op2												Store single data item
1	1	1	1	1	0	0	op1		0	0	1	Rn				Rt				op2												Load byte, memory hints
1	1	1	1	1	0	0	op1		0	1	1	Rn				Rt				op2												Load halfword, memory hints
1	1	1	1	1	0	0			1	0	1	Rn				x				op2												Load world
1	1	1	1	1	0	0	x	x	1	1	1					x	1	1	1	1												Undefined
1	1	1	1	1	0	1	0	op1				Rn				1	1	1	1					op2				Rm				Data processing (register)
1	1	1	1	1	0	1	1	0	op1			Rn				Ra								0	0	op2		Rm				Multiply, multiply accumulate, and absolute difference
1	1	1	1	1	0	1	1	1	op1			Rn												op2				Rm				Long multiply, long multiply accumulate, divide
1	1	1	1	1	1	1	op1					Rn				x				coproc						op						Coprocessor instructions

13.6 Instruction Decoding Example 1

We will show how to decode the following hex numbers into assembly instructions.

F04F, 0003, F04F, 0104, F04F, 0300, 2900
D003, 4403, F1A1, 0101, E7F9, 4618, E7FE

The first step is to divide all bits into instructions. If the most significant five bits of a half-word are 11101, 11110, or 11111, then this half-word starts a 32-bit instruction.

	15	14	13	12	11	10	9	8	7	6	5	4	3	2	1	0	16 or 32
0xF04F	1	1	1	1	0	0	0	0	0	1	0	0	1	1	1	1	32-bit
0x0003	0	0	0	0	0	0	0	0	0	0	0	0	0	0	1	1	instruction
0xF04F	1	1	1	1	0	0	0	0	0	1	0	0	1	1	1	1	32-bit
0x0104	0	0	0	0	0	0	0	1	0	0	0	0	0	1	0	0	instruction
0xF04F	1	1	1	1	0	0	0	0	0	1	0	0	1	1	1	1	32-bit
0x0300	0	0	0	0	0	0	1	1	0	0	0	0	0	0	0	0	instruction
0x2900	0	0	1	0	1	0	0	1	0	0	0	0	0	0	0	0	16-bit
0xD003	1	1	0	1	0	0	0	0	0	0	0	0	0	0	1	1	16-bit
0x4403	0	1	0	0	0	1	0	0	0	0	0	0	0	0	1	1	16-bit
0xF1A1	1	1	1	1	0	0	0	1	1	0	1	0	0	0	0	1	32-bit
0x0101	0	0	0	0	0	0	0	1	0	0	0	0	0	0	0	1	instruction
0xE7F9	1	1	1	0	0	1	1	1	1	1	1	1	1	0	0	1	16-bit
0x4618	0	1	0	0	0	1	1	0	0	0	0	1	1	0	0	0	16-bit
0xE7FE	1	1	1	0	0	1	1	1	1	1	1	1	1	1	1	0	16-bit

Table 13-3. Binary representation of the instructions

Decoding: 0xF04F, 0x0003 ⟹ MOV r0, #3

The most significant five bits of the first half-word is 11110, indicating this half-word and the next half-word form a 32-bit instruction. By looking up the opcode from the 32-bit decoding table (Appendix B), we know that this is an MOV instruction. According to the format of MOV instruction, we know that the destination register is 0000, i.e. r0, and the 11-bit immediate number is 00000000011, i.e. 3. In addition, the S suffix is 0, thus it is MOV, instead of MOVS. Therefore, this instruction is decoded as "MOV r0, #3".

	15	14	13	12	11	10	9	8	7	6	5	4	3	2	1	0
	1	1	1	op1		i	op2				S					
0xF04F	1	1	1	1	0	0	0	0	0	1	0	0	1	1	1	1

	15	14	13	12	11	10	9	8	7	6	5	4	3	2	1	0
	op	imm3			Rd				imm8							
0x0003	0	0	0	0	0	0	0	0	0	0	0	0	0	0	1	1

Decoding: 0xF04F, 0x0104 ⟹ MOV r1, #4

Similar to the previous instruction, we can decode this as "MOV r1, #4".

	15	14	13	12	11	10	9	8	7	6	5	4	3	2	1	0
	1	1	1	op1		i			op2			S				
0xF04F	1	1	1	1	0	0	0	0	0	1	0	0	1	1	1	1

	15	14	13	12	11	10	9	8	7	6	5	4	3	2	1	0
	op	imm3			Rd				imm8							
0x0104	0	0	0	0	0	0	0	1	0	0	0	0	0	1	0	0

Decoding: 0xF04F, 0x0300 ⟹ MOV r3, #0

Similar to the first instruction, we can decode this as "MOV r3, #0".

	15	14	13	12	11	10	9	8	7	6	5	4	3	2	1	0
	1	1	1	op1		i			op2			S				
0xF04F	1	1	1	1	0	0	0	0	0	1	0	0	1	1	1	1

	15	14	13	12	11	10	9	8	7	6	5	4	3	2	1	0
	op	imm3			Rd				imm8							
0x0300	0	0	0	0	0	0	1	1	0	0	0	0	0	0	0	0

Decoding: 0x2900 ⟹ CMP r1, #0

The most significant five bits is not 11101, 11110, nor 11111. Thus, it is a 16-bit instruction. The opcode is 001010, specifying it is a CMP instruction that compares a register with an 8-bit immediate number. The source operands are register r1 and an immediate number 0. Therefore, this instruction is decoded as "CMP r1, #0".

	15	14	13	12	11	10	9	8	7	6	5	4	3	2	1	0
	opcode						Rn			imm8						
0x2900	0	0	1	0	1	0	0	0	1	0	0	0	0	0	0	0

Decoding: 0xD003 ⟹ BEQ exit

Again, this is a 16-bit instruction. The condition code is listed as 0000, which represents EQ, according to Table 13-4.

	15	14	13	12	11	10	9	8	7	6	5	4	3	2	1	0
	1	1	0	1	cond				imm8							
0xD003	1	1	0	1	0	0	0	0	0	0	0	0	0	0	1	1

The 8-bit immediate number is 3. The immediate number is in two's complement format. Thus, the memory address offset can be negative and the branch instruction can jump backwards. The program counter (PC) is updated as follows if the branch is taken.

$$PC = PC + 4 + SignExtend\_to\_32Bits(imm8:'0')$$

In this example, we have $PC = PC + 4 + 3 \times 2 = PC + 10$, and the instruction that is branched to is 0x4618, to which we give a label "exit". Therefore, this instruction is decoded as "BEQ exit".

Condition Code	Suffix	Description
0000	EQ	EQual
0001	NE	Not Equal
0010	CS/HS	unsigned Higher or Same
0011	CC/LO	unsigned LOwer
0100	MI	MInus (Negative)
0101	PL	PLus (Positive or Zero)
0110	VS	oVerflow Set
0111	VC	oVerflow Clear
1000	HI	unsigned HIgher
1001	LS	unsigned Lower or Same
1010	GE	signed Greater or Equal
1011	LT	signed Less Than
1100	GT	signed Greater Than
1101	LE	signed Less than or Equal
1110	AL	ALways

Table 13-4. Condition code

Decoding: 0x4403 ⟹ ADD r3, r3, r0

This is a 16-bit instruction. The opcode shows it is "ADD". The destination register is DN:Rdn, *i.e.* 0011 (r3). Register r3 is also a source operand. For this instruction, the S suffice is fixed to 0. Therefore, it is decoded as "ADD r3, r3, r0", or "ADD r3, r0".

	15	14	13	12	11	10	9	8	7	6	5	4	3	2	1	0
	opcode								DN	Rm				Rdn		
0x4403	0	1	0	0	0	1	0	0	0	0	0	0	0	0	1	1

Decoding: 0xF1A1, 0x0101 ⟹ SUB r1, r1, #1

This is a 32-bit instruction. The opcode indicates that it is SUB. The S suffix bit is 0 and thus it is not SUBS. The 12-bit immediate number (i:imm3:imm8) is 1, thus we have "SUB r1, r1, #1".

	15	14	13	12	11	10	9	8	7	6	5	4	3	2	1	0
	1	1	1	op1					op2					Rn		
						i	0	1	1	0	1	S				
0xF1A1	1	1	1	1	0	0	0	1	1	0	1	0	0	0	0	1

	15	14	13	12	11	10	9	8	7	6	5	4	3	2	1	0
	op	imm3			Rd				imm8							
0x0101	0	0	0	0	0	0	0	1	0	0	0	0	0	0	0	1

Decoding: 0xE7F9 ⟹ B loop

This 11-bit immediate number in this branch instruction is two's complement, representing -7. The program counter $PC = PC + 4 + (-7) \times 2 = PC - 10$, pointing to the instruction 0x2900, *i.e.* "CMP r1,#0". We labeled the CMP instruction as "loop", and this instruction is decoded as "B loop".

	15	14	13	12	11	10	9	8	7	6	5	4	3	2	1	0
	opcode					imm11										
0xE7F9	1	1	1	0	0	1	1	1	1	1	1	1	1	0	0	1

Decoding: 0x4618 ⟹ MOV r0, r3

The destination register of this 16-bit instruction is D:Rdn, *i.e.* 0000 (r0).

	15	14	13	12	11	10	9	8	7	6	5	4	3	2	1	0
	opcode						opcode2			Rm				Rdn		
									D							
0x4618	0	1	0	0	0	1	1	0	0	0	0	1	1	0	0	0

Decoding: 0xE7FE ⟹ B stop

This is a branch instruction, the program counter $PC = PC + 4 + (-2) \times 2 = PC$, which points to the instruction itself and creates a dead loop.

	15	14	13	12	11	10	9	8	7	6	5	4	3	2	1	0
	opcode					imm11										
0xE7FE	1	1	1	0	0	1	1	1	1	1	1	1	1	1	1	0

In summary, the following bit stream in hex format is decoded into 10 assembly instructions.

F04F,0003,F04F,0104,F04F,0300,2900,D003,4403,F1A1,0101,E7F9,4618,E7FE

Address Offset	Label	Binary Instruction	Decoded Instruction
0		F04F0003	MOV r0,#3
4		F04F0104	MOV r1,#4
8		F04F0300	MOV r3,#0
12	loop	2900	CMP r1,#0
14		D003	BEQ exit
16		4403	ADD r3,r3,r0
18		F1A10101	SUB r1,r1,#1
22		E7F9	B loop
24	exit	4618	MOV r0,r3
26	stop	E7FE	B stop

This program actually multiplies two integers, stored in register r0 and r1, respectively. The product is temporally saved in register r3 during the execution and is moved to register r0 at the end. We can translate the above assembly program to a C program, which multiplies two integers via repeatedly adding the multiplicand to the product.

Assembly Program	C Program

`      MOV r0,#3  ; Multiplicand`
`      MOV r1,#4  ; multiplier`
`      MOV r3,#0  ; product`
`  `
`loop  CMP r1,#0`
`      BEQ exit`
`      ADD r3,r3,r0`
`      SUB r1,r1,#1`
`      B    loop`
`exit  MOV r0,r3`
`  `
`stop  B    stop`
	`int a = 3;`
	`int b = 4;`
	`int product = 0;`
	`  `
	`for(int i = b; i > 0; i--) {`
	`    product += a;`
	`}`
	`while(1);`

13.7 Instruction Decoding Example 2

In this example, we will convert the following machine instructions into an assembly program. We examine the most significant five bits of each half-word to check whether it is a 16-bit instruction or part of a 32-bit instruction.

We find that two words, 0xF8511020 and 0xF84D1020, stored at the memory address 0x080001D6 and 0x080001DA respectively, are 32-bit instructions. The rest half-words are 16-bit instructions.

Memory Address	HEX	Binary
0x080001C8	B08A	1011000010001010
0x080001CA	2100	0010000100000000
0x080001CC	4A06	0100101000000110
0x080001CE	6011	0110000000010001
0x080001D0	2000	0010000000000000
0x080001D2	E005	1110000000000101
0x080001D4	4905	0100100100000101
0x080001D6	F851	1111100001010001
0x080001D8	1020	0001000000100000
0x080001DA	F84D	1111100001001101
0x080001DC	1020	0001000000100000
0x080001DE	1C40	0001110001000000
0x080001E0	280A	0010100000001010
0x080001E2	DBF7	1101101111110111
0x080001E4	BF00	1011111100000000
0x080001E6	E7FE	1110011111111110
0x080001E8	0028	0000000000101000
0x080001EA	2000	0010000000000000
0x080001EC	0000	0000000000000000
0x080001EE	2000	0010000000000000

Table 13-5. Layout of instruction memory

The program also places two constants (0x20000028 and 0x20000000) in the binary instruction. They are the memory addresses of two variables in the data memory. The data memory layout is given as follows:

Memory Address	HEX
0x20000000	0
. . .	. . .
0x20000028	0x0001
0x2000002C	0x0002
0x20000030	0x0003
0x20000034	0x0004
0x20000038	0x0005
0x2000003C	0x0006
0x20000040	0x0007
0x20000044	0x0008
0x20000048	0x0009
0x2000004C	0x000A

Table 13-6. Layout of data memory

Following Appendix A and B, we can decode each binary instruction as following.

Address	HEX	Binary and Decoded Instruction	Explanation
0x080001C8	B08A	1011_00001_0001010 **SUB SP, SP, #40**	SUB SP, SP, #imm7<<2 #imm7 = 0001010$_2$ #imm7 << 2 = 40

0x080001CA	2100	00100_001_00000000
		MOVS r1, #0
			MOV Rd, #imm8
			#imm8 = 00000000$_2$
			Rd = 001$_2$

0x080001CC	4A06	01001_010_00000110
		LDR r2, [pc, #24]
			LDR Rt, [pc, #imm8<<2]
			#imm8 = 00000110$_2$
			#imm8 << 2 = 11000$_2$ = 24
			Rt = 010$_2$
			Target address = pc + 4 + #imm8<<2
			= 0x080001CC + 4 + 24
			= 0x80001E8
			Load the memory address of the integer array. As results, r2 = 0x20000028

0x080001CE	6011	01100_00000_010_001
		STR r1, [r2, #0]
			STR Rt, [Rn, #imm5<<2]
			#imm5 = 00000$_2$
			Rt = 001$_2$
			Rn = 010$_2$

0x080001D0	2000	00100_000_00000000
		MOVS r0, #0
			MOV Rd, #imm8
			#imm8 = 00000000$_2$
			Rd = 000$_2$

0x080001D2	E005	11100_00000000101 **B check**	B #imm11<<1 #imm11 = 00000000101 #imm11<<1 = 10 Target pc = pc + 4 + 10 = 0x080001D2 + 14 = 0x080001E0

0x080001D4	4905	01001_001_00000101
		loop LDR r1, [pc,#20]
			LDR Rt, [pc, #imm8<<2]
			#imm8 = 00000101$_2$
			#imm8<<2 = 10100$_2$ = 20
			Rt = 001
			Target address = pc + 4 + #imm8<<2
			= 0x080001D4 + 4 + 20
			= 0x080001EC
			Load the memory address of the total variable. As results, r1 = 0x20000000

0x080001D6	F851	111110000101_0001	This half-word is part of a 32-bit instruction.

0x080001D8	1020	0001_000000_10_0000
		LDR r1, [r1,r0,LSL #2]
			LDR Rt,[Rn,Rm, LSL #imm2]
			#imm2 = 10$_2$
			Rt = 0001$_2$
			Rn = 0001$_2$
			Rm = 0000$_2$

0x080001DA	F84D	111110000100_1101	This half-word is part of a 32-bit instruction.

0x080001DC	1020	0001_000000_10_0000
		STR r1, [sp,r0,LSL #2]
			STR Rt,[Rn,Rm, LSL #imm2]
			#imm2 = 10_2
			Rt = 0001_2
			Rn = 1101_2
			Rm = 0000_2

0x080001DE	1C40	0001110_001_000_000
		ADDS r0, r0, #1
			ADD Rd, Rn, #imm3
			#imm3 = 001_2
			Rd = 000_2
			Rn = 000_2

0x080001E0	280A	00101_000_00001010
		check CMP r0, #10
			CMP Rn, #imm8
			#imm8 = 00001010_2 = 10
			Rn = 000_2

0x080001E2	DBF7	1101_1011_11110111
		BLT loop
			B(cond) #imm8<<1
			Cond = 1011_2 = Less Than
			#imm8 = 11110111_2
			#imm8<<1 = 111101110_2 = -18
			Target pc = pc + 4 - 18
			= 0x080001E2 - 14
			= 0x080001D4

0x080001E4	BF00	1011111100000000 **NOP**	
0x080001E6	E7FE	11100_11111111110 **self B self**	B #imm11<<1 #imm11 = 11111111110_2 #imm11<<1 = 111111111100_2 = -4 Target pc = pc + 4 + #imm11<<1 = pc + 4 - 4 = pc

The final decoded assembly program and its corresponding C program are given in the following table. The program uses PC-relative addressing to access the integer array *a* and the integer variable *total*. It is inferred from the binary code that the memory address of the array starts at 0x20000028 and the total variable is stored at 0x20000000.

Binary Program	Assembly Program	C Program
Refer to the data memory	AREA myDATA, DATA total DCD 0 a DCD 1,2,3,4,5,6,7,8,9,10 AREA myCode, CODE EXPORT __main __main PROC	int total; int a[10] = {1, 2, 3, 4, 5, 6, 7, 8, 9, 10}; int main(void){
B08A	SUB sp, sp, #0x28	int i;
2100	MOVS r1, #0x00	int b[10];
4A06	LDR r2, [pc, #24]	total = 0;
6011	STR r1, [r2, #0x00]	for (i=0;i<10;i++){
2000	MOVS r0, #0x00	b[i] = a[i];
E005	B check	}
		while(1);
4905	loop LDR r1, [pc,#20]	}
F8511020	LDR r1, [r1,r0,LSL #2]	
F84D1020	STR r1, [sp,r0,LSL #2]	
1C40	ADDS r0, r0, #1	
280A	CMP r0, #0x0A	
DBF7	check BLT loop	
BF00	NOP	
E7FE	self B self	
0028 ; addr of a	DW 0x0028	
2000 ; 0x20000028	DW 0x2000	
0000 ; addr of total	DW 0x0000	
2000 ; 0x20000000	DW 0x2000	
	ENDP	
	END	

13.8 Exercises

1. Translate the following 16-bit binary instructions into assembly instructions
   240A, 3430, 7004, 2A00, 1E40, 1C49, 4288, BD30, 468D, 0000, 6568, 6C20, 7A61

2. Translate the following 32-bit binary instructions into assembly instructions
   FB01F000, FBB2F5F4, FB042415, F2430039, F0210107, E8AC09C0, EA4F2030, EA804130, F04F0001, F0000301, EA4F0050

3. Translate the following binary program into an assembly program. What does the program perform? Translate the assembly program back to a C program.

0x080001FC	4601
0x080001FE	2941
0x08000200	DB04
0x08000202	295A
0x08000204	DC02
0x08000206	F1010020
0x0800020A	B2C1
0x0800020C	2961
0x0800020E	D007
0x08000210	2965
0x08000212	D005
0x08000214	2969
0x08000216	D003
0x08000218	296F
0x0800021A	D001
0x0800021C	2975
0x0800021E	D101
0x08000220	2001
0x08000222	4770
0x08000224	2000
0x08000226	E7FC
0x08000228	4A08
0x0800022A	4614
0x0800022C	E007
0x0800022E	7813
0x08000230	4618
0x08000232	F7FFFFE3
0x08000236	B908
0x08000238	7023
0x0800023A	1C64
0x0800023C	1C52
0x0800023E	7810
0x08000240	2800

0x08000242	D1F4
0x08000244	7020
0x08000246	BF00
0x08000248	E7FE
0x0800024A	0000
0x0800024C	0000
0x0800024E	2000
...	...
0x20000000	6854
0x20000002	2065
0x20000004	7571
0x20000006	6369
0x20000008	206B
0x2000000A	7262
0x2000000C	776F
0x2000000E	206E
0x20000010	6F66
0x20000012	2078
0x20000014	756A
0x20000016	706D
0x20000018	2073
0x2000001A	766F
0x2000001C	7065
0x2000001E	7420
0x20000020	6568
0x20000022	6C20
0x20000024	7A61
0x20000026	2079
0x20000028	6F64
0x2000002A	0067

4. Convert the binary search assembly program given in Chapter 7.12 to machine code manually.

Generic-purpose I/O

This chapter illustrates how a processor uses a GPIO pin as digital input or digital output. Example applications presented include lighting an LED, interfacing a push button and scanning a keypad.

14.1 Introduction to Generic Purpose I/O (GPIO)

Since the number of pins available on a processor is usually limited, a pin that can be dynamically configured by software at runtime to perform various functions is called a general-purpose input/output (GPIO) pin. GPIO provides high flexibility of use and enormous convenience of system design. It enables a processor to meet the needs of a broad range of embedded system applications. However, the flexibility comes at a price tag. The software has to perform a sophisticated initialization.

A GPIO pin can be programmed as one of the following four different functions:

1. Digital input that detects whether an external voltage signal is higher or lower than a predetermined threshold
2. Digital output that controls the voltage of the pin
3. Analog functions that perform digital-to-analog or analog-to-digital conversion
4. Other complex functions such as PWM output, LCD driver, timer-based input capture, external interrupt, and interface of USART, SPI, I²C and USB communication

The last category of functions is called alternative functions (AF) in documents of Cortex-M3 processors. The software can dynamically change the function of a GPIO pin at runtime. In this chapter, we focus on the digital input and digital output, which are simply called input or output, and the other functions will be introduced in the later chapters.

A GPIO port consists of a group of GPIO pins, typically 8 or 16, which share the same data and control registers.

- When a GPIO port is configured as digital input, the binary data read from all pins of this GPIO group are combined into a word or half-word and saved in the input data register (IDR), with each bit of IDR holding the digital input of the corresponding pin.
- When a GPIO port is configured as digital output, the output data register (ODR) holds the output of all pins of this port. Therefore, when changing the output of a GPIO pin, the programmer should only change the value of the corresponding bit of ODR, without affecting the other bits of ODR. Chapter 4.6 introduces how to test, clear, set, and toggle a specific bit of a register in C and assembly.

14.2 GPIO Input Modes: Pull Up and Pull Down

When a GPIO pin is used as digital input, the pin has three states: high voltage, low voltage, or high impedance (also called floating or tri-stated). Pull-up and pull-down are used to ensure the input pin has a valid high (logic 1) or a valid low (logic 0) when external circuit does not drive the pin.

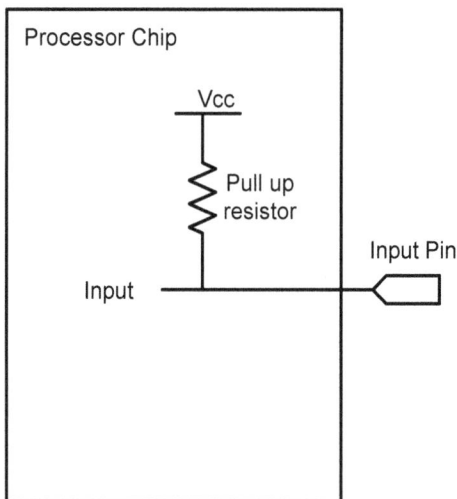

Figure 14-1. The input pin is pulled up internally.

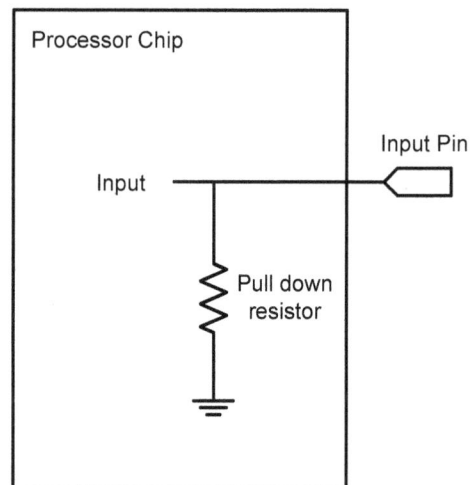

Figure 14-2. The input pin is pulled down internally.

When a pin is configured as pull-up, the pin is internally connected to the power supply via a resistor, as shown in Figure 14-1. The pin is always read as high (logic 1) unless the external circuit drives this pin to low. Similarly, when a pin is configured as pull-down, the pin is then internally connected to the ground via a resistor, as shown in Figure 14-2. The pin is always read as low (logic 0) unless the external circuit drives this pin to high. When a pin is neither pulled up nor pulled down internally, then the pin has high impedance and the analog signal on the GPIO pin cannot reliably represent a logic value. Software can change the pull-up and pull-down setting of a GPIO pin dynamically at runtime.

When a pin is internally pulled up but the external circuit drives the pin to low, a pull-up current is generated and is drawn internally from the processor chip. Similarly, when a pin is pulled down within the chip but the external circuit drives the pin to high, a pull-down current is drawn to the processor chip. In order to limit the pull-up/pull-down current, the internal resistors usually have large impedance (> 10KΩ).

When the external circuit connected to a GPIO pin has a fair amount of capacitance, the process of pulling the pin voltage to the level of logic high or logic low takes a long time because the impedance of the pull-up and pull-down resistors are too large. We call pulling via large resistors weak pull-up or weak pull-down. The internal pulling often does not meet the speed requirement for fast communication protocols, such as I²C. In order to change the pin voltage rapidly, a GPIO pin can be externally pulled up or down via a smaller resistor (several KΩ). Pulling via small resistors is often called strong pull-up or strong pull-down.

Strong vs Weak pull-up/pull-down

14.3 GPIO Output Modes: Push-Pull and Open-Drain

A GPIO output pin can be configured as either push-pull or open-drain. The push-pull mode allows the pin to supply and absorb current. However, a GPIO pin in the open-drain (also called collector) mode can only absorb current.

14.3.1 GPIO Push-Pull Output

A push-pull output consists of a pair of complementary transistors, as shown in Figure 14-3. Only one of them is turned on at any time.

- When logic 0 is outputted, the transistor connected to the ground is turned on to sink current from the external circuit, as shown in Figure 14-4.

- When the pin outputs logic 1, the transistor connected to the power supply is turned on, and it sources current to external circuit connected to the output pin, as shown in Figure 14-5.

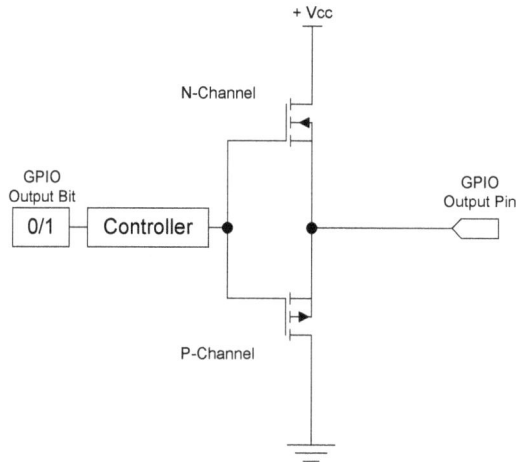

Figure 14-3. A push-pull output

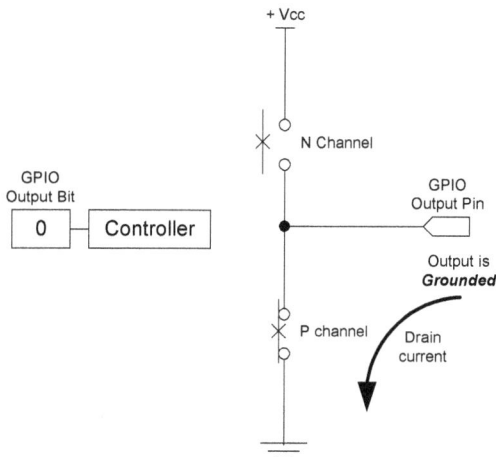

Figure 14-4. If the digital output is 0, then the GPIO output pin is pushed to the ground in a push-pull setting.

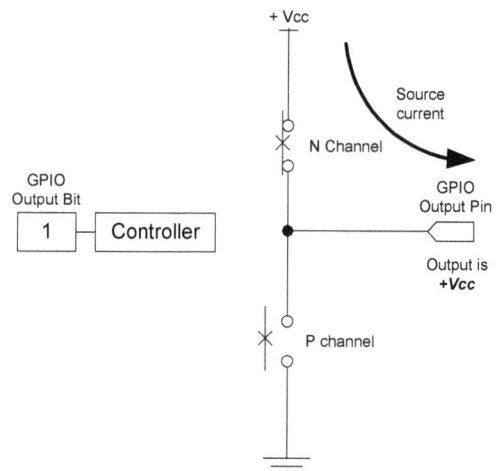

Figure 14-5. If the digital output is 1, then the GPIO output pin is pulled to the Vcc in a push-pull setting.

14.3.2 GPIO Open-Drain Output

An open-drain output consists of a pair of the same type of CMOS or transistors, as shown in Figure 14-6. An open-drain output can sink the electrical current when logic 0 is produced. However, when logic 1 is outputted, it cannot supply any current to the external circuit because the output pin is floating, connected to neither the power supply nor the ground. It has only two states: low voltage, and high impedance. An open-drain output often has an external pull-up resistor.

One important usage of open-drain outputs is to directly connect several outputs together and implement logic OR function in a simple way. If multiple open-drain output pins are connected and are pulled up via a shared resistor, any output pin can drive the output voltage to low. The pin voltage is high if and only if all pins output logic 1. This wired-OR function is useful to simplify circuit design. For example, the I2C communication protocol relies on wired-OR to allow multiple master devices to operate on the same bus.

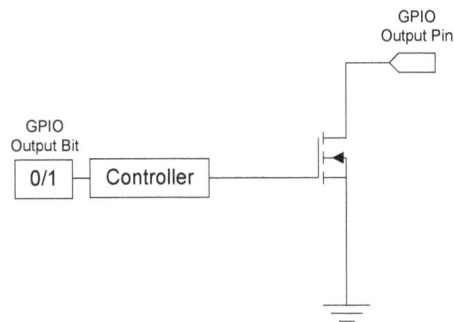

Figure 14-6. An open-drain output

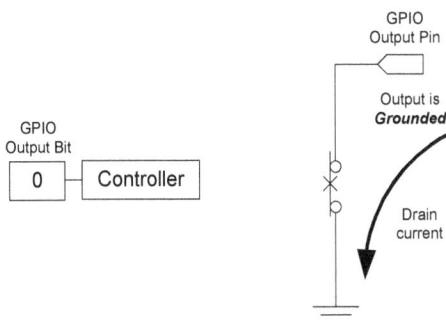

Figure 14-7. If the digital output is 0, then the GPIO output pin is pushed to the ground (drain) in an open-drain setting.

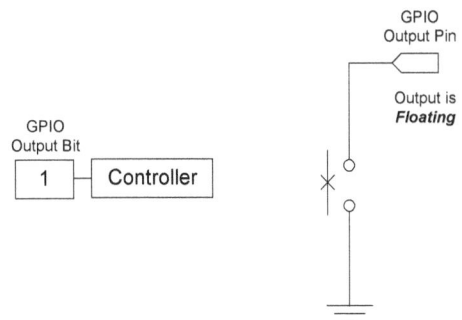

Figure 14-8. If the digital output is 1, then the GPIO output pin is floating (open) in an open-drain setting.

Compared to open-drain, the push-pull mode has the advantage of faster speed, since it can change the pin voltage faster if the external circuit has some capacitance. Another advantage is that it can supply current. For example, a push-pull output can directly control an external LED while an open-drain output cannot. However, the wired-OR characteristics can only be provided in open-drain outputs. Usually push-pull output pins cannot be directly connected, as it might cause a potential short circuit. In addition, open-drain output also allows the pin to be pulled up to any voltage, which can be helpful when this pin is used as an input to a system that requires a higher level of input voltage.

14.4 GPIO Output Speed: Slew Rate

The slew rate of a GPIO pin is the rate of change of its output voltage per unit of time, as defined as follows.

$$Slew\ Rate = \frac{\Delta V}{\Delta t}$$

If the logic value of a GPIO pin is changed from 0 to 1 and accordingly the voltage output of this pin rises from 0V to 3V in 3μs, then the slew rate is 1 volt per μs. Figure 14-9 shows an example of ΔV and Δt when the output voltage increases from low to high. The slew rate definition applies to both the rising edge and the falling edge of a voltage output.

The higher the slew rate, the shorter duration the output voltage takes to rise or fall to desired values. Therefore, a higher slew rate allows a faster speed at which the processor can toggle the logic level of a GPIO pin. Figure 14-9 also compares the desired square wave output and the real output when the logic output of a GPIO pin is toggled periodically. A shorter rise and fall time allows a GPIO pin to change its logic value more rapidly.

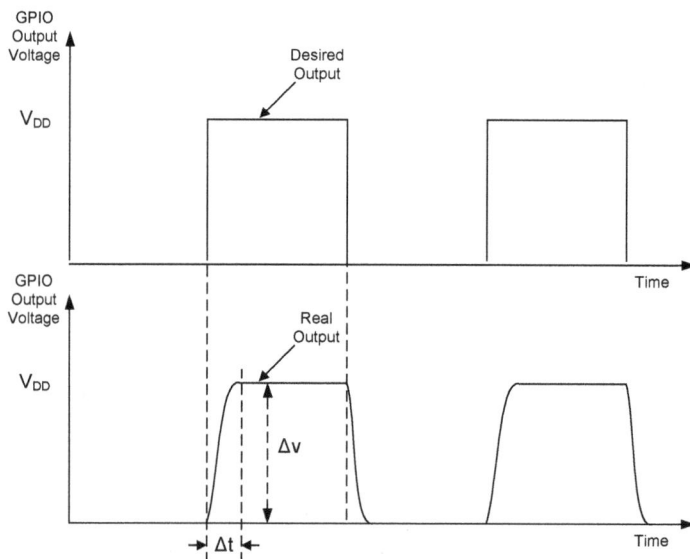

Figure 14-9. Comparing a desired square wave voltage output with the real GPIO output

However, a large slew rate often causes high electromagnetic interference (EMI), also called radio frequency interference (RFI) to neighbor electronic circuits. A fast rising and falling signal has large amplitude high frequency harmonics, which can transfer to a victim circuit via radiation, conduction, or induction, and may cause malfunctions. A slower valid slew rate is often preferred to minimize EMI disturbance. The slew rate of the GPIO circuit is programmable by setting the GPIO output speed. For example, the digital output speed of a GPIO pin can be 400 KHz, 2 MHz, 10 MHz or 40 MHz in the STM32L processors.

14.5 Lighting up an LED

The following shows the basic procedure to light up an LED. The GPIO data structure includes (1) RCC for enabling the clock of the GPIO port B, and (2) GPIO to configure the pin 6 of GPIO port B as general-purpose output with push-pull mode. To light up the blue LED, we need to output logic "1" to pin 6.

A GPIO port has ten control registers, such as the mode register, the output type register, and the output speed register. The memory address for each control register is pre-defined by the manufacturer during chip design. A GPIO port has 16 pins and each pin may take 1, 2, or 4 bits in a control register. Therefore, the size of these control registers can be 2, 4, or 8 bytes.

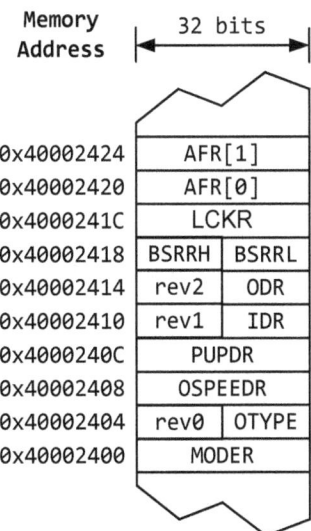

```
typedef struct{
  __IO uint32_t MODER;  // Mode register
  __IO uint16_t OTYPER; // Output type register
       uint16_t rev0;   // Padding two bytes
  __IO uint32_t OSPEEDR;// Output speed register
  __IO uint32_t PUPDR;  // Pull-up/pull-down register
  __IO uint16_t IDR;    // Input data register
       uint16_t rev1;   // Padding two bytes
  __IO uint16_t ODR;    // Output data register
       uint16_t rev2;   // Padding two bytes
  __IO uint16_t BSRRL;  // Bit set/reset register(low)
  __IO uint16_t BSRRH;  // Bit set/Reset register(high)
  __IO uint32_t LCKR;   // Configuration lock register
  __IO uint32_t AFR[2]; // Alternate function registers
} GPIO_TypeDef

#define GPIOB ((GPIO_TypeDef *) 0x4002400))
```

Figure 14-10. Casting a memory address to the GPIO structure.

In order to access each control register conveniently in C, we can cast the base memory address of a GPIO port to a data structure, as shown in Figure 14-10. Six bytes are padded in the *GPIO_TypeDef* structure into order to make the structure members to align with their pre-defined memory addresses. The following C statement casts the memory address defined by the chip manufacturer to the GPIO control structure.

```
#define GPIOB ((GPIO_TypeDef *) 0x4002400))
```

If we want to set the output the GPIO pin 6 to high, we can use the following C statement:

```
GPIOB->ODR |= 1<<6;    // Set bit[6] to 1
```

Note the pin number of a port starts with 0, instead of 1. In assembly, a load-modify-store sequence is required to change the register value stored in memory. The following gives corresponding implementation in assembly language.

```
LDR r7, =0x40020400     ; Load GPIO port B base address
LDR r1, [r7, #0x14]     ; Byte offset of ODR is 0x14
ORR r1, r1, #(1<<6)     ; Set bit 6
STR r1, [r7, #0x14]     ; Write ODR
```

We can use directive "EQU" to substitute a constant with a symbol, which makes the assembly program more readable and self-documenting. The assembly code can be rewritten as follows:

```
GPIOB_BASE EQU 0x40020400
GPIO_ODR   EQU 0x14

LDR r7, =GPIOB_BASE      ; Load GPIO port B base address
LDR r1, [r7, #GPIO_ODR]  ; r1 = GPIOB->ODR
ORR r1, r1, #(1<<6)      ; set bit 6
LDR r1, [r7, #GPIO_ODR]  ; Write GPIOB->ODR
```

In addition, we also need to enable the clock of GPIO port B. In order to save energy, the clock of all peripherals is turned off by default. We can enable the clock of a peripheral by set the corresponding bit of the clock control register defined in the reset and clock control (RCC) structure, as shown below.

```
// Reset and clock control
typedef struct {
  __IO uint32_t CR;        // Clock control register
  __IO uint32_t ICSCR;     // Internal clock sources calibration register
  __IO uint32_t CFGR;      // Clock configuration register
  __IO uint32_t CIR;       // Clock interrupt register
  __IO uint32_t AHBRSTR;   // AHB peripheral reset register
  __IO uint32_t APB2RSTR;  // APB2 peripheral reset register
  __IO uint32_t APB1RSTR;  // APB1 peripheral reset register
  __IO uint32_t AHBENR;    // AHB peripheral clock enable register
```

```
    __IO uint32_t APB2ENR;    // APB2 peripheral clock enable register
    __IO uint32_t APB1ENR;    // APB1 peripheral clock enable register
    __IO uint32_t AHBLPENR;   // AHB peripheral clock enable in low power mode register
    __IO uint32_t APB2LPENR;  // APB2 peripheral clock enable in low power mode register
    __IO uint32_t APB1LPENR;  // APB1 peripheral clock enable in low power mode register
    __IO uint32_t CSR;        // Control/status register
} RCC_TypeDef;

#define RCC ((RCC_TypeDef *) 0x40023800))
```

The following C statements enable the clock of GPIO port B.

```
#define RCC_AHBENR_GPIOBEN  (0x00000002)
RCC->AHBENR |= RCC_AHBENR_GPIOBEN;
```

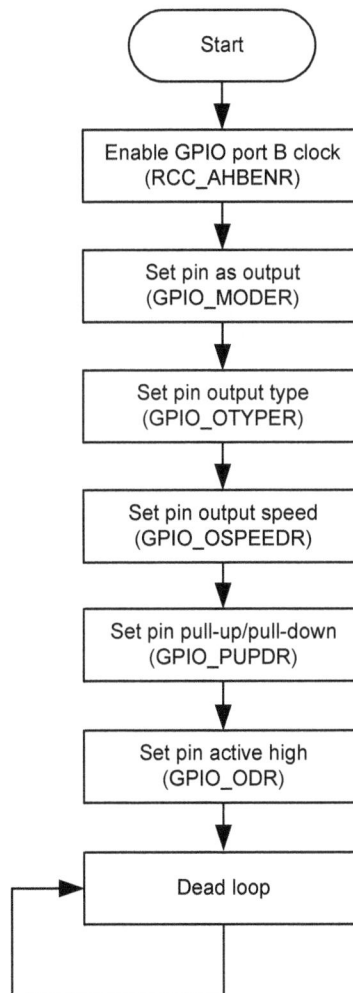

Figure 14-11. Flowchart of GPIO initialization

Figure 14-11 shows the flowchart of initializing a GPIO pin as digital output with push-pull. The following C program demonstrates how to set up a GPIO pin and light up the green LED in detail. The GPIO pin PB 6 is used to drive the green LED.

- When we change the value of specific bits of a register, we need to preserve the value of the other bits of this register in order to avoid creating unexpected negative impacts. For example, if we want to set the least significant bit of register R, "R = 0x1;" is not the correct approach since it also clears all the other bits. Instead, we should use a bitwise logical OR operation "R |= 0x1;".
- When we change the value of multiple bits, it is a good practice to reset these bits before updating them. For example, if we want to set the least significant four bits $b_3 b_2 b_1 b_0$ of register R to 1001, we need to clear these four bits first by running "R &= ~0xF; R |= 0x9;" If we do not clear these four bits first, we may fail to set the register correctly if their initial value is not 0. For example, if the value of $b_3 b_2 b_1 b_0$ is 0111 initially, "R |= 0x9;" will lead a binary value of 1111.
- Each GPIO port has a data output register (DOR) and a data input register (DIR). Each bit of the DOR register controls the output of a corresponding GPIO pin in this port. In a push-pull setting, if the bit value is 1, the output voltage on its corresponding GPIO pin is high; if the bit value is 0, the output voltage then is low. The DIR register records the input of all pins of a GPIO port.

```c
// Blue LED is connected PB 6 (GPIO port B pin 6)

void GPIO_Clock_Enable(){
    // Enable the clock to GPIO port B
    RCC->AHBENR |= 0x00000002;
}

void GPIO_Pin_Init(){
    // Set pin 6 I/O mode as general-purpose output
    // 00 = digital input(default),   01 = digital output
    // 10 = alternative function,     11 = analog
    GPIOB->MODER &= ~(0x03<<(2*6));      // Mode mask
    GPIOB->MODER |= 0x01<<(2*6);         // Set pin 6 as digital output

    // Set output type of pin 6 as push-pull
    // 0 = push-pull(0, default), 1 = open-drain
    GPIOB->OTYPER &= ~(1<<6);

    // Set I/O output speed
    // 00 = 400 KHz(00), 01 = 2 MHz, 10 = 10 MHz, 11 = 40 MHz
    GPIOB->OSPEEDR &= ~(0x03<<(2*6));    // Speed mask
    GPIOB->OSPEEDR |=  0x01<<(2*6);      // Set output as 2 MHz

    // Set I/O as no pull-up pull-down
```

```
    // 00 = no pull-up, no pull-down (default),
    // 01 = pull-up, 10 = pull-down, 11 = reserved
    GPIOB->PUPDR &= ~(0x03<<(2*6));          // no pull-up, no pull-down
}

int main(void){
  GPIO_Clock_Enable();
  GPIO_Pin_Init();
  GPIOB->ODR |= 1<<6;   // Set bit 6 of output data register (ODR)
  while(1);             // Dead loop & program hangs here
}
```

Example 14-1. Lighting up an LED in C

The implementation in assembly is similar to the above C program. In the program, the GPIO_BASE and RCC_BASE are pre-defined memory addresses, and GPIO_MODER, GPIO_OTYPER, GPIO_OSPEEDR, GPIO_PUPDR, and GPIO_ODR are byte offset of its corresponding variable in the data structure GPIO_TypeDef defined previously. It is a good practice to define a frequently used constant as some symbols associated with meaningful semantics. This can be achieved by using the "EQU" directive in assembly. This practice can effectively make a program easier to read and debug.

```
; Memory addresses of GPIO port B and RCC (reset and clock control) data
; structure. These addresses are predefined by the chip manufacturer
GPIOB_BASE      EQU    0x40020400
RCC_BASE        EQU    0x40023800

; Byte offset of each individual variable of the GPIO_TypeDef structure
GPIO_MODER      EQU    0x00
GPIO_OTYPER     EQU    0x04
GPIO_RESERVED0  EQU    0x06
GPIO_OSPEEDR    EQU    0x08
GPIO_PUPDR      EQU    0x0C
GPIO_IDR        EQU    0x10
GPIO_RESERVED1  EQU    0x12
GPIO_ODR        EQU    0x14
GPIO_RESERVED2  EQU    0x16
GPIO_BSRRL      EQU    0x18
GPIO_BSRRH      EQU    0x1A
GPIO_LCKR       EQU    0x1C
GPIO_AFR0       EQU    0x20 ;  AFR[0]
GPIO_AFR1       EQU    0x24 ;  AFR[1]
GPIO_AFRL       EQU    0x20
GPIO_AFRH       EQU    0x24

; Byte offset of variable AHBENR in the RCC_TypeDef structure
RCC_AHBENR      EQU    0x1C

; Enable the clock to GPIO port B
```

```
LDR r7, =RCC_BASE   ; Load address of reset and clock control (RCC)
; LDR is a pseudo-instruction and will be expanded to
; multiple real instructions
LDR r1, [r7, #RCC_AHBENR]     ; r1 = RCC->AHBENR
ORR r1, r1,  #0x00000002      ; Set bit 2 of AHBENR
STR r1, [r7, #RCC_AHBENR]     ; GPIO port B clock enable

; Set pin 6 I/O mode as General-purpose Output
LDR r7, =GPIOB_BASE           ; Load GPIO port B base address
LDR r1, [r7, #GPIO_MODER]     ; r1 = GPIOB->MODER
BIC r1, r1, #(0x03 << 12)     ; Direction mask pin 6, clear bit 13 and 12
ORR r1, r1, #(0x1 << 12)      ; Set mode as digital output (mode = 0b01)
STR r1, [r7, #GPIO_MODER]     ; Save the mode

; Set pin 6 the push-pull mode for the output type
LDR r1, [r7, #GPIO_OTYPER]    ; r1 = GPIOB->OTYPER
BIC r1, r1, #(1<<6)           ; Push-pull(0, default), open-drain(1)
STR r1, [r7, #GPIO_OTYPER]    ; Save output type

; Set I/O output speed value as 2 MHz
LDR r1, [r7, #GPIO_OSPEEDR]   ; r1 = GPIOB->OSPEEDR
BIC r1, r1, #(0x03<<12)       ; Speed mask for pin 6
ORR r1, r1, #(0x03<<12)       ; 400KHz(00), 2MHz(01), 10MHz(01), 40MHz(11)
STR r1, [r7, #GPIO_OSPEEDR]   ; Save output speed

; Set I/O as no pull-up pull-down
LDR r1, [r7, #GPIO_PUPDR]     ; r1 = GPIOB->PUPDR
BIC r1, r1, #(0x03<<12)       ; PUPD mask for pin 6
ORR r1, r1, #(0x00<<12)       ; No PUPD(00, reset), pull-up(01)
STR r1, [r7, #GPIO_PUPDR]     ; Save pull-up and pull-down setting

; Light up the LED
LDR r7, =GPIOB_BASE           ; Load GPIO port B base address
LDR r1, [r7, #GPIO_ODR]       ; r1 = GPIOB->ODR
ORR r1, r1, #(1<<6)           ; Set output of pin 6 to high
STR r1, [r7, #GPIO_ODR]       ; Write the output data register
```

Example 14-2. Lighting up an LED in an assembly program

14.6 Push Button

When a push button is pressed, two metal contacts bang together and immediately rebound a couple of times before setting. This produces multiple signals within a few milliseconds due to the bounce effects. Figure 14-12 shows the voltage signal across a push button when it is pressed at the time instant 0. Because the processor runs at a fast speed, the processor is able to observe these falling and rising transitions and mistakenly thinks the push button has been pressed multiple times.

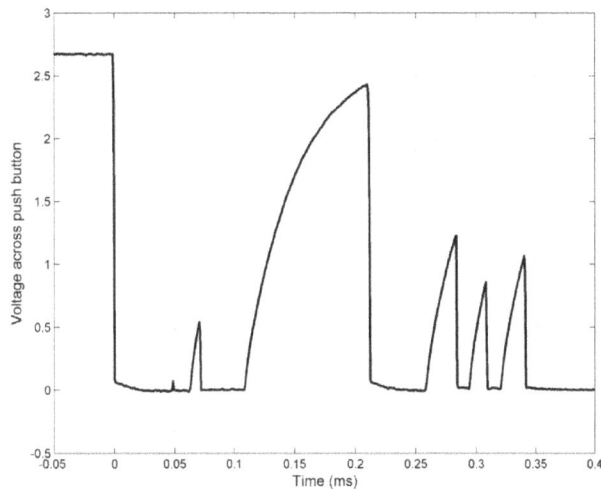

Figure 14-12. The voltage across a push button when there is no hardware debouncing

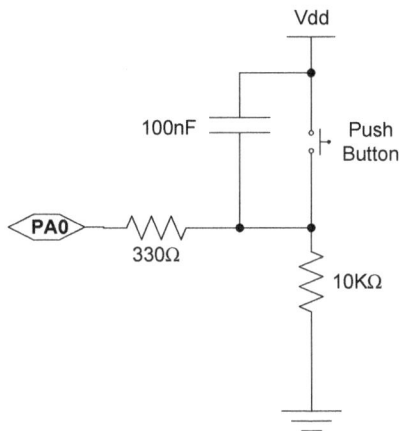

Figure 14-13. A push button with hardware debouncing

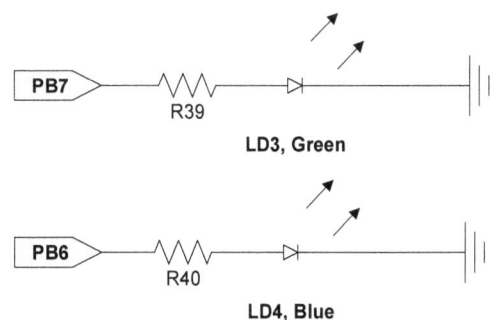

Figure 14-14. Blue and green LED

There are both hardware and software solutions to eliminate the bouncing effects. These solutions are called debouncing. The hardware debouncing usually uses a simple RC circuit, with the capacitor connected in parallel with the push button to filter out any high frequency signals, as shown in Figure 14-13. Figure 14-15 shows the voltage signals when the LED is lit up after the push button is pressed. It can see that the voltage on the pin (PA 0) that is connected to the push button rises up smoothly without generating any bouncing signals. In this example, the processor constantly checks whether the button is pushed. The latency between the event of detecting button pushed and lighting up the LED is approximate 12 μs in this example.

The software debouncing usually uses a time delay function. When a voltage transition from high to low is detected, the software re-examines the signal input after several milliseconds. If the signal is still low after the delay, the button is considered to be pushed.

The STM32L discovery kit has two push buttons on board, one for user, and the other for reset. The USER push button is connected to the GPIO Port A Pin 0 (PA 0) of the STM32L processor chip. The RESET push button is used to RESET the STM32L processor chip to restart the processor. We will use the USER push button to control the blue LED. When the button is pressed, the blue LED is toggled.

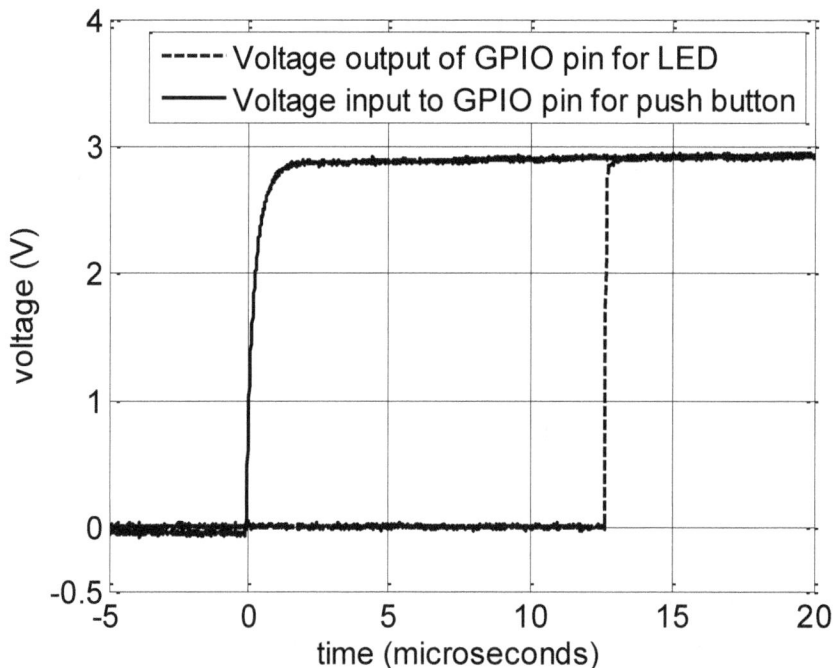

Figure 14-15. Voltage signals on the LED pin when the push button is pressed

The program uses a polling I/O method (*busy waiting*) that constantly queries the input of external devices. In this lab, it repeatedly checks whether the push button is pressed or not. Although the polling method is simple, it is inherently inefficient since the CPU wastes many cycles on querying or waiting for input. If there are many input devices, this method is not recommended since the time required to poll them can exceed the time available to service a given I/O input. A method based on interrupts will be more efficient than polling.

Suppose a push button is connected to the GPIO pin PA 0. We can set up the clock and the pin configuration as follows. The input of pin 0 is saved at bit 0 of the input data register (IDR) for GPIO port A. A low voltage input yields to a value of 0, and a high voltage generates a value of 1.

```
// Enable the clock to GPIO port A
RCC->AHBENR   |= RCC_AHBENR_GPIOAEN;

// Set pin 0 I/O mode as general-purpose input
// input(00, default), output(01), alternative function(10), analog(11)
GPIOA->MODER &= ~(0x03);         // Set mode as input (00)

// Set pin 0 the output type as push-pull
GPIOA->OTYPER &= ~(0x1);         // push-pull(0, reset), open-drain(1)

// Set I/O output speed value as 2 MHz
// 400 KHz(00), 2 MHz(01), 10 MHz(10), 40 MHz(11)
GPIOA->OSPEEDR &= ~(0x03);       // Speed mask
GPIOA->OSPEEDR |=  0x01;

// Set I/O as no pull-up pull-down
// No pull-up/pull-down (00, default),
// pull-up(01), pull-down(10), reserved(11)
GPIOA->PUPDR &= ~(0x03);         // Pull-up pull-down mask
```

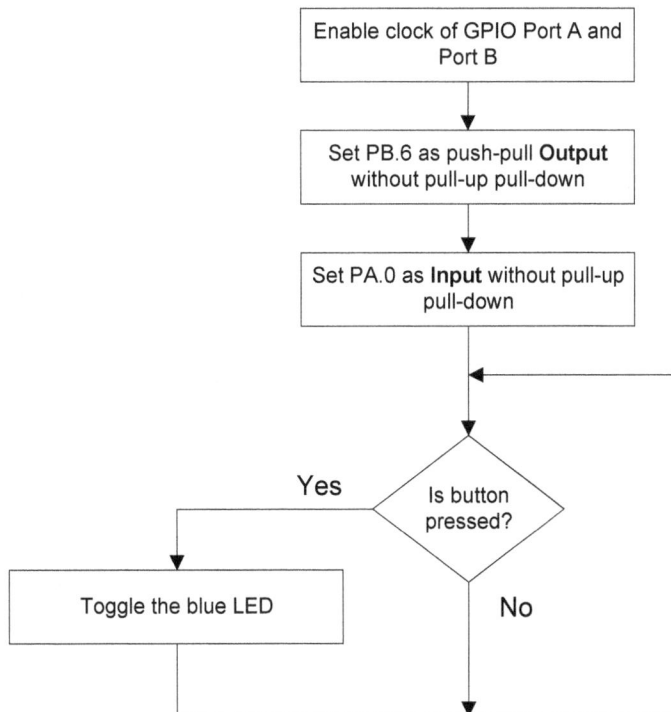

Figure 14-16. Flowchart of programming a push button to control an LED

14.7 Keypad Scan

Suppose we have a keypad that has 12 keys, as shown in Figure 14-17. One simple way is to interface each key in the same approach as a push button, with each key having a dedicated pin to detect whether it is pressed or not. However, this would require 12 I/O pins, which is not desirable for many applications since the total number of pins available for use on a microcontroller is limited. In order to reduce the number of pins required, a keypad is usually organized in a matrix, as shown in Figure 14-17 Figure 14-18. This will reduce the number of I/O pins from 12 to 7 in this example.

On STM32L processors, a GPIO pin provides only weak pull-up and weak pull-down internally. The internal pull-up and pull-down circuit consists of a 60KΩ resistor in series with a switchable PMOS/NMOS. The pull-up and pull-down configuration bits of a GPIO pin are used to turn on or turn off the PMOS and NMOS. When the load has a fair amount of capacitance, a strong pull-up or pull-down is often required by the application to shorten the rising or falling time of the voltage signal on a pin. To achieve strong pull-up or strong pull-down, the pin should be externally connected to the ground or a high voltage via a resistor with a much lower resistance than the internal pull-up and pull-down resistors. In the keypad example, each pin connected to the input port (C1, C2, and C3) is pulled up to 3.3V via a 2.2KΩ resistor. Because the pins connected to C1, C2 and C3 are externally pulled up, they should be configured as no pull-up and no pull-down internally.

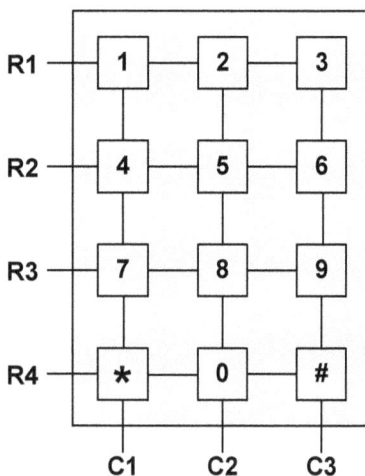

Figure 14-17. 3×4 keypad

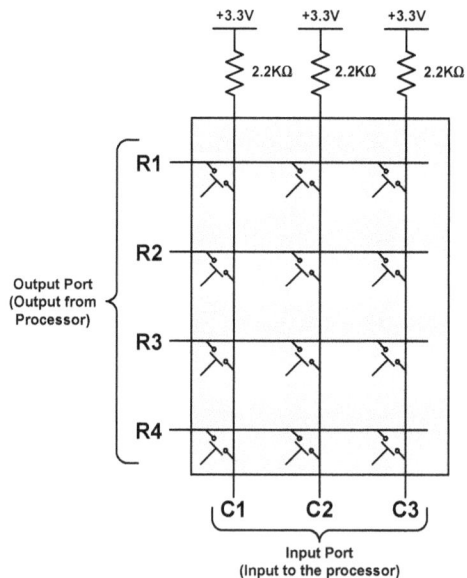

Figure 14-18. Input and output setting

Scanning algorithm is widely used to detect which key is pressed. The algorithm has two iterations of loops: looping over the row pins and then looping over the column pins. Suppose all row pins are set as output and all column pins are set as input. Each column pin is pulled up to a high-level voltage via a small resistor. The algorithm involves two steps.

1. Identify the column number of the pressed key. Set the output of all row pins as zero and read all column pins. If all columns are read as 1, then no key has been pressed. If one of them is zero, then at least one of the keys in that corresponding column is pressed down.
2. Identify the row number of the pressed key. Drive the output of the first row to low (zero) while keeping the other rows at high (one). For example, suppose the input of column C2 is read as zero. If the input of C2 is still zero when the output of row R1 is high, then the pressed key is not located in row R1. Otherwise, row R1 is the row in which the pressed key is located. We repeat the process for all the other rows until the row is successfully identified.

The following gives a simple example how the scanning algorithm works when the key "0" is pressed.

1. Before key "0" is pressed, the row output port is set as low, *i.e.* R1,R2,R3,R4 = 0000. If the input port is read now, C1, C2, and C3 are read as one, *i.e.* C1,C2,C3 = 111.
2. When key "0" is pressed, the column C2 is connected to the ground via the R4 pin (since R4 is set to 0). As a result, we have C1,C2,C3 = 101. Thus, we successfully identify that the pressed key is in the C2 column.
3. After the column is identified, we scan the output row by row.
   (1) Set the row output (R1,R2,R3,R4) as 0111, and read the column input. In this case, we have C1,C2,C3 = 111. The pressed key is not in row R1.
   (2) Set the row output (R1,R2,R3,R4) as 1011, and read the column input. In this case, we have C1,C2,C3 = 111. The pressed key is not in row R2.
   (3) Set the row output (R1,R2,R3,R4) as 1101, and read the column input. In this case, we have C1,C2,C3 = 111. The pressed key is not in row R3.
   (4) Set the row output (R1,R2,R3,R4) as 1110, and read the column input. In this case, we have C1,C2,C3 = 101. Since C2 is read as zero, the pressed key is in row R4.
4. After identifying that the pressed key is located in column C2 and row R4, we can loop up the pre-defined mapping table of the matrix keypad to find that key "0" has been pressed.

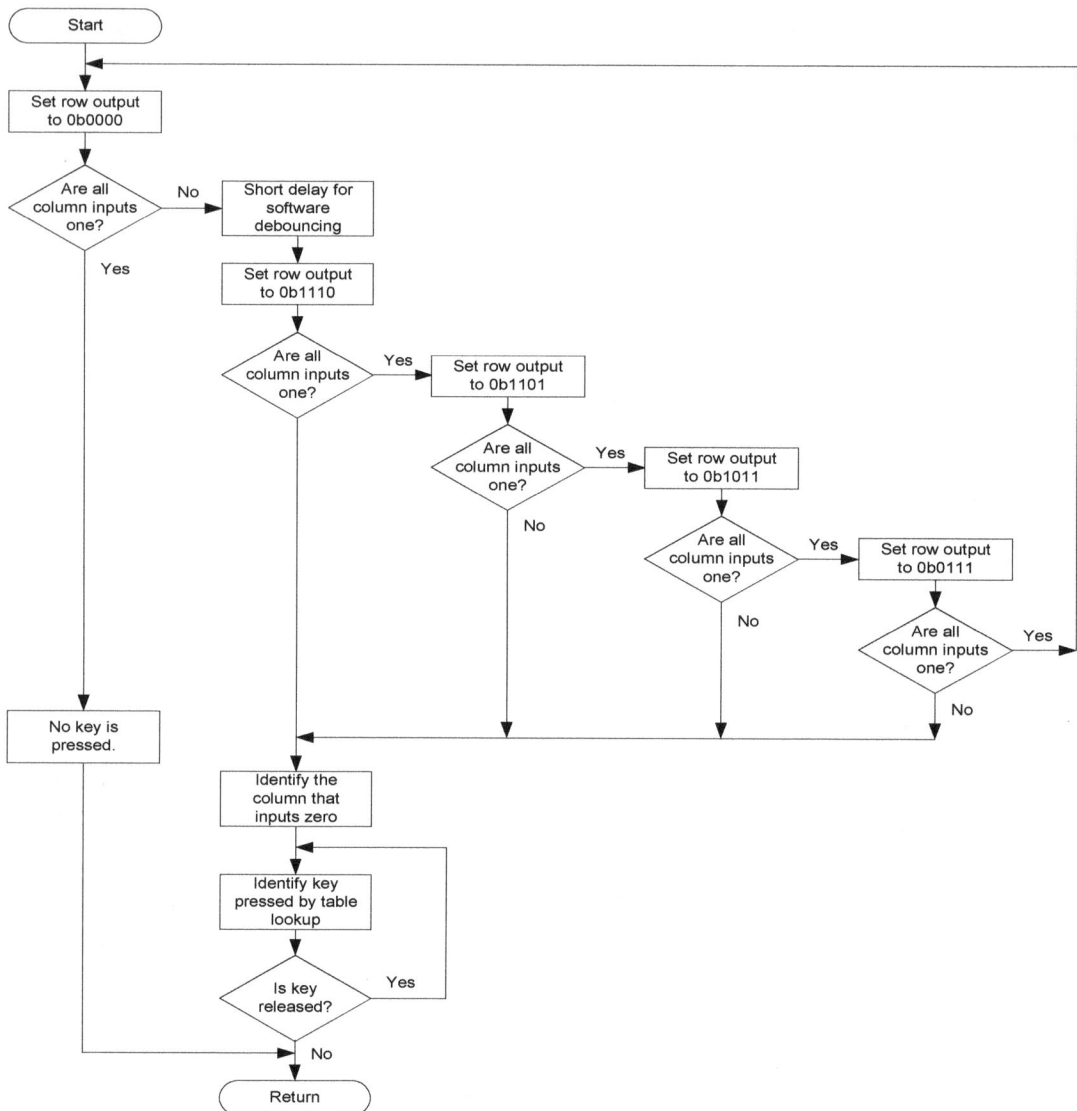

Figure 14-19. Keypad scanning algorithm.
All rows are set as output. All columns are set as inputs.

This approach is simple but not safe. During the second step, two row pins will be shorted if multiple keys on the same column are pressed simultaneously. Specifically the row pin that outputs 1 (*i.e.* 3 V) can be shorted to the row pins that output 0 (*i.e.* 0 V), thus potentially damaging the microcontroller. Figure 14-20 gives one example.

This issue can be resolved by either software or hardware. The hardware solution is to configure all output pins as open-drain, instead of push-pull. When a pin outputs one, the pin is then in HiZ state, and no circuit short can occur. The software solution is to switch the row pin from output to input when the rows are scanned. Specifically, when the output of a row pin is set to zero, the direction of the other row pins are changed from output to input. For example, when the third row is tested during the row locating process, row 3 is set as output and its output value is zero, but row 1, 2, and 4 are set as input, instead of output, to avoid a circuit short.

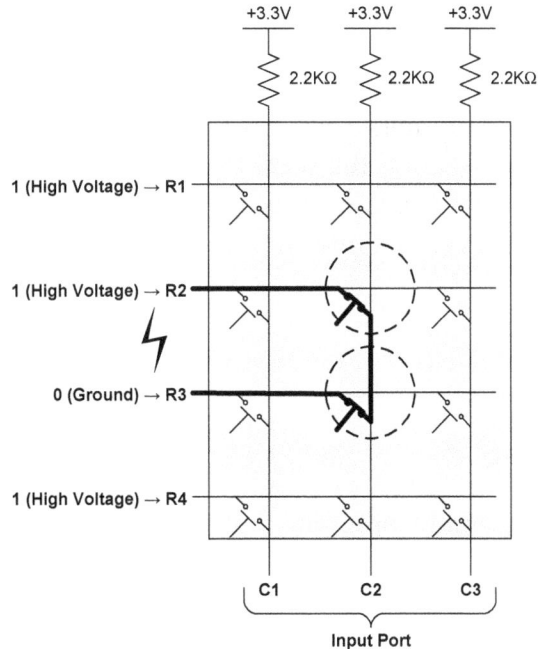

Figure 14-20. The GPIO pins connected to R2 and R3 are shorted if two keys marked by a circle are pressed simultaneously and the GPIO output is 1101.

Another method to avoid damage when multiple keys are pressed is to use reverse scanning algorithm. This method sets the row port and the column port alternatively as input and output to detect the row and the column of a pressed key. This method requires both the row pins and the column pins to be pulled up by some small resistors. This method involves two steps described below.

- During the first step, similar to the scanning algorithm described previously, it sets the row port as output and the column port as input and then reads the column input to identify the column.
- During the second step, it reverses the direction, sets the row port as input and the column port as output, and reads the row input to identify the row.

How does the microcontroller know when a keypad is pressed? There are two methods: polling or interrupt.

- The polling method scans the keypad periodically with a small time interval. This method is simple but causes a waste of time of microcontrollers. In addition, since the microcontroller usually has multiple tasks, other tasks may potentially delay the scanning process so the system is not responsive when a keypad is pressed.
- The interrupt method generates a signal to the processor when the keypad is pressed, which informs the processor to stop the current tasks and start to execute the scanning code. This method saves the microcontroller from periodically executing the scanning algorithm, thus saving the processor time. In addition, the interrupt reduces the latency in responding when a keypad is pressed. However, the interrupt program is more complex to write and debug than polling.

14.8 Exercises

1. Write an assembly program that toggles an LED when the push button is pressed.

2. Write an assembly program that blinks an LED with a time internal of one second.

3. Write an assembly program that scans the keypad to verify a four-digit password. The password is set as 1234. If the user enters the correct password, the blue LED will light up. Otherwise, the red LED will be on.

4. Write an assembly program to blink an LED to send out an SOS Morse code.
   - Blinking Morse code SOS ($\cdots - - - \cdots$) DOT, DOT, DOT, DASH, DASH, DASH, DOT, DOT, DOT.
   - DOT is on for ¼ second and DASH is on for ½ second, with ¼ second between them.
   - At the end of SOS, the program has a delay of 2 seconds before repeating.

5. Write an assembly program to implement software debouncing for push buttons.

6. Use the logic analyzer to measure the time latency between pressing a button and lighting up an LED.

CHAPTER

15

General-purpose Timers

General-purpose timers are complex but powerful. This chapter presents two example uses of timers: measuring the pulse lengths of input signals (input capture) or generating output waveforms (output compare and PWM).

15.1 Timer Organization and Counting Modes

A timer is a free-run hardware counter that increments or decrements once for every clock cycle. The frequency of the timer clock can be set by software. If it is used as output compare, as shown in Figure 15-1, the counter value is compared with some given constant, and an output is generated if they are equal.

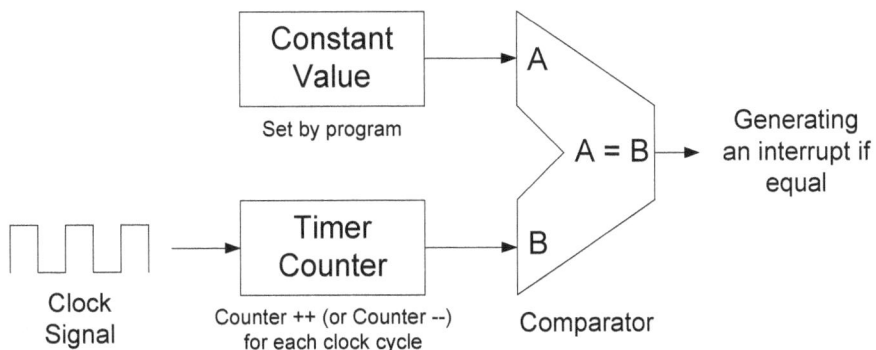

Figure 15-1. A timer is used as output compare. The frequency of the clock signal and the constant value are set by software. The timer counter is a hardware register, and it automatically increments or decrements once for each clock cycle.

If it is used as input capture as shown in Figure 15-2, the hardware automatically logs the counter value, and the software calculates the difference between two consecutively logged values and finds the time span of two consecutive events.

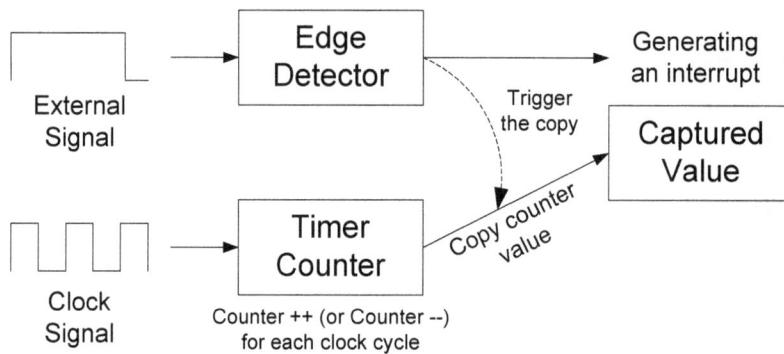

Figure 15-2. A timer is used as input capture. The edge detector triggers the copy from the timer counter register to the capture value hardware register (CCR). The interrupt service routine calculates the difference of two consecutively captured values to find the time span between two external events.

The hardware timer counter has three different counting modes: *upcounting*, *downcounting*, or *center-aligned counting*, as illustrated in Figure 15-3.

- In the upcounting mode, the counter starts from 0 to a constant and then restarts from 0. The constant is set by the program and stored in a special register called the auto-reload register (ARR). For example, if ARR is 4, the counter value is 0, 1, 2, 3, 4, 0, 1, 2, 3, 4 and so on.
- In the downcounting mode, the counter starts from the auto-reload value down to 0, and then restarts from the auto-reload value. For example, if ARR is 4, the counter value is 4, 3, 2, 1, 0, 4, 3, 2, 1, 0, and so on.
- The third mode is called center-aligned counting mode, which performs upcounting and downcounting alternatively. For example, if ARR is 4, the counter value is 0, 1, 2, 3, 4, 3, 2, 1, 0, and so on.

The timer counter forms a periodical saw tooth shape. The period is determined by both the clock frequency to the counter and the value stored in the ARR register. The timer resolution is defined as the minimum time unit that a timer can represent. It is determined by the driven clock and the number of bits that the hardware timer register has. A 16-bit counter can count 65,536 steps.

A timer counter has two update events: overflow and underflow.

- During the upcounting mode, overflow occurs when the counter is reset to 0.
- During the downcounting mode, underflow occurs when the counter is reset to ARR.

- During the center-aligned counting mode, both underflow and overflow can occur.

When using the timer to measure a large time span between the occurrences of two external events, the overflow and underflow have to be considered to avoid underestimating the time span.

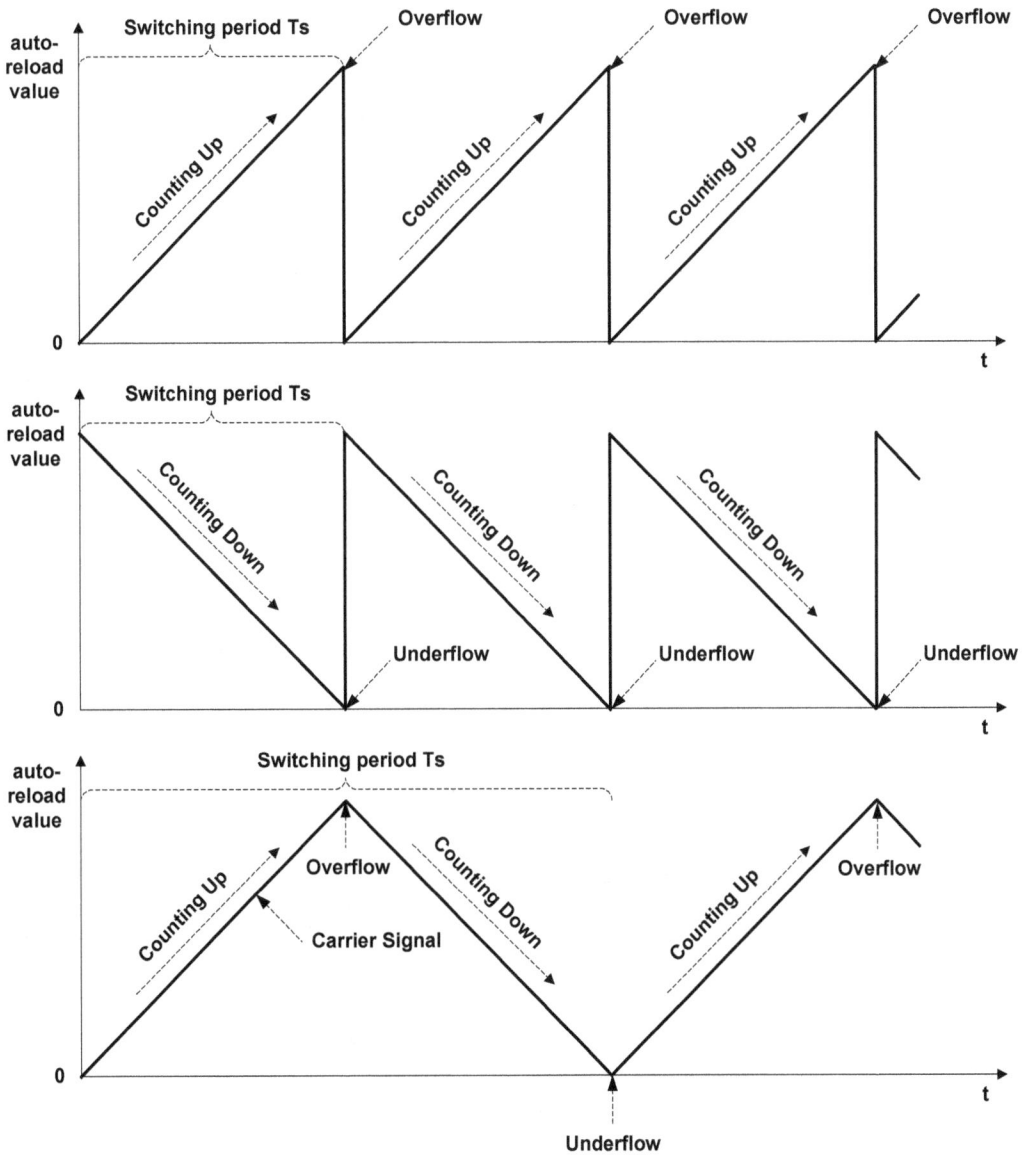

Figure 15-3. Three counting modes: upcounting, downcounting, and center-aligned counting

15.2 Compare Output

Figure 15-4 shows the basic diagram of output compare of a timer. The timer counter (CNT) has 16 bits. The value that is compared against the timer counter is stored in the capture compare register (CCR). In this example, four output channels share the same free-run timer counter. Therefore, the timer counter is compared with four CCR registers simultaneously, generating four outputs independently.

The clock driving the timer counter ($CLOCK\_CNT$) can be slowed down by a constant factor called *prescaler* in order to generate outputs that spans over a long time period.

$$f_{CLOCK\_CNT} = \frac{f_{CLOCK\_PSC}}{Prescaler + 1}$$

A large prescaler reduces the timer's resolution but decreases the chance of overflow and underflow and improves the energy efficiency.

Different clocks can be used to drive the timer, including built-in clocks within the processor chip, external crystal oscillators, or some internal trigger signal such as the output of another timer. External clocks are preferred over internal clocks since external clocks are more accurate.

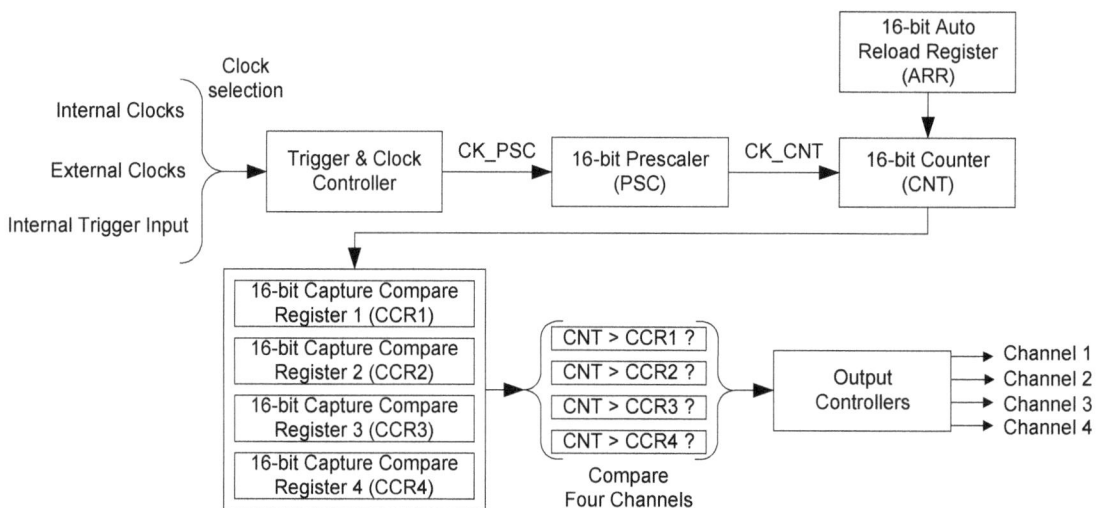

Figure 15-4. Basic diagram of the output compare of a timer that supports four channels

15.2.1 Setting Output Mode

When the timer counter (CNT) equals the compare value (CCR), the output of a channel (OCREF) can be set up as different values, depending on the configuration stored in the output compare mode (OCM) register, as shown in Table 15-1.

- The mode 000 leaves the output unchanged.
- The mode 011 toggles the output whenever CNT and CCR match, making the output switch between high and low alternatively.
- The mode 001 and 010 output high and low respectively when CNT matches CCR. In digital output, we have two different logical representation forms: active high and active low. In active high, a signal with a high voltage represents a logical 1, and a low voltage represents 0. On the contrary, a high voltage represents 0 and a low voltage represents 1 in active low. Selection of active high or active low is determined by the output polarity setting of the control register.
- The mode 100 and 101 forces the output to stay low and high, respectively. While the output is constant, the mode still updates the flags and generates interrupts if enabled.

Output Compare Mode (OCM)	Timer Output (OCREF)
000	Frozen
001	High if CNT = CCR
010	Low if CNT = CCR
011	Toggle if CNT = CCR
100	Forced low (always low)
101	Forced high (always high)

Table 15-1. Control of timer channel output

Figure 15-5 compares the channel output signal when the output mode is the toggle mode, the none-one-pulse high mode, and the one-pulse high mode. In this example, the counter is counting upward from 0 to ARR.

- In the toggle mode (011), the output is toggled whenever the free-run counter (CNT) equals the capture and compare register (CCR). In this mode, the output alternates between high and low for an equal amount of time as long as CCR is smaller than ARR.
- When the mode is in the high mode (001), the output is set as high whenever CNT matches CCR. The output is cleared if the timer is set as one pulse mode; otherwise, the output is not cleared. If it is not in the one-pulse mode, the output is not cleared automatically. The timer output has to be cleared either externally by using an input signal to the chip or internally by using another timer.
- In the one-pulse mode, the timer output is cleared automatically when the counter reaches the value of CCR during counting upward or 0 during counting

downward. The one-pulse mode can periodically generate a pulse with a programmable width, with the period programmable, too.

If interrupt of a timer is enabled, an interrupt is generated and its corresponding interrupt service routine is executed whenever (1) CNT matches CCR, or (2) CNT has an overflow (reset to 0 if counting up) or an underflow (reset to ARR if counting down). The interrupt service routine needs to check the timer status register to find what event has occurred. The update interrupt flag (UIF) is set upon overflow or underflow, and the capture and compare interrupt flag (CCIF) is set when CNT matches CCR. A separate DMA interrupt can also be generated to load efficiently a value stored in the data memory into ARR or CRR without involving the processor. DMA operations are introduced in Chapter 19.

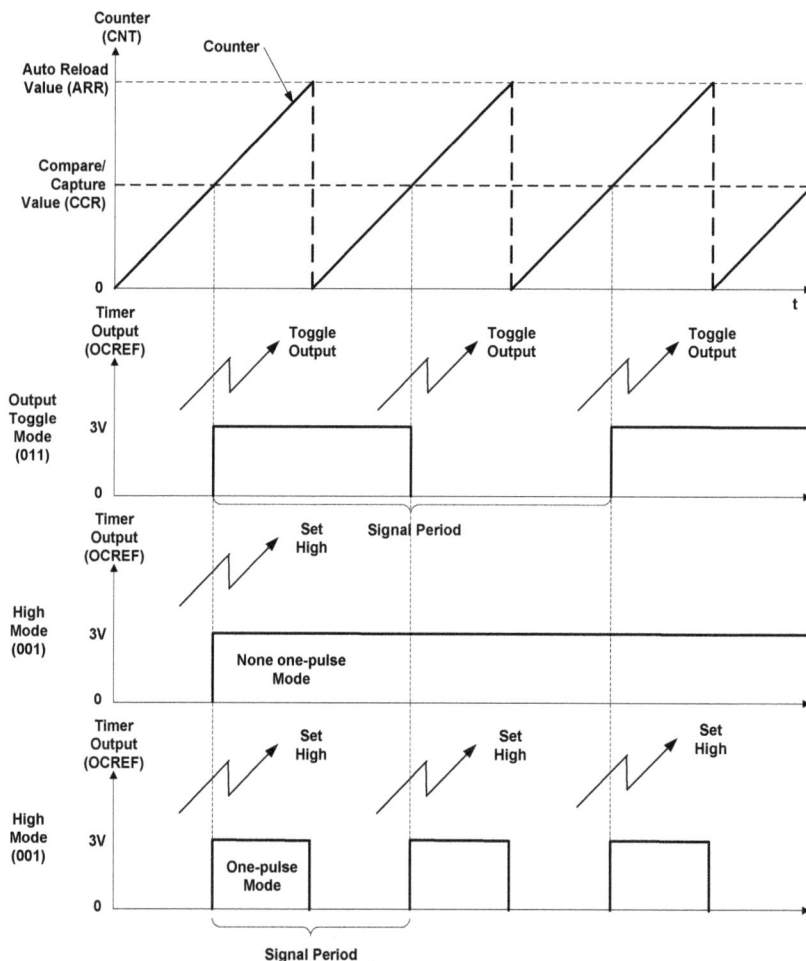

Figure 15-5. Timer output if the output compare mode is toggle (011), none one-pulse and one-pulse high mode (001).

15.2.2 Example of Toggling LED

This following example shows an LED is toggled every second by using the compare and output function of a timer. The output mode is set as toggling the output whenever the timer counter (CNT) equals the compare and capture register (CCR). Suppose the clock frequency to the timer is 2.097 MHz. We will slow down the clock to the counter to 1 KHz. Since we have

$$f_{CLOCK\_CNT} = \frac{f_{CLOCK\_PSC}}{Prescaler + 1}$$

We get

$$Prescaler = \frac{f_{CLOCK\_PSC}}{f_{CLOCK\_CNT}} - 1 = \frac{2.097MHz}{1KHz} - 1 = 2096$$

In order to turn an LED on for 1 second and then off for 1 second repeatedly, the auto-reload register (ARR) is then set to 1,000. The timer counts from 0 to 999 repeatedly, and CCR can be set as any integer value between 0 and 999.

GPIO Pin	Connection	Mode	AF	Output Type	Pull-up/Pull-down	Clock
Port B pin 6	Blue LED	AF	TIM4_CH1	Push-pull	No pull-up, no pull-down	40 MHz

Table 15-2. Setting of GPIO pin that uses a timer to toggle a LED

```
// PB 6 is connected to Blue LED externally and to TIM4_CH1 internally.

int main(void) {
  // Enable the clock to GPIO port B
  RCC->AHBENR    |= RCC_AHBENR_GPIOBEN;

  // Set pin 6 I/O mode as alternative function
  // input(00, reset), output(01), alternative function(10), analog(11)
  GPIOB->MODER   &= ~(0x03 << (2*6)); // Clear bit 13 and bit 12
  GPIOB->MODER   |= 0x02 << (2*6);
  // Pin PB 6 as alternative function 2 (TIM4)
  GPIOB->AFR[0]  |= 0x2 << (4*6);

  // Set I/O output speed value as 40 MHz
  // 400 KHz(00), 2 MHz(01), 10 MHz(01), 40 MHz (11)
  GPIOB->OSPEEDR &= ~(0x03<<(2*6));    // Speed mask
  GPIOB->OSPEEDR |=  0x03<<(2*6);

  // Set I/O output as push-pull
  // Push-pull(0, reset), open-drain(1)
  GPIOB->PUPDR   |= (0x00<<(2*6));
  GPIOB->OTYPER  &= ~(1<<6);
```

```
RCC->APB1ENR    |= RCC_APB1ENR_TIM4EN;   // Enable clock

// Default clock: MSI Range 5, 2.097 MHz
// Set the timer clock frequency as 1000Hz
// Timer clock = processor clock / (PSC[15:0] + 1).
TIM4->PSC       = 2097000/1000 - 1; // Prescaler Value

TIM4->ARR       = 1000;                 // Auto-reload value
TIM4->CCR1      = 500;                  // Compare and output register

// Set OC1M of channel 1 to 011: OC1REF toggles when CNT matches CCR1
TIM4->CCMR1     = TIM_CCMR1_OC1M_0 | TIM_CCMR1_OC1M_1;

TIM4->CCER      = TIM_CCER_CC1E;    // Enable compare output 1
TIM4->CR1       = TIM_CR1_CEN;      // Enable timer 4

while(1);
}
```

Example 15-1. Lighting up an LED by using the compare-output function of a timer

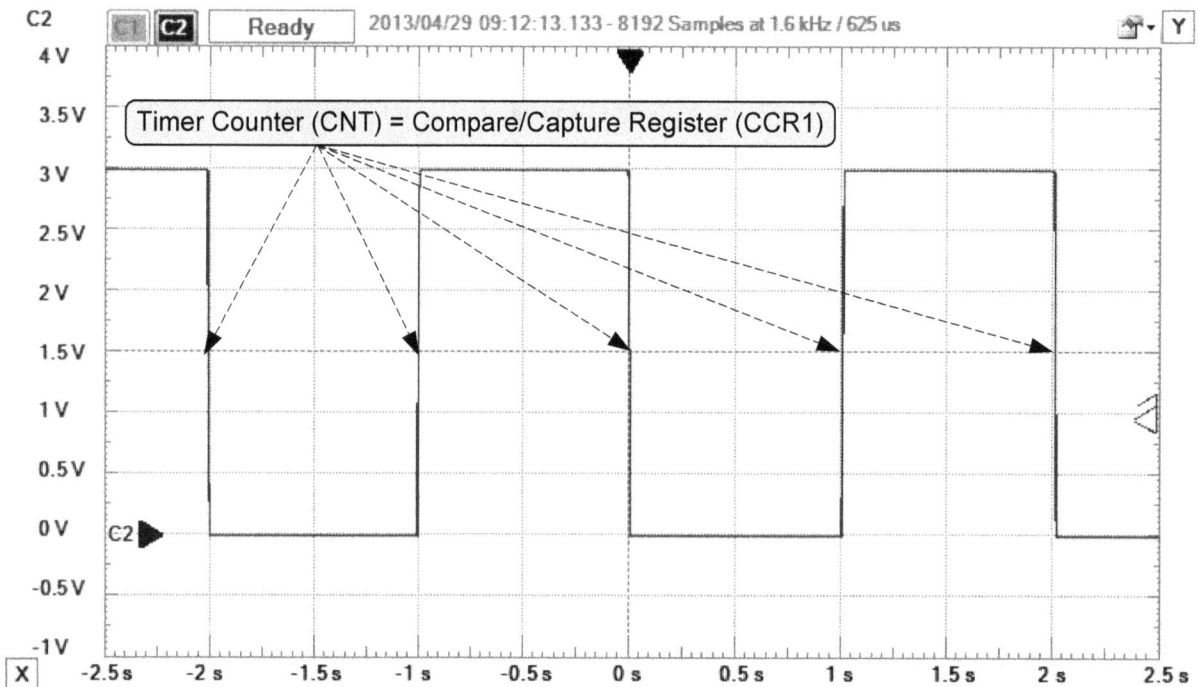

Figure 15-6. Voltage output signal of channel 1 of timer 4 (OC1REF)

15.3 PWM Output

Pulse width modulation (PWM) is a simple digital technique to control the value of an analog variable. PWM uses a fast rectangular pulse waveform to quickly switch a voltage source on and off to produce a desired average voltage output. The percentage of time spent on the on state within one period is proportional to the average value of the voltage output. Thus by changing or modulating the width of the on state or the switching frequency, the output voltage or the output power delivery is adjusted accordingly to emulate an analog signal.

PWM has been widely used in a variety of applications, such as motor speed and torque control, digital encoding in telecommunications, DC-to-DC power conversion, and audio amplification. In this lab, we will use the PWM technique to control the brightness of an LED.

The PWM switching frequency should be carefully selected to avoid serious negative impacts on applications. For example, the PWM switching frequency of an LED light must be at least 120Hz to avoid the flickering effects that can be seen by the human eyes.

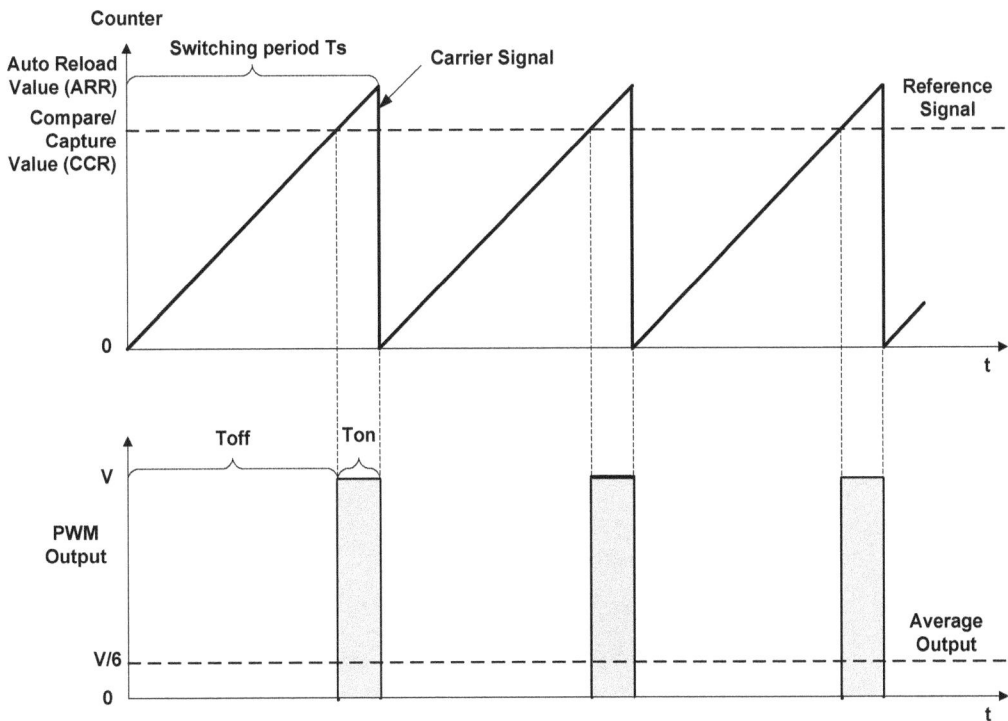

Figure 15-7. Example of simple PWM when duty cycle is 1/6

The average output value of a simple PWM that uses a saw-tooth carrier signal and a constant reference signal, as illustrated in Figure 15-7, Figure 15-8, and Figure 15-9, is linearly proportional to the **duty cycle**. The duty cycle is defined as follows:

$$duty\ cycle = \frac{pulse\ on\ time}{pulse\ switching\ period} \times 100\% = \frac{T_{on}}{T_s} \times 100\%$$

where

$$pulse\ switching\ period = \frac{1}{PWM\ switching\ frequency}$$

By controlling the duty cycle, we control this average value. In the LED example, the brightness is determined by the PWM duty cycle. Figure 15-7, Figure 15-8, and Figure 15-9 give three examples in which the average output is 1/6, 1/3, and 1/2 respectively.

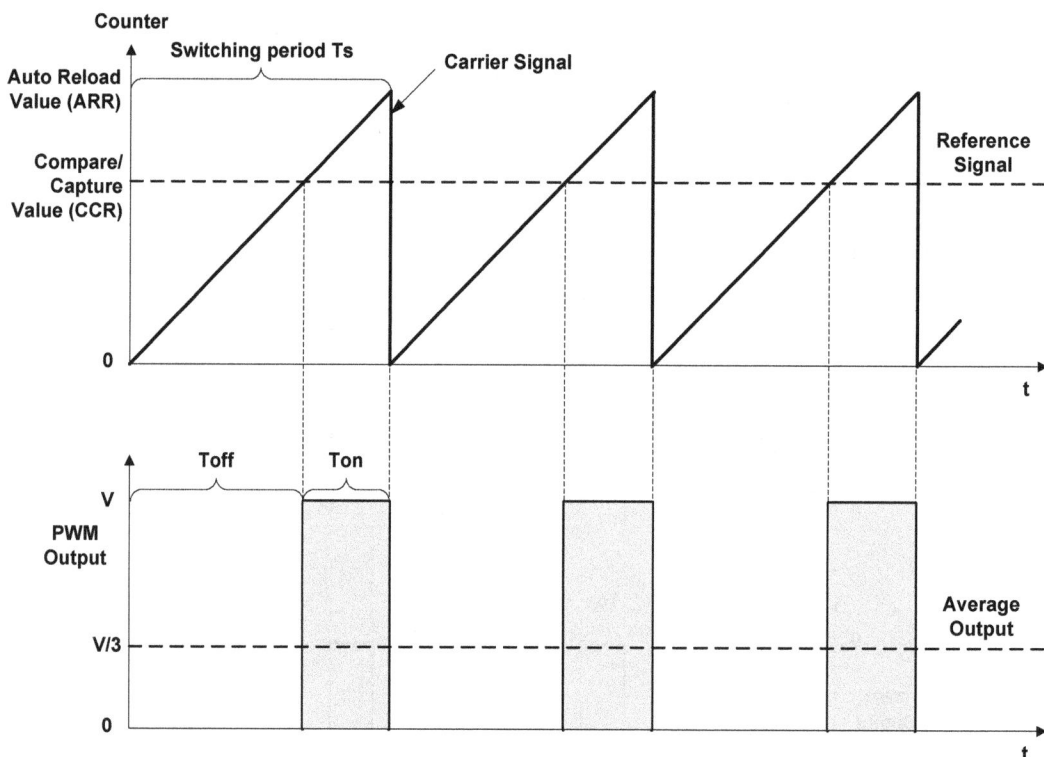

Figure 15-8. Example of simple PWM when duty cycle is 1/3

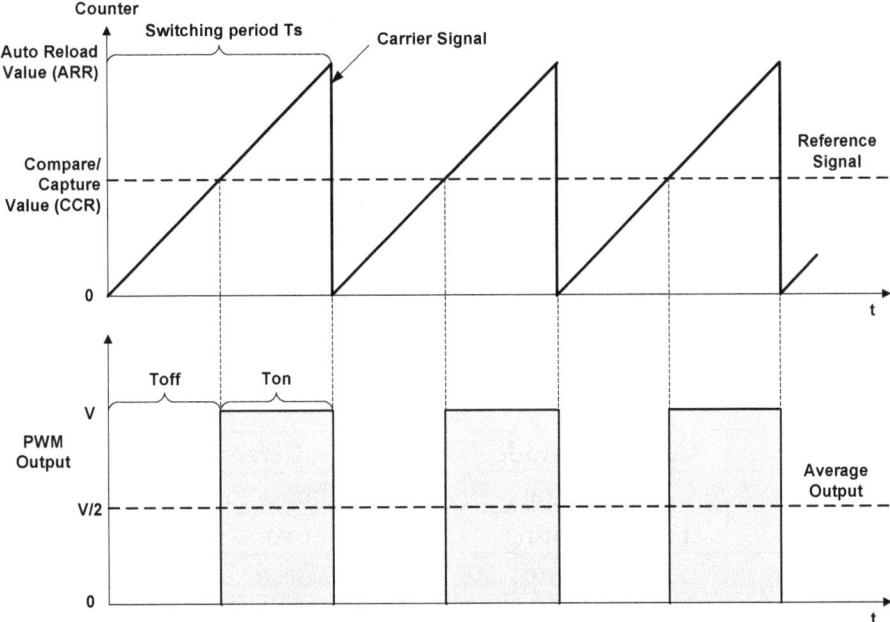

Figure 15-9. Example of simple PWM when duty cycle is 1/2

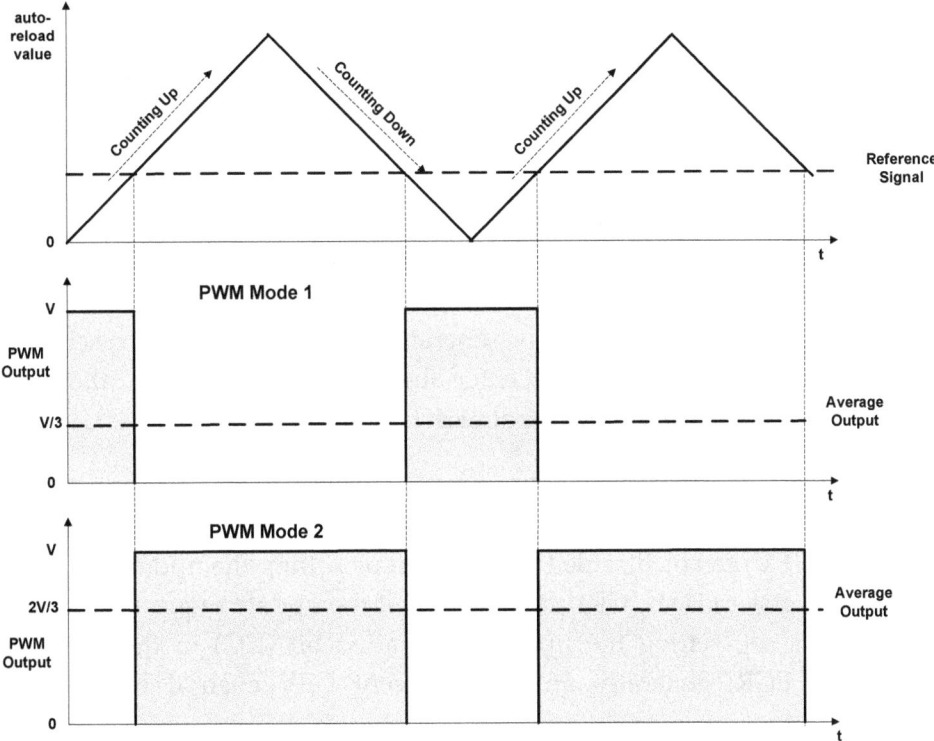

Figure 15-10. Comparison of PWM mode 1 and PWM mode 2

The PWM output is determined by comparing the counter and the given reference signal, as well as the PWM output mode. There are two PWM output modes, and the outputs in these two modes are opposite to each other.

- **PWM mode 1**: If the counter is less than the reference signal, the PWM output is then held at active; otherwise, it is held at inactive.
- **PWM mode 2**: The PWM output is the opposite of the output of the PWM mode 1. If the counter is greater than the reference signal, the PWM output is then held at active; otherwise, it is held at inactive.

In the center-aligned mode, the output logic scheme depends on the current counting direction, as shown in Figure 15-10.

Mode	Counting Mode	Counter < Reference	Counter ≥ Reference
PWM mode 1	Upcounting	Active	Inactive
	Downcounting	Active	Inactive
PWM mode 2	Upcounting	Inactive	Active
	Downcounting	Inactive	Active

Table 15-3. Two PWM output modes

The polarity of PWM output can be programmed by software as either active high or active low by software. In the active high, logic '1' outputs a high voltage and logic '0' outputs a low voltage. The output of active low is the opposite of active high.

15.3.1 PWM Output Events

An update event (UEV) can be generated depending on the counting mode. In the upcounting mode, the UEV is generated when the counter matches the reference constant stored in the auto-reload value register, *i.e.* a counter overflow occurs. In the downcounting mode, a UEV event is generated when the counter reaches zero, *i.e.* a counter underflow occurs. In the center-aligned counting mode, these events are generated at each counter overflow or at each counter underflow.

For STM32 processor, when an update event of timer x occurs, an interrupt is generated if the update interrupt flag bit (UIF) of the control register TIMx_CR1 is set to 1. The update event (UEV) can be disabled by software by setting the update disable bit (UDIS) in the control register (TIMx_CR1). In addition, if the update request selection bit (URS) of TIMx_CR1 is set, setting the update generation bit (UG) in the event generation register (TIMx_EGR) generates an update event UEV even if the UIF flag bit of TIMx_CR1 is not set.

15.3.2 PWM Programming Flowchart

The diagram given in Figure 15-11 uses the PWM output to gradually increase or decrease the brightness of the blue LED on the STM32L discovery kit. The blue and green LED is connected to the PB 6 pin and the PB 7 pin, respectively. Table 15-4 shows the alternative functions available for these two pins. On the chip, the PB 6 pin can be programmed to connect to channel 1 of timer 4, and the PB 7 pin can be connected to channel 2 of timer 4.

LED	Pin	Available Alternative Functions
Blue	PB 6	I2C1_SCL/TIM4_CH1/USART1_TX
Green	PB 7	I2C1_SDA/TIM4_CH2/USART1_RX/PVD_IN

Table 15-4. Alternative functions of pin PB 6 and 7

The default clock frequency that is used to drive the processor as well as each peripheral, including timers, is 2^{21} Hz $\approx$ 2.097 MHz. In this example, the prescaler factor is set as 63, thus the frequency at which the counter increments is

$$f_{CK\_CNT} = \frac{f_{CL\_PSC}}{Prescaler + 1} = \frac{2^{21}}{63 + 1} = 2^{15} \ Hz = 32.768 \ KHz$$

We set the ARR register as 199. Therefore, the timer generates a pulse in each period of

$$T_{PWM} = \frac{ARR + 1}{f_{CK\_CNT}} = \frac{200}{2^{15} Hz} = 6.1 \ ms$$

As a result, approximately 164 outputs are generated each second. This shows that the ARR register determines the frequency at which PWM outputs are generated. When the ARR register is fixed, the duty cycle is determined by the value of the compare and capture register (CCR).

In PWM mode 1, we have

$$duty \ cycle = \frac{CCR}{ARR+1} \times 100\%,$$

In PWM mode 2, we have

$$duty \ cycle = (1 - \frac{CCR}{ARR+1}) \times 100\%.$$

When the CCR gradually increases from 0 to 199, the duty cycle of PWM mode 1 is then gradually increases 0 to 1. Therefore, the brightness of the LED slowly increases 0% to 100%.

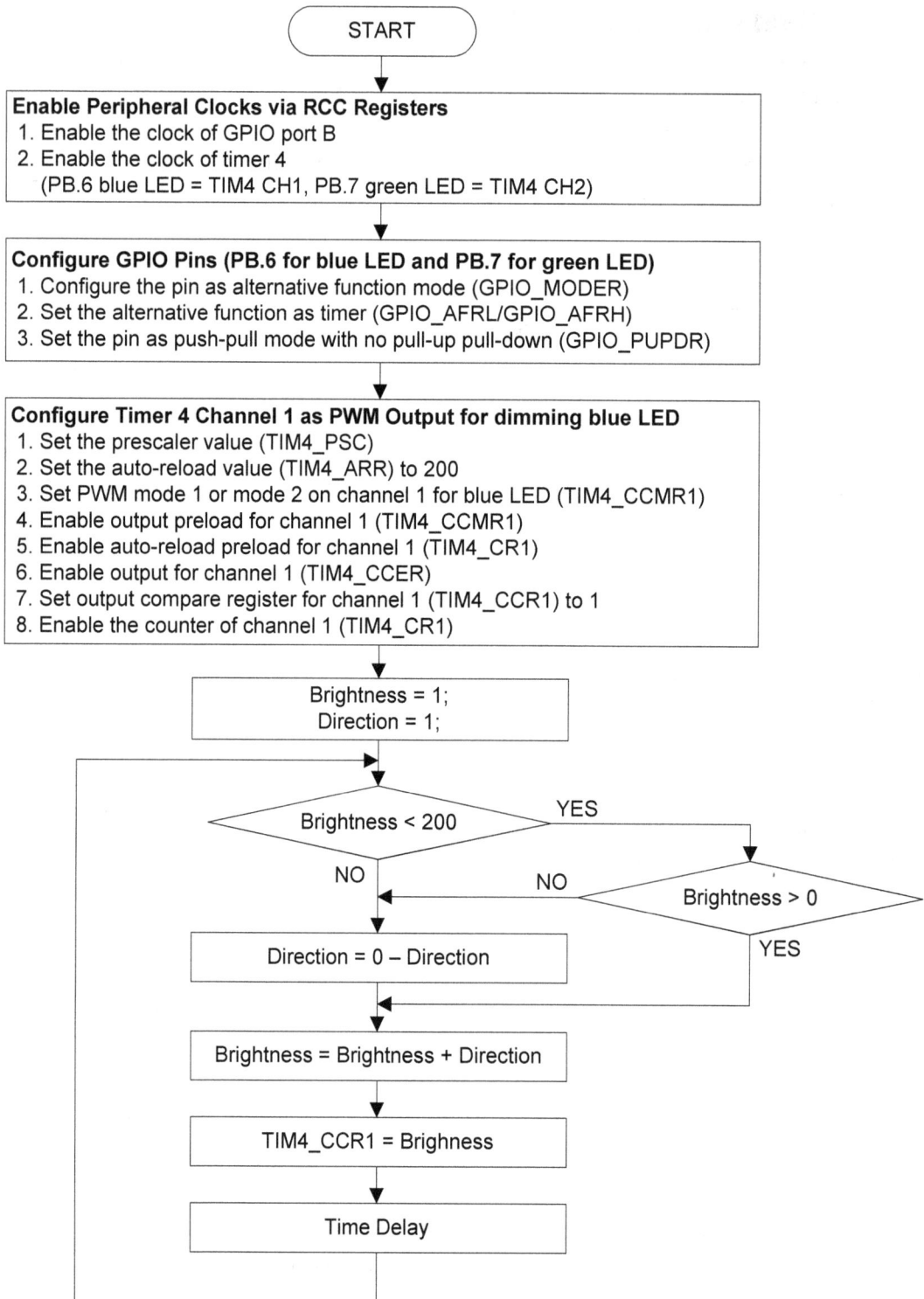

Figure 15-11. Flowchart for dimming an LED via PWM output of a timer

The following C programs, given in Example 15-2 and Example 15-3, show the initialization of channel 1 of timer 4 as PWM output and changing the duty cycle of the PWM output, respectively.

```c
void TIM4_Init() {
        RCC->APB1ENR |= RCC_APB1ENR_TIM4EN;      // Enable timer clock

        TIM4->PSC    = 63;                        // Prescaler = 63

        // Auto-reload: upcounting (0->ARR), downcounting (ARR->0)
        TIM4->ARR    = 200 - 1;

        // OC1M = 110 for PWM Mode 1 output on channel 1
        TIM4->CCMR1 |= TIM_CCMR1_OC1M_1 | TIM_CCMR1_OC1M_2;
        TIM4->CCMR1 |= TIM_CCMR1_OC1PE;    // Output 1 preload enable
        TIM4->CR1   |= TIM_CR1_ARPE;       // Auto-reload preload enable
        TIM4->CCER  |= TIM_CCER_CC1E;      // Enable output for channel 1
        TIM4->EGR   |= TIM_EGR_UG;         // Force update
        TIM4->SR    &= ~TIM_SR_UIF;        // Clear the update flag
        TIM4->DIER  |= TIM_DIER_UIE;       // Enable interrupt on update event
        TIM4->CR1   |= TIM_CR1_CEN;        // Enable counter
}
```

Example 15-2. Initialization program of PWM output in C

The following program shows the main function. Within the endless loop, the compare and capture register for channel 1 (CCR1) is increased or decreased gradually after a short delay.

```c
Void main(){
        int i;
        int brightness = 0;
        int stepSize = 1;
        ...  // Initialization codes, not shown here
        while(1) {
           if ((brightness >= 200) || (brightness <= 0))
              stepSize = -stepSize;      // Reverse direction
           brightness += stepSize;       // Change brightness
           TIM4->CCR1 = brightness;      // Set brightness for channel 1
           for(i = 0; i < 10000; i++);   // A short delay
        }
}
```

Example 15-3. Example program to change the brightness

The following program shows the initialization of channel 1 of timer 4 as PWM output in assembly program.

```asm
        ; Enable clock on timer 4
        LDR    r7, =RCC_BASE
        LDR    r0, [r7, #RCC_APB1ENR]
        BIC    r0, r0, #RCC_APB1ENR_TIM4EN
```

```
ORR    r0, r0, #RCC_APB1ENR_TIM4EN
STR    r0, [r7, #RCC_APB1ENR]
LDR r7, =TIM4_BASE

; Set prescaler
LDR    r0, [r7, #TIM_PSC]
MOV    r1, #0
STR    r0, [r7, #TIM_PSC]  ; Set prescaler to appropriate value

; Set auto-reload value
LDR    r0, [r7, #TIM_ARR]
MOV    r1, =TIM_ARR_ARR
BIC    r0, r0, r1
ORR    r0, r0, #199
STR    r0, [r7, #TIM_ARR]  ; Counts from 0 to 199 (200 steps)

; Set PWM mode on channel 1
LDR    r0, [r7, #TIM_CCMR1]
BIC    r0, r0, #TIM_CCMR1_OC1M
ORR    r0, r0, #TIM_CCMR1_OC1M_2
ORR    r0, r0, #TIM_CCMR1_OC1M_1

; Enable output preload on channel 1
BIC    r0, r0, #TIM_CCMR1_OC1PE
ORR    r0, r0, #TIM_CCMR1_OC1PE
STR    r0, [r7, #TIM_CCMR1]

; Enable auto-reload preload on channel 1
LDR    r0, [r7, #TIM_CR1]
BIC    r0, r0, #TIM_CR1_ARPE
ORR    r0, r0, #TIM_CR1_ARPE
STR    r0, [r7, #TIM_CR1]

; Enable output on channel 1
LDR    r0, [r7, #TIM_CCER]
ORR    r0, r0, #TIM_CCER_CC1E
STR    r0, [r7, #TIM_CCER]

; Enable output compare register for channel 1
LDR    r0, [r7, #TIM_CCR1]
LDR    r1, =TIM_CCR1_CCR1
BIC    r0, r0, r1
ORR    r0, r0, #0xFF
STR    r0, [r7, #TIM_CCR1]

; Enable counter on channel 1
LDR    r0, [r7, #TIM_CR1]
ORR    r0, r0, #TIM_CR1_CEN
STR    r0, [r7, #TIM_CR1]
```

Example 15-4. Initialization of PWM output in assembly

15.4 Input Capture

As presented previously, a timer can be used for triggering an output at a specified time to general output signals (PWM output, comparator output). In this section, we discuss the usage of timer as input capture, which finds the time space between the rising or falling transition events of an external signal, as shown in Figure 15-12. Depending on the application's need, captured events can be (1) either rising edges or falling edges, (2) only falling edges, or (3) only rising edges. Input capture timers are useful in many applications such as measuring motor speed and position, calculating time-of-flight for ultrasonic distance sensors, and communication between two remote devices.

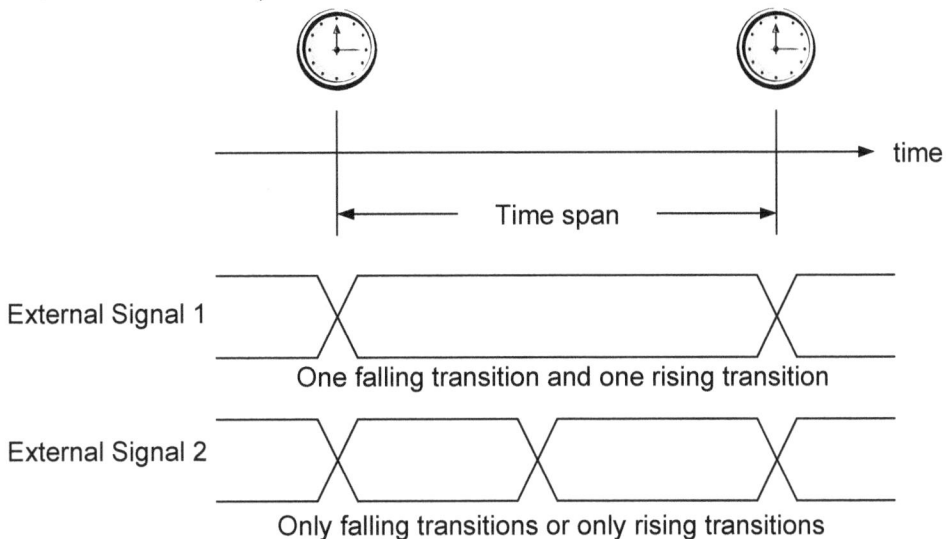

Figure 15-12. Input capture measures the time span between two consecutive events of an external signal. Timer can capture events (1) either rising or falling edges, (2) only rising edges, or (3) only falling edges, depending on the application's need. The time span is the product of the clock counter period and the difference of two consecutively captured values of the timer counter.

When a transition of an input signal occurs, the time instant is recorded by copying the value of the free-run counter to the compare and capture register. When a long time span is to be measured, the program needs to take care of the overflow of the free-running counter and a separate counter is needed to record the number of overflows. Each input capture channel has an input pin, a filter, a counter, and an edge detector configurable for detection of the falling edge, rising edge or both simultaneously. The timer counts according to a clock scaled by a prescaler constant. The 16-bit prescaler can be updated on the fly and is used to divide the counter clock frequency by any factor between 1 and 65536. If we wish to capture each valid transition, the external trigger filtering should be disabled by setting the External Trigger Filter (ETF) to zero.

Each input channel also has a simple digital input filter to remove noise pulses in an input signal. For example, if the input signal of a push button takes 10 internal clock cycles to become stable, then we can make the filter duration last longer than 10 clock cycles. We can validate the transition by repeatedly sampling the inputs. If a sequence of consecutive samples remain unchanged and stay at the same level, then this level is considered a stable input. If a noise spike occurs causing the input to change during any of the consecutive sampling points, the input is then considered not stable and is ignored, thus filtering out noisy transitions. The sampling frequency of the filter is configurable, and is typically two to four times the timer clock frequency. The number of consistent consecutive readings to validate a transition ranges from 0 to 8. If it is zero, then the noise filtering is disabled. Figure 15-13 shows an example in which the number of consistent readings is 2.

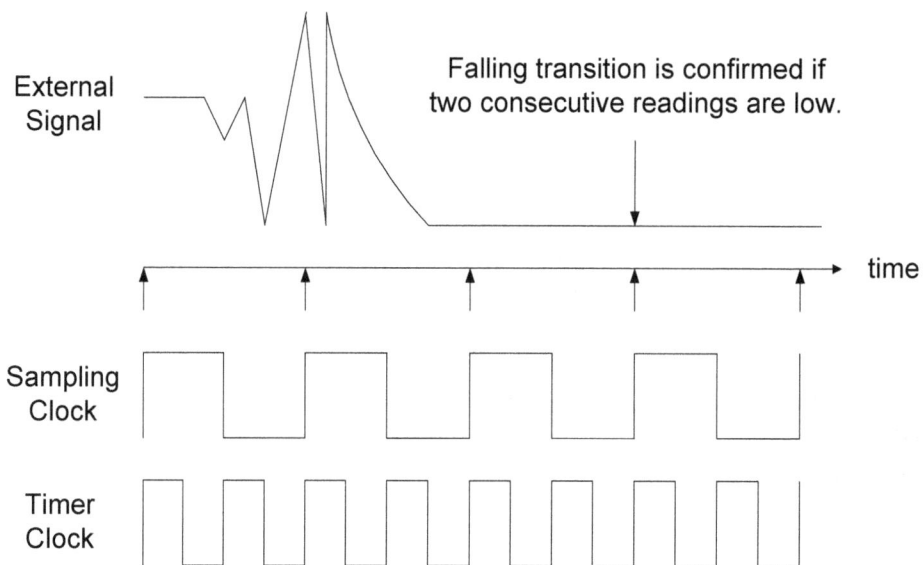

Figure 15-13. An example of filtering noise in external signal. The falling transition is confirmed if two consecutive sample readings are low. The sampling frequency is 1/8 of the timer frequency at which the timer counter is incremented or decremented.

The difference between two consecutive transitions can be used to measure an elapsed time span. If the input signal is periodic, the difference of the counters of two rising edge captures can measure the period of the waveform, and the difference of a rising edge and a falling edge can measure the pulse width. In this way, we can calculate the frequency and duty cycle of the input waveform.

15.4.1 Input Capture Timer Diagram

The 16-bit free-running counter can be driven by internal clocks, external clocks, or internal trigger input (such as another timer). The clock frequency can be divided by a 16-bit clock prescaler (PSC) to generate a desired frequency for the free-running counter.

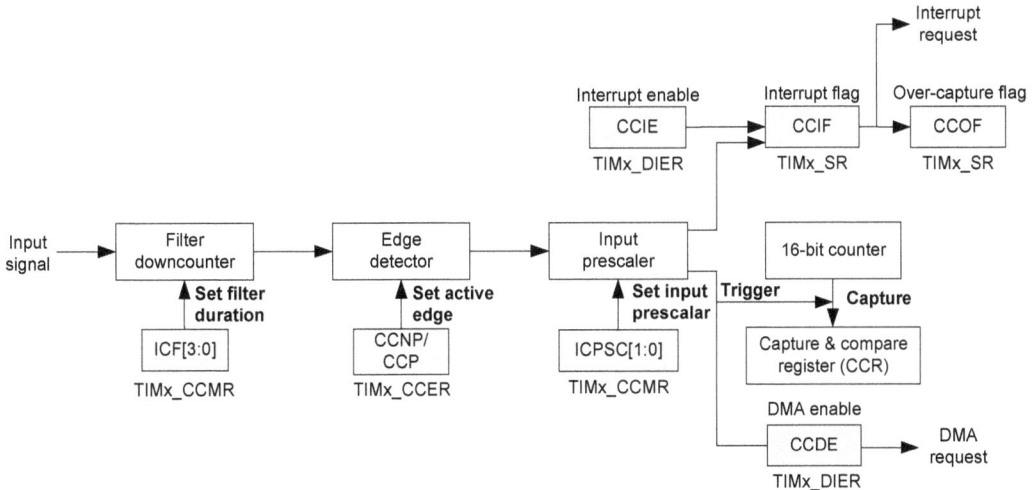

Figure 15-14. Diagram of input capture

Input capture: Figure 15-14 shows the timer diagram for input capture. When the number of external transitions on an input channel reaches the constant threshold defined by the *input capture prescaler* bits (ICPSC) of the capture/compare mode register (TIMx_CCMR), a capture takes places and the following operations are performed automatically by the microprocessor.

- It latches the value of the free-running counter to the capture/compare register (TIMx_CCR) corresponding to that channel. There is a 16-bit capture/compare for each capture channel (TIMx_CCR1 for channel 1, TIMx_CCR2 for channel 2, TIMx_CCR3 for channel 3, and TIMx_CCR4 for channel 4).
- In the status register (TIMx_SR), the capture/compare interrupt flag (CCIF) corresponding to that channel is set by hardware on a capture. If the CCIF flag has already been set, then corresponding capture/compare over-capture flag (CCOF) in the status register (TIMx_SR) is set by hardware. While the CCIF flag is cleared by software (writing it to 0) or by reading the corresponding CCR register, the CCOF flag can only be cleared by software.
- If the interrupt is enabled according to the capture/compare interrupt enable bit (CCIE) of the DMA and interrupt enable register (TIMx_DIER), an interrupt correspondingly to that channel is then generated.

- If DMA is enabled according to the capture/compare DMA request enable bit (CCDE) of the DIER register, a DMA request is then generated.

15.4.2 Configuring Input Capture

In the following, we use the channel 1 of timer 4 as an example to illustrate the basic procedure of capturing a rising edge transition of an external signal.

1. *Select the active input.* Each timer supports four capture/compare channels in the STM32L processor and each channel can be configured as a compare output or a capture input connected to one of the timer external input or internal trigger sources. The CC1S[1:0] bits in TIM4_CCMR1 register configures the direction of channel 1 (input or output) and the input source of channel 1. The usage of CC1S[1:0] bits are defined as follows:

   - 00: Channel 1 is configured as output.
   - 01: Channel 1 is configured as input, and it is mapped on timer input 1 (TI1).
   - 10: Channel 1 is configured as input, and it is mapped on timer input 2 (TI2).
   - 11: Channel 1 is configured as input, and it is mapped on TRC. The input of another timer is used as the input.

   Thus to link to the timer input 1 (TI1), we need to set CC1S bits to 01. Note if CC1S bits are 00, then the channel is configured as a compare output. When a channel is configured as capture input, its corresponding CCR register becomes read-only.

2. *Set the input filter.* The IC1F bits of the TIM4_CCMR1 register define the frequency used to sample TI1 and the length of digital filtering applied to TI1. The digital filtering is to check whether a number of consecutive readings of an input remain the same. If yes, the input is stable and the input transition is valid.

   a. For example, if IC1F is 0000, the digital filtering is disabled.
   b. If IC1F is 0010, the sampling frequency is the counter frequency and if four consecutive samplings remain the same, then the transition is valid.

3. *Set the active edge.* The CC1P bit and CC1NP bit in the TIM4 capture/compare enable register (TIM4_CCER) collectively determines the edge of an active transition on the TI1 channel.

   - If CC1NP = 0 and CC1P = 0, then the edge detection is configured to capture rising edges.

- If CC1NP = 0 and CC1P = 1, only falling edges are captured.
- If CC1NP = 1 and CC1P = 1, then both falling and rising edges are captured.

4. *Set the input prescaler.* If we wish to capture the event each time an edge is detected in channel 1, the prescaler, defined by the IC1PSC bits of the TIM1 capture/compare mode register 1 (TIM4_CCMR1), should be set to 00. When IC1PSC is 01, 10, and 11, the input capture is then performed once every 2, 4, and 8 events, respectively. Depending on applications, we might want to wait for multiple valid transitions before the counter is latched.

5. *Enable the input capture.* The input capture of channel 1 can be enabled by setting the CC1E bit of the TIM4 capture/compare enable register (TIM4_CCER).

6. *Enable interrupt and DMA if needed.* The related interrupt request is enabled by setting the CC1IE bit in the TIM4 DMA/interrupt enable register (TIM4_DIER). The DMA request is enabled by setting the CC1DE bit of the TIM4_DIER register. The TIE bit enables trigger interrupt and the UIE bit enables the update interrupt.

7. *Enable the timer counter.* Sets the counter enable bit (CEN) in the TIM4 control register 1 (TIM4_CR1).

```
           ┌─────────────┐
           │    START    │
           └─────────────┘
                  │
                  ▼
```

Configure GPIO Pin
1. Enable the clock for GPIO port B (RCC_AHBENR_GPIOBEN)
2. Set Pin PB.6 as alternative function 2 (TIM 4)
3. Note: PB.6 can be used as I2C1_SCL/TIM4_CH1/USART1_TX. When used as a generic timer, it is connected to channel 1.

Configure Timer 4 Input Capture (Channel 1)
1. Enable the clock of timer 4 (RCC_APB1ENR_TIM4EN)
2. Set the prescaler (TIM4_PSC) to configure frequency of free-run counter
2. Select the active input (TIM4->CCMR1)
3. Program the input filter duration (TIM4->CCMR1)
4. Select the edge of the active transition (TIM4->CCER)
5. Program the input prescaler (TIM4->CCMR1). To capture each valid transition, set the input prescaler to zero.
6. Enable capture from the counter (TIM4->CCER)
7. Enable the interrupt (TIM4->DIER)
8. Enable the counter (TIM4->CR1)

Enable Interrupt
1. Set the interrupt priority of TIM4_IRQn
2. Enable the interrupt TIM4_IRQn

```
           ┌─────────────┐
           │  Dead loop  │
           └─────────────┘
```

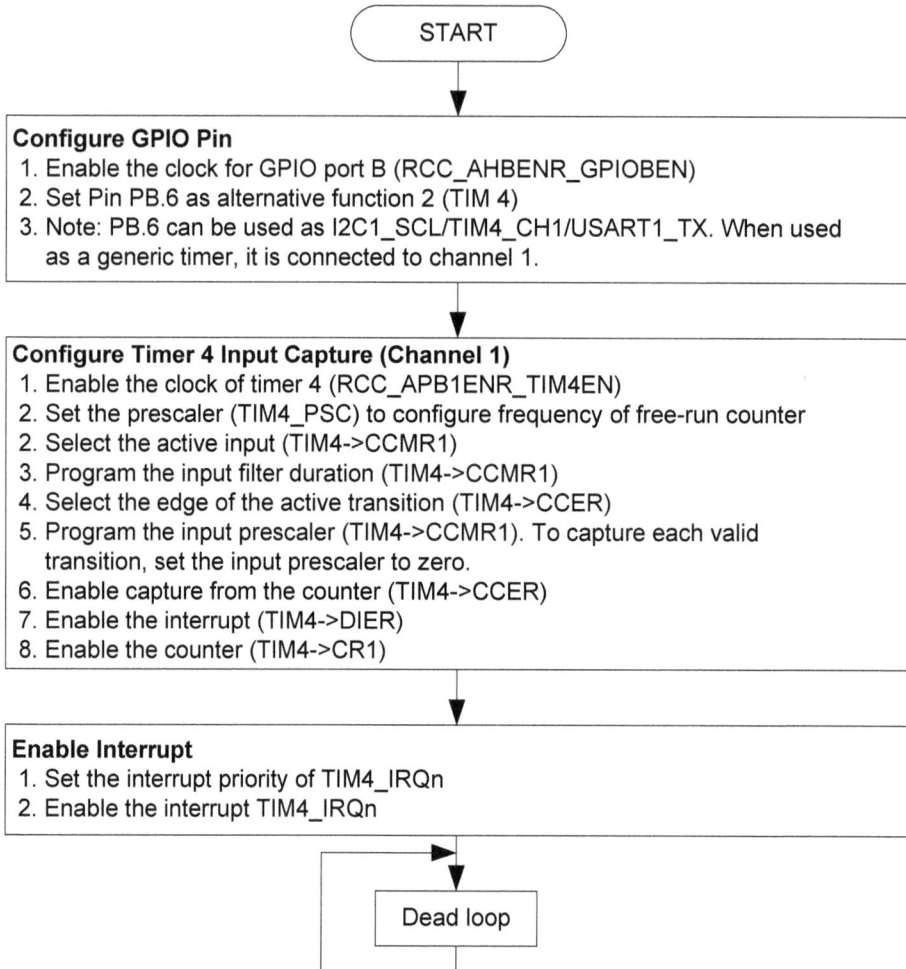

Figure 15-15. Flowchart to set the GPIO pin PB.6 as input capture

The following gives an example code of the interrupt service routine.

```c
void TIM4_IRQHandler() {
    if(TIM4->SR & TIM_SR_CC1IF != 0) {// If update flag is set
        // Calculate the time interval between two consecutive capture events
        current_value = TIM4->CCR1; // Reading CCR1 clears CC1IF interrupt flag
        time_interval = current_value - old_value; // if counting up
        old_value = current_value;
    }
}
```

Example 15-5. Timer interrupt handler in C

GPIO Pin	Connection	Mode	AF	Output Type	Pull-up/Pull-down	Clock
Port B pin 6	Blue LED	AF	TIM4_CH1	Push-pull	No pull-up, No pull-down	40 MHz

The following gives an example code of setting pin PB.6 as input capture.

```c
#include <stdint.h>
#include "stm32l1xx.h"

void TIM4_IRQHandler(void);

int value = 0;

int main() {

    // Blue LED   -> PB6/I2C1_SCL/TIM4_CH1/USART1_TX
    RCC->AHBENR  |=  RCC_AHBENR_GPIOBEN;  // Enable GPIOB clock

    // Configure GPIO port B pin 6 as AF function (i.e. TIM4_CH1)
    // with push-pull, and enable the clock of GPIO port B
    // Code is not give here.

    /*********************************************************************
     * Configure channel x to make input capture
     * (1) CCRx stores the value of the counter after a transition detected by
     *     corresponding ICx signal.
     * (2) When a capture occurs, CCxIF flag of TIMx_SR is set.
     *     If CCxIF is already set, then the over-capture flag CCxOF of
     *     TIMx_SR is set.
     * (3) CCxIF is cleared by software by writing it to 0 or
     *     by reading TIMx_CCRx.
     * (4) CCxOF is cleared by software by writing it to 0.
     *********************************************************************/

    // Enable the clock of timer 4
    RCC->APB1ENR |= RCC_APB1ENR_TIM4EN;

    // Set up an appropriate prescaler to slow down the clock of timer counter
    TIM4->PSC = 127;
    // Set the direction as input and select the active input
    TIM4->CCMR1  &= ~TIM_CCMR1_CC1S;     // CC1S[1:0] for channel 1:
    TIM4->CCMR1  |= 0x1; // 00 = output
                         // 01 = input, CC1 is mapped on timer Input 1
                         // 10 = input, CC1 is mapped on timer Input 2
                         // 11 = input, CC1 is mapped on slave timer

    // Program the input filter duration
    // Set as no filter by clearing IC1F[3:0] bits (input capture 1 filter)
    TIM4->CCMR1  &= ~TIM_CCMR1_IC1F;

    // Select the edge of the active transition
    // Detect only rising edges in this example
    // CC1NP:CC1P bits
    //    00 = rising edge, 01 = falling edge, 10 = reserved, 11 = both edges
```

```
    TIM4->CCER   &= ~(1<<1 | 1<<3);      // only rising edge

    // Program the input prescaler
    // To capture each valid transition, set the input prescaler to zero;
    // IC1PSC[1:0] bits (input capture 1 prescaler)
    TIM4->CCMR1 &= ~(TIM_CCMR1_IC1PSC);

    // Enable capture of the counter
    // CC1E: Capture/compare output enable for channel 1
    // 0 = capture disabled;  1 = capture enabled
    TIM4->CCER   |= TIM_CCER_CC1E;

    // if needed, enable the related interrupt
    // CC1IE: Capture/compare interrupt enable for channel 1
    TIM4->DIER   |= TIM_DIER_CC1IE;
    // CC1DE: Capture/compare DMA request enable for channel 1
    TIM4->DIER   |= TIM_DIER_CC1DE;

    // Enable the counter
    TIM4->CR1    |= TIM_CR1_CEN;

    NVIC_SetPriority(TIM4_IRQn, 1);      // Set priority to 1

    NVIC_EnableIRQ(TIM4_IRQn);           // Enable EXTI0_1 interrupt in NVIC

    while(1);
}
```

Example 15-6. Implementation of the initialization of a timer for input capture

15.4.3 Interfacing to Ultrasonic Distance Sensor

An ultrasonic distance sensor has one transmitter that can generate high frequency waves and one receiver that can detect the wave, as shown in Figure 15-16. Without contacting with the target, it measures the distance by calculating the difference in time between sending short bursts of ultrasonic waves and receiving the return waves reflected back from the target, as shown below:

$$Distance = \frac{Round\ Trip\ Time \times Speed\ of\ Sound}{2}$$

One example application is an automatic door opener, which opens a door when a person approaches. Compared with optical distance sensor, ultrasonic distance sensors are low cost but less accurate.

Figure 15-16. Ultrasonic distance sensor of HC-SR 04
(VCC = +5V DC, Trig = Trigger input to sensor, Echo = Echo time output of sensor)

To start a distance measurement, a high-pulse signal (≥3.2V) with a width of 10μs is sent to the Trig pin. The ultrasonic transmitter then sends out 8 cycles of 40-KHz ultrasonic waves (*i.e.* for 200 μs), which is greater than the upper limit of human hearing range (typically 20 KHz). When the ultrasonic receiver detects any waves reflected back within a predefined time window, it generates a high pulse (5V) on the echo pin. The pulse width is directly proportional to the distance of the nearest objects. Specifically, if the width of the pulse generated by the echo pin is in microseconds (μs), the distance, measured in centimeters, is calculated as the following:

$$Distance\ (cm) = \frac{Pulse\ Width\ (\mu s)}{58}$$

The sensor can measure a distance in 2 cm – 400 cm, with a resolution of 0.3 cm, and the corresponding echo pulse width is 150 μs – 25 ms. When no object is detected, the echo pulse width is 38 ms.

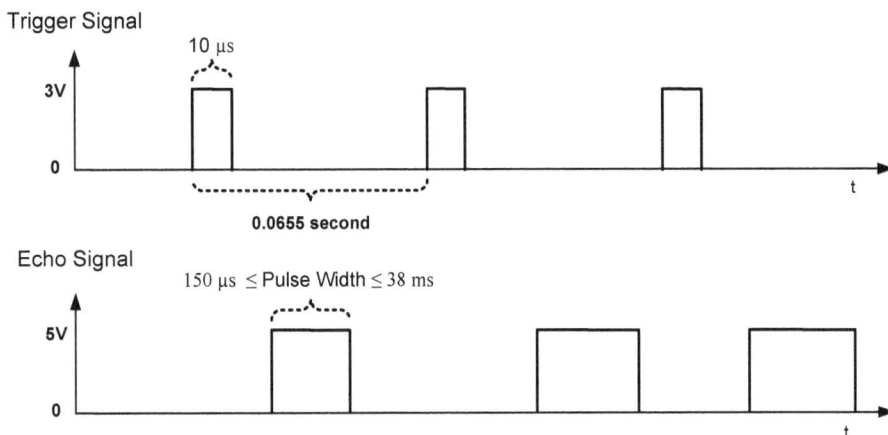

Figure 15-17. Trigger and echo signals

Suppose we want to measure the distance every 0.0655 second, as shown in Figure 15-17. We can use two timers to interface the ultrasonic distance sensor. The first timer, which is set as output compare and connected to the trigger pin of the sensor, generates a pulse signal with a width of 10 μs. The second timer, which is set as input capture and connected to the echo pin of the sensor, measures the pulse width of the echo signal. The second timer should be able to detect both the rising and falling edge of the echo signal.

Note the distance measured is only for one particular direction with limited angular resolution. Multiple ultrasonic sensors are often used to detect objects in several directions. It is also possible that an object reflects the ultrasonic waves away if the target surface is oriented at unfavorable angles, resulting in the object being undetected. In addition, objects with a soft or irregular surface might not reflect enough ultrasonic waves back and accordingly they may not be detected. In addition, sounds travel slower in colder air and thus calibration should be performed in order to achieve better accuracy.

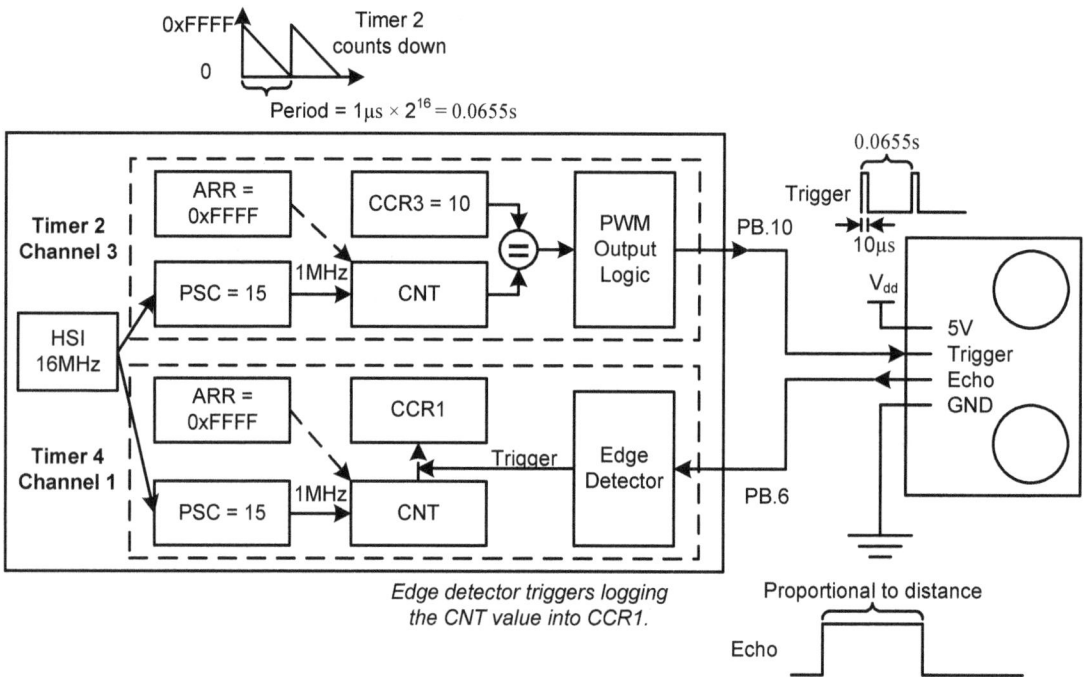

Figure 15-18. Setup of timers for interfacing the ultrasonic distance sensor.

On the STM32L discovery board, we can use pin PB.6 to perform input capture. Since PB.6 is also connected to the blue LED, we can use the brightness of the LED to observe the distance measured. We can also use pin PB.5 to periodically generate the trigger signal. The processor allows PB.6 has the function of I2C1_SCL, TIM4_CH1, and

USART1_TX, and PB.10 has the function of I2C2_SCL, USART3_TX, TIM2_CH3, and LCD_SEG10. We set PB.6 to be the input capture on channel 1 of timer 4 (TIM4_CH1), and PB.10 to be the output of channel 3 of timer 2 (TIM2_CH3). Figure 15-18 shows the setup of timer 2 and timer 4.

Suppose the 16-MHz HSI (high-speed internal) oscillator is selected as the system clock. Since the default system clock is MSI (multi-speed internal), we have to set up HSI, as shown in the following code.

```
; Select HSI (high-speed internal, 16 MHz, 1% accuracy) as the system clock.
HSI_init    PROC
            LDR     r0,   =RCC_BASE

            ; Turn on HSI oscillator
            LDR     r1, [r0, #RCC_CR]
            ORR     r1, r1, #RCC_CR_HSION
            STR     r1, [r0, #RCC_CR]

            ; Select HSI as system clock
            LDR     r1, [r0, #RCC_CFGR]
            BIC     r1, r1, #RCC_CFGR_SW
            ORR     r1, r1, #RCC_CFGR_SW_HSI
            STR     r1, [r0, #RCC_CFGR]

            ; Wait for HSI stable
WaitHSI     LDR     r1, [r0, #RCC_CR]
            AND     r1, r1, #RCC_CR_HSIRDY
            CMP     r1, #0
            BEQ     WaitHSI
            BX      LR
            ENDP
```

Timer 4 is used as input capture that records the time instant of a rising or falling edge of the external ECHO signal, as shown in Figure 15-18. We set up the update event (UIF) and capture event flags in the DMA/interrupt enable register (DIER) to allow them to generate interrupts. The timer 4 counter is set as counting upward. A counter overflow occurs when the 16-bit timer counter reaches 0xFFFF. Since the counter increments every 1µs, an overflow occurs every 0.0655s in this example. When an overflow occurs, the timer generates an interrupt and set up the UIF flag bit in the interrupt status register (SR).

Since it is possible that the counter can overflow when measuring the pulse width of the ECHO signal, we need a variable (named overflow in the following code) that counts the number of overflows has occurred during the time window of two external events. The time span can be calculated as the following:

$$Time\ Span\ (\mu s) = (Current\ Counter\ Value - Last\ Counter\ Value) +$$

$$65536 \times Number\ of\ Overflows$$

After the calculation, the program should use the current counter value to update the last counter value that is saved in memory.

The following assembly code shows the implementation of the interrupt handler for timer 4.

```
timespan        DCD      0    ; the pulse width
lastCounter     DCD      0    ; the timer counter value of last capture event
overflow        DCD      0    ; Counter the number of overflows

TIM4_IRQHandler PROC
                EXPORT   TIM4_IRQHandler
                PUSH {r4, r6, r10, lr}

                LDR r0, =TIM4_BASE
                LDR r2, [r0, #TIM_SR]
                AND r3, r2, #TIM_SR_UIF     ; Check update event flag
                CBZ r3, check_CC

                LDR r3, =overflow
                LDR r1, [r3]
                ADD r1, r1, #1              ; Increment overflow counter
                STR r1, [r3]

                BIC r2, r2, #TIM_SR_UIF     ; Clear update event flag
                STR r2, [r0, #TIM_SR]

check_CC        AND r2, r2, #TIM_SR_CC1IF   ; Check capture event flag
                CBZ     r2, exit

                ; Fetch the current CCR value
                LDR r0, =TIM4_BASE
                LDR r1, [r0, #TIM_CCR1]     ; Read the capture value

                LDR r2, =lastCounter
                LDR r0, [r2]                ; load the last counter value
                STR r1, [r2]                ; save the new counter value
                CBZ r0, clearOverflow

                LDR r3, =overflow
                LDR r4, [r3]                ; load the overflow value
                LSL r4, r4, #16             ; x 65536
                ADD r6, r1, r4
                SUB r10, r6, r0             ; r10 = timer counter difference
                LDR r2, =timespan
```

```
                STR r10, [r2]

clearOverflow   MOV r0, #0
                LDR r3, =overflow
                STR r0,  [r3]                 ; clear overflow counter

exit            POP {r4, r6, r10, pc}
                ENDP
```

In the above code, we use "LSL r4, r4, #16" instruction to replace multiplication with 65536 (*i.e.* 2^{16}). A shift instruction runs much faster than a multiplication instruction. In addition, the lastCounter variable is initialized to 0.

The code above calculates the time span between a rising edge and a falling edge. The code can be improved by only calculating the time span from a rising edge to a falling edge, and ignore the time span from a falling edge to a rising edge.

One common mistaken is that programmers often forget to clear the update event flag in the interrupt status register (SR). In the above code, the hardware will set up two flags in SR: the update flag when a counter overflow (or a counter underflow if the counter counts down) occurs and the capture flag when a rising edge or a falling edge of an external signal is detected. The hardware automatically clears the capture flag after the timer data register (DR) is read. However, the software has to clear the update flag in the interrupt service routine of the timer. If it were not cleared, the timer interrupt service routine would be repeatedly called, making the processor have no time to run other codes with a lower priority.

> *Software must clear the update flag.*

15.5 Exercises

1. Suppose we want to generate a PWM signal with a duty cycle of 0.25. The processor clock is 32 MHz. We want the PWM signal to have a fixed frequency of 320 Hz. How would you design the prescaler (PSC), auto-reload register (ARR), and compare and capture (CCR)? Show your calculation. The timer output mode is set as follows: the PWM output is high if the counter is larger than or equal to the content of CCR.

2. Use an oscilloscope to measure duty cycles. Suppose the default MSI clock is used, which is 2.097 MHz.

    a. What is the relationship between the system clock, the counter clock CK_CNT, the prescaler TIM4_PSC, and the pulse period measured?

    b. We want to keep TIM4_ARR fixed but set TIM4_CCR1 to three different values, as listed below. How would you set up the ARR, PSC and CCR register values? Calculate the duty measured and verify the correctness.
- Case 1: TIM4_CCR1 = 1/6 * (TIM4_ARR + 1)
- Case 2: TIM4_CCR1 = 1/3 * (TIM4_ARR + 1)
- Case 3: TIM4_CCR1 = 1/2 * (TIM4_ARR + 1)

Case	TIM4_CCR1	Pulse Width	Pulse Period
#1			
#2			
#3			

3. Suppose the HSE (high-speed external clock) of 16 MHz is selected as the clock of the timer. In order to generate a 1Hz square wave with duty cycle of 50%, how would you set up the timer? Indicate your counting mode and show the value of ARR, CCR, and PSC registers.

4. Write an assembly program that uses the output compare function of a timer to toggle an LED every second.

5. Write an assembly program that generates a PWM output signal to dim an LED periodically.

6. Write an assembly program that uses PWM to generate a square wave signal with a frequency of 440 Hz and a duty cycle of 50% (*i.e.* musical tone A).

7. Write an assembly program that uses PWM to control a stepper motor via micro stepping.

8. Write an assembly program that uses the input capture function to measure the frequency of an external signal. Use a function generator to generate a 1HZ square wave. Send the square wave to the STM32L board to verify the correctness of your assembly program.

9. Write an assembly program that uses the HC-SR04 ultrasonic distance sensor presented in Chapter 15.4.3 to measure the distance to an object.

CHAPTER

16

Stepper Motor Control

DC motors are often used in applications as diverse as robots, printers, machine tools, household appliances, medical equipment, automotive devices, and computer hard drives. DC motors can be classified into two major categories: servo motors and stepper motors.

- A *servo motor* operates in a closed loop system since it relies on continuous position feedback to control the motor to achieve some desired speed or position. Thus, they usually are more expensive than stepper motors.
- A *stepper motor* rotates to a specific position in discrete steps. The control of a stepper motor can be an open loop system, which requires no position feedback.

Compared with stepper motors, servo motors are more suitable for applications that require high speed or high torque, or applications that have dramatic load changes. Stepper motors tend to have lower torque capacity at high speeds, lose steps if overloaded, and have a higher level of vibration due to stepwise motion. However, stepper motors are less expensive due to the cost savings of the sensors and the controller and easier to interface with microprocessors. They are also suitable for applications that require low or medium accelerations or applications that have constant load.

16.1 Bipolar and Unipolar Stepper Motor

Stepper motors are either *bipolar* or *unipolar*. A bipolar stepper motor often requires a switchable polarity power source, such as a complicated H bridge (see Figure 16-3), in order to reverse the electric current and the electromagnetic polarity of each coil winding. A unipolar stepper motor requires only one power source, and the electric current does not reverse its direction in each coil winding (see Figure 16-4). The unipolar motor uses half of its winding coil to generate the electromagnetic field while a bipolar motor uses a full winding coil. Therefore, a bipolar stepper motor usually has a higher torque capacity than a unipolar one of the same weight. However, a unipolar stepper motor has a simpler control circuit.

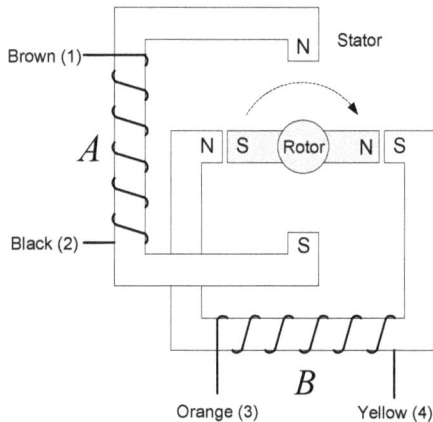

Figure 16-1. Bipolar stepper motor with two phases (A, B) on the stator, and two permanent-magnetic poles on the rotor

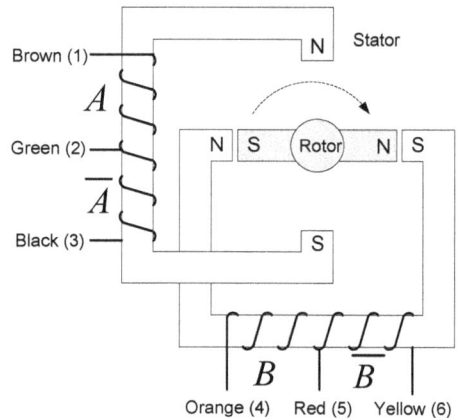

Figure 16-2. Unipolar stepper motor with two phases (A, B) on the stator, and two permanent-magnetic poles on the rotor

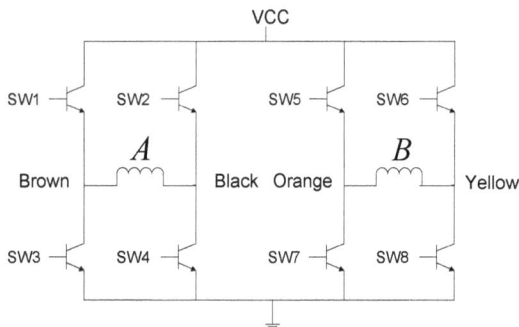

Figure 16-3. Circuit to drive a bipolar stepper motor. Each winding is fully utilized but its electrical current reverses the direction alternatively.

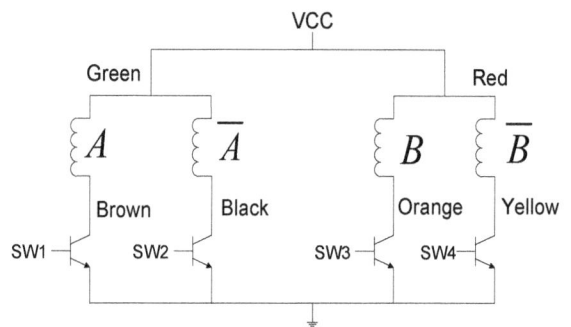

Figure 16-4. Circuit to drive a unipolar stepper motor. The electrical current always flows in one direction but only half of each winding is utilized.

In this chapter, we will use a *unipolar stepper motor*. The model is Mabuchi #PF35T, as shown in Figure 16-5. The motor has two phases and 48 steps per revolution, *i.e.* 7.5 degrees per step. The rotor has 10 teeth.

Figure 16-5. A six-lead unipolar stepper motor

16.2 Step Angle

For each pulse, the shaft of a stepper motor rotates a fixed angle. Depending on the activation sequence of coil windings, the shaft can rotate a full step, a half step, or a specific fraction of a full step. The corresponding activation sequence is called full stepping, half stepping, and micro stepping.

When the shaft rotates a full step, the angle it moves is called *step angle,* which can be calculated as the following:

$$Step\ Angle = \frac{360^{\circ}}{steps\ per\ revolution}$$

$$steps\ per\ revolution = P \times T$$

where P is the total number of phases on the stator, and T is the total number permanent-magnetic poles available on the rotor. In Figure 16-1 and Figure 16-2, there are only two poles on the rotor. In reality, there are more magnetic poles on the rotor in order to achieve a small step angle, as shown in Figure 16-6.

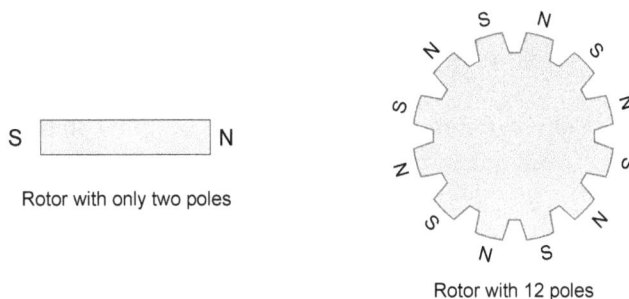

Rotor with only two poles

Rotor with 12 poles

Figure 16-6. Number of magnetic poles on the rotor of a stepper motor

Usually a stepper motor has two or three phases. Typical number of steps per revolution is 48, 72, 144, 180, and 200, resulting in step angle of 7.5°, 5°, 2.5°, 2°, and 1.8°. The motor shown in Figure 16-5 has 2 phases on its stator and 24 poles on its rotor. Thus its step angle is

$$Step\ Angle = \frac{360°}{2 \times 24} = 7.5°$$

For full stepping, a stepper motor rotates by a step angle for each input pulse. For half-stepping, it rotates half of a step angle. For micro stepping, the motor rotates a specific fraction of a step angle. This enables open loop position control. The number and rate of the pulses control the position and speed of the motor shaft.

16.3 Wave Stepping

As the simplest stepping method, wave stepping turns on one switch and energizes a single phase at a time. Figure 16-7 shows the control sequence of four switches of four winding coils (A, B, $\bar{A}$, and $\bar{B}$). For each switch, if its control signal is high, the switch is turned on and electric current flows through the corresponding winding coil. For example, when the signal of SW1 is high, the corresponding coil A is energized. All switches are turned on alternatively in this control sequence.

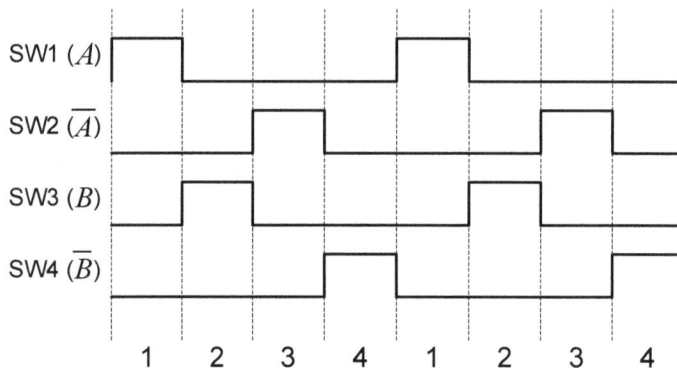

Figure 16-7. Sequence of wave stepping for two-phase unipolar stepper motors. The stator is energized in the sequence of A, B, $\bar{A}$, and $\bar{B}$.

In order to simplify the presentation, we assume the rotor has only two permanent-magnet poles, as shown in Figure 16-8. In reality, the rotor often has more poles in order to obtain a small step angle.

Therefore, the rotor rotates 90 degrees for each pulse in this simplified example. If the load on a stepper motor is not too large, the rotor is eventually locked at an angular position where the permanent-magnet rotor is aligned with the electromagnetic field of the activated coil winding. Figure 16-8 shows that the rotor is being pulled from the previously locked position when a new phase is energized.

This control sequence is called wave stepping.. At any time, there is only one coil winding is energized and thus it offers relatively small torque. Therefore, it is not widely used in real systems.

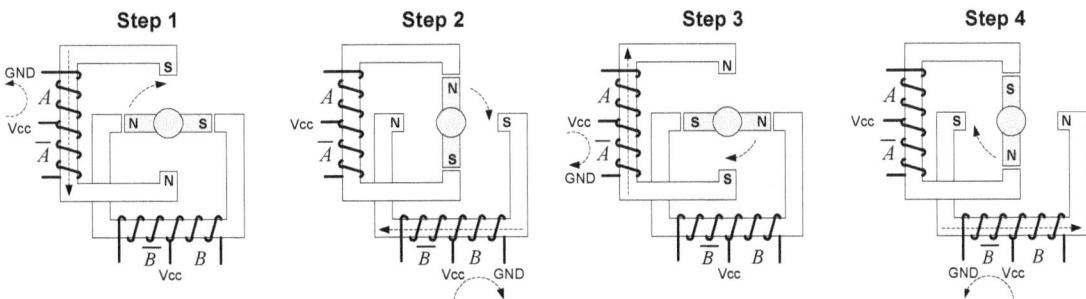

Figure 16-8. Wave stepping sequence of a bipolar stepper motor with two phases on the stator and two poles on the rotor (90° stepping)

16.4 Full Stepping

While wave stepping activates one coil winding each time, full stepping energizes two coil windings alternatively. To turn the shaft clockwise, the coil activation sequence is $A\bar{B}$, AB, $\bar{A}B$, and $\bar{A}\bar{B}$, as shown in Figure 16-9. Reversing the activation sequence makes the shaft to rotate counterclockwise. Both wave stepping and full stepping rotate the shaft a step angle each time and have the same number of steps in one revolution. However, the full stepping produces a higher torque than wave stepping since two coil windings push or pull the shaft simultaneously.

Figure 16-8 shows that the rotor starts to move from the angular position locked at the previous step. The rotation can be reversed by reversing the control sequence supplied to the switches. For clockwise rotation, the coil activation sequence is $A\bar{B}$, AB, $\bar{A}B$, and $\bar{A}\bar{B}$. For counter-clockwise rotation, the coil activation sequence is $\bar{A}\bar{B}$, $\bar{A}B$, AB, and $A\bar{B}$.

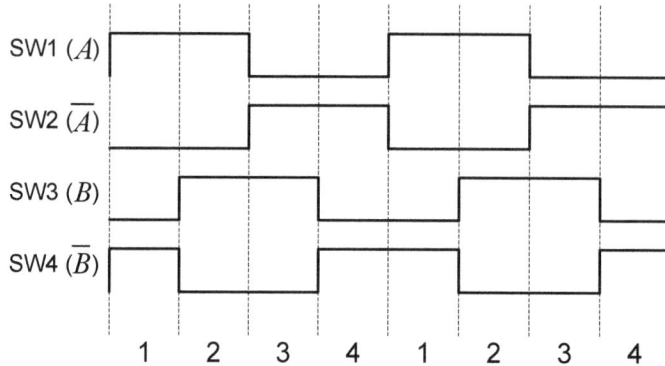

Figure 16-9. Sequence of full stepping for two-phase unipolar stepper motors

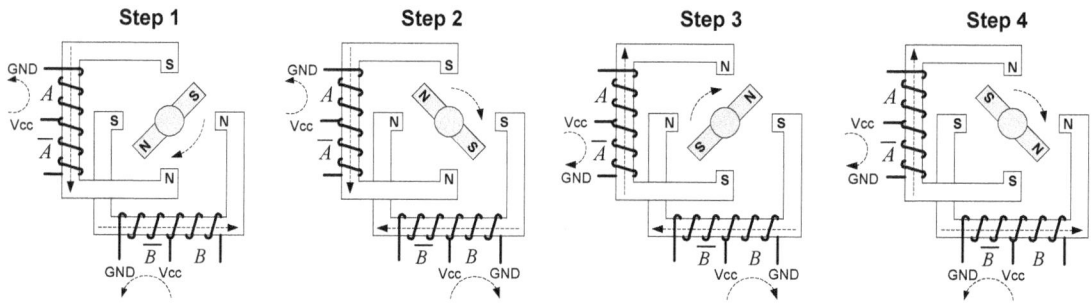

Figure 16-10. High torque full stepping sequence (90° stepping)

Example 16-1 and Example 16-2 show incomplete C programs that use full stepping to rotate a stepper motor 360 degrees clockwise and counter-clockwise, respectively.

```
// Full Step: 0b1001, 0b1010, 0b0110, 0b0101
// Each four-bit sequence represents the ON/OFF control of A, Ā, B, and B̄.
unsigned char FullStep[4] = {0x9, 0xA, 0x6, 0x5};

for(int j = 0; j < 48; j++){   // 48 steps × 7.5° per step = 360°
  for(int i = 0; i < 4; i++){
    for(int k = 0; k < 6000; k++);   // A short delay
    // Winding A = (FullStep[i] & 0x8) >> 3
    // Winding Ā = (FullStep[i] & 0x4) >> 2
    // Winding B = (FullStep[i] & 0x2) >> 1
    // Winding B̄ = FullStep[i] & 0x1
    // Set the value of the GPIO output data register (ODR)
  }
}
```

Example 16-1. Incomplete C program rotating a stepper motor clockwise by full stepping

```
// Full Step: 0b1001, 0b1010, 0b0110, 0b0101
// Each four-bit sequence represents the ON/OFF control of A, Ā, B, and B̄.
unsigned char FullStep[4] = {0x9, 0xA, 0x6, 0x5};

for(int j = 0; j < 48; j++){   // 48 steps × 7.5° per step = 360°
  for(int i = 3; i >= 0; i--){
    for(int k = 0; k < 6000; k++);   // A short delay
    // Winding A = (FullStep[i] & 0x8) >> 3
    // Winding Ā = (FullStep[i] & 0x4) >> 2
    // Winding B = (FullStep[i] & 0x2) >> 1
    // Winding B̄ = FullStep[i] & 0x1
    // Set the value of the GPIO output data register (ODR)
  }
}
```

Example 16-2. Incomplete program rotating counter-clockwise by full stepping

16.5 Half Stepping

Figure 16-11 shows the activation sequence of half-stepping: $A\bar{B}$, A, AB, B, $\bar{A}B$, $\bar{A}$, $\bar{A}\bar{B}$, and $\bar{B}$. It energizes one winding coil and two winding coils alternatively. Half stepping provides less torque but twice as much rotation resolution as full stepping. Half stepping can rotate the shaft more smoothly than full stepping. However, it sometimes has only one half-coil winding activated and produces less torque than full stepping.

Figure 16-12 shows the rotation sequence of a simplified motor with only two poles on the rotor. This sequence includes eight half steps and the shaft rotates 45° in each half step.

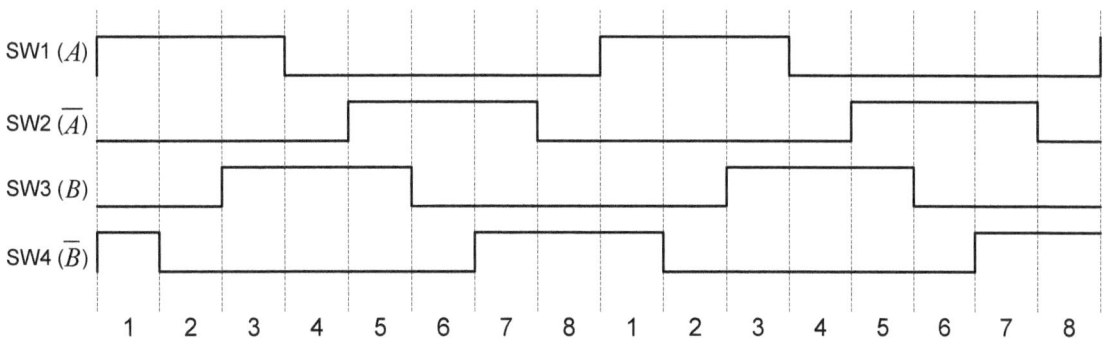

Figure 16-11. Sequence of half stepping for two-phase unipolar stepper motors

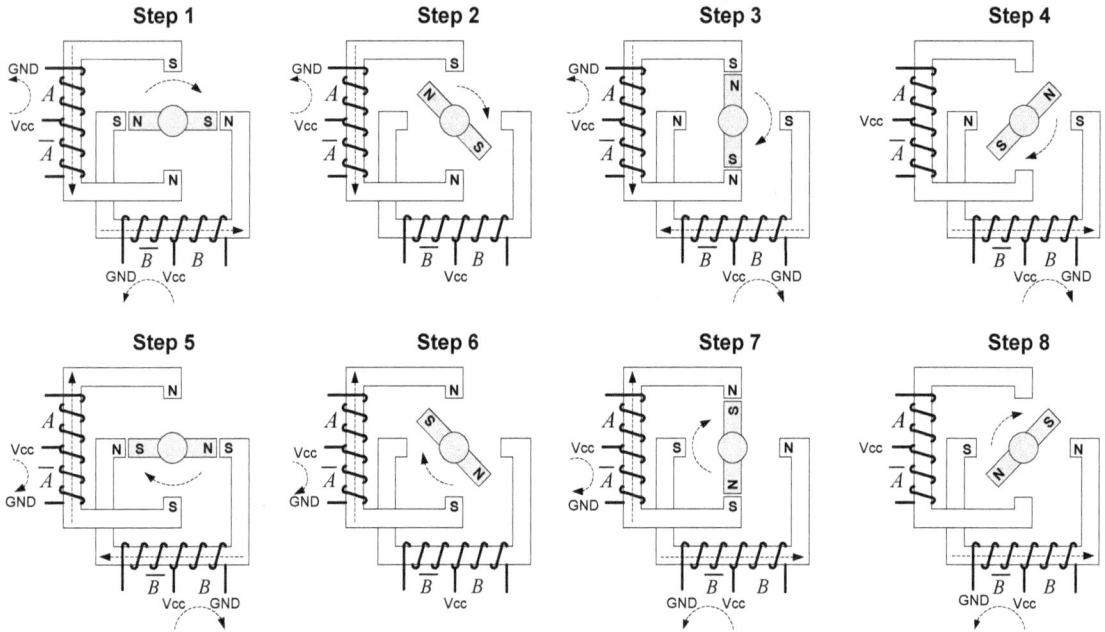

Figure 16-12. Half-stepping sequence for unipolar stepper motors (45° stepping)

Example 16-3 shows an incomplete C program that uses half-stepping to rotate a stepper motor 360 degrees clockwise.

```
// Half Step: 0b1001, 0b1000, 0b1010, 0b0010, 0b0110, 0b0100, 0b0101, 0b0001
// Each four-bit sequence represents the ON/OFF control of A, Ā, B, and B̄.
unsigned char HalfStep[8] = {0x9, 0x8, 0xa, 0x2, 0x6, 0x4, 0x5, 0x1};

for(int j = 0; j < 96; j++){   // 96 steps × 3.75° per step = 360°
  for(int i = 0; i < 8; i++){
    for(int k = 0; k < 6000; k++);   // A short delay
    // Winding A = (HalfStep[i] & 0x8) >> 3
    // Winding Ā = (HalfStep[i] & 0x4) >> 2
    // Winding B = (HalfStep[i] & 0x2) >> 1
    // Winding B̄ = HalfStep[i] & 0x1
    // Set the value of the GPIO output data register (ODR)
  }
}
```

Example 16-3. Incomplete C program that rotates a stepper motor clockwise by half stepping

16.6 Micro-stepping

As introduced previously, a microcontroller can use full stepping or half stepping to control a stepper motor. A stepper motor rotates exactly a full step angle or a half step angle in each excitation in full or half stepping, respectively, resulting in jerky and noisy movements of the motor. In this section, we will use the PWM to perform micro-stepping, which rotates a fraction of a full step angle in one excitation, such as 1/4, 1/8, 1/16, or 1/32 of a full step. Microstepping divides a full step into multiple smaller steps. It moves the shaft in a smaller angle increment, provides a much smoother movement, and reduces the problems of movement noise and vibration.

The goal of micro-stepping is to adjust the electrical current dynamically in each winding to make the acceleration or deceleration of the shaft less noticeable. We can use PWM to generate a fast binary signal with an appropriately chosen duty cycle to adjust the amplitude of the voltage across each winding dynamically. Usually the applied voltage on a winding is linearly proportional to the current generated.

Sine-cosine micro-stepping is a widely used method to adjust the amplitude of the voltage on each winding. When two windings a and b are excited simultaneously, the overall static magnetic torque generated by both windings is

$$T = -ki_a \sin \theta + ki_b \cos \theta$$

where k is a constant, θ is the shaft mechanical angle from the last full-step position, and i_a and i_b are the electrical current in windings a and b.

When the shaft remains at a stable angle, the torque force is balanced and thus we have $T = 0$. In sine-cosine micro-stepping, in order to make the overall torque force to be zero, we can set the electrical current in both windings as the following:

$$i_a = I_m \cos \theta$$

$$i_b = I_m \sin \theta$$

where I_m is a constant. Therefore, the overall static magnetic torque is

$$\begin{aligned} T &= -ki_a \sin \theta + ki_b \cos \theta \\ &= -kI_m \cos \theta \sin \theta + kI_m \sin \theta \cos \theta \\ &= 0 \end{aligned}$$

Microprocessors use discrete sine and cosine wave to drive both windings. Figure 16-13 shows the voltage signal of each phase of unipolar stepper motors if 1/4 micro-stepping is used. Figure 16-14 show the voltage signal across each coil winding.

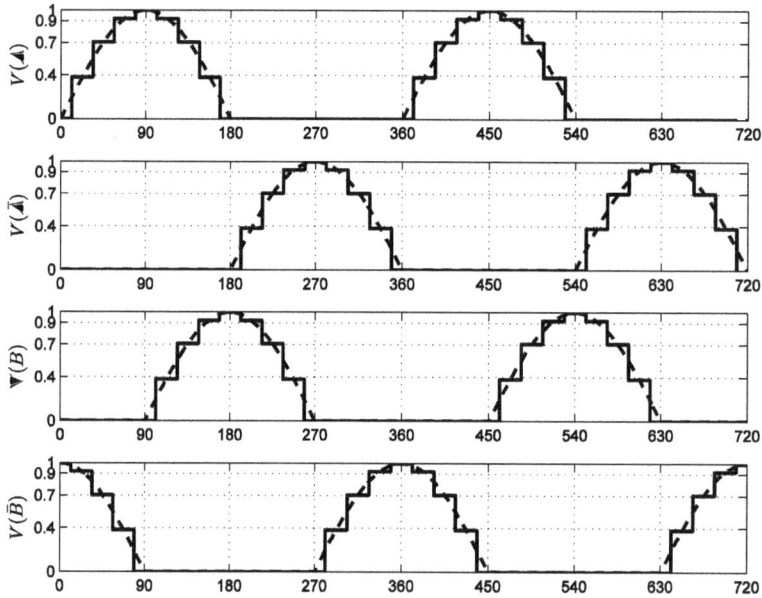

Figure 16-13. 1/4 sine-cosine micro-stepping for four-phase unipolar stepper motors

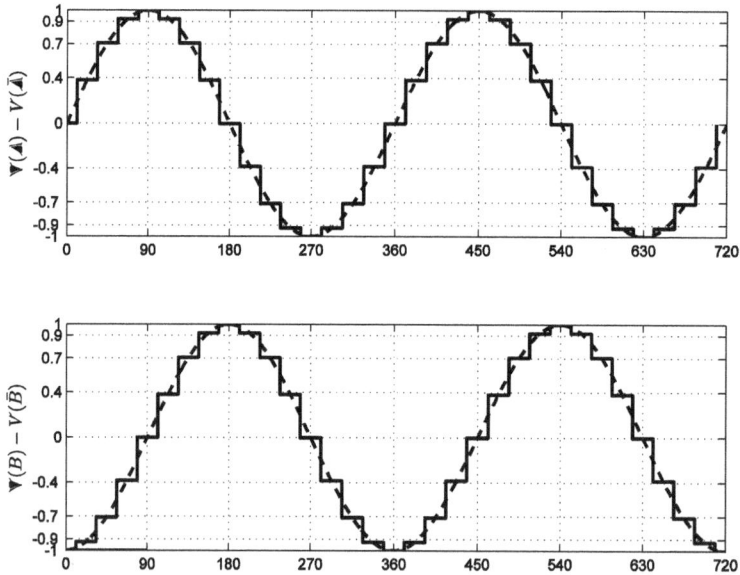

Figure 16-14. 1/4 sine-cosine micro-stepping for each coil winding of unipolar stepper motors

Suppose the auto-reload register (ARR) of a timer is $1,000 - 1$, i.e. 999, the compare and capture register (CCR) of the timer should be set as the following values for 1/4 micro-stepping.

```
uint16_t CCR_MicroSteping[] = {0, 383, 707, 924, 1000};
```

For 1/2 micro-stepping, the sequence of CCR should be

```
uint16_t CCR_MicroSteping [] = {0, 707, 1000};
```

For 1/8 micro-stepping, the sequence of CCR should be

```
uint16_t CCR_MicroSteping [] = {0, 195, 383, 556, 707, 832, 924, 981, 1000};
```

16.7 Driving Stepper Motor

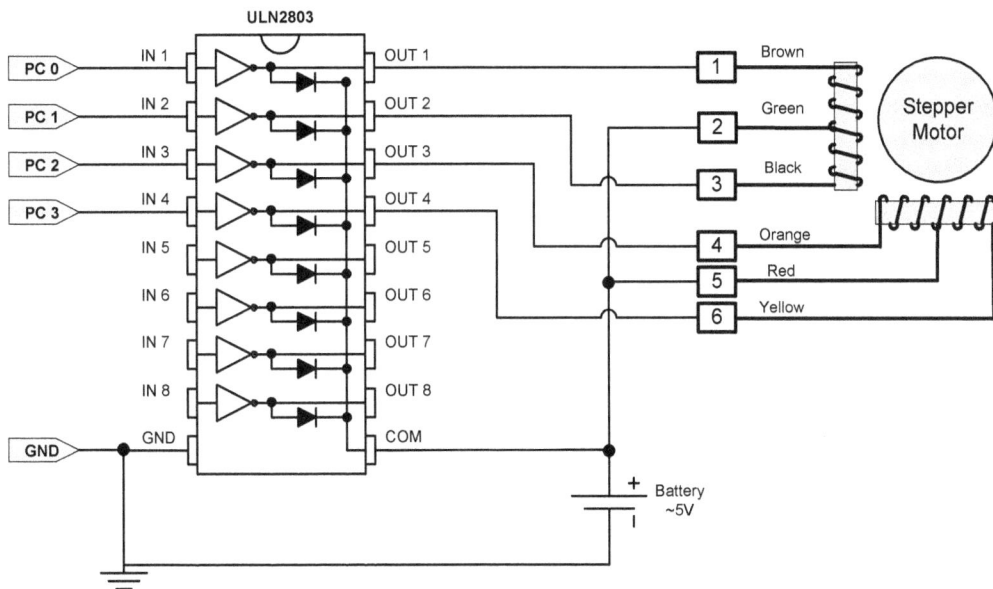

Figure 16-15. Connection diagram of driving a stepper motor

We cannot directly drive a stepper motor by using the GPIO pins of the microprocessor because the GPIO ports cannot provide sufficient electric current required by the stepper motor. The maximum electric current provided by a GPIO pin is approximately 10 mA. The stepper motor used in this lab has only 20 Ωs and it draws $3V/20\Omega = 150$ mA, which exceeds the maximum current that can be supplied by a GPIO pin. These GPIO pins should be configured as digital output with push-pull.

Another important reason for not using GPIO pins to drive the motor directly is that the motor may cause a back electromotive force in the circuit while it is accelerating or decelerating. This generates a voltage that pushes against the current that induces it, which could potentially damage the microprocessor.

We can use the 8-channel Darlington driver (ULN2803) to drive the stepper motor, as shown in Figure 16-15. The ULN2803 is a high-voltage, high-current Darlington transistor array, which consists of eight NPN Darlington pairs. Each Darlington pair can collect currents up to 500 mA. The output pin can withstand at least 50V in the off state. Suppression diodes are included for inductive load driving. Outputs may be paralleled for high current capability.

For each Darlington pair, if a positive high voltage is applied to the input pin, then the corresponding output pin is grounded and it can draw the electric current up to 500 mA. If the input pin has a low voltage supply, then the corresponding output pin cannot drain any current. An input pin takes ~1 mA current only.

16.8 Exercises

1. Write an assembly program that turns the stepper motor 360 degrees clockwise by using full stepping. What is the highest update frequency of the full-stepping control signals while the motor does not drop any steps? You might need to use an oscilloscope to find your update frequency.

2. Write an assembly program that turns the stepper motor 360 degrees counter-clockwise by using half-stepping. What is the highest update frequency of the half-stepping control signals while the motor does not drop any steps? You might need to use an oscilloscope to find your update frequency.

3. Write an assembly program that changes the rotation speed when the push button is pressed.

4. What would happen if the update frequency were higher than the maximum allowed in Question 1 and 2?

5. Write an assembly program that uses pulse-width modulated (PWM) to perform micro-stepping. Microstepping is a digital technique to turn a stepper motor smoothly.

CHAPTER
17

Liquid-crystal Display (LCD)

An LCD is a cost-effective interface to display information to users in a friendly way. LCD display modules are categorized into two groups:

- *External hardware driver*. These have an external LCD controller chip, such as Hitachi HD44780, Toshiba T6963 and Seiko-Epson SED1330. They use standard protocols to exchange data and commands between the microprocessor and the LCD controller chip. The advantage of using an external hardware driver is that fewer processor pins are required and the software to interface the LCD module is relatively easier.
- *Internal hardware driver*. These have a built-in hardware driver within the microprocessor chip. The STM32L Cortex-M3 processor on the STM32L discovery board has a built-in LCD driver. The advantage of having an internal hardware LCD driver is that the system can be made smaller. However, it uses many processor pins and requires complex software to drive the LCD display.

In this chapter, we only consider the processors that already have an on-chip LCD hardware driver. Interfacing off-chip (external) hardware driver usually is relative easy since it uses some serial communication protocol, such as I²C and USART, introduced in Chapter 5, to transfer the data to be displayed from the processor to the external LCD hardware driver. The application software does not need to worry about how to control each individual display pixels.

Specifically, this chapter will focus on two important aspects. (1) How does the on-chip LCD hardware driver generate voltage signals to turn a display pixel on or off? (2) How does a software driver to display a given character string on the LCD? The goal of the first aspect is to reduce the pin requirements, and the goal of the second aspect is to provide a flexible and easy-to-use interface to application developers.

17.1 Static Drive

When the amplitude of the segment voltage across is greater than a threshold voltage (V), the crystals of this segment are aligned, and this segment is visible (or turned on). Crystals themselves do not emit any light but aligned segments prevent light from passing through. The segment voltage is typically alternated to avoid damage. Usually each segment is driven by two square waveforms. There are two hardware techniques to drive an LCD: static drive and multiplexed drive.

Static drive is to use one dedicated pin to turn on or turn off an LCD display segment (also called a display pixel). Figure 17-1 shows an eight-segment display (including seven segments for the digit display and the dot). All segments share the same com signal. If the signals to drive the eight segment lines (SL i, i = 1 to 8) are shown below, then digit 2 is displayed. The voltage across segment lines 1, 2, 4, 5, 7 and 8 has an alternative voltage with amplitude larger than the threshold voltage V, while the voltage across segment 3 and 6 is a constant zero.

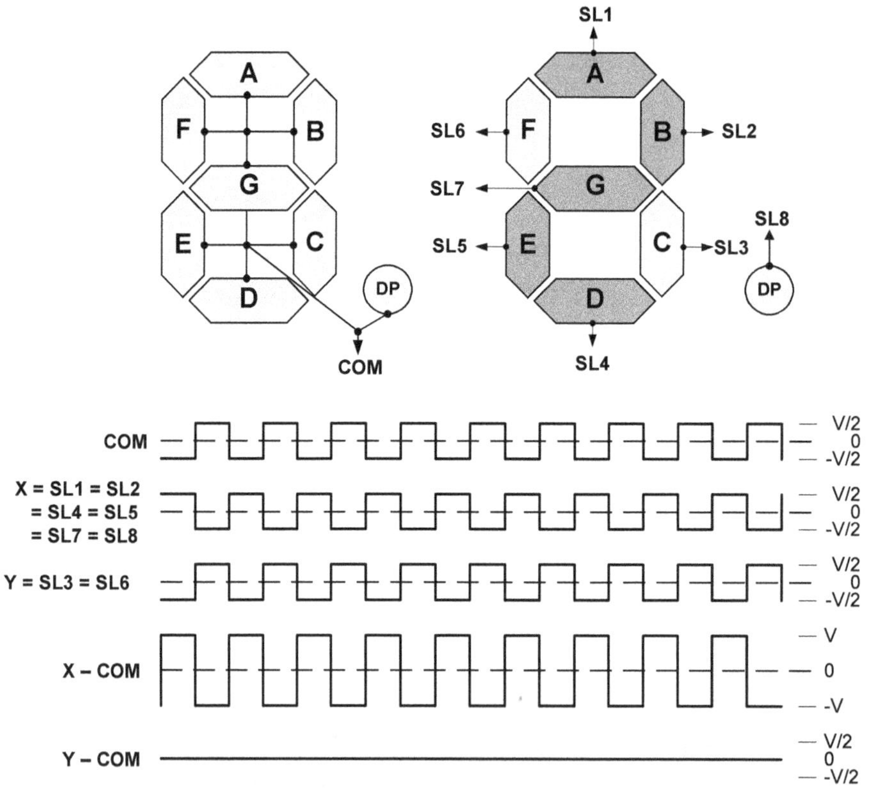

Figure 17-1. Static driving (Duty ratio = 1). There is only one common terminal in static driving. When a segment line has the same voltage waveform as the waveform of COM, this segment is turned on; otherwise, this segment line is turned off.

Static drive is simple but requires many pins. An LCD display usually has many pixel segments. For example, the LCD display on the STM32L kit can display six decimal numbers and have 96 pixel segments. If the processor uses one pin to drive each pixel segment, then 97 pins would be required. Unfortunately, the processor does not have many pins. Even if it did, it would not be desirable.

17.2 Multiplexed Drive

In order to reduce the number of pins required, a special hardware technology, called multiplexed drive, is developed. While all display segments in static drive have a single shared terminal, multiplexed drive shares two or more common terminal lines to reduce the number of pins.

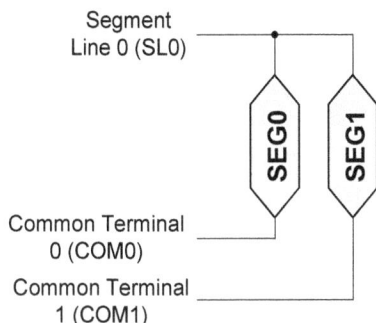

Figure 17-2. Example of duty ratio of 1/2. Each segment line drives two display segments.

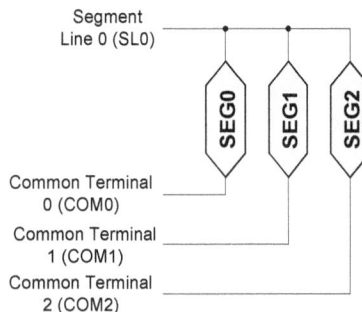

Figure 17-3. Example of duty ratio of 1/3. Each segment line drives three display segments.

One of the key concepts of multiplexed LCD drive is duty ratio and bias, which are defined below.

$$Duty\ Ratio = \frac{1}{Number\ of\ Common\ Terminals}$$

$$Bias = \frac{1}{Number\ of\ Voltage\ Levels - 1}$$

Figure 17-2 and Figure 17-3 give two examples in which the duty ratio is 1/2 and 1/3, respectively. In both examples, there are two and three common terminals, which are shared by all display segments.

In the static display given in Figure 17-1, nine pins are required, including one for the common terminal and eight for segments. If a multiplexed drive with a duty ratio of ½ is used to drive the same display, only six lines are required, as shown in Figure 17-4.

As discussed previously, static drive would require a total number of 97 pins. Multiplexed drive with a duty ratio of ¼ can reduce the total pins required to drive the LCD from 97 to 28, including 4 common terminals and 24 segment lines. In this setting, each segment line drives four display segments.

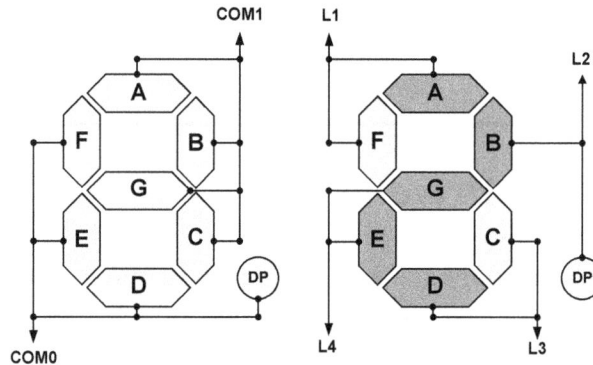

Figure 17-4. Multiplexed drive scheme of a segment digit display (Duty ratio = ½). It has two common terminal lines. Each segment line drives two display segments.

Compared with static drive, multiplexed drive reduces the total number of pins required at the cost of the brightness. The duty ratio represents the fraction of each time cycle that a segment is activated. In multiplexed drive, each visible display segment is switched on and off with a frequency typically larger than 30 Hz. Human eyes usually cannot notice fast switching between on and off alternatively. If the duty cycle is ½, each visible display segment is 50% time on and 50% time off. By contrast, static drive keeps each visible display segment on continuously.

We use a simple example with only two display segments to illustrate the basic concept of multiplexed drive when the duty ratio is ½. These two segments share the same segment line signal. The following presents four different cases: (1) light up both segments, (2) turn off both segments, (3) light up the first segment, and (4) light up the second segment. The signals for two common terminals and the segment line are shown for each case. Note there are three voltage levels $(0, \pm V/2, \pm V)$ for the voltage across each segment. Therefore, the bias is ½.

- When a segment is lit up, the voltage across this segment is either $V/2$ (less than the activation threshold V, thus the segment remains in the inactivate state) for half of the time, or V (activated state) for the other half of the time. The frequency of on and off is usually very fast so that naked eyes cannot detect the flashing. However, the brightness is reduced by half.
- When a segment is turned off, the voltage across it is either 0 or $V/2$, which are less than the activation threshold V. Thus, the segment is constantly off.

Case 1: Setup of signals to light up both segments

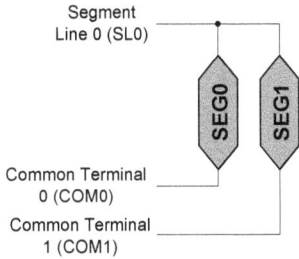

Segment Line 0 (SL0)

SEG0   SEG1

Common Terminal 0 (COM0)

Common Terminal 1 (COM1)

$$Duty\ Ratio = \frac{1}{2}$$

$$Bias = \frac{1}{2}$$

SEG 0 is visible.
SEG 1 is visible.
(Both are switched on and off quickly.)

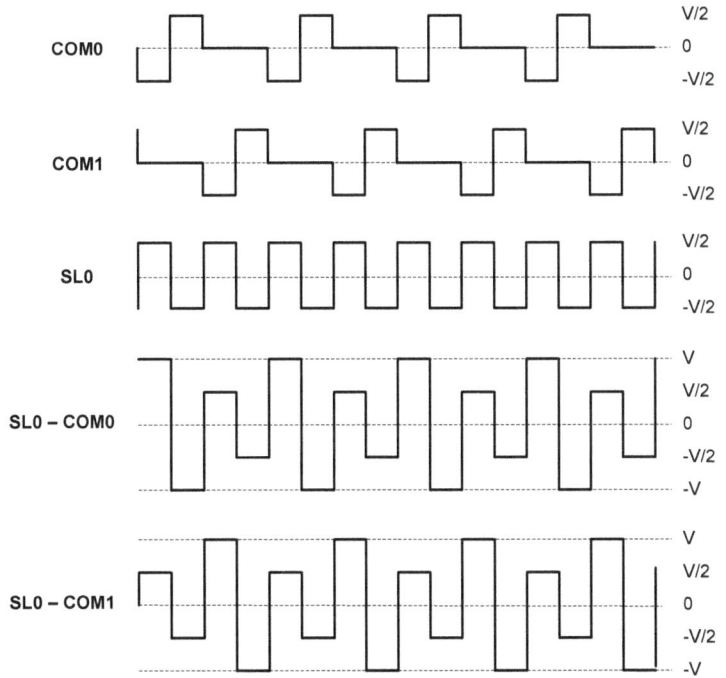

Case 2: Setup of signals to turn off both segments

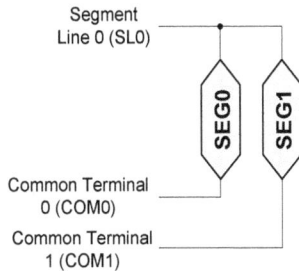

Segment Line 0 (SL0)

SEG0   SEG1

Common Terminal 0 (COM0)

Common Terminal 1 (COM1)

$$Duty\ Ratio = \frac{1}{2}$$

$$Bias = \frac{1}{2}$$

SEG 0 is invisible.
SEG 1 is invisible.

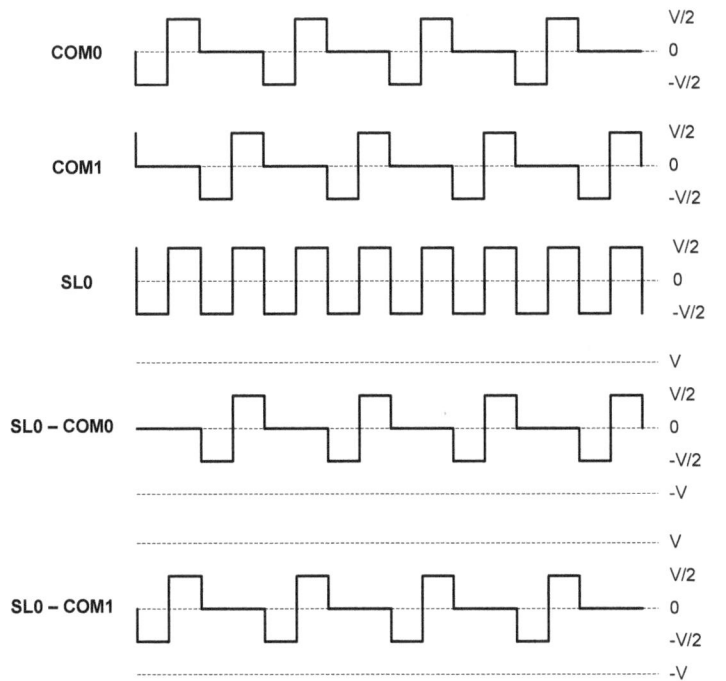

Case 3: Setup of signals to light up only SEG 0

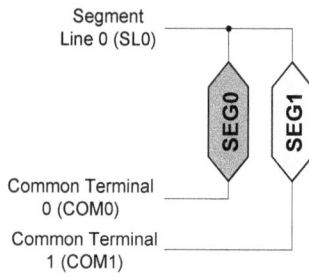

Segment Line 0 (SL0)

SEG0   SEG1

Common Terminal 0 (COM0)
Common Terminal 1 (COM1)

$$Duty\ Ratio = \frac{1}{2}$$

$$Bias = \frac{1}{2}$$

SEG 0 is visible.
SEG 1 is invisible.
(SEG 0 is switched on and off quickly.)

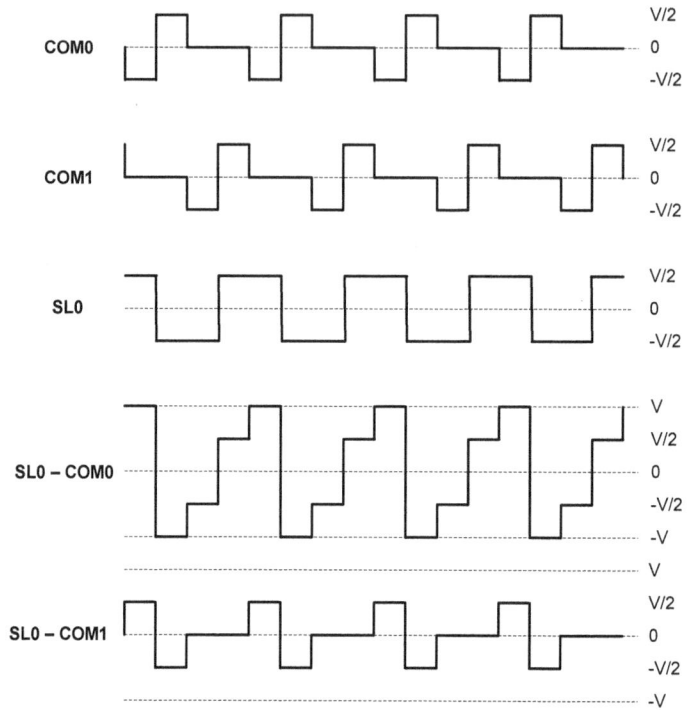

Case 4: Setup of signals to light up only SEG 1

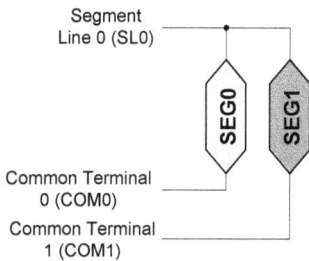

Segment Line 0 (SL0)

SEG0   SEG1

Common Terminal 0 (COM0)
Common Terminal 1 (COM1)

$$Duty\ Ratio = \frac{1}{2}$$

$$Bias = \frac{1}{2}$$

SEG 0 is invisible.
SEG 1 is visible.
(SEG 1 is switched on and off quickly.)

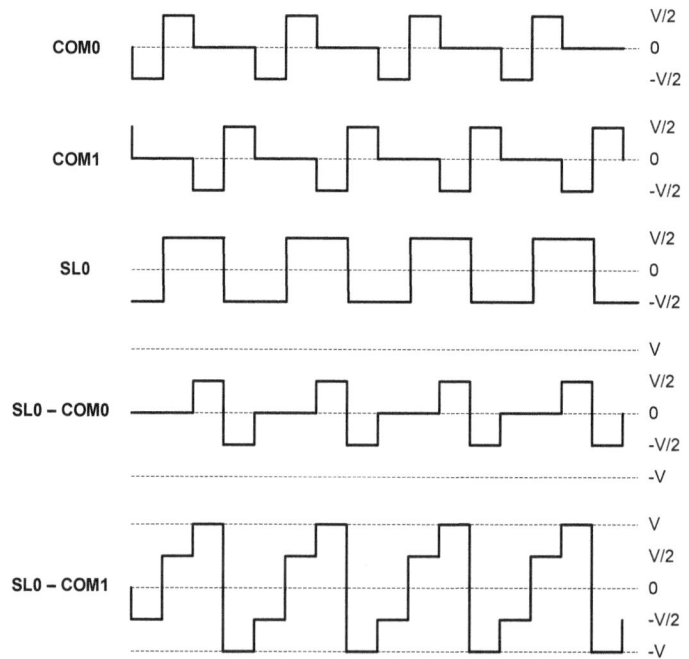

17.3 LCD Software Driver

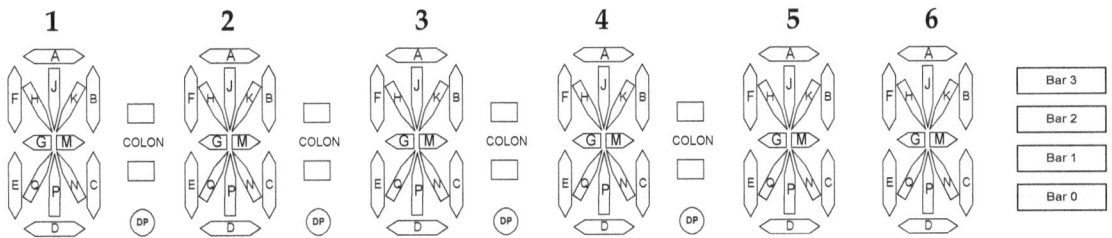

Figure 17-5 LCD display on board with 6 digits and 4 bars

Overview of the LCD of the STM32L discover kit:
- Drive method: multiplexed 1/4 duty, 1/3 bias
- 24 segment lines (SEG0 - SEG23) and 4 common terminals (COM0 - COM3). Thus, the duty is 1/4.
- The LCD has six digits and four bars. There are 14 segments in each digit. There are a total of 96 pixels (segments) and 24 segment lines. Each segment line drives four pixels (segments).
- The processor uses 28 I/O pins for LCD (24 segment lines plus 4 common terminals).

There are 96 segments on the LCD and each segment is turned on or off by one bit in the display memory. The mapping between segments and corresponding bits are given in Table 17-1 and Table 17-2. For example, in order to show "2" on the sixth character position, we need to turn on the segments 6A, 6B, 6G, 6M, 6E, and 6D.

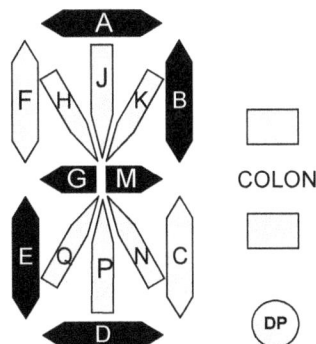

Figure 17-6. Display "2" by turning on segments 6A, 6B, 6G, 6M, 6E and 6D.

The LCD controller uses a total of 28 GPIO pins, and each GPIO pin has to be configured as alternative function (AF) mode, with an alternative function value of 0x0B (LCD function). The duty ratio of this LCD is 4 and therefore there are four common terminals (COM0 - COM3), which are connected to four GPIO pins. The other 24 GPIO pins are mapped to pixel bits stored in the internal LCD RAM, as given in Table 17-2.

STM32L		LCD				
Name	Pin	COM3	COM2	COM1	COM0	LCD_RAM
PA1	1	1N	1P	1D	1E	Bit 0
PA2	2	1DP	1COLON	1C	1M	Bit 1
PA3	3	2N	2P	2D	2E	Bit 2
PB3	4	2DP	2COLON	2C	2M	Bit 7
PB4	5	3N	3P	3D	3E	Bit 8
PB5	6	3DP	3COLON	3C	3M	Bit 9
PB10	7	4N	4P	4D	4E	Bit 10
PB11	8	4DP	4COLON	4C	4M	Bit 11
PB12	9	5N	5P	5D	5E	Bit 12
PB13	10	BAR2	BAR3	5C	5M	Bit 13
PB14	11	6N	6P	6D	6E	Bit 14
PB15	12	BAR0	BAR1	6C	6M	Bit 15
PB9	13	COM3				
PA10	14		COM2			
PA9	15			COM1		
PA8	16				COM0	
PA15	17	6J	6K	6A	6B	Bit 17
PB8	18	6H	6Q	6F	6G	Bit 16
PC0	19	5J	5K	5A	5B	Bit 18
PC1	20	5H	5Q	5F	5G	Bit 19
PC2	21	4J	4K	4A	4B	Bit 20
PC3	22	4H	4Q	4F	4G	Bit 21
PC6	23	3J	3K	3A	3B	Bit 24
PC7	24	3H	3Q	3F	3G	Bit 25
PC8	25	2J	2K	2A	2B	Bit 26
PC9	26	2H	2Q	2F	2G	Bit 27
PC10	27	1J	1K	1A	1B	Bit 28
PC11	28	1H	1Q	1F	1G	Bit 29

Table 17-1. Segment mapping between display and LCD_RAM

Accordingly, the LCD data memory (LCD_RAM) is set as follows. Note LCD_RAM[4] and LCD_RAM[6] are not modified since no segments represented by these two registers need to be turned on.

```
LCD_RAM[0] |= 0x0003C000
LCD_RAM[2] |= 0x00024000
```

	31	30	29	28	27	26	25	24	23	22	21	20	19	18	17	16	15	14	13	12	11	10	9	8	7	6	5	4	3	2	1	0
LCD_RAM[0]			1G	1B	2G	2B	3G	3A			4G	4B	5G	5B	6B	6G	6M	6E	5M	5E	4M	4E	3M	3E	2M					2E	1M	1E
															1	1	1	1														
LCD_RAM[2]			1F	1A	2F	2A	3F	3A			4F	4A	5F	5A	6A	6F	6C	6D	5C	5D	4C	4D	3C	3D	2C					2D	1C	1D
															1	0	0	1														
LCD_RAM[4]			1Q	1K	2Q	2K	3Q	3K			4Q	4K	5Q	5K	6K	6Q	1 Bar	6P	3 Bar	5P	4 Col	4P	3 Col	3P	2 Col					2P	1 Col	1P
															0	0		0														
LCD_RAM[6]			1H	1J	2H	2J	3H	3J			4H	4J	5H	5J	6J	6H	0 Bar	6N	2 Bar	5N	4 DP	4N	3 DP	3N	2 DP					2N	1 DP	1N
															0	0		0														

Table 17-2. Bit map of the display memory when displaying "2" on LCD. The display memory is a special memory region to hold the on/off setting of each individual display pixel. If a bit is set, the corresponding pixel is visible. Some LCD RAM registers (such as LCD_RAM[1], LCD_RAM[3], and LCD_RAM[5]) are not used because there are no display pixels on the STM32-L discovery kit associated with them.

The on-chip LCD controller uses a technique called double buffer (data memory and display memory) to ensure the coherency of the displayed information without having to interrupt the process of modifying LCD_RAM. When the application completes updating the data memory, the controller locks the data memory first to prevent any modification, then copies data from the LCD data memory to the second buffer (display memory), and frees up the clocks to allow modification to the data memory.

The LCD software driver should follow the above double buffer protocol to ensure the coherency of the displayed information. Specifically, the following is the procedure sequence to update the displayed information on the LCD.

1. Wait until the update display request (UDR) flag in the LCD status register (LCD_SR) is cleared. When UDR is set, the data stored in LCD_RAM has not been copied into the display memory yet and thus the driver should wait.
2. After the UDR flag is cleared by the hardware, the driver can write the on/off setting for each segment into LCD_RAM.
3. Set the UDR flag to inform the hardware that the data are ready to be copied into the display memory. The UDR flag stays set until the end of the update, and during this period, the LCD_RAM is write-protected. The controller then generates the signals of common terminals (COM0 - COM3) and segment lines (SEG0 - SEG43) to drive the external LCD.
4. After setting the UDR flag, the software driver should wait until the update display done (UDD) flag in the LCD status register (LCD_SR) is set.

```
                          ┌─────────────┐
                          │    START    │
                          └─────────────┘
                                 │
                                 ▼
┌──────────────────────────────────────────────────────────────────┐
│ LCD Clock Initialization                                           │
│ 1. Disable RTC clock protection (RTC and LCD share the same clock).│
│    Write 0xCA and 0x53 to RTC_WRP register to unlock the write     │
│    protection                                                      │
│ 2. Enable LSI clock (RCC_CSR)                                      │
│ 3. Select LSI as LCD clock source (RCC_CSR RTCSEL field)           │
│ 4. Enable LCD/RTC clock (RCC_CSR RTCEN field)                      │
└──────────────────────────────────────────────────────────────────┘
                                 │
                                 ▼
┌──────────────────────────────────────────────────────────────────┐
│ Configure LCD GPIO Pin as Alternative Functions                    │
│ 1. Enable the clock of GPIO port A, B, and C                       │
│ 2. Configure Port A Pin 1, 2, 3, 8, 9, 10, and 15 as AF 11 (0x0B)  │
│ 3. Configure Port B Pin 3, 4, 5, 8, 9, 10, 11, 12, 13, 14, and 15  │
│    as AF 11 (0x0B)                                                 │
│ 4. Configure Port C Pin 0, 1, 2, 3, 6, 7, 8, 9, 10, and 11 as      │
│    AF 11 (0x0B)                                                    │
└──────────────────────────────────────────────────────────────────┘
                                 │
                                 ▼
┌──────────────────────────────────────────────────────────────────┐
│ LCD Configuration                                                  │
│ 1. Configure BIAS[1:0] bits of LCD_CR and set the bias to 1/3      │
│ 2. Configure DUTY[2:0] bits of LCD_CR and set the duty to 1/4      │
│ 3. Configure CC[2:0] bits of LCD_FCR and set the contrast to max   │
│    value 111                                                      │
│ 4. Configure PON[2:0] bits of LCD_FCR and set the pulse on period  │
│    to 111, i.e., 7/ck_ps. A short pulse consumes less power but    │
│    might not provide satisfactory contrast.                        │
│ 5. Enable the mux segment of the LCD_CR                            │
│ 6. Select internal voltage as LCD voltage source                  │
│ 7. Wait until FCRSF flag of LCD_SR is set                         │
│ 8. Enable the LCD by setting LCDEN bit of LCD_CR                   │
│ 9. Wait until the LCD is enabled by checking the ENS bit of LCD_SR │
│ 10. Wait until the LCD booster is ready by checking the RDY bit of │
│     LCD_SR                                                        │
└──────────────────────────────────────────────────────────────────┘
                                 │
                                 ▼
                 ◇ Is the LCD_RAM protected? ◇ ──YES──┐
                 (If the UDR bit LCD_SR is set,        │
                    then RAM is protected.)            │
                                 │                     │
                                NO                     │
                                 ▼                     │
┌──────────────────────────────────────────────────┐  │
│ Set up the value of LCD_RAM[0], LCD_RAM[2],       │  │
│ LCD_RAM[4], LCD_RAM[6]                             │  │
└──────────────────────────────────────────────────┘  │
                                 │                     │
                                 ▼                     │
┌──────────────────────────────────────────────────┐  │
│ Set the UDR flag of LCD_SR register to request    │  │
│ update display                                     │  │
└──────────────────────────────────────────────────┘  │
                                 │                     │
                                 ▼                     │
                 ◇ Is the update done? ◇ ──NO──────────┘
                 (If the UDD bit LCD_SR is set,
                    then update is done.)
                                 │
                                YES
                                 ▼
                          ┌─────────────┐
                          │    STOP     │
                          └─────────────┘
```

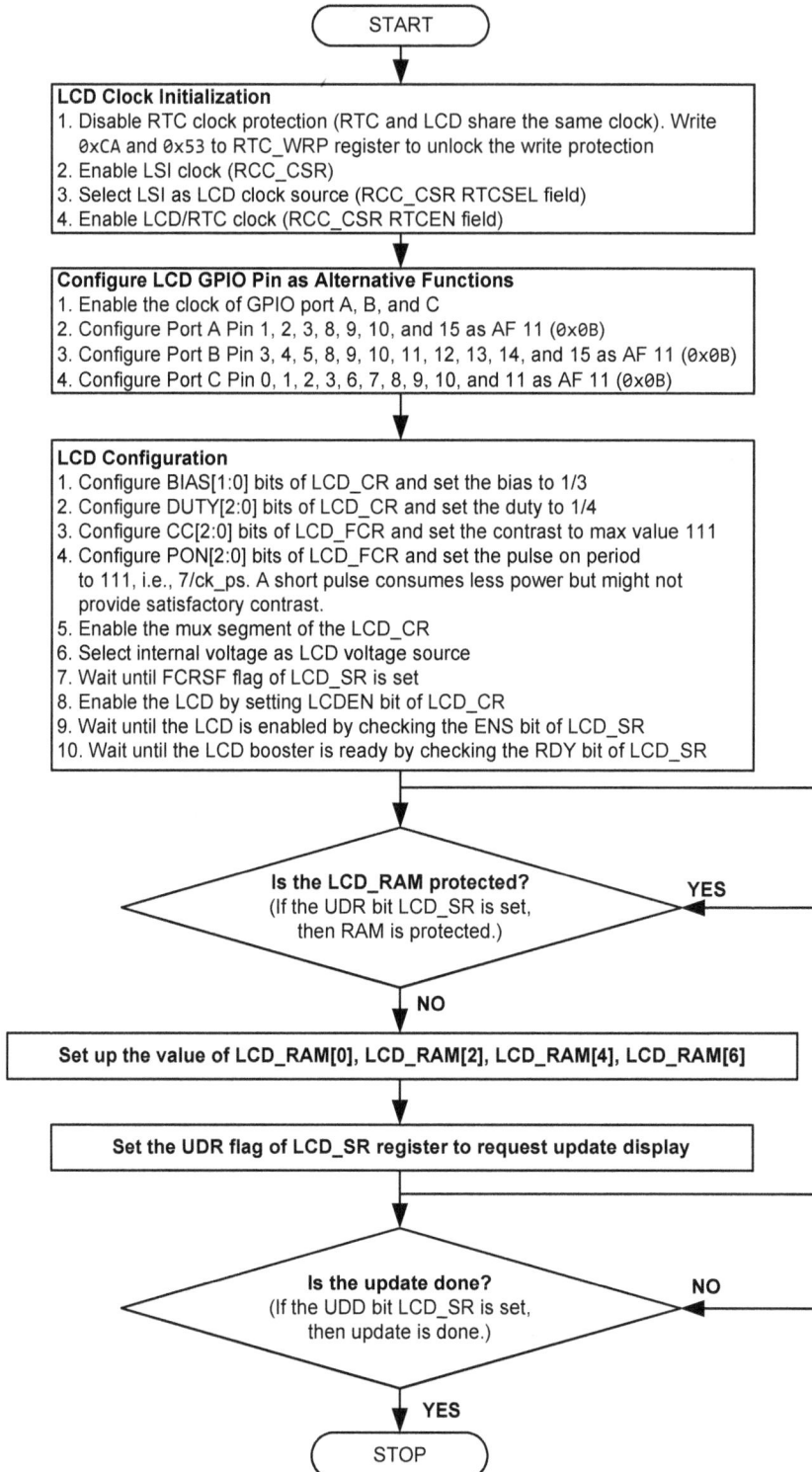

Figure 17-7 Program flowchart to drive the LCD

Figure 17-7 shows the flowchart of initializing and interfacing the LCD controller. The LCD clock is the same clock as the real-time clock (RTC).

Since the RTC clock domain is protected, to configure the LCD clock source, the RTC domain needs to be unlocked first by writing a special data sequence ("0xCA" and "0x53") to the RTC write protection register (RTC_WPR).

```c
void LCD_Clock_Init(void){
    RCC->APB1ENR |= RCC_APB1ENR_PWREN;      // Power interface clock enable
    PWR->CR      |= PWR_CR_DBP;             // Disable write protection
    RCC->CSR     |= RCC_CSR_RTCSEL_LSI;     // LSI used as RTC clock
    RCC->CSR     |= RCC_CSR_RTCEN;          // RTC clock enable

    // Disable the write protection for RTC registers
    RTC->WPR = 0xCA;   // RTC write protection register (WPR)
    RTC->WPR = 0x53;   // Write "0xCA" and "0x53" to disable protection

    // Enable the clock of LCD
    RCC->APB1ENR  |= RCC_APB1ENR_LCDEN;

    // Enable SYSCFG
    RCC->APB2ENR  |= RCC_APB2ENR_SYSCFGEN;

    // Enable LSI and wait until LSI ready
    RCC->CSR  |= RCC_CSR_LSION;
    while( (RCC->CSR & RCC_CSR_LSIRDY) == 0 );

    // Select LSI as LCD clock source
    RCC->CSR  &= ~RCC_CSR_RTCSEL_LSI;
    RCC->CSR  |= RCC_CSR_RTCSEL_LSI;        // Select LSI for RTC and LCD
    RCC->CSR  |= RCC_CSR_RTCEN;
}
```

Example 17-1. Program to initialize LCD clock initialization

17.4 Generic LCD Driver to Display Strings

This section is to understand the basic idea of writing a generic software function that can display any string. An LCD usually can display multiple numeric or alphabetic characters. The on-chip hardware driver maps each pixel of the LCD display to a binary bit in the display memory. The display memory is a special memory region used by the hardware driver to holds the on or off setting of each individual display pixel. If a bit in the display memory is set, the corresponding pixel should be visible. On the other hand, all string characters are stored as ASCII values (see Chapter 2.5) in data memory. Therefore, we need to create a function that sets up the display memory accordingly to two key inputs: (1) the ASCII value of a given letter or number, and (2) the location where this letter or number should be displayed on the LCD.

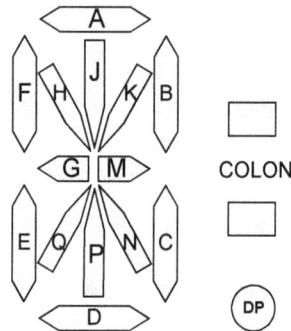

Figure 17-8. A display digit has 16 segments: 14 digit segments, 1 colon and 1 decimal point.

Each digit consists of 16 display segments: 14 segments for the digit, 1 segment of the colon, and 1 segment for the decimal point, as shown in Figure 17-8. We use a 16-bit binary value to encode an alphabetic letter and a digit number. When a segment is visible, the corresponding bit in its 16-bit code is set. If a segment is invisible, the corresponding bit is zero. For example, letter "A" can be encoded as 0xFE00, since it turns on segments G, B, M, E, F, A, and C. Similarly, number "2" can be encoded as 0xF500, making segments G, B, M, E, and A visible.

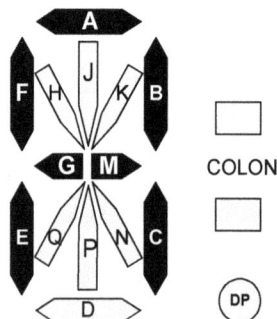

G	B	M	E	
1	1	1	1	0xF
F	A	C	D	
1	1	1	0	0xE
Q	K	Colon	P	
0	0	0	0	0x0
H	J	DP	N	
0	0	0	0	0x0

Encoding "A" as 0xFE00

Liquid-crystal Display (LCD)

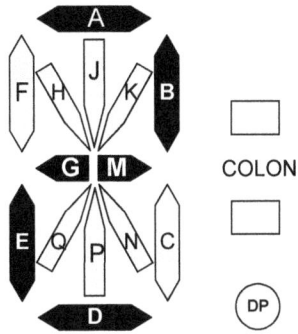

G	B	M	E	
1	1	1	1	0xF
F	A	C	D	
0	1	0	1	0x5
Q	K	Colon	P	
0	0	0	0	0x0
H	J	DP	N	
0	0	0	0	0x0

Encoding "2" as 0xF500

The following table gives more examples of encoding five letters (A-Z) and five numbers (1-5).

	15	14	13	12	11	10	9	8	7	6	5	4	3	2	1	0	
	G	B	M	E	F	A	C	D	Q	K	Col	P	H	J	DP	N	Coding
A	1	1	1	1	1	1	1	0	0	0	0	0	0	0	0	0	**0xFE00**
B	0	1	1	0	0	1	1	1	0	0	0	1	0	1	0	0	0x6714
C	0	0	0	1	1	1	0	1	0	0	0	0	0	0	0	0	0x1D00
D	0	1	0	0	0	1	1	1	0	0	0	1	0	1	0	0	0x4714
E	1	0	0	1	1	1	0	1	0	0	0	0	0	0	0	0	0x9D00
1	0	1	0	0	0	0	1	0	0	0	0	0	0	0	0	0	0x4200
2	1	1	1	1	0	1	0	1	0	0	0	0	0	0	0	0	**0xF500**
3	0	1	1	0	0	1	1	1	0	0	0	0	0	0	0	0	0x6700
4	1	1	1	0	1	0	1	0	0	0	0	0	0	0	0	0	0xEA00
5	1	0	1	0	1	1	1	1	0	0	0	0	0	0	0	0	0xAF00

Table 17-3. Encoding characters A, B, C, D and E, and numbers 1, 2, 3, 4 and 5

We use an array to store encoding of all capital letters.

```
uint16_t LetterCoding[26] = {
  // A       B       C       D       E       F       G       H       I
  0xFE00, 0x6714, 0x1D00, 0x4714, 0x9D00, 0x9C00, 0x3F00, 0xFA00, 0x0014,
  // J       K       L       M       N       O       P       Q       R
  0x5300, 0x9841, 0x1900, 0x5A48, 0x5A09, 0x5F00, 0xFC00, 0x5F01, 0xFC01,
  // S       T       U       V       W       X       Y       Z
  0xAF00, 0x0414, 0x5B00, 0x18C0, 0x5A81, 0x00C9, 0x0058, 0x05C0};
```

For any given capital letter, we can perform a simple look at the array to find its encoding. In addition, Chapter 2.5 gives functions to test for a lower-case or upper-case character in C, as well as the function to convert all alphabetic characters to their upper-case.

For example, since the ASCII value of letter 'A' is 0x40, the coding of 'D' is LetterCoding['D' – 'A'], i.e., LetterCoding[3].

The following C program is used to find the LCD display coding of a given alphabetic character. If the character is lower case, the LCD displays its corresponding upper case.

```c
// Suppose variable c points a letter and
// if *c is upper-case
if ( (*c < 0x5B) && (*c > 0x40) ) { // ASCII 'A' = 0x41, 'Z' = 0x5A
    coding = LetterCoding[*c - 'A'];
}

// if *c is lower-case; We cannot display lower case letters.
// Therefore, we display their upper case
if ( (*c < 0x7B) && ( *c > 0x60) ) { // ASCII 'a' = 0x61, 'z' = 0x7A
    coding = LetterCoding[*c - 'a'];
}
```

Similarly, the coding of 0-9 digits is stored in a separate array, as given below.

```c
uint16_t NumberCoding[10] = {
// 0       1       2       3       4       5       6       7       8       9
0x5F00,0x4200,0xF500,0x6700,0xEA00,0xAF00,0xBF00,0x04600,0xFF00,0xEF00};
```

Suppose variable *c* points to a numeric digit. Its LCD display coding can be found by looking up the above NumberCoding array, with the array index as the difference of the ASCII value of this number and the ASCII value of '0'. Chapter 2.5 gives a function to test for a decimal digit (0 through 9).

```c
coding = NumberCoding [*c - 0x30];   // ASCII '0' = 0x30
```

We can clear all information displayed on the LCD by turning off all segments.

```c
LCD->RAM[0] = 0;
LCD->RAM[2] = 0;
LCD->RAM[4] = 0;
LCD->RAM[6] = 0;
```

Suppose the coding of a number or a letter is stored in a character array C[4]. For example, the coding of letter "A" is 0xFE00, and we have C[3] = 0xF, C[2] = 0xE, C[1] = 0x0, and C[0] = 0x0. The following program displays it at different positions.

At the 1st position:

```c
LCD->RAM[0] |= ((C[3] & 0x0c)<<26) | (C[3] & 0x03); // 1G 1B 1M    1E
LCD->RAM[2] |= ((C[2] & 0x0c)<<26) | (C[2] & 0x03); // 1F 1A 1C    1D
LCD->RAM[4] |= ((C[1] & 0x0c)<<26) | (C[1] & 0x03); // 1Q 1K 1Col 1P
LCD->RAM[6] |= ((C[0] & 0x0c)<<26) | (C[0] & 0x03); // 1H 1J 1DP   1N
```

At the 2nd position:

```c
LCD->RAM[0] |= ((C[3] & 0x0c)<<24) | ((C[3] & 0x02)<<6) | ((C[3] & 0x01)<<2);
                                                        // 2G 2B 2M 2E
```

```
LCD->RAM[2] |= ((C[2] & 0x0c)<<24) | ((C[2] & 0x02)<<6) | ((C[2] & 0x01)<<2);
                                                         // 2F 2A 2C 2D

LCD->RAM[4] |= ((C[1] & 0x0c)<<24) | ((C[1] & 0x02)<<6) | ((C[1] & 0x01)<<2);
                                                         // 2Q 2K 2Col 2P

LCD->RAM[6] |= ((C[0] & 0x0c)<<24) | ((C[0] & 0x02)<<6) | ((C[0] & 0x01)<<2);
                                                         // 2H 2J 2DP 2N
```

At the 3rd position:

```
LCD->RAM[0] |= ((C[3] & 0x0c)<<22) | ((C[3] & 0x03)<<8); // 3G 3B 3M   3E
LCD->RAM[2] |= ((C[2] & 0x0c)<<22) | ((C[2] & 0x03)<<8); // 3F 3A 3C   3D
LCD->RAM[4] |= ((C[1] & 0x0c)<<22) | ((C[1] & 0x03)<<8); // 3Q 3K 3Col 3P
LCD->RAM[6] |= ((C[0] & 0x0c)<<22) | ((C[0] & 0x03)<<8); // 3H 3J 3DP  3N
```

At the 4th position:

```
LCD->RAM[0] |= ((C[3] & 0x0c)<<18) | ((C[3] & 0x03)<<10); // 4G 4B 4M   4E
LCD->RAM[2] |= ((C[2] & 0x0c)<<18) | ((C[2] & 0x03)<<10); // 4F 4A 4C   4D
LCD->RAM[4] |= ((C[1] & 0x0c)<<18) | ((C[1] & 0x03)<<10); // 4Q 4K 4Col 4P
LCD->RAM[6] |= ((C[0] & 0x0c)<<18) | ((C[0] & 0x03)<<10); // 4H 4J 4DP  4N
```

At the 5th position:

```
LCD->RAM[0] |= ((C[3] & 0x0c)<<16) | ((C[3] & 0x03)<<12); // 5G 5B 5M 5E
LCD->RAM[2] |= ((C[2] & 0x0c)<<16) | ((C[2] & 0x03)<<12); // 5F 5A 5C 5D
LCD->RAM[4] |= ((C[1] & 0x0c)<<16) | ((C[1] & 0x01)<<12); // 5Q 5K    5P
LCD->RAM[6] |= ((C[0] & 0x0c)<<16) | ((C[0] & 0x01)<<12); // 5H 5J    5N
```

At the 6th position:

```
LCD->RAM[0] |= ((C[3]&0x04)<<15) | ((C[3]&0x08)<<13) | ((C[3]&0x03)<<14);
                                                      // 6B 6G 6M 6E

LCD->RAM[2] |= ((C[2]&0x04)<<15) | ((C[2]&0x08)<<13) | ((C[2]&0x03)<<14);
                                                      // 6A 6F 6C 6D

LCD->RAM[4] |= ((C[1]&0x04)<<15) | ((C[1]&0x08)<<13) | ((C[1]&0x01)<<14);
                                                      // 6K 6Q    6P

LCD->RAM[6] |= ((C[0]&0x04)<<15) | ((C[0]&0x08)<<13) | ((C[0]&0x01)<<14);
                                                      // 6J 6H    6N
```

We can also display some special characters. The percentage sign needs two digits to display.

?	*	-	%
0x6084	0xA0DD	0x00C0	0xEC00, 0xB300

17.5 Exercises

1. Suppose the duty ratio of an LCD display is ¼ and it has 100 display segments (pixels). How many pins are required to drive this LCD?

2. Write an assembly program that displays the animation of moving a ball from left to right.

3. Write an assembly program to display your last name on the LCD screen.

4. Write an assembly program to display any A-Z character at any position.

5. Write a generic assembly function that can display a string of characters.

6. Write a generic assembly function that can display any integer less than 999,999.

7. Write an assembly function that can display a floating-point number.

CHAPTER
18

Real-time Clock (RTC)

A real-time clock (RTC) is a digital clock that provides calendar time and date. RTC has very low power consumption. It is usually powered separately by a lithium battery or a super-capacitor. Accordingly, even when the system is reset, in sleep mode, or even off, RTC does not stop and thus the system will not lose track of the current time. RTC has been widely used for calendar, alarm, periodical wakeup trigger, and time stamp.

18.1 UNIX Epoch Time

The calendar time and date are encoded in a signed 32-bit integer, which represents the number of seconds that have elapsed since the UNIX Epoch. The UNIX Epoch is defined as the time 00:00:00 (Mid-night) on January 1, 1970, Coordinated Universal Time (UTC). The number of days that have elapsed is the number of seconds divided by 86,400, which is the total number of seconds in a day.

> *"The future is something which everyone reaches at the rate of 60 minutes an hour, whatever he does, whoever he is."*
>
> C. S. Lewis, novelist

The farthest representable past time is 20:45:52 UTC on December 13, 1901 when the UNIX time number is -2^{31}. The farthest representable future time is 03:14:07 UTC on January 19, 2038 when the Unix time number is $2^{31} - 1$. If no remedy were taken, many systems would fail because January 19, 2018 would become December 13, 1901 due to the overflow of the signed 32-bit integer. This is called year 2038 problem.

The UNIX Epoch time number does not count leap seconds. In order to keep the time of day in phase with the rotation of Earth, the UTC time is added by one second at a rate of approximately once a year. This second that is added into the UTC is called a leap second. The goal of leap seconds is to ensure the Sun, on average over a year, is directly overhead on the Greenwich meridian. Since 1972, 25 leap seconds have been added to UTC by 2013.

Example of converting 2:07:39am, April 21, 2014 (UTC) to Unix Epoch number

There are 16181 days between April 21, 2014 and January 1, 1970. Note a day has 86400 seconds ($24 \times 60 \times 60 = 86400$).

$UNIX\ Epoch\ Number$

$$= 16181\ days \times \frac{seconds}{day} + 2\ hours \times \frac{seconds}{hour} + 7\ minutes \times \frac{seconds}{minutes} + 39$$

$$= 16181 \times 86400 + 2 \times 3600 + 7 \times 60 + 39$$
$$= 1398046059$$
$$= 0x53547D6B$$

18.2 RTC Frequency Setting

The UNIX time number is incremented at a frequency of 1 Hz. Therefore, we need to derive a 1-Hz clock from an input clock. The input clock can be one of three sources: internal low-speed clock, external low-speed clock, or external high-speed clock. External clocks are preferred over the internal clocks because of two important reasons: (1) internal clocks are less accurate and (2) internal clocks are stopped if the system is powered down.

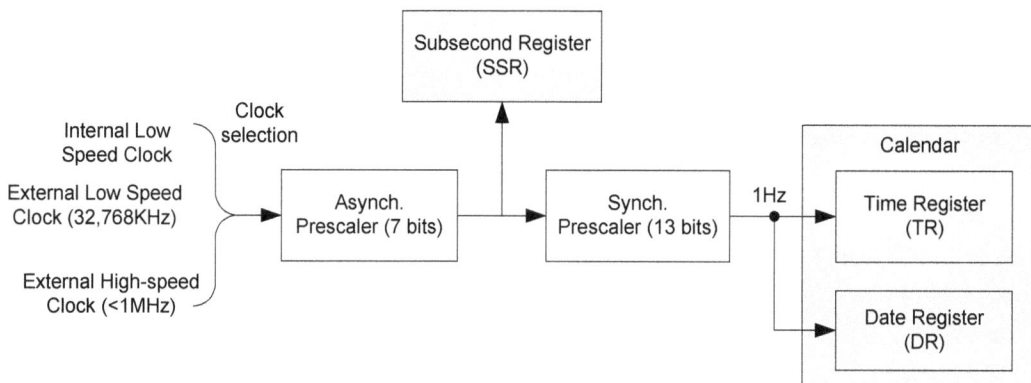

Figure 18-1. Diagram of real-time clock (RTC)

Figure 18-1 shows the frequency configuration of the RTC module. It uses two configurable prescaler registers (a 7-bit Asynchronous Prescaler and a 13-bit

Synchronous Prescaler) to slow down the frequency of the input clock to a frequency of 1 Hz. It is called asynchronous clock because the RTC input clock is usually a clock different from the processor clock.

Low-speed external crystal oscillators are highly recommended. A typical frequency is 32.768 kHz (2^{15} Hz), which is the same frequency widely used in quartz clocks and watches. Two prescalers are used to slow the input clock to 1 Hz, as shown below.

$$f_{1Hz} = \frac{f_{RTC}}{(Asynch\_Prescaler + 1) \times (Synch\_Prescaler + 1)}$$

If f_{RTC} is 32.768 kHz, *i.e.* 2^{15} Hz, then *Asynch_Prescaler* is 2^7-1, *i.e.* 127, and *Synch_Prescaler* is set as 2^8-1, *i.e.* 255, in many applications, as shown below.

$$
\begin{aligned}
f &= \frac{f_{RTC}}{(Asynch\_Prescaler + 1) \times (Synch\_Prescaler + 1)} \\
&= \frac{2^{15}}{(127 + 1) \times (255 + 1)} \\
&= \frac{2^{15}}{2^7 \times 2^8} \\
&= 1 Hz
\end{aligned}
$$

The real-time clock module is usually powered by a battery so that the processor will not lose any time and date information. Thereby, the energy efficiency is very important to real-time clock module. A larger *Asynch_Prescaler* value will make the real-time clock module more energy effiencient.

18.3 Binary Coded Decimal (BCD) Encoding

The time and date are encoded in BCD format. BCD encodes each digit (0 through 9) of a decimal number by using a fixed number of binary bits, typically four, as shown in Table 18-1.

The conversion between BCD and decimal is simple. For example, the decimal integer 29 is encoded as `00101001` in BCD, with `0010` representing the tenth digit 2, and `1001` representing the unit digit 9.

Note the BCD code is not the binary equivalent of a decimal. For example, the binary equivalent of 2013 is `111 1101 1101`, while the corresponding BCD code is `0010 0000 0001 0011`.

Decimal Digit	BCD
0	0 0 0 0
1	0 0 0 1
2	0 0 1 0
3	0 0 1 1
4	0 1 0 0
5	0 1 0 1
6	0 1 1 0
7	0 1 1 1
8	1 0 0 0
9	1 0 0 1

Table 18-1. Binary coded decimal (BCD)

In the RTC system, the date and time are encoded in BCD format. Specifically, the month, day, hour, minute, second, and last two digits of the year are encoded by two four-digit BCD codes, with four bits for the tens digit, and four bits the units digit. Only the first two digits of the year are not recorded in the date register.

Although BCD takes more bits to represent the date and time, it is more convenient to extract each individual digit of date and time and display them. For example, using 8-bit BCD to represent the minute does not require the program to perform the division or modular operations to get the tenths digit and the unit digit of the minute.

18.4 RTC Initialization

In STM32 processors, the RTC registers are protected from write to prevent malicious or accidental modification.

The following shows the RTC initialization in C code.

```c
void RTC_Init(void) {

  // Note from STM32L reference manual:
  // The RTC registers (RTC registers and RTC backup registers) are protected
  // against possible stray write accesses. To enable access to the RTC Registers,
  // proceed as follows:
  // 1. Enable the power interface clock by setting PWREN bits in RCC_APB1ENR register.
  // 2. Set the DBP bit in the PWR_CR register (see Chapter 4.4.1).
  // 3. Select the RTC clock source through RTCSEL[1:0] bits in RCC_CSR register.
  // 4. Enable the RTC clock by programming the RTCEN bit in the RCC_CSR register.

  RCC->APB1ENR |= RCC_APB1ENR_PWREN;   // Power interface clock enable
  PWR->CR      |= PWR_CR_DBP;          // Disable backup domain write protection

  // Disable the write protection for RTC registers
```

```
RTC->WPR = 0xCA;            // RTC write protection register (WPR)
RTC->WPR = 0x53;            // Write '0xCA' and '0x53' to unlock the write protection

// Select LSE clock
RCC->CSR |= RCC_CSR_RTCSEL_LSE;    // LSE oscillator clock used as RTC clock
RCC->CSR |= RCC_CSR_RTCEN;         // RTC clock enable

// Enable external low-speed oscillator, LSE clock = 32.768kHz (0x8000Hz)
RCC->CSR |= RCC_CSR_LSEON;

// Wait until LSE clock ready
while( (RCC->CSR & RCC_CSR_LSERDY) == 0 );

// Enter initialization mode to program time and date register (RTC_TR and RTC_DR)
RTC->ISR |= RTC_ISR_INIT;
while( (RTC->ISR & RTC_ISR_INITF) == 0);  // wait until INITF is set to 1

RTC->CR  &= ~RTC_CR_FMT;    // Hour format: 0 = 24 hour/day; 1 = AM/PM hour

// Generate a 1 Hz clock for the calendar counter
// The LSE crystal is a 32.768 kHz low-speed external crystal or ceramic resonator.
RTC->PRER |= (2<<7 - 1) << 16;        // Asynch_Prescaler = 127
RTC->PRER |= (2<<8 - 1);              // Synch_Prescaler  = 255

// Set time as 11:32:00 am
RTC->TR = 0<<22 | 1<<21 | 1<<16 | 3<<12 | 2<<8;

// Exit initialization mode
RTC->ISR &= ~RTC_ISR_INIT;

// Enable the write protection for RTC registers
RTC->WPR = 0xFF;
}
```

Example 18-1. Initialize RTC in C

```
        AREA RTC_Demo CODE, READONLY
        EXPORT __main
        INCLUDE      stm32l1xx_constants.s
        ALIGN
        ENTRY
__main
        ; Power interface clock enable
        LDR    r0, =RCC_BASE
        LDR    r1, [r0, #RCC_APB1ENR]
        ORR    r1, r1, #RCC_APB1ENR_PWREN
        STR    r1, [r0, #RCC_APB1ENR]

        ; Disable backup domain write protection
        LDR    r0, =PWR_BASE
        LDR    r1, [r0, #PWR_CR]
        ORR    r1, r1, #PWR_CR_DBP
        STR    r1, [r0, #PWR_CR]
```

```
            ; Write '0xCA' and '0x53' to unlock the write protection
            LDR     r0, =RTC_BASE
            MOV     r1, #0xCA
            STR     r1, [r0,  #RTC_WPR]
            MOV     r1, #0x53
            STR     r1, [r0,  #RTC_WPR]

            ; Select and enable LSE Clock
            LDR     r0, =RCC_BASE
            LDR     r1, [r0, #RCC_CSR]
            ORR     r1, r1, #RCC_CSR_RTCSEL_LSE
            ORR     r1, r1, #RCC_CSR_RTCEN
            ORR     r1, r1, #RCC_CSR_LSEON
            STR     r1, [r0, #RCC_CSR]

            ; Wait until LSE clock ready
Wait        LDR     r0, =RCC_BASE
            LDR     r1, [r0, #RCC_CSR]
            AND     r1, r1, #RCC_CSR_LSERDY
            CMP     r1, #0
            BEQ     Wait

            ; Generate a 1 Hz clock for the calendar counter
            LDR     r0, =RTC_BASE
            LDR     r1, [r0, #RTC_PRER]
            ORR     r1, r1, #0xFF
            ORR     r1, r1, #0x7F0000
            STR     r1, [r0, #RTC_PRER]

            LDR     r0, =RTC_BASE
            LDR     r1, [r0, #RTC_ISR]
            ORR     r1, r1, #RTC_ISR_INIT
            STR     r1, [r0, #RTC_ISR]

            ; Wait until INITF flag is set
Wait2       LDR     r0, =RTC_BASE
            LDR     r1, [r0, #RTC_ISR]
            AND     r1, r1, #RTC_ISR_INITF
            CMP     r1, #0
            BEQ     Wait2

            ; Set time as 11:32:00 am
            LDR     r0, =RTC_BASE
            MOV     r2, #0
            MOV     r1, #1              ; 1 = pm, 0 = am
            ORR     r2, r2, r1, LSL #22
            MOV     r1, #1              ; hr tens
            ORR     r2, r2, r1, LSL #21
            MOV     r1, #1              ; hr ones
            ORR     r2, r2, r1, LSL #16
```

```
        MOV    r1, #3                    ; min tens
        ORR    r2, r2, r1, LSL #12
        MOV    r1, #2                    ; min ones
        ORR    r2, r2, r1, LSL #8
        STR    r1, [r0, #RTC_TR]

        ; Exit initialization mode
        LDR    r0, =RTC_BASE
        LDR    r1, [r0, #RTC_ISR]
        BIC    r1, r1, #RTC_ISR_INIT
        STR    r1, [r0, #RTC_ISR]

        ; Enable the RTC protection
        LDR    r0, =PWR_BASE
        MOV    r1, #0xFF
        STR    r1, [r0, #PWR_CR]

stop    B stop

        END
```

Example 18-2. Initialize LCD in assembly program

18.5 RTC Alarm

The RTC module also provides alarm functions that allow the processor to execute a specific task at a scheduled time. For example, the RTC alarm can be used to wake up the processor at a certain time after it has entered a low-power mode.

STM32L RTC module has two alarm units, alarm A and alarm B. Their alarm time and date are saved in register RTC_ALRMAR for alarm A, and in register RTC_ALRMBR for alarm B. The alarm time and date are compared with the RTC date stored in register RTC_DR and the RTC time stored in register RTC_TR. An RTC alarm interrupt can be generated if the alarm date and time has come.

The alarm time and date comparison can be programmable. The day of week, the hour, the minute, and the second can individually selected by their mask bits to take part in the comparison. When a mask bit is 1, then its corresponding time component is ignored during alarm time comparison. Suppose the alarm time register is set to 21:25:37 on Monday. Table 18-2 shows a few examples of various settings of the mask bits.

MSK 4 (day of week)	MSK 3 (hour)	MSK 2 (minute)	MSK 1 (Second)	When does the alarm occur?
0	0	0	0	At 21:25:37 on each Monday
1	0	0	0	At 21:25:37 everyday
1	1	1	0	At the 37th second of every minute
0	0	0	1	At every second of 21:25 on each Monday
1	0	0	1	At every second of 21:25 everyday
0	0	1	1	At every second of the 21st hour on each Monday
0	1	1	1	At every second on Monday

Table 18-2. Example of mask bit setting for various alarm time comparisons

The following program sets up the alarm A, which occurs at the 30th second of each minute.

```
void RTC_Set_Alarm(void) {

  uint32_t AlarmTimeReg;

  // Remove write protection of RTC registers by writing "0xCA"
  // and then "0x53" into the RTC_WPR register
  RTC->WPR = 0xCA;              // WPR: write protection register
  RTC->WPR = 0x53;

  // Disable alarm A and its interrupt
  RTC->CR &= ~RTC_CR_ALRAE;     // Clear alarm A enable flag
  RTC->CR &= ~RTC_CR_ALRAIE;    // Clear alarm A's interrupt enable flag


  // Wait until access to alarm registers is allowed
  // Write flag (ALRAWF) is set by hardware if alarm A can be changed.
  while((RTC->ISR & RTC_ISR_ALRAWF) == 0);

  // Set alarm if the second is 30
  // Bits[6:4] = Second tens in BCD format
  // Bits[3:0] = Second units in BCD format
  AlarmTimeReg = 0x3 << 3;

  // Set alarm mask field to compare only the second
  AlarmTimeReg |= RTC_ALRMAR_MSK4;  // 1: Ignore day of week in comparison
  AlarmTimeReg |= RTC_ALRMAR_MSK3;  // 1: Ignore hour in comparison
  AlarmTimeReg |= RTC_ALRMAR_MSK2;  // 1: Ignore minute in alarm comparison
  AlarmTimeReg &= ~RTC_ALRMAR_MSK1; // 0: Alarm set if the second match

  // RTC alarm A register (ALRMAR)
  RTC->ALRMAR = AlarmTimeReg;
```

```
   // Enable Alarm A and its interrupt
   RTC->CR |= RTC_CR_ALRAE;        // Enable alarm A
   RTC->CR |= RTC_CR_ALRAIE;       // Enable alarm A interrupt

   // Enable the write protection for RTC registers
   RTC->WPR = 0xFF;

}
```

All RTC interrupts are connected to the EXTI controller. For example, the RTC alarm event is connected to the EXTI line 17, as shown in Table 12-5. In order to enable the alarm interrupt, we have to enable the EXTI line 17, which is connected to the RTC alarm events.

```
void RTC_Alarm_Enable(void){

   ...

   // Configure EXTI 17
   // rising edge trigger selection register
   EXTI->RTSR |= EXTI_RTSR_TR17; // 1 = Trigger at rising edge

   // interrupt mask register
   EXTI->IMR  |= EXTI_IMR_MR17;  // 1 = Enable EXTI 17 line

   // event mask register
   EXTI->EMR  |= EXTI_EMR_MR17;  // 1 = Enable EXTI 17 line

   // pending register
   EXTI->PR   |= (1<<17);        // Write 1 to clear pending interrupt

   // Enable RTC interrupt
   NVIC->ISER[1] |= 1<<9;        // RTC_Alarm_IRQn = 41

   ...

}
```

In this example, when an RTC_Alarm interrupt is triggered, we toggle the blue LED on the STM32L discovery kit. The RTC alarm interrupt service routine has to clean the interrupt pending flag of EXTI line 17 and the interrupt status flag of alarm A.

```
void RTC_Alarm_IRQHandler(void){

   // RTC initialization and status register (RTC_ISR)
   // Alarm A flag (ALRAF) is set by hardware when the time/date registers
   // (RTC_TR and RTC_DR) match the alarm A register (RTC_ALRMAR).

   if(RTC->ISR & RTC_ISR_ALRAF){
```

```
    // Toggle the blue LED
    GPIOB->ODR ^= 1<<6;   // Toggle GPIO pin PB.6

    // Clear the alarm A interrupt flag
    RTC->ISR &= ~(RTC_ISR_ALRAF);

}

// Clear the EXTI line 17
EXTI->PR |= (1<<17);   // write 1 to clear pending interrupt

}
```

18.6 Exercises

1. Write a C program that converts the UNIX Epoch time to a calendar date and time.

2. Write a C program that converts a given calendar date and time to the UNIX Epoch time.

3. Write an assembly program that sets up the RTC date and displays the current date on an LCD screen.

4. Write an assembly program that sets up the RTC time and displays the current time on an LCD screen.

5. Implement an assembly program to allow user to change the date and time via the keypad.

6. Write an assembly program that utilizes the RTC alarm to toggle an LED every five seconds.

CHAPTER 19

Direct Memory Access (DMA)

Direct memory access (DMA) is a useful technique to transfer data between peripherals and memory, or between memory and memory, without using many CPU cycles. For slow peripherals, DMA releases CPU from waiting for peripheral data and allows CPU to serve other tasks. For fast peripherals, such as ADC and DAC, DMA improves the data transfer throughput since memory accesses take place without the involvement of the CPU. For high-speed peripherals, DMA can help significantly reduce the rate at which interrupts are generated, and therefore decrease the performance overhead from interrupts. This chapter presents the implementation of bus matrix within the processor and gives an example code of programming DMA.

19.1 DMA Bus Matrix

Figure 19-1 and Figure 19-2 compare the operations when data is transferred from the serial port (USART) to the RAM memory without and with DMA. Without DMA, the processor needs to perform two operations explicitly: a load instruction that copies data of a peripheral data register into a register in the processor core, and then a store instruction that saves data into the memory. The processor needs to use either busy-waiting or interrupt methods to make sure that peripheral's data register is ready to use. Without DMA, data exchanges between different subsystems are inefficient since the load and store operations take useful CPU cycles.

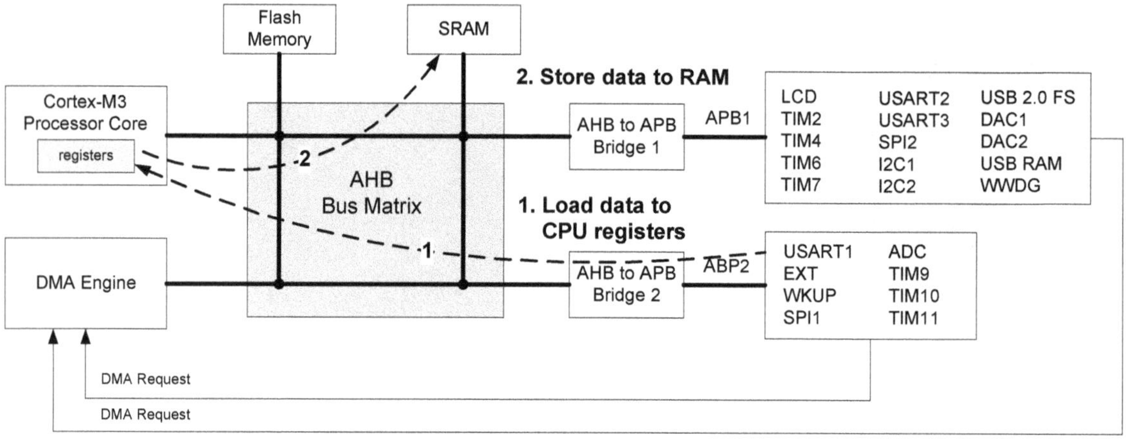

Figure 19-1. Receiving data from USART serial port without using DMA

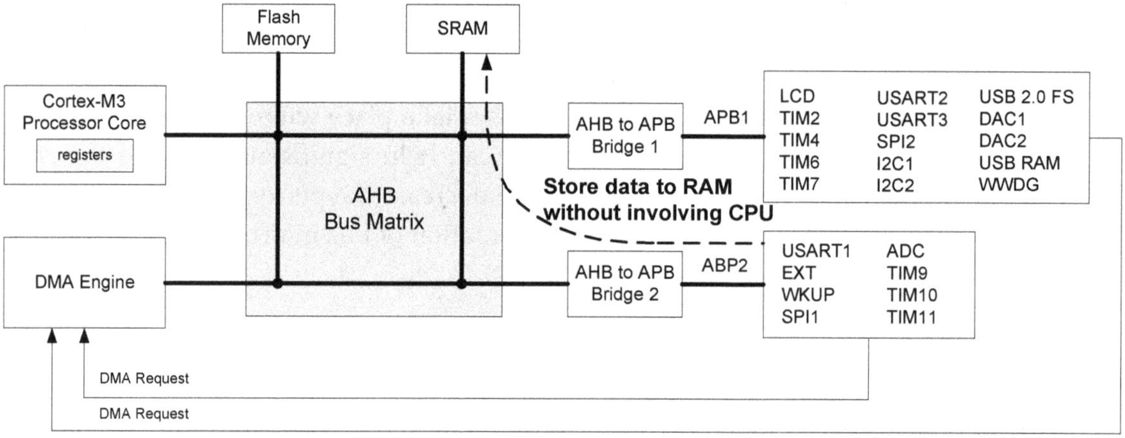

Figure 19-2. Receiving data from USART serial port using DMA

On the contrary, if DMA is used, after the processor configures and initiates the DMA channel, data in the peripheral register is automatically copied into the memory without processor intervention. The "write to" and "read from" operations are offloaded from the CPU to a dedicated hardware module called DMA engine or controller. The DMA engine can generate an interrupt at the end of each DMA transfer to inform the processor that data has been saved into the memory and is ready to be manipulated. In this way, DMA allows data computation and data transfer to take place in parallel, leading to a significant improvement in performance.

Peripherals	Channel 1	Channel 2	Channel 3	Channel 4	Channel 5	Channel 6	Channel 7
ADC1	ADC1						
SPI		SPI1_RX	SPI1_TX	SPI2_RX	SPI2_TX		
USART		USART3_TX	USART3_RX	USART1_TX	USART1_RX	USART2_RX	USART2_TX
I2C				I2C2_TX	I2C2_RX	I2C1_TX	I2C1_RX
TIM2	TIM2_CH3	TIM2_UP			TIM2_CH1		TIM2_CH2 TIM2_CH4
TIM3		TIM3_CH3	TIM3_CH4 TIM3_UP			TIM3_CH1 TIM3_TRIG	
TIM4	TIM4_CH1			TIM4_CH2	TIM4_CH3		TIM4_UP
TIM6 DAC_Ch1		TIM6_UP DAC_Ch1					
TIM7 DAC_CH2			TIM7_UP DAC_CH2				

Table 19-1. DMA channels connecting peripheral devices

19.2 Programming DMA

Each DMA channel is configured by four registers:
- DMA memory address register (CMAR)
- DMA peripheral address register (CPAR)
- DMA number of data register (CNDTR)
- DMA configuration register (CCR)

Once set, DMA takes care of memory address increment without disturbing CPU. DMA channels can generate three interrupts: transfer finished, half-finished, and transfer error. The type of a DMA interrupt can be identified by checking two shared registers: DMA interrupt status register (DMA_ISR) and DMA interrupt flag clear register (DMA_IFCR).

Channel configuration procedure. The following sequence is used to configure a DMA channel x (where x is the channel number).
1. Set the peripheral register address in the DMA_CPARx register. The data will be moved from this register to the memory or from the data memory to this register after the peripheral event.
2. Set the memory address in the DMA_CMARx register. The data will be written to or read from this memory after the peripheral event.
3. Configure the total number of data to be transferred in the DMA_CNDTRx register. After each peripheral event, this value will be decremented.
4. Configure the channel priority using the PL[1:0] bits in the DMA_CCRx register.

5. Configure data transfer direction, circular mode, peripheral and memory incremented mode, peripheral & memory data size, and interrupt after half and/or full transfer in the DMA_CCRx register.
6. Activate the channel by setting the ENABLE bit in the DMA_CCRx register.

As soon as the channel is enabled, it can serve any DMA request from the peripheral connected on the channel.

Once half of the bytes are transferred, the half-transfer flag (HTIF) is set and an interrupt is generated if the half-transfer interrupt enable bit (HTIE) is set. At the end of the transfer, the transfer complete flag (TCIF) is set and an interrupt is generated if the transfer complete interrupt enable bit (TCIE) is set.

```c
int main(void) {
   int i;
   for(i = 0; i < 8; i++)
      SRC_Const_Buffer[i] = i;

   // DMA1 clock enable
   RCC->AHBENR |= RCC_AHBENR_DMA1EN;

   // Enable memory to memory mode
   DMA1_Channel1->CCR |= DMA_CCR1_MEM2MEM;

   // Peripheral transfer size (PSIZE)
   DMA1_Channel1->CCR |= (0x2 << 8);   // 00:8-bits, 01:16-bits, 10:32-bits

   // Memory transfer size (MSIZE)
   DMA1_Channel1->CCR |= (0x2 << 10); // 00:8-bits, 01:16-bits, 10:32-bits

   // Enable memory increment mode
   DMA1_Channel1->CCR |= (0x1 << 7);

   // Enable peripheral increment mode
   DMA1_Channel1->CCR |= (0x1 << 6);

   // Disable circular mode
   DMA1_Channel1->CCR &= ~(0x1 << 5);

   // Set the transfer direction
   DMA1_Channel1->CCR &= ~(0x1 << 4);

   // Enable transfer complete interrupt
   DMA1_Channel1->CCR |= (0x1 << 1);

   // Set interrupt priority to very high
   DMA1_Channel1->CCR |= (0x3 << 12);
```

```
    // Channel priority level: 00: Low; 01: Medium; 10: High; 11: Very high

    // DMA channel x number of data register (DMA_CNDTRx)
    DMA1_Channel1->CNDTR = 8;

    // DMA channel x peripheral address register (DMA_CPARx)
    DMA1_Channel1->CPAR = (unsigned int) SRC_Const_Buffer;

    // DMA channel x memory address register (DMA_CMARx)
    DMA1_Channel1->CMAR = (unsigned int) DST_Buffer;

    NVIC_SetPriority(DMA1_Channel1_IRQn, 1);    // Set priority to 1
    NVIC_EnableIRQ(DMA1_Channel1_IRQn);

    // Enable EXTI0_1 interrupt in NVIC
    DMA1_Channel1->CCR |= 0x1;                  // Enable channel 1

    while( DMA1_Channel1 -> CNDTR != 0);

    while (1);  // dead loop
}

void DMAChannel1_IRQHandler(void) {

}
```

Example 19-1. Using DMA channel 1

19.3 Exercises

1. Write an assembly program that uses DMA to copy 256 bytes of data from one memory region to another memory region.

2. Write an assembly program that uses DMA to perform analog-to-digital conversion (ADC) conversion. (Requires the background of Chapter 21).

3. Write an assembly program that uses DMA to perform digital-to-analog conversion (DAC) conversion. (Requires the background of Chapter 21)

[This page is intentionally left blank.]

CHAPTER 20

Analog-to-Digital Converter

An analog-to-digital converter (ADC) produces a finite-precision signed or unsigned digital number to represent approximately the size of an analog voltage relative to a reference voltage. The reference voltage is a fixed voltage provided by the internal circuit of the microprocessor or by an external circuit connected to a pin of the microprocessor. It does not convert a voltage larger than the reference voltage. Three key performance parameters of ADCs are *sampling rate*, *resolution*, **and** *power dissipation*.

- The sampling rate indicates how many conversions can be performed in a second. ADC can perform up to several millions or billions of samples per second.
- The number of bits in the ADC output is called resolution. While typical resolutions vary between 6 to 24 bits, the resolution has not been improved much in the past few years since a 12-bit or 24-bit resolution is often sufficient for most modern applications.
- The power dissipation measures the power efficiency of ADC converters. In many mobile embedded systems, it is the power budget, not the hardware speed, which limits the throughput of ADC converters.

20.1 ADC Architecture

There are three most popular ADC architectures: *sigma-delta* ADC for low-speed applications, *successive-approximation* (SAR) ADC for low-power applications, and *pipelined* ADC for high-speed application.

- Sigma-delta ADCs are mostly used in applications requiring low sampling rates but high resolution, typically less than 100 kilo samples per second and 12 to 24-

bit resolution, such as voice band and audio applications. They have been widely used in modern cellphones.

- SAR ADCs have been widely used in low-power data acquisitions with moderate sampling rates, typically less than 5 million samples per second (MSPS).
- Pipelined ADCs are widely used for high-speed applications, such as digital oscilloscopes HDTV, and radar communication, requiring fast sampling rates greater than 5 MSPS and relatively low resolution less than 18 bits.

The ADC on STM32 microcontrollers is based on the *successive-approximation* (SAR) architecture, as shown in Figure 20-1. The architecture includes two major components: sample-and-hold amplifier (SHA), and SAR digital quantization.

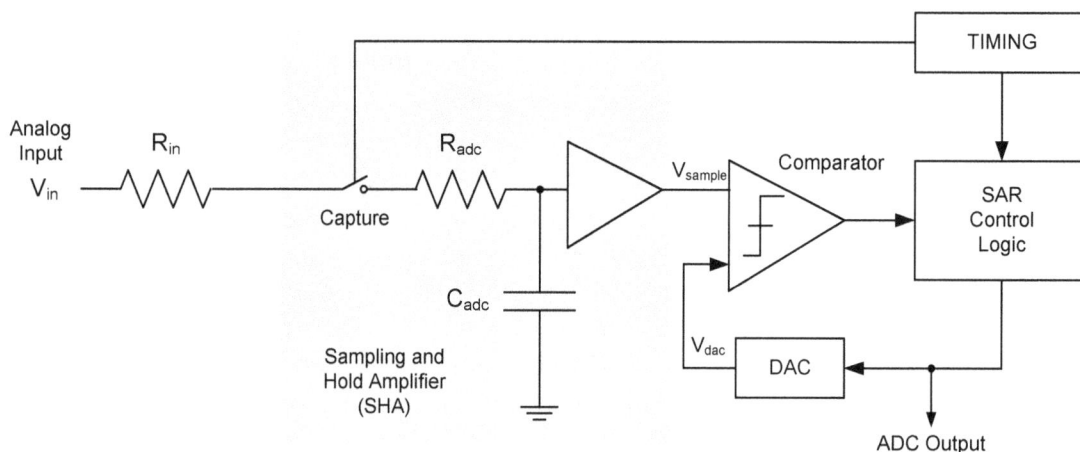

Figure 20-1. Basic architecture of successive-approximation (SAR) ADC

20.1.1 Digital Quantization

The digital quantization works as follows. The SAR control logic uses the binary search algorithm to find the digital number (ADC output) that represents the analog input most closely. The SAR control logic dynamically changes the ADC output so that the digital-to-analog converter (DAC) output V_{dac} gradually approaches the DAC input voltage V_{in}.

(1) The conversion starts with setting the internal DAC output V_{dac} to $\frac{1}{2}V_{REF}$ and then compares the DAC output V_{dac} with the ADC input V_{in}.

(2) If V_{in} is larger than $\frac{1}{2}V_{REF}$, the SAR logic controller sets the most significant bit (MSB) of the ADC conversion result to 1. Otherwise, the MSB of the ADC is set to 0.

(3) Next, the DAC output V_{dac} is set to either ¾V_{REF} or ¼V_{REF}, depending on the comparison result between V_{in} and V_{dac}.

(4) This process repeats until all bits of the ADC output have been determined.

If the ADC has a resolution of n bits, the successive-approximation conversion takes n steps to complete. This shows a tradeoff between the resolution and sampling rate. A higher resolution usually reduces the ADC conversion rate.

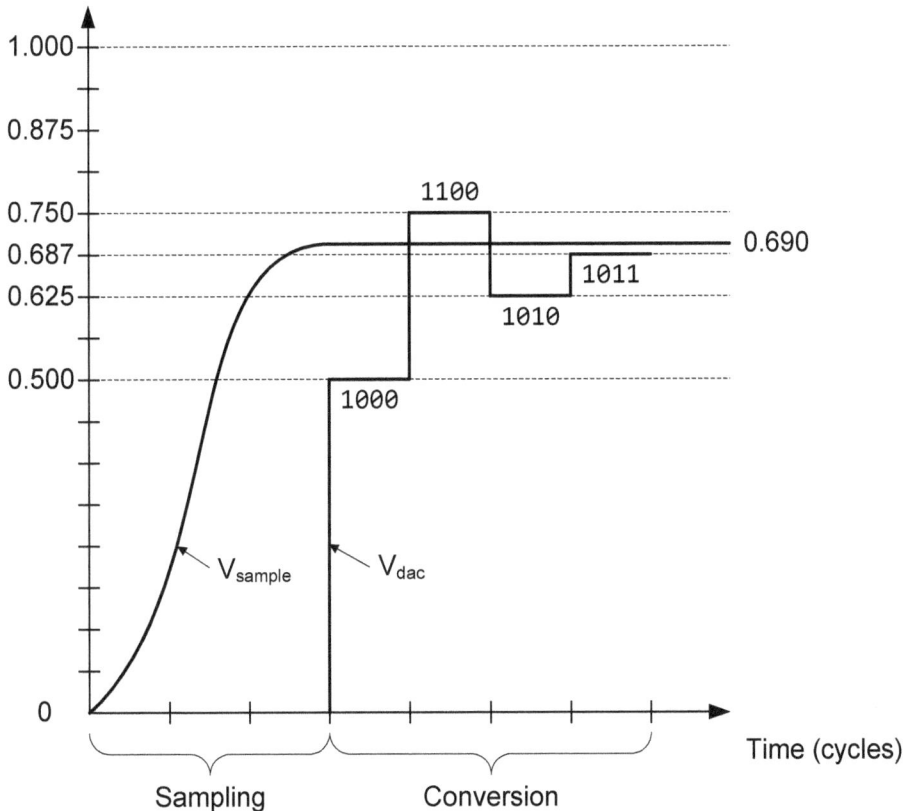

Figure 20-2. Example of four-bit successive-approximation (SAR) ADC. Suppose the input voltage is between 0 and 1 V.

Figure 20-2 shows an example of converting an input voltage of 0.690V into a 4-bit binary value by using SAR ADC. Suppose the range of the input voltage is between 0V and 1V.

- After the input voltage is sampled, the SAR control logic starts the conversion by setting the V_{dac} as 0.5V (*i.e.* the ADC output is 0b1000) and comparing it with V_{sample}.

- Since V$_{sample}$ is larger than V$_{dac}$, the control logic then sets V$_{dac}$ as 0.750V (*i.e.* the ADC output is 0b1100).
- Because V$_{sample}$ is smaller than V$_{dac}$, the control logic then sets V$_{dac}$ as 0.625V.
- The above process repeats and the final output of ADC is 0b1011. In this example, the conversion process takes four cycles.

20.1.2 Sampling and Hold

The sample-and-hold amplifier (SHA) includes a switched capacitor and one operational amplifier, which is used to sample the analog input voltage V$_{in}$ and hold the value over a certain amount of time for subsequent ADC processing. The sampling and hold circuit is a simple resistor-capacitor circuit. When the switch is closed, the voltage across the capacitor V_C increases exponentially according to the following equation:

$$V_C(t) = V_{in} \times \left(1 - e^{-\frac{t}{T_c}}\right)$$

where $T_c = (R_{in} + R_{adc}) \times C_{adc}$. This shows that the input voltage V$_{in}$ cannot be sampled instantly. For example, when the switch is closed for a time period of $3T_c$, the voltage across the capacitor V_C is only 95.02% of the input voltage V$_{in}$, as shown in Figure 20-3. As a result, in order to achieve precise analog-to-digital conversion, the capture switch should be closed for a sufficient amount of time. The amount of time that the capture switch remains closed is called *sampling time*.

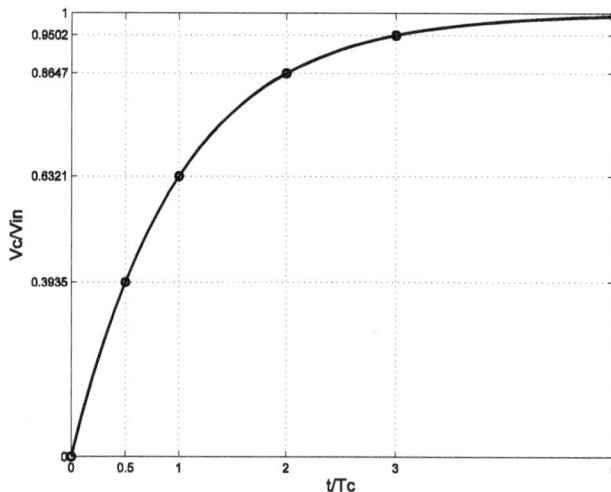

Figure 20-3. The change of the ratio of Vc to Vin over time

On STM32L processors, ADC uses the HSI as the default clock, no matter what clock the processor uses. ADC can use a clock divider to change ADC clock speed, either by 1 for full speed (16 MHz), by 2 for medium speed (8 MHz), or by 4 for low speed (4 MHz). Each ADC channel can select its own sampling time, determined by the SMP[2:0] bits of the corresponding SMPRx registers (x=1, 2, or 3).

The total ADC conversion time is as follows. Note if the ADC has a resolution of n bits, the conversion time of successive-approximation takes n cycles to complete.

$$T_{conversion} = Sampling\ Time + Channel\ Conversion\ Time$$

For 12-bit ADC conversion, if the sampling time is to set as 4 cycles and the ADC clock is set as 16 MHz, then we have

$$T_{conversion} = 4 + 12 = 16\ cycles = 1\mu s$$

A larger sampling time is recommended if the ADC meets the application's speed requirement. As discussed earlier, in order to achieve precise analog-to-digital conversion, the capture switch in the sample-and-hold component should be closed for a sufficient amount of time.

20.2 ADC Sampling Error

Suppose the ADC output has n bits, the ADC result of an input voltage V can be calculated as follows:

$$Digital\ Result = round\left(2^n \times \frac{V - V_{RL}}{V_{RH} - V_{RL}}\right)$$

where V_{RH} and V_{RL} are the high-reference voltage and the low-reference voltage, respectively. There are two conversion modes: single-end mode and dual-end mode. In the single-end mode, V_{RL} is 0 and the digital output is an unsigned number, then we have

$$Digital\ Result = round\left(2^n \times \frac{V}{V_{RH}}\right)$$

In the dual-end mode, V_{RL} is equal to $-V_{RH}$ often and the digital output is a signed number represented in two's complement format.

$$Digital\ Result = round\left(2^n \times \frac{V + V_{RH}}{2V_{RH}}\right) = round\left(2^{n-1} \times \frac{V + V_{RH}}{V_{RH}}\right)$$

The ADC output approximates the analog input signal in time and amplitude. While an analog signal is continuous in time and amplitude and has an infinite number of possible values, the output of ADC is sampling out with a fixed time interval and has only a limited number of possible values. The error can be reduced by using a higher sampling frequency or using more bits to represent the digital output.

The difference between the actual analog value and the analog value represented by the quantized digital value is called quantization error. In the single-end mode, assuming the input voltage is in the range [0, V_{REF}]. Figure 20-4 and Figure 20-5 show two different quantization methods in the single-end mode, in which V_{REF} is 5V. The digital ADC output in these examples has only three digits, which only represent a total of 8 possible values. Figure 20-4 uses the following quantization.

$$Digital\ Result = floor\left(2^3 \times \frac{V}{V_{REF}}\right)$$

Note the floor operation is actually to truncate all decimal part during the division, which is the default operation in integer divisions.

Figure 20-5 uses the quantization method introduced previously.

$$Digital\ Result = round\left(2^3 \times \frac{V}{V_{REF}}\right) = floor\left(2^3 \times \frac{V}{V_{REF}} + \frac{1}{2}\right)$$

Apparently, the average quantization error in Figure 20-5 is half of the quantization of Figure 20-4. The quantization result based on the round function can be achieved from the result of the floor function by shifting the input voltage toward left by $0.5 \times \frac{V_{REF}}{8}$.

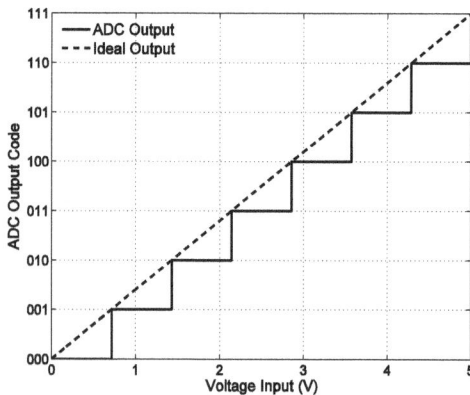

Figure 20-4. ADC output based on floor function in the single-end mode

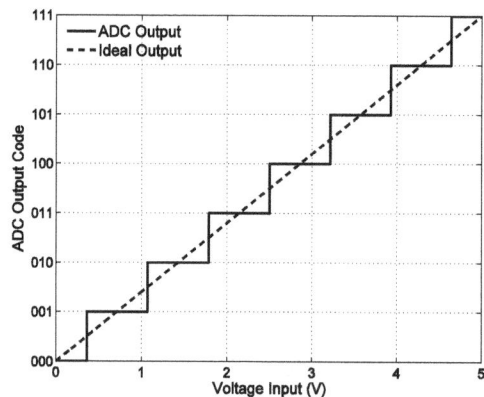

Figure 20-5. ADC output based on the round function in the single-end mode

In the single-end mode, if the ADC output has n bits, the output of an input voltage v can be calculated as the following:

$$V = \frac{Digital\ Value}{2^n - 1} \times V_{REF}$$

20.3 ADC Conversion Modes

The STM32 ADC module is a 12-bit converter that provides up to 42 multiplexed channels allowing it to measure 40 external and 2 internal analog signals. The resolution can be configured to 12, 10, 8 or 6 bits depending on the application requirements. The voltage input range of each channel is in $[V_{ref-}, V_{ref+}]$, where the V_{ref-} and V_{ref+} are two dedicated input pins on some processors and serves as external voltage reference.

The processor also provides internal reference voltage, which is individually measured in production. The internal reference voltage is 3 ± 0.01 V and its corresponding converted value is stored at a protected memory area during the manufacturing process.

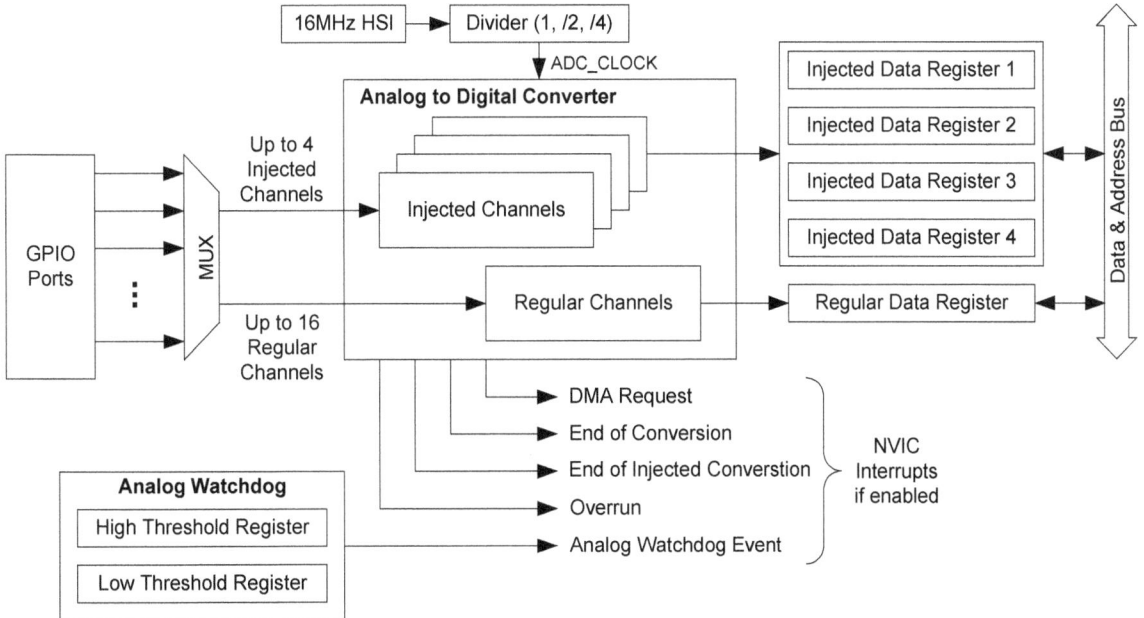

Figure 20-6. Analog-to-digital converter (ADC)

The ADC module operates by using the high-speed internal clock (HSI) after a specific clock divider. The divider is 1 for 16 MHz, 2 for 8 MHz, or 4 for 4 MHz. For a resolution of 12 bits, the STM32 takes at least 16 cycles of the ADC clock, including 4 cycles for sampling and 12 cycles for 12-bit sampling. Even at the low speed, a conversion will take only $4\mu s$ (16/4MHz).

For a selected conversion channel, the conversion can be performed in either *single* mode or *continuous* mode, as shown in Figure 20-7.

- For the single mode in the regular group, one of the input channels is selected by the SQ1[4:0] bits in the SQR5 register, and then sampled once. The conversion value is stored in the 16-bit ADC data register (ADC_DR). The end of conversion flag (EOC) is set, and an interrupt is generated if the EOCIE bit of the ADC control register 1 is set. For the injected group, the conversion channel is selected by the JSQ1[4:0] bits in the JSQR register, and the result is saved into the 16-bit ADC_JDR1 register.
- During the continuous mode, the ADC starts a new conversion immediately after it finishes one. The last conversion result is saved in the ADC data register (ADC_DR).

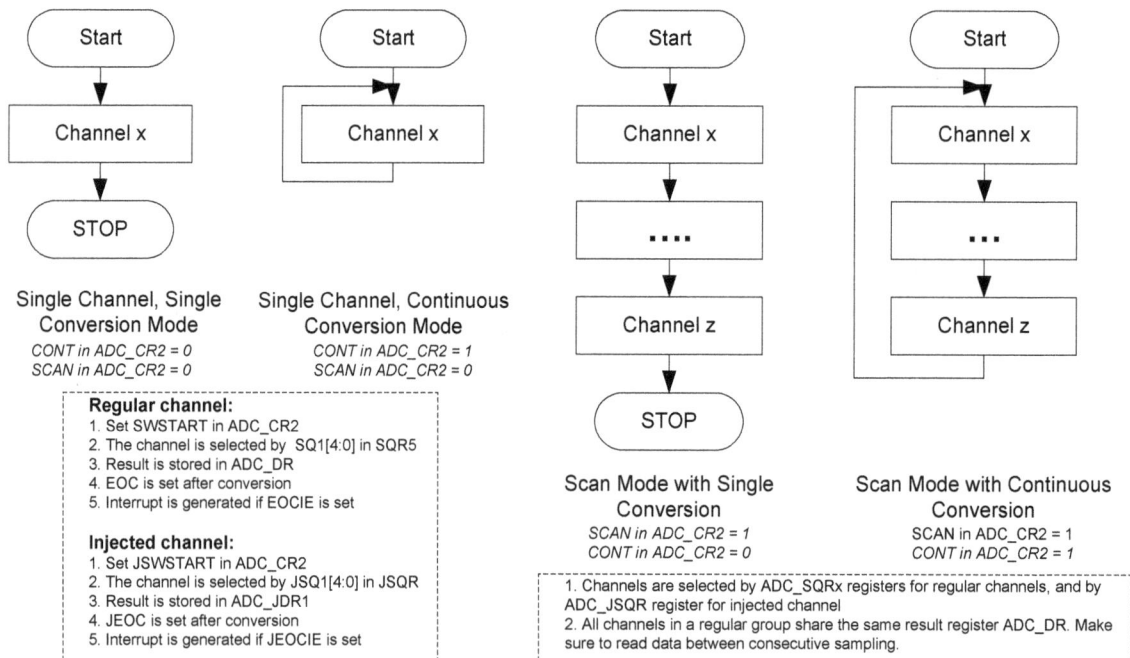

Figure 20-7 ADC Conversion Modes

For a group of conversion channels, the conversion can also be performed in a round-robin fashion and this is called *scan* mode. This mode scans all the channels selected in the ADC_SQRx registers for a regular group or in the ADC_JSQR register for an injected group. The ADC performs a single conversion for one channel of the group, and then continues successively for the other channels of the group in turn.

The conversion operation can be set up to perform only once or repeatedly, depending on the CONT bit in the ADC_CR2 register. For the injected group, there is one data register for each injected channel. However, there is only one data register that is shared for all channels in a regular group. Therefore, after each conversion, the software needs to read the data register between consecutive sampling. Since an interrupt or DAM request can be triggered at the end of each conversion, a read operation should be performed by the corresponding interrupt service routine or by the DMA operation.

A nice timesaving hardware feature is the analog watchdog. If the voltage input is below a user-defined lower threshold or above a user-defined higher threshold, the ADC can generate an interrupt to start or stop the conversion, or perform other user-specified tasks. Normally we could continuously perform DAC conversion and monitor the voltage input by software, wasting precious CPU cycles and battery energy. The STM32 microcontrollers directly implement the watchdog function in hardware, making them more time efficient. The analog watchdog can be set for all channels of a group of regular or injected channels, or specific channels within a group.

20.4 ADC Data Alignment

The ADC resolution can be configured by software. The resolution can be 12, 10, 8 and 6 bits, selected by setting the RES[1:0] bits of the ADC_CR1 register. The output data registers have 16 bits and can be either right-aligned or left-aligned.

Figure 20-8 shows different data out formats. The output of an injected channel is decreased by a user-defined offset specified in the ADC_JOFRx registers, the result can be a negative value. Therefore, sign extension must be performed for both right and left alignment. A sign extension operation duplicates the left-most bit of a signed number, *i.e.* the sign bit, to all bits to the left. For each regular channel, no subtraction is done to the output and thus each output value is positive.

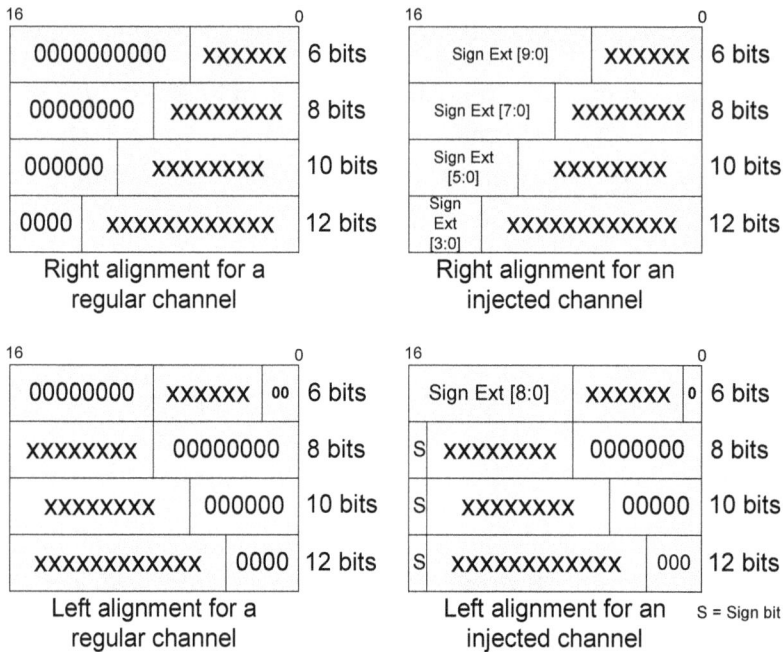

Figure 20-8 Data alignment of ADC data registers

All output data except 6-bit ones are aligned based on half-words, and their memory addresses are a multiple of 2. For 6-bit output, the alignment of the data portion is aligned at the byte boundary. Two zero bits are appended at the end of the 6-bit output for a regular channel, and one zero bit is appended for an injected channel.

20.5 ADC Triggers

The ADC conversion can be triggered by using software or external signals.

- *Software trigger.* The ADC conversion is started if the software set the SWTRIG bit. The SWTRIG flag is reset automatically by hardware once the conversion completes. If the continuous mode is selected, the ADC will repeatedly make ADC conversion.

- *External trigger.* The EXTEN[1:0] bits for regular channels and the JEXTEN[1:0] bits for injected channels configure the trigger edge detection, with a choice from rising edge, falling edge, or both rising and falling edges. The external trigger signal can be a specific channel output of a timer, the trigger output (TRGO) of a timer, or an external signal to a chip (EXTLINE).

When the software trigger is used, one common programming error is that the software does not set up the length of delay at the end of each regular conversion. As a result, the ADC conversion was only performed once, instead of continuously. In defaulting setting, there is no delay before a new regular conversion can start. If the system clock is slow, there is no enough time for the processor to read the ADC data register (DR) before a new

Tip: Insert some delay between conversions when the system clock is slow.

conversion completes. Therefore, it is a good practice to set the delay (DELS[2:0] bits of the ADC_CR2 register) as waiting until the ADC_DR register has been read or the EOC flag has been cleared by hardware. This delay setting is also called ADC freeze mode.

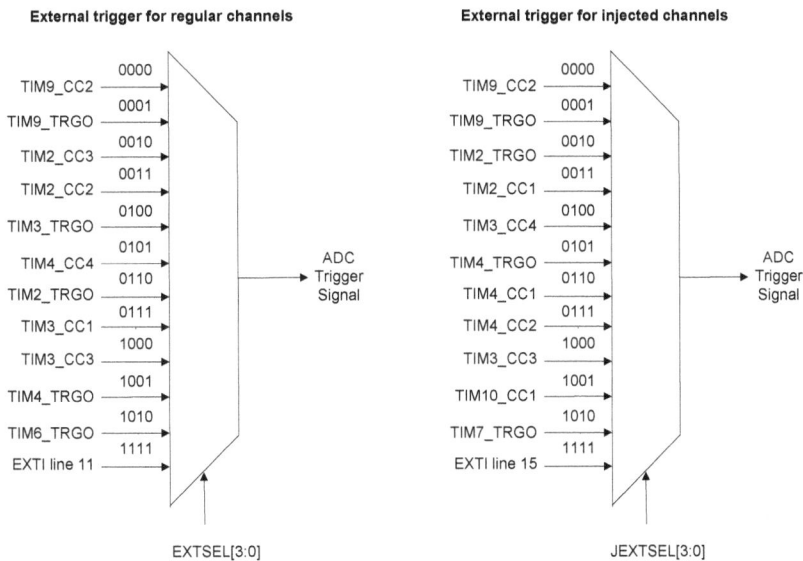

Figure 20-9. External trigger selection for regular and injected channels

A timer is often used as the ADC external trigger, as shown in Figure 20-9. In a STM32L processor, a timer has one TRGO output and four channel outputs (CC1, CC2, CC3 and CC4). The master mode selection bits (MMS[2:0]) of the control register 2 selects one of the following signals as the TRGO output of a timer:

- the update generation (UG) bit of the event generation register (EGR) register,
- the counter enable (CEN) bit of the control register (CR) 1, update event, or
- the output of four channels.

The following C program configures channel 1 output of timer 3, which will be used as the trigger signal of the ADC converter. Suppose the default 2.097MHz MSI is used as the system clock. The timer counter increases from 0 to 1000, incrementing by one for each millisecond. The output of channel 1 is a square wave with a frequency of 1 Hz and a duty cycle of 50%.

```
// Timer trigger setup
// Default MSI 2.097MHz, Time 3 counter clock 1 KHz,
// Time 3 channel 1 output 1 Hz
RCC->APB1ENR |= RCC_APB1ENR_TIM3EN; // Enable clock
TIM3->PSC = 2097-1;              // MSI / (1 + Prescaler)
TIM3->ARR = 1000-1;              // Auto-reload register

// OC1M = 110 for PWM Mode 1 output on channel 1
// Channel 1 is active if counter < CCR1, and inactive otherwise
// CC1P of CCER register: 0 = Active High (default);  1 = Active Low
TIM3->CCMR1 |= TIM_CCMR1_OC1M_1 | TIM_CCMR1_OC1M_2;

TIM3->CCMR1 |= TIM_CCMR1_OC1PE; // Enable preload for channel 1
TIM3->CR1    |= TIM_CR1_ARPE;     // Enable auto-reload preload
TIM3->CCER  |= TIM_CCER_CC1E;    // Enable output for channel 1
TIM3->CCR1   = 499;              // Output Compare Register for channel 1
TIM3->EGR   |= TIM_EGR_UG;       // Re-initialize the timer counter
TIM3->CR1    |= TIM_CR1_CEN;      // Enable counter
```

After configuring timer 3, we can select the channel 1 output (CC1) of timer 3 as the trigger signal of the ADC converter.

```
...

// Enable continuous conversion
ADC1->CR2 |= ADC_CR2_CONT;

// Turn on ADC conversion
ADC1->CR2 |= ADC_CR2_ADON;

// Select TIM3_CC1 as ADC trigger
// EXTSEL[3:0] = 0100: TIM3_TRGO event
// EXTSEL[3:0] = 0111: TIM3_CC1 event
// EXTSEL[3:0] = 1000: TIM3_CC3 event
ADC1->CR2 &= ~(ADC_CR2_EXTSEL);
ADC1->CR2 |= (0x7)<<24;

// Start the conversion of the regular channels by software
ADC1->CR2 |= ADC_CR2_SWSTART;

...
```

20.6 Measuring the Input Voltage

A potentiometer, informally a pot, is a three-terminal variable resistor. It uses a sliding contact and works as an adjustable voltage divider. When two outer terminals are connected to Vcc and the ground respectively, the center terminal will generate a voltage that varies from 0 to Vcc depending on the position of the sliding contact.

In the following sections, we use the internal voltage reference, which is approximately 3V. In this example, we measure the input voltage. If the input voltage V_{input} is larger than ½ of V_{cc}, then we turn on an LED. Another interesting application is that we use the potentiometer to adjust the brightness of an LED dynamically if the LED is controlled by a PWM. The V_{input} is then used to adjust the duty cycle of the PWM output signal.

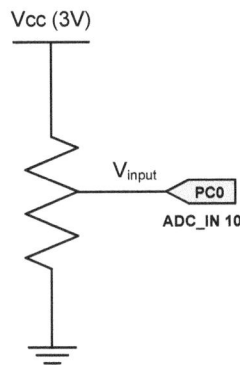

Figure 20-10. Measuring the voltage output of a potentiometer

Suppose the ADC result has 12 bits, then we have the following ADC conversion result:

$$ADC\ Result = \frac{V_{input}}{V_{REF}} \times 4096$$

20.7 ADC Configuration Flowchart

The STM32L processor contains only one ADC module. However, this ADC module can support multiple analog input channels simultaneously, including
- one channel for the built-in I_{DD} measurement circuit,
- one channel for the internal temperature measurement, and
- the remainder channels for analog input via the GPIO pins defined in Table 20-1.

Analog Input Signal	Pin	Analog Input Signal	Pin
ADC_IN 1	PA 1	ADC_IN 11	PC 1
ADC_IN 2	PA 2	ADC_IN 12	PC 2
ADC_IN 3	PA 3	ADC_IN 13	PC 3
ADC_IN 4	PA 4	ADC_IN 14	PC 4
ADC_IN 5	PA 5	ADC_IN 15	PC 5
ADC_IN 6	PA 6	ADC_IN 18	PB 12
ADC_IN 7	PA 7	ADC_IN 19	PB 13
ADC_IN 8	PB 0	ADC_IN 20	PB 14
ADC_IN 9	PB 1	ADC_IN 21	PB 15
ADC_IN 10	PC 0		

Table 20-1. Pin definition for analog input signal of STM32L processors

Up to four input channels can be selected by software to join the injected group. A channel in the injected group is called an injected channel. Each injected channel has its own ADC data register. Input channels can also be put by software into a regular group. An input channel in the regular group is called a regular channel. All regular channels share an ADC data register.

Figure 20-11 shows the flowchart of initializing the continuous ADC conversion for channel 10 (GPIO pin PC 0) with a software start of conversion. An interrupt will be generated at the end of each ADC conversion if the ADC interrupt is enabled.

- For a regular channel, the End of Conversion (EOC) flag is set by the hardware at the end of each conversion. The EOC flag can be cleared by software explicitly or be cleared implicitly by reading ADC_DR.
- For an injected channel, the injected end of conversion (JEOC) flag is set at the end of the conversion of all injected channels in the injected group. The JEOC can only be cleared by software.

On STM32L processors, the ADC needs to be driven by the 16-MHz high-speed internal (HSI) clock. Therefore, at the beginning of the flowchart, the program turns on the HSI clock and waits until it is ready. The processor clock is independent from the ADC clock and can be higher or lower than the HSI clock.

If ADC interrupts are enabled, an interrupt is generated at the end of converting a regular channel or at the end of converting all injected channels. As presented in Chapter 20.4, the data register can have up to 12 valid bits aligned right or left. Reading the data register (DR) will automatically clear the EOC flag in the ADC status register (SR). The regular channel interrupt and the injected channel interrupt have different flags in the ADC status register (SR).

Start

1. Turn on HSI (RCC_CR_HSION)
2. Wait for it is ready (RCC_CR_HSIRDY).

Configure GPIO PB.6 as output with push-pull for blue LED

Configure GPIO PC.0 as Analog Input
Note: PC.0 is connected the ADC Channel 10 (PC.0 = ADC_IN10)
1. Enable the clock of GPIO C
2. Set PC.0 as Analog Input (GPIO_MODER)

Analog to Digital Converter 1 (ADC1) Setup
Note: HSI (16MHz) is always used for ADC on STM32L.
1. Turn on the ADC clock (RCC_APB2ENR_ADC1EN)
2. Turn off the ADC conversion (ADC1->CR2)
3. Set the length of the regular channel sequence to 1 since we only perform ADC in Channel 10.
   (L[4:0] bits of register ADC1->SQR1)
4. Set Channel 10 as the 1st conversion in regular sequence
   (SQ1[4:0] bits of register ADC1->SQR5)
5. Configure the sample time register for channel 10 (SMP10[2:0] bits of register ADC1->SMPR2)
6. Enable End-Of-Conversion interrupt (EOCIE bit of register ADC1->CR1)
7. Enable continuous conversion mode (CONT bit of register ADC1->CR2)
8. Configure delay selection as delayed until the converted data have been read
   (DELS[2:0] bits in register ADC1->CR2)
9. Enable the interrupt of ADC1_IRQn in NVIC
10. Configure the interrupt priority of ADC1_IRQn
11. Turn on the ADC conversion (ADON bit of register ADC1->CR2)
    Note: Make sure that we should write to CR2 register before the next step since SWSTART
          cannot be updated if ADC is off.
12. Start the conversion of the regular channel (ADC_CR2_SWSTART)
    Note: If SWSTART only performs one conversion, then it is very likely that your code did not
          set up the delay correctly in step 8.

Dead Loop

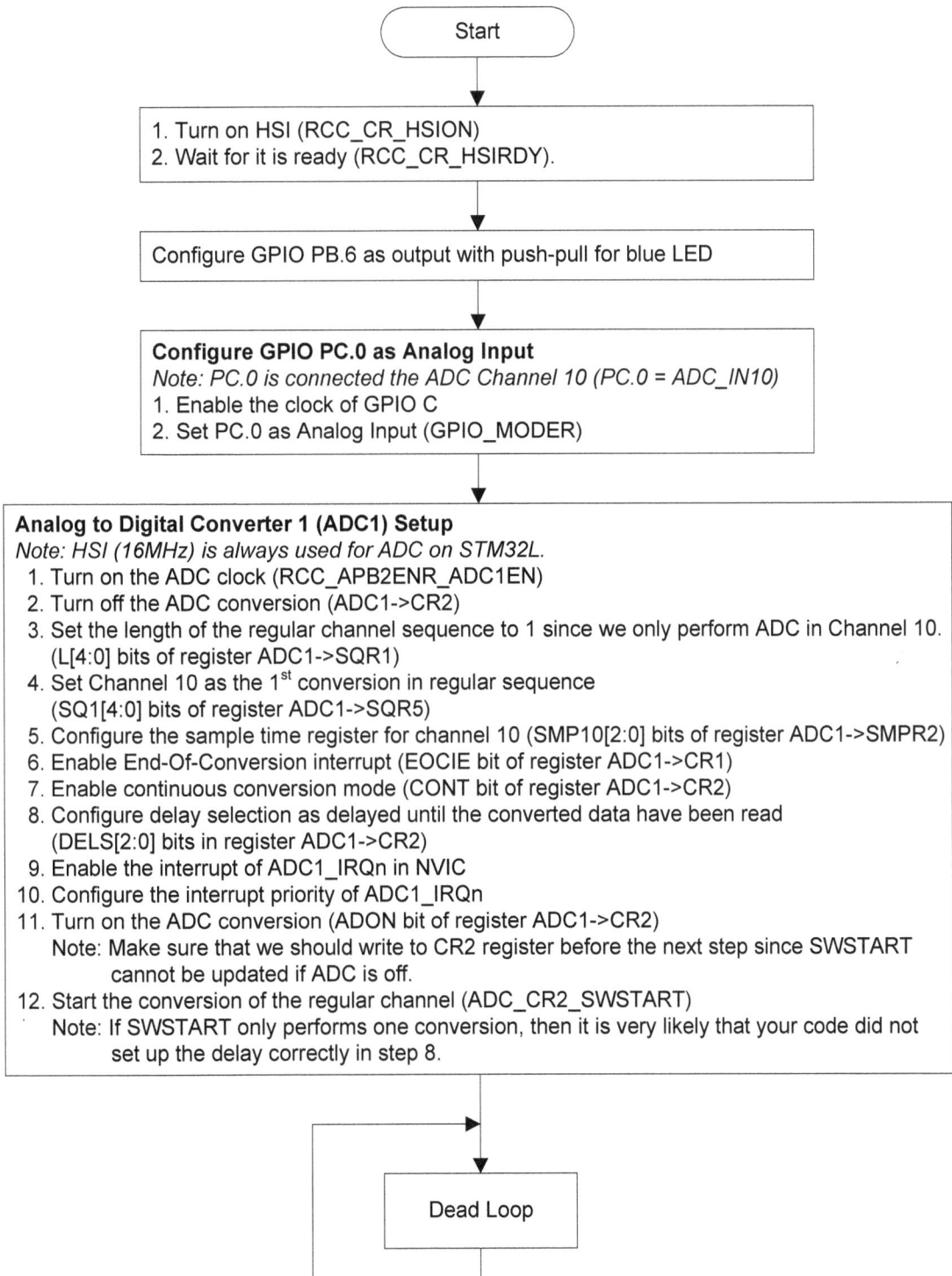

Figure 20-11. Flowchart of ADC conversion for channel 10 (GPIO pin PC 0)

The following is an example C code of the ADC interrupt handler.

```
void ADC1_IRQHandler (void) {
    if(ADC1->SR & ADC_SR_EOC) {
        // For a regular channel, check End of Conversion (EOC) flag
        // Reading ADC data register (DR) clears the EOC flag
        Result = ADC1->DR;
    } else if (ADC1->SR & ADC_SR_JEOC) {
        // For injected channels, check the JEOC flag
        // Reading injected data registers does not clear the JEOC flag
        // Each injected channel has a dedicated data register
        Result_1 = ADC1->JDR1;       // Injected channel 1
        Result_2 = ADC1->JDR2;       // Injected channel 2
        Result_3 = ADC1->JDR3;       // Injected channel 3
        Result_4 = ADC1->JDR4;       // Injected channel 4
        ADC1->SR & = ~(ADC_SR_JEOC); // Clear JEOC flag
    }
}
```

Example 20-1. Interrupt handler routine for ADC

Configuring the ADC regular sequence takes two steps: first set the total number of regular input channels, and then place the target input channels in the regular sequence registers (SQR), starting from SQR5 to SQR1. The following code shows the code to set up the ADC sequence that includes only one regular channel.

```
// Set the sequence length
// L[4:0] = 00000: 1 conversion in the regular sequence
ADC1->SQR1   &= ~ADC_SQR1_L;

// Specify the channel number of the 1st conversion in regular sequence
ADC1->SQR5   = 0;       // clear the register

// SQR5[4:0] bits (1st conversion in the regular sequence)
ADC1->SQR5  |= 10;
```

Suppose we want to perform a sequence of ADC conversion on three regular channels: channel 8 (PB 0), channel 9 (PB 1) and channel 10 (PC 0). We sample channel 8 first, then channel 9, and finally channel 10.

```
// Set the sequence length
// L[4:0] = 00010: 3 conversions in the regular sequence
ADC1->SQR1   &= ~ADC_SQR1_L;   // clear the sequence length
ADC1->SQR1   |= 1<<21;

// Specify the channel number of the 1st conversion in regular sequence
ADC1->SQR5   = 0;         // clear the register

// SQR5[4:0] bits (1st conversion in the regular sequence)
```

```
ADC1->SQR5 |= 8;           // channel 8 as the 1st conversion

// SQR5[9:5] bits (2nd conversion in the regular sequence)
ADC1->SQR5 |= 9 << 5;     // channel 9 as the 2nd conversion

// SQR5[14:10] bits (3rd conversion in the regular sequence)
ADC1->SQR5 |= 9 << 10;   // channel 10 as the 3rd conversion
```

Note when sampling a group of regular channels, the data register (ADC->DR) is shared for channels. Therefore, the interrupt handler needs to differentiate the results of these channels.

```
int counter = 0;

void ADC1_IRQHandler (void) {
   if(ADC1->SR & ADC_SR_EOC)    { // Check End of Conversion (EOC) Flag
      ADC_Result = ADC1->DR;
      counter++;
      if (counter % 3 == 0) {
          // channel 8
          counter = 0;    // reset counter to prevent counter overflow
          ...
      } else if (counter % 3 == 1) {
          // channel 9
          ...
      } else if (counter % 3 == 2) {
          // channel 10
          ...
      }
   }
}
```

20.8 ADC with DMA

As presented in Chapter 19, direct memory access (DMA) is a hardware technology that provides efficient and fast data exchange between peripheral data registers and the main memory, without involving the processor. As presented in Table 19-1, the ADC converted is managed by DMA channel 1.

Suppose the program uses three ADC regular channels: channel 8, 9, and 10. In the previous section, we give a short example code to set up a sequence of regular channels. In this section, we will demonstrate how to set up the DMA controller to copy the ADC results automatically into the memory when a ADC conversion completes.

```
...
// Suppose ADC runs three regular channels
uint16_t  ADC_Results[3];          // store results of three channels

// Enable DMA
ADC1->CR1 |= ADC_CR2_DMA;

// Set peripheral transfer size (PSIZE) to 16 bits
DMA1_Channel1->CCR |= (0x1<<8);  // 00:8-bits, 01:16-bits, 10:32-bits

// Set memory transfer size (MSIZE) to 16 bits
DMA1_Channel1->CCR |= (0x1<<10); // 00:8-bits, 01:16-bits, 10:32-bits

// Enable memory increment mode
DMA1_Channel1->CCR |= (0x1<<7);

// Disable peripheral increment mode
DMA1_Channel1->CCR &= ~(0x1<<6);

// Enable circular mode
DMA1_Channel1->CCR = (0x1<<5);

// Set the transfer direction: from peripheral to memory
DMA1_Channel1->CCR &=~(0x1<<4);   // 0: read peripheral 1: write peripheral

// Enable transfer complete interrupt
DMA1_Channel1->CCR |= (0x1<<1);

// Set interrupt priority to very high
// Channel priority level: 00: Low; 01: Medium; 10: High; 11: Very high
DMA1_Channel1->CCR |= (0x3<<12);

// DMA channel 1: number of data register (DMA_CNDTRx)
DMA1_Channel1->CNDTR = 1;

// DMA channel 1: address of source peripheral register (DMA_CPARx)
DMA1_Channel1->CPAR = (unsigned int) & (ADC1->DR);

// DMA channel 1: destination memory address (DMA_CMARx)
DMA1_Channel1->CMAR = (unsigned int) & (ADC_Results);

NVIC_SetPriority(DMA1_Channel1_IRQn, 1);    // Set priority to 1
NVIC_EnableIRQ(DMA1_Channel1_IRQn);         // Enable DMA interrupt

// Enable EXTI0_1 interrupt in NVIC
DMA1_Channel1->CCR |= 0x1;                  // Enable channel

...
```

The above code allows the ADC converter to make three conversions and then automatically store the conversion results in the array ADC_Results[3], with the result of channel 8 stored in ADC_Results[0], the result of channel 9 in ADC_Results[1], and the result of channel 10 in ADC_Results[2]. (In the previous section, we set the ADC conversion order as channel 8, 9, and 10.)

Since a single data register (ADC1->DR) is shared by all regular channels, as shown in Figure 20-6, the address increment mode for the peripheral is turned off. However, since each conversion result is saved in different memory addresses, the address increment mode for the memory has to be turned on. After each conversion, the destination memory address register is increased automatically by 2 since the memory transfer size is set as 16 bits.

In addition, the circular mode is turned on. This allows the processor to reuse the result array ADC_Results[3] repeatedly during each sequence of ADC conversions. In this specific example, at the end of the third ADC conversion, the destination memory address register (CMAR) is automatically reset by hardware to the address of ADC_Results[0], making the result array continuously serving DMA requests.

20.9 Exercises

1. Suppose V_{REF} = 1.5V, what is the minimum number of bits required to achieve a resolution of 1mV?

2. Successive-approximate (SAR) ADC is widely used. Suppose the ADC has a resolution of 14 bits, and the time for sampling and hold is set as 6 clock cycles. How many clock cycles are required to complete one analog-to-digital conversion?

3. Write an assembly program that monitors an input voltage, as shown in Figure 20-10. When the voltage input is higher than Vcc/2, the LED is lit up. When the voltage is lower than Vcc/2, the LED is off. The input voltage can be controlled manually by using a potentiometer.

4. Write an assembly program that uses a potentiometer to control the brightness of an LED.

5. Write an assembly program that uses a potentiometer to control the rotation speed of a stepper motor.

6. Write an assembly program that uses a timer to trigger the ADC periodically.

7. Write an assembly program that uses the potentiometer to control the brightness of a LED.

8. Write an assembly program that shows the ADC measurement on an LCD.

9. Write an assembly program that uses the potentiometer to control the rotation speed of a stepper motor.

CHAPTER

21

Digital-to-Analog Converter

A digital-to-analog converter (DAC) transforms a finite-precision digital number to an analog voltage or current. For example, DAC is used in music players that generate audio signals from digital values encoded in a music file. This chapter introduces DAC architecture and programming, and presents an example application that uses DAC to synthesize music.

21.1 DAC Architecture

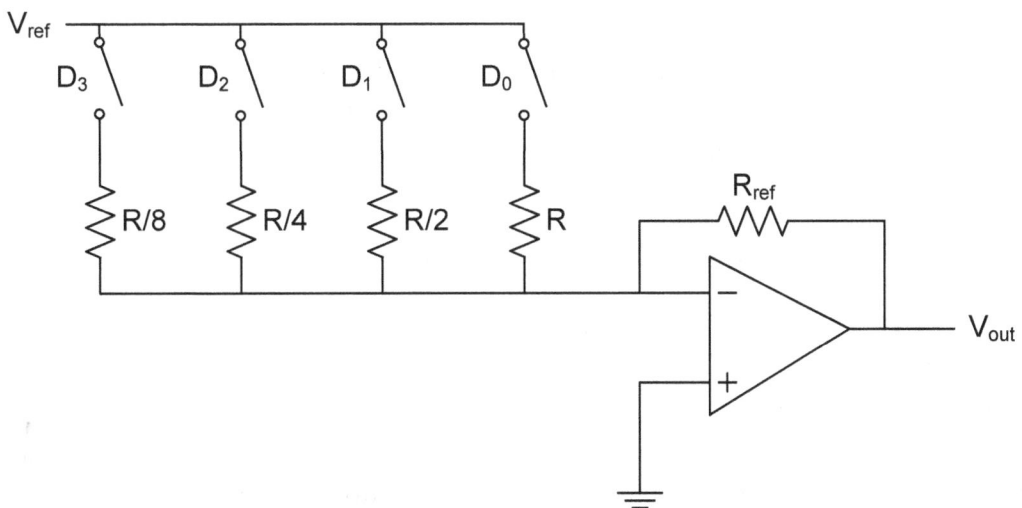

Figure 21-1. Basic architecture of a four-bit digital-to-analog converter (DAC)

Figure 21-1 shows a simple implementation of a four-bit DAC. Suppose the digital value to be converted to an analog voltage has four bits in binary: $D_3 D_2\ D_1 D_0$, with D_3 being the most significant bit. D_i is either 0 or 1, for i = 0, 1, 2, and 3. If D_i is 0, the corresponding switch is open. Otherwise, the corresponding switch is closed. Then the analog voltage output V_{out} can be calculated as follows:

$$V_{out} = -V_{ref} \times \left(\frac{D_3}{R/8} + \frac{D_2}{R/4} + \frac{D_1}{R/2} + \frac{D_0}{R}\right) \times R_{ref}$$

This can be rewritten as the following:

$$V_{out} = -V_{ref} \times \frac{R_{ref}}{R} \times (D_3 \times 2^3 + D_2 \times 2^2 + D_1 \times 2 + D_0)$$

As we can see in the above equation, the voltage output is linearly proportional to the digital value to be converted. The output ranges between 0 and V_{ref}. For a 12-bit DAC, the conversion is performed as follows:

$$DAC_{output} = V_{ref} \times \frac{DOR}{4095}$$

The performance of DAC is often evaluated by its resolution and maximum sampling rate.

- *Resolution* is the smallest change that can occur in the analog output as the digital input varies. For an n-bit DAC, the total number of possible output levels is 2^n. If the output voltage range is between 0 and 5V, then the minimum change in the output of an 8-bit DAC is $5/2^8 = 0.0195V = 19.5mV$. For simplicity, we sometimes use the number of bits in the DAC input to represent its resolution.
- *Maximum Sampling Rate* describes the maximum speed at which the digital-to-analog conversion can be performed. It is determined by the conversion time. According to the Nyquist–Shannon sampling theorem, the maximum frequency of the analog output is less than half of the maximum sampling rate.

21.2 DAC on STM32L Processors

The STM32L processor has two independent DAC converters, with one channel in each converter. Both converters can be configured as a resolution of 8 bits or 12 bits. The two converters can update their output signals independently or synchronously. The synchronous mode can be useful for some applications. For example, a stereo audio player needs the outputs of the left and right channels to be synchronized in order to avoid double talk.

As shown in Figure 21-2, the DAC module includes the data holding registers (DHR), control logic, the data output register (DOR) and the DAC converter. The DAC converter needs the analog power supply (V_{DDA}) the analog ground (V_{SSA}) and the voltage reference (V_{REF}). The analog output range is from 0V to V_{REF}.

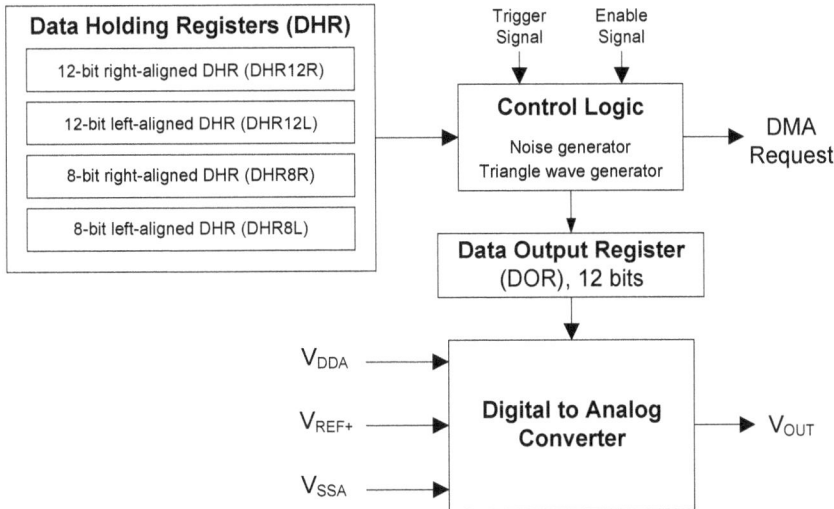

Figure 21-2. Digital to Analog Converter (DAC)

The control logic can add white noise and triangle wave to the output voltage V_{OUT}. White noise is a serially uncorrelated random disturbance with zero mean, and constant and finite variance. White noise has many applications. It is often used in the production of electronic music to emulate instruments such as cymbals that have a lot of noise in their frequency band. The triangle wave can be used for device testing and digital music.

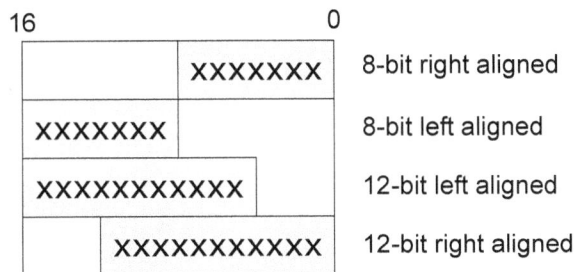

Figure 21-3 Data registers in single DAC channel mode

Each DAC channel has four data registers, listed below:

- 12-bit right-aligned data holding register (DAC_DHR12Rx)
- 12-bit left-aligned data holding register (DAC_DHR12Lx)
- 8-bit right-aligned data holding register (DAC_DHR8Rx)
- 8-bit left-aligned data holding register (DAC_DHR8Lx)

where x = 1 or 2. The data are could be left- or right- aligned, as shown in Figure 21-3. When using dual channels, two data values to be converted need to be stored on a shared dual-channel register, including DAC_DHR8RD for 8-bit right alignment, DAC_DHR12LD for 12-bit left alignment, and DAC_DHR12RD for 12-bit right alignment.

21.3 Conversion Trigger

The DAC conversion can be triggered by software triggers, external timers, and internal timers. When a conversion is triggered, the data stored in one of the data holder registers (DAC_DHR12Rx, DAC_DHR12Lx, DAC_DHR8Rx, and DAC_DHR8Lx) is transferred to the DAC data output register (DAC_DORx, x = 1 or 2) to generate a corresponding output voltage.

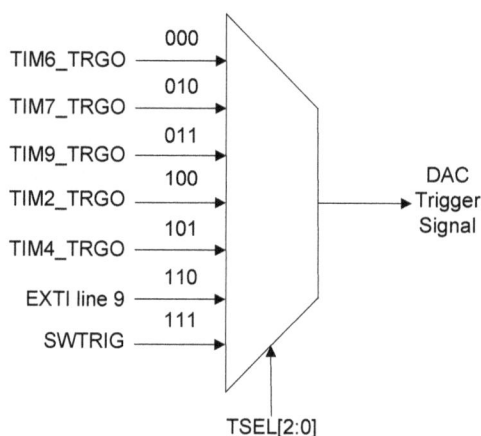

Figure 21-4. TSEL bits in the control register DAC_CR to select DAC trigger signal

When an internal timer is selected as the trigger, the DAC converter starts the conversion after detecting a rising edge on the selected timer trigger output (TIMx_TRGO). When software is used as the trigger, the conversion starts after the trigger bit in DAC_SWTRIGR is set by software. The trigger bit in DAC_SWTRIGR is reset automatically by the hardware once the data content of DAC_DHR has been loaded into DAC_DOR.

The trigger is controlled by the TSEL[2:0] bits in the control register DAC_CR. When both DAC converters are triggered by the same source (*i.e.* the TSEL1 and TSEL2 select the same trigger source), these two channels are synchronized, performing conversions at the same time.

21.4 Buffered Output

When the DAC output is used to drive some external load directly, such as earphones, the voltage output may be lower than the desired value due to loading effects, as shown in Figure 21-5. For example, when the input of DAC data output register DOR is 0xFFF, the desired output should be 3V, and in reality the output voltage V_{OUT} is only 1.5V if the external load has exactly the same impedance as the DAC, *i.e.* $R_{DAC} = R_{LOAD}$.

$$V_{OUT} = \frac{R_{LOAD}}{R_{DAC} + R_{LOAD}} \times V_{OUT}^{desired}$$

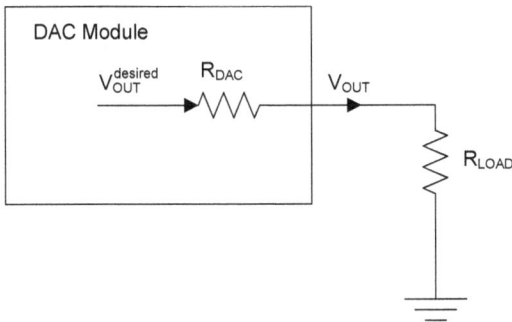

Figure 21-5. Load effects of DAC Module

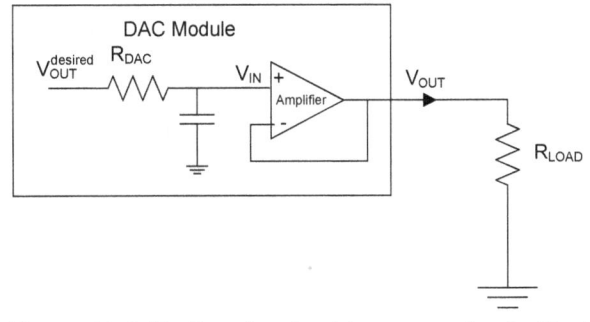

Figure 21-6. Buffered output to remove load effects.

We can use an internal output buffer to avoid the load impedance problem. As shown in Figure 21-6, the voltage output buffer is implemented by using an amplifier. The amplifier has high input impedance (close to infinity) so that the impact of R_{DAC} is diminished. The amplifier also has low output impedance (close to zero) so that the effect of R_{LOAD} is removed. As a result, the output voltage V_{OUT} will be kept close to the voltage desired.

$$V_{IN} = \frac{R_{IN,Amplifier}}{R_{DAC} + R_{IN,Amplifier}} \times V_{OUT}^{desired} \approx \frac{\infty}{R_{DAC} + \infty} \times V_{OUT}^{desired} = V_{OUT}^{desired}$$

$$V_{OUT} = \frac{R_{LOAD}}{R_{LOAD} + R_{OUT,Amplifier}} \times V_{IN} \approx \frac{R_{LOAD}}{R_{LOAD} + 0} \times V_{IN} = V_{IN} \approx V_{OUT}^{desired}$$

The output buffer can be enabled or disabled by the DAC_CR_BOFF bit in the control register DAC_CR.

21.5 Generating a Sinusoidal Wave via Table Lookup

Many microcontrollers do not have a floating-point unit (FPU) and rely on software that uses integer operations to implement a floating-point arithmetic function. While the software approach reduces the silicon cost, its main disadvantage is slow performance. While FPU takes two to ten clock cycles to complete a typical floating-point operation, a software library requires 50-100 or even more cycles.

If there is no FPU available on the processor, a popular software approach to improve the floating-point performance is to use a lookup table. The lookup table is an array that stores pre-calculated values of a floating-point operation with different inputs. In order to find the result of a given input, instead of performing expensive computations, we simply look up the table and find the approximate result. This method takes more memory and reduces the computation precision, but it can reduce the CPU computation requirements significantly.

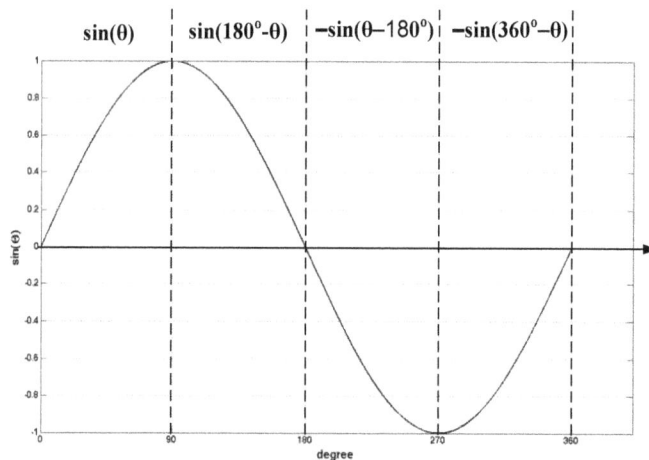

Figure 21-7. Converting θ into the range [0°, 90°]

We will use a lookup table to find the value of $\sin(x)$. Typically, we can use the following Taylor series to compute the value of $\sin(x)$.

$$\sin(x) = \sum_{n=0}^{\infty} \frac{(-1)^n}{(2n+1)!} x^{2n+1} \approx x - \frac{x^3}{6} + \frac{x^5}{120} - \frac{x^7}{5040}$$

Fortunately, the math C library has a function **sin** that can be directly used. The following program shows how to build a table if the result is limited to 12 bits (The data registers of DAC is limited to 12 bits). The program also offsets the output by 2028, because the DAC module cannot output a negative value.

$$TableValue\ (x) = \left(1 + \sin(\frac{x}{180}\pi)\right) \times 2^{11}$$

where the input x is in degrees. Because the value of the sine function is between [-1, 1], the table values are between [0, 4096]. When the sine function returns zero, the corresponding value in the table is 2048. In addition, 4096 has 13 bits in binary and it cannot be represented by using 12 bits. Therefore, we use 4095, *i.e.* 0xFFF, to approximate 4096 in the table.

```c
#include <stdio.h>
#include <string.h>
#include <math.h>

main(void){
  int i;
  signed int sine_table[91];
  float sf;

  // for 12-bit ADC, [0, 2047(0xFFF)];
  for (i = 0; i <= 90; i++){
    sf = sin(M_PI * i /180);
    sine_table[i] = (1 + sf) * 2048;
    if(sine_table[i] == 0x1000)
        sine_table[i] = 0xFFF; // sin(90) is out of range
  }

  printf("Sine_Table");
  for (i = 0; i < 90; i += 5){
    printf("\tDCD\t");
    printf("0x%03x,0x%03x,0x%03x,0x%03x,0x%03x\n",
            si[i], si[i+1], si[i+2], si[i+3], si[i+4]);
  }
  printf("\tDCD\t0x%03x\n", si[90]);
}
```

Example 21-1. C program to generate sine table

The following program shows how to use the pre-calculated table to find the value of sin(x), where x is in degrees. The DAC output voltage is between 0 and 3 V. It cannot output a negative voltage. The value found in the following program is used to set up the data register of the DAC module. When the data register is 0, the DAC analog output voltage is 0V. When the data register is 0xFFF, the DAC output voltage is 3V. For the sine wave, we have the following setting:

- When sin(x) is -1, the DAC data register is 0;
- When sin(x) is 0, the DAC data register is 2048;
- When sin(x) is 1, the DAC data register is 4095.

```
unsigned int lookup_sine(int x){
    // x is the input in degrees
    x = mod(x, 360); // x might be larger than 360
    if (x < 90)  return sine_table[x];
    if (x < 180) return sine_table[180-x];
    if (x < 270) return 4086 - sine_table[x-180];
    return 4096 - sine_table[360-x];
}
```

Example 21-2. C program that table lookup method to calculate the sine value

The following assembly program shows how to use the table lookup method to calculate the sine value in assembly. Note the assembly program follows the standard of embedded application binary interface (EABI), which takes the input argument in degrees in register r0 and returns the table lookup results in register r0 too. Note r1 is not required to be preserved.

```
; Input:
;       r0: x input argument in degrees
; Return:
;       r0: value of (1 + sin(x))*2^11
; Register used:
;       r1 = sine input argument (in degrees)
;       r4 = starting address of sine table
;       r6 = copy of the sine input argument (in degrees)

sine    PROC
        PUSH  {r4,r6,lr}            ; preserve used registers in stack
        MOV   r6, r0               ; make a copy of x (in degrees)
        MOV   r1, r0               ; make a copy of x (in degrees)
        LDR   r4, =sine_data       ; load address of sine table
        CMP   r1, #90              ; determine quadrant
        BLS   retvalue             ; first quadrant (0 < x ≤ 90)
        CMP   r1, #180
        RSBLS r1, r1, #180         ; second quadrant (90 < x ≤ 180)
        BLS   retvalue
        CMP   r1, #270
        SUBLE r1, r1, #180         ; third quadrant (180 < x ≤ 270)
        BLS   retvalue
        RSB   r1, r1, #360         ; fourth quadrant (270 < x ≤ 360)

retvalue
        LDR   r0, [r4, r1, LSL #2] ; get sin value from table
                                   ; memory address = sin_data + r1 * 4
        CMP   r6, #180             ; if 180 < x < 360
        RSBGT r0, r0, #4096        ; 4096 - 2048*abs(sin(x))
        pop   {r4,r6,pc}           ; recovery environment
        ENDP
```

```
        ALIGN
sine_data       ; DAC has 12 bits. DCD = allocate words (4 bytes)
        DCD     0x800,0x823,0x847,0x86b,0x88e,0x8b2,0x8d6,0x8f9,0x91d,0x940
        DCD     0x963,0x986,0x9a9,0x9cc,0x9ef,0xa12,0xa34,0xa56,0xa78,0xa9a
        DCD     0xabc,0xadd,0xaff,0xb20,0xb40,0xb61,0xb81,0xba1,0xbc1,0xbe0
        DCD     0xc00,0xc1e,0xc3d,0xc5b,0xc79,0xc96,0xcb3,0xcd0,0xcec,0xd08
        DCD     0xd24,0xd3f,0xd5a,0xd74,0xd8e,0xda8,0xdc1,0xdd9,0xdf1,0xe09
        DCD     0xe20,0xe37,0xe4d,0xe63,0xe78,0xe8d,0xea1,0xeb5,0xec8,0xedb
        DCD     0xeed,0xeff,0xf10,0xf20,0xf30,0xf40,0xf4e,0xf5d,0xf6a,0xf77
        DCD     0xf84,0xf90,0xf9b,0xfa6,0xfb0,0xfba,0xfc3,0xfcb,0xfd3,0xfda
        DCD     0xfe0,0xfe6,0xfec,0xff0,0xff4,0xff8,0xffb,0xffd,0xffe,0xfff
        DCD     0xfff
        ; sin(90) = 1. However, 1 cannot be represented in Q12 notation
        ; thus we set sin(90) = 0xFFF
        END
```

Example 21-3. Generate sine wave output by using table lookup

The following program generates a sawtooth waveform on both DAC output channels.

```c
// DAC channel 1:  DAC_OUT1 = PA 4;  DAC channel 2:  DAC_OUT2 = PA 5
int main(void){
   unsigned int i, output;

   // Enable the clock of GPIO port A
   RCC->AHBENR  |= RCC_AHBENR_GPIOAEN;

   // Enable the clock of DAC
   RCC->APB1ENR |= RCC_APB1ENR_DACEN;

   // Set I/O mode as analog
   GPIOA->MODER &= ~(0x0F<<(2*4));        // Clear mode bits of pin 4 and 5
   GPIOA->MODER |= 0x0F<<(2*4);           // Set the mode as analog (11)

   // Disable DAC output buffer for channel 1 and 2
   DAC->CR |= DAC_CR_BOFF1 | DAC_CR_BOFF2;  // 0: enabled; 1: disabled

   // Enable DAC trigger for channel 1 and 2
   DAC->CR |= DAC_CR_TEN1 | DAC_CR_TEN2;   // 0: disable; 1: enabled

   // Select DAC trigger signal
   DAC->CR |= DAC_CR_TSEL1 | DAC_CR_TSEL2;  // 111:Software trigger

   // Enable DAC converter 1 and 2
   DAC->CR |= DAC_CR_EN1   | DAC_CR_EN2;    // 0: disable; 1: enabled

   output = 0;

   while(1){
       // Data in DAC_DHRx are automatically transferred to DAC_DORx
       // after one APB1 clock cycle, if no hardware trigger is selected.
```

```
    DAC->DHR12R1  = output;     // Channel 1 12-bit right-aligned data
    DAC->DHR12R2  = output;     // Channel 2 12-bit right-aligned data

    // Set flags for software trigger. The flags are cleared by hardware
    // once DAC_DHRx is copied to DAC_DORx.
    DAC->SWTRIGR |= DAC_SWTRIGR_SWTRIG1 | DAC_SWTRIGR_SWTRIG2;

    for(i = 0; i <= 10; i++); // Software delay

    output++;    // Increment the DAC analog output voltage

    if (output >= 0xFFF) output = 0;
  }
}
```

Example 21-4. Using C program to generate a sawtooth analog output

21.6 Using Timer as a Trigger to DAC

This section shows how to configure timer 4 as a master trigger to the DAC converter. The MMS bits in the TIM4_CR2 register controls the trigger output (TIM4_TRGO). For example, when MMS bits are 010, the TRGO signal has a rising edge each time an update event occurs. When MMS bits are 100, 101, 110, and 111, the OC1REF, OC2REF, OC3REF and OC4REF is selected as the TRGO output, respectively.

In digital audio, a common sampling frequency is 44,100Hz, *i.e.* 44.1kHz. That means an analog audio signal is recorded as 44,100 digital values per second. Human ears can hear up to 20,000Hz. According to the Nyquist–Shannon sampling theorem, the sampling frequency must be at least twice the maximum frequency of signals audible to human ears. Most compact discs (CD) are recorded with this rate.

Timer 4 needs to generate an interrupt with a frequency of 44.1kHz. If the 16-MHz HSI is used, the prescaler (PSC) and the auto-reload register have to meet the following requirement.

$$\frac{f_{HSI}}{(1 + PSC)(1 + ARR)} = f_{sampling} = 44.1Khz$$

A large PSC is recommended to slow down the counter clock frequency. This will reduce the energy consumption of the timer hardware.

For example, if we select $PSC = 18$, and $ARR = 18$, then the DAC is performed at a rate of 44.3kHz, which is only 0.5% off from 44.1Khz.

$$\frac{f_{HSI}}{(1 + PSC)(1 + ARR)} = \frac{16MHz}{(1 + 18)(1 + 18)}$$
$$= 44.3kHz$$

Once the DAC conversion is fixed to 44.1Khz, the frequency of the sine wave generated is determined by the step size of the sine variable during each time interrupt. Since the sine function should increase from 0° to 360° in order to complete one cycle of the sinusoidal waveform, if the frequency of a music tone is f, the step size of the angular variable in the in TIM4_IRQHandler can be calculated as the following:

$$Step\ Size = \frac{360°}{Number\ of\ DAC\ outputs\ in\ one\ sinusoidal\ cycle}$$
$$= 360° \div \frac{Period\ of\ Sine\ Wave}{Time\ Interval\ of\ DAC\ Outputs}$$
$$= 360° \div \left(\frac{1}{f} \div \frac{1}{44.3KHz}\right)$$
$$= 360° \div \frac{44.3KHz}{f}$$

For example, if f is 440 Hz (music tone A), we have

$$Step\ Size = 360° \div \frac{44.3KHz}{440Hz}$$

$$\approx 3.576°$$

However, Cortex-M3 processors do not have a FPU and they do not support floating-point instructions. Therefore, we have to use a fixed-point format. The following gives a simplified C implementation to illustrate the basic idea.

```
int StepSize = 3576;    // Multiply by 1000
angle += StepSize;
sine_value = sine_table_lookup(angle/1000);
```

Figure 21-8 shows the flow chart of configuring GPIO port A pin 4 and 5 as analog output triggered by Timer 4. The Interrupt is enabled for Timer 4. The STM32 discovery kit has to use the 16MHz HSI (high-speed internal clock) to drive DAC. Therefore, the clock of HSI has to be turned on. We also select HSI as the system clock. The program uses two wait loops to make sure that HSI is ready and HSI has been successfully selected as the system clock.

Start

1. Turn on HSI (RCC_CR_HSION) , HSI = 16MHz
2. Wait until HSI is ready (RCC_CR_HSIRDY).
3. Select HSI as the system clock (RCC_CFGR_SW_HSI)
4. Wait until HSI is selected system clock (RCC_CFGR_SWS_HSI)

Configure GPIO PA.4 and PA.5 as Analog
Note: DAC_OUT1 = PA.4, DAC_OUT2 = PA.5
1. Enable the clock of GPIO port A (RCC_AHBENR_GPIOAEN)
2. Set the mode of pin PA.4 and PA.5 as analog (GPIO_MODER)

Configure TIM4 as Master Trigger
1. Enable the clock of TIM4 (RCC_APB1ENR_TIM4EN)
2. Set the prescaler (TIM4->PSC)
3. Set the auto-reload value (TIM4->ARR)
4. Set the compare register (TIM4->CCR1)
5. Set OC1M bits of TIM4->CCMR1 for channel 1 to toggle OC1REF
   when TIM4_CNT=TIM4_CCR1
6. Enable compare output 1 (TIM_CCER_CC1E)
7. Enable the update (TIM_EGR_UG)
8. Clear the update flag (TIM_SR_UIF)
9. Enable the TIM4 interrupts (TIM_DIER_UIE and TIM_DIER_CC1IE)
10. Select the master mode as OC1REF signal as trigger output TRGO
    (TIM_CR2_MMS)
11. Enable timer 4 (TIM_CR1_CEN)

Configure DAC (DAC_OUT1 = PA.4, DAC_OUT2 = PA.5)
1. Enable DAC clock (RCC_APB1ENR_DACEN)
2. Enable DAC output buffer (DAC_CR_BOFF1 and DAC_CR_BOFF2)
3. Select TIM4 TRGO as trigger for both outputs (DAC_CR_TSEL1 and
   DAC_CR_TSEL2)
4. Enable DAC1 and DAC2 (DAC_CR_EN1 and DAC_CR_EN2)

NVIC Interrupt
1. Enable TIM4_IRQn
2. Set priority for TIM4_IRQn

Dead loop

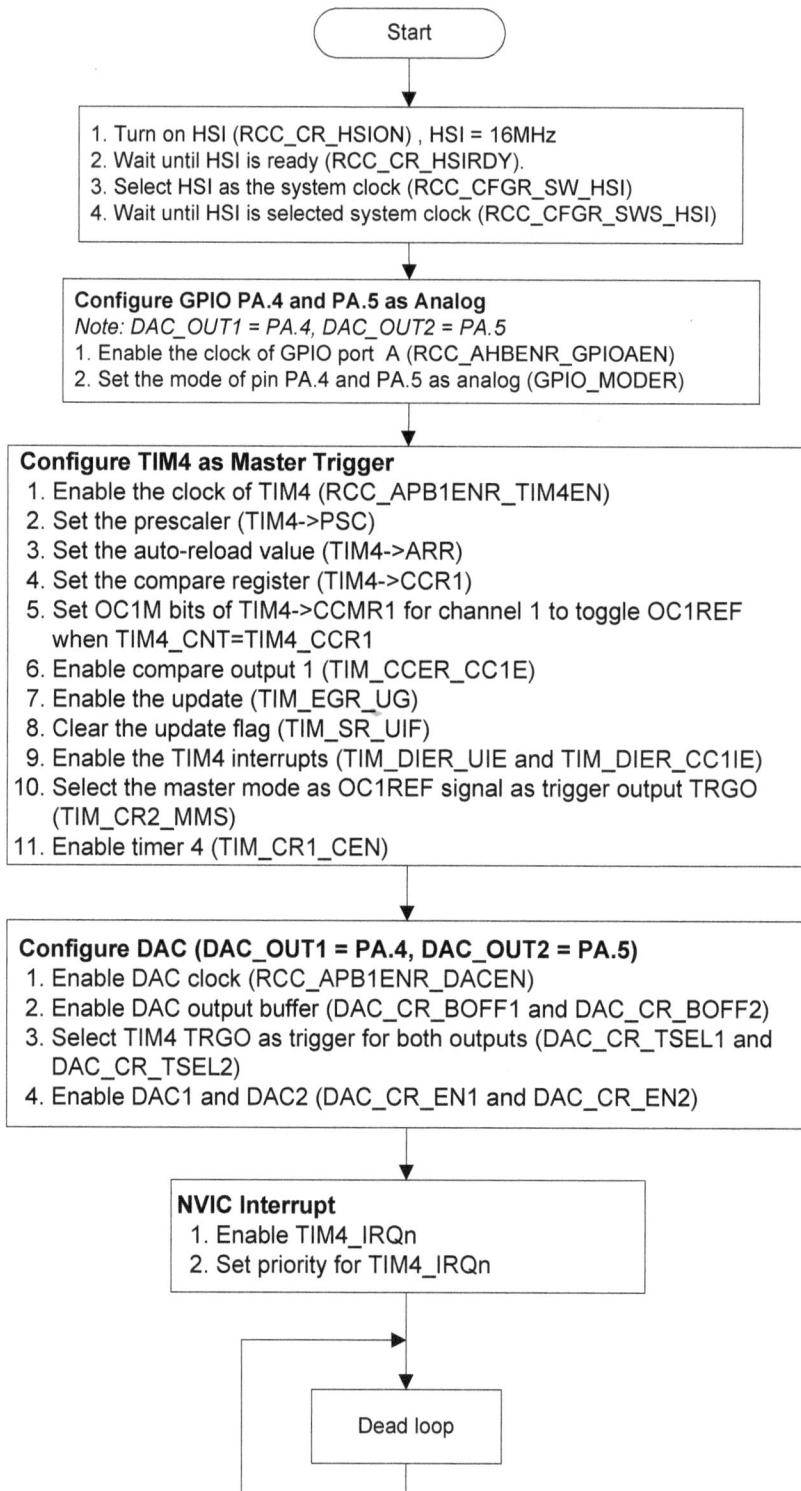

Figure 21-8. Flowchart of configuring DAC

```
// Enable TIM4 clock
RCC->APB1ENR  |= RCC_APB1ENR_TIM4EN;

// The clock frequency of counter CK_CNT equals f / (PSC[15:0] + 1).
TIM4->PSC = 18;

// Set the auto-reload value
TIM4->ARR = 18;

// Set the compare and capture register for channel 1
TIM4->CCR1 = 9;

// Set OC1M of channel 1 to 011: Toggle - OC1REF toggles
// when TIMx_CNT=TIMx_CCR1.
TIM4->CCMR1 |= TIM_CCMR1_OC1M_0 | TIM_CCMR1_OC1M_1;

// Enable compare output 1
TIM4->CCER |= TIM_CCER_CC1E;

// Master mode selection
// 100: Compare - OC1REF signal is used as trigger output (TRGO)
TIM4->CR2  &= ~ TIM_CR2_MMS;
TIM4->CR2  |= TIM_CR2_MMS_2;

// Enable timer 4
TIM4->CR1  |= TIM_CR1_CEN;
```

Note *DAC1_IRQHandler* does not provide *End-of-Conversion* interrupt. The only interrupt available for DAC is the DMA under-run.

The following is an example implementation of TIM4_IRQHandler. You need to change this sample code according to the desired output since-wave frequency.

```
void TIM4_IRQHandler() {
  if( (TIM4->SR & TIM_SR_ CC1IF) != 0) {
    // Data stored in the DAC_DHRx register are automatically transferred
    // to the DAC_DORx register after one APB1 clock cycle.

    // When using dual channels, the values stored in a shared register
    DAC->DHR12RD  = sin(v)<<16 | sin(v);

    // When not using dual channels, they are set separately
    //DAC->DHR12R1 = sin(v);  // DAC channel-1 12-bit Right aligned data
    //DAC->DHR12R2 = sin(v);  // DAC channel-2 12-bit Right aligned data

    // Note: v++ is not your solution.
    // Adjust v appropriately for desired sine waveform frequency.
    v += degrees_desired;  // You need to calculate degrees_desired.
```

```
    if (v >= 360) v = 0;

    // Clear CC1IF flag to prevent mistakenly re-entering the interrupt
    // CC1IF is cleared (1) by software or (2) by hardware if CCR1 is read
    // Since CCR1 is read in this application, software has to clear CC1IF.
    TIM4->SR &= ~(TIM_SR_ CC1IF);
  }
}
```

Example 21-5. The interrupt service handler of timer 4

21.7 Musical Synthesizing

A musical tone is a fundamental element of music. A tone is a periodic waveform, and its major attributes include duration, pitch (frequency), loudness (amplitude), and timbre (spectrum and envelope). If a piano and a guitar play the same pitch at the same loudness with the same duration, they differ in timbre since they have different spectral content of the sound over time. An experienced listener can distinguish the instruments according to their timbres.

The sinusoidal waveform has been widely used for digital music due to its simplicity and flexibility. In addition, instruments, such as the guitar, flute and piano, are often mathematically modeled by sinusoids due to their fundamental physical characteristics and harmonics, and thus it is nature to use sinusoidal waveforms to synthesize digital music.

21.7.1 Musical Pitch

The pitch of a music tone is determined by the frequency of the sinusoidal waveform. The musical note A above middle C, often noted as '$A4$' or '$A440$', has been standardized to 440 Hz. It is often used as a reference in musical instrument tuning. The musical instrument digital interface (MIDI) standard assigns the A note as pitch 69. In addition, for a pitch p, its frequency f can be calculated as follows:

$$f = 440 \times 2^{(p-69)/12}$$

In other words, for a given frequency f, its pitch p can be calculated as follows:

$$p = 69 + 12 \times \log_2 \left(\frac{f}{440} \right)$$

Table 21-1 shows the frequency of different musical notes with consecutive pitches. When the pitch increases by 12, the frequency is doubled. In this table, each column, called an octave, has exactly 12 musical notes. The octave is numbered from 0 to 8. The note 'A4' denotes A in the fourth octave. The frequency of a musical note in the nth octave is the double of the corresponding note in the $(n\text{-}1)^{th}$ octave.

	0	1	2	3	4	5	6	7	8
C	16.352	32.703	65.406	130.813	261.626	523.251	1046.502	2093.005	4186.009
C#	17.324	34.648	69.296	138.591	277.183	554.365	1108.731	2217.461	4434.922
D	18.354	36.708	73.416	146.832	293.665	587.330	1174.659	2349.318	4698.636
D#	19.445	38.891	77.782	155.563	311.127	622.254	1244.508	2489.016	4978.032
E	20.602	41.203	82.407	164.814	329.628	659.255	1318.510	2637.020	5274.041
F	21.827	43.654	87.307	174.614	349.228	698.456	1396.913	2793.826	5587.652
F#	23.125	46.249	92.499	184.997	369.994	739.989	1479.978	2959.955	5919.911
G	24.500	48.999	97.999	195.998	391.995	783.991	1567.982	3135.963	6271.927
G#	25.957	51.913	103.826	207.652	415.305	830.609	1661.219	3322.438	6644.875
A	27.500	55.000	110.000	220.000	**440.000**	880.000	1760.000	3520.000	7040.000
A#	29.135	58.270	116.541	233.082	466.164	932.328	1864.655	3729.310	7458.620
B	30.868	61.735	123.471	246.942	493.883	987.767	1975.533	3951.066	7902.133

Table 21-1. Musical frequency (note pitch) table based on A4 = 440 Hz

21.7.2 Musical Duration

The duration is the amount of time a musical tone takes, which determines the number of beats per minute (BPM) the song should be played. For example, a BPM of 60 provides a beat each second and a BPM of 120 is twice as rapid. Typical BPM is between 40 and 200. A slow tempo (68-80 BPM) makes listeners relaxed, while a faster tempo (BMP 120-140) can energize listeners. In most songs, a standard 4-4 time signature is used. What this means is that there are four notes per measure, and a quarter note will get the beat.

Computer software can easily identify the time instants of each musical beat, and use it to synchronize other devices, such as LED light, drum machine, and audio effects to the audio source. The BPM is also an important criterion to identify the type of music a specific listener likes most.

21.7.3 Amplitude Modulation of Tones

The amplitude of a tone determines its loudness or volume. Most musical instruments do not generate tones with steady amplitude. They do not build up its volume to its maximum amplitude instantly nor fall to zero amplitude suddenly. The attack, decay, sustain, and release (ADSR) envelope model has been widely used to modulate the amplitude of a tone over time to emulate how a tone is played on a musical instrument. It divides a tone into four different phases, as shown in Figure 21-10.

- **Attack.** The attack phase usually is fast, and a tone quickly reaches its peak intensity when a key is pressed on the real instrument. For most mechanical instruments, the duration of this phase is short.
- **Decay.** After reaching peak amplitude, the tone starts to fade gradually from the peak.
- **Sustain.** After the decay phase, the amplitude is maintained nearly at a constant level while a key is held or a sustain pedal is pressed.
- **Release.** After the music key or pedal is released, the amplitude decreases from the sustained level to zero. While the duration of the release phase is typically short, it can last relatively long, such as eight seconds for a foghorn, and two seconds for a bell.

By changing the amplitude and duration of each phase, ADSR can be used for computers to emulate different musical instruments. For example, a guitar is the loudest immediately after a string is plucked and it fades quickly after that. In contrast, when a key of a pipe organ is pressed, its corresponding tone has almost constant amplitude.

The digital signal of a sinusoidal waveform with a frequency f, denoted as $S(n)$, can be generated according the following formula:

$$S(n) = \sin\left(2\pi \frac{n \times f}{f_s}\right)$$

where f_s is the sampling frequency to this sinusoidal wave, and $n = 0, 1, 2, \cdots, f_s - 1$.

Thus, the modulated sinusoid signal $\tilde{S}(n)$ is the product of the generated sample value $S(n)$ and the ADSR modulated amplitude $ADSR(n)$.

$$\tilde{S}(n) = ADSR(n) \times S(n)$$

The ADSR modulated amplitude $ADSR(n)$ can be generated by using a simple digital filter,

$$ADSR(n) = g \times \overrightarrow{ADSR} + (1 - g) \times ADSR(n - 1)$$

where $\overrightarrow{ADSR}$ is the target modulated amplitude value, and g is the gain parameter. The filter gradually increases or decreases to the target value at a pace determined by the gain parameters.

ADSR has four different phases, and there are three parameters associated with each phases: the duration, the target amplitude value, and the gain parameter. For a given sampling frequency f_s, the duration of each phase is expressed by the number of samples in this phase. The total number of samples in all four phases should equal the total number of samples of the musical tone.

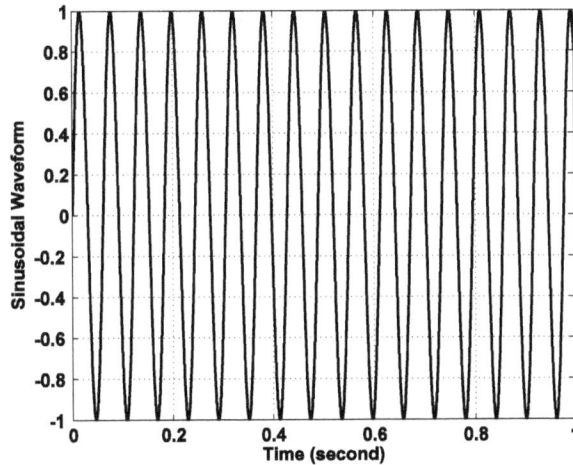

Figure 21-9. Sinusoidal waveform for musical note C0 (16.325Hz)

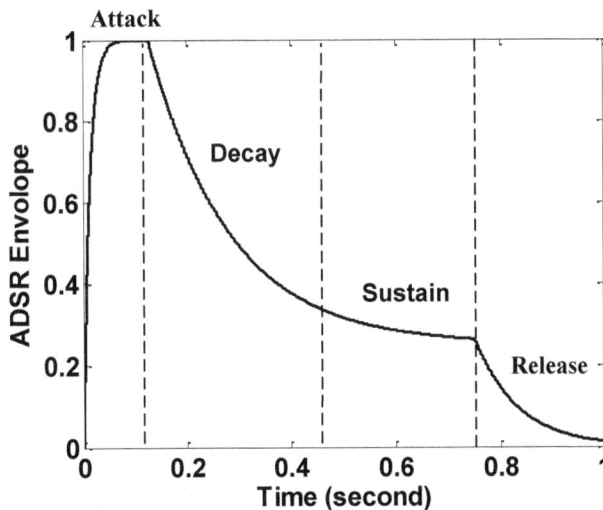

Figure 21-10. Attack, decay, sustain, and release (ADSR) envelope signal

Let us assume BPM is 60. Accordingly, each note is played for duration of one second. Figure 21-9 shows periodical waveform of the musical note C0, which has a frequency of 16.325Hz. Figure 21-9 shows the amplitude-modulating signal based on the ADSR envelope. Figure 20-11 presents the final modulated sinusoidal wave signal used to drive a speaker or headphones.

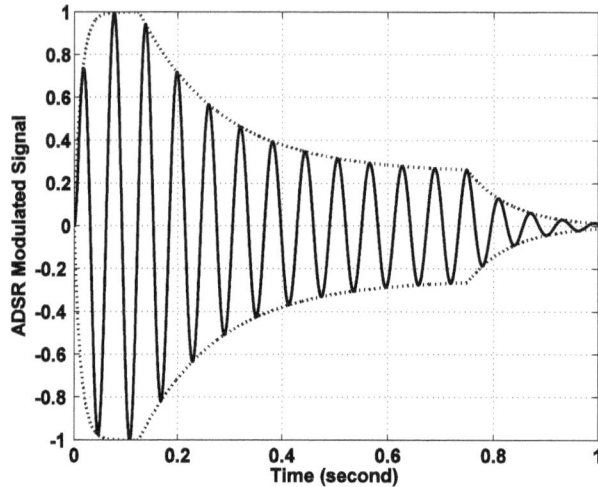

Figure 21-11. Modulated sinusoidal waveform for musical note C0 (16.325Hz)

In digital audio, a common sampling frequency is 44,100Hz, *i.e.* 44.1kHz. That means an analog audio signal is recorded as 44,100 digital values per second. Human ears can hear up to 20,000Hz. According to the Nyquist–Shannon sampling theorem, the sampling frequency must be at least twice the maximum signal frequency that is audible to human ears. Most compact discs (CDs) are recorded with this rate.

If the music data is not compressed, the date rate of CD audio is as follows:
  2 channels × 2 bytes/sample × 441,000 samples/channel/second = 176,400 bytes/second

A CD with 74 minutes of music has a total of 777 MB music data if it is uncompressed, as calculated below:
        176,400 bytes/second × 60 seconds/minute × 74 minutes = 777 MB

Note the DAC voltage output is always positive on STM32L processors. In order to filter out the DC component, a large capacitor is used. In addition, a resistor is added to reduce the current to protect your earphone, as shown in Figure 21-12.

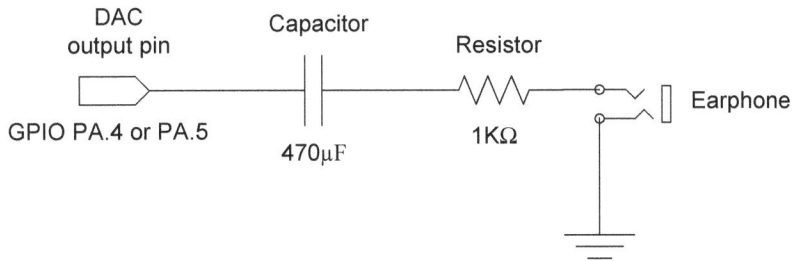

Figure 21-12. Filtering DC component of DAC output via a capacitor

```
        AREA myMusic, DATA
        ALIGN


        ; Size, frequency, time duration of "Twinkle Twinkle Little Star"
TT_S    DCD   42   ; Number of notes
TT_F    DCD 262, 262, 392, 392, 440, 440, 392   ; Twinkle twinkle little star
        DCD 349, 349, 330, 330, 294, 294, 262   ; How I wonder what you are
        DCD 392, 392, 349, 349, 330, 330, 294   ; Up above the world so high
        DCD 392, 392, 349, 349, 330, 330, 294   ; Like a diamond in the sky
        DCD 262, 262, 392, 392, 440, 440, 392   ; Twinkle twinke little star
        DCD 349, 349, 330, 330, 294, 294, 262   ; How I wonder what you are!
        ; Set beats per minute (BMP) as 120
TT_T    DCD 1, 1, 1, 1, 1, 1, 2                  ; Twinkle twinkle little star
        DCD 1, 1, 1, 1, 1, 1, 2                  ; How I wonder what you are
        DCD 1, 1, 1, 1, 1, 1, 2                  ; Up above the world so high
        DCD 1, 1, 1, 1, 1, 1, 2                  ; Like a diamond in the sky
        DCD 1, 1, 1, 1, 1, 1, 2                  ; Twinkle twinkle little star
        DCD 1, 1, 1, 1, 1, 1, 2                  ; How I wonder what you are!


        ; Size, frequency, time duration of "Happy Birthday"
HB_S    DCD   25
HB_F    DCD 392, 392, 440, 392, 523, 494        ; Happy Birthday to You
        DCD 392, 392, 440, 392, 523, 494        ; Happy Birthday to You
        DCD 392, 392, 784, 659, 523, 494, 440   ; Happy Birthday to Dear (name)
        DCD 349, 349, 330, 262, 294, 262        ; Happy Birthday to You
        ; Set beats per minute (BMP) as 240
HB_T    DCD 1, 1, 2, 2, 2, 4                     ; Happy Birthday to You
        DCD 1, 1, 2, 2, 2, 4                     ; Happy Birthday to You
        DCD 1, 1, 2, 2, 2, 2, 6                  ; Happy Birthday to Dear (name)
        DCD 2, 2, 2, 2, 2, 4                     ; Happy Birthday to You
        END
```

Example 21-6. Note frequency and time duration of two simple songs

21.8 Exercises

1. Assume an audio is recorded at a rate of 44,100 Hz, and the DAC is driven by the timer trigger output (TGRO). What is the time interval between two consecutive triggers? If the timer is driven by the HSI clock (16 MHz), how do you set the timer prescaler register (PSC) and the auto-reload register (ARR)? Show your calculations.

2. Assume we are required to generate a sinusoidal waveform of 293.665 Hz (music tone D) and the DAC converter is triggered by TIM4 TRGO with a frequency of 44,100Hz.

   a. How many DAC outputs should we produce during one cycle of sinusoidal waveform?
   b. The angle of the sine function should increase from 0° to 360° in order to complete one cycle of the sinusoidal waveform. How many degrees should the angle variable be increased in timer interrupt handler each time?
   c. The processor only supports integer arithmetic. If the angle degree to be increased is not an integer, what can you do to get around this issue?

3. Write an assembly program that uses a table-lookup method to generate a sinusoidal wave. The built-in *logic analyzer* in MDK-Keil can only show the value stored in the data memory. The value stored in a register cannot be analyzed. In order to solve this problem, we create a variable named "output" in the data area. In your main program, within the loop over different x values, make sure to store the lookup value into the memory address "output" so that the logic analyzer can display the value.

   ```
             AREA myData, DATA
             ALIGN
   output    DCD    0x000
   ```

   In the logic analyzer, you can click "Setup" and add a variable "(signed int) output" to observe. Make sure to adjust the data display range to show the curve. Logic analyzer can only monitor global variable. Thus, you need to add "EXPORT output" after the "EXPORT __main" to make the output as a global variable.

4. Write an assembly program that generates a sinusoidal waveform with a frequency of 440 Hz and use an oscilloscope to verify the frequency.

5. Write an assembly program to play the song of "Twinkle Twinkle Little Star."

CHAPTER
22

Serial Communication Protocols

This chapter introduces three serial communication protocols, including universal asynchronous receiver and transmitter (UART), inter-integrated circuit (I²C) and serial peripheral interface (SPI). Serial communication transfers a single bit each time and uses either a single wire for each communication direction or a shared wire for both directions. It differs from parallel communications, which use multiple communication wires and can transfer several bits at the same time. Compared with parallel communications, serial communications provide lower speed, but allow longer cable length and are less expensive.

22.1 Universal Asynchronous Receiver and Transmitter

One of the most common usages of universal asynchronous receiver and transmitter (UART) is to communicate a microprocessor and a PC serial port to exchange data for software debugging or system monitoring. UART stands for universal asynchronous receiver transmitter, and it has been widely used for various peripherals, such as printers, terminals, and modems. The keyword "universal" means the serial interface is programmable. UART is often configured to communicate synchronously, which is then called USART.

The asynchronous transmission allows bits to be transmitted in a serial fashion without requiring the sender to provide a clock signal to the receiver. However, senders and receivers must agree on the transmission rate to be used by both sides. Baud rate is used in UART to set up the clock agreement between the sender and the receiver. In digital systems, the baud rate is actually the bit rate, *i.e.* the number of bits transmitted per second. Usually the UART interface can tolerate 10% clock shift during the transmission. In some analog systems such as modem, a baud rate is larger than the corresponding bit rate when there are more than two voltage levels and a voltage signal transmitted can represent multiple bits.

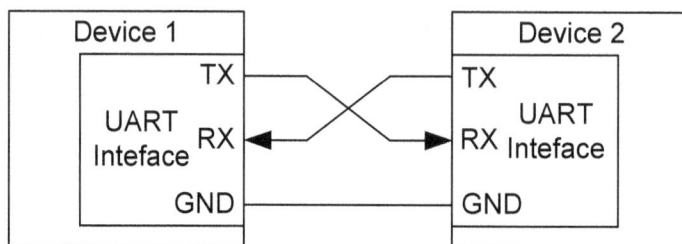

Figure 22-1. Connection between two UART devices

The transmission involves two communication lines (TX and RX), as shown in Figure 22-1. The data is always transmitted out bit by bit from the TX line and is received by the other device on its RX line. The receiver reassembles bits received into bytes. For synchronous serial communications, the clock (CLK) pin of the devices must be connected together. In addition, the clear to send (CTS) line must be connected to the request to send (RTS) line of the other device.

22.1.1 Communication Frame

UART divides data to be transmitted into frames and a frame is the smallest unit that can be exchanged, as shown in the following figure.

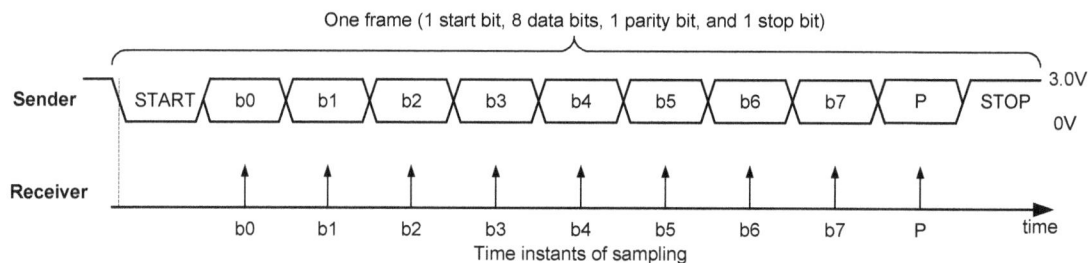

Figure 22-2. A frame of UART communication

Each frame begins with a start bit, represented by a low-level voltage. After the start bit, the individual bits of each frame is shifted out or in of the UART interfaces, with the least significant bit being sent first. For example, when 0xE1 is transmitted, the bit stream 10001111 is seen in order on the transmission line. The number of bits in the data can be programmed to be either 8 or 9 on STM32 processors.

When an entire frame has been sent, the sender may calculate the parity of this frame and send the parity bit to the receiver for error checking. This helps improve the data integrity. The parity bit is optional. The parity bit uses a high-level voltage to represent logic 0 and a low-level voltage to represent logic 1. Additionally logic 1 on the parity bit can be configured to represent either an odd or even number of ones in the data to be transmitted.

Each frame ends by a stop bit, represented by a high voltage. If no further data is transmitted, the voltage of the transmission line remains high. If the receiver does not obtain the stop bit, this frame is considered corrupted and will be discarded. In addition, the number of stop bit in each frame is usually one by default. However, it can be programmed to have 2 stop bits, 0.5 stop bit, and 1.5 stop bits.

22.1.2 Baud Rate

Historically baud rate was used in telecommunication to represent the number of pulses physically transferred per second. In digital communication systems, since each pulse represents a binary bit, baud rate is the number of bits physically transferred per second, including the actual data content and the protocol overhead.

For example, if the baud rate is 9,600, and each frame consists of a start bit, 8 data bits, a stop bit, and no parity bit, then the transmission rate of actual data is not 9600/8 = 1200 bytes/second, instead it is 9600/(1 + 8 + 1) = 960 bytes/second. The start and stop bits are the protocol overhead.

STM32 microcontrollers used a fractional baud rate register (BRR) to set up the baud rate.

$$Baud\ Rate = \frac{f_{PCLK}}{8 \times (2 - OVER8) \times USARTDIV}$$

where f_{PCLK} is the clock frequency of the processor. The $USARTDIV$ is stored in the BRR register and the $OVER8$ bit flag indicates: (1) the oversampling rate, and (2) how many bits in the BRR register are used for the fractional part of the $USARTDIV$.

- If $OVER8$ is 0, then the signal is oversampled by 16, and 4 bits are used for the fractional part.
- If $OVER8$ is 1, then the signal is oversampled by 8, and 3 bits are used for the fractional part.

The oversampling method is used to provide flexibility between transmission speed and the tolerance of clock deviation.

For example, if BRR is `0x1BC` and $OVER8$ is 0, then `0x1B` is the integer part and `0xC` is the fractional part.

$$USARTDV = 0x1B + \frac{0xC}{0x10} = 27 + \frac{12}{16} = 27.75$$

Suppose the processor clock f_{PCLK} is 16MHz and the system is oversampled by 16 ($OVER8 = 0$), then we have

$$USARTDIV = \frac{f_{PCLK}}{8 \times (2 - OVER8) \times Baud\ Rate}$$
$$= \frac{16 \times 10^6}{8 \times (2 - 0) \times 9600}$$
$$= 104.1667$$

The integer part is 104 and the fractional part is 0.1667. In this case, four binary bits are used to represent the fractional part. The nearest integer to the fractional part is 3 because $16 \times 0.1667 = 2.6672$. Using 3 gives a fraction value of $3/16 = 0.1875$. Thus, *USARTDIV* is 104.1875, which is encoded as `0x683`. The actual baud rate set up is 9,598, as shown as follows. This has only 0.02% deviation to the desired baud rate 9,600 and the receiver usually can tolerate such a small baud rate error.

$$Baud\ Rate = \frac{16 \times 10^6}{8 \times (2 - 0) \times 104.1875}$$
$$= 9598$$

Voltage signals of UART are defined in different standards, such as RS-232, RS-422, and RS-485. While the voltage of the TX and RX line in RS-422 and RS-485 is differential, with two separate wires for each line, RS-232 uses a single-end voltage with a shared ground. In RS-232, a voltage signal between +5V and +15V represents a logic one being transmitted, whereas a signal between -5V and -15V represents a logic zero. The receiver must interpret a voltage with +3V and +25V as logic one, and a voltage with -3V to -25V as logic zero. Any voltage signals between -3 and + 3 is invalid data. When the line is idle, the line has to be driven to logic zero.

Standard	Voltage signal	Max distance	Max speed	Number of devices supported per port
RS-232	Single end (logic 1: +5 to +15V, logic 0: -5 to -15 V)	100 feet	115Kbit/s	1 master, 1 receiver
RS-422	Differential (-6V to +6V)	4000 feet	10Mbit/s	1 master, 10 receivers
RS-485	Differential (-7V to +12V)	4000 feet	10Mbit/s	32 masters, 32 receivers

Table 22-1. Various UART standards

Most computers have at least one RS-232 serial port. However, we cannot directly connect STM32 processor to the RS-232 port of a computer due to the voltage incompatibility. The STM32 processors can only tolerate voltage signals under 5V. In addition, STM32 uses 0V to represent logic zero and 3V to represent logic one.

FT232R chip converts the UART port of STM32 to a standard USB interface, as shown below.

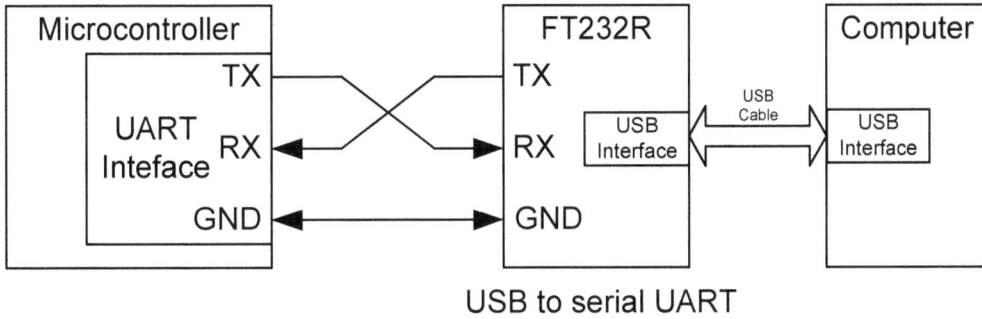

USB to serial UART

Figure 22-3. Serial communication via a USB-to-UART converter

The following diagram shows the voltage signal of the UART port when transmitting two data bytes, 0x32 and 0x3C. Each data frame includes one start bit, 8-bit data, and one stop bit. No parity bit is used in this example. After the start bit, the least significant bit of the data is transmitted first. For example, the binary value of 0x32 is 0b00110010 and the bit sequence seen on the transmission (TX) line is 01001100. The baud rate is set as 9,600 and thus each bit takes approximately 0.104ms. When the TX line is idle, it is set to 3V. The start bit has 0V while the stop bit has 3V.

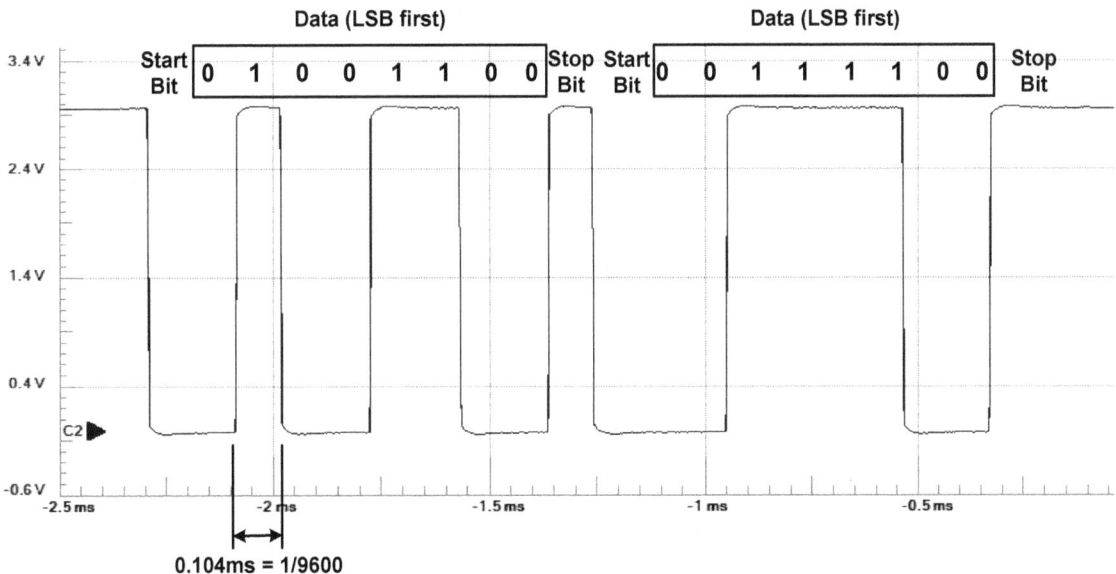

Figure 22-4. Voltage signal when transmitting 0x32 and 0x3C via UART
(1 start bit, 1 stop bit, 8 data bits, no parity, baud rate = 9,600)

22.1.3 Example Program Code in C

The GPIO pins for USART 1 and USART 2 are set up as follows:

Pin	Connection	Mode	AF	Output Type	Pull-up/Pull-down	Clock
PA.9	USART1_TX	AF	USART 1	Push-pull	No pull-up, no pull-down	40 MHz
PA.10	USART1_RX	AF	USART 1	Open-drain	No pull-up, no pull-down	40 MHz
PA.2	USART2_TX	AF	USART 2	Push-pull	No pull-up, no pull-down	40 MHz
PA.3	USART2_RX	AF	USART 2	Open-drain	No pull-up, no pull-down	40 MHz

Table 22-2. Setting of GPIO pins of USART 1 and 2 for asynchronous communication

Since we are using asynchronous communication, we only need to set up the GPIO pins for the TX and RX lines. If synchronous communication is used, then we also need to configure GPIO pins for the CTS, RTS, and CK lines.

Pin	Connection	Mode	AF	Output Type	Pull-up/Pull-down	Clock
PA.11	USART1_CTS	AF	USART 1	Push-pull	No pull-up, no pull-down	40 MHz
PA.12	USART1_RTS	AF	USART 1	Push-pull	No pull-up, no pull-down	40 MHz
PA.8	USART1_CK	AF	USART 1	Push-pull	No pull-up, no pull-down	40 MHz
PA.0	USART2_CTS	AF	USART 2	Push-pull	No pull-up, no pull-down	40 MHz
PA.1	USART2_RTS	AF	USART 2	Push-pull	No pull-up, no pull-down	40 MHz
PA.4	USART2_CK	AF	USART 2	Push-pull	No pull-up, no pull-down	40 MHz

Table 22-3. Setting of GPIO pins of USART 1 and 2 for synchronous communication

The following shows the main program that USART 1 sends 32 bytes of data to USART 2, and vice versa. The USART1 and USART2 are two pre-defined pointers, referring to a data structure that consists of all registers of a USART port.

```
#define BufferSize 32

uint8_t USART1_Buffer_Tx[BufferSize] = {
    0x01,0x02,0x03,0x04,0x05,0x06,0x07,0x08,
    0x09,0x0A,0x0B,0x0C,0x0D,0x0E,0x0F,0x10,
    0x11,0x12,0x13,0x14,0x15,0x16,0x17,0x18,
    0x19,0x1A,0x1B,0x1C,0x1D,0x1E,0x1F,0x20
};
```

```
uint8_t USART2_Buffer_Tx[BufferSize] = {
    0x51,0x52,0x53,0x54,0x55,0x56,0x57,0x58,
    0x59,0x5A,0x5B,0x5C,0x5D,0x5E,0x5F,0x60,
    0x61,0x62,0x63,0x64,0x65,0x66,0x67,0x68,
    0x69,0x6A,0x6B,0x6C,0x6D,0x6E,0x6F,0x70
};

uint8_t USART2_Buffer_Rx[BufferSize] = {0xFF};
uint8_t USART1_Buffer_Rx[BufferSize] = {0xFF};

uint8_t Rx1_Counter = 0;
uint8_t Rx2_Counter = 0;

int main(void) {
    RCC_Init();
    GPIO_Init();

    USART_Init(USART1);
    USART_Init(USART2);

    NVIC_SetPriority(USART1_IRQn, 1);    // Set priority to 1
    NVIC_EnableIRQ(USART1_IRQn);         // Enable interrupt of USART1

    NVIC_SetPriority(USART2_IRQn, 2);    // Set priority to 1
    NVIC_EnableIRQ(USART2_IRQn);         // Enable interrupt of USART2

    USART_Write(USART1, USART1_Buffer_Tx, 32); // Send 32 bytes to USART 2
    USART_Write(USART2, USART2_Buffer_Tx, 32); // Send 32 bytes to USART 1

    while(1);
}
```

The following code enables the clock the clock of USART 1 and USART 2.

```
Void RCC_Init(void) {

    // Turn on HSI (16MHz)
    RCC->CR |= RCC_CR_HSION;

    // Wait until HSI is ready
    while( (RCC->CR & RCC_CR_HSIRDY) == 0);

    // Select HSI as system clock
    RCC->CFGR &= ~RCC_CFGR_SW_HSI;
    RCC->CFGR |= RCC_CFGR_SW_HSI;
    while( (RCC->CFGR & RCC_CFGR_SWS)!=RCC_CFGR_SWS_HSI ); // Wait till HSI

    // Enable the clock of GPIO A
    RCC->AHBENR    |= RCC_AHBENR_GPIOAEN;
```

```
    // Enable the clock of USART 1 & 2
    RCC->APB2ENR  |= RCC_APB2ENR_USART1EN;      // Enable USART 1 clock
    RCC->APB1ENR  |= RCC_APB1ENR_USART2EN;      // Enable USART 2 clock
}
```

The initialization of USART is given below. It configures the USART port as 8 data bits, no parity, one start bit and one stop bit, with a baud rate of 9600.

```
void USART_Init (USART_TypeDef * USARTx) {

    // Configure word length to 8 bit
    // M = 0: 8 data bits,
    // M = 1: 9 data bits
    USARTx->CR1 &= ~USART_CR1_M;

    // Configure oversampling mode
    // 0 = oversampling by 16
    // 1 = oversampling by 8
    USARTx->CR1 &= ~USART_CR1_OVER8;

    // Configure stop bits to 1 stop bit.
    // 00: 1 Stop bit;    01: 0.5 Stop bit
    // 10: 2 Stop bits;   11: 1.5 Stop bit
    USARTx->CR2 &= ~USART_CR2_STOP;

    // Configure baud rate as 9,600 bits per second.
    USARTx->BRR  = 0x683;

    // Enable transmitter and receiver
    USARTx->CR1  |= (USART_CR1_RE | USART_CR1_TE);

    // Enable USART
    USARTx->CR1  |= USART_CR1_UE;

    // Enable received data ready interrupt
    USARTx->CR1  |= USART_CR1_RXNEIE;
}
```

When USART transfers a byte out, make sure to wait until the TXE (transmission data register empty) flag is set in the status register. The TXE flag is set by hardware when the content of the transmission data register (TDR) has been transferred into the shift register. In addition, writing USART data register (DR) automatically clears the TXE flag. After exiting the *for* loop, wait for the transmission complete (TC) flag to ensure the last byte has been sent out.

```
void USART_Write(USART_TypeDef * USARTx, uint8_t * buffer, int nBytes) {
   int i;
   for (i = 0; i < nBytes; i++) {

     while (!(USARTx->SR & USART_SR_TXE));   // Wait until TXE is set

     USARTx->DR = (buffer[i] & 0x1FF);       // Read data register

   }
   while (!(USARTx->SR & USART_SR_TC));     // Wait until TC flag is set
   USARTx->SR &= ~USART_SR_TC;              // Clear the TC flag
}
```

An USART interrupt can be generated by several events, such as transmission data register empty (TXE), transmission complete (TC), received data ready to be read (RXNE), overrun error detected (ORE), idle line detected (IDLE) and parity error (PE).

To receive data, the USART interrupt service routine checks whether the RXNE flag (read data register not empty) in the status register (SR) is set. The RXNE flag is set by hardware when the received data has been transferred to the USART data register (DR). The interrupt service routine should also clear the RXNE flag. This can be done implicitly by clearing the RXNE flag or explicitly by writing a "0" to it.

```
void USART_IRQHandler(USART_TypeDef * USARTx,
                      uint8_t * buffer,
                      uint8_t * pRx_counter){

   if(USARTx->SR & USART_SR_RXNE) {      // check whether data is received
       buffer[*pRx_counter] = USARTx->DR;
       // Reading USART_DR automatically clears the RXNE flag
       (*pRx_counter)++;
       if((*pRx_counter) >= BufferSize )  // avoid buffer overflow
           (*pRx_counter) = 0;
   }
}

void USART1_IRQHandler(void) {

   USART_IRQHandler(USART1, USART1_Buffer_Rx, &Rx1_Counter);

}

void USART2_IRQHandler(void) {

   USART_IRQHandler(USART2, USART2_Buffer_Rx, &Rx2_Counter);

}
```

22.1.4 Serial Communication to Bluetooth Module

Bluetooth is a low-power, low-cost wireless communication protocol operating at 2.4GHz band, which is a globally unlicensed radio frequency band for industry, science and medical (ISM).

Bluetooth is based on a master-slave model. A master device can connect up to seven active slave devices to form a local network (called *piconet*), while potentially there may be other inactive slave devices in the piconet. The disadvantages of Bluetooth include that it has a short communication range (15-30 feet) and it is relatively insecure.

Bluetooth uses a technique of time division duplex (TDD) to coordinate the access to the physical channel. It divides the time into a fixed length interval (625 microseconds) called *slots*. Each second is divided into 1,600 slots. The master sets the ratio frequency and initiates a data communication.

- *Master sets frequency hopping sequence.* Bluetooth divides the 2.4GHz band into 79 channels with their frequencies 1 MHz apart. In order to avoid interference on one specific channel, in each slot both the master and the slave device switch to a different channel. Such frequency hopping generally is performed 1,600 times per second, which allows a retransmission to occur soon at a different channel, hopefully on a clean one without any interference. This technique is called FHSS (frequency hopping spread spectrum). The master sets the frequency hopping sequence, and slave devices follow the hopping sequence by using a special algorithm.
- *Master initiates communication.* The master transmits data to a slave in even numbered slots and receives data from a slave in odd numbered slots. A slave device is only allowed to transmit data in a given slot if the master has polled it or sent a data packet to it in the preceding slot. The slave then responds to the master by sending a data packet or a NULL packet if the slave has nothing to send.
- Each Bluetooth device has a unique fixed 48-bit address, which is assigned at manufacture time. Two communicating devices need to know each other's address, which is either explicitly supplied by programmers or automatically discovered during the device discovery process. The discovery process searches all devices nearby and identifies the one that matches a user-friendly name such as "Joe's Phone."

Bluetooth Transfer Protocols

There are many transfer protocols available between two Bluetooth devices. A standardized set of protocols designed for a specific type of devices is called Bluetooth device profile. The following gives a few examples.

- The radio frequency communication (RFCOMM) profile emulates the serial cable line and guarantees reliable delivery of every packet. It is used for devices such as PC, printers, and moderns.
- The generic audio/video distribution profile (GAVDP) is used to stream video or audio data to devices such as stereo headphones and laptops.
- The audio/video remote control profile (AVRCP) provides a standard interface to control audio or video devices. Example devices include headphones, speakers, and TVs.

In this section, we will focus on the RFCOMM profile designed for serial communication. There are inexpensive Bluetooth-UART modules such as HC-05 (master or slave) and HC-06 (slave only) that supports the RFCOMM profile. They include a UART interface for serial communication between the Bluetooth module and microprocessors, and a Bluetooth interface for wireless communication between two Bluetooth modules, as shown in Figure 22-5.

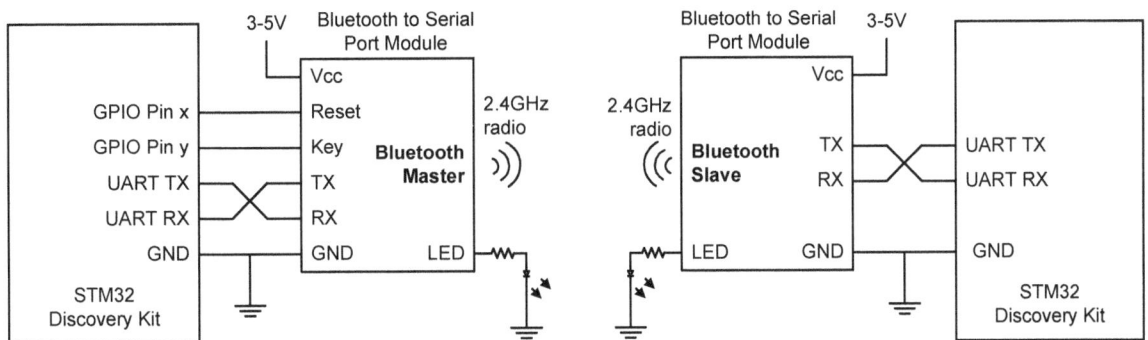

Figure 22-5. Serial port Bluetooth modules. One Bluetooth modules connects with each other via wireless communication. The Bluetooth modules transfer data to or from the processor via UART.

Pairing Bluetooth Modules

Two Bluetooth modules need to be paired and bound together before they can exchange data. The master device has to know the 48-bit address of the slave device and the paring password set by the slave device.

The microprocessor needs to send string commands via the serial interface to the Bluetooth master device to complete the paring and binding process. These string commands start with "AT" (abbreviation of attention) and end with a terminator "Return", *i.e.* with ASCII values of "0x0D,0x0A". Therefore, they also called "AT commands"

The following shows the procedure and the AT commands that the microprocessor performs to set up the Bluetooth master module.

In this example, we assume the slave Bluetooth blue has a MAC address of "0018,e4,0c680a" and a pairing password of "1234".

```
Pull the KEY pin high to set the Bluetooth master device to command mode

Pull the RESET pin low for a short time and then pull it high to reset the
Bluetooth master module

"AT+RESET\r\n"           ; add a return, i.e. "0x0D,0x0A", to the end
                         ; ASCII 0x0D = CR (carriage return)
                         ; ASCII 0x0A = NL (new line),

"AT+UART=57600,0,0\r\n" ; Baud rate: 57,600 bits/s, 1 stop bit, no parity bit
                         ; 1st parameter: baud rate
                         ; 2nd parameter: 0 = 1 stop bit, 1 = 2 stop bits
                         ; 3rd parameter: 0 = no parity bit, 1 = parity bit

"AT+ROLE=1\r\n"          ; A Bluetooth module can be either master or slave.
                         ; Set the module as a Bluetooth master.
                         ; 0 = Slave, 1 = Master, 2 = Slave Loop

"AT+PSWD=1234\r\n"       ; Password code for paring. The password is set by a
                         ; Bluetooth slave module.

"AT+PAIR=0018,e4,0c680a\r\n" ; Paired with a 48-bit slave address

"AT+BIND=0018,e4,0c680a\r\n" ; Bound with the target slave device

"AT+CMODE=0\r\n          ; 0 = Connect specified address a
                         ; 1 = Connect any address
                         ; 2 = Slave loop

Pull the KEY pin low to let the Bluetooth master device exit command mode and
enter communication mode

Pull the RESET pin low for a short time and then pull it high to reset the
Bluetooth master module
```

Table 22-4. Process of using AT commands to pair two Bluetooth devices

22.2 Inter-Integrated Circuit (I²C)

Inter-integrated circuit (I²C) is a standard bus protocol, originally developed by Philips in late 1980s, to enable the communication between microprocessors and their peripheral devices by using two wires: a serial data line (SDA) and a serial clock line (SCL). The two-wire design reduces the number of physical pins, making it inexpensive and simple to interface. The data transfer rate of I²C can be up to 100 Kbit/s in the standard mode, up to 400 Kbit/s in the fast mode, and up to 3.4 Mbit/s in the high-speed mode.

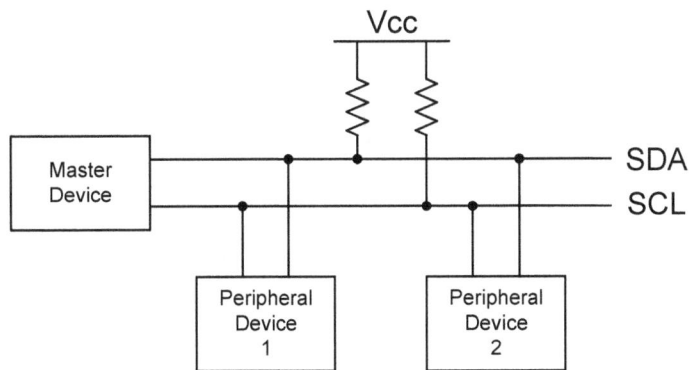

Figure 22-6. An example of I²C bus that connects one master and two peripheral devices. It uses two bidirectional open-drain wires: serial data (SDA) and serial clock (SCL). Both wires are pulled up to a positive voltage supply. The open-drain and external pull-up realize a Boolean and logic.

Each device, including master devices and peripheral devices, has a unique address, which typically has 7 bits, 10 bits, or 16 bits. Depending on the function, each device can serve as a transmitter, a receiver, or both. For example, a digital temperature may operate only as a transmitter, an LCD driver may operate only as a receiver, and a memory device can be both a transmitter and a receiver.

The master device initializes a data transfer on the bus, and then generates the clock signals to permit that data transfer, and finally terminates the transfer after receiving all requested data. The device addressed by the master is called a slave. Note multiple masters can co-exist on the same I²C bus. When multiple masters want to control the bus, an arbitration procedure is then performed. The number of devices that can be connected to the bus is limited by the bus capacitance.

The pins of the master and peripheral devices connected to the SDA and SCL lines have to be internally configured as *open-drain* or called open collector. An open-drain is a common type of output that connects to a positive voltage source if an active high (logic 1) is outputted but is in a high impedance state if a low (logic 0) is outputted. The high impedance is often achieved by keeping the output floated, *i.e.* not connected to either the ground or the positive voltage source.

Although the SDA and SCL pins of the microprocessor can be configured as open-drained internally, the microprocessor pull-up resistor is too large, often in the order of 100 kΩ, resulting in a pull-up power too weak for I²C. In order to reduce the rise time when pulling the voltage up to a high voltage, external pull-up circuits via a smaller resistor, such as 3 kΩ, are often used.

As shown in Figure 22-6, the SDA and SCL lines are connected to a positive supply voltage via two small pull-up resistors. Recommended resistance is 4.7 kΩ for low speed, 3 kΩ for standard mode, and 1 kΩ for fast mode.

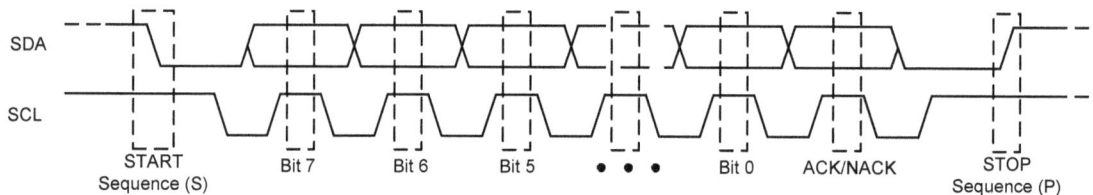

Figure 22-7. Timing diagram of sending N bits with the start bit (S) and the stop bit (P)

The communication begins with a START (s) setting and terminates by a STOP (P) setting. A START setting is defined as a high-to-low transition on the SDA line while the SCL line is high, whereas a STOP setting is a low-to-high transition on SDA while SCL is high. The master generates both START and STOP settings. The I²C interfacing hardware of all peripheral devices is capable of detecting START and STOP.

After the START setting, the master begins to send data byte by byte. For each byte, the most significant bit is transferred first. The slave will send an acknowledge bit to the Master to indicate that a byte has been successfully received.

After a byte is transferred, the receiver should answer the transmitter with either an acknowledge (ACK) bit or a not acknowledge (NACK) bit, as shown in Figure 22-8. The transmitter release the SDA line during the acknowledge clock period (the ninth clock period) so that the receiver can pull SDA to low. If the SDA is low in the ninth clock period, a ACK takes place. If the SDA is high in the ninth clock period, a scenario we call NACK occurs.

- When a master is transferring to a slave, an NACK answered by the slave means that the communication fails and the master needs to either generate a STOP to abort the current transfer or generate a START to restart the transfer.
- When a slave is transferring to a master, an NACK answered by the master means that the master will send a stop bit to terminate the communication after the current byte is transferred.

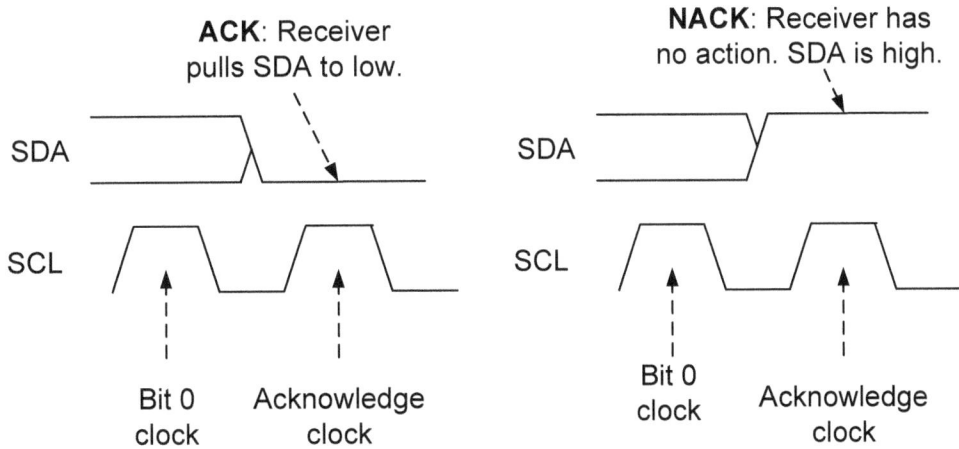

Figure 22-8. Comparison of ACK and NACK

While the master generates the transfer clock, the slave can control the transfer speed, too. If the slave is too busy to receive another byte, it will hold the SCL line low to force the master to wait. Data transfer continues after the slave releases SCL to high.

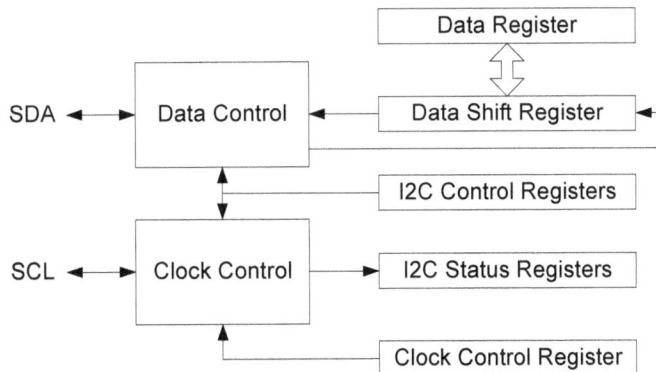

Figure 22-9. Simplified diagram of I²C

The STM32L processor has two I²C modules. Figure 22-9 shows the simplified data and clock control of one I²C module. The bytes stored in the data register are shifted in or out to the SDA line through an internal data shift register, with the most significant bit in or out first.

- When the master is transmitting a byte to a slave, the I²C hardware automatically sets the *TxE* (transmitter buffer empty) flag in the status register if an acknowledge pulse is received from the slave.
- On the other hand, when the master is receiving a byte from a slave, the I²C hardware then automatically sets the *RxNE* (receiver buffer not empty) flag in the status register if a byte has been successfully received.

For an I²C master, an interrupt can be generated if a start bit is sent, a slave address is sent, transfer of a data byte completes, the TxE flag is set, or the RxNE flag is set. For an I²C slave, an interrupt can be generated if the address received matches its own address, a stop bit is received, the TxE flag is set, or the RxNE flag is set.

When there are multiple master devices on the I²C bus, clock synchronization and arbitration are required. The SCL interface of all devices performs a logic AND operation. When one master pulls SCL low, no other masters can pull it high. During data transfer, the master constantly checks whether the SDA voltage level matches what it has sent. When two masters generate a START setting concurrently, the first master, which detects SDA low while it has actually intended to set SDA high, will lose the arbitration and let the other master complete the data transfer.

Example message protocols between a master and a slave with a 7-bit address or 10-bit address are given in Table 21-1 and Table 22-6. For a 7-bit slave, the basic procedures are listed as the following:

1. The master begins with sending a start bit, the slave address, and a single bit $(R/\overline{W})$ representing the data transfer direction. The slave whose address matches the address sent by the master will answer with an ACK bit.
2. The data transfer direction is represented by a single bit $(R/\overline{W})$. If the $R/\overline{W}$ bit is 0, then the master requests to receive data from the slave. After the address transfer completes, the slave sends data to the master and the master answers with either an ACK or NACK bit for each byte received. On the other hand, if the $R/\overline{W}$ bit is 1, then the master requests to send data to the slave. The slave then answers with an ACK/NACK bit for each byte sent by the master.
3. The master ends the message by sending a STOP bit to the slave.

Communication with a slave with a 7-bit address

S	Slave Address	R/$\overline{W}$	A	Data	A	Data	A	P
1 bit	7 bits	1 bit	1 bit	8 bits	1 bit	8 bits	1 bit	1 bit

Table 22-5. Example communication protocol for 7-bit slave address
(S = Start, P = Stop, A = Acknowledge)

Communication with a slave with a 10-bit address

S	Slave Address (higher 2 bits)	R/$\overline{W}$	A1	Slave Address (lower 8 bits)	A2	Data	A	Data	A	P
1 bit	11110xx (7 bits)	1 bit	1 bit	8 bits	1 bit	8 bits		8 bits	1 bit	1 bit

Table 22-6. Example communication protocol for 10-bit slave address
(S = Start, P = Stop, A = Acknowledge)

When the slave address has 10 bits, the communication protocol is changed slightly. After the start bit, the byte sent out by the master consists of a five-bit binary constant (11110), the most significant two bits of the slave address, the R/$\overline{W}$ bit. The next byte sent by the master is the least significant eight bits of the slave address.

When the first byte is sent out, all slave devices compare it with their own address. It is possible that more than one device finds a match between the most significant two bits of the 10-bit address. Therefore, multiple ACK bits might be generated during the A1 clock period. After the master sends out the lower 8 bits of the slave address, at most one device finds an address match and thus no multiple ACK bits are generated during the A2 clock period. The I²C slave remains as addressed until the master sends out the stop bit.

22.2.1 Interfacing Serial Digital Thermal Sensors via I²C

We will give an example in which the microprocessor interacts with multiple simple digital sensors via the I²C bus. In this example, we use TC74 digital thermal sensors from Microchip Technology, which provide 8-bit temperature measurements, with a resolution of 1°C and a conversion rate of 8 samples per second. The sensor has five pins, as listed in Table 22-7.

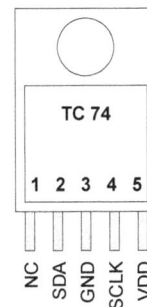

Figure 22-10. TC74 temperature sensor

Pin No.	Symbol	Type	Description
1	NC	None	No internal connection
2	SDA	Bidirectional	I²C serial data line
3	GND	Power	System ground
4	SCL	Input	I²C serial clock line
5	Vdd	Power	Power supply input

Table 22-7. Pin connection of TC74 digital temperature sensor

The address of TC sensors has 7 bits and TC74 has eight different binary addresses (from 1001000 to 1001111), depending on the part number of the device. The sensor provides two commands: (1) command code 0x00, which reads the temperature register, and (2) command code 0x01 to read/write the configuration register. The temperature measurement, represented in two's complement binary format, is stored in the 8-bit temperature register in units of Celsius degrees. For example, a reading of 0x00 represents $0°C$ and a reading of 0xFF represents $-1°C$. The most significant bit of the 8-bit configuration register is used to switch the sensor between standby and normal state, and bit 7 indicates whether the temperature data is ready or not.

Register Address (Command)	Description
0x00	Temperature register
0x01	Read/write configuration register

The read/write configuration register

7	6	5	4	3	2	1	0
Read/Write	Read-only	Reserved					
1 = standby	1 = ready						
0 = normal	0 = not ready						

Writing a Byte

S	Address	R/$\overline{W}$	ACK	Command	ACK	Data	ACK	P
1 bit	7 bits	1 bit	1 bit	8 bits	1 bit	8 bits	1 bit	1 bit

- The R/$\overline{W}$ bit is 0 for writing data to the configuration register of the sensor.
- The command byte selects to which register the data is written.
- The data byte specifies the data content to be written to the target register.
- The ACK bit is sent by the sensor to the microcontroller to acknowledge the receipt of each byte.

Reading a Byte

S	Address	R/$\overline{W}$	ACK	Command	ACK	S	Address	R/$\overline{W}$	ACK	Data	NACK	P
	7 bits	0		8 bits			7 bits	1		8 bits	1 bit	

- The first R/$\overline{W}$ bit is 0 for transmitting command to the sensor and the second R/$\overline{W}$ bit is 1 for receiving data from the sensor.
- The command byte selects which register is to be read.
- The address is repeated due to the change of data flow direction.
- The ACK bit is sent by the sensor to the microcontroller to acknowledge the receipt of each byte.
- The NACK (a bit of 1) is sent from the master to inform the slave to stop.

Reading a Byte

S	Address	R/$\overline{W}$	ACK	Data	NACK	P
1 bit	7 bits	1 bit	1 bit	8 bits	1 bit	1 bit

- The R/$\overline{W}$ bit is 1 for reading data from the sensor.
- The data received is from the register specified by the last command.
- The ACK bit is sent by the sensor to the microcontroller to acknowledge the receipt of each byte.

The address of the digital sensor depends on the part number provided on the chip.

Part Number	Address
A0	1001 000
A1	1001 001
A2	1001 010
A3	1001 011
A4	1001 100
A5	1001 101 (default)
A6	1001 110
A7	1001 111

22.2.2 I²C Clock Control

The frequency of the serial clock (SCL) determines the data transfer rate. The I²C clock must be at least 2MHz to achieve standard mode I²C frequency, and 4MHz to achieve fast mode I²C frequencies. The I2C_CCR clock control register controls the SCL clock. Assuming the 16MHz HSI is used to drive the I²C module, *i.e.* we have $f_{CLK} = 16MHz$.

Clock Configuration for Fast Mode. For fast mode, the duty control bit of the I²C clock control register (I2C_CCR) can be configured as either 0 or 1.

If the duty bit is zero, then we have

$$T_{high} = CCR \times T_{CLK} = CCR \times \frac{1}{f_{CLK}}$$

$$T_{low} = 2 \times CCR \times T_{CLK} = CCR \times \frac{2}{f_{CLK}}$$

Then

$$f_{SCL} = \frac{1}{T_{high} + T_{low}} = \frac{f_{CLK}}{3 \times CCR}$$

Thus, we have

$$CCR = \frac{1}{T_{high} + T_{low}} = \frac{f_{CLK}}{3 \times f_{SLK}}$$

For instance, in order to generate a 400 KHz SCL signal (*i.e.* $f_{SLK} = 400KHz$), CCR must be programmed with the following value:

$$CCR = \frac{16MHz}{3 \times 400KHz} \approx 13$$

If the duty bit is 1, then we have

$$T_{high} = 9 \times CCR \times T_{CLK} = CCR \times \frac{9}{f_{CLK}}$$

$$T_{low} = 16 \times CCR \times T_{CLK} = CCR \times \frac{16}{f_{CLK}}$$

Then

$$f_{SCL} = \frac{1}{T_{high} + T_{low}} = \frac{f_{CLK}}{25 \times CCR}$$

Thus, we have

$$CCR = \frac{1}{T_{high} + T_{low}} = \frac{f_{CLK}}{25 \times f_{SLK}}$$

Clock Configuration for Standard Mode. In standard mode, in order to generate a 100-KHz SCL frequency, the CCR must be configured as follows:

$$CCR = \frac{f_{CLK}}{3 \times f_{SLK}} = \frac{16MHz}{3 \times 100KHz} = 53$$

22.2.3 I²C Maximum Rising Time

According to the I2C standard, the maximum SCL rise time is $1000ns$ for standard mode and $300ns$ for fast mode. For standard mode, we have

$$T_{rise} = \frac{f_{CLK}}{10^6} + 1$$

For example, when $f_{CLK} = 16MHz$, then we have $T_{rise} = 17$.

For fast mode, we have

$$TRISE = \frac{300 \times 10^{-9} s}{\frac{1}{16MHz}} + 1 = 0.3 * 16 + 1 = 4.8 + 1 = 5.8$$

22.2.4 Sending Data to I²C Slave

During idle, both SCL and SDA lines are pulled to high. When the master wants to send data to a slave, the master first sends a start bit by pulling SDA to low and places the clock signal on SCL. Then the master sends the address frame, with the least significant bit being 0 to indicate that the master is the transmitter. After data frame, the master waits for the I2C_SR_TXE flag. This flag is set by the hardware after the master receives the acknowledgement bit from the slave. The master stops the data transfer by terminating the clock on SCL and pulling SDA to high.

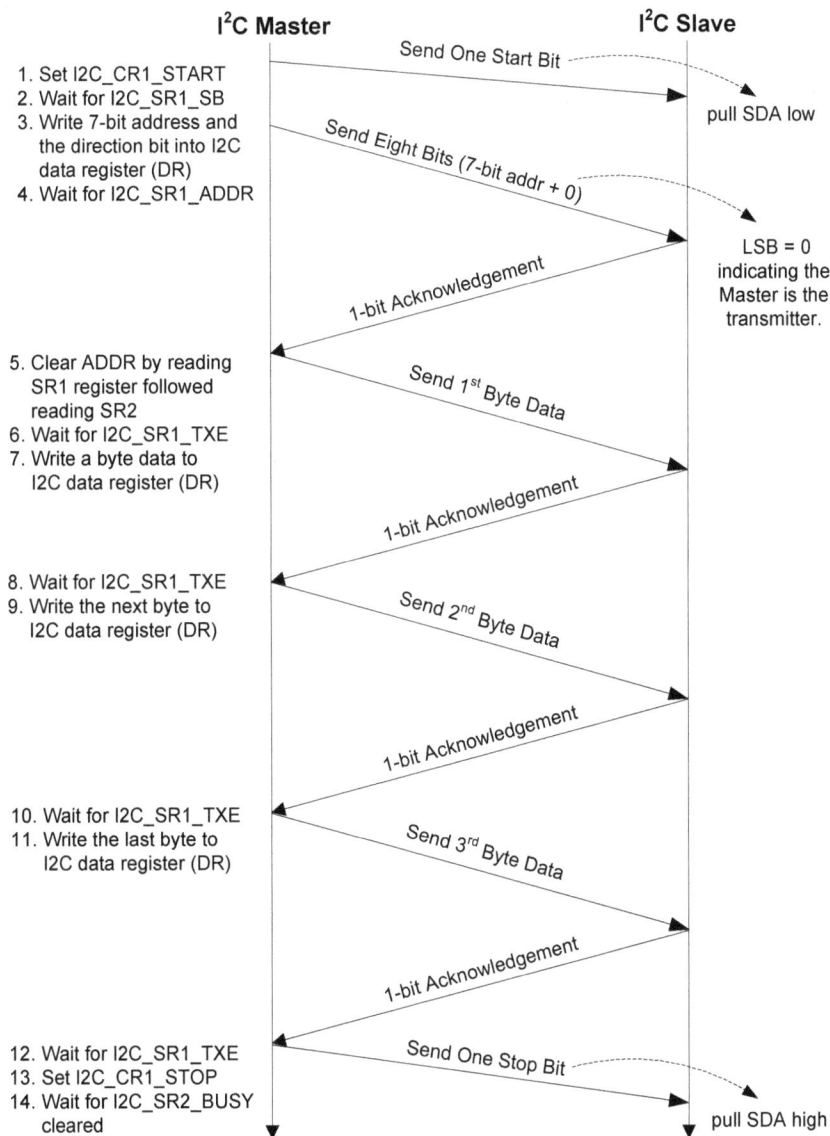

Figure 22-11. Time diagram when a master sends three bytes to a slave

22.2.5 Receiving Data from I²C Slave

When a master receives one byte, two bytes, and more than two bytes from a slave, the corresponding procedures are differs from each other slightly, as shown in Figure 22-12, Figure 22-13, Figure 22-14. When receiving one or two bytes, the master uses NACK (*i.e.* the ACK is disabled) for each data frame received, which is to inform the slave to release the control of the SCL and SDA lines. When the master receives more than two bytes, the master sends an ACK bit (*i.e.* the ACK bit is set to 1) for all data bytes except the last two. In addition, when receiving more than two bytes, the data register (DR) is read twice at the end. The first read is to retrieve the data from the data register and the second read is to retrieve the last byte stored in the shift register.

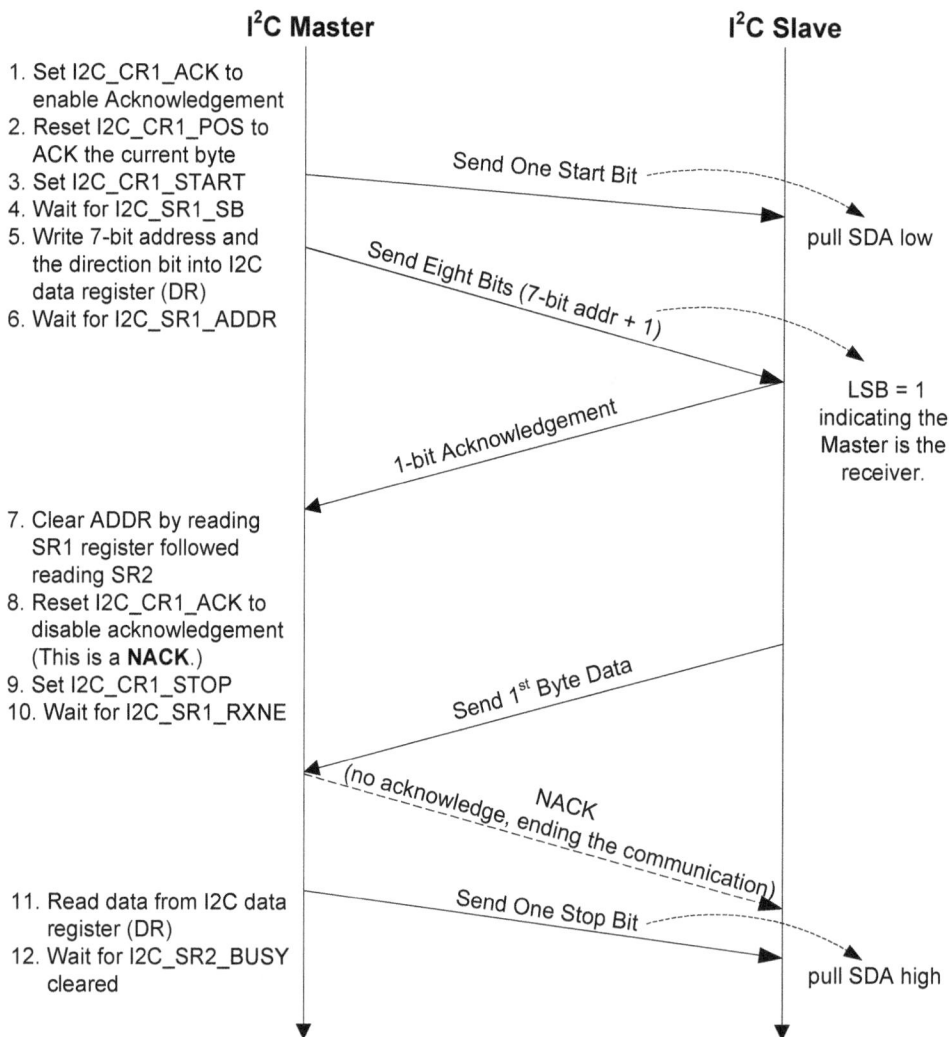

Figure 22-12. Time diagram when the master receives one byte from a slave

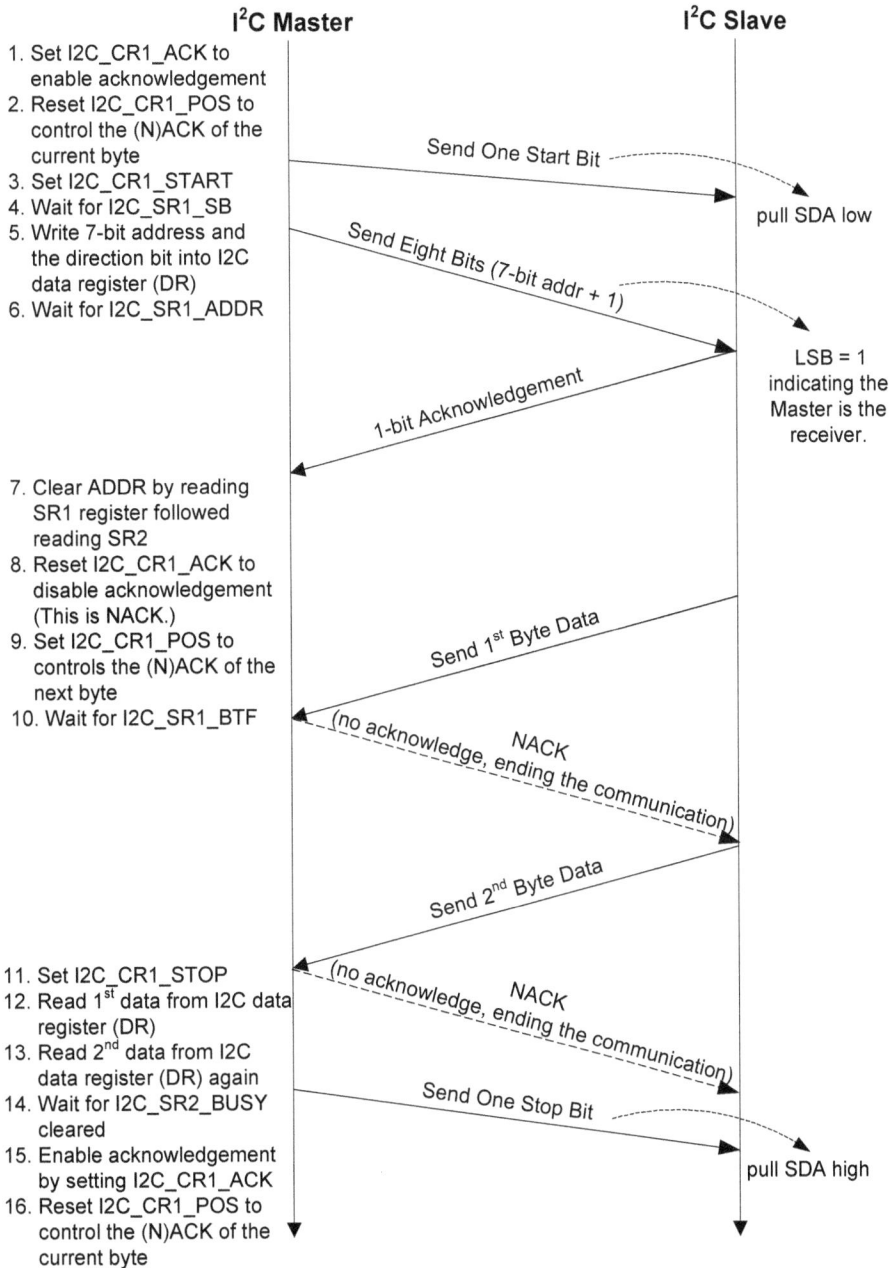

I²C Master

1. Set I2C_CR1_ACK to enable acknowledgement
2. Reset I2C_CR1_POS to control the (N)ACK of the current byte
3. Set I2C_CR1_START
4. Wait for I2C_SR1_SB
5. Write 7-bit address and the direction bit into I2C data register (DR)
6. Wait for I2C_SR1_ADDR

7. Clear ADDR by reading SR1 register followed reading SR2
8. Reset I2C_CR1_ACK to disable acknowledgement (This is NACK.)
9. Set I2C_CR1_POS to controls the (N)ACK of the next byte
10. Wait for I2C_SR1_BTF

11. Set I2C_CR1_STOP
12. Read 1st data from I2C data register (DR)
13. Read 2nd data from I2C data register (DR) again
14. Wait for I2C_SR2_BUSY cleared
15. Enable acknowledgement by setting I2C_CR1_ACK
16. Reset I2C_CR1_POS to control the (N)ACK of the current byte

I²C Slave

Send One Start Bit ·····
pull SDA low

Send Eight Bits (7-bit addr + 1)
LSB = 1 indicating the Master is the receiver.

1-bit Acknowledgement

Send 1st Byte Data
(no acknowledge, ending the communication) NACK

Send 2nd Byte Data
(no acknowledge, ending the communication) NACK

Send One Stop Bit ·····
pull SDA high

Figure 22-13. Time diagram when the master receives two bytes from a slave

Note: In step 12 and 13, the I²C data register (DR) is read twice consecutively. When the byte transfer finished (BTF) flag is set, one byte is stored in DR and the second byte is stored in the shift register. After reading the first byte in step 12, the data in the shifter register is automatically copied to DR. Therefore, we need read DR again to retrieve the second byte.

I²C Master   **I²C Slave**

1. Set I2C_CR1_ACK to
   enable acknowledgement
2. Reset I2C_CR1_POS to
   control the (N)ACK of the
   current byte   *Send One Start Bit*
3. Set I2C_CR1_START
4. Wait for I2C_SR1_SB   pull SDA low
5. Write 7-bit address and
   the direction bit into I2C   *Send Eight Bits (7-bit addr + 1)*
   data register (DR)
6. Wait for I2C_SR1_ADDR
                                                               LSB = 1
                                                               indicating the
                                                               Master is the
                                    1-bit Acknowledgement   receiver.

7. Clear ADDR by reading
   SR1 register followed
   reading SR2   *Send 1st Byte Data*
8. Wait for I2C_SR1_BTF

9. Read 1st byte data from
   I2C data register (DR)   *Send 1-bit Acknowledgement*
10. Set I2C_CR1_ACK to   This repeats for
    send acknowledgement   the first (n-2)
                                                               bytes.

                                    Send (n-1)th Byte Data

11. Reset I2C_CR1_ACK to   *(no acknowledge, NACK*
    disable acknowledgement   *ending the communication)*
    (This is NACK.)
12. Set I2C_CR1_POS to
    controls the (N)ACK of the
    next byte
13. Wait for I2C_SR1_BTF
                                    Send nth Byte Data

14. Set I2C_CR1_STOP
15. Read 1st data from I2C data   *(no acknowledge, NACK*
    register (DR)   *ending the communication)*
16. Read 2nd data from I2C
    data register (DR) again
17. Wait for I2C_SR2_BUSY   *Send One Stop Bit*
    cleared.
18. Enable acknowledgement
    by setting I2C_CR1_ACK   pull SDA high
19. Reset I2C_CR1_POS to
    control the (N)ACK of the
    current byte

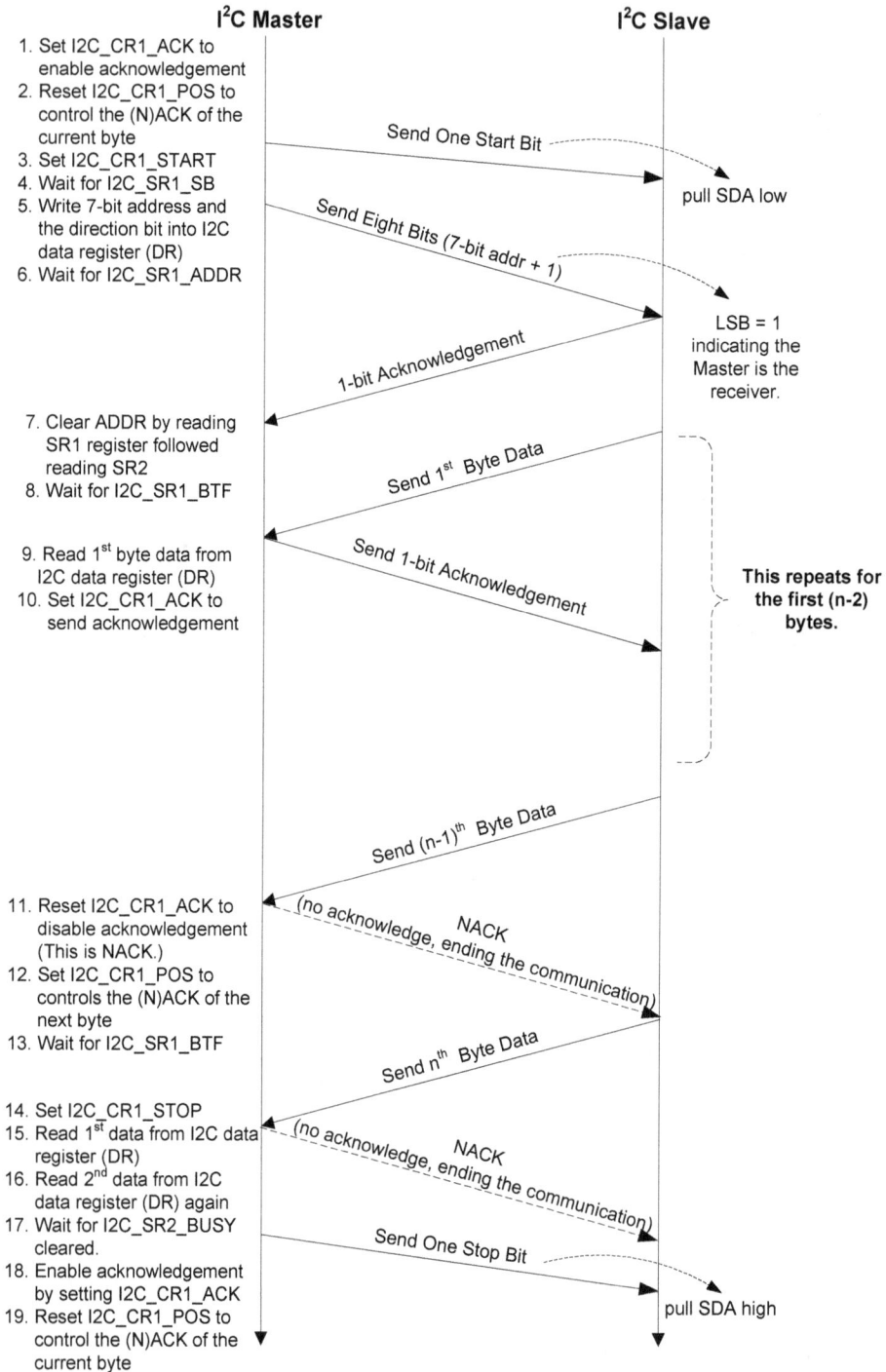

Figure 22-14. Time diagram when the master receives three bytes from a slave

Note in step 15 and 16, the I²C data register (DR) is read twice consecutively.

22.2.6 Example Program Code in C

In the section, we will show the C example program that interfaces with TC74 digital temperature sensors. Make sure that the VDD of the TC74 temperature sensor is connected to 5V, as shown in Figure 22-15.

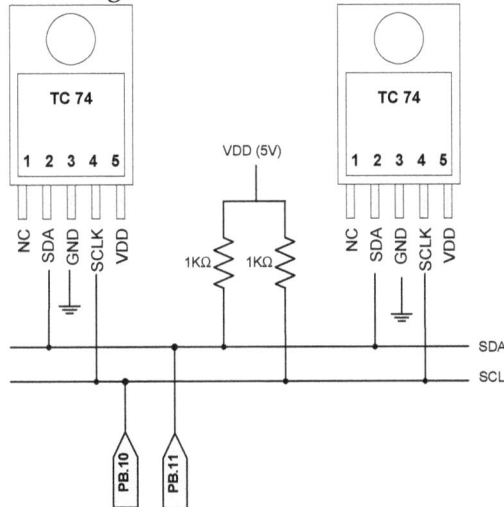

Figure 22-15. Connecting two TC74 digital temperature sensors via the I²C bus.

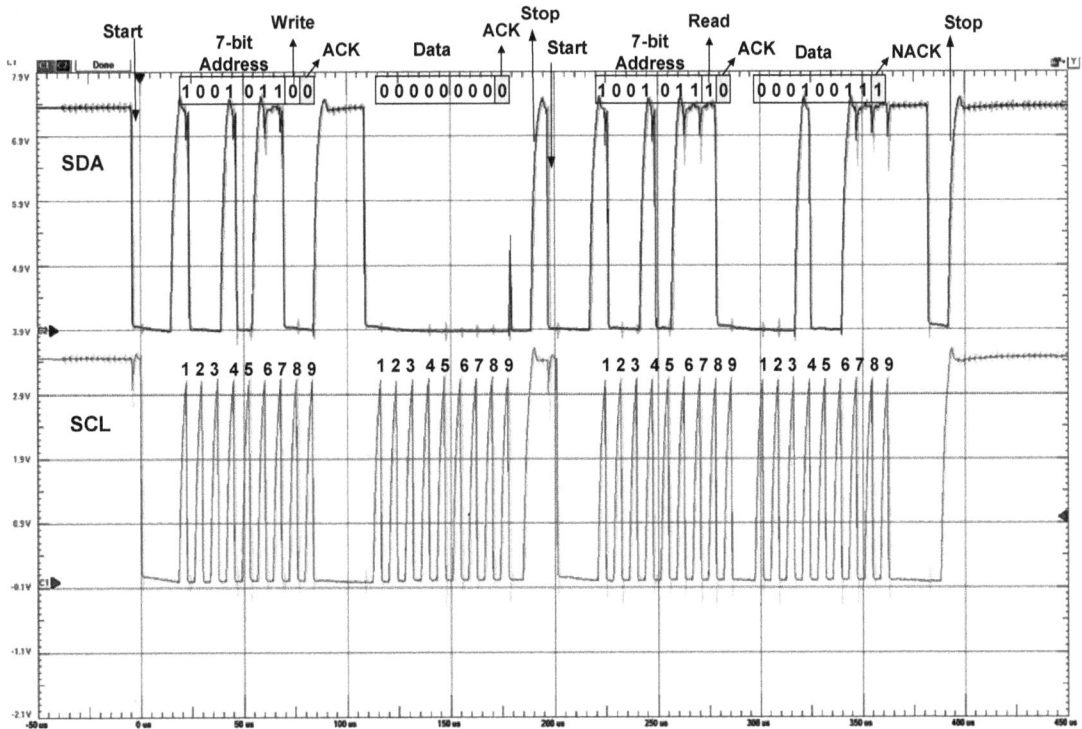

Figure 22-16. Analog signal capture on the SDA (the top signal) and SCL pin (the bottom signal).

There are two I²C modules on the STM32L processors. In this example, we use the second I²C module, which consists of the following two pins.

Pin	Connection	Mode	AF	Output Type	Pull-up/Pull-down	Clock
PB.9	I2C2_SCL	AF	I2C2	Open-drain	Pull-up	40 MHz
PB.10	I2C2_SDA	AF	I2C2	Open-drain	Pull-up	40 MHz

The initialization of the second I²C module is given as the following:

```
void I2C_Initialization(void){
  // Enable the clock of I2C
  RCC->APB1ENR  |= RCC_APB1ENR_I2C2EN;          // I2C 2 clock enable

  // Reset the I2C (set and reset by software)
  RCC->APB1RSTR |= RCC_APB1RSTR_I2C2RST;
  RCC->APB1RSTR &= ~RCC_APB1RSTR_I2C2RST;

  // I2C Control registers
  // ACK is set and cleared by software and cleared by hardware when PE=0.
  I2C2->CR1 |= I2C_CR1_ACK;         // 1 = Acknowledge after a byte is received
                                    // 0 = No acknowledge returned
  I2C2->CR1 &= ~I2C_CR1_SMBUS;      // Mode: 0 = I2C; 1 = SMBus

  I2C2->CR2 &= ~I2C_CR2_FREQ;       // Clear peripheral CLK frequency FREQ[5:0]
  I2C2->CR2 |= I2C_CR2_FREQ_1;      // Set peripheral clock frequency as 2 MHz

  I2C2->CR2 |= I2C_CR2_ITEVTEN;     // Event interrupt enable
  I2C2->CR1 &= ~I2C_CR1_PE;         // Disable I2C to configure TRISE

  // Set up the maximum rise time
  I2C2->TRISE &= ~I2C_TRISE_TRISE;  // Clear maximum rise time
  I2C2->TRISE |= 17;                // Set maximum rise time for standard mode

  // Set up I2C own address registers
  // Before the STM32 sends its start sequence it sits listening to the I2C
  // lines waiting for its address. This is helpful if STM32 is used as slave
  I2C2->OAR1 %= ~(0x01);
  I2C2->OAR1 = 0x00;   // Set up the address byte to select the slave device
  I2C2->OAR2 = 0x00;   // Set up the I2C own address

  // I2C Clock control register
  I2C2->CCR &= ~I2C_CCR_FS;             // 0 = Standard mode ((up to 100 kHz));
                                        // 1 = Fast mode (up to 400 kHz)
  I2C2->CCR &= ~I2C_CCR_CCR;
  I2C2->CCR |= 0x08;                    // Set up the SCL clock speed

  // Enable I2C module
  I2C2->CR1 |= I2C_CR1_PE;              // PE: peripheral enable
}
```

The following *I2C_Start*() subroutine generates a start bit. First, it clears the control flag for generating a stop bit and sets the control flag for generating a start bit. The start-bit control flag is cleared by hardware when the start bit is sent. After the start bit has been generated, the hardware sets up the start bit status flag (SB) of the status register. Software has to reset the SB status flag for future transfers by reading the status register (SR1) followed by writing the I²C data register (DR).

```
void I2C_Start(void) {
  uint32_t dump;

  // Clear the control flag of stop bit generation
  I2C2->CR1 &= ~I2C_CR1_STOP;

  // Set the control flag of start bit generation.
  I2C2->CR1 |= I2C_CR1_START;

  // Wait until the I2C module has entered the master mode.
  // Master/Slave (MSL) flag: 0 = slave mode; 1 = master mode
  while( (I2C2->SR2 & I2C_SR2_MSL) == 0);

  // Clear the start bit status flag by reading the SR1 register
  // followed by writing the DR register.
  dump = I2C2->SR1;

  return;
}
```

The following *I2C_Addr*() subroutine allows a master to send out the slave address. When the least significant bit (LSB) of the data address frame is 0, the data transfer direction is from a slave to a master. Otherwise, the data transfer direction is from a master to a slave.

For a master, the hardware sets the address sent status flag (ADDR) of the data status register if the address transmission has been successfully acknowledged by an I²C slave. For a slave, the hardware sets the ADDR status flag if the received slave address matched with the own address register (OAR).

Note *I2C_Addr*() should not wait on the TxE flag to check the completion of sending address because TxE is set during the address phase. Software must clear the ADDR status flag by first reading the status register 1 (SR1) and then reading the status register 2 (SR2).

```
void I2C_Addr(uint8_t DeviceAddress, uint8_t direction){
  uint8_t Address;
  uint32_t dump;

  // Set the transfer direction
  // LSB = 0: sending data to the slave
  // LSB = 1: receiving data from the slave
  Address  = (DeviceAddress << 1) | direction;

  // Send the address
  I2C2->DR = Address;

  // Wait until the address is acknowledged by an I2C slave
  while( (I2C2->SR1 & (I2C_SR1_ADDR ) ) == 0 );

  // Clear ADDR status flag by reading SR1 and SR2
  dump = I2C2->SR2;
}
```

The *I2C_SendData*() sends multiple bytes to a target slave. It first waits until the SDA and SCL lines are idle (*i.e.* the voltage of both lines are high), then sends a start bit and the slave address, and finally starts to send out the data byte by byte. When the master successfully sends a byte to the target slave, the transmitter register empty (TxE) flag is set by hardware. Before sending the next byte, normally the master should wait until TxE is set. Writing to the data register (DR) automatically clears the TxE flag.

In order to ensure the last byte is successfully sent out, the subroutine should wait until the Byte Transfer Finished (BTF) flag is set before it exits. The BTF flag, instead of the TxE flag, is checked because TxE is not set if a NACK is received or the next byte to be transmitted is packet error checking (PEC).

At the end of the subroutine, the subroutine sends a stop bit and waits until the SDA and SCL lines are idle. If the stop control bit is set, a master will generate a stop bit after the current byte or the current start bit is sent. The stop control bit is automatically cleared by hardware after a stop bit is generated. TxE and BTF are cleared by hardware by the stop bit.

```
void I2C_SendData(uint8_t DeviceAddress, uint8_t *Data, uint8_t Size) {

  int i, dump;

  if (Size <= 0) return;

  // Wait for I2C bus ready.
  // The BUSY flag is set by hardware on detection of SDA or SCL low
  // and is cleared by hardware on detection of a stop bit.
```

```
    while( (I2C2->SR2 & I2C_SR2_BUSY) == 1 );   // If busy, wait

    // Send the start bit
    I2C_Start();
    // Send the device address
    I2C_Addr(DeviceAddress, 0); // Direction: 0 = from master to slave

    // Send the first byte of data
    I2C2->DR = Data[0];

    for (i = 1; i < Size; i++) {
      // Wait until Transmitter Register Empty (TXE) flag is set
      while( (I2C2->SR1 & I2C_SR1_TXE) == 0 );

      // TXE is cleared by software writing to the DR register.
      I2C2->DR = Data[i];
    }

    // Make sure that the last byte has been sent before stop.
    while( (I2C2->SR1 & I2C_SR1_BTF) == 0 );   // Byte Transfer Finished (BTF)

    // Send a stop bit
    I2C2->CR1 |= I2C_CR1_STOP;

    // Wait until no communication
    while( (I2C2->SR2 & I2C_SR2_BUSY) == 1 );
}
```

The *I2C_ReceiveData*() subroutine receives data from an I²C slave. The program enables the acknowledgement and sets up the acknowledgement position so that an acknowledgement bit is sent for each byte received. As shown in Figure 22-12, Figure 22-13, and Figure 22-14, the sequence of receiving one byte, two bytes, and more than two bytes differs from each other slightly.

- When only one byte is to be received, the master makes an NACK for the current byte and sets up the stop control flag before reading the data register (DR).
- When two bytes are to be received, the master makes an NACK for the next byte, sends out a stop bit, and reads the data register (DR) twice consecutively.
- When more than two bytes are to be received, the master receives the first N-2 bytes by checking the byte transfer finished (BTF) flag and sending an ACK bit for each byte received. The master then uses a special sequence to retrieve the last two bytes.

```
void I2C_ReceiveData(uint8_t DeviceAddress, uint8_t *Data, uint8_t Size){
  int i;
```

```
if(Size <= 0)  return;

while( (I2C2->SR2 & I2C_SR2_BUSY) == 1 ); // Wait until bus is available
I2C2->CR1 |= I2C_CR1_ACK;        // Enable acknowledgement

// Set up the acknowledgement position
// 0 = ACK/NACK the current byte being received in the shift register
// 1 = ACK/NACK the next byte that will be received in the shift register
I2C2->CR1 &= ~I2C_CR1_POS;

I2C_Start();                     // Send out a start bit
I2C_Addr(DeviceAddress, 1);      // Direction = 1: receive data from slave

// Receive Data
if ( Size == 1 ){                // Receive only one byte
   I2C2->CR1 &= ~I2C_CR1_POS;    // ACK currently received byte
   I2C2->CR1 &= ~I2C_CR1_ACK;    // NACK
   I2C2->CR1 |= I2C_CR1_STOP;    // Send out a stop bit
   // Wait for Receiver Register Not Empty (RXNE) flag
   while( (I2C2->SR1 & I2C_SR1_RXNE) == 0 );
   Data[0] = I2C2->DR;           // Read the data
   I2C2->CR1 |= I2C_CR1_ACK;     // Reset ACK setting
} else if (Size == 2){           // Receive two bytes
   I2C2->CR1 &= ~I2C_CR1_ACK;    // NACK
   I2C2->CR1 |= I2C_CR1_POS;     // NACK the next byte
   // Wait on Byte Transfer Finished (BTF) flag
   while( (I2C2->SR1 & I2C_SR1_BTF) == 0 );
   I2C2->CR1 |= I2C_CR1_STOP;    // Send a stop bit
   Data[0] = I2C2->DR;           // Read 1st byte from data register (DR)
   Data[1] = I2C2->DR;           // 2nd byte was in the shifter register
   I2C2->CR1 |= I2C_CR1_ACK;     // Reset ACK setting
   I2C2->CR1 &= ~I2C_CR1_POS;    // Reset POS and ACK current byte received
} else {                         // Receive more than two bytes
   for(i = 0; i < Size-2; i++){  // Receive the first N-2 bytes
      // Wait on Byte Transfer Finished (BTF)
      while( (I2C2->SR1 & I2C_SR1_BTF) == 0);
      Data[i] = I2C2->DR;
      I2C2->CR1 |= I2C_CR1_ACK;  // Send an ACK bit to slave
   }
   I2C2->CR1 &= ~I2C_CR1_ACK;    // NACK
   I2C2->CR1 |= I2C_CR1_POS;     // NACK the next byte
   // Wait on Byte Transfer Finished (BTF)
   while( (I2C2->SR1 & I2C_SR1_BTF) == 0 );
   I2C2->CR1 |= I2C_CR1_STOP;    // Set up a stop bit
   Data[Size-2] = I2C2->DR;      // read the (N-1)th byte
   Data[Size-1] = I2C2->DR;      // read the Nth byte
   I2C2->CR1 |= I2C_CR1_ACK;     // Reset ACK setting
   I2C2->CR1 &= ~I2C_CR1_POS;    // Reset POS
}
}
```

22.3 Serial Peripheral Interface Bus (SPI)

Serial peripheral interface (SPI) is a synchronous serial communication interface widely used to exchange data between a microprocessor and peripheral devices with four wires. For example, a digital camera often uses SPI to control its lens and save photos to an MMC or SD media. SPI is simple, has low power requirement, and supports high throughput. Disadvantages of SPI include that it does not support multiple masters, and slaves cannot start the communication and control data transfer speed. All communications are initiated and controlled by the master.

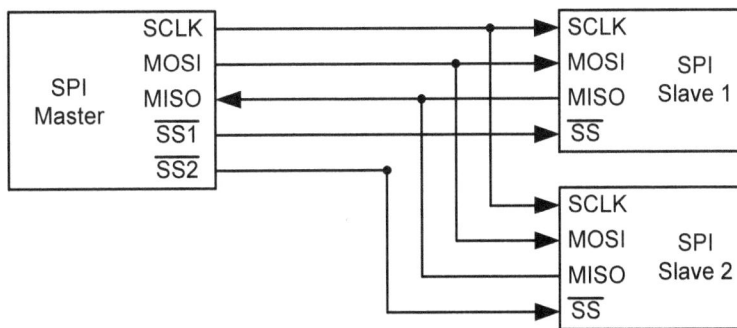

Figure 22-17. A SPI master device connecting to multiple SPI slave devices

A SPI interface consists of four lines: a master-in-slave-out data line (MISO), a master-out-slave-in data line (MOSI), a serial clock line (SCLK), and an active-low slave select line ($\overline{SS}$), as shown in Figure 22-17. SPI is also called four-wire serial interface.

SPI only supports a single master communicating with multiple slave devices. As shown in Figure 22-19, when the master wishes to exchange data with a specific slave, it pulls down the corresponding select line (SS_N). The master then generates clock pulses to coordinate the data transmission on the MOSI and MISO lines. Data exchange can take place in both directions simultaneously and this two-way serial channel is often called *full duplex*. Data bits are transmitted on both the MOSI line and the MISO line synchronously, with the flow direction opposite to the other. Note the SCLK line has only one direction and only the master can generate the clock signal. The slave devices cannot control the clock line.

When there are multiple slave devices, the master decides which slave device it wants to communicate. There is a dedicated slave select (SS) line for each slave device. The master selects the target slave device by pulling the corresponding SS line to a low voltage prior to data transfer. The selected slave device then listens for the clock and MOSI signals. When there is only one slave device, the SS line can be directly connected to the ground physically or the slave can be programmed by software to be constantly selected.

22.3.1 Data Exchange

SPI is a synchronous protocol and the slave devices must send and receive data based on the clock provided by the master. It differs from an asynchronous protocol in which no clock signal is provided physically and the data are sent and received at the same predetermined speed rate.

The master and a slave perform data exchange at synchronized time steps according to the clock signal generated by the master. As a bit is being shifted out from the data register to the output line in one clock period, a new bit is shifted into this register from the input line in the same clock period, as shown in Figure 22-18. When one device writes a data bit to the data line at the rising or falling edge of the clock, the other device

SPI master provides clock signal (SCLK) to SPI slaves.

then reads the data bit at the opposite edge of the same clock. The data transfer is usually a byte or half-word (16 bits).

Communication from master and slave and communication from slave to master are always take place concurrently. In each communication link (either MISO or MOSI), each device sends out a data item and at the same time receives a new data item. No devices can just be a transmitter or a receiver.

Therefore, when a slave wants to send some data to the master via the MISO line, it must wait for the clock signal, and the master must send some dummy data out via the MOSI line in order to generate the clock signal to initiate the data transfer, as shown in Figure 22-18.

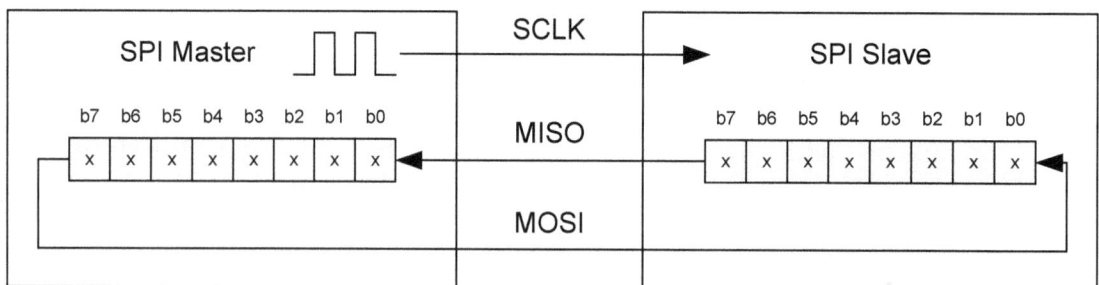

Figure 22-18. A byte is shifted out and in simultaneously via MOSI and MISO.

When a master exchanges data with slave n, the master must set the $\overline{SS_N}$ to low in order to select slave n, as shown in Figure 22-19. During the communication, the most significant bit of both data registers is sent out first.

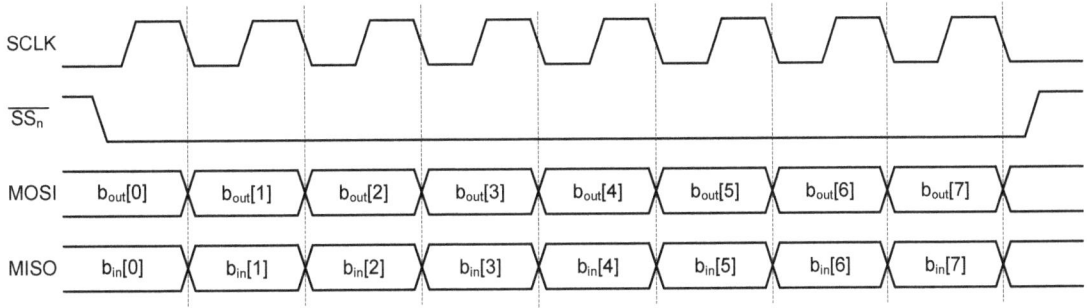

Figure 22-19. Communication signals between a master and slave n. In this example, the most significant bit is transferred first.

Figure 22-20 shows the signal of SCLK and MOSI when two bytes (0xAA and 0x3C) are sent out. In this example, the least significant bit (LSB) of each data is sent out first.

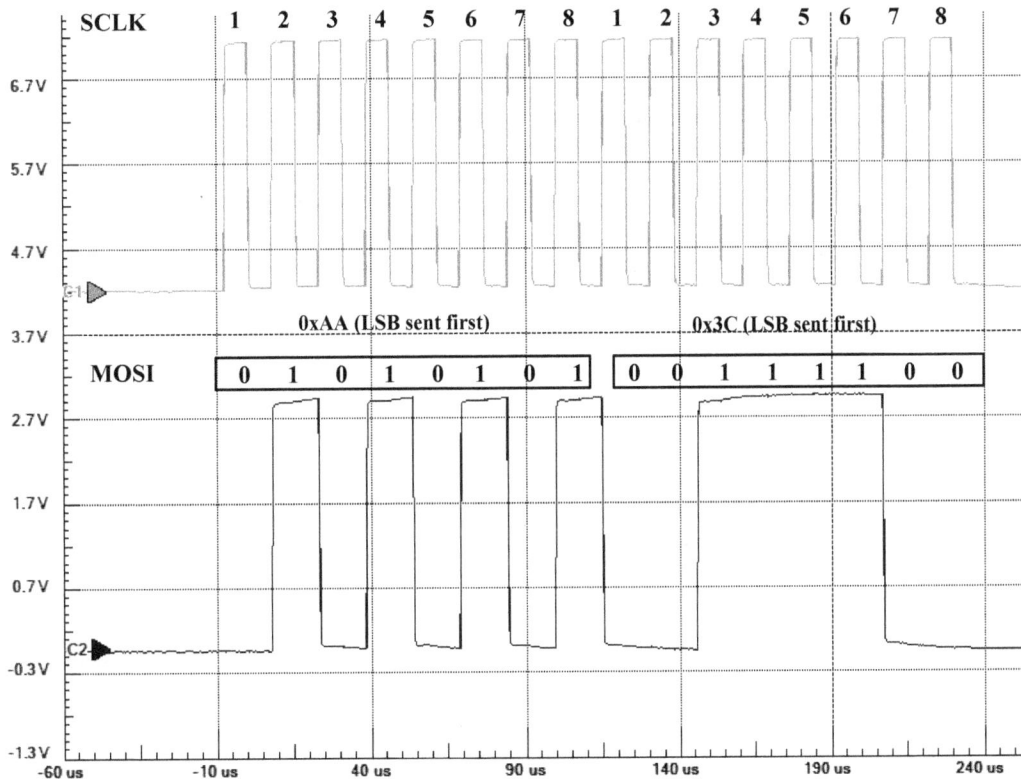

Figure 22-20. SCLK and MOSI signals when the master sends two bytes: 0xAA and 0x3C

22.3.2 Clock Configuration

The clock speed determines the data transfer rate. The data rate ranges from 1 to 20 megabits per second. The master can change the clock speed by programming the clock prescaler register. The clock frequency is usually between 100 KHz to 16 MHz. The SCLK clock frequency is programmed by setting the baud rate control factor.

$$f_{SCLK} = \frac{f_{system}}{constant}$$

For STM32L processors, the baud rate control factor is stored in the BR[2:0] bits of the SPI control register (CR1). The constant can be calculated as $2^{1+BR[2:0]}$.

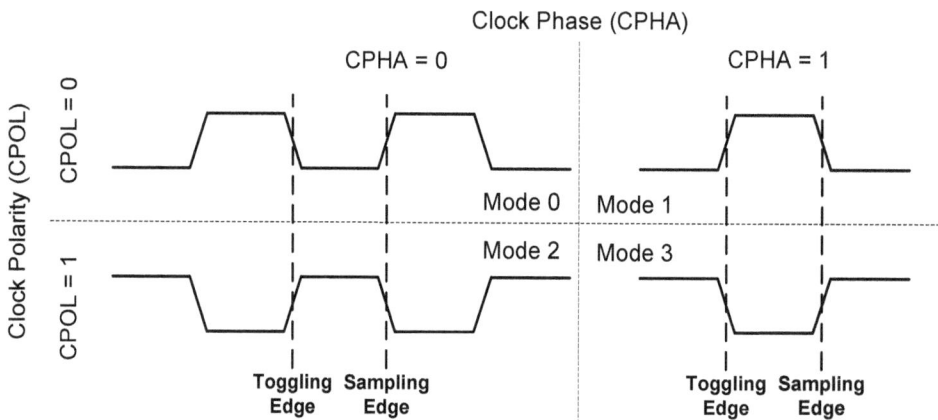

Figure 22-21. Configuration of clock phase and clock polarity

In addition to setting the clock frequency, four possible clock modes are available to program the clock edge used for data sampling and data toggling, as shown in Figure 22-21. The clock modes are determined by two parameters: clock phase (CPHA) and clock polarity (CPOL).

- When CPOL is 0, the SCLK line is pushed to low during idle. When CPOL is 1, the SCLK line is pulled to high during idle.
- When CPHA is 0, the first clock transition (either rising or falling) is the first data capture edge. When CPHA is 1, the second clock transition is the first data capture edge.

The combination of CPOL and CPHA selects the clock edge for transmitting data and the clock edge for receiving data. For example, in mode 0 (CPOL = 0, CPHA = 0), the data is toggled (*i.e.* transmitted) at the clock falling edge and is sampled (*i.e.* received) at the rising edge. Note the reception of the first bit is delayed one-half cycle in Mode 0 and 2.

22.3.3 Example Program Code in C

In this section, we give example codes that use SPI to exchange data between two SPI interfaces of a STM32 processor. The following initialization program configures SPI 1 as a master and SPI 2 as a slave.

```c
void SPI_Init(SPI_TypeDef * SPIx){

  if(SPIx == SPI1){ // Set SPI1 as master
      RCC->APB2ENR  |= RCC_APB2ENR_SPI1EN;      // Enable SPI1 clock
      RCC->APB2RSTR |= RCC_APB2RSTR_SPI1RST;    // Reset SPI1
      RCC->APB2RSTR &= ~RCC_APB2RSTR_SPI1RST;   // Clear reset of SPI1
      SPIx->CR1 |= SPI_CR1_MSTR;   // Master selection: 0 = slave, 1 = master
      SPIx->CR1 |= SPI_CR1_SSI;    // Manage slave selection by software
  } else if(SPIx == SPI2){ // Set SPI2 as slave
      RCC->APB1ENR  |= RCC_APB1ENR_SPI2EN;      // Enable SPI2 Clock
      RCC->APB1RSTR |= RCC_APB1RSTR_SPI2RST;    // Reset SPI2
      RCC->APB1RSTR &= ~RCC_APB1RSTR_SPI2RST;   // Clear reset of SPI2
      SPIx->CR1 &= ~SPI_CR1_MSTR;  // Master selection: 0 = slave, 1 = master
      SPIx->CR1 &= ~SPI_CR1_SSI;   // Manage slave selection by software
  }

  // Configure duplex or receive-only
  // 0 = full duplex (transmit and receive);  1 = receive-only
  SPIx->CR1 &= ~SPI_CR1_RXONLY;    // full duplex

  // Data frame format
  // 0 = 8-bit frame; 1 = 16-bit frame
  SPIx->CR1 &= ~SPI_CR1_DFF;         // frame size = 8 bits

  // Frame format
  // 0 = MSB transmitted first;  1 = LSB transmitted first
  SPIx->CR1 |= SPI_CR1_LSBFIRST;

  // Software slave management (SSM)
  // 1 = software slave management enabled
  // 0 = software slave management disabled
  // When enabled, SSI is forced onto the NSS, and the GPIO of NSS is ignored
  SPIx->CR1 |= SPI_CR1_SSM;

  // Clock phase (CPHA)
  // 0 = The first clock transition is the first data capture edge
  // 1 = The second clock transition is the first data capture edge
  SPIx->CR1 |= SPI_CR1_CPHA;

  // Clock polarity  (CPOL)
  // 0 = Set clock to low when idle
  // 1 = Set clock to high when idle
  SPIx->CR1 &= ~SPI_CR1_CPOL;
```

```
  // Baud rate control:
  // 000: f_PCLK/2   001: f_PCLK/4    010: f_PCLK/8    011: f_PCLK/16
  // 100: f_PCLK/32  101: f_PCLK/64   110: f_PCLK/128 111: f_PCLK/256
  SPIx->CR1 |= 4<<3;

  // Bidirectional data mode enable
  SPIx->CR1 &= ~SPI_CR1_BIDIMODE;
  // 0: 2-line unidirectional data mode selected

  // Output enable in bidirectional mode
  // 0: Output disabled (receive-only mode)
  // 1: Output enabled (transmit-only mode)
  SPIx->CR1 |= SPI_CR1_BIDIOE;

  // Enable RX buffer not empty interrupt
  SPIx->CR2 |= SPI_CR2_RXNEIE;

  // Enable error interrupt
  SPIx->CR2 |= SPI_CR2_ERRIE;

  // Enable SPI
  SPIx->CR1 |= SPI_CR1_SPE;
}
```

The following subroutine is for SPI master (*i.e.* SPI 1 in this example) to send the data to a SPI slave. It checks the transmission buffer empty flag (TXE) and waits until TXE is set by the hardware. If TXE is set, the transmission register is ready to accept the next data to be transmitted. Writing to the SPI data register (DR) automatically clears the TXE flag. The subroutine also waits until the busy flag is cleared to ensure the last data has been successfully sent.

```
void SPI_Write(SPI_TypeDef * SPIx, uint8_t *buffer, int size) {
  int i = 0;

  for (i = 0; i < size; i++) {
    while(!(SPIx->SR & SPI_SR_TXE )); // Wait for TXE (transmit buffer empty)
    SPIx->DR = buffer[i];
  }

  while( SPIx->SR & SPI_SR_BSY );      // Wait for not busy
}
```

The following subroutine shows how the SPI slave sent the data to the master. Note only the master can initiate the data transfer and controls the communication clock (SCLK). Therefore, the master has to send a dummy byte data to the slave to start the clock.

```
void SPI_Read(SPI_TypeDef * SPIx, uint8_t *buffer, int size) {
  int i = 0;
  for (i = 0; i < size; i++) {
    // Wait for TXE (transmit buffer empty)
    while(!(SPIx->SR & SPI_SR_TXE ));
    SPIx->DR = buffer[i];

    // Wait for TXE
    while(!(SPI1->SR & SPI_SR_TXE ));
    SPI1->DR = 0xFF;        // A dummy byte
  }

  // Wait until SPI is not busy
  while( SPI1->SR & SPI_SR_BSY );
}
```

The following configures GPIO pins for SPI interfaces.

Pin	Connection	Mode	AF	Output Type	Pull-up/Pull-down	Clock
PA.4	SPI1_NSS	AF	SPI1	Push-pull	No pull-up pull-down	40 MHz
PA.5	SPI1_SCK	AF	SPI1	Push-pull	No pull-up pull-down	40 MHz
PA.11	SPI1_MISO	AF	SPI1	Push-pull	No pull-up pull-down	40 MHz
PA.12	SPI1_MOSI	AF	SPI1	Push-pull	No pull-up pull-down	40 MHz

Table 22-8. GPIO pin configuration for SPI 1

Pin	Connection	Mode	AF	Output Type	Pull-up/Pull-down	Clock
PB.12	SPI2_NSS	AF	SPI2	Push-pull	No pull-up pull-down	40 MHz
PB.13	SPI2_SCK	AF	SPI2	Push-pull	No pull-up pull-down	40 MHz
PB.14	SPI2_MISO	AF	SPI2	Push-pull	No pull-up pull-down	40 MHz
PB.15	SPI2_MOSI	AF	SPI2	Push-pull	No pull-up pull-down	40 MHz

Table 22-9. GPIO pin configuration for SPI 2

The following is the main function that exchanges data between two SPI interfaces.

```
#define BufferSize 32

uint8_t SPI1_Buffer_Tx[BufferSize] = {
      0x01,0x02,0x03,0x04,0x05,0x06,0x07,0x08,
      0x09,0x0A,0x0B,0x0C,0x0D,0x0E,0x0F,0x10,
      0x11,0x12,0x13,0x14,0x15,0x16,0x17,0x18,
      0x19,0x1A,0x1B,0x1C,0x1D,0x1E,0x1F,0x20
};

uint8_t SPI2_Buffer_Tx[BufferSize] = {
      0x51,0x52,0x53,0x54,0x55,0x56,0x57,0x58,
      0x59,0x5A,0x5B,0x5C,0x5D,0x5E,0x5F,0x60,
      0x61,0x62,0x63,0x64,0x65,0x66,0x67,0x68,
```

```
        0x69,0x6A,0x6B,0x6C,0x6D,0x6E,0x6F,0x70
};

uint8_t SPI1_Buffer_Rx[BufferSize] = {0xFF};
uint8_t SPI2_Buffer_Rx[BufferSize] = {0xFF};

uint8_t Rx1_Counter = 0;
uint8_t Rx2_Counter = 0;

int main(void) {
  GPIO_Init();
  NVIC_SetPriority(SPI1_IRQn, 1);      // Set Priority to 1
  NVIC_EnableIRQ(SPI1_IRQn);           // Enable interrupt of SPI1 peripheral
  NVIC_SetPriority(SPI2_IRQn, 2);      // Set Priority to 1
  NVIC_EnableIRQ(SPI2_IRQn);           // Enable interrupt of SPI2 peripheral
  SPI_Init(SPI1);                      // Initialize SPI 1
  SPI_Init(SPI2);                      // Initialize SPI 2
  SPI_Write(SPI1, SPI1_Buffer_Tx, 32); // SPI 1 writes data out
  SPI_Read(SPI2, SPI2_Buffer_Tx, 32);  // SPI 2 reads data
  while(1);
}
```

Example 22-1. Sending data between two SPI interfaces

The SPI interrupt handler is implemented as the following. It checks whether the receiver buffer not empty (RXNE) flag of the status register is set. If RXNE is set, then there are valid data received and the program then reads the data register (DR). Reading SPI data register automatically clears the RXNE flag.

```
void SPIx_IRQHandler(SPI_TypeDef * SPIx, uint8_t *buffer, uint8_t *counter) {

  if(SPIx->SR & SPI_SR_RXNE) { // if SPI Receive Register is not empty
    buffer[*counter] = SPIx->DR;
    // Reading SPI_DR automatically clears the RXNE flag
    (*counter)++;
    if( (*counter) >= BufferSize )
        (*counter) = 0;
  }
}

void SPI1_IRQHandler(void) {

  SPIx_IRQHandler(SPI1, SPI1_Buffer_Rx, & Rx1_Counter);

}

void SPI2_IRQHandler(void) {

  SPIx_IRQHandler(SPI2, SPI2_Buffer_Rx, & Rx2_Counter);

}
```

Example 22-2. Interrupt service handler for SPI interface

22.4 Universal Serial Bus (USB)

Universal serial bus (USB) is a widely used industry standard to connect multiple peripheral devices to a host (typically a computer). Compared to other serial or parallel communication standards, USB has the advantage of ease of use (such as plug and play, hot-swapping without rebooting, and no power supply required), low cost, low power consumption, and fast data transfer. USB 1.0, 2.0 and 3.0 specifications were officially released in 1996, 2000, and 2008, respectively. They are backward compliant. USB 2.0 also includes USB OTG (on-the-go) protocol, which allows a USB device to perform both the master and slave roles. For example, a printer is a USB slave to a host PC, but it can also be a master when a USB flash drive is plugged in. In this chapter, we only cover the fundamental concepts of USB 1.0 and 2.0. USB OTG and USB 3.0 are not covered in this chapter.

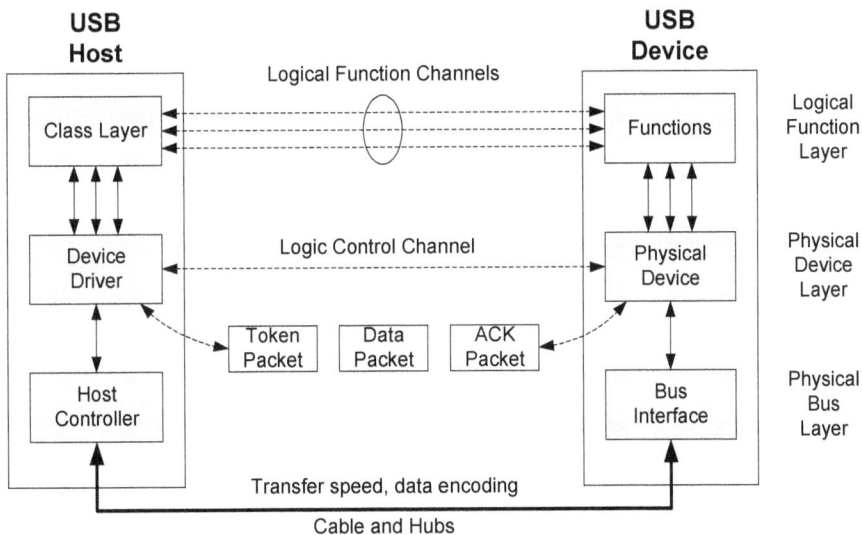

Figure 22-22. USB protocol stack

The USB protocol can be divided into three hierarchical layers.
- The bus layer takes care of wire connections, power supply to peripheral devices, transfer speed, and data signal encoding.
- The device layer establishes a logic control channel (endpoint 0) for the host to control and set up the device, detects errors in a packet, and breaks a high-level request into multiple packets.
- The logic function layer establishes multiple logical function channels between a host and a USB device. A USB device might have multiple functions. For example, a printer may have fours functions: printing, photocopy, scan, and fax.

A logical channel allows the host to read data from or write data to a specific function of a USB device.

22.4.1 USB Bus Layer

USB supports four transmission speeds:

- low speed (1.5 Mbit/s = 187 KB/s)
- full speed (12 Mbit/s = 1.5 MB/s)
- high speed (480 Mbit/s = 60 MB/s)
- super speed (4.8 Gbit/s = 600 MB/s)

A standard USB cable has four shielded wires: ground, Vbus (5 volts), data plus (D+) and data minus (D-). The Vbus can provide power supply to USB devices. The D+ and D- wires are physically twisted to cancel out external electromagnetic interference. A voltage under 0.3V on a wire is considered low and a voltage over 2.8V is high.

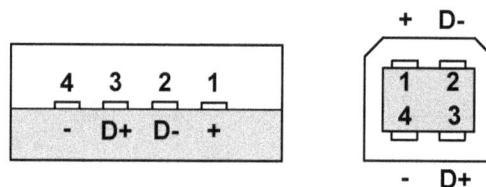

Figure 22-23. USB Connector type A plug (left) and type B plug (right)

Every high-speed USB device must support a data rate of 480Mb/s, with a clock accuracy of ±500 PPM (part per million). One PPM is 0.0001% or 1E-6. A PPM of 12 means a maximum error of approximately one second after one day has past. 500 PPM implies the clock is off by up to 43 seconds per day. The internal clocks of a microprocessor often do not provide such high accuracy and therefore an external crystal oscillator is often used to drive the USB peripheral. For example, the internal clocks of the STM32L processor only provide an accuracy of ±1000 PPM at room temperature, which implies up to 8.6 seconds off per day and up to 14 minutes off per month. A cheap external crystal oscillator is within ±20 PPM.

Data are transmitted via the D+ and D- wires using differential signals.. One of them must be high and the other must be low. For example, for a full-speed connection, the wires are either in the "J" state (D+ = high and D- = low) or the "K" state (D+ = low and D- = high). When no data is transferred (*i.e.* idle state), the wires are in the J state. The states for a low-speed are the opposite of the full-speed. Non-return-to-zero inverted (NRZI) is used to encode a sequence of binary bits. A binary 1 bit is represented by maintaining the current state. A binary 0 is represented by switching from the J state to

K state or from the K state to J state (also called change-on-zero). Figure 22-24 gives an example of encoding a binary bit string.

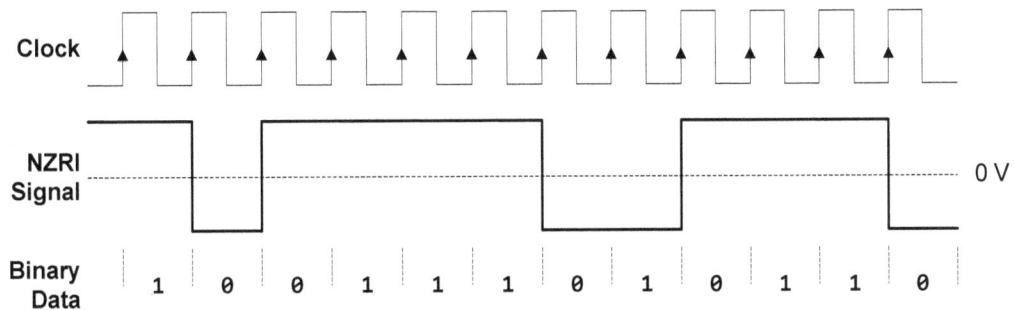

Figure 22-24. Example of NRZI data encoding for full speed

USB also uses the D+ and D- to transmit single-ended signals. We call the bus in the SE0 (SE stands for single-ended) state when both are low, and in the SE1 state when both are high. SE0 is used in ending a transfer, disconnecting or resetting USB devices. SE1 is an illegal state except for battery charging.

In addition, USB uses a technique called *bit stuffing* to ensure enough state transitions on D+ and D- for clock synchronization between the transmitter and the receiver. More specifically, an additional 0 bit is inserted into the bit streams after six consecutive ones.

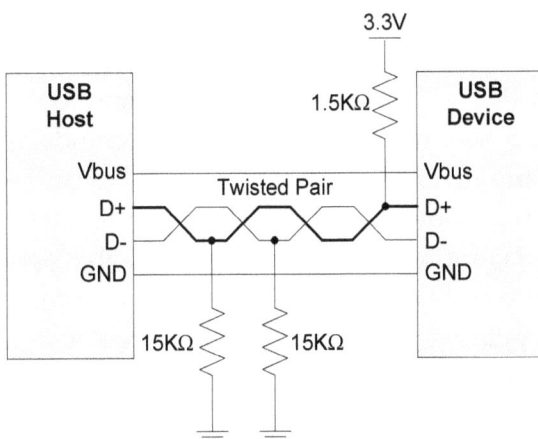

Figure 22-25. Full-speed mode (12 Mbits/s) identified by 3.3KΩ pull-up on D+

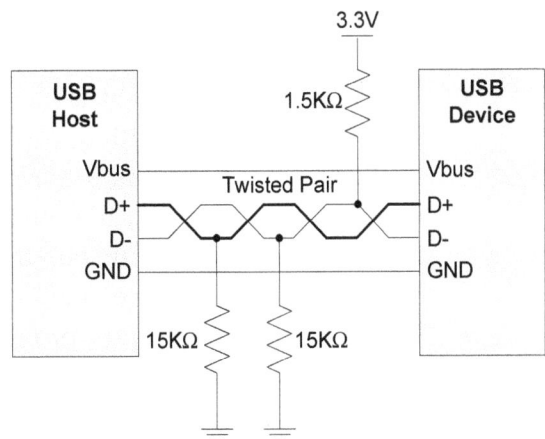

Figure 22-26. Low-speed mode (1.5Mbits/s) identified by 3.3KΩ pull-up on D-

The USB speed is determined by pulling up the D+ or D- wire. When neither of them is pulled up, the host assumes no devices are connected to the bus. If the D+ is pulled up via a 1.5KΩ resistor to 3.3V, the host assumes a high-speed USB device is connected. The same pull-up on D- indicates a low-speed device. A high-speed device is identified by initially pulling up D+. The host attempts to send or receive packets at high speed. If the communication is successful, the host assumes the device is high speed and the device should remove the pull-up afterward. If the communication fails, the host assumes it is full speed.

22.4.2 USB Device Layer

USB is a token-based data transfer protocol in which only a host can initiate the transfer. Each token has a target USB device address. The USB device with a matching address responds to the token packet issued by the host. The token packet also includes a target endpoint and the data transfer direction. A USB device might have multiple endpoints. Each endpoint is a predefined buffer in the USB device's memory.

The transfer direction can be either IN or OUT, from the perspective of the host. An IN token packet indicates that the host is requesting to read data from the target endpoint of the USB device. An OUT token packet indicates that the host is requesting to write data to the target endpoint of the device.

A data transfer takes place between a host and the endpoint of a USB device. USB provides four different types of data transfers: *control, bulk, interrupt*, and *isochronous*. The last three provide different tradeoffs between bandwidth, response time and reliability.

- The host uses control transfers to obtain basic information (called descriptors) of a USB device and to read or set the status and address of the device. All USB devices must support control transfers.
- The bulk transfers are designed to deliver relatively large but bursty data. It provides high bandwidth but requires the application to tolerate a long delay if the busy is busy. Printers, scanners, and mass storage devices use bulk transfer.
- For interrupt transfers,, the host periodically queries a USB device for data. It provides less bandwidth but the maximum latency is limited to the period between two consecutive queries. Mice and keyboards use interrupt transfer.
- The isochronous transfers provide guaranteed latency but are unreliable (no error detection code). Microphones and web cameras often use isochronous transfers.

At the low level, a transfer consists of multiple packets. There are three different packet formats: token packet, data packet and acknowledge packet. Figure 22-27 shows the packet structure of full/low speed. Each packet includes at least a SYNC byte, a PID byte, and EOP field.

- **Synchronization field (SYNC).** The SYNC byte is the first byte of a packet. It is used to ensure that the receiving clock is synchronized to the transmitting clocks in a packet transfer. The value of the SYN byte is `0b00000001`. For full speed, since the idle state is the J state, the D+ and D- wires are in a sequence of "KJKJKJKK" when the SYNC byte is transmitted.

- **Packet identification field (PID)**. The PID byte identifies the type of the packet being sent. The lower four bits the PID bytes are the inversion of the upper four bits. This is designed for error checking. In addition, the least-significant bit (LSB) is sent out first. For example, if the PID field is `0b10000111`, the actual PID code is `0b0001`.
- **Address field (ADDR)**. An ADDR that has 7 bits can address 127 devices (address 0 is reserved). The address is assigned by the host. A device uses address 0 during the initial communication until the host assigns the device an address.
- **Endpoint field (ENDP)**. It has four bits and can identify 16 endpoints within a USB device.
- **Data field**. The length of the data field varies from 0 to 1,023, depending on the transfer type and the USB speed. For example, the data field size is limited to typically 8 bytes in low-speed devices, and to 8, 16, 32 or 64 bytes for control transfers and 64 bytes for interrupt transfer in full-speed devices.
- **Cyclic redundancy check (CRC) field**. CRC is used to detect payload corruption arising from transmission error. A five-bit CRC secures the address and endpoint information (a total of 11 bits) in a token packet and a 16-bit CRC checks the validity of the data payload (up to 1024 bytes) in a data packet. The basic idea of CRC calculation involves three steps: first treat the data to be protected as a binary number, then divide it by another predefined binary number, and finally make the remainder of the division as the CRC code. The receiver performs the same steps to compare the remainder calculated and the remainder received (*i.e.* CRC code). CRC are typically calculated by hardware circuits for fast performance. In communication, a contiguous sequence of erroneous data bits is called burst errors. An n-bit CRC can detect all single- and double-bit errors, and any single burst error that is shorter than or equal to n bits. It can also detect a fraction $1-2^{-n}$ of all longer burst errors.
- **End of packet field (EOP)**. EOP consists of SEC0 for two time units of a bit and a J-state for one time unit.

A transaction is completed in three steps: a token packet, a data packet and a acknowledge packet.

- First, the host sends a token packet, indicating the recipient, *i.e.* a specified endpoint (ENDPOINT field) of the target USB device (ADDR field), and the transfer direction of the next data packet (packet ID).

- Second, if the packet ID of the token packet is OUT or SETUP, the host sends a data packet to the specified endpoint of the target USB device, and the device must also send an acknowledge packet back to the host to inform the host whether the data packet has been successfully received. If the token packet is an IN packet, the device sends the data packet and the host replies an acknowledge packet.

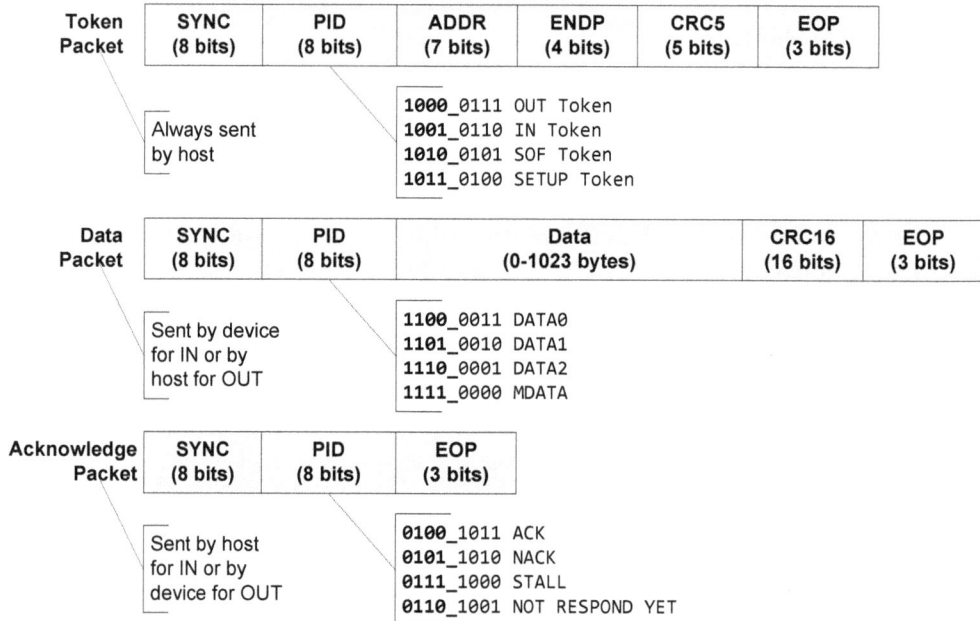

Token Packet	SYNC (8 bits)	PID (8 bits)	ADDR (7 bits)	ENDP (4 bits)	CRC5 (5 bits)	EOP (3 bits)

Always sent by host

```
1000_0111 OUT Token
1001_0110 IN Token
1010_0101 SOF Token
1011_0100 SETUP Token
```

Data Packet	SYNC (8 bits)	PID (8 bits)	Data (0-1023 bytes)	CRC16 (16 bits)	EOP (3 bits)

Sent by device for IN or by host for OUT

```
1100_0011 DATA0
1101_0010 DATA1
1110_0001 DATA2
1111_0000 MDATA
```

Acknowledge Packet	SYNC (8 bits)	PID (8 bits)	EOP (3 bits)

Sent by host for IN or by device for OUT

```
0100_1011 ACK
0101_1010 NACK
0111_1000 STALL
0110_1001 NOT RESPOND YET
```

Figure 22-27. A transaction starts with a token packet sent by the host, then a data packet, and finally a handshake packet.

The USB host broadcasts a start-of-frame (SOF) packet every 1ms for a full-speed bus and every 125μs for a high-speed bus. The host does not expect any USB devices to return any packet. The SOF packets provide time stamps for USB devices to schedule data transfers. For example, the host can use the SOF to inform a USB device to prepare receiving or transmitting one data packet for an isochronous transfer.

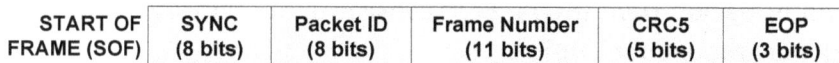

START OF FRAME (SOF)	SYNC (8 bits)	Packet ID (8 bits)	Frame Number (11 bits)	CRC5 (5 bits)	EOP (3 bits)

Figure 22-28. Format of start-of-frame (SOF)

Receiving a packet is usually handled automatically by the USB architecture hardware. The USB architecture automatically detects or generates the SYNC field, identifies the packets addressed to this USB device, performs CRC error checking, and detects or generates the end of packet (EOP) field to conclude a packet.

The architecture hardware automatically generates interrupts for software to handle corresponding events. For example, when CRC checking fails or the response expected from the host has not been received for a long time, the USB hardware generates an interrupt and sets the ERR bit of the USB interrupt status register to 1.

22.4.3 USB Function Layer

A USB device many have multiple functions. For example, a web camera may have three functions: microphone, camera, and storage. A printer may have the functions of printing, scanning, and photocopying. Endpoints are the interface between a function of a USB device and the USB host. Data are transferred between the host and an endpoint. A USB device can have multiple endpoints. All USB devices must support endpoint 0, which is a special endpoint for the host to control USB devices.

A logic communication that takes place between the host and an endpoint is called a pipe or channel. An endpoint contains the endpoint number, transfer type (control, isochronous, bulk, and interrupt), transfer direction (IN and OUT), maximum packet size, and polling intervals in terms of the number of start-of-frames.

22.4.3.1 USB Descriptors

The properties of a USB device are defined in a hierarchy of descriptors. Figure 22-29 shows example descriptors of a USB device. Each device has one and only one device descriptor; each device can have one or more configurations; and each configuration can have multiple interfaces.

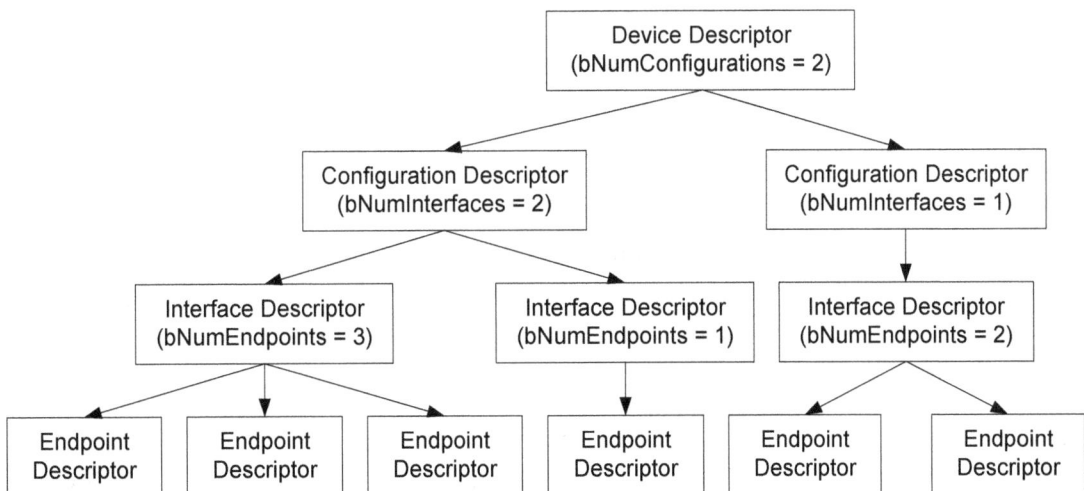

Figure 22-29. An example of hierarchical descriptors

- The device descriptor presents important information of the whole USB device, such as the vendor ID (signed by USB.org) and the product ID (assigned by the manufacturer), the total number of configurations, and the maximum packet size for endpoint 0.

- Although it is uncommon, a device might have multiple configuration descriptors. For example, a USB device might have a configuration for USB power supply and another configuration for battery power supply. When there are multiple configuration descriptors, the USB host must select one. A configuration descriptor contains information such as the total number of interfaces used for this configuration and power requirements.
- An interface descriptor is associated with a specific function of the USB device. A configuration can include a set of interfaces. For example, a web camera can have one interface for its microphone and another interface for its camera. An interface descriptor describes information such as the number of endpoints for this interface, and the class and subclass codes (assigned by USB.org).

The format of each descriptor is shown in Figure 22-30. All descriptors have three common fields:

(1) The *bLength* field specifies the number of bytes in the descriptor.
(2) The *bDescriptor* field indicates the type of descriptor (0x01 = Device, 0x02 = Configuration, 0x04 = Interface, 0x05 = Endpoint).
(3) The *bcdUSB* field states the highest USB version of the device supports in BCD code. For example, `0x0110` is USB 1.1, `0x0200` is USB 2.0, and `0x0300` is USB 3.0. The BCD code is shown in Chapter 18.3.

The *bDeviceClass, bDeviceSubClass* and *bDeviceProtocols* are defined by USB.org. For example, a device class code of 0x09, 0xDC and 0xFF specifies a USB hub, a diagnostic device and a vendor specific device, respectively. When the device class code is 0x00, the interface class code is used to determine the device class.

The *bInterfaceClass* is also predefined by USB.org. For example, the following are some example codes of interface class: audio (0x01), human interface device (0x03), physical interface device (0x05), image (0x06), printer (0x07), mass storage (0x08), smart card (0x0B), content security (0x0D), video (0x0E), personal healthcare (0x0F), and wireless controller (0xE0).

There is also a string descriptor, which defines an array of strings. The *iManufacturer, iProduct, iSerialNumber, iConfiguration, iFunction* and *iInterface* used in the above descriptors are the index to the string array.

Device Descriptor

Field Name	Size	Offset
bLength	1	0
bDescriptorType	1	1
bcdUSB	2	2
bDeviceClass	1	4
bDeviceSubClass	1	5
bDeviceProtocol	1	6
bMaxPacketSize	1	7
idVendor	2	8
idProduct	2	10
bcdDevice	2	12
iManufacturer	1	14
iProduct	1	15
iSerialNumber	1	16
bNumConfigurations	1	17

Configuration Descriptor

Field Name	Size	Offset
bLength	1	0
bDescriptorType	1	1
wTotalLenght	2	2
bNumInterfaces	1	4
bConfigurationValue	1	5
iConfiguration	1	6
bmAttributes	1	7
bMaxPower	1	8

Interface Descriptor

Field Name	Size	Offset
bLength	1	0
bDescriptorType	1	1
bInterfaceNumber	1	2
bAlternateSetting	1	3
bNumEndpoints	1	4
bInterfaceClass	1	5
bInterfaceSubClass	1	6
bInterfaceProtocol	1	7
iInterface	1	8

Endpoint Descriptor

Field Name	Size	Offset
bLength	1	0
bDescriptorType	1	1
bEndpointAddress	1	2
bmAttributes	1	3
wMaxPacketSize	2	4
bInterval	1	6

String Descriptor

Field Name	Size	Offset
bLength	1	0
bDescriptorType	1	1
wLANGID[0]	2	2
wLANGID[1]	2	4
wLANGID[x]	2	6

Field Name	Size	Offset
bLength	1	0
bDescriptorType	1	1
bString	n	2

Figure 22-30. Format of device, configuration, interface and endpoint descriptor

22.4.3.2 Endpoint-Oriented Communication

A transfer over USB can be identified by a three-tuple: device address, endpoint, and direction. Every device must support endpoint 0, which is for the host to control and set up the device.

As shown in Figure 22-31, the web camera has four endpoints in the first configuration.

- Endpoint 0 is for the host to control the device.
- Endpoint 1 forms a channel to access the microphone, endpoint 1 is to access the camera.
- Endpoint 2 is to access the storage.

In order to meet time constraints, isochronous transfers are used to transmit audio and video signals from endpoint 1 and 2 to the host. Bulk transfers are used for endpoint 3 IN and OUT to store and retrieve data. The web camera can have a second configuration, which includes another set of functions. The host decides which configuration is to be used.

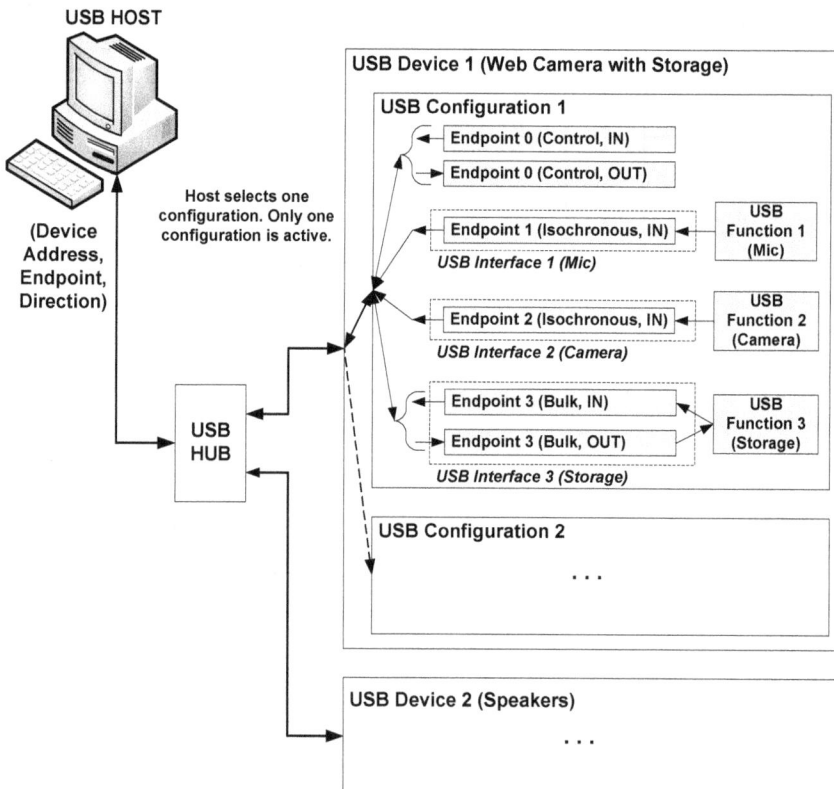

Figure 22-31. A configuration can have multiple functions (such as microphone, camera, and storage). All communications take place between the host and the endpoints of the device.

22.4.3.3 USB Enumeration

USB enumeration is a process of detecting and identifying a USB device. During a USB enumeration, the host performs the following steps:

1. Detecting a device has been connected. When a USB device is plugged into a host, there is a change on the USB D+ or D- line since one of them is pulled up by the device.
2. Determining the USB speed. As introduced previously, pulling up D- via 1.5KΩ pull-up to 3V indicates a low-speed device. The same pull-up on D+ specifies a high-speed device.
3. Retrieving the device descriptor and determining what device is attached.
4. Retrieving all configuration descriptors. This process may take milliseconds to complete. The host selects one configuration.
5. Retrieving all interface descriptors.
6. Loading the corresponding device driver. This is typically handled by the operating systems on the host. The host typically uses *idVendor* and *idProduct* to match a driver.

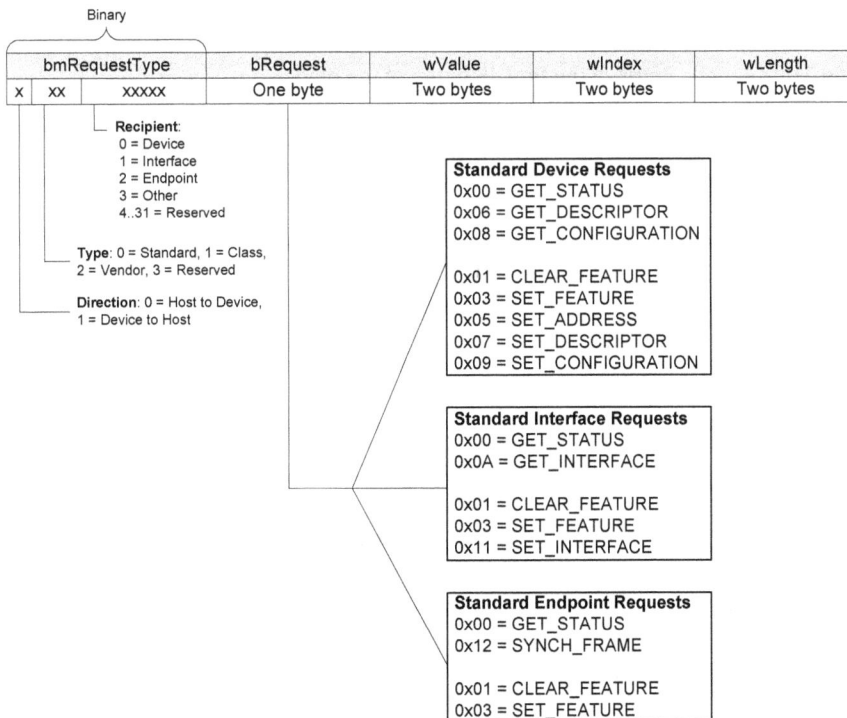

Figure 22-32. Format of setup request

The host sends a series of setup requests to complete the above enumeration process. The device responds to each setup request. Figure 22-32 shows the standardized format of a setup request. Figure 22-33 shows the procedures of retrieving the device description. Note the setup request is encapsulated into the data packet as its payload.

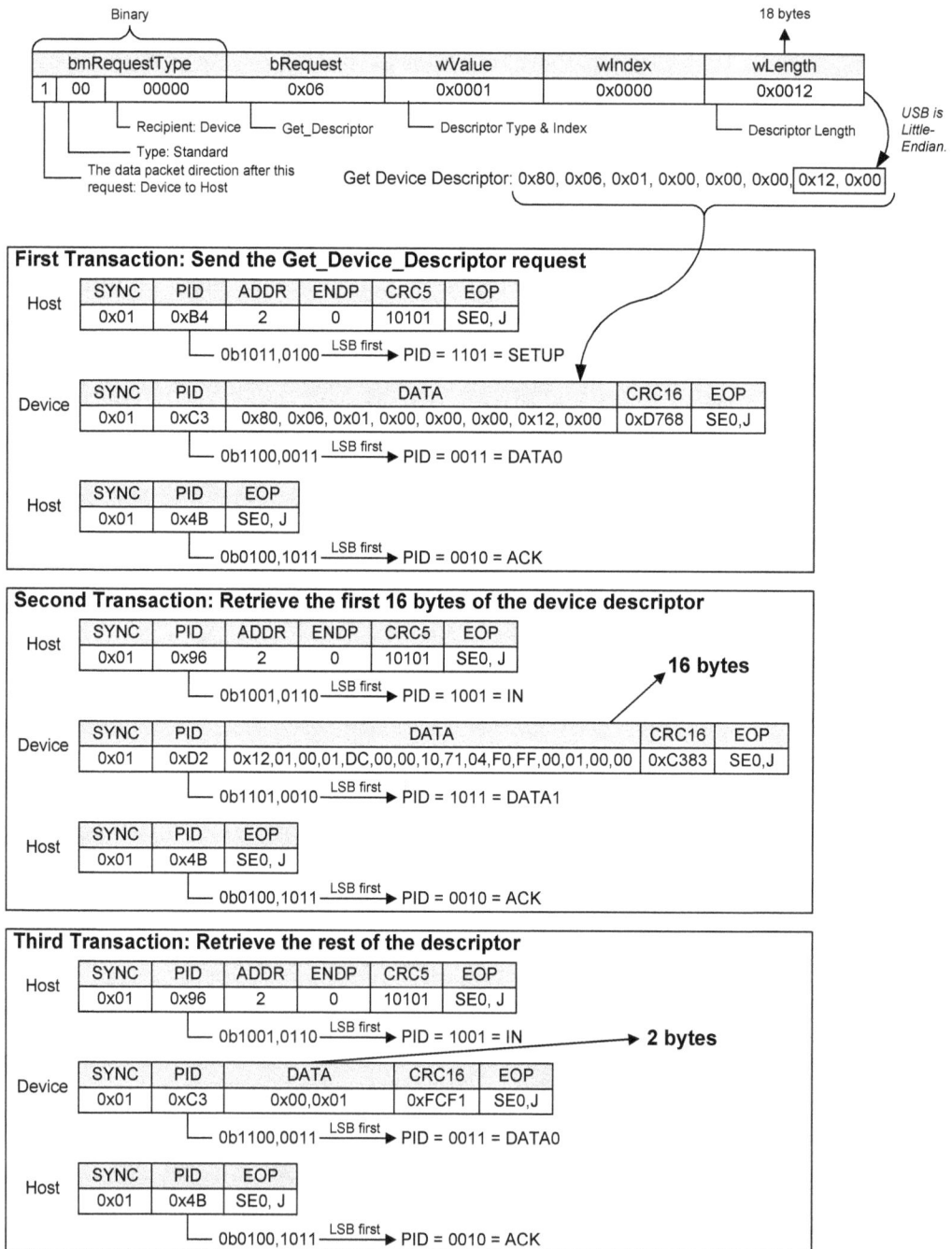

Figure 22-33. Example of sending a get_device_descriptor by using three transactions. Assume the maximum data size is 16 bytes. The request is sent as the payload of the first transaction.

After detecting a USB device is attached, the host waits for at least 100 *ms* to allow the completion of USB device plugging and then issues a reset request. The reset request sets the device into the default state. Initially the default address of a USB device is 0. Each USB device should respond to all requests addressed to 0 before it is assigned a unique address.

It is the host's responsibility to assign a unique address to the USB device. The host sends a SET_ADDRESS request, which includes the assigned address, to the device, as shown in Figure 22-34. The device shall respond to all requests targeted to the assigned address.

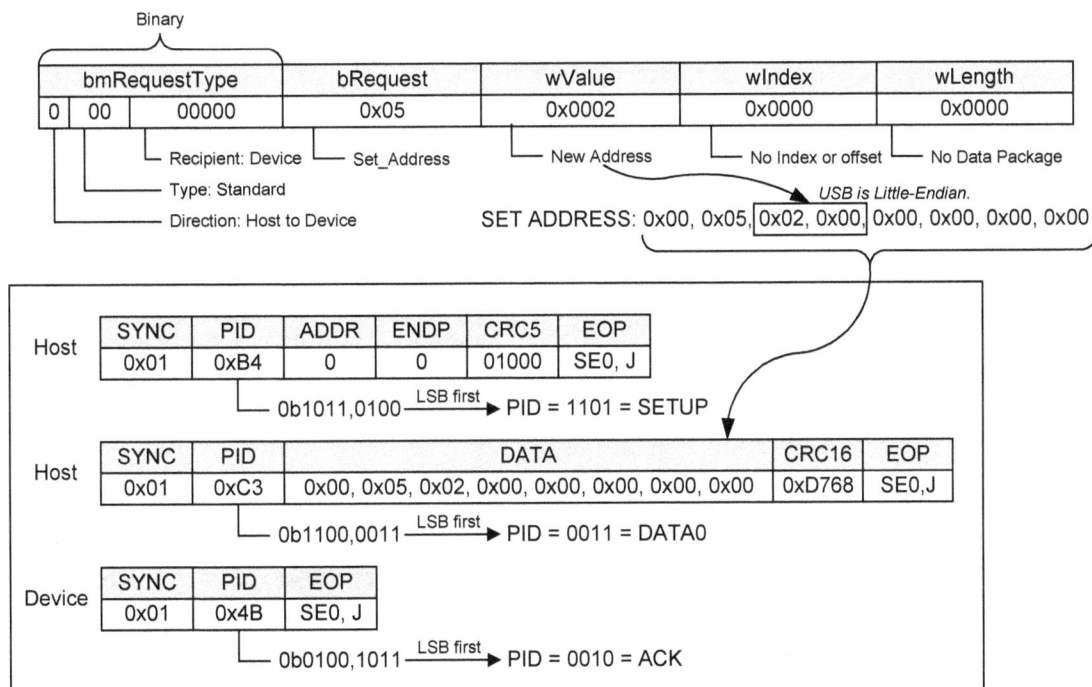

Figure 22-34. Example of sending a set_address request by using one transaction

The enumeration process in Windows operating systems is given in Figure 22-35. The host first uses a simple debouncing technique to wait for the USB device to plug in successfully and become stabilized. Then the host issues a reset request by using the default USB address 0. Since the host initially does not know the packet size supported by the control endpoint (*i.e.* endpoint 0) of the USB device, the host issues two GET_DESCRIPTOR requests for the device descriptor. The first device descriptor request is to find the packet size supported by the device. Before issuing the second device descriptor request, the host sends another reset request to eliminate any confusion that the device may have. Some devices get confused if the host does not let the response to the first device descriptor request complete.

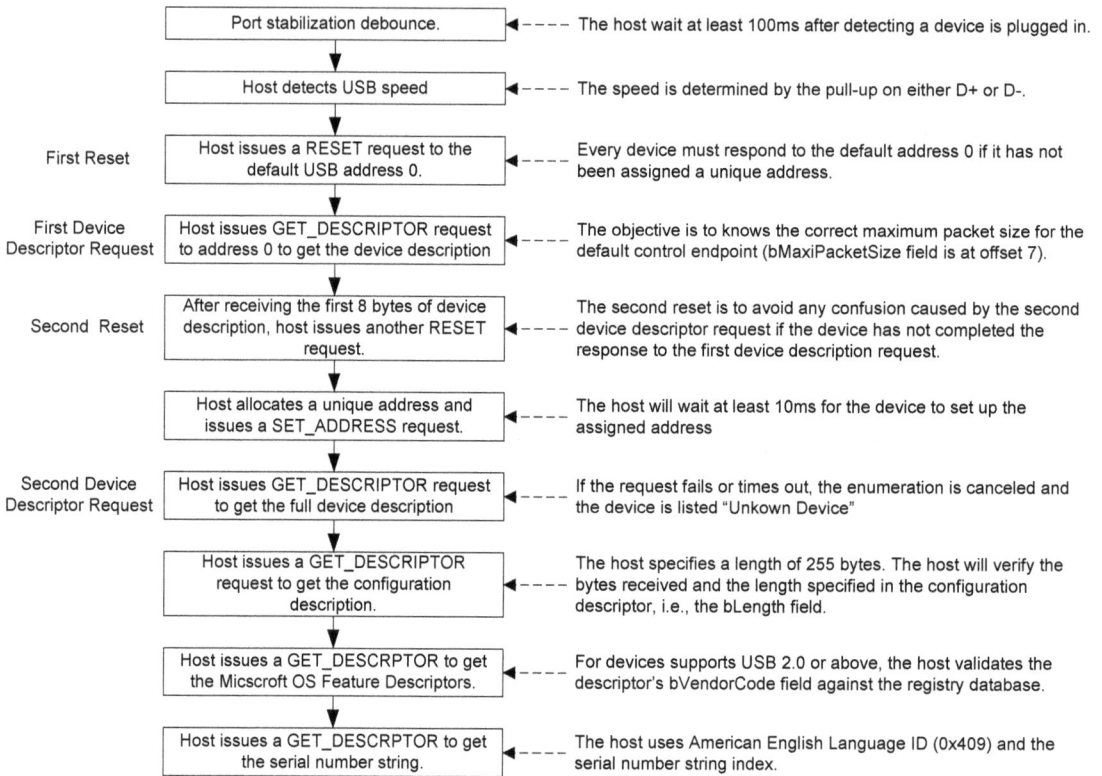

Port stabilization debounce.	◄ – – – – The host wait at least 100ms after detecting a device is plugged in.
Host detects USB speed	◄ – – – – The speed is determined by the pull-up on either D+ or D-.
First Reset — Host issues a RESET request to the default USB address 0.	◄ – – – – Every device must respond to the default address 0 if it has not been assigned a unique address.
First Device Descriptor Request — Host issues GET_DESCRIPTOR request to address 0 to get the device description	◄ – – – – The objective is to knows the correct maximum packet size for the default control endpoint (bMaxiPacketSize field is at offset 7).
Second Reset — After receiving the first 8 bytes of device description, host issues another RESET request.	◄ – – – – The second reset is to avoid any confusion caused by the second device descriptor request if the device has not completed the response to the first device description request.
Host allocates a unique address and issues a SET_ADDRESS request.	◄ – – – – The host will wait at least 10ms for the device to set up the assigned address
Second Device Descriptor Request — Host issues GET_DESCRIPTOR request to get the full device description	◄ – – – – If the request fails or times out, the enumeration is canceled and the device is listed "Unkown Device"
Host issues a GET_DESCRIPTOR request to get the configuration description.	◄ – – – – The host specifies a length of 255 bytes. The host will verify the bytes received and the length specified in the configuration descriptor, i.e., the bLength field.
Host issues a GET_DESCRPTOR to get the Micscroft OS Feature Descriptors.	◄ – – – – For devices supports USB 2.0 or above, the host validates the descriptor's bVendorCode field against the registry database.
Host issues a GET_DESCRPTOR to get the serial number string.	◄ – – – – The host uses American English Language ID (0x409) and the serial number string index.

Figure 22-35. USB enumeration process in Windows

Windows operating systems (OS) also define proprietary descriptors for USB 2.0 and above, which allow the OS to automatically install and configure the device, and make the process of plug and play smooth for users. The OS descriptors contain a variety of vendor-specific information, such as the identification code of a new type of device that incorporates new features of a standard USB device class or subclass. Figure 22-36 shows the format of the request that retrieves a vendor-specific OS descriptor.

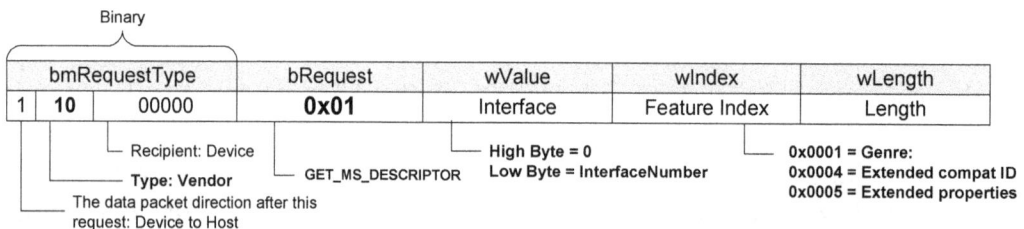

Binary			bRequest	wValue	wIndex	wLength
bmRequestType						
1	10	00000	**0x01**	Interface	Feature Index	Length

Recipient: Device
Type: Vendor
The data packet direction after this request: Device to Host

GET_MS_DESCRIPTOR

High Byte = 0
Low Byte = InterfaceNumber

0x0001 = Genre:
0x0004 = Extended compat ID
0x0005 = Extended properties

Figure 22-36. Format of the request to retrieve an OS descriptor

22.4.4 USB Class Layer

As introduced previously, a USB device can perform multiple logical functions. The device layer allows a host to send a USB request to a given function via endpoints. Each function follows a predefined class protocol to handle USB requests. Examples of standardized USB class protocols include the human interface device (HID), the communications device class (CDC), the personal healthcare device class (PHDC), the mass storage class (MSC), the audio, and the video. The USB class protocols can also be customized by vendors.

The HID class specifies the interactions to human interface devices such as keyboards, mice, and game controllers. This chapter will introduce HID in detail.

The CDC class emulates a virtual UART to interconnect with a serial communication port such as RS-232 COM port. As serial ports are being gradually eliminated on personal computers, more applications rely on the CDC function of USB to communicate devices such as modems, fax machines, and telephony devices.

The PHDC class specifies the standards to interact with personal health devices such as blood pressure monitors, glucose meter, cardiovascular fitness monitor, and weight scales. The protocols are grouped into three themes: health and wellness, disease management, and aging independently. Since low latency and high reliability are very critical to some applications, this class defines meta-data along with the message data so that the host can determine how to transfer data over USB to meet the latency and reliability requirements.

The MSC class is a protocol to access a USB storage device. Modern USB storage devices use bulk transfers in order to achieve high bandwidth. Another important specification is the bootability, which allows a computer to boot from an external USB storage device, instead of an internal hard drive.

The audio class uses isochronous data transfers to stream audio data at a constant rate. For full-speed USB devices, a data frame spans 1 *ms* and a device can transfer 0-1023 bytes per data frame, depending on the application's need. As introduced previously, isochronous transfers have no acknowledge packet and no error-checking ability. Thus transmission error may occur.

The video class provides the function of streaming video in real time like web cameras. Similar to the audio class, the video class also uses isochronous transfers. A video device shall complete a bandwidth negotiation process with the host. This allows the host to determine preferred stream parameters to the device. After the device reports to the host, the maximum bandwidth usage based on given parameters, the host uses the bandwidth information to identify alternate interfaces. An alternative interface is an interface that the device provides to replace the default interface. For example, a video device with various resolutions provides different alternative interfaces that have different bandwidth requirements.

22.4.5 Human Interface Device (HID)

The HID class consists of devices that are used by humans to interact with a computer, such as a mouse, keyboard, touch screen, or game controller.

- One advantage of HID is that the host probably already has device drivers and thus a programmer might not need to write any software for the host.
- One disadvantage of HID is that its bandwidth is relatively low since its maximum packet size for full speed is limited to 64 bytes. Since there is one data transfer per frame (1 *ms*), the bandwidth of HID is limited to 64KB/s.

HID is the interface descriptor and it is not the device descriptor. HID specifies the class information.

- A class code of 0x03 in the interface descriptor indicates that the device is a HID device.
- ALL HID devices must have a control endpoint (endpoint 0), an interrupt IN endpoint, and an optional interrupt OUT endpoint.
- The device data, such letters pressed on a keyboard, are sent to the host via the interrupt IN endpoint.

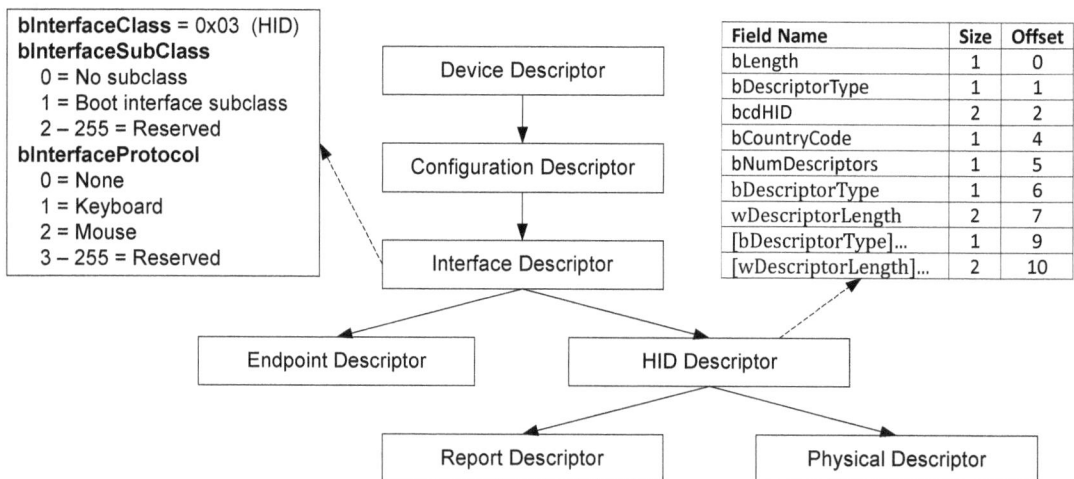

blnterfaceClass = 0x03 (HID)
blnterfaceSubClass
  0 = No subclass
  1 = Boot interface subclass
  2 – 255 = Reserved
blnterfaceProtocol
  0 = None
  1 = Keyboard
  2 = Mouse
  3 – 255 = Reserved

Field Name	Size	Offset
bLength	1	0
bDescriptorType	1	1
bcdHID	2	2
bCountryCode	1	4
bNumDescriptors	1	5
bDescriptorType	1	6
wDescriptorLength	2	7
[bDescriptorType]...	1	9
[wDescriptorLength]...	2	10

Device Descriptor

Configuration Descriptor

Interface Descriptor

Endpoint Descriptor

HID Descriptor

Report Descriptor

Physical Descriptor

Figure 22-37. HID Descriptor

The format of the input data to the host and the output data from the host are defined in a special descriptor called *HID descriptor*.

- Example input data include the pressed key on a keyboard, and the X and Y data from a mouse.
- Example output data include LEDs indicating power status, caps lock or the number lock on a keyboard.

The host requests the HID descriptor during the USB enumeration process. An HID descriptor can include both report and physical descriptors.

- A report descriptor specifies the structure (data size, data type and data meaning) of all data items that a device generates.
- A physical descriptor is optional and describes the part or parts of the human body used to activate the controls.

The objective of both descriptors is to help the USB host parse received data. Two example HID descriptors (a keyboard and a mouse) are given in this section.

The following gives an example report descriptor of a keyboard. The ":" sign is to declare a bit-field inside a structure. Three padding bits are defined in the LED structure to make the length of the structure to be one byte.

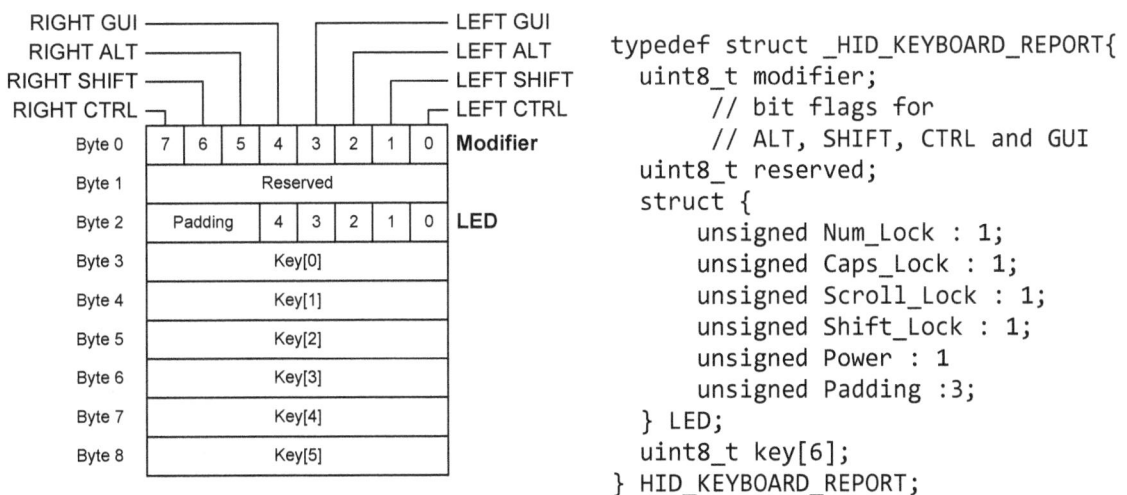

```
typedef struct _HID_KEYBOARD_REPORT{
    uint8_t modifier;
        // bit flags for
        // ALT, SHIFT, CTRL and GUI
    uint8_t reserved;
    struct {
        unsigned Num_Lock : 1;
        unsigned Caps_Lock : 1;
        unsigned Scroll_Lock : 1;
        unsigned Shift_Lock : 1;
        unsigned Power : 1
        unsigned Padding :3;
    } LED;
    uint8_t key[6];
} HID_KEYBOARD_REPORT;
```

Figure 22-38. Report format of a keyboard

HID class-specific requests are used during the enumeration. Supported class-specific requests for HID devices include GET_REPORT, SET_REPORT, GET_IDLE, SET_IDLE, GET_PROTOCOL, and SET_PROTOCOL. Figure 22-39 shows an example of GET_REPORT request to retrieve HID report descriptor.

Get HID Descriptor: 0x81, 0x06, 0x00, 0x22, 0x03, 0x00, 0x72, 0x00

Binary

bmRequestType			bRequest	wValue	wIndex	wLength
1	00	00001	0x06	0x2200	0x0003	0x0072

- Recipient: Interface
- Type: Standard
- The data packet direction after this request: Device to Host
- Get_Descriptor
- Descriptor Type & Index
- Descriptor Length

Figure 22-39. A GET_REPORT request to retrieve HID report descriptor

```
const uint8_t HID_Keyboard_ReportDescriptor[] = {
    0x05, 0x01,     // Usage page (generic desktop)
    0x09, 0x06,     // Usage (keyboard)
    0xA1, 0x01,     // Collection (application)
    0x75, 0x01,     //   Report size (1 bit)
    0x95, 0x08,     //   Report count (8): for 8 modifier bits
    0x05, 0x07,     //   Usage page (key codes)
    0x19, 0xE0,     //   Usage minimum (keyboard left control)
    0x29, 0xE7,     //   Usage maximum (keyboard right GUI)
    0x15, 0x00,     //   Logical minimum (0)
    0x25, 0x01,     //   Logical maximum (1)
    0x81, 0x02,     //   Input (data, variable, absolute)
    0x95, 0x01,     //   Report count (1): for reserved byte
    0x75, 0x08,     //   Report size (8 bits)
    0x81, 0x03,     //   Input (const, variable, absolute)
    0x95, 0x05,     //   Report count (5), for 5 LED outputs from the host
    0x75, 0x01,     //   Report size (1 bit)
    0x05, 0x08,     //   Usage page (LEDs)
    0x19, 0x01,     //   Usage minimum (number lock)
    0x29, 0x05,     //   Usage maximum (kana)
    0x91, 0x02,     //   Output (data, variable, absolute)
    0x95, 0x01,     //   Report count (1) : LED report padding
    0x75, 0x03,     //   Report size (3 bits)
    0x91, 0x03,     //   Output (const, variable, absolute)
    0x95, 0x06,     //   Report count (6): Key arrays (6 bytes)
    0x75, 0x08,     //   Report size (8 bits)
    0x15, 0x00,     //   Logical minimum (0)
    0x26, 231, 0,   //   Logical maximum (231)
    0x05, 0x07,     //   Usage page (keyboard)
    0x19, 0x00,     //   Usage minimum (reserved)
    0x29, 231,      //   Usage maximum (keyboard application)
    0x81, 0x00,     //   Input (data, array, absolute)
    0xC0            // End collection
};
```

Table 22-10. HID keyboard report descriptor

Each row item in the HID descriptor includes a predefined type and value. For example, the second row in the HID keyboard report descriptor givein in Table 22-10 has a type-value pair "0x09, 0x06",

- 0x09 represents the data type, and
- 0x06 represents the value.

The type 0x09 means the upper byte of the usage definition and the value 0x06 represents keyboard or keypad. The values are predefined, such as 0x02 for mouse, 0x0B for telephony devices, 0x0D for digitizer, and 0x80 for monitor devices.

The HID descriptor defines a report data structure with a total of eight bytes, as shown in Figure 22-38. The first byte of the data structure is a bit map, which includes eight logical flags. It is defined by the following two lines:

```
0x75, 0x01,   //   Report size (1 bit)
0x95, 0x08,   //   Report count (8)
```

The second byte is a reserved byte. The third byte defines five LED outputs from the USB host and three unused padding bits.

```
0x95, 0x05,   //   Report count (5), for 5 LED outputs from the host
0x75, 0x01,   //   Report size (1 bit)
...
0x95, 0x01,   //   Report count (1): LED report padding
0x75, 0x03,   //   Report size (3 bits)
```

Following the LED byte is a byte array, which is used to hold six key values. Note a keyboard does not send an ASCII value to the host when a key is pressed. Instead, it sends the HID key code, as shown in Appendix C.

Note it is often that two key inputs share the same key code. For example, the key code of "a" and "A" is 0x04. They are differentiated by the modifier byte shown in Figure 22-38. For example, when Key[0] = 0x04, it represents "A" if the LEFT SHIFT or RIGHT SHIFT bit is set as 1 in the modifier, and it represents "a" if none of these two bits are set.

The device needs to inform when a key is released. This can be done in two different forms. The first one is that the device sends a report in which all key values are zero. The second one is that the device sends a report in which different key values are stored, implying that previous keys have been released and new keys are pressed.

The following gives an example report of a mouse with three buttons and a wheel. To create a mouse "click", two reports are needed: one is to report the button down (set the corresponding bit of the first byte to 1) and the other is to report the button release (set the corresponding bit of the first byte to 0).

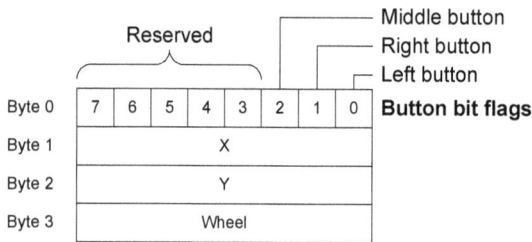

Figure 22-40. Report format of a mouse

```
typedef struct _HID_MOUSE_REPORT{
    struct {
        unsigned Left : 1;
        unsigned Right : 1;
        unsigned Middle : 1;
        unsigned Padding : 5;
    } Buttons;
    uint8_t X;
    uint8_t Y;
    uint8_t Wheel;
} HID_MOUSE_REPORT;
```

```
const uint8_t HID_ReportDescriptor[] = {
    0x05, 0x01, // Usage page (generic desktop)
    0x09, 0x02, // Usage (mouse)
    0xA1, 0x01, // Collection (application)
    0x09, 0x01, //   Usage (pointer)
    0xA1, 0x00, //   Collection (physical)
    0x05, 0x09, //     Usage page (buttons)
    0x19, 0x01, //     Usage minimum (button #1)
    0x29, 0x03, //     Usage maximum (button #3)
    0x15, 0x00, //     Logical minimum (0)
    0x25, 0x01, //     Logical maximum (1)
    0x95, 0x03, //     Report count (3), for middle, right and left buttons
    0x75, 0x01, //     Report size (1 bit)
    0x81, 0x02, //     Input (data, variable, absolute)
    0x95, 0x01, //     Report count (1)
    0x75, 0x05, //     Report size (5 bits), five padding bits
    0x81, 0x01, //     Input (const, variable, absolute)
    0x05, 0x01, //     Usage page (generic desktop)
    0x09, 0x30, //     Usage (X)
    0x09, 0x31, //     Usage (Y)
    0x09, 0x38, //     Usage (wheel)
    0x15, 0x81, //     Logical minimum (-127)
    0x25, 0x7F, //     Logical maximum (127)
    0x75, 0x08, //     Report size (8 bits)
    0x95, 0x02, //     Report count (3), for x, y, and wheel
    0x81, 0x06, //     Input (data, array, absolute)
    0xC0        //   End collection
    0xC0        // End collection
};
```

Table 22-11. HID mouse report descriptor

22.5 Exercises

1. Write an assembly program that periodically collects temperature readings from two TC74 digital temperature sensors. The sensors use I²C protocol.

2. Write an assembly program that periodically collects information from a Wii Nunchuk controller, which uses the I²C standard mode (100 Kbps). A Nunchuk has two push buttons (labeled as C and Z), an 8-bit 2-axis analog joystick (X, Y) and a 10-bit 3-axis accelerometer sensor (X, Y, and Z). It has two slave addresses, 0xA4 for writing and 0xA5 for reading. The data returned from a Nunchuk consists of 6 bytes. Note the communication is encrypted. One possible decoding is

    Data = (Received data XOR 0x17) + 0x17

Address	Data							
0x00	Joystick X							
0x01	Joystick Y							
0x02	Accelerometer X (bit 9 to bit 2)							
0x03	Accelerometer Y (bit 9 to bit 2)							
0x04	Accelerometer Z (bit 9 to bit 2)							
0x05	Accel. Z (bit 1)	Accel. Z (bit 0)	Accel. Y (bit 1)	Accel. Y (bit 0)	Accel. X (bit 1)	Accel. X (bit 0)	C button	Z button

The initialization command has two bytes (0x40, 0x00) and a conversion command has only one byte (0x00). The conversion command is to ask the Nunchuk to collect the data from all of its sensors and make the data ready to transfer. All commands should be sent to the slave address 0xA4. After the conversion command, the six-byte data can read out from the slave address 0xA5.

Joystick X	0x80 = Center, 0x00 = Full left, 0xFF = Full right
Joystick Y	0x80 = Center, 0x00 = Full up, 0xFF = Full down
Acceleration	0 – 1023.
Button	0 = pressed, 1 = released

3. Use the SPI protocol to interact with 3-axis gyroscope (Parallax L3G4200D Module). The gyroscope provides the rate of change in rotation on its X, Y and Z axes.

4. Use the SPI protocol to read a SD memory Card.

5. Implement a HID keyboard device. When the user button of the discovery kit board is pressed, the host PC automatically plays a YouTube video.

6. Implement a HID mouse device. The device automatically draws a picture on the host screen (such as drawing a circle in Paint in Windows).

CHAPTER 23

Multitasking

23.1 Cortex-M3 Processor Mode and Privilege

Cortex-M3 processors have two modes: handler mode and thread mode. On reset, the processor defaults to the thread mode. The processor enters the handler mode when an exception occurs.

The stack pointer r14 (SP) is a shadow of two registers: the main stack pointer (MSP) and the process stack pointer register (PSP). In the handler mode, the push and pop stack operations use MSP. In the thread mode, the push and pop operations can use either MSP or PSP. On reset, MSP is the default active stack.

There are two approaches to select MSP or PSP in the thread mode. First, bit[1] of the control register can select either MSP or PSP. If bit[1] is 0, then MSP is used in the thread mode. Otherwise, PSP is used in the thread mode. Second, when returning from an interrupt service routine, setting the LR register to different values can make the process to choose MSP or PSP. When exiting an interrupt service routine, the processor transits from the handler mode to the thread mode. At this time, MSP is selected as the current active stack if LR has a value of 0xFFFFFFF9, and PSP is selected if LR is 0xFFFFFFFD.

In addition, the processor can be either in a privileged or unprivileged state. While in the privileged state all resources can be accessed by the software, the unprivileged state presents the software from accessing some resources. The handler mode is always in the privileged state. However, the thread mode can be either privileged or unprivileged depending on the bit 0 of the control register. When the processor is reset, the processor enters the privileged thread mode by default.

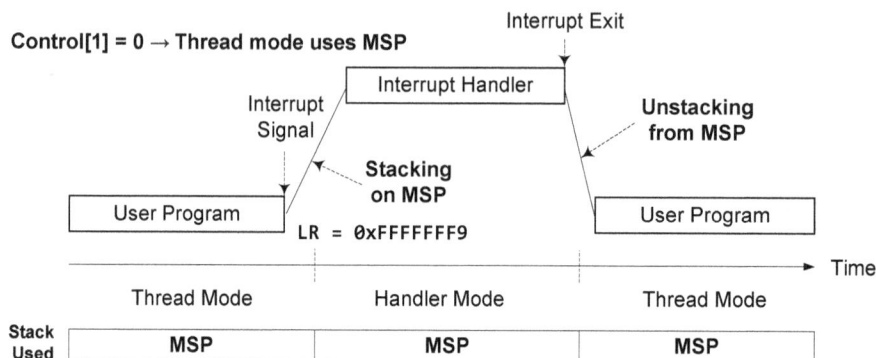

Figure 23-1. If control[1] = 0, then SP = MSP in thread mode, and SP = MSP and LR = 0xFFFFFFF9 in interrupt handler

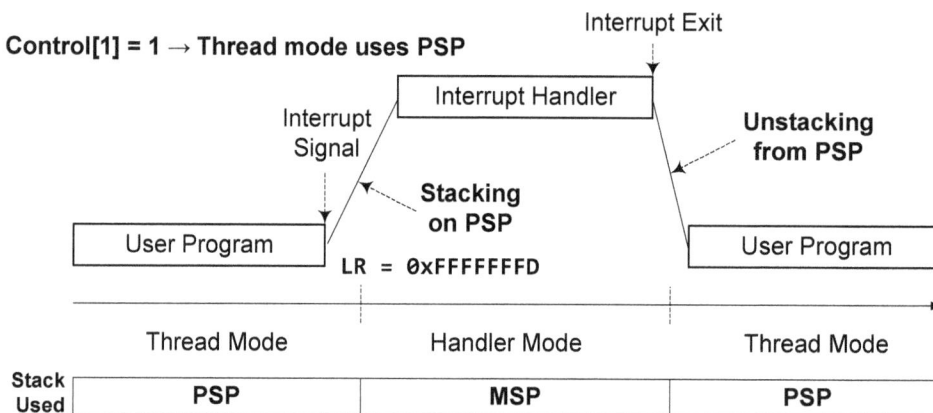

Figure 23-2. If control[1] = 1, then SP = PSP in thread mode, and SP = MSP and LR = 0xFFFFFFFD in interrupt handler

When the control[1] is 0, MSP is used as the stack for both the user program and the interrupt handler. When entering the interrupt handler, the link register (LR) is initialized as 0xFFFFFFF9 to indicate that the automatic unstacking should use MSP on interrupt exit.

	0	1
Bit 0 of Control Register	Thread mode is privileged.	Thread mode is unprivileged.
Bit 1 of Control Register	Thread mode uses MSP as the current stack pointer.	Thread mode uses PSP as the current stack pointer.

Table 23-1. Change privilege of thread mode

However, when the control[1] is 1, PSP is used in the thread mode and MSP is used in the handler mode. The automatic stacking and unstacking for the interrupt handler are performed based on PSP. If the interrupt handler uses push or pop instructions, these instructions then use MSP. LR is initialized to 0xFFFFFFFD to indicate that the automatic unstacking on interrupt exit should use PSP.

The following program gives an example how to change the processor stack and privilege for the thread mode.

```
// Return the content of the control register
__asm uint32_t get_CONTROL(void) {
    MRS r0, control   ; Move to register from status register
    BX lr
}

// Set the content of the control register value
__asm void set_CONTROL(uint32_t control) {
    MSR control, r0   ; Move to status register from register
    BX lr
}
```
Example 23-1. Change the processor's default stack and the privilege of thread mode

23.2 Supervisor Call (SVC)

A software program can be run at the privileged state or user (unprivileged) state. When the processor is in the unprivileged state, the program cannot directly execute privileged instructions and has limited access to processor resources. For example, the program cannot change the processor state via the CPS instruction, it cannot change the system timer, and it has restricted access to memory, peripherals, or the processor status registers.

Supporting privileged and user states enhances the reliability and security of embedded systems. For example, certain areas of memory address space or peripheral I/O registers can only be accessed when the code is run in the privileged state. In addition, a user program running in the unprivileged state cannot change the processor to the privileged state, thus these restrictions cannot be bypassed. However, in order to allow a user program running at the unprivileged state to request some system level service that requires the processor to be at the privileged state, software interrupts enable a user program to call for a privilege service without violating the restrictions.

The user program uses the supervisor call (SVC) instruction to execute privileged instructions. SVC can generate an exception, which immediately turns the processor into the privileged state. The user program can pass parameters to the SVC handler.

One important parameter is the SVC number, which provides a convenient approach to the SVC handler to run different services. For example, the instruction "SVC #0x01" passes the immediate number 1 to the SVC handler. Following the standard of packing and unstacking, eight registers, including the program counter (PC), are pushed into the stack before *SVC_Handler* runs, and popped out from the stack when the SVC handler exits, as shown below.

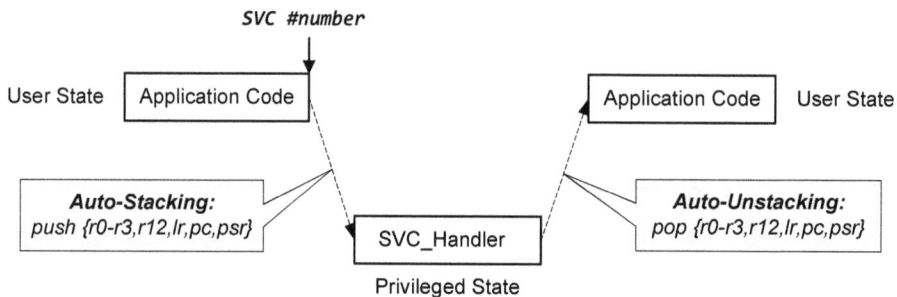

Figure 23-3. Process of stacking and unstacking when SVC interrupt handler is called

If the SVC interrupt performs critical operations, such as accessing some shared resources or data, all interrupts should be disabled when the processor is serving a SVC interrupt. This is to prevent the SVC interrupt handler from been temporally stopped by some interrupt with higher urgency. The pseudo instruction "CPSID I" is executed on the entry to the SVC interrupt handler to disable all interrupts excluding hard faults and non-maskable interrupts. When the SVC handler exits, it runs the pseudo instruction "CPSIE I" to enable all interrupts. CSPID and CPSIE instructions are introduced in Chapter 12.3.3.

> "Don't interrupt me while I'm interrupting."
>
> Winston Churchill,
> British politician

The SVC handler can retrieve the previous PC from the stack, which points to the instruction before the SVC handler starts. In this case, it is the SVC instruction. After retrieving PC, the SVC handler can retrieve the SVC instruction and obtain the 8-bit SVC number directly from the SVC instruction. Table 23-2 shows the format of the SVC instruction.

Instruction	15	14	13	12	11	10	9	8	7	6	5	4	3	2	1	0
SVC	1	1	0	1	1	1	1	1				imm8				

Table 23-2. Instruction format of SVC instruction

In the following example, the SVC handler selectively executes two different kernel functions based on the SVC number. In addition, the user program can pass parameters to the kernel functions via registers (r0 - r3), following the standard protocol of a procedure call.

In addition, this example uses the process stack (PSP) for all assembly codes running in the unprivileged mode. The instruction "MSR psp, r0" sets the content of PSP. The user program uses the instruction "MSR control, r0" to switch the processor to the unprivileged mode. Once the processor is in the unprivileged mode, a user application is not capable of changing the processor back to the privileged mode.

Note there is no corresponding statement in standard C language to call the SVC instruction. Inline assembly is used to make supervisor calls.

```
PSP_Stack_Size   EQU      0x00000400

       AREA    PSP_STACK, NOINIT, READWRITE, ALIGN=3

PSP_Stack_Mem SPACE    PSP_Stack_Size

       AREA    main, CODE, READONLY
       EXPORT  __main
       ENTRY

__main PROC
       ; Initialize PSP
       LDR     r0, =PSP_Stack_Mem
       MSR     psp, r0

       ; Use PSP and set state as unprivileged
       MOV     r0, #0x3            ; bit 0: 0 = privileged, 1 = unprivileged
                                   ; bit 1: 0 = MSP, 1 = PSP
       MSR     control, r0

       ; Prepare arguments for kernel functions
       MOV     r0, #1              ; First argument to kernel function
       MOV     r1, #2              ; Second argument to kernel function
       MOV     r2, #3              ; Third argument to kernel function
       MOV     r3, #4              ; Fourth argument to kernel function

       SVC     0x01                ; Call kernel function 1

       SVC     0x02                ; Call kernel function 2

stop   B       stop
       ENDP
```

```
SVC_Handler PROC
        EXPORT SVC_Handler
        ; Enter handler mode: MSP is used, processor is in privileged state
        CPSID I                 ; Set PRIMASK to disable IRQ
        PUSH  {r4-r8,lr}        ; Those are pushed into MSP

        ; Processor automatically pushes r0-r3, r12, LR, PC, and PSR
        ; into the PSP stack. It is PSP because the processor was using PSP
        ; immediately before the interrupt.
        MRS   r7, psp
        LDR   r8, [r7, #24]     ; read saved PC from the stack
        LDRH  r8, [r8, #-2]     ; load half-word
        BIC   r8, r8, #0xFF00   ; Extract SVC number
                                ; SVC instruction has 16 bits: 0xDF,#imm8
        CMP   r8, #0x01         ; if SVC number = 1, call kernel function 1
        BLEQ  kernel_func_1
        CMP   r8, #0x02         ; if SVC number = 2, call kernel function 2
        BLEQ  kernel_func_2
        POP   {r4-r8, lr}       ; Pop from MSP
        CPSIE I                 ; Clear PRIMASK to enable IRQ
        BX    lr
        ENDP

kernel_func_1 PROC
        ; The processor is in privileged state and MSP is used.
        ; Run privileged instructions
        ; ...
        BX    lr                ; Exit the function
        ENDP

kernel_func_2 PROC
        ; The processor is in privileged state and MSP is used.
        ; Run privileged instructions
        ; ...
        BX    lr                ; Exit the function
        ENDP
        END
```

Example 23-2. Using inline assembly to make supervisor calls

23.3 CPU Scheduling

Many embedded systems use real-time operating systems (RTOS), and one of the fundamental functions of RTOS is to schedule multiple computation tasks on the processor. When there are two or more tasks running at the same time, the scheduling algorithm is a mechanism required to share a processor across multiple threads of execution. Round robin is a simple and widely used scheduling algorithm that processes each task for a fixed period in circular order.

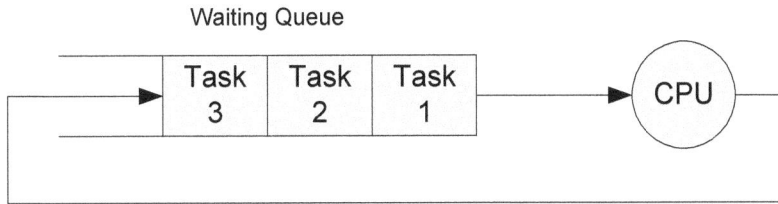

Figure 23-4. Basic concept of CPU scheduling

This section illustrates the implementation of a round-robin scheduling algorithm by using system timers (SysTick), which generates an interrupt after each fixed time interval. In the SysTick handler, the processor stops the current running task and starts to execute the next task.

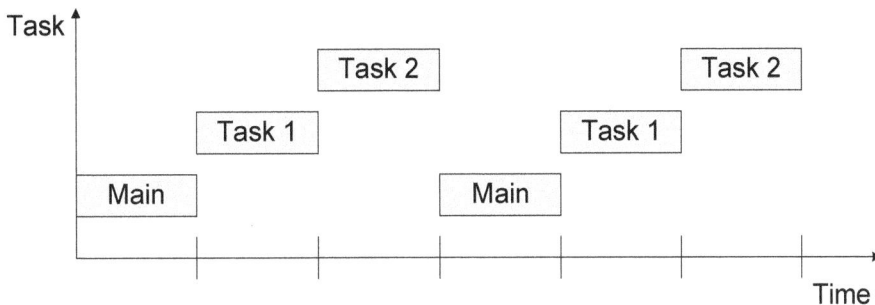

Figure 23-5. Time slices are assigned to tasks in circular order

The processor's time is divided into time slices (small time units with a fixed length), which are assigned to each task in circular order, as shown in Figure 23-5. If the time slice is too small, frequent context switches lead to significant overhead. If the time slice is too large, time-critical tasks might experience a long delay. A generic time slide has 10 to 100 *ms*. When a time slice expires, the processor switches to the next task.

The SysTick handler performs the following two operations during context switch:

(1) The registers, such as the program counter and the stack pointer, used by the current task are stored into the stack so that it can be restarted from the same point at a later time, and

(2) The registers to be used by the new task are restored from the stack to recover the running environment.

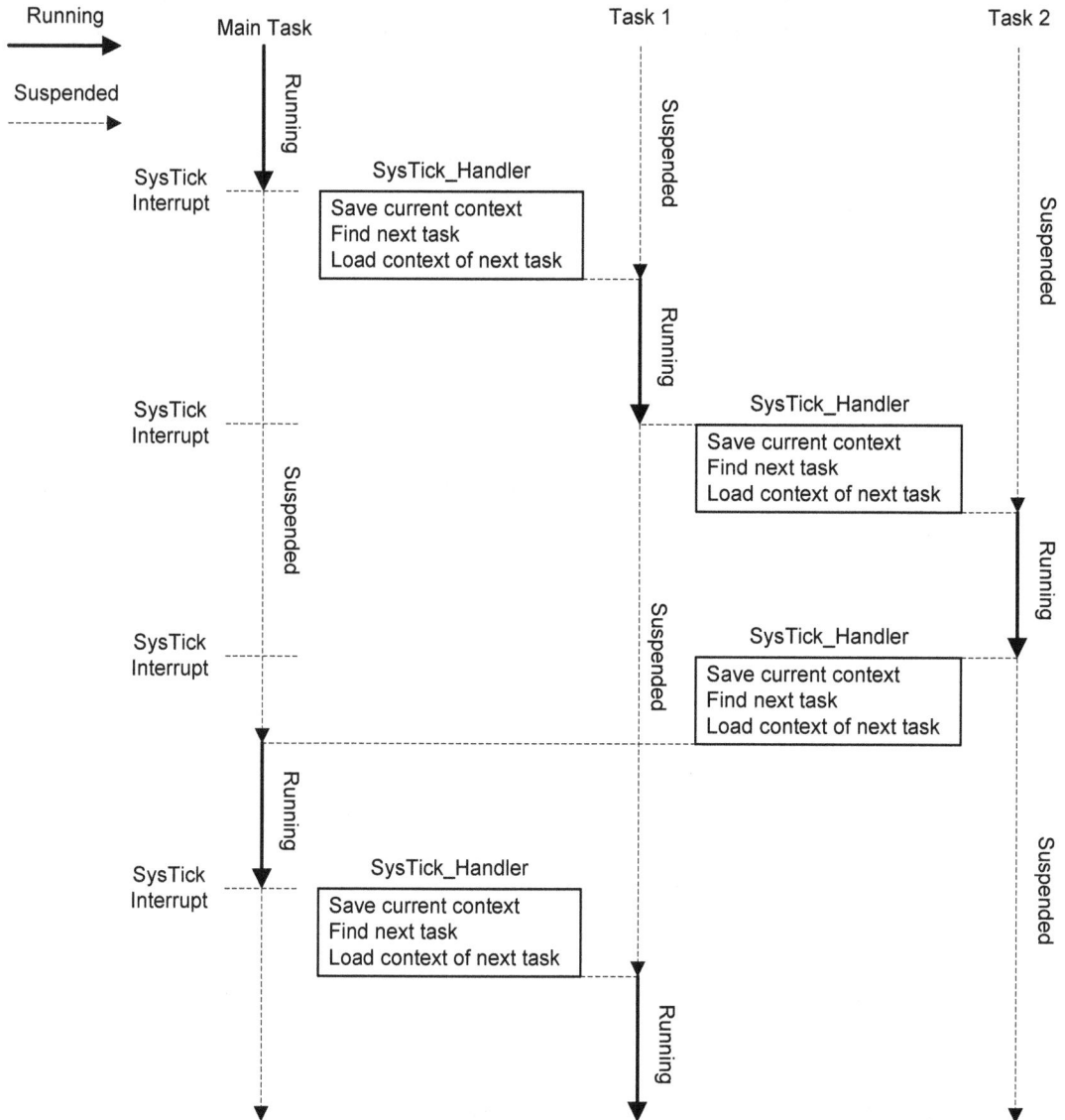

Figure 23-6. The SysTick interrupt service routine performs context switch.

As shown below, each task has an infinite loop and keeps incrementing a global counter after a short time delay. Each task does not exist and never voluntarily give up the control of the processor to other tasks. In fact, in most embedded systems, a task constantly monitors inputs from external sensors, push buttons, or keyboards, updates outputs to the external display or to other systems via communication, or performs computation in response to sensed data or external events. Typically, a task has an infinite loop and never exits.

```
int counter_main = 0;
int counter_task1 = 0;
int counter_task2 = 0;

int main(void){
  int k;

  // Initialization code is not shown here

  while(1){
    counter_main++;              // increase a global counter
    for(k = 0; k < 1000; k++);   // time delay
  }
}

void my_task_1(void *data){
  int i;
  while(1){
    counter_task1 ++;            // increase a global counter
    for(i = 0; i < 1000; i++);   // time delay
  }
}

void my_task_2(void * data){
  int j;
  while(1){
    counter_task2++;             // increase a global counter
    for(j = 0; j < 1000; j++);   // time delay
  }
}
```

Example 23-3. Three endless jobs

This example has a mix of C and assembly languages. We have to uses assembly instructions because some necessary machine operations do not have corresponding C statements. This shows the importance of assembly programming languages.

When serving an interrupt, the processor automatically pushes eight registers:

- the lowest four registers (r0, r1, r2, and r3) , and
- the highest four registers (r12, LR, PSR, and PC).

The processor also automatically pops them back when exiting that interrupt handler. As a result, software only needs to preserve the rest eight registers (r4 - r11) during a context switch. In the following, we assume software pushes eight registers (r4 - r11) into the stack in decreasing order, with r11 being the first and r4 the last.

```
typedef struct {
    // Pushed by software
    uint32_t r4;      // 16ᵗʰ item
    uint32_t r5;      // 15ᵗʰ item
    uint32_t r6;      // 14ᵗʰ item
    uint32_t r7;      // 13ᵗʰ item
    uint32_t r8;      // 12ᵗʰ item
    uint32_t r9;      // 11ᵗʰ item
    uint32_t r10;     // 10ᵗʰ item
    uint32_t r11;     //  9ᵗʰ item
    // Pushed by hardware
    uint32_t r0;      //  8ᵗʰ item
    uint32_t r1;      //  7ᵗʰ item
    uint32_t r2;      //  6ᵗʰ item
    uint32_t r3;      //  5ᵗʰ item
    uint32_t r12;     //  4ᵗʰ item
    uint32_t lr;      //  3ʳᵈ item
    uint32_t pc;      //  2ⁿᵈ item
    uint32_t psr;     //  1ˢᵗ item
} stack_frame_t;
```

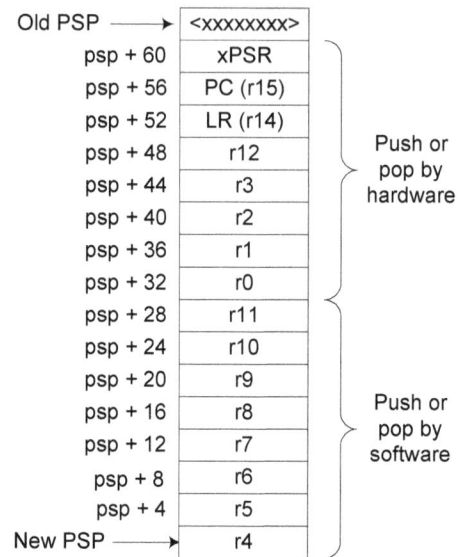

Figure 23-7. Memory layout of a stack frame

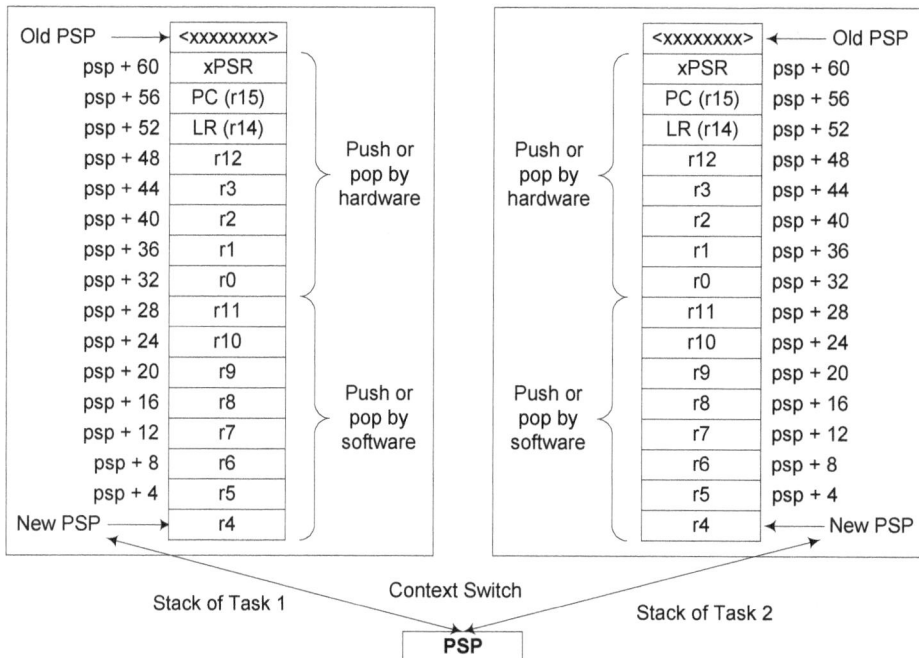

Figure 23-8. The process stack pointer (PSP) can switch between two stacks to perform a context switch.

The *stack_frame* casts a stack frame pointer into a data structure pointer in C language, for the convenience of accessing the content of each individual register pushed in the stack. Note the data structure and the stack grow in opposite directions. When a data item is pushed into the stack, the stack pointer is decremented. However, when a data item is added into a data structure definition, the memory address offset increases. Since the program status register (PSR) is pushed first, the PSR content has the highest memory address and thus it is the last item in the data structure.

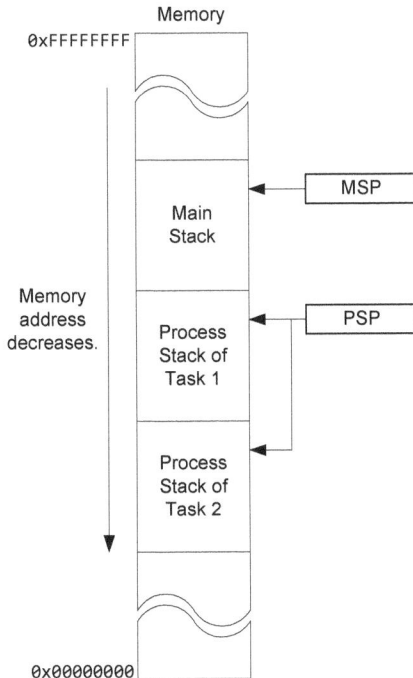

Figure 23-9 Stack allocation

```
// Structure of task_table
typedef struct {
    uint32_t  sp;     // Task stack pointer
    int flags;        // Task status flags
} task_table_t;

// Allocate the task table
task_table_t task_table[3];
// task_table[0]: stack of the main task
// task_table[1]: stack of task 1
// task_table[2]: stack of task 2

// Keep track of which task is running
int current_task = 0;
```

The program has a global task table, recording the stack pointer and status flags for each task, as shown above. Figure 23-9 shows the task allocation of these three tasks. These three stacks are allocated in the memory contiguously. It is assumed that *task_table*[0] is for the main task, *task_table*[1] is for task 1, and *task_table*[2] is for task 2. As introduced in Chapter 23.1, the processor has two stack pointers. We use the main stack (MSP) for the main task and the process stack (PSP) for task 1 and 2.

The following code shows how to cast the stack pointer to a stack frame pointer and access the content of a register stored in the stack directly.

```
stack_frame_t * frame;
frame = (stack_frame_t *)( task_table[i].sp - sizeof(stack_frame_t) );
frame->r0 = 0;
frame->pc = ((uint32_t)func);
task_table[i].sp = (uint32_t) frame;
task_table[i].flags = TASK_FLAG_EXEC | TASK_FLAG_INIT;
```

One important procedure in the above code is to set the saved PC as the memory address of the task function. During the context switch, the SysTick interrupt service routine copies this PC value saved in the stack of this task to the PC register, which instructs the processor to start to execute this task function.

The following is the code of the main task, which initializes the stack and stack table for two tasks, sets up and enables the system timer, keeps incrementing a global variable (*counter_main*) in an infinite loop, and never exits.

```
int main(void){
  int k;
  uint32_t var = 1;

  tasks_init();
  new_task(my_task_1, (uint32_t)&var);  // Initialize task 1 and one argument
  new_task(my_task_2, (uint32_t)&var);  // Initialize task 2 and one argument

  SysTick_Init();                        // See Chapter 12.4 for SysTick
  NVIC_EnableIRQ(SysTick_IRQn);          // Enable SysTick interrupt in NVIC

  while(1){
    counter_main++;                      // Increase the global counter
    for(k = 0; k < 1000; k++);           // Delay
  }
}
```

Since MOV cannot access special-purpose registers, the program has to use MRS and MSR to read or write the PSP and MSP registers, as shown below.

```
__asm uint32_t  get_MSP(void){  // Read main stack pointer
  MRS r0, msp      ; copy msp to r0
  BX  lr           ; r0 holds result returned
}

__asm void set_MSP(uint32_t topStackPointer){  // Write main stack pointer
  MSR msp, r0      ; copy r0 to msp
  BX  lr           ; r0 holds result returned
}

__asm uint32_t  get_PSP(void){  // Read process stack pointer
  MRS r0, psp      ; copy psp to r0
  BX  lr           ; r0 holds result returned
}

__asm void set_PSP(uint32_t topStackPointer){  // Write process stack pointer
  MSR psp, r0      ; copy r0 to psp
  BX  lr           ; r0 holds result returned
}
```

The following shows the function of creating and initializing a new task. The task can take one input argument.

```
void new_task(void (*func)(void*), uint32_t args){
  int i;
  stack_frame_t * frame;
  for(i=1; i < MAX_TASKS; i++){
    if( task_table[i].flags == 0 ){
      frame = (stack_frame_t *)( task_table[i].sp - sizeof(stack_frame_t) );
      frame->r4  = 0;
      frame->r5  = 0;
      frame->r6  = 0;
      frame->r7  = 0;
      frame->r8  = 0;
      frame->r9  = 0;
      frame->r10 = 0;
      frame->r11 = 0;
      frame->r0  = (uint32_t)args;
      frame->r1  = 0;
      frame->r2  = 0;
      frame->r3  = 0;
      frame->r12 = 0;
      frame->pc  = ((uint32_t)func);
      frame->lr  = 0;
      frame->psr = 0x21000000;      // Set default PSR value
      task_table[i].flags =  TASK_FLAG_EXEC | TASK_FLAG_INIT;
      task_table[i].sp    = (uint32_t) frame
      set_PSP(task_table[i].sp);
      break;
    }
  }
}
```

The system timer (SysTick) generates an interrupt after a fixed time interval. The key mission of the SysTick interrupt handler is to perform a context switch, which allows all tasks to take over the control of the processor in a circular order. The handler first disables all interrupts to prevent interrupt overrun, and then checks bit[2] of the link register to identify whether PSP or MSP should be used. After pushing registers r4 to r11, *update_sp()* is called to update the stack table. The subroutine *get_next_task()* uses the round-robin scheduling algorithm to identify the next task to be executed.

The context switch takes the following five steps:
1. Save the registers of the current task (r0 - r15, and psr). Registers from r4 to r11 are pushed into the stack by the instruction "STMDB r0!, {r4-r11}". The other eight registers, including r0 - r3, r12, LR, PSR, and PC, are automatically pushed in to the main stack (MSP) or the process stack (PSP) by the processor during the

auto-stacking process. When an interrupt occurs, if SP is MSP, then these eight registers are automatically pushed into the main process stack. Otherwise, these eight registers are automatically pushed into the process stack.

2. Update the stack pointer and status flag of the stack table for the current task.
3. Search the task table, and identify the next task that is ready to run.
4. Set MSP or PSP to the stack pointer saved in the task table.
5. Recover the registers (r4 - r11) from the stack of the next task. Note the other eight registers are automatically recovered from the stack by hardware when the SysTick handler exists.

```
__asm void SysTick_Handler(void){
    IMPORT get_next_task
    IMPORT update_sp

    ; Before entering the handler, eight registers (r0-r3, r12, LR, PSR, and
    ; PC) have already been pushed automatically into the stack into the main
    ; stack or the process stack.

    CPSID   I                   ; Set PRIMASK to disable IRQ

    ; save the context of current task
    TST     lr, #0x04           ; LR=0xFFFFFFF9 -> MSP; LR->0xFFFFFFFD -> PSP
    MRSEQ   r0, msp             ; Get MSP if LR = 0xFFFFFFF9
    MRSNE   r0, psp             ; Get PSP if LR = 0xFFFFFFFD
    STMDB   r0!, {r4-r11}       ; Save partial context (r4-r11) into the stack
    MSREQ   msp, r0             ; Update MSP if LR = 0xFFFFFFF9
    MSRNE   psp, r0             ; Update PSP if LR = 0xFFFFFFFD

    BL      update_sp;
    BL      get_next_task       ; r0 =  0xFFFFFFF9 or 0xFFFFFFFD
    MOV     lr, r0              ; Set the link register

    ; load the context of new task
    TST     lr, #0x04           ; LR=0xFFFFFFF9 -> MSP; LR->0xFFFFFFFD -> PSP
    MRSEQ   r0, msp             ; Get MSP if LR = 0xFFFFFFF9
    MRSNE   r0, psp             ; Get PSP if LR = 0xFFFFFFFD
    LDMFD   r0!, {r4-r11}       ; Load partial context (r4-r11) from the stack
    MSREQ   msp, r0             ; Update MSP if LR = 0xFFFFFFF9
    MSRNE   psp, r0             ; Update PSP if LR = 0xFFFFFFFD

    CPSIE   I                   ; Clear PRIMASK to enable IRQ
    BX      lr                  ; Trigger unstacking (r0-r3, r12, LR, PSR, PC)
}
```

Either MSP (for the main task) or PSP (for the task 1 and 2) is saved into the stack table.

```
// Update the stack table
void update_sp(void) {
  //Save the current task's stack pointer
  if (current_task == 0) {
    task_table[current_task].sp = get_MSP();
  } else if ( (task_table[current_task].flags & TASK_FLAG_INIT) == 0 ) {
    task_table[current_task].sp = get_PSP();
  }
}
```

The following is the round-robin scheduler, which selects the next task in circular order. The return value is used by the interrupt handler to set up the link register (LR), indicating whether either the main stack or the process stack should be used for automatically unstacking.

```
// Identify the next task to be executed
uint32_t get_next_task(void) {
    current_task++;
    if (current_task == MAX_TASKS){
        current_task = 0;
        set_MSP( task_table[current_task].sp );
        return 0xFFFFFFF9;      // Exit interrupt by using the main stack
    } else if (task_table[current_task].flags & TASK_FLAG_EXEC){
        set_PSP(task_table[current_task].sp);
        if (task_table[current_task].flags & TASK_FLAG_INIT)
            task_table[current_task].flags &= ~TASK_FLAG_INIT;
        return 0xFFFFFFFD;      // Exit interrupt by using the process stack
    }
}
```

23.4 Exercises

1. Immediately after the instruction "SVN #0x01" is executed, draw a memory diagram that shows the stack content.

2. Explain why the interrupts are usually disabled after entering the software interrupt handler.

3. If multiple concurrently running tasks increase the same counter variable, will the counter be incremented correctly? If not, how would you solve this issue?

4. When the processor starts to execute the interrupt handler, the processor automatically performs stacking. How does the processor identify whether MSP or PSP is used immediately before the interrupt handler is executed?

Appendix A: Cortex-M3 16-bit Thumb-2 Instruction Encoding

Instruction	15	14	13	12	11	10	9	8	7	6	5	4	3	2	1	0
LSL Rd, Rm, #imm5	0	0	0	0	0	imm5					Rm			Rd		
LSR Rd, Rm, #imm5	0	0	0	0	1	imm5					Rm			Rd		
ASR Rd, Rm, #imm5	0	0	0	1	0	imm5					Rm			Rd		
ADD Rd, Rn, Rm	0	0	0	1	1	0	0	Rm				Rn			Rd	
SUB Rd, Rn, Rm	0	0	0	1	1	0	1	Rm				Rn			Rd	
ADD Rd, Rn, #imm3	0	0	0	1	1	1	0	imm3				Rn			Rd	
SUB Rd, Rn, #imm3	0	0	0	1	1	1	1	imm3				Rn			Rd	
MOV Rd, #imm8	0	0	1	0	0	Rd			imm8							
CMP Rn, #imm8	0	0	1	0	1	Rn			imm8							
ADD Rdn, #imm8	0	0	1	1	0	Rdn			imm8							
SUB Rdn, #imm8	0	0	1	1	1	Rdn			imm8							
AND Rdn, Rm	0	1	0	0	0	0	0	0	0	0	Rm			Rdn		
EOR Rdn, Rm	0	1	0	0	0	0	0	0	0	1	Rm			Rdn		
LSL Rdn, Rm	0	1	0	0	0	0	0	0	1	0	Rm			Rdn		
LSR Rdn, Rm	0	1	0	0	0	0	0	0	1	1	Rm			Rdn		
ASR Rdn, Rm	0	1	0	0	0	0	0	1	0	0	Rm			Rdn		
ADC Rdn, Rm	0	1	0	0	0	0	0	1	0	1	Rm			Rdn		
SBC Rdn, Rm	0	1	0	0	0	0	0	1	1	0	Rm			Rdn		
ROR Rdn, Rm	0	1	0	0	0	0	0	1	1	1	Rm			Rdn		
TST Rm, Rn	0	1	0	0	0	0	1	0	0	0	Rm			Rn		
RSB Rd, Rn, #0	0	1	0	0	0	0	1	0	0	1	Rn			Rd		
CMP Rm, Rn	0	1	0	0	0	0	1	0	1	0	Rm			Rn		
CMN Rm, Rn	0	1	0	0	0	0	1	0	1	1	Rm			Rn		
ORR Rdn, Rm	0	1	0	0	0	0	1	1	0	0	Rm			Rdn		
MUL Rdm, Rn	0	1	0	0	0	0	1	1	0	1	Rn			Rdm		
BIC Rdn, Rm	0	1	0	0	0	0	1	1	1	0	Rm			Rdn		
MVN Rd, Rm	0	1	0	0	0	0	1	1	1	1	Rm			Rd		
ADD Rdn, Rm	0	1	0	0	0	1	0	0	DN	Rm			Rdn			
Unpredictable	0	1	0	0	0	1	0	1	0							
CMP Rm, Rn	0	1	0	0	0	1	0	1	N	Rm			Rn			
MOV Rd, Rm	0	1	0	0	0	1	1	0	D	Rm			Rdn			
BX Rm	0	1	0	0	0	1	1	1	0	Rm			(000)			
BLX Rm	0	1	0	0	0	1	1	1	1	Rm			(000)			
LDR Rt, [pc, #imm8<<2]	0	1	0	0	1	Rt			imm8							
STR Rt, [Rn, Rm]	0	1	0	1	0	0	0	Rm				Rn			Rt	
STRH Rt, [Rn, Rm]	0	1	0	1	0	0	1	Rm				Rn			Rt	
STRB Rt, [Rn, Rm]	0	1	0	1	0	1	0	Rm				Rn			Rt	
LDRSB Rt, [Rn, Rm]	0	1	0	1	0	1	1	Rm				Rn			Rt	
LDR Rt, [Rn, Rm]	0	1	0	1	1	0	0	Rm				Rn			Rt	
LDRH Rt, [Rn, Rm]	0	1	0	1	1	0	1	Rm				Rn			Rt	
LDRB Rt, [Rn, Rm]	0	1	0	1	1	1	0	Rm				Rn			Rt	
LDRSH Rt, [Rn, Rm]	0	1	0	1	1	1	1	Rm				Rn			Rt	
STR Rt, [SP, #imm8<<2]	1	0	0	1	0	Rt			imm8							
LDR Rt, [SP, #imm8<<2]	1	0	0	1	1	Rt			imm8							
STR Rt, [Rn, #imm5<<2]	0	1	1	0	0	imm5					Rn			Rt		
LDR Rt, [Rn, #imm5<<2]	0	1	1	0	1	imm5					Rn			Rt		
LDRH Rt, [Rn, #imm5<<1]	0	1	1	1	0	imm5					Rn			Rt		

Instruction	15	14	13	12	11	10	9	8	7	6	5	4	3	2	1	0
LDRB Rt, [Rn, #imm5<<1]	0	1	1	1	1	imm5					Rn			Rt		
STRH Rt, [Rn, #imm5<<1]	1	0	0	0	0	imm5					Rn			Rt		
LDRH Rt, [Rn, #imm5<<1]	1	0	0	0	1	imm5					Rn			Rt		
CPS iflags	1	0	1	1	0	1	1	0	0	1	1	im	0	0	I	F
ADD SP, SP, #imm7<<2	1	0	1	1	0	0	0	0	0	imm7						
SUB SP, SP, #imm7<<2	1	0	1	1	0	0	0	0	1	imm7						
CB{N}Z Rn, label	1	0	1	1	0	0	0	1	imm5					Rn		
CBZ i:#imm5:0	1	0	1	1	0	0	i	1	imm5					Rn		
SXTH Rd, Rm	1	0	1	1	0	0	1	0	0	0	Rm			Rd		
SXTB Rd, Rm	1	0	1	1	0	0	1	0	0	1	Rm			Rd		
UXTH Rd, Rm	1	0	1	1	0	0	1	0	1	0	Rm			Rd		
UXTB Rd, Rm	1	0	1	1	0	0	1	0	1	1	Rm			Rd		
REV Rd, Rm	1	0	1	1	1	0	1	0	0	0	Rm			Rd		
REV16 Rd, Rm	1	0	1	1	1	0	1	0	0	1	Rm			Rd		
REVSH Rd, Rm	1	0	1	1	1	0	1	0	1	1	Rm			Rd		
CBNZ i:#imm5:0	1	0	1	1	1	0	i	1	imm5					Rn		
POP registers	1	0	1	1	1	1	0	P	register list							
PUSH registers	1	0	1	1	0	1	0	M	register list							
BKPT #imm8	1	0	1	1	1	1	1	0	imm8							
IT{x{y{z}}} firstcond	1	0	1	1	1	1	1	1	firstcond				mask			
NOP	1	0	1	1	1	1	1	1	0	0	0	0	0	0	0	0
YIELD	1	0	1	1	1	1	1	1	0	0	0	1	0	0	0	0
WFE	1	0	1	1	1	1	1	1	0	0	1	0	0	0	0	0
SEV	1	0	1	1	1	1	1	1	0	1	0	0	0	0	0	0
B(cond) #imm8<<1	1	1	0	1	cond				imm8							
SVC #imm8	1	1	0	1	1	1	1	1	imm8							
B #imm11<<1	1	1	1	0	0	imm11										

The condition codes for the branch instruction B are listed as follows:

Condition	Suffix	Description
0000	EQ	EQual
0001	NE	Not Equal
0010	CS/HS	unsigned Higher or Same
0011	CC/LO	unsigned LOwer
0100	MI	MInus (Negative)
0101	PL	PLus (Positive or Zero)
0110	VS	oVerflow Set
0111	VC	oVerflow Clear
1000	HI	unsigned HIgher
1001	LS	unsigned Lower or Same
1010	GE	signed Greater or Equal
1011	LT	signed Less Than
1100	GT	signed Greater Than
1101	LE	signed Less than or Equal
1110	AL	ALways

Appendix B: Cortex-M3 32-bit Thumb-2 Instruction Encoding

Data processing (register)

31 - 24	23	22	21	20	19 - 16	15 - 12	11 - 8	7	6	5	4	3 - 0	Instruction
11111010	0	0	0	S	Rn	1111	Rd	0	0	0	0	Rm	LSL{S} Rd, Rn, Rm
11111010	0	0	1	S	Rn	1111	Rd	0	0	0	0	Rm	LSR{S} Rd, Rn, Rm
11111010	0	1	0	S	Rn	1111	Rd	0	0	0	0	Rm	ASR{S} Rd, Rn, Rm
11111010	0	1	1	S	Rn	1111	Rd	0	0	0	0	Rm	ROR{S} Rd, Rn, Rm
11111010	0	0	0	0	Rn	1111	Rd	1	0	rotate		Rm	SXTAH Rd, Rn, Rm, rotation
11111010	0	0	0	0	1111	1111	Rd	1	0	rotate		Rm	SXTH Rd, Rm, rotation
11111010	0	0	0	1	Rn	1111	Rd	1	0	rotate		Rm	UXTAH Rd, Rn, Rm, rotation
11111010	0	0	0	1	1111	1111	Rd	1	0	rotate		Rm	UXTH Rd, Rm
11111010	0	0	1	0	Rn	1111	Rd	1	0	rotate		Rm	SXTAB16 Rd, Rn, Rm, rotation
11111010	0	0	1	1	Rn	1111	Rd	1	0	rotate		Rm	UXTAB16 Rd, Rn, Rm, rotation
11111010	0	0	1	1	1111	1111	Rd	1	0	rotate		Rm	UXTB16 Rd, Rm, rotation
11111010	0	1	0	0	Rn	1111	Rd	1	0	rotate		Rm	SXTAB Rd, Rn, Rm, rotation
11111010	0	1	0	0	1111	1111	Rd	1	0	rotate		Rm	SXTB Rd, Rm
11111010	0	1	0	1	Rn	1111	Rd	1	0	rotate		Rm	UXTAB Rd, Rn, Rm, rotation
11111010	0	1	0	1	1111	1111	Rd	1	0	rotate		Rm	UXTB Rd, Rm, rotation

- rotate: 00 = no rotation; 01 = ROR #8; 10 = ROR #16; 11 = ROR #24;

Data processing with shifted register

31 - 25	24	23	22	21	20	19 - 16	15	14 - 12	11 - 8	7	6	5	4	3 - 0	Instruction
1110101	0	0	0	0	S	Rn	0	imm3	Rd	imm2	type			Rm	AND{S} Rd, Rn, Rm, shift
1110101	0	0	0	0	1	Rn	0	imm3	1111	imm2	type			Rm	TST Rn, Rm, shift
1110101	0	0	0	1	S	Rn	0	imm3	Rd	imm2	type			Rm	BIC{S} Rd, Rn, Rm, shift
1110101	0	0	1	0	S	Rn	0	imm3	Rd	imm2	type			Rm	ORR{S} Rd, Rn, Rm, shift
1110101	0	0	1	1	S	Rn	0	imm3	Rd	imm2	type			Rm	ORN{S} Rd, Rn, Rm, shift
1110101	0	0	1	1	S	1111	0	imm3	Rd	imm2	type			Rm	MVN{S} Rd, Rm, shift
1110101	0	1	0	0	S	Rn	0	imm3	Rd	imm2	type			Rm	EOR{S} Rd, Rn, Rm, shift
1110101	0	1	1	0	S	Rn	0	imm3	Rd	imm2	0	T		Rm	PKHBT Rd,Rn,Rm,LSL #imm
1110101	0	1	1	0	S	Rn	0	imm3	Rd	imm2	1	T		Rm	PKHTB Rd,Rn,Rm,ASR #imm
1110101	1	0	0	0	S	Rn	0	imm3	Rd	imm2	type			Rm	ADD{S} Rd, Rn, Rm, shift
1110101	1	0	0	0	1	Rn	0	imm3	1111	imm2	type			Rm	CMN Rn, Rm, shift
1110101	1	0	1	0	S	Rn	0	imm3	Rd	imm2	type			Rm	ADC{S} Rd, Rn, Rm, shift
1110101	1	0	1	1	S	Rn	0	imm3	Rd	imm2	type			Rm	SBC{S} Rd, Rn, Rm, shift

- shift amount (5 bits) = imm3:imm2
- shift type: 00 = LSL, 01 = LSR, 10 = ASR, 11 = ROR (if shift amount is non-zero), 11 = RRX (if shift amount is 0)
- PKHBT, PKHTB: A Pack Half-word instruction combines one half-word of its first operand with the other half-word of its shifted second operand. B stands for the bottom half. T stands for the top half.

Data processing (modified immediate)

31 - 25	24	23	22	21	20	19 - 16	15	14 - 12	11 - 8	7 - 0	Instruction
11110i0	0	0	0	0	S	Rn	0	imm3	Rd	imm8	AND{S} Rd, Rn, #const
11110i0	0	0	0	0	1	Rn	0	imm3	1111	imm8	TST Rn, #const
11110i0	0	0	0	1	S	Rn	0	imm3	Rd	imm8	BIC{S} Rd, Rn, #const
11110i0	0	0	1	0	S	Rn	0	imm3	Rd	imm8	ORR{S} Rd, Rn, #const
11110i0	0	0	1	0	S	1111	0	imm3	Rd	imm8	MOV{S} Rd, #const
11110i0	0	0	1	1	S	Rn	0	imm3	Rd	imm8	ORN{S} Rd, Rn, #const
11110i0	0	0	1	1	S	1111	0	imm3	Rd	imm8	MVN{S} Rd, #const
11110i0	0	1	0	0	S	Rn	0	imm3	Rd	imm8	EOR{S} Rd, Rn, #const
11110i0	0	1	0	0	1	Rn	0	imm3	1111	imm8	TEQ Rn, #const
11110i0	1	0	0	0	S	Rn	0	imm3	Rd	imm8	ADD{S} Rd, Rn, #const
11110i0	1	0	0	0	1	Rn	0	imm3	1111	imm8	CMN Rd, Rn, #const
11110i0	1	0	1	0	S	Rn	0	imm3	Rd	imm8	ADC{S} Rd, Rn, #const
11110i0	1	0	1	1	S	Rn	0	imm3	Rd	imm8	SBC{S} Rd, Rn, #const
11110i0	1	1	0	1	S	Rn	0	imm3	Rd	imm8	SUB{S} Rd, Rn, #const
11110i0	1	1	0	1	1	Rn	0	imm3	1111	imm8	CMP Rn, #const
11110i0	1	1	1	0	S	Rn	0	imm3	Rd	imm8	RSB{S} Rd, Rn, #const

- imm12 = i:imm3:imm8
- #const = ThumbExpandImm(imm12, carry_in)

```
ThumbExpandImm(imm12, carry_in){
  if imm12<11:10> == '00' {
    switch(imm12<9:8>){
      case '00':
        imm32 = ZeroExtend(imm12<7:0>, 32);
      case '01':
        imm32 = '00000000' : imm12<7:0> : '00000000' : imm12<7:0>;
      case '10':
        imm32 = imm12<7:0> : '00000000' : imm12<7:0> : '00000000';
      case '11':
        imm32 = imm12<7:0> : imm12<7:0> : imm12<7:0> : imm12<7:0>;
    }
    carry_out = carry_in;
  else {
    unrotated_value = ZeroExtend('1':imm12<6:0>, 32);
    (imm32, carry_out) = ROR_C(unrotated_value, UInt(imm12<11:7>));
  }
  return (imm32, carry_out);
}
```

Multiply, multiply accumulate, and absolute difference

31 - 23	22	21	20	19 - 16	15 - 12	11 - 8	7	6	5	4	3 - 0	Instruction
111110110	0	0	0	Rn	Ra	Rd	0	0	0	0	Rm	MLA Rd, Rn, Rm, Ra
111110110	0	0	0	Rn	1111	Rd	0	0	0	0	Rm	MUL Rd, Rn, Rm
111110110	0	0	0	Rn	Ra	Rd	0	0	0	1	Rm	MLS Rd, Rn, Rm, Ra
111110110	0	0	1	Rn	Ra	Rd	0	0	0	0	Rm	SMLABB Rd, Rn, Rm, Ra
111110110	0	0	1	Rn	Ra	Rd	0	0	0	1	Rm	SMLABT Rd, Rn, Rm, Ra
111110110	0	0	1	Rn	Ra	Rd	0	0	1	0	Rm	SMLATB Rd, Rn, Rm, Ra
111110110	0	0	1	Rn	Ra	Rd	0	0	1	1	Rm	SMLATT Rd, Rn, Rm, Ra
111110110	0	0	1	Rn	1111	Rd	0	0	0	0	Rm	SMULBB Rd, Rn, Rm
111110110	0	0	1	Rn	1111	Rd	0	0	0	1	Rm	SMULBT Rd, Rn, Rm
111110110	0	0	1	Rn	1111	Rd	0	0	1	0	Rm	SMULTB Rd, Rn, Rm
111110110	0	0	1	Rn	1111	Rd	0	0	1	1	Rm	SMULTT Rd, Rn, Rm
111110110	0	1	0	Rn	Ra	Rd	0	0	0	0	Rm	SMLAD Rd, Rn, Rm, Ra
111110110	0	1	0	Rn	Ra	Rd	0	0	0	1	Rm	SMLADX Rd, Rn, Rm, Ra
111110110	0	1	0	Rn	1111	Rd	0	0	0	0	Rm	SMUAD Rd, Rn, Rm
111110110	0	1	0	Rn	1111	Rd	0	0	0	1	Rm	SMUADX Rd, Rn, Rm
111110110	0	1	1	Rn	Ra	Rd	0	0	0	0	Rm	SMLAWB Rd, Rn, Rm, Ra
111110110	0	1	1	Rn	Ra	Rd	0	0	0	1	Rm	SMLAWT Rd, Rn, Rm, Ra
111110110	0	1	1	Rn	1111	Rd	0	0	0	0	Rm	SMULWB Rd, Rn, Rm
111110110	0	1	1	Rn	1111	Rd	0	0	0	1	Rm	SMULWT Rd, Rn, Rm
111110110	1	0	0	Rn	Ra	Rd	0	0	0	0	Rm	SMLSD Rd, Rn, Rm, Ra
111110110	1	0	0	Rn	Ra	Rd	0	0	0	1	Rm	SMLSDX Rd, Rn, Rm, Ra
111110110	1	0	0	Rn	1111	Rd	0	0	0	0	Rm	SMUSD Rd, Rn, Rm
111110110	1	0	0	Rn	1111	Rd	0	0	0	1	Rm	SMUSDX Rd, Rn, Rm
111110110	1	0	1	Rn	Ra	Rd	0	0	0	0	Rm	SMMLA Rd, Rn, Rm, Ra
111110110	1	0	1	Rn	Ra	Rd	0	0	0	1	Rm	SMMLAR Rd, Rn, Rm, Ra
111110110	1	0	1	Rn	1111	Rd	0	0	0	0	Rm	SMMUL Rd, Rn, Rm
111110110	1	0	1	Rn	1111	Rd	0	0	0	1	Rm	SMMULR Rd, Rn, Rm

- **SMLA<x><y>** Rd, Rn, Rm, Ra   ; Signed Multiply Accumulate (half-words)
- **SMUL<x><y>** Rd, Rn, Rm   ; Signed Multiply Accumulate (word by half-word)
- **SMLAW**<y> Rd, Rn, Rm, Ra   ; Signed Multiply Accumulate (word by half-word)
- **SMULW**<y> Rd, Rn, Rm   ; Signed Multiply (word by half-word)
  - If <x> is B, then the bottom half (Rn[15:0]) is used as the first multiply operand.
    If <x> is T, then the top half (Rn[31:16]) is used as the first multiply operand.
  - If <y> is B, then the bottom half (Rm[15:0]) is used as the second multiply operand.
    If <y> is T, then the top half (Rm[31:16]) is used as the second multiply operand.
- **SMLAD{X}** Rd, Rn, Rm, Ra   ; Signed Multiply Accumulate Dual
- **SMLSD{X}** Rd, Rn, Rm, Ra   ; Signed Multiply Subtract Dual
- **SMUAD{X}** Rd, Rn, Rm   ; Signed Dual Multiply Add
- **SMUSD{X}** Rd, Rn, Rm   ; Signed Multiply Subtract Dual
  - If X is present, then the multiplication results are Rn[15:0] × Rm[31:16] and Rn[31:16] × Rm[15:0].
  - If X is omitted, then the multiplication results are Rn[15:0] × Rm[15:0] and Rn[31:16] × Rm[31:16].
- **SMMLA{R}** Rd, Rn, Rm, Ra   ; Signed Most Significant Word Multiply Subtract
- **SMMUL{R}** Rd, Rn, Rm   ; Signed Most Significant Word Multiply
  - If R is present, then the multiplication result is rounded.
  - If the R is omitted, then the multiplication result is truncated.

Long multiply, long multiply accumulate, divide

31 - 23	22	21	20	19 - 16	15 - 12	11 - 8	7	6	5	4	3 - 0	Instruction
111110111	0	0	0	Rn	RdLo	RdHi	0	0	0	0	Rm	SMULL RdLo, RdHi, Rn, Rm
111110111	0	0	1	Rn	1111	Rd	1	1	1	1	Rm	SDIV Rd, Rn, Rm
111110111	0	1	0	Rn	RdLo	RdHi	0	0	0	0	Rm	UMULL RdLo, RdHi, Rn, Rm
111110111	0	1	1	Rn	1111	Rd	1	1	1	1	Rm	UDIV Rd, Rn, Rm
111110111	1	0	0	Rn	RdLo	RdHi	0	0	0	0	Rm	SMLAL RdLo, RdHi, Rn, Rm
111110111	1	0	0	Rn	RdLo	RdHi	1	0	0	0	Rm	SMLALBB RdLo, RdHi, Rn, Rm
111110111	1	0	0	Rn	RdLo	RdHi	1	0	0	1	Rm	SMLALBT RdLo, RdHi, Rn, Rm
111110111	1	0	0	Rn	RdLo	RdHi	1	0	1	0	Rm	SMLALTB RdLo, RdHi, Rn, Rm
111110111	1	0	0	Rn	RdLo	RdHi	1	0	1	1	Rm	SMLALTT RdLo, RdHi, Rn, Rm
111110111	1	0	0	Rn	RdLo	RdHi	1	1	0	0	Rm	SMLALD RdLo, RdHi, Rn, Rm
111110111	1	0	0	Rn	RdLo	RdHi	1	1	0	1	Rm	SMLALDX RdLo, RdHi, Rn, Rm
111110111	1	0	1	Rn	RdLo	RdHi	1	1	0	0	Rm	SMLSLD RdLo, RdHi, Rn, Rm
111110111	1	0	1	Rn	RdLo	RdHi	1	1	0	1	Rm	SMLSLDX RdLo, RdHi, Rn, Rm
111110111	1	1	0	Rn	RdLo	RdHi	0	0	0	0	Rm	UMLAL RdLo, RdHi, Rn, Rm
111110111	1	1	0	Rn	RdLo	RdHi	0	1	1	0	Rm	UMAAL RdLo, RdHi, Rn, Rm

- **SMLAL<x><y>** RdLo, RdHi, Rn, Rm   ; Signed Multiply Accumulate Long (half-words)
    - <x> = B → Rn[15:0] is used.   <x> = T → Rn[31:16] is used.
    - <y> = B → Rm[15:0] is used.   <y> = T → Rm[31:16] is used.
- **SMLALD{X}** RdLo, RdHi, Rn, Rm   ; Signed Multiply Accumulate Long Dual
- **SMLSLD{X}** RdLo, RdHi, Rn, Rm   ; Signed Multiply Subtract Long Dual
    - If X is present, then the multiplication results are Rn[15:0]) × Rm[31:16] and Rn[31:16] × Rm[15:0].
    - If X is omitted, then the multiplication results are Rn[15:0] × Rm[15:0] and Rn[31:16] × Rm[31:16].

Branches and miscellaneous control

31 - 27	26	25 - 22	21	20 - 16		15 - 12	11 - 8			7 - 0		Instruction
11110	0	1110	0	Rn		1000	mask	0	0	SYSm		MSR
11110	0	1110	1	0	1111	1000	0000			00000000		NOP
11110	0	1110	1	0	1111	1000	0000			00000001		YIELD
11110	0	1110	1	0	1111	1000	0000			00000010		WFE
11110	0	1110	1	0	1111	1000	0000			00000011		WFI
11110	0	1110	1	0	1111	1000	0000			00000100		SEV
11110	0	1110	1	0	1111	1000	0000			1111	option	DBG
11110	0	1110	1	1	1111	1000	1111			00101101		CLREX
11110	0	1110	1	1	1111	1000	1111			0100	option	DSB
11110	0	1110	1	1	1111	1000	1111			0101	option	DMB
11110	0	1110	1	1	1111	1000	1111			0110	option	ISB
11110	0	1110	1	0	1111	1000	Rd			SYSm		MRS
11110	S	cond	imm6		1 0 J1 0	J2				imm11		B
11110	S	imm10			1 0 J1 0	J2				imm11		B
11110	S	imm10			1 1 J1 1	J2				imm11		BL

- Unconditional Branch:
    - I1 = NOT(J1 EOR S);   I2 = NOT(J2 EOR S);   PC = PC + SignExtend32(S:I1:I2:imm10:imm11:'0');
- Conditional Branch and Branch and Link (BL)
    - I1 = NOT(J1 EOR S);   I2 = NOT(J2 EOR S);   PC = PC + SignExtend32(S:I1:I2:imm10:imm11:'0');

Load/store multiple

31 - 25	24	23	22	21	20	19 - 16	15	14	13	12 - 0	Instruction
1110100	0	1	0	W	0	Rn	0	M	0	register_list	STM Rn{!},<registers>
1110100	0	1	0	W	1	Rn	P	M	0	register_list	LDM Rn{!},<registers>
1110100	0	1	0	1	1	1101	P	M	0	register_list	POP <registers>
1110100	1	0	0	W	0	Rn	0	M	0	register_list	STMDB Rn{!},<registers>
1110100	1	0	0	W	0	Rn	0	M	0	register_list	STMFD Rn{!},<registers>
1110100	1	0	0	1	0	1101	0	M	0	register_list	PUSH <registers>
1110100	1	0	0	W	1	Rn	P	M	0	register_list	LDMDB Rn{!},<registers>
1110100	1	0	0	W	1	Rn	P	M	0	register_list	LDMEA Rn{!},<registers>

- registers = '0':M:'0':register_list or registers = P:M:'0':register_list.
- If W (writeback) = 1, R[n] = R[n] + 4*BitCount(registers).
- LDMIA and LDMFD are pseudo-instructions for LDM.
- STMEA and STMIA are pseudo-instructions for STM.

Load/store dual or exclusive, table branch

31 - 25	24	23	22	21	20	19 - 16	15 - 12	11 - 8	7	6	5	4	3 - 0	Instruction
1110100	0	0	1	0	0	Rn	Rt	Rd			imm8			STREX Rd, Rt, [Rn, #imm8 << 2]
1110100	0	0	1	0	1	Rn	Rt	1111			imm8			LDREX Rt, [Rn, #imm8 << 2]
1110100	1	U	0	0	0	Rn	Rt	Rt2			imm8			STRD Rt, Rt2, [Rn, #+/-imm8<<2]
1110100	0	U	1	0	0	Rn	Rt	Rt2			imm8			STRD Rt, Rt2, Rn, #+/-imm8<<2
1110100	1	U	1	1	0	Rn	Rt	Rt2			imm8			STRD Rt, Rt2, [Rn, #+/-imm8<<2]!
1110100	1	U	0	0	0	1111	Rt	Rt2			imm8			LDRD Rt, Rt2, [Rn, #+/-imm8<<2]
1110100	0	U	1	0	0	1111	Rt	Rt2			imm8			LDRD Rt, Rt2, Rn, #+/-imm8<<2
1110100	1	U	1	1	0	1111	Rt	Rt2			imm8			LDRD Rt, Rt2, [Rn, #+/-imm8<<2]!
1110100	0	1	1	0	0	Rn	Rt	1111	0	1	0	0	Rd	STREXB Rd, Rt, [Rn]
1110100	0	1	1	0	0	Rn	Rt	1111	0	1	0	1	Rd	STREXH Rd, Rt, [Rn]
1110100	0	1	1	0	1	Rn	1111	0000	0	0	0	0	Rm	TBB [Rn, Rm]
1110100	0	1	1	0	1	Rn	1111	0000	0	0	0	1	Rm	TBH [Rn, Rm, LSL #1]
1110100	0	1	1	0	1	Rn	Rt	1111	0	1	0	0	1111	LDREXB Rt, [Rn]
1110100	0	1	1	0	1	Rn	Rt	1111	0	1	0	1	1111	LDREXH Rt, [Rn]

- If U = 1, then the memory address is [Rn, #imm8 << 2]. Otherwise, it is [Rn, #-imm8 << 2].

Store single data item

31 - 24	23	22	21	20	19 - 16	15 - 12	11 - 6	5	4	3 - 0	Instruction
11111000	1	0	0	0	Rn	Rt		imm12			STRB Rt, [Rn, #imm12]
11111000	0	0	0	0	Rn	Rt	000000	imm2		Rm	STRB Rt, [Rn, Rm, LSL #imm2]
11111000	1	0	1	0	Rn	Rt		imm12			STRH Rt, [Rn, #imm12]
11111000	0	0	1	0	Rn	Rt	000000	imm2		Rm	STRH Rt, [Rn, Rm, LSL #imm2]
11111000	1	1	0	0	Rn	Rt		imm12			STR Rt, [Rn, #imm12]
11111000	0	1	0	0	Rn	Rt	000000	imm2		Rm	STR Rt, [Rn, Rm, LSL #imm2]

Load byte, memory hints

31 - 25	24	23	22 - 20	19 - 16	15 - 12	11	10	9	8	7	6	5	4	3 - 0	Instruction
1111100	0	U	011	1111	Rt				imm12						LDRB Rt, #+/-imm12
1111100	0	1	011	Rn	Rt				imm12						LDRB Rt, [Rn, #imm12]
1111100	0	0	011	Rn	Rt	1	1	1	0			imm8			LDRBT Rt, [Rn, #imm8]
1111100	0	0	011	Rn	Rt	0	0	0	0	0	0	imm2		Rm	LDRB Rt, [Rn, #imm12]
1111100	1	U	011	1111	Rt				imm12						LDRSB Rt, #+/-imm12
1111100	1	1	011	Rn	Rt				imm12						LDRSB Rt, [Rn, #imm12]
1111100	1	0	011	Rn	Rt	1	1	1	0			imm8			LDRSBT Rt, [Rn, #imm8]
1111100	1	0	011	Rn	Rt	0	0	0	0	0	0	imm2		Rm	LDRSB Rt, [Rn, #imm12]
1111100	0	0	001	Rn	1111	0	0	0	0	0	0	imm2		Rm	PLD [Rn, Rm, LSL #imm2]
1111100	0	0	001	Rn	1111	1	1	0	0			imm8			PLD [Rn, #-imm8]
1111100	0	U	001	1111	1111				imm12						PLD #+/-imm12
1111100	0	1	001	Rn	1111				imm12						PLD [Rn, #imm12]
1111100	1	0	001	Rn	1111	1	1	0	0			imm8			PLI [Rn, #-imm8]
1111100	1	0	001	Rn	1111	0	0	0	0	0	0	imm2		Rm	PLI [Rn, Rm, LSL #imm2]
1111100	1	U	001	1111	1111				imm12						PLI #+/-imm12
1111100	1	1	001	Rn	1111				imm12						PLI [Rn, #imm12]

- If U = 1, use #imm12. Otherwise, use #-imm12.
- PLD (Preload Data) and PLI (Preload Instruction) are the only memory hint instructions

Load half-word

31 - 25	24	23	22 - 20	19-16	15-12	11 - 8			7	6	5	4	3 - 0	Instruction
1111100	0	U	011	1111	Rt		imm12							LDRH Rt, #+/-imm12
1111100	0	1	011	Rn	Rt		imm12							LDRH Rt, [Rn, #imm12]
1111100	0	0	011	Rn	Rt	0 0 0	0	0 0			imm2		Rm	LDRH Rt, [Rn, Rm,LSL #imm2]
1111100	0	0	011	Rn	Rt	1 0 1	0				imm8			LDRHT Rt, [Rn]
1111100	0	0	011	Rn	Rt	1 1 U	0				imm8			LDRHT Rt, [Rn,#imm8]
1111100	0	0	011	Rn	Rt	1 0 U	1				imm8			LDRHT Rt, Rn,#imm8
1111100	0	0	011	Rn	Rt	1 1 U	1				imm8			LDRHT Rt, [Rn,#imm8]!
1111100	1	1	011	Rn	Rt		imm12							LDRSH Rt, [Rn, #imm12]
1111100	1	U	011	1111	Rt		imm12							LDRSH Rt, #+/-imm12
1111100	1	0	011	Rn	Rt	0 0 0	0	0 0			imm2		Rm	LDRH Rt, [Rn, Rm,LSL #imm2]
1111100	1	0	011	Rn	Rt	1 1 1	0				imm8			LDRSHT Rt, [Rn,#imm8]

- If U = 1, use #imm; oherwise, use #-imm.

Load word

31 - 25	24	23	22 -20	19 - 16	15-12	11 - 8			7	6	5	4	3 - 0	Instruction
1111100	0	1	101	Rn	Rt		imm12							LDR Rt, [Rn, #imm12]
1111100	0	0	101	Rn	Rt	1 1 1	0				imm8			LDRT Rt, [Rn, #imm8]
1111100	0	0	101	Rn	Rt	0 0 0	0	0 0			imm2		Rm	LDR [Rn, Rm, LSL #imm2]
1111100	0	U	101	1111	Rt		imm12							LDR Rt, #imm12

- Load Register Unprivileged (LDRT)

Coprocessor instructions

31 - 26	25	24	23	22	21	20	19-16	15-12	11 - 8	7-5	4	3-0	Instruction
111011	0	P	U	N	W	0	Rn	CRd	coproc	imm8			STC
111111	0	P	U	N	W	0	Rn	CRd	coproc	imm8			STC2
111011	0	P	U	D	W	1	Rn	CRd	coproc	imm8			LDC (immediate)
111111	0	P	U	D	W	1	Rn	CRd	coproc	imm8			LDC2 (immediate)
111011	0	P	U	D	W	1	1111	CRd	coproc	imm8			LDC (literal)
111111	0	P	U	D	W	1	1111	CRd	coproc	imm8			LDC2(literal)
111011	0	0	0	1	0	0	Rt2	Rt	coproc	opc1		CRm	MCRR
111111	0	0	0	1	0	0	Rt2	Rt	coproc	opc1		CRm	MCRR2
111011	0	0	0	1	0	1	Rt2	Rt	coproc	opc1		CRm	MRRC
111111	0	0	0	1	0	1	Rt2	Rt	coproc	opc1		CRm	MRRC2
111011	1	1	0	opc1			CRn	CRd	coproc	op2	0	CRm	CDP
111111	1	1	0	opc1			CRn	CRd	coproc	op2	0	CRm	CDP2
111011	1	0	opc1			0	CRn	Rt	coproc	op2	1	CRm	MRC
111111	1	0	opc1			0	CRn	Rt	coproc	op2	1	CRm	MRC2
111011	1	0	opc1			1	CRn	Rt	coproc	op2	1	CRm	MRC
111111	1	0	opc1			1	CRn	Rt	coproc	op2	1	CRm	MRC2

- Store Coprocessor (STC)
- Load Coprocessor (LDC)
- Move to Coprocessor from two ARM Registers (MCRR)
- Move to two ARM Registers from Coprocessor (MRRC)
- Move to Coprocessor from ARM Register (MCR)
- Move to ARM Register from Coprocessor (MRC)
- Example Instruction formats:
    - MRC coproc, opc1, Rt, CRn, CRm,opc2
    - LDC{L} coproc, CRd, [Rn,#+/-imm}]   ; Offset. P = 1, W = 0.
    - LDC{L} coproc, CRd, [Rn,#+/-imm>]!   ; Pre-index. P = 1, W = 1.
    - LDC{L} coproc, CRd, [Rn],#+/-imm   ; Post-index. P = 0, W = 1.
    - LDC{L} coproc, CRd, [Rn],   ; Unindexed. P = 0, W = 0, U = 1.
    - LDC{L} coproc, CRd, label   ; Normal form with P = 1, W = 0
    - LDC{L} coproc, CRd, [PC,#-0]   ; Alternative form with P = 1, W = 0

Appendix C: HID Codes of a Keyboard

Code	Usage Name	Code	Usage Name	Code	Usage Name	Code	Usage Name	Code	Usage Name
0x00	Reserved	0x23	6 and ^	0x46	Print Screen	0x69	F14	0x8C	International 6
0x01	Error Roll Over	0x24	7 and &	0x47	Scroll Lock	0x6A	F15	0x8D	International 7
0x02	POST Fail	0x25	8 and *	0x48	Pause	0x6B	F16	0x8E	International 8
0x03	Error Undefined	0x26	9 and (	0x49	Insert	0x6C	F17	0x8F	International 9
0x04	a and A	0x27	0 and)	0x4A	Home	0x6D	F18	0x90	LANG1
0x05	b and B	0x28	Return	0x4B	Page Up	0x6E	F19	0x91	LANG2
0x06	c and C	0x29	ESCAPE	0x4C	Delete Forward	0x6F	F20	0x92	LANG3
0x07	d and D	0x2A	Backspace	0x4D	End	0x70	F21	0x93	LANG4
0x08	e and E	0x2B	Tab	0x4E	Page Down	0x71	F22	0x94	LANG5
0x09	f and F	0x2C	Spacebar	0x4F	Right Arrow	0x72	F23	0x95	LANG6
0x0A	g and G	0x2D	- and _	0x50	Left Arrow	0x73	F24	0x96	LANG7
0x0B	h and H	0x2E	= and +	0x51	Down Arrow	0x74	Execute	0x97	LANG8
0x0C	i and I	0x2F	[and {	0x52	Up Arrow	0x75	Help	0x98	LANG9
0x0D	j and J	0x30	] and }	0x53	Keypad Num Lock and Clear	0x76	Menu	0x99	Alternate Erase
0x0E	k and K	0x31	\ and |	0x54	Keypad /	0x77	Select	0x9A	SysReq Attention
0x0F	l and L	0x32	Non-US # and ~	0x55	Keypad *	0x78	Stop	0x9B	Cancel
0x10	m and M	0x33	; and :	0x56	Keypad -	0x79	Again	0x9C	Clear
0x11	n and N	0x34	' and "	0x57	Keypad +	0x7A	Undo	0x9D	Prior
0x12	o and O	0x35	` and ~	0x58	Keypad Enter	0x7B	Cut	0x9E	Return
0x13	p and P	0x36	Keyboard, and <	0x59	Keypad 1 and End	0x7C	Copy	0x9F	Separator
0x14	q and Q	0x37	. and >	0x5A	Keypad 2 and Down Arrow	0x7D	Paste	0xA0	Out

0x15	r and R	0x38	/ and ?	0x5B	Keypad 3 and Page Down	0x7E	Find	0xA1	Oper
0x16	s and S	0x39	Caps Lock	0x5C	Keypad 4 and Left Arrow	0x7F	Mute	0xA2	Clear/Again
0x17	t and T	0x3A	F1	0x5D	Keypad 5	0x80	Volume Up	0xA3	CrSel/Props
0x18	u and U	0x3B	F2	0x5E	Keypad 6 and Right Arrow	0x81	Volume Down	0xA4	ExSel
0x19	v and V	0x3C	F3	0x5F	Keypad 7 and Home	0x82	Locking Caps Lock	0xE0	Left Control
0x1A	w and W	0x3D	F4	0x60	Keypad 8 and Up Arrow	0x83	Locking Num Lock	0xE1	Left Shift
0x1B	x and X	0x3E	F5	0x61	Keypad 9 and Page Up	0x84	Locking Scroll Lock	0xE2	Left Alt
0x1C	y and Y	0x3F	F6	0x62	Keypad 0 and Insert	0x85	Keypad Comma	0xE3	Left GUI
0x1D	z and Z	0x40	F7	0x63	Keypad . and Delete	0x86	Keypad Equal Sign	0xE4	Right Control
0x1E	1 and !	0x41	F8	0x64	\ and |	0x87	International 1	0xE5	Right Shift
0x1F	2 and @	0x42	F9	0x65	Application	0x88	Internationa 2	0xE6	Right Alt
0x20	3 and #	0x43	F10	0x66	Power	0x89	International 3	0xE7	Right GUI
0x21	4 and $	0x44	F11	0x67	Keypad =	0x8A	International 4		
0x22	5 and %	0x45	F12	0x68	F13	0x8B	International 5		

Bibliography

1. STMicroelectronics. Reference manual, STM32L151xx, STM32L152xx and STM32L162xx Advanced ARM-based 32-bit MCUs, July 2012

2. STMicroelectronics. UM1079 User Manual, STM32L-DISCOVERY, Doc ID 018789 Rev 2, June 2011

3. STMicroelectronics. STM32L151xx STM32L152xx Data Sheets, January 2012

4. ARM Limited. Cortex-M3 Technical Reference Manual, Revision: r1p1, 2006

5. ARM Limited. ARMv7-M Architecture Reference Manual, Fourth release, 2010

6. ARM Limited. Cortex-M3 Devices, Generic User Guide, 2010

7. ARM Limited. ELF for the ARM Architecture, ARM IHI 0044D, 10/28/2009

8. ARM Limited. Application Binary Interface for the ARM Architecture, The Base Standard, ARM IHI 0036B, 11/30/2010

9. ARM Limited. Procedure Call Standard for the ARM Architecture, ARM IHI 0042D, 8/16/2009

10. ARM Limited. ARM Compiler Toolchain, Version 5.02, Assembler Reference, ARM DUI 0489H (ID070912), 2010-2012

11. ARM Limited. ARM Compiler Toolchain, Version 5.02, Compiler Reference, ARM DUI 0491H (ID070912), 2010-2012

12. ARM Limited. ARM Developer Suite, Version 1.2, Developer Guide, ARM DUI 0056D, 1999-2001

13. Peter Wegner, "A Technique for Counting Ones in a Binary Computer," Communications of the ACM, Page 322, 1960

14. IEEE Std 754 – 2008, IEEE Standard for Floating-Point Arithmetic, IEEE Computer Society, 2008

15. USB Device Class Definition for Human Interface Devices (HID), Firmware Specification, 6/27/2001, Version 1.11, www.USB.org

16. USB HID Usage Tables, 10/28/2004, Version 1.12, www.USB.org

17. Universal Serial Bus Specification, Revision 2.0, 5/27/2000, www.USB.org

18. USB in a Nutshell. Making Sense of the USB Standard. www.beyondlogic.org, 3/10/2014

19. Jan Axelson, USB Complete, The Developer's Guide, Fourth Edition, ISBN 978-1931448086, June 2009

20. ATMEL Application Note, AVR065: LCD Driver for the STK502, Rev. 2530E-AVR-07/08

21. Microchip, AN907 Stepping Motors Fundamentals, DS00907A, 2004

22. Texas Instruments, Data Sheet of ULN2803N Darlington Transistor Array, July 2007

23. STMicroelectronics. AN2604 Application note, STM32F101xx and STM32F103xx RTC calibration, August 2007

24. STMicroelectronics. AN3371 Application note, Using the hardware real-time clock (RTC) in STM32 F0, F2, F3, F4 and L1 series of MCUs, Doc ID 018624 Rev 5, September 2012

25. Robert H. Walden, Analog-to-Digital Converter Survey and Analysis, IEEE JOURNAL ON SELECTED AREAS IN COMMUNICATIONS, VOL. 17, NO. 4, APRIL 1999

26. Walt Kester, ADC Architectures II: Successive Approximation ADCs, Analog Devices, MT-021 Tutorial, Rev.A, 10/08, WK

27. ATMEL, Atmel AVR127: Understanding ADC parameters, Application Note Rev. 8456A-AVR-11/11, 2011

28. Walt Kester, Which ADC Architecture Is Right for Your Application? Analog Dialogue 39-06, June, 2005

29. STMicroelectronics. AN3126 Application note, Audio and waveform generation using the DAC in STM32 microcontroller families, Doc ID 16895 Rev 1, May 2010

30. Walt Kester, Basic DAC Architectures II: Binary DACs, Analog Devices MT-015 Tutorial, Rev.A, 10/08, WK, 2008

31. Phillip L. De Leon, Computer Music in Undergraduate Digital Signal Processing, Annual Conference on Interactive Learning in Engineering Education, Session 76A3, 2000

32. Miller Puckette. The Theory and Technique of Electronic Music. World Scientific Publishing Co., Inc., River Edge, NJ, USA. 2007

33. Leens, F., An introduction to I2C and SPI protocols, Instrumentation & Measurement Magazine, IEEE , vol.12, no.1, pp.8,13, February 2009

34. STMicroelectronics. AN2824 Application note, STM32F10xxx I2C optimized examples, Doc ID 15021 Rev 4, June 2010

35. Microchip, TC74 Datasheet, Tiny Serial Digital Thermal Sensor, DS21462C, 2002

36. NXP Semiconductors, UM10204 I2C-bus specification and user manual, Rev. 6, 4 April 2014 User manual

37. UBICOM, Serial Peripheral Interface (SPI) and Microwire/Plus implementation Using the SX Communications Controller, Application Note 20, November 2000

38. Motorola, Inc. SPI Block Guide V03.06, Original Release Date: 21 JAN 2000, Revised: 04 FEB 2003

39. STMicroelectronics. AN2159 Application note, SPI protocol for STPM01/STPM10 metering devices, Doc ID 11400 Rev 3, July 2010

40. FTDI Chip. FT232R USB UART IC Datasheet Version 2.09, Document No.: FT_000053, 2010

41. Microchip, Section 18. USART, DS31018A, 1997
42. STMicroelectronics. AN3155 Application note, USART protocol used in the STM32 bootloader, Doc ID 17066 Rev 2, April 2010
43. Joseph Yiu and Andrew Frame, ARM Cortex-M3 Processor Software Development for ARM7TDMI Processor Programmers, White Paper, July 2009
44. Tyler Gilbert, Make the most out of Cortex-M3's preemptive context switches, EE Times-India, 2011
45. Micriµm. µC/OS-II and ARM Cortex-M3 Processors, Application Note AN-1018, 2006
46. Albert Huang and Larry Rudolph, Bluetooth for Programmers, http://people.csail.mit.edu/rudolph/Teaching/Articles/BTBook.pdf, Retrieve in Jan. 2014
47. connectBlue, AT Command Specification - Bluetooth EPA, http://www.connectblue.com, 2009
48. HC, HC-03/05 Embedded Bluetooth Serial Communication Module AT command set, http://www.wavesen.com/, April, 2011
49. STMicroelectronics. xxxx-TOUCH-LIB, STMTouch library, DocID023933 Rev 4, February 2014
50. Cytron Technology, Product User's Manual – HCSR04 Ultrasonic Sensor, V1.0, May 2013
51. Gutierrez-Osuna, R.; Janet, J.A; Luo, R.C., "Modeling of ultrasonic range sensors for localization of autonomous mobile robots," Industrial Electronics, IEEE Transactions on , vol.45, no.4, pp.654,662, Aug 1998
52. Microsoft, Keyboard Scan Code Specification, Revision 1.3a — March 16, 2000
53. Silicon Laboratories, AN249 Human Interface Device, Rev. 0.5 3/11
54. Robert Murphy, AN57294 USB 101: An Introduction to Universal Serial Bus 2.0, Document No. 001-57294 Rev. *D, www.cypress.com
55. STMicroelectronics. STM32L Discovery Firmware Pack V1.0.2, www.stm.com
56. MacKenzie, S., "A structured approach to assembly language programming," Education, IEEE Transactions on , vol.31, no.2, pp.123,128, May 1988
57. Barry Donahue. 1988. Using assembly language to teach concepts in the introductory course. In Proceedings of the nineteenth SIGCSE technical symposium on Computer science education (SIGCSE '88), Herbert L. Dershem (Ed.). ACM, New York, NY, USA, 158-162.
58. E. Dijkstra. 1979. Go to statement considered harmful. In Classics in software engineering, Edward Nash Yourdon (Ed.). Yourdon Press, Upper Saddle River, NJ, USA 27-33.

Index

C

www.ingramcontent.com/pod-product-compliance
Lightning Source LLC
Chambersburg PA
CBHW060953210326
41598CB00031B/4811